For Carol Doty
with best wishes
Eugene Davidson

THE
Unmaking
OF
ADOLF
HITLER

THE
Unmaking
OF
ADOLF
HITLER

Eugene Davidson

University of Missouri Press
Columbia and London

Copyright © 1996 by
Eugene Davidson
University of Missouri Press, Columbia, Missouri 65201
Printed and bound in the United States of America

5   4   3   2   1   00   99   98   97   96

Library of Congress Cataloging-in-Publication Data

Davidson, Eugene, 1902–
     The unmaking of Adolf Hitler / Eugene Davidson.
       p.   cm.
     Includes bibliographical references and index.
     ISBN 0-8262-1045-7 (alk. paper)
       1. Hitler, Adolf, 1889–1945.   2. National socialism—Germany.   3. Germany—Politics
   and government—1933–1945.   4. Heads of state—Germany—Biography.   I. Title.
DD247.H5D384   1996
943.086—dc20   95-53092
                                                                                CIP

∞™ This paper meets the requirements of the
American National Standard for Permanence of Paper
for Printed Library Materials, Z39.48, 1984.

Designer: Kristie Lee
Typesetter: BOOKCOMP
Printer and Binder: Thomson-Shore, Inc.
Typefaces: Miniona and Futura Condensed

Jacket photographs are courtesy of Süddeutscher Verlag.

To the German Resistance

Contents

Acknowledgments

This book has taken a long time to put together; it was begun in 1977 when its predecessor, *The Making of Adolf Hitler,* was published. Maria Abbadi typed the early chapters, some of them far removed from where they were written, and her ability to decipher convoluted changes was uncanny. Evie Sullivan has been responsible not only for typing the latter part of a similarly cluttered manuscript but for checking sources and bibliographies and readying the entire project in its final phases.

I am deeply indebted to the late Harold C. Deutsch for his critical reading of the manuscript. Professor Deutsch generously provided me with the hitherto unpublished text of his interview with the former German Foreign Minister Richard von Kühlmann containing Kühlmann's illuminating account of how Hitler dared take the enormous gamble of sending his token forces into the Rhineland despite the overwhelming superiority of the French troops confronting them.

Professor Robert H. Ferrell from the beginning has concerned himself with forwarding the progress of the book. He has attentively read the entire typescript, making many perspicacious suggestions for improvements, and taken endless pains to expedite its publication.

I am most grateful to the Director and Editor in Chief of the University of Missouri Press, Beverly Jarrett, for her abiding interest in the manuscript and to the Press's sharp-eyed editor Annette Wenda.

THE
Unmaking
OF
ADOLF
HITLER

1

The Grasp for Power

A few hours after he was sworn in as chancellor by the president on January 30, 1933, Adolf Hitler called his cabinet together. It was a somewhat stilted but outwardly harmonious session in keeping with the pronouncements of the new, decorous, conciliatory Hitler of the last weeks before Hindenburg had overcome his aversion to making the man he called the "Bohemian corporal" head of the government. At the opening of the cabinet meeting Hitler immediately reset the tone of toleration and common purpose he had lately adopted—the manner of outward bonhomie and propriety that had greatly helped his predecessor, Franz von Papen, to persuade the president to name Hitler chancellor. Hitler said politely, at the opening of the meeting, that he hoped the members of the cabinet would lend him the same confidence that he had in them.

Even rank and file Communists were not excluded from the atmosphere of benignity. The government, Hitler told his ministers, could perhaps consider forbidding the Communist Party, deprive its deputies of their mandate, and thus achieve a majority in the Reichstag. But such a measure, he said, would be pointless. Domestic upheaval would follow and then a general strike. The economy needed a period of quiet, and a general strike was a far greater danger than new elections would be, despite the uncertainty and disturbances they would entail. In any event, Hitler said, it was impossible to exclude from public life the 6 million people who stood behind the Communist Party.

As for the Center Party, the cabinet members all agreed it had to be approached circumspectly. Its deputies' votes would be needed if the Reichstag was to adopt the course Hitler most favored and voluntarily prorogue itself. His right-hand man, Hermann Göring, told the cabinet that the chancellor had been in touch with the Centrist leaders and while they were aggrieved by having been left out of political negotiations, he had the impression they were waiting for some sort of signal from the new government to which they might respond favorably.

It was plain to everyone in the cabinet that the imminent danger to the just-sworn-in government lay in a general strike. It was a general strike that had put an end to the right-wing Kapp putsch of 1920, and if the Communists and the Social Democrats joined forces as the National Socialists and the Communists had done just before the November 1932 election in backing the strike of the Berlin transport workers, the whole waterlogged economy would be in danger of sinking and the government with it.

There was no doubt that the Communists would call a general strike; the only question was whether the Social Democrats would join them. Everyone knew the two Left parties were further apart in their practical politics from one another than they were from the National Socialists. The Communists not only had allied with the Nazis to support the transit workers' wildcat strike, but the two parties had worked together repeatedly as the chief activist, revolutionary parties in Germany—to bring down republican governments of any kind, whether they were led by the Center, the right wing, or the Social Democrats. It was unlikely, as Göring remarked, that the two workers' parties would ally in a general strike.

The immediate task, as Hitler and his cabinet—including his chief German National opponent, the industrialist Alfred Hugenberg—saw it, was to make certain that the Communists were prevented from spearheading an active opposition. That was all the coalition could readily agree upon. From there on the paths diverged. Hitler was determined to hold new elections, which he was certain would at least greatly increase the number of National Socialist deputies in the Reichstag and possibly, given the key positions they already held in the government, allow them to win a majority.

New elections were very nearly the last thing in the world Hugenberg wanted. In a campaign waged with Hitler in the chancellor's seat, the Nationals were unlikely to fare well against their Nazi rivals. But Hugenberg could not logically oppose the elections if the hope of a functioning right-wing coalition government was to be kept alive. So at the end of the first cabinet meeting it was decided that Hitler would get in touch with the Centrist leaders whose votes were essential if the Reichstag were to dissolve itself. The Centrists, Hugenberg agreed, must not be alienated, and he was comfortingly reminded by Göring and Hitler that, whatever the outcome of new elections, the members of the present government would keep their posts. Hitler had already told him that before the cabinet was sworn in, and the pledge was now repeated.

Nothing contentious came up at the meeting. The only act that might have given pause to the non-Nazis in the government was one with which the cabinet agreed. Göring told them that he had forbidden a demonstration scheduled a few hours hence by the Communist Party. He did not believe, he added, that the Social Democrats would join the Communists in declaring a general strike, but obviously they would not be given an opportunity, if they were so disposed, to join in the forbidden Berlin demonstration. Even in the matter of the general strike, Hitler was mindful of the sensibilities of his ministerial colleagues. He would not, he assured General Werner von Blomberg, the man President Paul von Hindenburg had named minister of Defense before he swore Hitler in as chancellor, call on the Reichswehr to put down a strike, and Blomberg, who held the conventional view of Reichswehr officers that the army must be used only against a foreign enemy, never against its own people, thanked him.

Thus it was a civil, peaceful meeting, as would be true of those immediately following it. Baron Constantin von Neurath, the new foreign minister, told Sir Horace Rumbold, the British ambassador to Berlin, that Hitler's behavior at these sessions was exemplary. Neurath said Hitler even voted against the positions of his two National Socialist comrades at times in the cabinet meetings, and it was plain that this was indeed a coalition government far removed from the one-party dictatorship the Nazis had long proclaimed as their goal.

The dream of the non-Nazi members of the government of a working, mutually tolerant right-wing coalition, a 1931 Harzburg front in operation, was to last a few days, or weeks, or months, depending on how long the dreamer needed to stay within his nighttime world.[1] For the country at large the outlook did not seem much more hazardous than it had been for a long time. The Communists called the general strike on January 30, the day the Hitler government took office, denouncing the "fascist dictatorship" of Hitler, Papen, Hugenberg, and Franz Seldte, the Stahlhelm leader. The strike call was addressed to the Social Democratic Party (SPD), the Center, and all the workers' organizations, but except for the Communists it went unheeded. As Göring had prophesied, there was no general strike. The SPD, in its manifesto for the coming election, would call on its members to vote against the enemies of the workers and of socialism and for the appropriation of large estates and providing land for workers and peasants, but it wanted no part of a common front with the Communists. The general strike never really got started.

The country at large took the political developments in stride. The *Frankfurter Allgemeine*, Rumbold noted with approval, wrote how incredible it was that the man who had congratulated the murderers of the Communist stomped to death at Potempa in 1932 (a heinous murder committed by Nazi storm troopers) could now be chancellor of Germany; Rumbold also observed that this was a government of the minority ranged against the great majority of the German people and its organizations. Against the now-dominant National Socialists were the Church, the army, the intellectuals, and two-thirds of the population. And the Nazi one-third of the nation was a movement, Rumbold wrote, made up mostly of men and women under thirty.

Few people, aside from its own supporters, expected the government to survive much longer than had most of its predecessors. It was another incompatible coalition, this time of the Harzburg front that had failed before to maintain any kind of unity, and considering the forces already deployed against it would have little more chance of survival than had Papen's or Kurt von Schleicher's or any of the other minority governments that had staggered through the recurrent Weimar crises. Papen and Hugenberg had been convinced that it was they who held Hitler in check, not the other way around.[2]

It was this version of the balance of political power, together with Papen's plea that the new Hitler could be brought within the framework of a conventional government, that had persuaded the reluctant president that a government led by Hitler might be able to find solutions for the infinite problems confronting the nation.

On January 31, the day following the first cabinet meeting, Hitler invited the chiefs of the Center Party, Monsignor Kaas and Heinrich Brüning, to meet with him.[3] Brüning was ill and his place was taken by Ludwig Perlitus, chairman of the Center Reichstag deputies, who kept a record of the conversations. Kaas was an upright, devoted Catholic prelate whose chief aim in political life was to safeguard the position of the Church and to preserve the Catholic political heritage in a society threatened by both far Right and far Left, by Nationalist Prussian Protestants as well as by Communists and Social Democrats. But he was scarcely a match in political acumen or ruthlessness for Hitler. Kaas was cautious and circumspect: "We have come," he told Hitler, "to receive information from you, for the moment we have ourselves nothing to say." Hitler, in turn, was all Austrian courtesy and outward friendliness. He immediately began to work from the one point he and Kaas shared in common—anti-Communism. After assuring Kaas of his loyalty and unwaveringly honorable intentions in dealing with the Center Party, Hitler went on to say that Communism had to be destroyed; it was a foreign body within the German people. But he assured Kaas he did not want to force the representatives of millions of Germans out of the Reichstag. He had been confronted with a difficult decision: Either he had to accept the office of chancellor or there would have been a military dictatorship. When Kaas protested that the Center had been offered no posts in the new government, Hitler disarmingly replied that this was not his fault. He had been ready to work together with the Center but what could he do with the Nationals infected as they were with a *furor protestanticus?* The Nationals were unwilling to see Centrists in the coalition cabinet, a quirk Hitler pointed out that was shared by Papen. The reference was, no doubt, intended to emphasize another animus shared by the two men. Kaas had felt himself vilely betrayed by Papen who had faithfully promised that he would not accept the chancellorship to replace his fellow Centrist, Brüning, and then, only a few hours later, had taken the post. But with that passing remark Hitler had exhausted his examples of any *politique* he shared with Kaas, and Kaas told Hitler the Center would not be content with the dregs of the coffee. He wanted to know what Hitler intended to do before agreeing to support his government. Kaas had in mind a list of questions that, since the matter was urgent, he proposed to place in Hitler's hands that afternoon. Hitler's answers would enable Kaas and the other Centrist leaders to decide whether they could support Hitler's demand that the Reichstag be dissolved for a year—a period, Hitler said, that would provide a respite from parliamentary haggling and give him time to deal with the fearful perils confronting the nation.

Kaas's list of ten questions was duly delivered to Hitler by 5 P.M. on January 31. They were typical of the methodical, plodding, upright Kaas and his notion of the kind of assurances that would protect his party and the Reich itself from the excesses of which the National Socialists would be capable. What assurances, Kaas asked in his questionnaire, could the government give that its measures would come within the framework of the constitution? Could it give binding assurances that no measures contrary to the constitution would be undertaken during the so-called state emergency? Was the government ready to return to normal constitutional procedures in Prussia (where the Landtag was prorogued and Papen was acting as Reichskommissar), and in what way would such normalization take place? There were other questions about social programs and Hitler's plans to continue a coalition government and to prevent another inflation. They were weighty questions and made good sense in a normal political context, but Hitler never tried to answer them.

On the next day he could readily wave the whole questionnaire aside, for he had been able to secure from Hindenburg the essential decree dissolving the Reichstag and calling for new elections.[4] Hitler wrote again in an outwardly courteous fashion, assuring Kaas that he had read his letter with the greatest interest; Hitler repeated that the respite from parliamentary incompetence was the only possible way in which he could constitutionally preserve the German state and its people. He wrote that the questions Kaas had raised would only make sense if they could be answered in the context of the year's indispensable interval.

Hitler dealt with Kaas with the practiced moves of a born political pitchman and gave him nothing at all: no seats in the cabinet, no assurances, no answers to his questions. Kaas could only reply helplessly that he had rushed to present his questions as Hitler had asked him to do. He repeated that he and his party had been shut out of the government, though their participation might have made for a government majority in the Reichstag and that answers to his questions, even if only in principle, might have provided the means for his collaborating in good conscience. Negotiations, he complained, had been suddenly broken off and contrary to the president's statement in his order of dissolution that a majority government could not be formed, such a government would, in fact, have been possible. And Kaas added, he thought it his duty to send a copy of his letter to the president. But Hitler, for the time being at least, had no more use for Kaas or the Center or any need to reply to the accusations. The Reichstag was dissolved and new elections would be held.

On February 1, the same day Hitler and Kaas exchanged letters, the coalition government issued a wide-ranging manifesto to the electorate designed to win votes from every segment of the population to the right of the Communists.

It was an unmistakably Hitlerian document: self-dramatizing, overblown, using phrases that had appeared over and over again in his speeches. It declared that the National government had taken over a frightful inheritance; the task they had to deal with was the most difficult that German statesmen had been assigned in the memory of mankind. But the government promised to foster Christianity as the basis of all morality and the family as the nuclear cell of the people and state, to restore the consciousness of German *Volkisch* and political unity above all class distinction, and, by restoring reverence for the great Germanic past and pride in its traditions, to provide a basis for the education of German youth.

The manifesto declared ruthless war on political and cultural nihilism and declared the government was resolved to prevent the Reich from sinking into "anarchic communism." The economy would be reorganized with two vast four-year plans. The old order, in fourteen years, had ruined the farmer and had created an army of millions of unemployed. Within four years the German farmer would be delivered from his misery, the economy would blossom, and unemployment finally would be overcome. In international affairs the government would see its highest mission in upholding the people's right to life and regaining German freedom. It was ready to work together with the community of nations as their equal to secure and maintain peace. And deeply as it loved the army as the nation's weapon bearer and symbol of its great past, the government would be happy if the rest of the world, by cutting down on its armaments, would not make an increase in German arms necessary. The men of the government, the manifesto declared, felt themselves responsible before German history for restructuring an orderly body politic and, with that accomplished, for finally overcoming class warfare. It saw itself responsible not to classes but to the German people who would either win their struggle together or go under together. "Now, German people," it said, "give us four years' time and then judge and pass sentence on us." True to the order of Field Marshal von Hindenburg they wanted to make a beginning. They asked God's help and the people's faith, for they wished to fight not for themselves but for Germany. The manifesto was signed by the entire cabinet, including Hitler, Papen, Neurath, Blomberg, and the others, and it was the first and last document they were ever to sign together in a show of solidarity that lasted no longer than the start of the election campaign.

While on the surface all was peace and harmony in the Hitler cabinet in those first days of the new government, the streets were the scenes of battle. The Communist demonstration was forbidden for Berlin, but clashes between Communists and National Socialists erupted and scores were arrested—eighty-two people, mostly Communists, in Berlin alone on February 1. In Hamburg four people were killed, and there were dead and wounded in other cities. Sometimes it was Nazis who were picked up by the police as a result of brawls, but mainly it was the members of the Left parties who filled the jails after these encounters. The disturbances were nothing new in the cities of the Reich; what was new was that the balance of power had patently shifted to the National Socialists. It was Göring who, as minister of Interior for Prussia, controlled the police there, and even in areas of the country where the National Socialists were not able to give the police orders it was likely to be their opponents who were locked up. At the very least the police could read the newspapers or hear the radio to learn which way the wind was blowing.

Popular reactions to the new government were mixed. The National Socialist paper, *Der Angriff,* called on the German people to show their solidarity with the Hitler government by beflagging their homes, and while flags did appear in cities such as Munich and Berlin, the workers' districts were bare of them. National Socialist papers reported that five hundred thousand men had marched in the torchlight procession that, on the night of January 30, filed past Hindenburg standing alone at a lighted window of the Reichschancellery, with Hitler and Göring at a neighboring window. But non-Nazi observers, the British ambassador among them, considered the figures grossly exaggerated. Rumbold reported that the Nazi figure was on the face of it impossible; his military attaché calculated it would take four hours for five thousand men marching ten abreast to pass a given point, and he thought no more than fifteen thousand men had taken part. But the procession had been joined by Stahlhelm forces as well as the Brownshirts and other National Socialist formations, and the *Münchner Neueste Nachrichten,* which had never been overly friendly to the Nazis, reported that modest houses in Berlin were blazing with color and that an entire people had lived to experience the fulfillment of a long-cherished dream after the years of national indignities and supineness.[5]

For the non-Nazi newspapers the mixed mood of wary expectancy and grave suspicion could only last a few days. Under emergency powers granted the government by Hindenburg on February 4, the Socialist paper *Vorwärts* was suspended for two days, the *Rheinische Zeitung* for three days, and the Communist *Rote Fahne* was shut down by the police. Soon similar penalties were imposed on almost any non-Nazi, including Center papers for adverse reporting on the state of the economy, or for printing allegedly false statements on the questionable behavior of the party or government, or for any other reason that came readily to hand. On February 19 the main newspaper of the Center Party, *Germania,* formerly controlled by Papen, was suspended for three days as were the *Thüringen Volkswacht* and the pro-Nationalist *Münchner Neueste Nachrichten.*[6] Hitler could talk of toleration in the cabinet meetings and to selected journalists, but the National Socialists in the streets showed no signs whatever of exhibiting it, nor did it appear where the Nazis were in control of the police.

But Hitler had to tread warily. The newspaper suspensions gave rise to protests. The Reichs Society of the German Press, representing newspapermen from all over the country, sent a telegram to President Hindenburg asking him to prevent any further interferences with the freedom of the press, prompting Hitler to go out of his way to reassure the opposition papers. On February 8 he held a most conciliatory press conference, telling a group of editors in Berlin that he and his government in no way wished to gag the press; what it wanted was cooperation, the recognition that men of goodwill were doing the best they could for *Volk* and fatherland. Criticism was necessary and useful, but the government had the right to demand that it be factual and free of personal attacks. He repeatedly emphasized that criticism was essential if often unpleasant to take, but it moved things ahead and kept the government on its toes. What could not be tolerated, however, were the attacks of those who wanted to damage the Reich, and he would take measures of the utmost severity against their perpetrators.[7] It was the very voice of reason, and it was persuasive to more people than the newspapermen and the cabinet.

Hindenburg's reply to Kaas and to a remonstrance from the chairman of the Bavarian Volksparty, who, like Kaas, said his party was willing to participate in the national coalition, had been to issue the decree of February 4, countersigned by Hitler, Minister of Interior Wilhelm Frick, and Minister of Justice Franz Gürtner, "For the Protection of the People." The decree gave the government the power to suppress almost any political gathering. It provided that political parties must announce any rally at least forty-eight hours before it was to be held, and, when such a meeting or demonstration threatened to imperil public security, it could be forbidden. Meetings could be dispersed by the police if they might lead to disobedience against any law or legal decree, or if a speaker calumniated any official or organ of the state. The police were to send observers to all political meetings, and the minister of the Interior was empowered to ban the wearing of uniforms or regalia that identified a political party. Similarly, periodicals or brochures containing material that might threaten public security could be confiscated and newspapers and magazines shut down for prescribed periods.

Hindenburg had very likely agreed to issue this decree on the ground that the general strike called by the Communists and the continued bloodshed in the cities of the Reich made it imperative for the government to act firmly to prevent disorders from spreading as the election campaign grew more heated. But its effect was to give the National Socialists—with their hold on the chancellorship and the Ministries of the Interior of the Reich and of Prussia—the power to suppress political meetings and newspapers of their opponents all over the Reich. The National Socialists now not only had the means of shutting off the opposition press and their speakers but they were also in charge of the government radio, which, linked with the local stations, was the only kind of radio the Reich had. Rumbold reported on February 7 that the government radio repeated Hitler's inaugural manifesto three times on the same day. It was almost impossible not to hear him. His speeches were recorded, loudspeakers were set up in city squares, and before the election on March 5 he and the other speakers for the coalition of the National Socialist German Workers' Party (NSDAP), the German National Volksparty, and the Stahlhelm (called the Battlefront Black-White-Red) were the only political voices to be heard on the airwaves. The hail of orders suspending newspapers continued, the *Augsburger Postzeitung* reported on February 23, and though, the paper complained, the courts often declared such measures illegal, in many cases their decisions came too late to prevent the suspensions that in the beginning lasted only three or four days.

The National Socialists were in a commanding position. Minister of Volks Enlightenment and Propaganda Josef Goebbels exulted in his diary of February 3 that to conduct the electoral battle they had all the means of the state at their disposal—radio, press, and government money. The one trouble, Goebbels wrote, was that in many of the radio stations the hacks of the old system *(Systembonzen)* were still at their posts and should be gotten rid of as quickly as possible. He planned to concentrate the Reich propaganda section in Berlin where he could direct it. Two days later Goebbels rejoiced that the prohibitions of newspapers such as *Vorwärts* and *8 Uhr Abendblatt* and of the "Jewish" organs that had given the Nazis so much trouble in the past had resulted in their disappearance from the newspaper stands in Berlin; Göring was getting rid of one unwanted official after another; a pro-Nazi, Rear Admiral von Levetzow, was the Berlin police president, and other pro-Nazis had similar posts in Hannover and in Dortmund.[8]

Along with the official acts of repression against their enemies were to be noted the toleration on the part of police and government authorities of almost anything the Nazis did. At a meeting of the Center Party in Krefeld on February 21, at which former Reichsminister Adam Stegerwald was the chief speaker, a firecracker exploded in the gallery when Stegerwald, as he was criticizing Papen's policies, mentioned Hitler's name. This was followed by a concerted attack of Nazis who had infiltrated the meeting that developed into a free-for-all. People in panic flooded over the platform to get to the emergency exits, and when the police arrived no one was left in the room except the chiefs of the Center Party and the Nazi intruders. Stegerwald had been struck in the face, two other Centrists were slightly injured, and the meeting was cautiously described in the press as the *Saalschlacht,* the battle of the lecture hall.

The government of national unity was a sham, much as it had been from the start. Nothing of substance held it together; it was an expedient to persuade Hindenburg to accept Hitler as chancellor where he would be surrounded by Papen, Hugenberg, Seldte, Neurath, the paper tigers of the Right who had nothing in common but an aversion to marxism and a desire to hold office. What Hitler planned to do was revealed by him in a speech in Berlin on February 20 to a group of twenty-five industrialists headed by Krupp von Bohlen und Halbach.[9] Hitler was accompanied by Göring and Frick and by the banker Hjalmar Schacht whose services he could use on this occasion.

He might have talked in the cabinet of mutual trust and of his devotion to the other ministers, but the content of his speech was quite different. Before he was appointed chancellor he had spoken to much the same group in Düsseldorf, and again he presented a program industrialists could scarcely find fault with. In the same words he had used in his previous talk he told them that private enterprise could not survive in a democracy, that private enterprise is only conceivable when a people have a sustaining concept of authority and of personality. Everything in the world that is positive and good and valuable in the realm of economics and culture is based solely on the significance of the individual, of the personality—something that majority rule can only destroy. Everything of value, he told the leading men in German industry who would have no trouble believing him, emerges from the battle waged on their behalf by a selected few. With an allusion to Goethe, he said the German people never sufficiently recognized they had two souls in their breasts fighting for survival; it was impossible for one part of a people to accept private enterprise while the other part rejects it.

> The communist principle cannot be sustained. It is not a matter of
> chance that one man performs better than another. In this fact private

enterprise is rooted. It is not enough to say "We don't want communism in our economy and if we continue as we have in the past we will perish." . . . Social democracy has steadily gained strength in the last forty years since Bismarck and Bismarck shortly before his dismissal said: "If that continues it will be Marx who triumphs." . . . I was advised when I wanted to take action to wait.

But he said he had to regain what has been lost in the last fourteen years.

We have refused to accept the Center's grace of toleration. . . . Hugenberg has only a small movement and he has greatly slowed up our development. We must first have all the means of power in our hands if we want to pin the opposition to the ground. . . . We now stand before the last election. It may turn out as it will but there will be no retracing our steps ever again even if the election decides nothing. In one way or another, if the vote is not decisive then the decision must be made in another way. I have taken the position that the people should once again be given the opportunity to decide its own fate.

Then he lifted the veil high enough to reveal a hint of the future.

If this election brings no solution, good. Germany will not perish. As never before it is incumbent on all of us to work for a success. Never has the need for sacrifice been greater than it is at this time. For the economy I have only one wish, that it move parallel with the inner reconstruction toward a peaceful future. The question of creating a Wehrmacht will be decided not in Geneva but in Germany, when through inner peace we have regained our inner strength. There can be no inner peace though until Marxism is done away with, and this is the decisive point that we must confront no matter how hard the battle. For this battle, I put my own life daily on the line like all the others who have joined with me in the battle. There are only two possibilities: either the adversary is driven back by constitutional measures, which is the purpose of this election, or the battle will be waged with other weapons which will perhaps demand greater sacrifices. I would be glad to avoid that. Let us hope the German people will grasp the momentousness of this hour which will be decisive for the next ten or even hundred years. . . . It will be a turning point in German history to which I devote myself with flaming energy.

Göring then added his own solacing words, promising there would be no economic experiments, and he cautioned that it would be essential to penetrate the circles infected by marxism; the storm troopers had to go into the marxist quarters of the big cities to battle for every soul. At the end of the meeting Schacht proposed that funds be collected from those present, which he said would be divided with the other parties in the coalition—in other words, with the German Nationals and the German National Volksparty—in proportion to their strength in the Reichstag. Two days later, Krupp von Bohlen und Halbach wrote a note of thanks to Hitler saying that he and the other industrialists present at the meeting agreed with him that it was high time to bring clarity to German domestic political policies—to place the interest of the entire German people ahead of any single calling or class—and that he and his friends were also convinced that only in a strong, independent state could the economy and industry develop and flourish.

Thus the occasion was a success. Hitler's was a well-crafted speech, tailor-made like its predecessors to the same audience of capitalists mired in the depression, fearful of the Left and uncertain of the future. Antimarxism and the need for a government favorable to a free economy, which would recognize the talents of the individual entrepreneur as well as the failures of the socialist measures taken by former governments, could only bring enthusiastic agreement. Even the derogatory mention of Hugenberg had the right tone. A good man, obviously, since he was a member of the coalition government, and a percentage of the funds collected would be apportioned to his German Nationals, but a man who could recruit only a small following and who was a burden on Hitler's back. Then, too, Hitler would act as the industrialists and the president wanted him to act—he would follow the constitution. That is, what he was doing by calling the election was to give the country the opportunity to make the best of its good fortune in having Hitler as chancellor by producing a majority for the government. In any case, he would rescue the fatherland; if the Reich did not give him a majority, he was determined to use extraconstitutional means to purge it of the marxist poison. As Göring explained, one of the jobs of the National Socialists was to trap marxism in its own lair; if there were to be street battles they would be waged in the good cause.

All the bases were covered; the cause was the Reich, free enterprise, the cult of the individual, and the unity of a purified, revitalized Germany. Hitler repeated the call uttered in a great moment of national unity in the nineteenth century—the call of "Deutschland, Deutschland über Alles," or the fatherland over the parochialism of class and profession: it would provide order after twelve years of misrule and it would provide for economic recovery based on domestic peace. Hitler's words confirmed the amputation of socialism from National Socialism, and the industrialists were certain that the course he set was the promising way to defeat the Great Depression, the very way they themselves had always wanted to go. With domestic peace and economic recovery a militarily strong Germany would emerge; a Reich whose strength would be determined not by foreigners but by itself. They liked that too.

The speech had different overtones from what he told the cabinet. In the speech, it was Hitler and the National Socialists, not the coalition, that were here to stay. It was Hitler and his party who constitutionally or otherwise would succor the country. The coming election was important, but, if need be, it would be overridden on behalf of the transcendent cause of the fatherland.

It was also a speech in the true Hitler tradition, of the kind he had made to the Munich Court in 1923 after his failed putsch and like the one he made on behalf of three young officers accused of high treason because they had joined the Nazi Party. It also had traces of the letter he had written to the Austrian authorities in Linz when, in 1913, they had threatened to draft him into the Austrian army. Again he was the self-sacrificing hero, ready day after day to risk his life for the great cause. Now it was for the salvation of the fatherland; as a youth trying to keep out of the Austrian army it had been for his own moral salvation, which arose from his dedication to his art for which he steadfastly had endured poverty and temptation. He offered the electorate no detailed plan; he asked them to judge him by what he did, and in order for them to make the judgment he had to be given full power to govern.

He would, in fact, get rid of organized marxism, but he would also impose iron regulations on industry that would be as inhibiting to the free market as anything devised by the Kremlin. The worth of the personality that he cherished so warmly was the worth of his own personality and not that of any industrialist nor of any banker such as Schacht who had passed the hat at the gathering and who would before long be cast aside. And the vague mention of extraconstitutional means that would, if necessary, be used to maintain the Hitler government in power was a bland euphemism. He had also promised, ever since he began his political career in 1919, to destroy the Weimar Constitution, the parliamentary system, and the "November criminals." Any means that served these ends he would use before and during and after the election. The only obstacle to this course was the president.

Hitler's rapid progress toward the absolute power he sought was greatly accelerated by agencies and events completely outside his control. He never would win a majority in a free or nearly free election, but he could win the means of controlling the government and the electorate without one. One psychological factor favoring his purposes was the continued refusal of the French government to permit the Reich the arms equality France had joined with Britain in promising a few months before or to reduce its own armaments as provided for in the Versailles treaty.[10] The negative attitude of the French government toward the possibility of a rearmed Germany under Hitler is, no doubt, understandable, but the utterances of Premier Edouard Daladier in Paris and of the French emissaries led by Joseph Paul-Boncour in Geneva were well designed to buttress public support for Hitler's promise that not foreigners but Germans would determine the strength of their defenses. France would neither disarm nor agree to permit Germany to increase the numbers of armament of the Wehrmacht. The French representatives in Geneva and the government in Paris would continue for many months to issue the most elaborate pronouncements as to why they could not agree to any practical plan for permitting Germany to begin to achieve the arms equality that had been promised in 1932 in Geneva. Theoretical arms equality was the farthest the French had been prepared to go after thirteen years of German demands for a start on the general disarmament promised in the Versailles treaty; any concrete suggestion for an increase in the manpower of the Wehrmacht, or a decrease in that of the victors, whether proposed by Socialist or Centrist or right-winger, always raised a storm of protest in France. With Hitler in power actual equality was unthinkable. No substantive proposal by Britain, the Reich, or any other country was ever acceptable to Paris or would ever persuade France to make concrete what it had granted in principle.

Another aid to Hitler was the stirring, in the depth of the depression, of a latent anti-Semitism not only in Germany but in other countries as well. What had long been regarded as crackpot explanations of the catastrophic slump that no society seemed able to deal with became as reasonable to hopeless people long out of work and barely subsisting as any other. Hitler did not mention the Jews when he spoke to the German industrialists; he talked about the marxists throughout his speech but made no direct mention of Jews. Goebbels, on the other hand, made a direct attack threatening the "Jewish press" with dire penalties if they transgressed the new press decree. Almost any paper he shut down he could call a Jewish paper; it was the code name for the opposition. But even as objective an observer as Rumbold took a not-unsympathetic attitude to a moderate degree of German anti-Semitism.

> Ever since the revolution, Jews have been given fair play in every walk of life in this country with the result that their racial superiority was asserting itself, at least in German eyes, to an almost alarming extent. It is obvious to any observer that the average German, while superior to the Jew in many respects and while endowed with remarkable qualities of tenacity, industry and sobriety, is distinctly inferior in an artistic sense and even in a purely intellectual sense to the German Jew. Whenever imagination, financial acumen or even business flair comes into play, the Jew tends to outdistance his German rival, and in every domain of intellectual effort the achievements of the Jews are out of all proportion to their numbers.

In a country where they hardly amount to two percent of the population, they have practically monopolized some professions and have obtained the plums of a great many others. . . . It is only natural that the academic youth of this country should bitterly resent the success of the Jews, especially at a moment when the learned professions are hopelessly overcrowded. . . . Jewish financiers . . . lay firm hands on the financial machinery of the country. The ostentatious mode of life of Jewish bankers and financiers—a tradition from the days when the ex-Emperor ennobled Jews who built ocean-going yachts or set up large racing stables—inevitably aroused envy when unemployment became general.

Rumbold also pointed out that Russian and Galician Jews had migrated to Germany after the 1918 revolution, and there had been notorious scandals. "Immigrants like Sklarek and Barmat with a natural bent for crooked finance became the center of great financial and political scandals, which seriously discredited the Left parties and still serve as classic examples of the kind of Jew abhorrent to the 'Nordic' or Nazi mind."[11]

Rumbold's report to the British foreign secretary in London, Sir John Simon, well states what was undoubtedly the going opinion among large numbers of moderate, tolerant people far removed from the rabid anti-Semites among the Nazi hoodlums. He made the same kind of summary that might have been written by any number of polite, well-bred critics in the Western nations who declared they admired Jews, or some of them, though they might confess they were put off by certain differences from their own norms and self-images. The great burden of the Jews despite all their attempts to assimilate was that they were always perceived as different—plainly distinguishable from the indigenous populations of the countries to which they had emigrated no matter how long they had been there or how fluently they spoke the native language. The photographs of German-Jewish soldiers killed in action, which were collected in an album published by Munich Jews after World War I, depicts what many Germans saw as incongruously Ashkenazic faces under German helmets, faces of young men who died for the same fatherland that was now preparing to reject them. Then, too, Jews were intelligent; for historical as well as for practical reasons they had flocked to professions such as medicine, journalism, and law for which they appeared to have higher aptitudes than the Germans themselves and, as Rumbold pointed out, in the endless depression they seemed to many Germans to be doing as well as they had before the economic collapse. German writers had long ridiculed the absurdities of the nouveaux riches, the oversuccessful, rising businessmen who, clumsily aping the nobility, far outdid them in conspicuous displays. When Christians filled their fishponds with champagne it was put down to a class vulgarity, the antics of the philistine with too much money and no idea of how it should be used. But when the Jewish arriviste did the same thing he was lampooned as a member not of a class but of a race. An enormously civilized man such as Walter Rathenau, a former foreign minister who was murdered in 1922, could scarcely be faulted for such bizarreries, but while he had tried desperately to see the Jews as merely another Germanic tribe, he could never get away from his sense of separation from the other Germans he loved so well. He tried to deal with this feeling with his general categories of the *Mut-Menschen* and the *Furcht-Menschen,* of the blond warrior northern races as opposed to the dark-haired, creative, fear-men of the south, but he never felt himself other than a second-class citizen despite his high office, his friendship with the Kaiser, and his entrée into the society of the Hohenzollern court. No matter what he accomplished for the Reich or for anyone who, like Hugo Stinnes, was irritated by his policies, he could never escape being a *fremdrassige Seele,* a soul of foreign race.

Germans were readier in 1933 than they had been for a long time to tolerate overt anti-Semitism, which had gone entirely out of fashion and had, in fact, been obliterated from the political scene by the start of World War I. Russian émigrés almost unanimously placed the blame for the Bolshevik revolution on the Jews, though Jews had been a small minority in the party and of its leadership, but even a man such as Rumbold said he could well sympathize with German resentment of the Jews as the depression laid bare the crude realities of the struggle for existence.

None of these issues nor all of them together, however, would be powerful enough to enable Hitler to win a majority in a free election. He was forced to turn to the other measures he had talked about outside the parliamentary system. On the night of February 24–25 the Berlin police raided the Communist headquarters in the Karl Liebknecht House; they discovered printing presses and masses of propaganda material all aimed, the newspapers reported, at over-throwing the government. The *Deutsche Allgemeine Zeitung* told how labyrinths of underground passages had been found that had enabled Communists on the run to escape from the police. It was a lurid story. It was also—as Diels, who was police president, later admitted—greatly exaggerated.[12] Diels declared in 1945 that the material found was interesting but not sensational. That the Communists had planned and worked for a revolution was known to every German, but that experienced party leaders would be foolish enough to leave really incriminating evidence of treason for the Berlin police, under Göring's control, to find would have been most implausible. The raid and others like it that took place outside Berlin only produced additional ammunition for Nazi speakers and press to use in a campaign that they did not need to wage in order to incite their own followers and that was useless against the Communists except to justify continued prohibitions of their meetings and publications.

What effect it might have had on the general public is not known because the real bomb exploded on the night of February 27–28 when the Reichstag burned. It was one of the most fateful fires in the history of the Reich. No one knows for certain how many arsonists set the blaze, though everyone is agreed that a confused, left-wing to anarchist former bricklayer, Marinus van der Lubbe, who had once been a member of the Dutch Communist Party, took a main part in it. The mighty fire illumined the night sky over Berlin; huge crowds watched it consume the great dome of the building, crowds that included Hitler, Göring, Papen, and Goebbels along with squads of police and the fire companies of Berlin. But the all-important result of the fire was to give Hitler the opportunity he needed to persuade his cabinet and the president to agree to grant his government the far-reaching powers he had been seeking since 1919.

He and the other chieftains of the party knew at once that it was the Communists who had set the blaze. Hitler told the cabinet they had to act immediately and ruthlessly against the Communist Party without regard to legal considerations. He had no doubt after the fire that the government could win at least 51 percent of the vote, and he proposed to issue an emergency decree for the protection of the society against the Communist danger. Göring said the blaze had not been set in retaliation for the raid on the Karl Liebknecht House but because of the documents that had been found showing Communist plans for setting fire to other public buildings, poisoning public food kitchens, taking hostages from the families of prominent officials, destroying power stations and subways—the fire was the signal for the start of the marxist revolution. Göring even named the leader of the plot—Willi Münzenberg—and he said two other Communists had already been arrested. He had ordered precautionary measures of public safety: closing museums and castles, prohibiting the publication of Communist and Social Democratic newspapers, shutting Communist centers, and ordering the arrest of all Communist Reichstag deputies and functionaries.

Some of his charges he lifted from van der Lubbe's confession. Van der Lubbe, though he denied that anyone else had been involved, declared he had set the blaze in the Reichstag as the first of a series of fires; it would be followed by the destruction of more public buildings and was intended to lead the workers to rise against the regime of oppression. He also said he believed the government of national concentration would not be tolerated by other countries and would lead to war. Van der Lubbe had been arrested at the scene of the crime; he promptly made a full confession admitting everything, and he showed a detective who interrogated him precisely where and how he had entered the building; how he had carried his incendiary materials—lighters for igniting coal fires; how he had used his shirt, vest, and jacket as torches; and how he had gone from room to room setting fire to draperies, curtains, an upholstered sofa and chair, furniture coverings, stacks of paper towels in the washroom, and anything else that would burn.

Few people, however, were satisfied with van der Lubbe's story. It seemed impossible that one man could have set such a widespread blaze without accomplices, and official announcements declared that the help had been provided by the Communists and Social Democrats. The entire National Socialist apparatus went into action. Communists and Social Democrats were arrested by the hundreds, all their newspapers shut down, and their meetings forbidden. The Communists retaliated by accusing the Nazis themselves of having set the fire after elaborate planning, and Communist propagandists set about with far more success than the National Socialists were ever to have to convince the world that they were revealing the true identity of the perpetrators. It was alleged that the underground passage where a man-high corridor, designed for heating pipes, that led from Göring's office in the Reichschancellery to the Reichstag, had been used by an arson squad of storm troopers, or SA men, along with van der Lubbe. It was on the face of it a much more plausible story than the one the Nazis told. Why should Communists have set fire to the Reichstag, thus giving Hitler the pretext he needed to arrest all the leaders the police could find? On the other hand, the Nazis obviously had every incentive to burn down anything in Berlin if it would give them the opportunity to get rid of their marxist enemies before the election.

Both sides set about with all their resources to prove the other was guilty. In the Reich four thousand Communists and left-wing intellectuals were arrested in wholesale roundups. Four Communists—Ernst Torgler (a member of the Reichstag who had voluntarily surrendered to the Berlin police) and three Bulgarian party members: Georgi Dimitrov, Simon Papov, and Vasili Tanev—and van der Lubbe were accused of carrying out the crime and were to be the central figures in a spectacular trial. The Communists responded with one of the most successful propaganda campaigns against National Socialism and all its works that would ever be waged. One of the Comintern's most skillful operators, the forty-four-year-old German-born Willi Münzenberg, who had been one of the youngest deputies in the Reichstag, organized a "World Committee for the Victims of Hitler Fascism" with branches in Europe and the United States—a committee, as Arthur Koestler said, that had only two well-known communist sympathizers, Henri Barbusse and J. B. S. Haldane, in a long list of internationally celebrated people, none of whom was a communist.[13] Münzenberg also founded, under the aegis of the world committee, a "Committee for the Investigation of the Background of the Reichstag Fire," which recruited another international group of well-known jurists. Among them was former Italian Premier Francesco Nitti; Arthur Garfield Hays, the defender of Sacco and Vanzetti in the United States; a Swedish jurist, George Branting; Gaston Bergery from France; and D. N. Pritt from England. The first session of this committee met in London, in the courtroom of the London

Law Society, under the chairmanship of the eminent British liberal, Sir Stafford Cripps.

Münzenberg, who had succeeded in crossing the border to Switzerland on the night of the fire, two weeks later moved to Paris where he established a headquarters from which he produced a series of remarkable documents and witnesses. One of the former was a profusely illustrated 382-page *Brown Book on the Reichstag Fire and Hitler Terror,* which was published in August 1933 in Basel and Paris. It was written by one of Münzenberg's close collaborators, Otto Katz (alias André Simonne), and was translated into seventeen languages. It had a foreword by Lord Marley, a distinguished member of the House of Lords and chairman of the world committee.[14] Lord Marley was highly respected, strongly anti-Hitler, and not a communist, but, according to a former Communist Party deputy in the Reichstag, Maria Reese, who knew both Münzenberg and Marley, he was paid a most-generous honorarium for his short introduction. The *Brown Book on the Reichstag Fire and Hitler Terror* not only documented the Nazi responsibility for the fire, describing how van der Lubbe had belonged to a homosexual ring together with leading Nationalists, but also described the concentration camps that had already been set up for the handling of thousands of political prisoners. One of the documents produced by Münzenberg was an alleged memorandum from Ernst Oberfohren who had been chairman of the German National Volksparty delegation in the Reichstag but had resigned as a result of a dispute with Hugenberg about the course the party should take.[15]

The statement attributed to Oberfohren was supposed to have been written in March 1933 just before he killed himself. It described how an arson squad under the leadership of SA leader Schlesiens and Nazi Reichstag Deputy Heines had used the approximately 140-yard underground passage from Göring's office to enter the Reichstag and set the fire that had been planned by the "morphinist" Göring and Goebbels. Schlesiens and his men had been joined by van der Lubbe who, along with his Dutch passport, had been supplied with a Communist leaflet and a paper identifying him as belonging to a splinter communist group.

Later, in connection with the propagandistic opportunities presented by the murders of Röhm and other SA leaders, still another version was produced under Münzenberg's direction. A deposition by SA Gruppenführer Karl Ernst presented a detailed account of how he, Count Helldorf (a leading Nazi and the police president of Potsdam), Edmund Heines (the SA Obergruppenführer and police president of Breslau), and others had, on Goebbels's and Göring's orders, planned the entire operation and how Ernst, with two trusted SA comrades and van der Lubbe, had set the fire.[16]

The stories were enormously successful; the Nazis were put on the defensive from the time Münzenberg set to work in Paris, and, despite the staging of a grand trial in Leipzig of the alleged Communist perpetrators, very nearly the entire press of the world swallowed the Communist version. It was widely accepted in both the East and the West by large numbers of people who recognized from the beginning that it was the Nazis who had the most to gain from the fire. They all knew from abundant evidence that the Nazis were capable of any crime that promised to advance their cause.

The Communist countercharge was so effective that it appeared years later at the Nuremberg trial of Göring, where the prosecution quoted witnesses who said that Göring had admitted on more than one occasion that it was he who had destroyed the Reichstag. It even resurfaced in the seventies under the auspices of another international committee.

Subsequent investigations have made both the Communist and the National Socialist versions of what went on unlikely. Göring explained at Nuremberg that since the foreign press had accused him of being the chief perpetrator he had joked that he would soon be in competition with Nero; people would say that while wearing a red toga he had stood across the way playing a lyre while the Reichstag burned. But he admitted he had thought little of the Reichstag architecture and wasn't sorry when the legislative chamber had burned up—he had hoped to build a better one. As for the tales told in the documents supposedly written by the Hugenberg defector Oberfohren and the SA man Ernst, they were probably not true either.[17] The Soviet secret police and propaganda apparat were old hands at manufacturing evidence and confessions for anything they wanted to prove, as they demonstrated in the remarkable trials staged in Moscow later in the thirties where former, highly placed Soviet government and party leaders abjectly admitted to crimes they could not possibly have committed. The Oberfohren and Ernst stories were concocted, and Arthur Koestler and Erich Wollenberg, both of whom were members of the group around Münzenberg, have since described the operation in some detail. And as the German writer Fritz Tobias points out, the perpetrators did not even bother in producing some of the documents to use official Nazi stationery, which they had in their possession, but instead merely typed them without a letterhead.

It now appears, ironically enough, that in the case of the Reichstag fire both the Communists and the Nazis may have been innocent. The Leipzig court that tried the four Communists was still made up of old-line German judges, and Torgler and Dimitrov, along with the other Bulgarians, were acquitted. The case against the Bulgarians was in fact so weak that the chief prosecutor himself asked for their acquittal. Only van der Lubbe was convicted and sentenced to death.[18] Dimitrov, who later became general secretary of the Comintern, had been more than a match for Göring who appeared as a witness at the trial; in fact, so striking was Dimitrov's success that the transcript of the exchange between him and Göring has been preserved and, until 1992, was to be heard on a tape played for the benefit of visitors to the city of Leipzig in the German Democratic Republic.[19]

The Communist-directed investigation committee that became an "International Jurists Commission" in London would also make its findings. Eight members from France, the United States, Britain, Denmark, Belgium, and Sweden dutifully found that van der Lubbe had not acted alone, that there was no shred of evidence that the Communist Party had been involved in the plot, and that the Communists accused in the Leipzig trial were all innocent. The committee reported that the evidence showed that the arsonists had used the underground passage connecting the presidential palace with the Reichstag, and it said truly that such a fire had been of the utmost use to the National Socialists. It also found that there was strong suspicion that high-ranking members of the Nazi Party had been involved. Part of the report said that Göring had prevented the sounding of a main general alarm for the Berlin Fire Department, that van der Lubbe had become a fascist, and that his name appeared on a list of homosexuals leading to Röhm. Also, the commission reported, a Stahlhelm leader, Elhard von Morozowicz, had stated that the fire was intended to provoke the Communists out of their inertia so they could be knocked out.[20]

Since that February night in 1933, the origins of the fire have been diligently investigated by criminologists, political scientists, historians, journalists, technicians, and others, and while they are far from agreed, it now seems not implausible that van der Lubbe was telling the truth when he said he was alone in setting it.[21] A minute-by-minute account of the sending of the successive fire alarms and the arrival of the many fire brigades checked against van der Lubbe's timetable has been worked out by one investigator, and it shows that it may indeed have been possible for one man to have covered the ground. Van der Lubbe may have done what he said he had—gone from room to room using his lighters (his vest, shirt, jacket, overcoat, as well as a tablecloth, draperies, and hand towels he picked up on his way), finally setting fire to the hangings and curtains in the chamber, shreds of which he pulled down to spread a blaze no one was able to put out. The huge room with its unusual height and open approaches apparently generated a draft like that of a gigantic elevator shaft.

Thus there may be nothing inherently implausible in van der Lubbe's account, though the question of how such a great fire could have spread without chemicals and outside help remains open.[22] Van der Lubbe had been, up to 1929, a member of the Dutch Communist Party but he had not remained in it, and his sentiments were more those of a lone anarchist than of a disciplined party member. During his trial he was apathetic and made no attempt to defend himself, to retract his confession, or to implicate anyone else. His story may well be true despite the fact that no one believed it at the time and that many people are still not convinced of it.

Certainly the fire was a mighty beacon, lighting the way for Adolf Hitler and his party. On the following day, February 28, President von Hindenburg issued a Decree for the Protection of the People and State, which effectively suspended the Weimar Constitution. The decree set aside the constitutional guarantees for freedom of the person, of speech, of the press, of association and assembly, and of the privacy of the mails and of telephone and telegraph. It permitted the Hitler government to invade personal rights, to conduct house searches, and to confiscate private property and restrict its uses. It could override the authority of the local officials, intervene if any *Land* failed to take the necessary measures for the restoration of law and order, and the death penalty could be imposed for crimes formerly punishable by life imprisonment, such as high treason; poisoning; arson; damage to railroads; or for any attempt on the life of the president of the Reich, of a Reichskommissar, or of an official of the state or central governments.

Nevertheless, despite the decree, the wholesale arrests of Communists and Social Democrats, the shutting down of opposition newspapers, and the mounting evidence that it was dangerous to life and limb to conduct any kind of active opposition to the Hitler government, the National Socialists won only 43.9 percent of the vote in the March 5 election. But with their temporary allies, the Battlefront Black-White-Red, which won 8 percent of the vote, the Hitler government had a slim majority—51.9 percent in the Reichstag. The Communists went down 12 percent—apparently a considerable number of them switched their vote to National Socialist—while the SPD, the Center Party, and the Bavarian Volksparty recorded minor losses. It was far from a major victory, but the National Socialist vote exceeded by three and one-half million its high-water mark of July 1932, and it was enough to allow Hitler to take the next steps toward total control of the government. He had promised industrialists that one way or another he would end the parliamentary system. Göring, in a talk on March 3 in Frankfurt, was even more explicit. He told an audience of National Socialists that in taking the measures he planned after the election, he would not be troubled by juridical considerations or by the bureaucracy. He said, in speaking about the marxists,

I have no need here for any kind of legality. I only have to destroy and exterminate, that's all. This battle, my Volkscomrades, will be a battle against chaos and I will not wage such a battle with police power. A bourgeois state might have done that. Of course I'll make use of the police and state power to the utmost but, meine Herren Communists, just so you don't draw any false conclusions, this battle to the death where I plant my fist against your neck I will conduct with those down there, with the Brown

Shirts . . . In the future, Gentlemen, only those will be admitted into this state who come from the ranks of the nationalist forces.

And as for the talk about justice, Göring told his audience he measured with a double standard. "It would not be just," he said, "if at long last I did not drive the red *Bonzen* to the devil." And that he did not have just Communists in mind he made clear by addressing his enemies as "You Red and Pink Gentlemen," a phrase broad enough to accommodate a moderate man such as the Social Democrat Severing who was also mentioned in his speech.

So there could be little doubt in the minds of anyone in the Reich who read the newspapers or listened to the radio of how the Nazis intended to govern once they had the power. Their pronouncements played on the old themes of a cleansing, *Volkisch, Machtpolitik* to come, and since they had been repeating them for a long time they could not be dismissed as mere election propaganda. Still, almost 57 percent of the electorate voted for parties other than the Nazis and the 8 percent of those who voted for the German National Volksparty and the Stahlhelm, such as Hugenberg himself, were pro-Hitler only insofar as they too were antimarxist, fed up with the parliamentary muddles, and nostalgic for a powerful Reich. But the trouble with the opposition was what it had always been—it could unite on no alternative; Communists and Social Democrats could agree on nothing resembling an operational common front, the Centrists and the other moderate parties, suspicious as they were of Hitler, nevertheless were reluctantly willing to collaborate with him. They had run out of stock of their own medicaments for the Reich's recovery, and they had lost the will to resist those Hitler offered. What they resented, as Kaas told Hitler, was that they had been ignored when they were ready to cooperate with him if he would only guarantee his support of the constitution and of a Christian state.

The almost 6 million vote increase for the National Socialists, since the November 1932 election, came from disparate sources, seemingly from every spectrum of the electorate, 88.04 percent of which voted as compared with 79.93 percent in 1932. The Communists lost more than a million votes, and it was the Nazis who won them. Millions of voters, mainly young men and women, urgently demanded radical solutions for their own plight, which seemed to them that of the Reich, and like Lieutenant Richard Scheringer they could move from one extreme to the other without great difficulty.[23] What they were sure of was that the Weimar system and the traditional economic and political establishments were moribund, and a revolutionary way had to be found for themselves and the society. The continued refusal of France and the former Allies at the disarmament conference at Geneva to implement the promised arms equality was the very symbol of the implacable tyranny of the Versailles treaty, of the hypocrisy of the victors, of the Reich's continued humiliation and weakness, and of the inanition of the Weimar coalitions. Even a paper that was far from pro-Hitler had commented on the sense of national regeneration that Hitler brought with him to the chancellorship. When Hitler promised that no foreign countries but Germany herself would determine the future strength of the Reichswehr, he was addressing the sentiments of every German from the Communists to the industrialists of the Ruhr.

Side by side the accounts of the campaign speeches and the turbulent domestic scene of the Reich, the newspapers told how the Geneva disarmament conference was playing the same record with the refrain: "Not yet," with Paul-Boncour, France's representative, providing one explanation after another as to why the promise of equality was still in force but had to remain unfulfilled. That Hitler's chancellorship had stimulated French skepticism of German reformation and reinforced the conviction that France's security was in mortal jeopardy was, of course, true and understandable enough, but it was also true that no German government, whether leftist or center or right wing, had fared any better in trying to persuade any French government to carry out either the disarmament promised in 1919 or to take a first step toward the arms equality promised in 1932. It was a frozen position of which Hitler could make ready use. In an interview with a British colonel, Edgerton, reported in the press on February 14, Hitler said a precondition for the return of peace was disarmament; the world could not be divided forever between victims and vanquished, the conditions of 1919 were no longer supportable, and the Polish Corridor was "a horrible injustice." Such statements, however appalling to the French, fell on willing ears in the Reich, and, whatever effect they might have had in Geneva, they could lose no votes in Germany.

They were part of the theme of the mortal danger besetting the Reich—the machinations of the marxists who burned down the Reichstag, of the November criminals who had surrendered Germany to the enemy and who were plainly still at work in Geneva, Moscow, Paris, and Wall Street to keep Germany impotent and bankrupt.

Not all the perils were imaginary. On March 6, the day after the election, the Polish president, Josef Pilsudski, ordered a battalion of 120 Polish marines to land at dawn at the Westerplatte, situated at the mouth of Danzig harbor.[24] They were ordered to reinforce the Polish garrison stationed there, an order that violated the Polish-Danzig agreement confirmed by the League of Nations. Under the agreement the Poles were permitted to station a limited body of troops at the Westerplatte—in 1925 that meant two officers, twenty noncommissioned officers, and sixty soldiers—to protect stores of munitions but were not to increase their number without the approval of the League of Nations high commissioner for Danzig. Pilsudski acted on his own without consulting the high commissioner, and numerous Polish sources, including the ambassador to Berlin, Józef Lipski, have openly stated that Pilsudski gave the order as a deliberate first step in what he envisaged as a preventive war against the Reich. What Pilsudski apparently had in mind—his pretext was an alleged plot by "Hitlerite gangs" to attack Polish installations on the Westerplatte—was to provoke a reaction from Hitler either in the form of reprisals by the Danzig SA or similar groups, which would enable him to call on France to fulfill her obligations under the terms of the Polish-French military alliance. Thus Poland would put an end to the threat posed by the election of Hitler and his ultranationalist government before it assumed too large proportions.

Hitler, however, did not react.[25] Nor did France, except to join Britain in a protest against Pilsudski's unilaterally determined test of Hitler's bellicosity. The League of Nations high commissioner, Helmer Rosting, declared the battalion's landing had been made without his consent, and the League of Nations Council ended the matter with a "compromise"—the reinforcements were withdrawn. But a few weeks later Pilsudski tried again.

In mid-April British Prime Minister Ramsay MacDonald and Foreign Secretary Simon journeyed to Rome where Mussolini had prepared the draft of a four-power pact of Britain, Italy, France, and Germany with a view to agreeing on a formula on disarmament and even a possible rectification of frontiers within the framework of the League of Nations Covenant. Such a pact was anathema to the Poles and the Little Entente because it threatened to strengthen German territorial claims against them, and again Pilsudski endeavored to persuade the French that this was the time to join with him in a preventive war against the Reich. Anti-German demonstrations were organized in Poland, a parade of thirty-five thousand demonstrators marched before Pilsudski in Vilna, and he had prepared a decree for a state of war. But Paris was not inclined to go to war on Pilsudski's urging, and Polish fears of what Hitler intended to do were appeased when, in May, Hitler told the Polish minister to Berlin, Alfred Wysocki, that the Reich would make no attempt to obtain territorial revisions as a result of the four-power pact.

There would be one other attempt by Pilsudski to call up French military assistance in a war against Germany; that would come toward the end of the year as the Poles discussed a nonaggression pact with Hitler and the talks seemed stalled. But again the French declined what they regarded as the incessant Polish efforts to embroil them in a war for Polish interests. And while Pilsudski, whose army was enormously superior to the German army in numbers and equipment, could in theory easily defeat Germany with his own resources, the Polish plan of campaign was based on the alliance with France and a two-front war. The Poles were not prepared to fight a war alone; when they had been forced to do so, as in the case of the war against Soviet Russia in 1920–1921, they had fared badly after initial successes. In alliance with an anti-Soviet Ukranian government the Poles had captured Kiev, but then came military disaster as the Bolsheviks mounted an offensive; France had been called on then, too, for help. General Maxime Weygand had been sent with a staff of officers to bolster the Polish high command when Warsaw was threatened. With their aid Pilsudski was able to mount a counteroffensive and eventually to annex fifty-one thousand square miles of territory formerly in the hands of the Soviet Union. Not much had changed in the Poles' military structure in the last decade, and Pilsudski himself declared in 1933 that the chief Polish military weakness lay in the high command.

With a slim majority in the Reichstag and an insignificant army of one hundred thousand men, Hitler would have to tread warily in foreign affairs. Outside of the "brother" German state of Austria with its sizeable contingent of National Socialists, any kind of hard line had to be put aside until he had succeeded in bringing the Reich's military strength nearer the numbers and material of his heavily armed neighbors. What he needed for this was time, and it was clear that his mood was as close to appeasement as it would ever come when, two months after the election, he began his talks with the Poles that would lead to a nonaggression pact. On May 2, in a conciliatory conversation with Wysocki that lasted for forty minutes, Hitler offered to foster the conditions of a Polish-German détente.

The situation on the domestic front was very different; there the Nazi revolution immediately went into high gear. Hitler, with his coalition partners, had a majority in the Reichstag, and he would soon seek what amounted to the Enabling Act in the Hindenburg decrees. His Brownshirts were spoiling to swing into action, their fists against the neck of the enemy as Göring had promised.

The anti-Semitism that had been relatively restrained before the election was officially unleashed on April 1 by SA contingents who stood howling in front of Jewish stores and businesses to intimidate any possible customers. The boycott of Jewish businesses, lawyers, doctors, and shops ordered by Hitler under the leadership of Julius Streicher, Gauleiter of Franconia and editor of *Der Stürmer,* was ostensibly a counteraction to the anti-German articles appearing in the foreign press.[26] It was accompanied by a wave of repressions, purges, and assaults that, despite short-lived remissions, were never to end while Hitler was in power. Anti-Semitism had always been the core of the Nazi movement in the minds of the leadership and of most of their ardent followers. From now on it would dominate not only the party but also the Reich.

The first steps were taken to get rid of Jews in newspaper offices, in government and private enterprises, and in the innumerable trade and professional associations of the Reich so as to cut down their numbers in schools and universities and to split them off wherever possible from the rest of the population. The anti-Semitic action was triggered from the top and the bottom of the party.

The SA street fighters had been hunting down Jews and marxists for a long time, as had Goebbels, Göring, and the Führer himself. But Hitler had been muting the anti-Semitic notes in what he said to the industrialists, and Jews often went unmentioned in solemn public pronouncements such as the speech in Potsdam when he, along with Hindenburg, made their appeals for German unity and regeneration. On such occasions Hitler was, as always, adapting his tactics to the audience to evoke the response he wanted. Simultaneously, however, with such pleas and exhortations, the vise from top and bottom was closing.

A few people showed their contempt for the Nazi measures by continuing to buy in Jewish stores. But the great majority stayed away as the pressures mounted. Photographs of customers entering the stores were snapped; in some villages the medieval custom of erecting forms of pillories was revived, and lists of those who patronized Jewish stores appeared on the pillories and in the newspapers. The campaign could spread rapidly. An old-line diplomat such as Neurath would have indignantly denied that he was an anti-Semite, and no one in London, for example, where he had been ambassador for two years, thought of him as Nazi-minded. But Neurath took a complacently optimistic view of the early days of the revolution. He told the British ambassador, Rumbold, that Hitler would not long be able to rely on the emergency decrees that put dictatorial power in his hands. They would be in effect for only a short period, he thought, and then as had happened in the past the government would have to revert to the normal observance of law. Nothing in the career of a man such as Neurath had stamped him as an anti-Semite. Like Hindenburg he was a conservative: not enthusiastic perhaps about Jews, but no SA fanatic either.[27] But by September, as the boycott of Jewish enterprises had set off counterboycotts in Britain, Western Europe, and especially in the United States, Neurath made a speech that was published in the *Völkischer Beobachter* in which he denounced foreign reactions to the Nazi measures. "The stupid talk about purely internal affairs," he said, "as for example the Jewish question, will quickly be silenced if one realizes that the necessary cleaning up of public life must temporarily entail individual cases of personal hardship but that nevertheless it only serves to establish all the more firmly the authority of justice and law in Germany."[28]

The political anti-Semitism of the nineteenth century, which had disappeared from German life for lack of popular support by 1914, now made its reappearance in respectable circles. At the start of World War I the anti-Semites as a party no longer had any representatives in the Reichstag, and years later in 1928, even with Hitler constantly beating the drum for their resurgence, he could win no more than 2.6 percent of the electorate. But by 1933 the years of defeat and frustration, of buffeting and turmoil, had taken their toll. Even Hindenburg, with his initial revulsion to the brawling street fighters and to Hitler, was not immune to their effects.

Only a few months before he appointed Hitler as chancellor, on October 3, 1932, he had written a tribute to the Jews who had died in World War I in the form of a letter to the head of the Reichs Society of Jewish Front Line Soldiers, Dr. Löwenstein. Hindenburg wrote: "I express my heartfelt thanks to the Reichs Society of Jewish Front Line Soldiers for their congratulations on my 85th birthday as well as for the beautiful flowers and the memorial book. In reverential memory of the comrades who from your ranks, too, fell for the Fatherland I accept the book and will place it on the shelves of my war library. With comradely greetings. von Hindenburg."[29]

It was the kind of tribute Hindenburg was always ready to make to any comrades in arms who had fought for the Reich, and his sentiments were echoed by the army high command and, far more dimly, even by the summary decrees the government issued. When, in mid-November, Lieutenant Colonel Ott, chief of the Wehrmacht Defense Section, made the acceptance speech in the book-presentation ceremonies in Berlin, he said: "Gentlemen, I have the honor on behalf of the Minister of Defense to tell you here in this solemn hour that we will keep this memorial book of our Jewish comrades who fell in the World War in a high place of honor as a remembrance of these devoted and true sons of our German people."[30] Ott had felt it necessary to assure the presentation committee that Jews too were "genuine" [he used the word *echt*] "sons of the Reich," but such sentiments, up to the time Hitler came to power, were always given at least lip service on ceremonial occasions, and they were so evident in Hindenburg that the Hitler government had to tailor its anti-Semitic decrees to them.

When the Law for the Restoration of Career Officialdom was issued on April 7, 1933, a decree that aimed to get rid of Jews and other undesirables among public officials, exemptions were made in the case of "non-Aryans" who had fought for the Reich or whose fathers or sons had been killed in the war; any such were permitted to remain at their posts.[31] Otherwise, Jewish officials and employees were to be retired. In addition, a note of Nazi puritanism was added—anyone who had been appointed to government service (which included railways and government banks) after November 9, 1918, without the credentials required before that date, was to be dismissed with loss of their official titles as well as any claim to retirement pay. Their salaries and allowances were to be continued for three months. Furthermore, any official whose political activity could not guarantee that he had favored the nationalist state could also be dismissed, though he might retain three-fourths of his retirement pay, providing he had been in government for ten years or more. The law regarding career officials was followed by the decree of April 22, 1933, that limited the number of Jews in the technical schools and universities to their proportion in the population. This law, too, did not apply to those whose fathers had fought in the world war for Germany or its allies.

Such dams against the anti-Semitic deluge that was flooding over the Reich were few, and when they held firm it was only because of President von Hindenburg. But Hindenburg, now eighty-six years old, was himself far from a mighty fortress of resistance. Brüning later said that at the time he was Reichschancellor, Hindenburg often did not recognize him when he called at the presidential palace to discuss matters of state, Once, as early as 1930, when Brüning and a member of his cabinet, Gottfried Treviranus, had met the train of the president and his son when it arrived in Berlin, Hindenburg had not known them. Hindenburg's son, Oskar, had to keep repeating: "Here is the Herr Reichschancellor and Minister Treviranus" to try to bring his father out of his mental fog.

Hindenburg in early 1933 no longer had either the strength or much desire to hold in check the man he called the "Bohemian corporal" and had promised never to appoint chancellor.[32] Only where his most deeply held, life-long convictions were touched did he resemble the old granite conservative his supporters had counted on to keep Hitler from the excesses Hindenburg had so strongly reacted to in years past. And Hitler, when he and the president appeared on the same platform, played on the themes he knew would impress Hindenburg with the consummate skill that he had long used when he directed his oratory at other uncommitted but vulnerable audiences.

The first meeting of the new Reichstag was to be held on March 21, 1933, the sixty-second anniversary of Bismarck's opening of the first German Reichstag. That morning a solemn ceremony of national renewal, rededicating the Reich to the restoration of its might and unity, was held at Potsdam. The staging of the great scene of national solidarity, called "The Day of Potsdam" was in the hands of Goebbels, who on March 13 was appointed minister for Volks Enlightenment and Propaganda. Goebbels had for years been the party propaganda chief, and no one knew better than he how to produce a spectacular mass ceremony of waving flags, uniformed marchers, and cheering crowds as a background to Hitler's oratory, even in the days when he could draw solely on the resources of the party. Now he had a cast of notables—the president, generals with detachments of the Reichswehr, and the Reichschancellor—to work with, and he made the most of his opportunity. The radio network of the Reich was to carry a running account of the ceremonies into the remotest German village; the entire country, Goebbels wrote in his diary, must be called on to participate in this day, to stamp its significance indelibly on the people's memory.[33] The radio announcer was Baldur von Schirach, head of the Nazi Youth Movement and party poet, author of innumerable flat verses that could be seriously recited only by his untutored young charges. The proceedings were orchestrated as a ceremony of nostalgia and vast promise, summoning memories of the glitter and power of the Second Reich with the presence of the men who promised to restore its glories, and it took place in the city where the spirit of old Prussia was immanent and perceptible to the faithful far more than in cosmopolitan Berlin.

It had rained the night before, but on the morning of March 21, in storybook fashion, the skies cleared and the sun was warm in the city beflagged with swastikas and the black, white, and red banners that Hindenburg, on March 12, had restored as the state colors in place of the black, red, and gold of the Weimar Republic. There were far more of the black, white, and red flags being flown in this nationalist stronghold than there were of the swastika banners, and the impartial church bells tolled as the uniformed or top-hatted dignitaries, including the veterans of 1864, 1866, and 1871, leaning on canes or sitting in wheelchairs escorted by the Stahlhelm, converged on the Garrison Church where Frederick the Great and the other Hohenzollern princes lay buried. Hindenburg, on his way, stopped at the Nicolai Church where the well-known Protestant ecclesiastic Otto Dibelius was preaching, while Heinrich Himmler, along with Kaas and Brüning—but without his fellow coreligionists, Hitler and Goebbels— stopped to worship at the Catholic church of St. Peter and Paul.

No room was left for the *Volk* as the Reichstag deputies, the diplomatic corps, the newly appointed National Socialist leaders of the *Länder*, along with the chief government and party officials took their seats in the Garrison Church. Only in the broad plaza in front of the church was there place for the rank and file. The top brass of the new order was all there but not all the Reichstag deputies were. The Communist deputies had been excluded (most of them were in jail), and the Social Democrats refused to attend. But the members of the former royal family were present: The crown prince, wearing his uniform of the Death's Head Hussars, was seated on the platform with his wife, Crown Princess Cecilie, and his sons and brothers. Only the Kaiser was missing, and for his absence an empty chair spoke eloquently.

A little before noon Hindenburg, accompanied by Hitler, entered the church. Hindenburg was wearing his spiked helmet with his Prussian uniform and carrying his field marshal's baton, which he raised in salute as he paused before the chair where the Kaiser he had counseled to abdicate and leave Germany should have been seated. It had been an act Hindenburg had never been able to fully digest, this sending into exile the liege lord to whom he had sworn his allegiance. But whatever thoughts he may have had as he saluted, he continued his solemn march to his seat, his uniform a little tight as the French ambassador André François-Poncet noted, but still a formidable figure of striking presence and dignity. Brüning thought Hindenburg looked deathly pale and seemed under emotional stress, occasionally wiping a tear from his eyes with his brown gloves. Brüning also thought Hindenburg had reason to be emotionally upset: Thousands of people who had voted for him against Hitler were in jail or concentration camps, thanks to his decrees giving Hitler emergency powers.

And alongside Hindenburg, as François-Poncet also noted, in marked contrast to the towering old gentleman, walked Hitler, looking, in his ill-fitting frock coat, a good deal like a funeral director. On Hitler's left side walked Papen, while behind them marched Göring and Goebbels, both of whom paused to raise their arms in the Nazi salute as they arrived before the princely guests.

Hindenburg, who in January had insisted that Papen be present when he met with Hitler, was ready, by the end of March, to place his full confidence in the Reichschancellor without the presence of Papen or anyone else. In his proclamation for the war dead preceding the ceremonies, Hindenburg had delivered his set remarks about the heroism of those who had given their lives for the fatherland, whom he now felt would at long last be fittingly memorialized in the government of national unity.

As the choir finished "Now, Praise My Soul, Master" Hindenburg rose, and his state secretary, Otto Meissner, handed him his speech, which Hindenburg began to read with what one observer called a deathly earnest face. The speech had been written in part by Meissner, and in it Hindenburg trustfully put the fate of the Reich in the hands of Hitler. He said that the regime he had appointed had, on March 5, received a clear majority, which provided the constitutional basis for the work of the new government. Then turning to Hitler and his cabinet, the president said:

> Heavy and manifold are the tasks that you, Herr Reichschancellor, and you, my Herren Ministers, have before you. . . . I know with what resolution the Chancellor and his government have approached these tasks and I hope that you, the deputies of the newly formed Reichstag, in the clear knowledge of the situation and its necessities, will for your part put yourselves behind the regime and do everything to support its work. The place in which we have gathered today bids us to look back on an old Prussia that in fear of God, never-failing courage and self-sacrificing love of Fatherland, has become great and on this fundament united the German peoples. May the old spirit of this hallowed place bless, too, the race of today, may it free us from selfishness and the disputes of parties and in national self-consciousness and renewal of soul lead us together again to the blessing of a united, free, proud Germany.

With these words Hindenburg turned the lectern over to Hitler.

With his plea for the deputies to unite behind the Hitler government it was far more than the lectern he was about to surrender to the Reichschancellor; he was putting his considerable weight on the side of Hitler's demand for the Enabling Act that would authorize him to bypass the Reichstag and make his own laws for the Reich. And, as always, Hitler, wooing an audience that was not wholly converted to National Socialism, was careful to say nothing with which his critics could take issue. There were no tirades against the Jews, or Social Democrats, or even Communists. What he had to say was intended to appeal to the sentiments of almost any German, especially to those of a man such as Hindenburg, who believed that righteous living and hard work led, despite all hardships, to the Lord's approval and blessing. Hitler recited the litany Hindenburg had repeated all his life; the fatherland was great and good and eternal, and only foreign and domestic enemies had confounded it. It was an echo of his old speeches, of one he made in August 1920 when he had said Germany had never been conquered from without but only from within its borders. Hitler repeated that despite unparalleled industry and willingness to work, despite energy, a rich store of knowledge, and the best of will, millions of people were seeking jobs in vain. He liked to deal in round numbers and he said the German people for two thousand years had been the victims of a fickle fate, the causes always the same—the disunity of the Reich. No wonder Germans had turned inward to become singers, poets, and thinkers. True to the Kaiser's proclamation, the German people had taken their part in increasing the goods of peace, of culture, of human civilization. They had never lost sight of their deep responsibility to the common life of the nations of Europe. For neither the Kaiser, nor the German government, nor the people had wanted the war. Only the fall of the nation, the general collapse, had compelled a weak contingent against their own better judgment and against their most holy inner convictions to accept the charge of war guilt. The collapse had affected all sectors of communal life. Germans had lost faith in their own strength, their traditions had been degraded, and the rest of the world had not been made happier or richer by the political and economic dissolution of an essential part of their community. Out of the superstition of eternal victors and vanquished came the folly of reparations and with it catastrophe for the world economy. Hitler and his government sought to restore the unity of spirit and will of the German nation; to protect "the eternal fundament of our life, our *Volkstum,* and the strength and values bestowed upon it. We want to restore faith in the healthy precepts of leadership . . . and in place of eternal vacillations form a government that will restore an unshakable authority to our people." Germany wanted to be a true friend of a peace that would heal the wounds of everyone. "The regime of national renewal is determined to fulfill the task assigned it by the German people. It therefore appears today before the Reichstag with the fervent wish to find through it the support for the fulfillment of its mission." And this mission was to build a genuine community made up of all Germans, out of all ranks, professions, and former classes.

The speech had echoes in it of most of the main addresses Hitler had ever made. There were no specifics, only words such as unity, strength, authority, and the restoration of values, and the promise that they, as well as something resembling a classless society, would be achieved through him and the party of the German National Socialist workers.

Hitler never for a moment lost sight of Hindenburg. He said:

> Today in our midst is a gray-haired chief of state. We rise before you, Herr General Field Marshal. Three times you have fought on the field of honor for the existence and future of our people. . . . You were present at the founding of the Reich, you saw before you the work of the great Chancellor, the wonderful rise of our people and finally led us in the great period when fate allowed us, too, to live and fight through with you. Today, too, may Providence permit you to be the protector of the new rising of your people. Your wonderful life is a symbol for all of us of the indestructible vitality of the German nation. Therefore the youth of the German people thank you today, as do we all who seek the blessing of your assent to the work of national renewal. May this strength be imparted, at the present inauguration, to the new representatives of the people. May Providence lend us, too, the courage and tenacity that we perceive around us in this place holy to every German as we strive for the freedom and greatness of our people at the foot of the bier of its greatest king.[34]

His speech ended, Hitler walked over to the president, shook his hand, and bowed low in an actor's reverence before the man who had commanded the German armies in the war where Hitler himself had been only a lance corporal. Only now, though Hindenburg could not know that, the roles were about to be reversed.

Hindenburg, followed by two officers bearing large wreaths, then walked heavily down to the entrance of the vault where the Prussian kings lay buried. The wreaths were laid on the coffins of Frederick the Great and his father, and after a few minutes Hindenburg climbed up the steps, greeting the crown prince and taking his place for the final ceremony—the review of the troops. The military parade led by the Reichswehr marched briskly past the church door: army formations, the police, the SA and the SS, and finally the veterans of the great war, the Stahlhelm. As François-Poncet wrote, all this was only the prelude, intended to create the atmosphere for the main act: the turning over of unlimited power by the Reichstag to the Leader.

The Enabling Act (or, as it was euphemistically titled, the Law for the Removal of Distress from People and Reich) permitted Hitler's government to issue laws without the participation of the Reichstag or Reichsrat for a period of four years or until it was replaced by another government. It was duly approved by the new Reichstag on the twenty-third, when it passed the required three readings with more than a two-thirds majority. It was formally approved even by men such as Brüning and Kaas, who were under few illusions as to its import but who saw no way to prevent its passage. Brüning called it "the most monstrous act ever presented to any parliament," but, like the other last-ditch opponents in the democratic, middle-class parties, he felt himself helpless in the running tide of the Nazi takeover. No one in those parties or among the Nationalists felt himself able to do much more than meet behind closed doors to protest the law. Hugenberg, whose party provided Hitler with the slim majority in the Reichstag and who had at long last become convinced of the overwhelming dangers in the Enabling Act, was among those who quietly protested. He had met with Brüning to devise some saving clauses, mainly for the protection of civil rights and to reaffirm the provisions of the constitution, but he got no further. Because of the intervention of the president's son, Oskar von Hindenburg, Hugenberg declared he was unable to reach the president to present their proposals to the only man in Germany in a position to hold Hitler to an accounting.

But the ground had slipped away from under all of them. Hugenberg had from the beginning joined the other conservatives in the cabinet, Neurath and Krosigk, in approving the draft of the act; Kaas and the other leaders of the Center Party felt themselves no longer able to resist it if their party was to have a chance for survival. A psychic avalanche was rolling over them, forming itself not so much out of mass and weight as of fanaticism and will. The Nazis were certain now that they alone would win control of Germany and get rid not only of the Communists but also of any opposition.

Hitler, Göring, Goebbels, the SA, and the SS used every means of pressure open to them for getting votes in favor of the Enabling Act—any promise or threat that was needed to cajole, coerce, or otherwise persuade the non-Nazis that they must vote for the act. They succeeded with everyone but the Social Democrats, who were the only ones to vote against it. All the others, including the Center Party, the Bavarian Volksparty, the democratic German State Party (headed by Reinhold Maier), and the Nationalists, however reluctantly, joined the National Socialists in placing all power in the hands of Adolf Hitler.

Enabling acts in one form or another were by no means new in the Reich; at the start of World War I, in mid-August 1914, the upper chamber of the parliament, the Bundesrat, had been given the right to take any necessary steps to alleviate the economic damage resulting from the war and had made use of its powers in measures going far beyond the purely economic sphere. In 1923, with the French invasion of the Ruhr and accelerating inflation, the Stresemann government had been authorized to adopt any economic, financial, and social measures that it regarded as essential and urgent, without participation of the Reichstag. In the years of continued crisis and the worsening depression, 1931 and 1932, more laws were issued by way of such emergency presidential decrees than there were by normal parliamentary processes. In 1932 the balance was overwhelming in favor of the emergency decrees—sixty compared with five laws passed by the Reichstag.[35] In 1933 the practice had continued, as we have seen, with the presidential order of February 28 in which, under the assumed threat of a Communist rising, the Hitler government was given the authority to abridge personal freedom and freedom of expression, including freedom of the press and assembly, and to invade the privacy of the mails, telephone, and domicile, giving the government, in short, the right to take almost any measures it deemed necessary to protect itself and the state. That decree resulted from the Reichstag fire, but Hitler aimed at more than emergency powers. From the start of his political career he had promised to get rid of the Reichstag and the parliamentary debates that inhibited the Leader's freedom of action; furthermore, he aimed to rule on his own, not by the limited grace of a presidential decree. At the first cabinet meeting, held on January 30, he told the ministers that once the Communists were dealt with it would be possible for the Reichstag to pass such a law, and no one in the cabinet, none of them friends of parliamentary government, made any objection.[36]

The barriers to such a law were only superficially formidable. Under the constitution two-thirds of the deputies would have to vote to end their participation in German political life. In the last completely free election, in November 1932, only one-third of the electorate had voted for the Nazis; in the March 1933 election, 43 percent voted for them. Nevertheless, Hitler was absolutely confident from the beginning that no matter what the hurdles or statistics, he would get what he wanted. And to achieve his goal he was ready to make any promise or any threat to win the votes he needed.

The president was still a threat in his own right, especially if he got the wrong advice and might be persuaded of what he had once been convinced: that Hitler would not be a reliable user of such powers as he was demanding. But Hindenburg had been worn down by age and the burdens of office. Hitler seemed to him now more a promising young man than a menace, and the pleas of anyone warning him of the dire consequences of a Hitler takeover fell on deaf ears. If he heard about the Nazi excesses, he showed no sign of it. Nor did he care what happened to the Communists who, he was convinced (the Reichstag fire was final proof) had been plotting revolution not only against the government but also against the fatherland.

While the storm troopers in the Reichstag and on the streets yelled their imprecations at the opposition, Hitler promised Kaas in their personal talks and in his speeches that his government would be based on Christianity, that he would make a concordat with the Vatican, that the president's prerogatives would never be invaded, that church and state would live together in peace and amity, and, as important as anything, that Centrist government officials would keep their jobs and receive their pensions. Kaas was eager to believe all this—promises were all he had to go on. Despite Brüning's plea that they were not enough, he accepted them.

When Kaas was told by Hitler that he looked forward to arranging a concordat with the Vatican that would regularize the relations between Germany and the Holy See and when he was assured that the Christian ethic would be the basis of the new state in which religious organizations would be undisturbed, he was impressed. These were powerful instruments of persuasion to a man who was far more clergyman than politician. Kaas was more skeptical of German Nationalists, such as Hugenberg, who were mainly Protestant and who brought back memories of the long struggle of the *Kulturkampf* than he was of Hitler who was, nominally at least, Catholic and who had as his vice chancellor a devout if politically aberrant Catholic, Papen.[37]

Brüning was astonished and depressed to hear as early as March 21 that 70 percent of the Center Party was ready to vote for the Enabling Act. Only a small fraction of the party was ready to range itself behind him to oppose the act, and there would be no point in opposing it if it would go through one way or another, as Hitler promised it would, and if those who voted against it lost their jobs and their pensions. Despite the minority status of the Nazis, the divided opposition was split into still smaller minorities.

Of the 644 deputies elected to sit in the Reichstag, eighty-one of them were Communists, who by March 1933 were shut out of political activities not only because of the wholesale arrests but also because of their own intransigence.

In all of this the Communists behaved stupidly. The Social Democrats, not the National Socialists, had long been their chief enemy. Gregori Zinoviev, president of the Comintern, had, in 1924, called the Social Democrats "a wing of fascism" and "an open battle organization of the counter revolution." Stalin said that fascism and social democracy were not "opposites" but "twin brothers."[38] One Communist Party interpretation said fascism was a necessary preliminary to the proletarian revolution; a phrase often used in party circles to describe the Social Democrats was *social fascists*. It was widely believed in the party that Hitler's taking power would be a greater blow to the Social Democrats than to the Communists, who would then be the sole alternative to fascism. No accusation was too bizarre for the party line. The Social Democrats were denounced for their alleged aid to the "imperialist interventions" against the Soviet Union, and, since the Socialist Democrats favored a reconciliation with France, many Communists regarded them as more dangerous to Russia than was Hitler, who could be expected to perpetuate the tension between Berlin and Paris but leave Moscow unscathed.

After Hitler's seizure of power the central committee of the German Communist Party was belatedly ready to make some tactical concessions to the Social

Democrats.[39] They were willing to propose a combined appeal to their followers to organize against the "fascist reaction" so as to obtain the release of people of both parties who had been arrested; to demand the cancellation of the newspaper closings; to conduct mass protests, demonstrations, and strikes; to work together against wage cuts and dismissals; and to demand the exclusion of both the police and the SA from factories.

But all this was too little and too late. Brüning and others have suggested that the Communists might have combined forces in the March 5 elections, placing their eighty-one deputies at the disposal of the Social Democrats. But that would have been of little help to the anti-Hitler movement, with Communist deputies imprisoned and excluded from the Reichstag. It would have merely confirmed in the eyes of the middle and right-wing parties the charge that Communists and Social Democrats were both of them marxists and traitors. All the Communists could do now was to operate as an underground party. They had become as much prisoners of their own ideology as of the Nazis.

After the March 5 elections the Nazis were in de facto control of the government, not only of the Reich but also of the *Länder,* and they also ruled the streets where the police now seldom interfered if the Nazis beat up their enemies. In the Reichstag they made use of the same tactics of intimidation, but they were exercised with more prudence. Foreign observers noted that the proceedings in the Kroll Opera House to which the deputies had repaired were much more decorous than they had been in the former Reichstag, where the Brownshirts had shouted down their opponents and often attacked them physically. With a Nazi in the chair the voting was orderly, and with the SA not only represented in a bloc in the chamber but also lined up as guards against the walls, any recalcitrant deputy could be readily escorted from the room on the chairman's order.[40]

When Social Democrat Otto Wels got up to oppose the Enabling Act, he read his speech without flair or passion, as though it was gesture enough to make it, and he was an easy target for Hitler's flaming reply accusing the Social Democrats of responsibility for all the ills of the Weimar period. The Nazis would obviously stop at nothing to get the law they demanded. Frick declared that any deputy whose absence was unexcused would be counted as present. Göring said at one cabinet meeting that he could expel enough Social Democrats from the chamber to ensure a two-thirds majority, and he made plain that he was uninterested in any legalities. In a speech in Essen on March 11, Göring said he was grateful to his Creator that he did not know what "objective" meant; the enemies of the party need not call for justice, the Center would be driven out of its key political position, and he denounced the Catholic hierarchy, "the black smear" that, he said, had always appeared when the Reds were stealing from Germans. The three internationals—that of the church, of the Reds, and of Jewish finance capital—had to be conquered, and he would see to it that the Reichstag had a law laid before it that not only got rid of undesirable officials without their receiving a pension but also required some officials to pay back what they had improperly received in the past.[41]

Such were the threats, and along with them were the promises Hitler made in his addresses to the Reichstag and in his conversations with Kaas. Hitler told the Reichstag on March 23 that he needed the Enabling Act to help him, together with the Nationals, to fulfill his tasks. He had no intention, he said, of doing away with the Reichstag; on the contrary, it would be convened from time to time, and the government would make use of this law only to enable it to carry out measures necessary for the life of the society. Neither the existence of the Reichstag nor of the Reichsrat was threatened. The position and the powers of the president would remain untouched, the *Länder* would not be ignored, and the rights of the church would be undiminished and its relationship to the state unchanged.[42] What the regime of national reconstruction was offering the parties, Hitler said, was the possibility of a peaceful German development and the way to future understanding.

Brüning for one was not satisfied with such generalizations, and he persuaded Kaas that Hitler must write a letter that would spell out the limitations of the powers bestowed on the government. This letter, too, Hitler promised to send; not only did he promise to write it, but he also said the letter was in fact written and was on its way to the Reichstag. But it never came, and Kaas and Brüning, too, had nothing left but to vote for the law. So did 441 deputies; only 94—all of them Social Democrats—voted nay. After the vote Brüning walked toward the exit; he was greeted by a battalion of SS men lined up in front of the door with shouts of "Down with Brüning. Knock him dead."[43] But Brüning walked on; the shouts died down, and the SS were silent as he went grimly past them to get into his car.

Hitler was disarming the opposition, dealing with it section by section. In early February, just after he took power, he told the military leaders precisely what he knew they wanted to hear—that the Reichswehr would be the sole bearers of arms in Germany; that his battle would henceforth be waged solely against the Versailles treaty and the military limitations on Germany and that every penny he could lay his hands on would be used to build up the armed forces. He assured the generals that the Reichswehr in the future as in the past would be kept out of politics; nor would the SS and the SA be absorbed into the army as rumormongers said they would. He had fulsome praise for Hindenburg and promised he would do all in his power to maintain peace with England.[44]

Although no officer would be likely to disagree with any of the points he made, there were skeptical voices. General Wilhelm von Leeb remarked that a merchant offering good wares need not sell them in such shrill tones. Other critics, among them Generals Bussche-Ippenburg, Adam, Gienanth, and Boehm-Tettelbach, were unimpressed; they agreed he was trying "to smear their mouths with pap."[45]

But little came of the dissidents. Hitler's words were certainly designed to be reassuring to military men, but what he said would not long comport with what he actually ordered. On April 11 Blomberg informed the Reichswehr that, contrary to former rules forbidding its participation in political activities, it henceforth was to demonstrate publicly that it made common cause with the "national movement" and supported all efforts on behalf of nationalist goals. For the May 1 celebration that the Nazis called the Day of National Work and "the most powerful expression of a unified people," which was designed to counter the traditional marxist May Day demonstrations, Blomberg issued a decree on the Participation of the Reichswehr in Ceremonies Outside the Defense Forces. He declared that the Hitler regime had so fundamentally changed German political life that the Wehrmacht was now to be completely identified with the state. The attitude of every soldier had to be determined by the feeling for unity and common purpose shared "with every national thinking and striving German." On May 4, after Hitler had called for the establishment of a foundation for aiding the families of incapacitated workers, Blomberg ordered that the Reichswehr arrange its own gatherings "to demonstrate its solidarity with the thinking of the Reichschancellor." On May 15 Blomberg ordered that Reichswehr personnel were to reciprocally salute national party formations as a sign of their comradely alliance, and in any public meeting members of the armed forces were to manifest their solidarity with the national movement.[46]

Blomberg had gone over to the regime. On May 27 he extended the Law for the Restoration of Career Officialdom to apply to officials, employees, and workers of the Reichswehr, and on July 20 he ordered that soldiers' brides "must be of Aryan descent" and come from reputable families that are "not inclined to be enemies of the state" *(Die Braut muss arischer Abstammung [und] einer nicht staatsfeindlichen gesinnten Familie angehören)*. On August 11 he ordered that all army bookstores stock *Mein Kampf* and recommended that soldiers buy a copy for private use. On October 20 he announced that it was the national duty of every career soldier who had served his term in the armed forces to put himself at the disposal of the National Socialist movement.[47] This could be done by joining the SA, where they would be indoctrinated in the spirit of National Socialism.

Hitler's speeches were designed for what he knew to be a critical audience, and many, especially among the younger officers, were attracted not only to the nationalist sentiments of the party but also to the possibilities of rapid advancement under its auspices. The army, like the rest of the country, was not of one mind with regard to Hitler and his Nazis. Some of those such as General

Ludwig Beck, who in the beginning took a favorable view of Hitler, soon came to be his most bitter opponents; others, such as General Alfred Jodl who thought him a charlatan, came to be convinced of his genius. The minister of Defense was one of the few among the senior officers who was pro-Nazi even before Hitler became chancellor. Brüning said Blomberg was the only Nazi general in the army and had suggested to General Wilhelm Groener, who was the minister of Defense at that time, that Blomberg, after a fall from a horse, was suffering from a nervous affliction and should be dismissed.[48] Until Hitler took power, men like Blomberg were few in the higher echelons of the army. But after Hitler became chancellor there were more of them, despite the attempts of men such as General Kurt von Hammerstein-Equord (chief of the Army Command) to keep the pro-Nazis out of key military positions. It was not Hammerstein but Blomberg who was in the seat of power, and Blomberg wanted men under him in key positions who took the same view of the party that he did.

Again, Hitler's tactics were designed to offer something to everyone; to everyone, that is, except the Left and the Jews. Actually he gave nothing substantial to anyone, nothing but reassuring promises like those he made to Kaas about a concordat, an uplift for a Christian society, and no losses of government jobs or pensions. And such assurances were sufficient for his purposes. The bourgeois parties were demoralized. They could no longer wage a political battle—they could only accept what he promised them and hope for the best. One by one decrees were issued getting rid of the opposition parties, or they dissolved themselves. First the Communists and the Social Democrats were banned; then the German and Bavarian Volksparties, the German Nationals, and the Center voted their own dissolutions. Hugenberg had to resign his cabinet post; he had no party, and the need for him had disappeared. Hitler knew all the principles of politics; they had been part of his stock-in-trade since he discovered that he could speak and that when he did people listened to him. His promises to the Centrists in the Reichstag, to Hugenberg, to the president, and to the army generals were designed for an immediate purpose, and they were kept only insofar as they remained part of a program he wished to keep.

Anti-Semitism was the one theme he would cling to all his life. He could be silent about that too, refrain from mentioning it when he spoke to industrialists from whom he was seeking support. He could even forget or at least leave anti-Semitism out of his conversation for days at a time as he talked with someone such as Albert Speer, who noted that Hitler rarely mentioned the subject. But the anti-Semitic rage was always there below the surface, ready to erupt as soon as the right button was pushed. And after the Enabling Act, the button was pushed, perhaps by the rank-and-file Nazis in the so-called seizure of power from below. The old street fighters of the SA and the SS had their turn after the Enabling Act was passed, and they owned the streets. Throughout the Reich they paraded in front of Jewish-owned stores and businesses yelling "Death to the Jews," and they meant it. German Jews reaching foreign countries told how Jews hauled into SA barracks were compelled to flog one another, and a *New York Times* correspondent reported that as a group of Jews came out of one Berlin restaurant they were forced to run a gauntlet of SA men who beat them up.[49]

The instruments of government were set to work against the Jews. The Law for the Restoration of Career Officialdom provided for the ousting of Jews from their offices, and it was in effect soon extended to every business and profession in the Reich. It was not just a campaign to diminish Jewish influence in the German economy, to limit, as it was said, their participation to their percentage of the population; it was also a deliberate campaign of harassment and humiliation that spared no Jew however eminent or useful to the state. In Stuttgart a Jewish businessman, Fritz Rosenfelder, shot himself after writing a letter to his friends saying he could not bear as a German Jew to live knowing that the movement to which nationalist Germany looked for rescue regarded him as a traitor.[50]

In Cologne, Jewish lawyers practicing in the courts were admitted to the courthouse, then arrested and brought to the front of the building where they were forced to take off their robes, after which they were led away. Rumbold reported to London that one of the foremost Jewish physicians in the Reich, Dr. Fürstenberg, was driven to suicide after he read a virulent anti-Semitic article in a medical journal and that another Jew, the orientalist Friedrich Rosen, who had served as minister for Foreign Affairs under Chancellor Wirth, had not only received notice that his pension would be reduced but also that he owed eighteen thousand marks in alleged overpayments. Rumbold said Rosen was actually a poor man who had no way of paying such a considerable sum. Artists and newspapermen, lawyers, judges and businessmen, writers and musicians, many of them world renowned, were forced to quit their jobs or to try to cling to them desperately in the forlorn hope that things might soon change.

Thousands of Germans were deeply disturbed by what was happening. Neurath, a helpless witness of the Nazi bullying tactics, though nominally foreign minister, was one of them. When the Austrian minister to Berlin, Tauschitz, was forced to listen to a Hitler tirade against the Dollfuss government, Neurath was a silent witness. When it was over Neurath went into the next room with Tauschitz, closed the door, buried his face in his hands, and said, "It is all too terrible." But he remained at his post, the British thought charitably, to have some braking effect on what was going on, and all across the Reich men like Neurath would stay in their jobs, giving similar reasons while the Nazis continued on their same paths. There can be no doubt that the Nazi behavior was deeply resented, but reactions had to be mute or the reactors would join the other "enemies of the state." Wilhelm Solf, the former ambassador to Japan, and General Hans von Seeckt (former chief of the army high command), were appalled by the events,

Rumbold wrote, and Seeckt said he felt the stigma of what the Nazis were doing so deeply he was leaving the country for a time.

There were limits to what Hitler and his party could do. Hindenburg again intervened on behalf of former Jewish soldiers. In a letter to Hitler on April 4, he wrote:

> In the last days a number of cases have been reported to me in which judges, lawyers and court officials wounded in the war, with unblemished records have been forced to retire and later have been discharged because they are of Jewish descent. For me, who with the explicit agreement of the government on the day of national awakening, on March 21, issued the proclamation to the German people in which I said I bowed reverentially before the dead and thought with gratitude on the survivors of the war, on the wounded and my old front-line comrades, such treatment of wounded Jewish officials is personally, absolutely insupportable.

Hindenburg went on to repeat that former front-line soldiers and their sons must be allowed to continue to work. If they were deemed worthy to fight and bleed for Germany, then they were equally worthy to serve the fatherland in their professions.[51]

But the effect of such a remonstrance was formal and temporary. Nothing changed in Hitler's purposes. On April 7, in an effort to make his tactics more circumspect and to effect the exceptions demanded by Hindenburg for Jews who had served as front-line soldiers or who had lost a father or son in World War I, the new laws were promulgated as to who could remain as government officials and who could be admitted to practice law. These anti-Jewish measures were soon widened to embrace other professions and to impose a *numerus clausus* on German schools and universities and on Jewish doctors whose practices were henceforth limited to private patients. And while the boycott was officially called off, the harassment of Jews in businesses and professions continued as did individual acts of terrorism.

All the while Jewish organizations themselves instructed foreigners not to intervene. Jewish war veterans on March 24 addressed a letter protesting the anti-German propaganda appearing in the United States to the American Embassy. The letter referred to "the alleged atrocities against the Jews," and while it admitted some excesses it said authorities had intervened energetically against their perpetrators. In any event, the letter said, such events had been the products of irresponsible elements, and the Jewish veterans assured the Americans that the German government sharply disapproved of such outrages. They wished to distance themselves from the blatant campaign undertaken by so-called Jewish intellectuals in foreign countries that was being conducted by people who for the most part had never regarded themselves as German, had fled to foreign countries, and, in a most critical moment, left their fellow religionists in the lurch. These people assumed the right to mix in German-Jewish affairs, and "the arrows they shoot from their secure hiding places," the veterans wrote, "certainly damage Germany and the German Jews. . . ." But they added, "Their reports are filled with exaggerations." The veterans said they would be thankful if the American Embassy would cable their protest immediately to the United States, and they offered to assume the costs. The Jewish Front Line Fighters of Hannover declared: "We German Jews have been unshakably bound for generations to the German fatherland, the German people and German honor and in the future, too, we will do everything possible in love and devotion, to serve the German fatherland. In addition, we want no foreign interference." They were joined by the Executive Committee of the Jewish Community in Berlin and by the collegium of Rabbis of the Berlin Jewish Community, as well as by other Jewish organizations, including the Central Society of German Citizens of Jewish Faith, the Association of National German Jews, and the Society for the Defense against Anti-Semitism. The German Advance Guard, a society of young Jews referring to themselves as "national German Jews," attacked the eastern and the left-wing Jews who had emigrated, declaring they had no right whatever to mix in German affairs. Among the more than a dozen Jewish organizations denouncing the anti-German campaign was the statement of a group of rabbis to the Episcopal bishop, William Manning, in New York, deploring the protest demonstrations in the United States.

The protests of German Jewish organizations in retrospect seem incredible. The *Israelitisches Familienblatt,* published in Hamburg, quoted the saying: "God protect me from my friends, I can protect myself against my enemies," in protesting "exaggerated" attacks on "our fatherland." It said everyone knew what had happened in Germany in the last weeks, a revolution had occurred and brought to the surface elements that the government itself most sharply condemned. Other newspapers—the *Jüdische Rundschau,* the *Jüdische Zeitung,* and the *C. V. Zeitung* published by the Central Society of Germans of Jewish Faith—expressed similar sentiments. Rabbi Leo Baeck was one of them. Baeck wrote that the Hitler government had two aims: to wage the battle against bolshevism and to renew Germany. He averred that the German Jews joined with the regime on both counts. Baeck, who would decide to remain in the Reich (though before the start of the war he accompanied transports of Jewish children to England where he was urged to remain), was joined by bankers, businessmen, lawyers—a cross section of German-Jewish leaders.[52]

The wish to take part in rebuilding the Reich was undoubtedly shared by thousands of non-Jews who had come to the end of their rope in the collapse of the Weimar society and who, like the Jewish veterans, were ready to gloss over or ignore the violence that one could believe was part of any revolution. They had a good deal to ignore. The Nazis were sweeping with an iron broom. Jews and any artists or writers suspected of marxist or left-wing sympathies, such as Käthe Kollwitz and Thomas Mann (who was chairman of the Academy of Letters), were forced to resign from the cultural organizations. Their pictures and books were soon banned everywhere in the Reich.

In May one of the most bizarre events of the early stages of the Hitlerian revolution took place when books that generations of Germans had revered were ceremoniously burned in a twentieth-century auto-da-fé. In 1634 heretical books had been burned in Madrid, but book burning had a precedent in Germany, too, when in 1817 in the patriotic euphoria following the war of liberation, books considered by some hundreds of students who took part in the ceremony to be "reactionary" and unpatriotic were symbolically burned.[53] In fact, however, no books had actually been destroyed—only old paper was consigned to the flames inscribed with the titles and names of authors. The year 1933 resembled 1634 as individual books were not only destroyed by fire but the works of blacklisted authors were combed out of bookstores and libraries throughout the Reich as well.

In mid-March, Goebbels and his Ministry of Volks Enlightenment and Propaganda ordered a campaign against the un-German spirit of the books and art of Jews and marxists, and two months later the antibook mission was thoroughly carried out in almost all institutions of higher learning by two competing student organizations. One was the *Deutsche Studentenschaft* founded in 1919 to which all students were obliged to belong, the other the rival *National Socialist Studentenbund* founded in 1926 and directly controlled by the party. Both organizations were run by National Socialists, but as in the case of other competing organizations in the Reich it was predictable that before long only one of them would be deemed worthy, in the eyes of the party and the government, to represent the activist students of National Socialist Germany; each was determined to be the survivor.[54]

On the nights of May 10 and May 11 throughout the Reich torchlight processions of students, wearing the colors of their corps, made their solemn way, often to the music of SA and SS bands, through university towns and cities.[55] The marches ended when the students hurled their torches onto the pyre where books on the Nazi blacklists, brought in by truckloads, were cast into the flames. In the presence of the professoriat and the entire student body, whose participation was compulsory, the titles and authors of the condemned books were intoned. The ceremony in Cologne was described in the *Neu Kölnischer Tageblatt* of May 12, 1933. "Against class warfare and materialism; for the volks community and an idealistic lifestyle, I deliver to the flames the works of Marx and Kautsky," announced one "caller." Then came the turn of the second one:

"Against decadence and moral decay; for discipline and morality in family and state, I deliver to the flames the works of Heinrich Mann, Ernst Glaeser and Erich Kästner."[56] The books of Heinrich Heine were among those destroyed as were those of Karl Marx, Thomas Mann, Stephan Zweig, Lion Feuchtwanger, Emil Ludwig, Erich Maria Remarque—anyone who was Jewish or regarded as leftist or pacifist, no matter what his or her literary reputation had been. According to the Bonn newspaper *General Anzeiger,* twenty thousand volumes were destroyed in that city alone on the night of May 10.

Little resistance was evident among the students, and only in Württemberg, Danzig, and Stuttgart did they fail to cooperate. In Württemberg the commissar for the student groups, Gerhard Schumann, a man who later became a well-known Nazi poet, for unknown reasons refused to permit the march to take place; in Stuttgart the excuse was made that the hilly terrain was not suitable for a procession; in Danzig, nominally under the governance of a League of Nations commissioner, the students reported the political situation would be unfavorable for such a demonstration. Otherwise, the students either actively or passively participated in the burnings.

How far they had departed from the norms by which they had lived until only a few months before may be seen in the protest of a British visitor. It was addressed to the executive committee of the *Deutsche Studentenschaft,* to the students who had written twelve theses against the un-German Jewish spirit, demanding of a government censor that books by Jews should be permitted to be printed only in Hebrew and that if such books were to appear in German they must be called translations. Only Germans were to be permitted to publish in German, and the un-German spirit, the theses declared, would be eradicated from bookstores. The English visitor was a physician as well as a member of the House of Commons, and he declared that he was writing "in deep contempt," that he and his colleagues were not agreed on a diagnosis of the sickness the authors of the theses suffered from, whether lues, paralysis, brain tumor, or destruction of the cerebral cortex. The German Jews, he wrote, who had contributed so much to medicine, referring, as German historian Hans-Wolfgang Strätz remarks, to Ehrlich, Wassermann, and other Nobel laureates, had not written in Hebrew but in German. He and his friends intended to publish the students' call to action in the foreign press so as to set before world opinion the evidence of German ignominy and what it would mean to be healed through German ways. Not a single German newspaper made any objection to the vandalism. The consequences of such an act doubtless would have been not only foolhardy but also disastrous.

The episode was unmistakable confirmation of what the opponents of National Socialism had long characterized as its essential nihilism. Nothing that the dadaists had written a few years before in their manifestos (printed in

France, Italy, and Germany), as they made a wholesale assault on the traditional bourgeois cultures of Europe, seemed as insane as this gratuitous destruction of a cultural heritage. The dadaists had seemed to be aesthetic dilettantes or, at worst, far-out experimentalists; these marchers represented the establishment itself, those who had been the supposed conservators of a tradition: the faculties of universities, students of higher learning, the duly constituted German government. They were turning against everything the universities had thitherto stood for and that they had been brought up to revere: the community of the spirit of creativity and learning, intellectual tolerance, and freedom of inquiry and expression that had made Germany and Austria foremost Western centers of erudition through the nineteenth century and the time of the Weimar Republic.

In this distemper the book-burning students were joined by some of the most distinguished members of the academic community. One of them was a founder of existentialism, the philosopher and metaphysician Martin Heidegger, a student of the German-Jewish founder of phenomenology, Edmund Husserl, and one of the most abstruse and influential among contemporary philosophers. He was world renowned for the range and originality of his thinking, for his bold attempt to create a fresh vocabulary to break through to far metaphysical regions. Just appointed rector of the University of Freiburg, he made an address on July 19 that strongly implied approval of the book burning. In it he praised the student body for their "determination to stand firm with German destiny in its hour of deepest need." He was scornful of "the much sung 'academic freedom,'" which he said would be driven out of the German universities. It was not a genuine freedom because it was merely a negation: "it meant above all else noninvolvement, a negligent choosing of purposes, a following of inclinations; it meant indifference in deeds and in letting things go their own way. The concept of the freedom of German students is being brought back now to its true meaning. From it the future commitment and service of the German student will evolve."

Heidegger was an enthusiast. "The first student commitment is to the volks community," made manifest in the *Arbeitsdienst,* the work service. "The second commitment is to the honor and fate of the nation among the other nations" requiring of those "secure through knowledge and ability and tempered through discipline, to be prepared to engage themselves to the uttermost." In the future, he said, this commitment would infuse the student's entire being and would lead to the defense service, the *Wehrdienst.* "The third commitment is to the spiritual task of the German people"—the service of knowledge. It demanded a youth that dared, early in life, to plunge into manhood and whose volition included the future destiny of the nation. For them learning could no longer be "the hollow and quick training for a prestigious profession." Because the statesman and teacher, the physician and judge, and the priest and the architect guide this essential being of the German *volkisch* state—or watch over and uphold it in its fundamental relation to the world-forming powers of human existence—these professions and the education leading to them must therefore be surrendered to the service of learning. Knowledge does not stand in the service of the professions but the other way around. The professions bring about and govern the highest and most essential knowledge of the *Volk* concerning its entire existence. "The three commitments—through the volk to the destiny of the state in its spiritual task—are all basic to the German being. The three services springing from it, the work service, defense service, and the service of knowledge are equally essential and of equal rank."[57]

Heidegger was repeating in his murky and elevated language what the student "caller" was saying when the latter threw the books into the fire with the incantation: "Against class warfare and materialism; for the volks community and an idealistic life-style." Some things obviously had to be destroyed if the nation was to get rid of the accumulated debris of past errors and to rededicate itself to eternal Germanic, spiritual values. And thus the eminent, esoteric philosopher came to much the same view as did an untutored crackpot Gauleiter such as Julius Streicher.

The revolution spared nothing and no one. It was not just books that were being destroyed. As Heine had written a century before: "There where books are burned, in the end people too are burned."[58] Jews and anyone suspected of having been an enemy of the Nazis were already being hounded from their posts to end up, if they could not emigrate, in concentration camps. A man such as Brüning soon thought it imprudent to sleep at his house, spending his nights in the apartments of one friend after another before he could manage to emigrate.

A good many people refused to believe that this was happening on a large scale or, like the Jews who protested against the reports in the foreign press, they preferred to believe that even if it was happening it would not last for long. Still, many non-Nazis, including Rumbold, agreed that there were too many Jews in the German learned professions and that the influx of Jews from the East, especially from Poland where Barmat and Sklarek had come from, was abrasive to both Christians and German Jews. Frick reported that 48 percent of the doctors, 54 percent of the lawyers, and 80 percent of theater directors in the Reich were Jews and that in Prussia the percentage of Jews in leading positions in industry and business was ten times that of the Aryan Germans. The truth was that Hitler's anti-Semitic campaign took hold in a society in disarray. Up to that time the percentage of Jews in this or that profession might be attributed to the intelligence and work ethic of the Jews, who might be resented but were not considered candidates for expulsion from the society. After disappearing from the German political scene in 1914 to return only in small clusters up to 1930, by the spring of 1933 the anti-Semites were back and running the country.

While some Nazis were finding jobs because it was politically expedient to hire them, Hitler was dealing directly with the problem of unemployment, which in February had reached a peak of over 6 million. In two decrees issued on May 31 and September 21 he ordered public works projects on a larger scale than previous, fiscally prudent governments had undertaken—the building of autobahns, housing, utility facilities, canals, dikes—up to a billion marks to be financed through treasury notes. Women working in industry and business were to be encouraged to quit and return to domestic jobs and, with the aid of government loans, to marry. A commission under the president of the Reichsbank was to work out wider financing of the make-work program, which, until rearmament provided thousands of jobs, was to be the key to the German economic recovery. It was an inflationary program, and the rise in prices could only be controlled or masked through wage and price restrictions.

On July 6, in a speech that avoided specific instructions, Hitler told a conference of *Reichsstatthälter*, governors of the provinces, that the revolution was over.[59] The decisions of individuals must replace the ineptitudes of the democratic state. Revolution was not a permanent condition nor should it become one—it must be diverted to an evolution where the most important task would be the education of people about National Socialist ideas. Therefore, said Hitler, no economist should be discharged because he was not yet a National Socialist providing he was a good economist, especially not if the National Socialist replacing him knew nothing of economics. Our job, said Hitler, is to provide work, work, and again work. The party had now become the state, and all authority was vested in the concept of the *Volk*. Again the words were fair and promising—a competent workman, even if he was not a Nazi, might keep his job if he had one, and if he did not, the government was on the way to providing one. The Reich was centralized, the *Länder* were governed by National Socialists, *Statthälter* were appointed as proconsuls to administer them—a beginning had been made to get rid of any potential opposition to the Nazi Party.

The political parties had finally been dissolved, and it remained only to sweep away the democratic debris. The pretense of a coalition government had vanished. Hitler, far from being contained by the conservatives, had made them his prisoners. He still made his moves with a degree of caution until he was ready to strike down or assimilate the non-Nazis, but when he was ready he struck with deadly precision. The Enabling Act had given the entire cabinet, not just the Reichschancellor, the power to enact laws, and the act declared the power would lapse when the government was replaced. That provision could apply to a change of cabinet as well as to a new chancellor, and Hitler for a time had to be careful to prevent the German Nationals from becoming an opposition party. But they were no longer a cohesive party and some members, such as Hans Bernd Gisevius and Axel von Freytagh-Loringhoven, were leaning toward Hitler.

By early July every party other than the National Socialists was dissolved either by government decree, as in the case of the Communists and Socialists, or by its own decision, as in the case of the Centrists, the German Nationalist Volks Party and the other middle-class parties. With them the nationalist, patriotic formations were declared illegal on the pretext that Communists had been flocking to their banners to continue their work of sabotaging the government, and the Stahlhelm, against which the same charges had been made, placed itself under the leadership of Hitler. Hugenberg, finding himself increasingly isolated and powerless, had resigned from the cabinet even before his party voted to dissolve itself, though Hitler urged him to stay on. After he quit, Hitler told one of the National's leaders, Freytagh-Loringhoven, that if the Nationals went into opposition (which both Hugenberg and Freytagh-Loringhoven assured him they had no intention of doing), thousands of members who were government officials would find themselves on the street the next morning, and he added piously that he could do nothing to prevent it.[60] The executive committee of the German National Volksparty thereupon voted fifty-six to four to dissolve, and as soon as that happened Hitler had State Secretary Meissner tell Hugenberg that he had not, after all, invited him to remain in the cabinet—the putative invitation was a misunderstanding.

In one day, July 14, the Hitler government enacted more than twenty-five laws, including one to permit the confiscation of goods of "enemies of the people and the state" and another to establish courts to oversee a program designed to keep the race strong and healthy "for the prevention of tainted progeny." A long list of *volkisch* legislation was enacted on that day—a law limiting the use of machinery in manufacturing cigars, another forbidding the founding of new parties, another permitting the withdrawal of German citizenship from naturalized aliens, others on price controls, the admission of court and patent lawyers to practice, and on the limited conditions under which new farm holdings might be acquired.

In foreign affairs Hitler was moving to widen the breach in the ranks of his divided enemies. He was the only one who could revive an Allied front, and he took pains to avoid it. Despite the anti-Communist measures in the Reich, relations with the Soviet Union remained outwardly normal and correct. Foreign Commissar Maxim Litvinov stopped off in Berlin on his way back to Moscow after making a tour of Western capitals, and Arthur Rosenberg, writing in the *Völkischer Beobachter*, declared that the representatives of the Soviet Union were to be treated like those of any foreign power. Germany, so Hitler and his ministers Goebbels and Neurath told French representatives, had no claims against France, no thought of revanche. Nothing was at issue that could lead to war in Europe. The one outstanding problem, that of the Saar, would be solved when the obligatory plebiscite was held in 1935, and while Hitler thought it might be a good idea for France to return the territory to Germany without awaiting the results of the vote, which was bound to go heavily against her, the Reich was willing to await the scheduled referendum.

Hitler had to deal with his opponents present, past, and future one at a time and ad hoc. His Reich had territorial claims on almost all the neighboring states: Lithuania (Memel), Czechoslovakia (the Sudetenland), Poland (Danzig, the Corridor, Upper Silesia), Austria, France, Belgium, not to mention his ambitions in the East, in the Soviet Union, but he could only deal with them separately. He would soon conclude a nonaggression pact with Poland at the cost of renouncing, for the time being at least, one of the most pressing claims the Reich had on revising the Versailles treaty. His options were limited, and he played the cards at his disposal with considerable skill.

Nevertheless, the way was made easier for him in winning popular support in Germany by the transparent subterfuges of the former Western Allies as they attempted to make a plausible case for maintaining their own huge military superiority and to avoid allowing the Reich to catch up.

In a speech to the Reichstag on May 17, Hitler told the cheering deputies and a skeptical world of the peaceful intentions of Germany and recited the well-known but always emotionally inciting list of the wrongs committed at Paris in 1919. The necessity for the revision of the Versailles treaty, he said, was recognized even by those who had drawn it up. A new configuration was needed among the European powers so the blood sacrifice of both victors and vanquished would not have been in vain. Ranged against a disarmed Germany were the French air force with over 3,000 planes, plus 350 Belgian, 700 Polish, and 670 Czech planes, not to mention the tanks and battle wagons of which the Reich had none. Germany, he said, was ready to consider both the English and the American disarmament proposals.[61]

The Reich was ready to renounce all aggressive weapons if other countries would destroy theirs; it had no thought of attacking any country—its only concern was its own security. In his speech Hitler even agreed with the pacifists that no genuine international reconstruction was possible without disarmament, and the Reich was ready, he said, to undertake unselfishly any obligation that would secure the peace of the world. He pointed out that the massive Polish and French armaments could scarcely be attributed to fear of a German invasion; Germany had no weapons of attack, no heavy artillery, no tanks, no bombers, no poison gas. The only country that had reason to fear invasion was Germany, which was without even weapons of defense. The Reich wanted nothing better than to assist in the final healing of the wounds of the war and of the Versailles treaty. But it would not accept the perpetuation of a permanent disqualification. It might, against all the principles of justice and morality, be possible to rape Germany, but it would not be possible to get her approval of such an act. He warned that with the continuing defamation of the Reich in foreign countries it would be difficult for Germany to remain in the League of Nations, and if the one-sided practices continued they would only lead to political and economic catastrophe. The Versailles treaty had brought misery to Germany, destroyed the existence of millions of people, ruined entire professions, and brought into existence an army of unemployed. A total of 224,900 Germans had committed suicide; they were the incorruptible complainants against the spirit and fulfillment of the treaty. The task at hand was to find a way to final understanding among all the peoples of Europe on the basis of equal rights.[62]

Hitler made no mention of Austria, where that country's National Socialists were preparing a coup against the Dollfuss government. The time for such a matter would come later—in the case of Austria not much later—when on May 27, as a reprisal against forbidding the display of National Socialist emblems in Austria and the expulsion of Hans Frank, the Bavarian minister of Justice, for an inflammatory speech on the Austrian radio, Hitler set a fee of one thousand marks for a travel visa to be paid by any German wishing to visit Austria. It was intended as a blow against an already staggering Austrian economy whose main source of income was tourism. What he said in his speech was most persuasive for domestic consumption but far less so for France and Britain. He had, however, a cautiously sympathetic listener in Premier Benito Mussolini who continued to be on the revisionist side against France and her allies in the Little Entente but who remained adamant on the independence of Austria and whose Germanic inhabitants and territory in the Tirol had been one of the few acquisitions Italy had made from participation in the war.

The speech, like so many of his polemics before he became chancellor, was no more than a propaganda piece imperfectly designed to allay the fears of his enemies but well directed to mobilize German public opinion behind him. Amid all the talk of his love for peace he did mention one thing he really had in mind—the possibility of Germany leaving the disarmament conference and the League of Nations. That is what he was soon to do—on October 14, when, after a year and a half of intermittent meetings, the conference had wrangled its way to nowhere.[63]

And so from what appeared to be weakness in foreign policy came strength. His enemies had dealt him high cards to play in an activist policy. When, at the disarmament conference, the Reich proposed that it be permitted an army of three hundred thousand men to serve shorter terms than the one-hundred-thousand-man army, France would have none of it. As a result of the war and the peace treaties, almost all the Reich's neighbors had German and other minorities living reluctantly under the sovereignty of foreign powers that often used rough methods to keep them in subordinate places. In Austria the whole country appeared to be on the dole, with a German population barely surviving on foreign loans, reduced from a high standard of living and self-evaluation to a state of economic and psychic poverty. France obviously had not the slightest intention of relinquishing any fraction of its armaments superiority over the Reich, and while British officials spoke often of the urgent need for a disarmament agreement, what they proposed somehow always had unequal applications. President Franklin D. Roosevelt added his words on the need to abide by treaties that disarmed only the powers defeated in the world war; Hitler could deal with their rhetoric not only by words but also by deeds.

Everything turned to Germany's advantage. Hitler quit both the disarmament conference and the League of Nations and soon stepped up clandestine rearmament of the Reich.[64] He cut through all the diplomatic verbiage and the complicated reasons the Allies had given for more than a year to show why Germany could not have the same armed forces they themselves were permitted to have by bypassing the devices of collective security that had never, in either Hitler's or Mussolini's opinion, served any but the victorious powers. And rearmament itself served many purposes, not least of all that of providing a solution for unemployment. When on September 23 the first autobahn was officially opened between Frankfurt and Heidelberg, it was seen as a dramatic start in Hitler's accelerated make-work program, and by the end of the year unemployment was in fact down by 2 million from its high of over 6 million. But it was only rearmament that would end the problem for Germany as it would for the United States when years later, after the New Deal's own make-work program had made only moderate dents in unemployment, the United States started to build up its armaments on a grand scale. Germany's public works program, like the concordat Hitler concluded with the Vatican, was a minor way station on his road to reestablishing the Reich as a power to be reckoned with.

On the day that Germany left the League of Nations, Hitler rediscovered the Reichstag, calling for new elections and a plebiscite to approve his policies. With no opposition parties, full control of the government, the newspapers and radio, the army, and the police, including the secret police—the Gestapo, established in May to combat any antistate activity—he could be certain now of an overwhelming majority to approve his dynamic courses by a people that had few if any other choices. From his *volkisch* and antiparliamentary point of view plebiscites were preferable to elections, but with only his own party appearing on the ballot and a popular issue at hand he could readily combine the two. Again he continued to play on surefire popular leitmotiv such as the one-sided disarmament of the Reich, the patent discrimination that had so disturbed even such an internationalist as Stresemann that he, Stresemann, had threatened in 1929 to take the Reich out of the League of Nations of which he had been one of the chief supporters, unless the Allies carried out their treaty obligations.

The German government and the German people, Hitler said in his proclamation announcing the forthcoming vote, believed force to be an impermissible means of resolving differences among nations. The German government and the German people would destroy the last machine gun and discharge the last man from the army if other nations would do the same. They would join at any time in nonaggression pacts to secure the peace of Europe; they would foster its economic well-being and take part in its cultural rebuilding. The German government and the German people shared the same concept of honor that considered granting of equality to Germany an indispensable moral and factual precondition for taking part in any international organizations or treaties. They were, therefore, unanimous in the decision to leave the disarmament conference and the League of Nations until this equality was achieved, and they would never in the future sign any treaty that would perpetuate the distress and misery of the Versailles treaty. They did not want an arms race, they sought only the tranquility and freedom that guaranteed the peaceful right to work. They wished to ensure these justifiable demands of the German nation through negotiations and treaties.

The government asked the German people whether they approved this policy as an expression of their own conception and would solemnly profess their belief in it. Posters were produced with quotations from recent speeches of David Lloyd George who had once campaigned on slogans of "Hang the Kaiser" and making Germany pay "until the pips squeak." Now Lloyd George was lashing out at the Allies' position on disarmament. "The most abominable breach of treaty obligations in the history of the world," the Welshman said. "The right is on Germany's side." He had asked rhetorical questions: "Could any self-respecting nation do otherwise than Germany is doing?" "How long would we English tolerate such a humiliation in similar circumstances?" Other signs urged Germans toward a better world: "We want honor and equality." "Vote for Hitler against the insanity of rearmament." "Vote for Hitler and peace." Or they were sentimental: "We do not want to be a second-class nation." "Germany's dead demand your vote." "Vote for those who died for you." War cripples sitting in wheelchairs spread out placards: "Have you cast your vote for Hitler? If not our sacrifice has been in vain."[65] Posters identified Hitler with Hindenburg. One, "The Marshal and the Corporal," showed photographs of both men and urged the voter to "Fight with us for peace and equality."

Hindenburg made a speech supporting Hitler, peace, honor, and equality, and Hitler himself went all out on a platform made to order for him. In his closing speech given two days before the election held on November 12, he addressed the workers at the Siemens plant in Berlin and a nationwide radio audience. The speech began with the same tall story he had told in *Mein Kampf* and that over the years had become a stock item in any oration addressed to a mass audience. Only part of what he said was true, but it was skillfully mixed with statements that were accepted as true by the entire population and thus could be very effective.

"My German workers," he said, "when I speak to you today and to millions of other German workers I have more right than anybody else to do so. I have come out of your ranks, once stood among you, fought for four and a half years in your midst and now speak to you, to whom I belong, with whom I feel at one, and for whom in the long run I am fighting. . . . I lead the battle for millions of our upright, industrious, working and creative people." Therefore, he said, he turned to them in this historic hour. They had, however, he reminded them, failed once with terrible consequences, and they must not fail a second time; the results would again be appalling for a long time to come. He repeated that like them he had been a worker in his youth: "Then through diligence and study, and I can also say through hunger, I slowly worked my way upwards. But in my innermost being I have always remained what I was before"—that is, a worker. He said he had been no more responsible for the war than anyone among them for like them he was unknown at the time, one of the millions at the mercy of fate. But he had not been one of those who had ranged themselves against their own nation.

He reminded them of the infamies of the Versailles treaty and its twin theses that there could always be the privileged victors ranged against the conquered who had no rights; and that if one people was disadvantaged the other was better off. These were doctrines that had had disastrous consequences, not only for Germans but also for other peoples; they had brought not peace but enmity to the world, and he was as determined to replace such ideas as he was to alter the class structure of the Reich, for class war and international war were of the same stripe. One class no more than one nation is better off because another is worse off. Conflicts between peoples are fostered by "a rootless, international clique," by those who are nowhere at home and have no soil of their own, as opposed to the *Volk* who are linked to the soil as the worker is to his work.

The strength of the German people was to be found not in a phantom of international solidarity but in the homeland itself. His goal from the first had been to awaken and strengthen this force. Therefore, Hitler said, citing the liturgy he had used for fourteen years, his movement was something entirely new; he had wanted to create a nation with the *Volk* as its source—its eternal source—where class, birth, and money had little meaning. First he would provide work and bread, but the program to combine nationalism with socialism could only be accomplished over a period of time, through education. He had begun with six or seven men, and now his movement was the largest in Germany; and all this had been achieved not by chance but through ideas—ideas that were right. He had needed great tenacity and an indomitable will just to begin this work, and the strength for accomplishing his task had not been given him by intellectuals. He had had the courage to move forward because "I, myself, knew the German worker and the German farmer." It was a gigantic program he had planned, and he had only one wish: to bring it to completion. What would a title mean to him? "I need no title. My name, which I have forged out of my own strength, is my title. . . . I told you," he said, "you must give me four years' time," and even in a short period, he reminded them, he had done pretty well. In nine months he had reduced unemployment from 6.2 million to 3.7 million. The German middle class must not believe they were doing well if the workers are doing badly. On the contrary, if people have work they also have buying power. The strength of a people is an entity.

There were those who liked to think that he was insane enough to want war. On the contrary, he assured his listeners, "I don't know how many among foreign statesmen fought in the war as soldiers but I have fought in it. I know it. And from among those who today are reviling Germany and calumniating the German people, I know this much—not one of them has ever heard the sound of a bullet." He had never, in these nine months, done anything to damage any foreign statesmen or country, and they in turn should leave Germany alone.

> We will not mix in the affairs of other countries, and they should not mix in ours. If for that matter, any people in the world should feel themselves threatened, we are that people. We want peace and understanding, nothing more. We want to stretch out our hands to our opponents to put an end to one of the most tragic times in world history.
>
> If the world wants to dictate to Germany then it will do so without my signature. And if the world says it can't trust the German people, how can that be? When had the German people ever broken its word? On the contrary, they had kept it too obstinately and loyally. If we had not kept faith with our allies in the war so stubbornly and loyally, Germany might have had an easier time of it. We protest against judging the character of a country by its emigrants. . . . The really worthy ones are those who stay in a country and work and create, and not the international gypsies.

The speech was well received not only in Germany but in some foreign countries as well. The English diplomat Sir Eric Phipps called it "a masterpiece. . . . worded in such a way that even the illiterate could grasp it."[66] It was made out of the grab bag of stock ideas Hitler carried with him, and it was well pitched to stir the emotions of a dispirited people who had tried the remedies prescribed for them by the victorious powers and by the democratic statesmen who had led the Reich since 1918 and still had found themselves suffering from the same diseases. Hitler's pattern of mixing half-truths and outright lies remained what it had always been. He was the worker who had fought his way upward against enormous odds. He, too, like millions of Germans, had suffered from hunger and deprivation. They could see in him a comrade, a brother who understood them and cared deeply for them because he was one of them. No matter that he had been a worker in their sense for only a few days, he had no opponents who could point that out. His title of worker, or former worker, was self-bestowed.[67] He had never worked for more than a few days at a time at any gainful employment, other than painting or selling picture postcards, until he joined the army and after that began a political career. The iniquities of the Versailles treaty were surefire, and so was the fact that at long last he was moving to undo their last vestiges by demanding equality and telling the Allies that without such equality he would participate in none of their international conferences.

Also, he had actually reduced unemployment. He had done it by ignoring the economic doctrines followed by his predecessors terrified of fueling another inflation with costly government projects. Armed with his own doctrine of the primacy of politics over economics he had far less fear of deficit spending than they had. People, the *Volk,* produced values, gave the mark (as they did all symbols of government) its value, and if they worked as the Germans were eager to do and produced as no people could do better than they, he would strangle any inflation with his iron controls.

Germany, he said, wanted merely to be left alone to carry out its high purposes; it wanted peace and work and would not interfere in the affairs of others. Even as he spoke, the National Socialists in Austria were preparing a coup in the country where he was born, which he planned to take over as soon as possible. But he gave no hint of such plans. Similarly he made only indirect mention of the Jews when he talked of a rootless, international clique. He addressed no threats to his enemies. He was simply presenting his German people with the opportunity to redeem their past through him, to be able to work and prosper again and look the world in the eye as equals.

On November 12, 95.7 percent of those eligible to vote cast their ballots for the single list of candidates put forward by the National Socialists, who received 92 percent of the vote and elected 639 deputies. Of the eligible voting population 96.3 percent took part in the plebiscite; 40.6 million voted "yes" on the question of whether they approved of the government's policies, and 2.1 million voted "no."[68]

It seemed to be an overwhelming vote of confidence, but was it? The voting admittedly was a bit skewed in favor of the Hitler supporters. What, as a British observer asked, had become of the 5 or 6 million Communists and the 10 million Socialists who had voted against Hitler only nine months before? Some of them undoubtedly were among the abstainers and the "no" voters, but thousands of them must have voted for the National Socialists. As foreign observers noted, Hitler had undoubtedly restored a sense of confidence and dignity to millions of Germans who for years had been living on handouts. And there was also fear, coercion, and time-serving, as may be seen in what should have been the embarrassing 100 percent vote of the inmates of Dachau in favor of his policies. The party apparatus saw to it that people voted even if they had to be carried to the polling places on stretchers. And, though the balloting was secret, how people voted could often be checked, as local party leaders watched the polls closely and were able to spot a bloc of abstainers or anti-Nazi voters. In some smaller polling places even the vote of an individual might be checked. So it was very dangerous for anyone in public employment to vote "no"; not only his job but also his pension could be lost. In one Rhineland town voters even avoided going into the voting booths but took care to cast their ballots in full sight of the officials.

Other factors encouraged the "yes" voters. There was hope in Hitler's program for those on relief. The Winter Help Movement, through the collection boxes of the SA, provided more than 350 million marks to supplement the meager subsistence of more than 6.6 million needy people. And there were circuses as well as bread. At the party rally in Nuremberg, called the Party Day for Victory and the Triumph of Belief—belief of the people, of the party fighters, and especially of Hitler—150,000 officials participated on the Zeppelin Field, and 100,000 SA, SS, and Stahlhelm men paraded past Hitler, who spoke about race: culture and race and *Volk* and race. The spectacular trial of the four Communists accused of setting the Reichstag fire, which he had not mentioned in his last speech, took place in Leipzig between September 21 and December 23. It was continuing evidence of the dangers besetting the Reich and also of its high quality of justice, for to Hitler's indignation only van der Lubbe was found guilty and beheaded. The others were released.

It was clearly a threadbare society in motion toward a promise of better days. For those accepted as a part of it there was evidence of a will for mutual aid and communality of which there had been few signs since the end of the world war. For the "no" voters, the abstainers, there was either outer or inner emigration.

2

Röhm

The Early Disenchanted

Hitler's luck while it lasted was extraordinary. He had come to power in 1933 by way of successive calamities over which he had little or no control but all of which he could promise to exorcise. In 1934 he was to magnify and consolidate that power beyond anything a Hohenzollern emperor might have dreamed of by way of three tragedies that, like the consequences of the Reichstag fire, he was able to divert to his purposes. He was operating as he had been since 1919 with a people shaken by one crisis after another, and when things had gone better, as they did for a few years in the late twenties, his movement had dwindled to an insignificant splinter group. After four years of the ever-deepening depression, he had come on strongly to win the approval of one-third of the electorate and then, with the short-lived collaboration of former and later opponents, the chancellorship itself. After that his run of luck and the flounderings of the postwar world continued to work for him, and no one knew better than he how to move into the troubled waters with a wide-flung net.

The militant arm of the party had been from the early days the SA, to which Hitler often said the movement owed everything. Founded in August 1921 the SA was headed first by former navy lieutenant Klintzsch, who was recommended to Hitler by Captain Ehrhardt to whose Free Corps brigade Klintzsch had belonged. Then, after a succession of leaders, including Göring, Hitler twice named Ernst

Röhm as chief. A former captain in the Reichswehr, he was a swashbuckling career soldier and a homosexual who made no secret of his sexual preferences or of his intellectual limitations, which he obviously considered an essential ingredient in his soldierly qualities.

In the foreword to his autobiography Röhm wrote: "I am a soldier, I see the world from my soldierly standpoint. Consciously one-sided."[1] He was eighteen years old when, after what he rightly called an undistinguished nine years in the royal humanistic Maximilian Gymnasium in Munich, he became an ensign *(Fähnrich)* in the Royal Bavarian Tenth Infantry Regiment, Prince Ludwig, and the dream of his youth was fulfilled. A military career, the only one that ever interested him, was not in his blood; his father was a railroad official, and the one soldier in his family was an uncle who served in the Franco-Prussian war. Röhm, however, was one of those Bavarians more Prussian than the Prussians, a man who believed soldiers should be preeminent in the state, and in a country where they were not so privileged, he wrote, "there is no peace and wars are lost." He was a man formidably circumscribed by the qualities that made him a good front-line soldier: simplistic, driving, embattled on behalf of his purposes, contemptuous of anyone who disagreed with them.

Röhm served throughout the world war as an infantry officer and was twice badly wounded, the second time requiring months of convalescence after which, since he was not able to return to his front-line duties, he was assigned to the staff of his old regiment. He was awarded three decorations, including the Iron Cross first and second class, and the commendations of his superior officers. Like Hitler he blamed the defeat of 1918 wholly on the failure of the home front and rear echelons to support the front-line fighters for whom he had nothing but praise. They, like his Royal Bavarian Tenth Infantry Regiment, which by September 1914 had lost 80 percent of its officers and 70 percent of its men, were a race apart and chosen among the peoples of the Reich and of every other country. They were the victors and the victims of the war, undefeated in the field, subjected to the humiliations of the armistice and peace by the same "November criminals" who, along with the Jews, headed Hitler's list of the infamous betrayers of the nation.

Early in 1919 Röhm had joined the Freikorps von Epp, a Bavarian formation headed by Colonel Franz Ritter von Epp that in October was inducted into the new Reichswehr. It was Röhm who was put in charge of the Bavarian ordinance department, the Feldzugmeisterei, and who in 1923 was thus able to provide the arms from Reichswehr stores for Hitler and the patriotic right wing, *Verbände,* a number of whom together with the SA were to attempt to take over the government in November. From 1918 Röhm was wholly devoted to the radical right-wing, free-corps formations. While he was still in the army, before he was forced to resign his commission for his blatant antigovernment activity, he was a founder of one such formation, the Reichskriegsflagge. When Hitler proclaimed his revolution in November 1923, Röhm took part in the uprising and for a few hours occupied the Ministry of War in Munich with his Reichskriegsflagge before he could be persuaded by Epp and Ludendorff to surrender.

Like many officers in the free-corps movement Röhm was a convinced monarchist. He had hoped to win over the crown prince of Bavaria, Ruprecht (whom he referred to as "King"), to the nationalist revolutionary cause, and in the first and second editions of his memoirs a passage occurs that was omitted from the later versions, which appeared under the imprint of the official National Socialist publisher, Franz Eher. In the earlier editions Röhm wrote that he wanted to bring "His Majesty the King closer to the undertakings of the *Kampfbund*." He described how with the black, white, and red and swastika banners fluttering in the wind the "King," along with General von Lossow and other high officers, had stood in front of the royal residence to review the march-past of the free-corps troops during the memorial-day services for the dead on November 4, 1923, in Munich. "These and similar thoughts moved us officers, above all our soldierly leader, First Lieutenant Kreibel who led the Kampfbund before the King. A considerable number of our young fighters, who here with measured tread marched past the rightful king of Bavaria, were workers. Many communists, too, stood in our ranks. Again an historical hour appeared to be nearing its end. But nothing happened."[2]

This passage is omitted from the 1933 edition of the Röhm memoirs, because obviously the chief of the SA could have no leaders in mind other than Hitler. But Röhm had chosen Hitler only because he could not persuade Ruprecht to head the Kampfbund. After the putsch failed Röhm was tried with Hitler, Ludendorff, and the others. He was found guilty of high treason and sentenced to a year and three months' imprisonment. But since the trial ended in April and he had been arrested in November, he was immediately freed for time served.

Hitler, following his own release from Landsberg prison, had entrusted Röhm with the reorganization of the SA, but the two had soon broken on the issue of incorporating into the SA still another paramilitary troop founded by Röhm, the Frontbann. Röhm wrote in his memoirs that he had intended for the Frontbann, which he organized during Hitler's imprisonment, to serve as a substitute for the SA, which was declared illegal in Bavaria after the putsch, and that Hitler had made no objection to his plan when he had told him about it during a visit to Landsberg. But after Hitler's departure from the prison he would have none of the Frontbann. He did not readily tolerate foreign bodies incorporated in National Socialist formations; the Frontbann had to be dissolved and its membership assimilated into the SA. The cantankerous Röhm thereupon resigned his posts as leader both of the SA and of the Frontbann.

Disappointed in Hitler and despairing of a republican Germany where impeccable patriots like himself were jailed, Röhm emigrated in 1928 to Bolivia where, as a lieutenant colonel, he helped train the Bolivian army. During his exile he conducted a lively correspondence with old friends in the Reich, a correspondence that included highly erotic letters expressing nostalgia for the Berlin turkish baths and their male clientele. He never made any attempt to conceal his predilections, and Hitler, while Röhm was useful to him, chose either to accept or ignore them. And by the end of 1930 Hitler could make use of him again. After Röhm had spent two years in Bolivia, Hitler sent him a cable late in 1930 asking him to become chief of staff of both the SA and the SS.

The then-current leader of the SA, Franz von Pfeffer, had, after five years' service, quit the post because of political differences with Hitler, who thereupon took over the command of the SA and the SS and needed a chief of staff. Hitler was obviously unruffled by Röhm's sexual habits. As always he had his eye on what needed to be done for himself and the party, and Röhm's homosexuality was rejected only when Röhm seemed to have become disobedient and dangerous. On February 3, 1931, soon after Röhm's appointment, Hitler issued a decree to the SA, the SS, and party leaders, which plainly expressed his Olympian disregard of any moral failings of which critics had complained. He wrote:

> The leadership of the SA have before them a collection of reports and charges directed against SA leaders and men, containing especially attacks on the private lives of these personalities. Examination reveals that for the most part these have had to do with matters completely outside the framework of SA service. . . . It is demanded of the SA leadership that it make decisions regarding these matters which are purely of a private nature. I sharply reject these unreasonable demands on principle. . . . The SA is a gathering of men for a determined political goal. . . . It is no moral institute for the education of young ladies but an association of rugged fighters. . . . The task of any inquiry can only be to determine whether or not an SA leader or man fulfills his service obligations. Private life can only be an object of inspection when it is opposed to the essential principles of National Socialism. . . . In the future the higher SA leadership when they receive such charges will first have to examine whether a complainant creating discord and discontent in the SA is not himself to be held to account and under some circumstances to ask that he be dismissed from the SA and the party.[3]

Hitler may have had the drunkenness and high living of a number of the SA and party leaders in mind when he issued the decree, but it defends no one more eloquently than Röhm, the just-appointed chief of staff of the SA and the SS, about whose private life there were many rumors, most of which had substance.

But, as Hitler said, it was not the private lives of the SA and party leadership that were important to him. He needed men who unconditionally accepted his decisions and reverently carried them out, and for Röhm, as for Pfeffer before him, this unquestioning obedience held up only to a point. Pfeffer was, like Röhm, a *Haudegen,* a broadsword wielder, who broke with National Socialism because he did not like Hitler's cautious policy of legality that had grown out of the aborted 1923 putsch. As for Röhm, he along with thousands of SA men expected a good deal more than they were given after the seizure of power. The SA was made up mainly of younger men in their teens, twenties, and early thirties, and hundreds of thousands of them were still unemployed in 1934. When jobs turned up it was mainly heads of families who got them, leaving the rank and file in much the same situation they had found themselves during the Weimar Republic, despite the torchlight parades, the chants of victory, and the heady sense of power they experienced when they could throw their enemies in the improvised concentration camps. Hitler at the hour of this triumph could not do much more than praise and review them without risking his own position with Hindenburg and with the army. When he made his February 3 speech to the commanders of the armed forces he had spoken of the great conscript army to come, the people's army that would be purged of pacifism, marxism, and bolshevism. Röhm too wanted a people's army, but it would take the form of a *Volksmilitia* to be recruited through the SA and that would one day dominate the army. His notions were shared by a good many SA leaders, especially former Reichswehr officers who had not been retained in the army. Many of them were envious of those who had been kept in service; they yearned for their old military status plus the promotions due them for their services in the front line of the National Socialist revolution.

When Hitler took power in 1933 the SA numbered less than a million men. A year later, with additions from the Stahlhelm and the splinter *Verbände* that had been dissolved, it numbered more than 4 million men, a motley conglomerate of street fighters: unemployed, nationalist-minded youths along with thousands of men who had been marxists and who flocked to the SA in the hope of getting jobs or at least a place on the bandwagon. The domestic victory had been won and the enemy driven from the streets, and the Schutz Abteilung, the protection staff that had long shielded Hitler and the party orators from marxist onslaughts, was no longer needed. As Röhm wrote in an article published in June 1933, shortly before he was murdered, narrow-minded people were asking what the SS and the SA still wanted.[4] Wasn't Hitler in power? Weren't the police maintaining law and order and the army protecting the frontiers? Röhm's answer was that the SA and the SS were the cornerstones of the Nationalist Socialist state, the fighting front of the National Socialist revolution. But only Hitler could flesh out his rhetoric, give the word for the rearmament of the Reich and the establishment of a people's militia that would be the SA blown large.

Hitler, though, could not give the word Röhm was waiting for. The generals, with few exceptions, such as Blomberg and Walter von Reichenau, had seldom been favorably disposed toward the Nazis, and a number of them reacted unfavorably to what Hitler told them in February 1933—even though he promised the Wehrmacht what they all believed to be essential to the defense of the Reich. They remained suspicious of Hitler, of the gruel, as they said, he spread on their mouths and the strident pitch he made for goals they otherwise accepted. It is unlikely that many of them took seriously his remarks about the need for acquiring territory and "germanizing" the east. It was the kind of line, like *agrarian reform,* that politicians might easily throw out as a catchphrase. The speech was designed to win the support of the high command, and thus Hitler said nothing that would give aid or comfort to his critics, no word of a role for the SA, no suggestion that the people's army to come would be anything but the Reichswehr's army. It was Hindenburg and the high command of the armed forces that had to be won over; the former enemy was silent or underground, the dissidents and opposition had disappeared as organized entities—all that remained were pockets of resistance, and some of that resistance was in the ranks of the SA and the party itself. A totalitarian state, or a state in the process of becoming totalitarian, cannot permit a rallying point for opponents, and that is why Stalin had the personally harmless Trotsky murdered by the NKVD in a country thousands of miles from Russia. Trotsky had no way to lead a liberation movement against Stalin's Soviet Union, but while he remained alive he would be a rallying point for those inside and outside Russia who wanted an end to Stalin's rule. Similarly, Hitler had to prevent his enemies and victims from combining against him, and the brutal tactics of his takeover had made it clear even to some of his supporters, such as Franz von Papen, how dangerous he could be.

By 1934 the list of people who had once supported Hitler and who now wanted him curbed or superseded had grown considerably. The opposition now ranged from the disenchanted ranks of the SA and the party—from men such as Gregor Strasser who resented the absence of socialism in Hitler's economic program—to members of the proscribed parties and, especially, of the Catholic and Protestant churches. Despite Hitler's comforting words addressed to the Catholic bishop Berning at a meeting on April 26, 1933, despite his assurances given before a session of the Reichstag in March 1933 of his devotion to the principles of Christian government, and despite the concordat with the Vatican concluded on July 23, many religious leaders and laymen of both confessions became increasingly skeptical of his purposes.[5] Whatever Hitler might promise, he and the party spokesmen—such as Alfred Rosenberg, Goebbels, Rudolf Hess, and Göring—were patently indisposed to tolerate any competition from churches of any denomination in National Socialism's drive for the bodies and souls of the German people. The only portions immediately clear in the blurred texts of Rosenberg were those where he attacked the church. And it was what Rosenberg had written, not what Hitler had promised, that was borne out as Catholic newspapers were banned along with Catholic youth organizations—this when Hitler, Göring, and Nazi-minded clerics attempted to organize the Protestant churches into a government-dominated Reichs church.

The National Socialists made use of the Faith Movement of German Christians, which was founded in 1932 before Hitler came to power, to infiltrate the Protestant *(Evangelisch)* Church. The German Christians recruited from the ranks of Nationalist racist church groups were antimarxist, anti-Semitic, and they utterly rejected the traditional Christian doctrine of the brotherhood of man. They were led by a fanatical Nazi pastor, Joachim Hossenfelder, who referred to his followers as the "SA of Jesus Christ." The German Christians backed the candidacy of Ludwig Mueller, a Wehrmacht pastor from the Königsberg district who was an adviser to Hitler on matters dealing with the Protestant church and Hitler's choice to become Reichsbishop. After Hitler became chancellor, the legal Reichsbishop elected by the representatives of the *Landeskirchen,* the regional churches, Fritz von Bodenschwung, was forced to resign his post when Hitler refused to receive him. Mueller then became the titular head of the Lutheran *(Evangelisch)* Church.

The new Reichsbishop and the German Christians ran into stiff opposition from leading clerics such as Martin Niemoeller, Karl Barth, and Dietrich Bonhoeffer, an opposition as relentless in its resistance to what the German Christians were trying to do as the Nazis were in their determination to take over the Evangelical Church. When, at a meeting at the Berlin Sport Palace a spokesman for the German Christians demanded that pastors who refused to accept the new doctrines be dismissed and the Old Testament be excised from the Bible, even some of the German Christians were appalled. The uproar was so loud and prolonged that Mueller had to forbid further political activity on the part of churchmen while a third of the clergy joined the Pastors' Emergency Association, founded by Niemoeller to range themselves against the heresy. Despite the heavy political support Hitler and the party could bring to the German Christians, support that sometimes led to the arrest of dissident pastors, the German Christians were unable to subdue the embattled wing of the Protestant clergy.[6] Hitler was of no mind to engage in another protracted religious controversy, especially one where the opposition could and did appeal to Hindenburg on behalf of the traditional church, and the Faith Movement of German Christians soon began to fall apart.

As for the Catholics, though the bishops of the ecclesiastical province of Cologne declared in 1931 that Catholics recognized no religion of race, and in June 1933 the bishops of the diocese of Germany further declared that Jesus was the Redeemer of all God's kingdom on earth regardless of race or nation, the Catholic church as a body went a long way to accommodate itself to National Socialism. Almost as soon as Hitler came to power the bishops had moved toward reconciliation with the Nazis, declaring at a meeting at Fulda on March 28 that the previous warnings against joining the National Socialists were rescinded. Not much in the Nazis' anti-Semitism seems to have disturbed either Protestants or Catholics; bishops, priests, and pastors were generally silent on the subject. Pastor Niemoeller, to be sure, expressed his disapproval of racism as divisive of Christianity; twenty-two ministers in Berlin declared the Aryan paragraph could not be applied to Protestantism; and in May 1934 the Lutheran Confessional Synod declared the doctrine that the state was the sole orderer of human life was false. The German Catholic bishops carefully denied that participation in the life of the state could be solely a matter of race and blood. This would lead, they said, to injustices and impose a burden on the Christian conscience, especially in cases where a person had been reborn through the sacrament of baptism.[7] Their pronouncements were placating, too. They made clear how much they approved of authority, German unity, and other tenets of the Nazi state, and like the Protestants they made no reference to the plight of the Jews in general. What roused Catholic protests were the attacks on church institutions and such measures as the law for the Protection of Future Generations from Inherited Disease, which permitted the sterilization of anyone determined by a court to suffer from schizophrenia, epilepsy, inherited blindness or deafness, feeblemindedness, Saint Vitus' dance, a misshapen body, or alcoholism.[8] Anti-Semitism per se was apparently not a primary moral issue for either confession. The nuncio, Cardinal Pacelli, deplored the persecution of the Jews and the Nazi reign of terror when he talked with the British diplomat Ivone Kirkpatrick in August 1933, but the Catholic church was officially silent on the subject. During his conversation with Bishop Berning, Hitler was able to point out that the church, too, had always recognized how damaging the Jews were to Christian society. That was the reason, he said, the Jews historically had been segregated in ghettoes from the German population.

On one issue the position of the Catholic and Protestant prelates was clear. They both rejected the new heathenism preached by Rosenberg and the heretical assertions that when a man put on the uniform of the Reich he ceased being a Catholic or a Protestant or that one could profess a positive Christianity without belief in Christ. In such matters the responses were unequivocal. Religious conviction was not something to be put on and taken off to hang on a nail, the bishops said in their pastoral letter of June 1934; there could be no Christianity without Christ, and the Nazi assertion that what was moral was whatever benefited the race was false. What was moral, the bishops declared, was what corresponded to the will and commands of God. The bishops said further: "You have heard and read that Christianity has been a misfortune for the German people, blemishing their ancestors. We the bishops, however, say unto you the introduction of Christianity to the Germans was the most precious gift of heaven."[9]

If such were the unmistakable replies when church doctrines were transgressed, the church fathers were ready to accept a good deal outside the theological absolutes. Any Catholic organization that might remotely be considered a political trades union, youth group, and the like was proscribed. The church had traded its right to such organizations and its right to foster a Center Party for a detailed list of prerogatives that Cardinal Pacelli, who signed the accord on behalf of the Vatican, said were far more inclusive than the church had ever been able to win from the Weimar Republic.[10]

The concordat never led to the modus vivendi that Papen, Kaas, and some of the bishops had hoped for. The church was attempting to blunt the Nazi attack with the weapons it had wielded for centuries. There was Cardinal Faulhaber's memorable address made on the last day of December 1933 in which he told his Munich parishioners that it was Christianity that had united the ancient Germans, made them a *Kulturvolk,* persuaded them to beat their swords into plowshares and renounce blood revenge. It was not the Ur-German heroes but Christianity that renewed the German earth and remade the hearts of the German people. But the attacks on the church and its organizations continued and intensified. The Catholic press practically ceased to exist, and, as a Vatican remonstrance pointed out, where a church publication was still published it was even harassed for defending Catholic doctrine. Pamphlets were confiscated. Priests were taken into protective custody for opposing some government regulation, under the pretext that they were engaging in politics. The clergy, the Vatican complained in May 1934, was worse off than before the concordat was negotiated.

What Hitler was trying to do was to keep the churches quiescent while he revolutionized the Reich. He had no idea of permitting them to interfere with his course, whatever reassurances he might address to the Reichstag or to Bishop Berning on the essential need for Christianity in any society, especially one fighting marxism, godlessness, and bolshevism.

It was this growing evidence that the National Socialists would tolerate no ideological claims outside of its own that roused Papen to make his memorable speech in Marburg on June 17, 1934, a speech that very nearly cost him his life and did result in the murder of the man who drafted it, a conservative Munich lawyer and publisher, Edgar Jung. Papen was not a man of deep convictions nor was he of the stuff of martyrs. But at Marburg he spoke out in what would be his finest hour.[11] He wrote in his memoirs that he made his speech as a matter of conscience after Hindenburg, disturbed by Nazi excesses, had begged him to help bring things into order. Hitler's increasing invasions of press and church and what had been the private as well as public sector had become intolerable, and as one of the individuals most responsible for bringing Hitler to power it was his duty, Papen wrote, either to convince Hitler that he must return to the paths of moderation and legality, or Papen would quit his post. He chose the University of Marburg as the scene of the address because a large number of German intellectuals would be there who were waiting for the clarion call he intended to make. He said he had prepared the speech carefully over a long period of time, but he made no mention of Jung, the man who prepared it. A more likely story is that Papen felt himself to be increasingly isolated, ignored in any serious decisions and unable to explain to himself or his friends what role he was playing as vice chancellor. At the time Hindenburg appointed Hitler, the president had insisted that Papen always be present whenever he met with his chancellor, but that condition soon went into limbo along with Hindenburg's doubts about Hitler's capacity to be a proper Reichschancellor. Hindenburg soon not only received Hitler without Papen but also routinely approved any of Hitler's proposed measures without asking Papen or anyone else whether they were advisable. So Papen—who had lost his post of Reichskommissar for Prussia to Göring two weeks after he was given it, with the concordat he had negotiated in shreds, and with no perceptible influence—was ready to protest.

Let it be said that Papen was a believer. He was a devout Catholic, and the plight of the church, which he had convinced himself he could alleviate by bringing the Hitler movement within a framework of conservative Christian government, had, like his own position, only worsened. And not only did his political advisers, such as Jung, who proposed as he once said to use Papen as Papen thought he could use Hitler, deplore the Hitlerian incursions into church and state; Papen's reverenced church hierarchy, too, was deeply disquieted.

In his memoirs, incidentally, Papen wrote that he told his Marburg audience that Hitler had come to power by democratic means, a Papenesque distortion since it was his own devious behind-the-scenes activity rather than a popular vote that had persuaded Hindenburg. But what Papen wrote in his memoirs did not appear in his speech. The only mention of democracy at Marburg occurred when Papen said Hitler's immediate contact with the masses, after the failure of the parliamentary system, made for a kind of direct democracy that had succeeded in rewinning the derailed masses for the state. That Papen had ever entertained the idea that Hitler could be made to see the error of his ways through a public address of his vice chancellor was but another sign of Papen's political and psychological naïveté. He was goaded into making the attempt because without making it he had no hope of regaining a position of importance either in the government or on the sidelines. It was Papen who had believed that Hitler was safely in the hands of the conservatives and that Hitler, once the children's sicknesses of the revolution were overcome, would proceed to govern a Christian Germany, uniting the forces of the Right and of righteousness. Thus what Papen had done would be justified.

The tension between the SA and the Reichswehr that might well erupt into armed conflict—in Silesia, for example, they had engaged in not-infrequent brawls—led some conservatives to expect and hope for such civil unrest that Hindenburg would be forced to declare a state of emergency, and a state of emergency could lead to the restoration of the monarchy. Papen at bottom shared such nostalgic wishes; in fact, his speech referring to the need for a better regime seemed itself to hint at such an eventuality—but the full charge was aimed no further than at the Führer himself, to urge him toward Papen's Christian state with a critical press and a responsible opposition.

The speech at Marburg had precisely the opposite effect. Only parts of the text appeared in the afternoon edition of the *Frankfurter Allgemeine* before Goebbels forbade its publication. The rest was silence. The party press completely ignored the speech and while Papen's audiences at Marburg and wherever surreptitious copies circulated were enthusiastic, not many people were able to get a copy. The secret police reported how outraged party members who were present at Marburg had been; the mayor had called the speech "devastating," and at least two SA leaders had stalked out of the auditorium while it was being delivered. The police reported the speech had been well received by former Centrists, left-wingers, and reactionaries in the audience; when Papen appeared a few days later at a Hamburg racetrack the police report was confirmed when he was greeted by shouts of "Heil Marburg." Although the threat of the Catholic and non-Catholic dissidents Papen spoke for was abundantly clear to the Nazis, the meanings the party leaders read into the speech were far from those Papen intended to convey.

Papen gave his talk on June 17, 1934, and by the end of the month Hitler had set out to liquidate any focus of opposition in the SA or in political life. The question of whether Röhm had actually planned a putsch has long been debated, and the consensus of opinion among historians is that he did not. But the story is unclear. There can be no doubt that he was bitter over the restrictions on the SA and the minor role assigned him and that Hitler was well aware of his discontent.

To all observers Hitler was pleased with Röhm. In December 1933 he had made him a minister without portfolio, and in a New Year's message he had assured Röhm, one of the few people to whom he used the intimate "Du," that the revolution had been made possible only through the SA's defeat of the marxist terror. As the army had the task of protecting the nation from foreign perils, Hitler wrote, so the SA had assured the victory of National Socialism within the country. Röhm, Hitler said, had taken over the SA at a critical time and after a few years had made it a political instrument that had enabled the party to win the battle for power by conquering the marxist enemy. He closed his effusion with words of warm gratitude: "At the end of the year of National Socialist Revolution," he wrote, "I am moved to thank you, my dear Ernst Röhm, for the unforgettable service you have rendered the National Socialist movement and the German people and to assure you how grateful I am to the Fate that enabled me to call men like you my friends and fellow warriors."

It was fulsome praise, but a few days later Hitler instructed Göring and the then-chief of the secret police, Rudolf Diels, to compile a dossier on the private lives of Röhm and other suspect SA leaders. It was the first time Hitler had ever displayed any interest in the subject other than to reprimand those who complained of the behavior of those he now wanted investigated.

Röhm was completely unsuspecting. Until the first months of 1934 he seems to have cherished the hope that he and the other SA leaders were slated for high military office as the Reich rearmed. This could come about by way of his militia plan and the peoples' army in which the top SA echelons would be generals and the lesser ones Reichswehr officers or by simply, as Röhm also proposed, moving four thousand SA officers into the army. On one occasion in January 1934, in answer to a question about whether his SA officers were capable of leading an army division or corps, he said people would have a better understanding of the matter when he became minister of Defense. He intended when he assumed that position to appoint an experienced army officer as chief of staff to any SA leader he named to such a high Reichswehr post.

Röhm clung tenaciously to such dreams, but Hitler could not have named him minister of Defense even if he had wanted to. Not even pro-Nazi officers such as Blomberg and his chief of staff, Reichenau, would hear of Röhm as minister of Defense or of the SA moving en masse, with its officers, into the Reichswehr, nor would Hindenburg for a moment have countenanced such an invasion of the army. The fact was that Hitler simply had no place for the more than 4 million SA in a Germany about to rearm under the Reichswehr. In the late spring of 1933 he had resolved upon the introduction of conscription, but until that was announced and accepted by the former Allies the Reich was dependent on the SA for manpower. In July a training program was set up under Röhm with the immediate command given to SA Obergruppenführer Friedrich Wilhelm Krüger to prepare 250,000 young men as a reserve for the Reichswehr. Reichenau arranged for Krüger to be assigned as an army officer on active service as chief of staff so that the army would be in close touch with the premilitary training.

Other decisions were cutting down the importance of the SA. Its defense role on the eastern borders was minimized when late in January 1934 Hitler concluded the nonaggression pact with Poland, which made any Polish invasion of East Prussia or Silesia most unlikely. And toward the end of February he told British Undersecretary of State for Foreign Affairs Anthony Eden that the ranks of the SA would be reduced by two-thirds. Although he never made any public announcement of this decision, it is more than likely that this is what he planned to do—and news of what he had in mind certainly reached Röhm.

Hitler now threw all his weight on the side of the army. Although on February 1 Röhm cockily announced that the defense of the country was the domain of the SA, and a little later on February 21 he met with François-Poncet probably in an effort to win French support for his never-abandoned plan for a militia, Hitler late in February ordered Blomberg and Röhm to work out a plan for placing the SA under the control of the minister of Defense. The announcement declared that the Wehrmacht in every instance relating to defense took precedence and deprived Röhm of any leading role in the Reich's rearmament. The sports program would be supervised by the Reichswehr; the SA would run it in a subordinate capacity and provide the young men with target-practice rifles before the army trained them with more formidable weapons. This was the main task of the old street fighters and of the swollen ranks of what had long considered itself the spearhead of the National Socialist revolution. Now it had become a heterogeneous conglomerate with a majority of older men, thousands of whom had never been in the least attracted by National Socialism. Hitler could dispense with it and would have to if he was to gain the full support of the army.

It was an assignment (since it was under the control of the Ministry of Defense) admirably suited for the YMCA—a fitness program that would include men who had already served in the Reichswehr and enable them to keep in shape—and Röhm had nothing but contempt for it and for the future political role Hitler planned for the SA. Röhm, however, did as he was told, but as soon as the agreement was signed he declared he had no intention of keeping it. He was furious enough, after having gone through the charade of sharing a breakfast of reconciliation with high army officers, to refer to Hitler to his SA comrades as "an ignorant corporal of the World War."[12]

Röhm began to push his irritation. On March 2 Blomberg protested to Hitler that SA units, the Stabswachen that represented the main armed force of the Stabschef, Röhm, were provided with heavy machine guns and had plans to appear in public with their weapons. Since on no subject was the army more touchy than on its traditional claim to be the sole bearer of arms in the Reich, Hitler knew that it could not possibly agree to tolerate a rival armed force in Röhm's Stabswach.[13] Furthermore, the Reichswehr and Hitler were waging a running battle with the SA that flowed beyond the Reich's border. Not only did Röhm meet with the French ambassador to try to win his support but also Rohm's military adjutant, Max Jüttner, testified years later at Nuremberg that Röhm had discussed his plans for recruiting three hundred thousand militiamen with the French military attaché in Berlin, General Redondeau. François-Poncet was apparently noncommittal, but, according to Jüttner, Redondeau made no objection despite the chronic French nervousness over any increase in German military strength. It is not an unlikely story since—with Hitler certain to build up the Reich's military forces—a militia would be vastly preferable to new battle divisions under the Reichswehr.

In a speech he made on April 18 to the Berlin diplomatic corps Röhm pursued his attack on Hitler's courtship of the army. He denounced the "reactionaries" who wrote monarchy on their shields, referring, as his hearers well understood, to the generals among others "who hang onto our coattails and to whom the SA was an immovable bulwark of the revolution."

The reports from many sources including military intelligence, some of them originating in former members of the Stahlhelm and from the SA itself, were disquieting. Not only did Röhm and other SA leaders speak publicly of the need for a second revolution but also in private Röhm continued to denounce Hitler and the army. He talked of the "stupid and dangerous councillors" around Hitler from whom the Führer must be freed, and on one occasion he even called Hitler "a weakling who should have been taken off our necks." Over and over again he attacked the generals and his "Dutz" friend. Even in 1933 before his grievances accumulated, he told Hermann Rauschning that Hitler was "lowdown" *(gemein)*. "He betrays us all," he said and added that he had warned him that the coming army must not be a replica of the Kaiser's. It must be a revolutionary force. Röhm now told his SA lieutenants that Hitler had been completely taken in and that the SA alone would put National Socialism back on the right track. The SA fighter, the true bearer of the revolution, would not deviate "by a hair's breadth until he reached the end goal."[14] For Röhm the ostensible end goal was what Hitler had lost sight of as he wooed big business and the army. The end goal meant achieving the *volkisch* state with a people's army under Röhm's command, and it meant socialism.[15]

When Hitler told Röhm and other SA leaders in mid-March 1934 that he would energetically oppose any second wave of revolution, which could only end in chaos, it had no more effect on Röhm than had any of Hitler's other warnings. Röhm continued to remind his followers and Hitler, too, that they had made a socialist as well as a national revolution, and the only security against the reactionaries who would always reject it was the SA. By May, as Hitler later revealed, he was collecting his own anti-Röhm dossier, scrutinizing lists of SA promotions, and the results, he said, horrified him. He found that men were raised to high rank regardless of their service records, solely because they were homosexuals and completely under Röhm's domination.

So by May both Hitler and the army high command, allied with Heinrich Himmler and the latter's new and ambitiously growing organization, the SS, had come to the same conclusion. The embattled Röhm, over 4 million men under his command and stores of armaments, was far more than a potential danger. Part of this weaponry to be sure had been furnished by the Reichswehr itself for the limited role the army foresaw for the SA in defense of the eastern borders, but the SA was securing weapons from foreign sources as well, not the most modern ones to be sure, but nevertheless armament for undisclosed purposes that conceivably could be used against the Reichswehr and the government.[16]

Hitler's response to the unbudging Röhm was to open a propaganda campaign against him and the other "croakers." On May 1, the national day of celebration of the German worker, after a rousing account of the party's accomplishments, he addressed a huge gathering said to number 2 million people, at the Tempelhof airfield.[17] He told them that only constructive criticism was justified, not the nihilistic criticism of those who attacked the essential authority of the state. This, he said, was criticism for its own sake and could only result in chaos. The SA, the SS, the workers, and the Reichswehr would be the sources of the new Germany to be forged from their ranks, and what this generation failed to accomplish toward the goal of the *volks* community the next generations would complete. It was a relatively low-keyed attack, and on May 11 Goebbels went further. He made a speech in the Berlin Sportpalast aimed at the same targets—Röhm and the dissident SA—but he widened the range to bracket Centrists and protesting clergy, men such as Cardinal Faulhaber as well. He too denounced the "croakers" who regarded the patience of the party leaders as a sign of weakness. But neither they nor the reactionaries would prevent the party from completing its task, and the government would take steps to deal with them if an attempt was made through the churches to continue the battle against National Socialism. Goebbels at this time had mollifying words for the SA. When people asked him why it continued to exist he answered that it was there because it had rescued France as well as Germany from bolshevism. The SA was not a war but a peace troop, a form of order and discipline and a guarantee that domestic and foreign political tensions would be overcome. So a bone was thrown to the SA, but it had little nourishment on it for the voracious appetites of Röhm and his SA chiefs.

Hitler, or so he said later after Röhm had been shot, made one last attempt to make Röhm see the light. Hitler told a meeting of the Reichstag on July 13 that in early June 1934 he had summoned Röhm to a nearly five-hour talk that lasted until midnight.[18] He told Röhm that he knew irresponsible elements in the SA were calling for what he called "a national-bolshevik action" that could only bring Germany into unfathomable disaster. Despite what he had told Eden about reducing the SA by two-thirds he assured Röhm that it was a base lie that the SA was to be dissolved and that while he could not deny publicly that he intended to take measures against it, he would nevertheless prevent any attempt to produce chaos in Germany, and anyone who attacked the state was to be counted among his enemies. He begged Röhm to disassociate himself from this national bolshevik movement, and again he urged him to put a stop to the "impossible" excesses in the SA and to get rid of their perpetrators. Although the rumors about them were in part untrue, in part exaggerated, Röhm had left the meeting with the promise he would do his best to put things right. Such was Hitler's self-serving account of the meeting that took place a few weeks before Röhm and some hundred others were shot, and there is no way of knowing what really went on because Hitler's Reichstag speech contains the only record.

In any event the result of their talk was that Röhm agreed to go on leave, and a few days later on June 7 the SA press bureau announced he would take a cure ordered by his doctor that would last some weeks. And then came the cryptic sentence: "To dispel any possible misunderstandings . . . the *Stabschef* declared that with the restoration of his health he would continue to carry out the full duties of his office." The SA, too, would go on "a well-earned leave" in July, after which "newly strengthened and unchanged it would fulfill its great task in the service of the Führer and movement."[19]

The next day Röhm's anger surfaced, and he reacted as he had after he signed the agreement forced on him with Blomberg. He issued an order of the day to the SA that was a call to arms as well as a dark promise of retribution to his enemies. He said that following the advice of his doctor he would take a cure in the next weeks for his painful rheumatism, and he would return with his strength fully restored. He recommended that the SA leaders also go on leave and that the rank and file take July as a time for relaxation and recuperation to return to duty rested and fortified for the "honorable and difficult tasks" entrusted to them by *Volk* and fatherland. His order of the day ended with portentous words: "If the enemies of the SA lull themselves with the hope that the SA, in whole or in part, will not return from their leave to resume their posts, we will let them have the pleasure of this short-lived hope. They will find out in the time and form that seems necessary to us what the proper answer is. The SA is, and remains, the fate of Germany." No mention of Hitler, no assurances of eternal loyalty, the promises were only to *Volk* and fatherland.

The significance of Röhm's words was certainly not lost on Hitler, but he held his fire, and for some weeks it seemed as though he might continue to avoid a showdown. It may well have been Papen's speech that exploded him into action. The recalcitrants inside and outside the movement were gathering strength and courage. Once he was convinced of this he had only one sure way to deal with them; they had to be made harmless by any means at his command, and in the case of Röhm he had a large number of willing hatchet men at his service. Röhm had scores of enemies in the party hierarchy, for he had been at no pains to conceal his contempt for these civilian pen pushers any more than he had for the reactionary generals. Even in the organizations under his command, which at this time included not merely the SA but also the SS, there were powerful antagonists who wished him nothing but ill—one of them was Heinrich Himmler. In theory Himmler's SS took orders from Röhm, but actually Himmler ran the SS as his own domain, and, much as Hitler had lost control over the SA, Röhm had lost it over the SS.

Röhm's order of the day was followed, a week and a half later, by Papen's speech, and on the same day—June 17—Hitler spoke in Gera at the party day of the Thuringian Gau. He had just returned from a meeting in Venice with Mussolini that had not turned out very auspiciously. He had looked like a seedy supplicant in the presence of his swaggering, well-uniformed host who had been in power for a decade, a forlorn figure in his raincoat amid the pomp and ceremony of the Fascisti turned out in his honor. His speech at Gera reflected his discontent. He denounced "the little dwarfs, the little worms" who had tried to prevent his victory and who now thought they ought to be heard from. It was as though he knew, which he certainly did not, what Papen was saying at the same time in Marburg. Papen was undoubtedly one of the dwarfs and worms he had in mind.

After the speech in Marburg the Hitler propaganda apparatus went into high gear. Goebbels spoke on June 21, Hess on June 25, and Göring on June 26. Goebbels, like Hitler, addressed himself to Papen and the "little clique" of grumblers and "croakers" who wanted to destroy the work of construction, who talked of the loss of élan in the revolution for which they had never in any event had any enthusiasm. They had not been able to prevent the seizure of power but now they would like to be able to hinder its use. Echoing Hitler he called them "ridiculous pygmies." They were untroubled by the low wages of workers but tried to rouse them against the National Socialist state.

> Thank God intelligence isn't limited to those gentlemen in club armchairs. The people have not forgotten the time when these gentlemen ruled and if they were too weak to win power then how are they strong enough to win it today? We assumed power because no one else had a claim to it, no crown prince, no councillor of commerce, no big bankers, no parliamentary chieftains. These nonentities say: "Yes Hitler is fine," but there are the little party functionaries who have no competence, the uneducated people to whom we're supposed to be subordinate. . . . Well, these little people

whom they now want to do in have conquered Germany. If we had relied on these superior gentlemen we'd have been lost. In the future too, we will win through if we remain true to ourselves and rely on our own strength. Then we'll deal with these carpers and nothing will be left of their fantasy. These people only dare criticize when no one confronts them. Get after them, move in on them and you'll see in what cowardly fashion they'll pull back. . . . Don't put up with them, call them to order. Brace yourselves against any nullity who decries the constructive work of our movement. We can assert with pride we are the better youth of another Reich and we alone have the right to represent it. Forward with us into the new era!

Hitler's deputy Hess addressed himself directly to the disquiet of the SA. He told a mass audience in a radio talk that he urged a special caution on the idealistic but gullible party members who sometimes, in memory of the heroism and comradeship of the days of battle, turned toward provocateurs who tried to incite mutual hostility in the *volk* society and who called this criminal game "a second revolution." "Believe me," he said, speaking of the time before the seizure of power, "the Führer could have played out a bloody game regardless of the practical realities," but with his profound sense of responsibility he had avoided a catastrophe that the dilettantes of revolution would not have been aware of, for they would be standing before the ruins they were guilty of producing. "The Führer has made us, his old liegemen, ripe for the constructive work transmitting at the right time our revolutionary will to the daily tasks, to make us ripe for the molding of the state. Once before in the developing stages of the National Socialist revolution there were enough party comrades who with limited understanding thought they could improve on what the Führer was doing and one day they were to learn better."[20]

Hess made everything clear. The Führer's liegemen all had to acknowledge that the Führer was the instrument of a higher will and that he consciously or unconsciously had gone the right way. "He alone can finish what he has begun. He alone can give us what we all yearn for." Maybe some day Hitler would again believe it necessary to give impetus to the movement by revolutionary means, but it would be a revolution steered by him and he would call on his old revolutionists when he knew it was necessary.

The order of the Führer, to whom we have sworn loyalty, alone has validity. Woe to them who would break their oath of allegiance in the belief they have been chosen to serve the revolution by a revolution. . . . Adolf Hitler is the great strategist of the revolution. He knows the limits, with the given means and circumstances, of what is attainable. . . . Woe to him who clumsily breaks through the fine threads of his strategy in the insane belief he can do things more quickly. He is an enemy of the revolution even though he is acting with the best intentions. Those who would benefit would be the enemies of the revolution whether under the sign of reaction or of communism. No one watches over his revolution more than the Führer. . . . It is after all his very own child and on its account he has placed his life at hazard and it was for that he went to prison.[21]

The line was continued in a speech the next day by Göring, who denounced the self-serving clique, the monarchists and reactionaries, and he promised one day, when they had gone too far, they would feel the weight of his fist.

Those were the speeches and behind them Hitler was coiling to strike. On June 7 he had written to Papen warmly thanking him for his services in arranging for the Saar plebiscite to be held in January 1935. Hitler had held off announcing his plan for military conscription until the League of Nations Council set the date, the earliest that could have been chosen under the provisions of the Versailles treaty, and he told Papen what a fine job he had done in a spirit of "sacrifice and tireless work." To Papen's Marburg speech he responded with not much more than a light slap—he had Edgar Jung arrested and refused to receive Papen when he came to protest. Hitler had also praised Röhm and his works before setting the police on his trail, but in his treatment of Papen there were other considerations to take into account. Hindenburg was critically ill and could scarcely last much longer; but while he lived he was the only man in the world who could keep Hitler from becoming commander in chief of the Wehrmacht and assuming total civil power.[22]

Under no circumstances could the president be antagonized at this last moment. Hindenburg had a high regard for Papen. He had presented Papen with his photograph when Papen was forced to resign as chancellor. The inscription in heavy black ink scrawled across it was: "Ich hatte einen Kameraden," the traditional tribute to a fallen comrade, and Hindenburg undoubtedly shared the hope of many conservatives who were enthusiastic about Papen's speech for a return to the monarchy.[23]

Hitler had to tread warily as far as Papen was concerned, but against Röhm he could do almost anything he wanted. The rumors of an SA putsch grew from day to day, some of them probably planted by Himmler and Reichenau who wanted finally to be rid of Röhm and the SA but many of them coming from other sources—including the SA itself.[24] General Franz Halder reported later that he had been visited at his command post in Münster by an SA Obergruppenführer who wanted to be told about the general's assignments because he was designated for Halder's post when the SA took over. Duty officers were assigned in army barracks to secure the stores of arms and ammunition, and General Jodl later said the Ministry of Defense was armed to the teeth against an imminent SA attack. Conservative, anti-Nazi generals such as Beck and Fritsch were convinced an SA putsch was about to begin; Beck said he had his pistol ready at hand and ordered his officers to do the same. In late June, General Ewald von Kleist, who was commanding the troops in Silesia, said he was warned by the chief of the high command of a forthcoming attack by the SA. Furthermore, Kleist said, reports were reaching him from all sides—including those from former Stahlhelm men, the SA, and civil authorities—of feverish SA preparations for an attack. Kleist also had a talk with SA Obergruppenführer Edmund Heines who told him he knew all the preventive measures Kleist had taken, said he believed them to be a prelude for a Reichswehr attack on the SA, and swore the SA planned none on the army. On June 28 or 29 Heines telephoned Kleist to say he had learned the army planned to move against the SA throughout the Reich, and he was flying to Munich to confer with Röhm, whereupon Kleist also flew to Munich to report to Generals Beck and Fritsch. He told them he had the impression the army and the SA were being incited to hostilities by third parties. Fritsch then called in Reichenau to whom Kleist repeated his story. Reichenau listened and then laconically replied: "That may be, but now it is too late." The security police and the armed forces' counterintelligence, the Abwehr, were now exchanging information they had received on the coming SA coup, and it was arranged that when it occurred for the Reichswehr to furnish arms to the SS as Himmler had urged.

The rumors involved circles other than Röhm and his SA followers. An army captain, Hermann Höfle, who was also an SA leader, wrote to Röhm that General von Schleicher was making no secret of his anti-Nazi views, telling his military friends that National Socialism would not last long, a remark that was confirmed by Meissner, the president's state secretary. Meissner told in his memoirs of other witnesses who heard Schleicher say Hitler would be done in by frondeurs within the party.[25] Meissner, too, believed Schleicher to be in touch not only with Röhm but also with anti-Hitler generals such as Hammerstein, Bussche-Ippenburg, and Haase, who were also known to be critical of Röhm, and Schleicher, Meissner thought, was attempting to dispel their "prejudices." Schleicher was also, Meissner had heard, in touch with François-Poncet.

SA Obergruppenführer Victor Lutze, a Reichstag deputy from Hannover, was another source of inflammatory, but on the whole accurate, information. Lutze was a stolid follower of the Führer's, he was well satisfied with his youth-training job, and in Berlin where he had his headquarters he kept in close touch with the Reichswehr. He had gone to Berchtesgaden in February to tell Hitler that Röhm had no intention of keeping his agreement with Blomberg, and Hitler had laconically replied, "We've got to let things ripen." Lutze had also shown General Reichenau a letter in mid-June in which he had warned Röhm against carrying out his designs against the Reichswehr.[26]

At the same time, Lutze was discussing with Hitler what individuals in the SA were to be shot. Reinhard Heydrich of the SS and Werner Best of the SD, the Security Service, had their own hit lists prepared. Lutze apparently wanted only Röhm to be liquidated, but Heydrich, Himmler, and the SD leaders had many more victims in mind, so lists of undesirables slated to be gotten rid of went the rounds. The SA too was said to have compiled the names of enemies to be killed; one report, perhaps instigated by Himmler, said all the higher army officers were on it.

Hitler prepared his counterputsch with considerable skill. On June 28, the day before Blomberg placed the army in a state of alert against an SA rising, Hitler and Göring left Berlin for Essen to attend the wedding of Gauleiter Terboven, the man to whom six years later he would assign the governance of Norway. After the wedding Göring returned to Berlin where he was to be in charge of the action to come in that city, while Hitler paid a formal visit to the Krupp works, under the guidance of Herr Krupp, accompanied by Heinrich Hoffmann, Hitler's personal photographer. Hoffmann took pictures that appeared in the German press showing an unruffled Führer on a routine inspection trip. That evening Hitler, through Röhm's adjutant Bergmann, summoned by telephone a meeting of SA leaders to be held at Bad Wiessee where Röhm was taking his cure.

The plan thus went forward. On June 29 Hitler visited a regional school for leaders of the work service and then went on to one of his favorite stopping places, the Hotel Dreesen at Bad Godesberg. There he was joined by Goebbels and Sepp Dietrich of the SS. At four o'clock in the afternoon he listened to a concert given by a band of the work service; at midnight he reviewed a march-past of the band, while across the Rhine six hundred men of the work service formed a flaming swastika with their torches. Then at two o'clock in the morning of June 30, Hitler drove to the Bonn airport where, accompanied by Goebbels, Obergruppenführer Lutze, and two aides, he boarded a Junker 52 waiting on the airstrip for a night flight to Munich. A second plane with a commando of SS men flew with them. They landed at Munich as dawn was breaking and in a cavalcade of three cars drove to the Ministry of the Interior in the Theatinerstrasse. There Hitler leaped out of the car, a whip which he had long used as a kind of dashing swagger stick in his hand, and immediately had SA Obergruppenführer August Schneidhuber and Gruppenführer Wilhelm Schmidt arrested, stripped of their insignia of rank, and taken off to prison by two policemen with drawn pistols.[27] Some fifteen minutes later the three black Mercedes set out for Röhm at Bad Wiessee.

The automobile trip to arrest Röhm on the morning of June 30 was a tense affair, and Hitler spoke little. Just before the entrance to the Hotel Hanselbauer where the SA men were staying, Hitler told his chauffeur, Erich Kempa, to drive up to the hotel entrance silently and to go on farther if an SA man was on guard.

There was none, and Hitler, Goebbels, the aides, and two drivers together with the SS men and the police brought along from Munich stormed into the hotel. Whip in hand, Hitler burst into Röhm's bedroom, two police officials behind him with drawn guns. "Röhm, you are arrested," he shouted. Röhm, roused from a deep sleep, saw Hitler and dutifully and no doubt automatically replied, "Heil, Mein Führer." "You are arrested!" Hitler yelled at him again, and both times he used "Du": "Du bist verhaftet."

A police officer then reported to Hitler that the police president of Breslau, Obergruppenführer Heines, who had a room across the corridor from Röhm, refused to get out of bed. Hitler thereupon rushed into Heines's room where he found the police president, who, long before holding that office, had marched with Hitler in the Beer Hall Putsch in 1923, in bed with a young SA man. Hitler shouted at Heines that if he was not dressed in five minutes he would have him shot.

Up and down the hotel corridors went the SS and the police, ordering the SA men out of their rooms. Hitler asked one after the other if they had anything to do with Röhm's machinations. They all denied any complicity, but in most cases Hitler merely said: "Arrested!" A few, such as Röhm's doctor, Ketterer, who was also an Obergruppenführer for whom Lutze vouched, he let go free. He asked Ketterer and his wife to leave the hotel, which, as Kempa later said, was not a pleasant place to stay on that day. The arrested SA men were shipped off to Munich in a hired bus. Hitler sharply ordered one group of heavily armed SA just arriving from Munich to return to the city and told them if they were stopped on their way by the SS to surrender their arms without resistance. Röhm, who was taking his third cup of coffee before being driven off to jail, watched the proceedings and said not a word, though these were his own armed men, and he might have called on them to resist.

Then they all drove away, leaving the hotel to the guests who had survived the Führer's visitation. Hitler's entourage had now swollen to some twenty cars, and as they drove toward Munich they encountered other SA men en route to the meeting at Bad Wiessee. They were all stopped and either arrested or sent back to the city. Hess was one of those driving to the Bad Wiessee conference; he too was stopped, and Hitler turned to him to ask whether he had anything to do with Röhm's activities. Hess merely smiled, and Hitler shook his hand. But according to Kempa, Hitler personally ordered the arrest of twenty SA men who were on their way to the meeting at Bad Wiessee that morning.

Most of the arrested men, along with others arrested from prepared lists, were shot. The victims included not only once highly esteemed party comrades such as Gregor Strasser, who now represented some kind of threat, but also others such as the ex-army captain Rohrbein and the engineer Ballerstedt, both of whom had been active in the early days of the movement and seem to have been victims of some local, private pogrom. Old enemies were also liquidated, such as Gustav von Kahr who had helped defeat the 1923 putsch; Schleicher's adjutant Bredow, along with well-known Catholic laymen such as Erich Klausener, head of the Catholic Action in Berlin; and the Catholic youth leaders Adalbert Probst and Friedrich Beck, along with Fritz Gerlich who in 1932 had attacked the Nazis in a publication he edited titled *Der Gerade Weg.*

In Berlin the counterputsch was directed by Göring, Himmler, and Heydrich. There General von Schleicher and his wife were gunned down by a commando of men who burst into Schleicher's study wearing civilian clothes. Frau von Schleicher died as she threw herself between the gunmen and her husband in a vain attempt to save his life. On the evening of the same day, June 30, the official announcement declared that Schleicher had been connected with enemies of the state in the SA and foreign countries; he had resisted arrest and been killed in an exchange of fire.

The list of those murdered was never to be known, but it is certain that the victims included many who had nothing whatever to do with Röhm and his SA followers. One man, Willi Schmidt, the music critic of the *Münchner Neueste Nachrichten,* was killed because of a confusion of names, and a former Jesuit priest, Bernhard Stempfle, who had been on the staff of the anti-Semitic *Miesburger Anzeiger* and had been associated with the publication of the first edition of *Mein Kampf,* was apparently killed without Hitler's knowledge. Hitler was later quoted by his photographer, Heinrich Hoffmann, as having called the men who killed Stempfle "swine," and one German historian believes it possible that they were the three SS men who appeared on the list of those shot "for shameful mishandling of prisoners under protective arrest." Two of Papen's conservative associates, Herbert von Bose and Edgar Jung, were shot, and three other members of his staff were arrested. Papen himself was placed under house arrest with SS guards by Göring, his telephone was cut off, and he was released only three days later.[28] When his telephone service was restored he was called by Göring, who blandly asked him why he had not appeared at the cabinet meetings.

Everything was duly approved by the cabinet, by Hindenburg, by the Reichstag, and, according to reports from the secret police, by a majority of the population. That a plot against Hitler and the state had been uncovered and put down was openly doubted by no one.

Hitler told the cabinet on July 3, and in a long speech to the Reichstag ten days later, how patient he had been, how loyal to the highest principles of statesmanship, and how he had been forced to act to save the nation. It was the kind of self-heroizing he had long made his own; the pattern was the same one he had used many years before to explain to the Austrian authorities why he had neglected to register for army service. In both explanations were echoes of the strenuous trials of the Germanic hero. Like Siegfried the young Hitler had had to struggle against sinister forces of turpitude, but he had kept his heart unsullied and selflessly tried to fulfill his high mission. In June 1934 he again had overcome the cohorts of evil—the neomarxists, the reactionaries. What he was battling against was an international phenomenon; the Jews were at work. Most nations of the world, he said, were experiencing mass terrorism, tumult in the streets, battles on the barricades. In Germany, too, fools and criminals were spreading destruction. Since National Socialism overcame the Communist Party, other communist, subversive, anarchistic elements had attempted to found new diversive parties. They were joined by a second group, by those who had previously failed in political leadership and whose incapacity had been forgotten by many. Added to them was a third destructive element, that of the uprooted revolutionaries—revolutionaries for the sake of revolution, the deserters and mutineers of 1918, who had lost their ties to the state and to any human society. But for the National Socialists who had destroyed the Second Reich, the revolution they had made was a powerful birthright that had called the Reich to life, a Reich the people could love, to whose authority they gladly submitted. "Revolution for us," Hitler said, "is not a permanent condition. . . ." The task of the restoration of the *Volk* could only be accomplished when the German people lived in inner tranquility.

The plot came down to specific personalities: Röhm had been in league with Schleicher who in turn had been in contact with foreign governments. Schleicher and Röhm had intended to arrest Hitler, to keep him on temporarily as chancellor, with Schleicher as vice chancellor in Papen's place. Röhm was to be minister of Defense, in charge of the Wehrmacht and the nationalist military organizations.

Hitler said he could only be unalterably opposed to any such plan, he could never have permitted Röhm to be minister of Defense or the SA to be more than the political instrument it had been for fourteen years. The chief of the SA could not lead the army, the army must be nonpolitical, and that is why, in 1923, he had proposed placing at its head an army officer and not the then-commander of the SA, Göring.[29]

The explanation was nothing if not careful. The commander in chief of the army, to whom he had sworn allegiance, was the field marshal and president whose person was inviolable. Any thought of accepting General Schleicher's plans would have been a breach of faith not only against the field marshal and the minister of Defense but also against the army. Still wooing the generals as well as Hindenburg, he said again that the army was the sole bearer of arms in the Reich as the party was the sole extension of its political will. He could not demand that army officers become party members. Blomberg and all the other officers had kept faith with the National Socialist state, and he had kept faith with them. Loyalty has its duties that may not be avoided, and certainly the man (himself) who had brought the nation together could under no circumstances behave perfidiously. If he did, all confidence in loyalty and faith would disappear. Hitler had tried to talk sense with Röhm in their five-hour interview, and as a result Röhm had intended to do away with him later on as the hit man Standartenführer Uhl had confessed to Hitler before he was shot.[30]

The extent of the danger was to be seen through the news coming to Germany from foreign sources. English and French newspapers gave increasing space to the forthcoming coup in the Reich and its foreign support. Bredow was working for Schleicher as a foreign agent to this end.

Therefore, to prevent the blood of ten thousand innocent people being shed and with tension that had become insupportable, Hitler had decided to deprive Röhm of his office and to arrest him and the other SA conspirators at the Bad Wiessee meeting. By midday on June 29 the preparations for the uprising were threatening Hitler, who had been forced to break off his inspection trip to be ready for all contingencies. For at this point, Hitler reported, Obergruppenführer Ernst had not gone to Bad Wiessee but had remained in Berlin to lead the putsch in that city. And the SA had been placed in a state of alarm in Munich. The men were not allowed to go home but were ordered to emergency stations. "That," said Hitler, "is mutiny. I and no one else am the Commander of the SA." "Only a ruthless and bloody intervention" could prevent the spread of the revolt. It was better that a hundred mutineers, traitors, and conspirators be destroyed than for tens of thousands of innocent SA men and others to shed their blood. "For if the action planned by the criminal Ernst in Berlin began to unroll, the consequences were unthinkable." The conspirators had planned to carry out their coup in Hitler's name, and it was therefore finally clear to him that only one man could and must confront Röhm. "He had broken faith with me and I alone must call him to account. . . . Mutiny has always been broken by the same eternal, iron laws. . . . At that hour I was responsible for the fate of the German nation and with it the German people, and thus the country's highest legal authority. . . . In every age mutineers' divisions have been brought to order by being decimated." Only one state—Germany—had failed to make use of its articles of war and therefore that state collapsed: "I did not want to deliver the young Reich to the fate of the older one," said Hitler.[31] So he had restored the balance and will to act that had been lacking in 1918.

The nation must know, he said, that its existence cannot be threatened, unpunished, by anyone. Certain death was the lot of whoever raised a hand against it, and no rank or high place would prevent his being held to personal responsibility and punishment. A foreign journalist, the correspondent of the *Daily Express,* Sefton Delmer, had protested in the names of the wives and children of those shot, but Hitler said women and children are always the innocent victims of the criminal behavior of their men. He, too, sympathized with them, but the pity he felt was but a tiny fraction of what he otherwise must have felt for the tens of thousands of German women had the coup been successful. François-Poncet declared that of course his meetings with Röhm and Schleicher had been harmless, but Hitler said, "When three men bent on high treason in Germany meet with a foreign statesman on a mission they themselves describe as 'official,' exclude everyone else, and take every precaution for secrecy, I have such men shot."[32]

He added up the numbers of those who had been killed, including three who committed suicide. There were seventy-four, he said, plus the three SS men who had been shot for "shameful mishandling of prisoners in protective custody." In addition a number of acts of violence unconnected with the revolt would be tried in the regular courts, he announced; but this never took place.[33]

By Hitler's count seventy-seven people had been shot, but the official list had eighty-three names on it; both totals were certainly underestimated. Like many other statistics on murders committed by the Nazis, they will remain incomplete. Hitler announced the restoration of tranquility. To prevent political passions from turning into lynch justice, he had ordered the killings to stop on July 1.

The speech was a classic Hitlerian performance: ingratiating those he thought he had to convince; rigorous against traitors; made up of some truths, half-truths, and bald-faced lies. It contained the trigger words needed to appeal to Hindenburg and the generals: "the betrayal of 1918," "unshakable loyalty," the overwhelming precedence of *Volk* and fatherland. The dreadful perils were there too: subversion, foreign enemies, civil war, breach of trust. But the hard evidence for the alleged crimes was either lacking or contrived. No solid evidence was ever brought to light to bear out Hitler's account of an imminent rising. Nor was there anything to connect Schleicher to Bredow with a coup involving a foreign power. Röhm and his SA men were in bed in a Kur hotel, without armed guards, awaiting a meeting Hitler had called, far removed from any armed rising in the streets of Berlin and Munich. Ernst had not remained in Berlin to head any coup there; he had gone with his wife to Bremen to board a ship bound for the Canary Islands to spend his SA leave. The Munich SA had, as Hitler said, been placed in a state of alarm, but it is not clear by whom. The alarm may well have been sounded by the minister of the Interior, Wagner, and all that is certain is that the SA quietly dispersed to their homes when Wagner sent them home. Nowhere was a shot fired against the Hitler forces. The killings were all one-sided.

Hitler's story was completely successful, perfectly designed for the purpose of convincing those who wanted to believe. Even before Hitler had presented his case Blomberg thanked him for what he had said in a directive to the defense forces on July 1: "The Wehrmacht as the bearer of arms of the entire people, far [removed] from domestic political strife, expresses its gratitude with devotion and loyalty." At the cabinet meeting on July 3 the minister renewed his homage. Now he thanked Hitler in the name of the cabinet and the Wehrmacht for his "decisive and courageous action which had spared the German people a civil war" and added, "The Führer as statesman and soldier has demonstrated a greatness that has awakened in the hearts of the cabinet and the whole German people a solemn vow of performance, devotion and loyalty in these difficult hours." Hindenburg in a telegram of July 2 solemnly congratulated Hitler for his "decisive action" and for courageously risking "your own person in stifling the treasonable machinations at their source." Even the British ambassador, Phipps, accepted the Hitlerian version, at least in its outlines, though Phipps was certain neither France nor Ambassador François-Poncet was involved as Hitler had implied they were. Neurath told Phipps that Röhm had planned the coup for August but upon learning that Hitler had wind of the plot had moved the date up to June 30. Röhm intended, Neurath said, to take over the government with Schleicher as vice chancellor in order to rescue Hitler from his evil counselors and to induce him to remain as chancellor. The minister of Justice, Franz Gürtner, approved too, though no trials or hearings had been held—in fact, there had been no legal proceedings of any kind. Hitler declared he had acted against high treason as the highest judge in the Reich, a post to which he had just appointed himself, on behalf of the security of the state, and Gürtner completely agreed, though what he assented to was a violation of every principle he had been brought up to honor and defend. Gürtner was no Nazi, he was a member of the cabinet because he was one of the conservatives Papen and Hindenburg had believed would help to control Hitler, and now he declared that what Hitler had done was not only legal but also the performance of a statesmanlike duty. Gürtner was joined by other German legal scholars. Professor Carl Schmitt, an eminent juridical authority, gave it as his opinion that Hitler had protected the law "before its worst misuse," when "in the moment of danger, on the strength of his leadership as the highest judge of the state, he had directly created law. The real leader is always a judge, too."[34]

Although many army officers were deeply disturbed by the savage executions, only two of them, General Adam, commander of the Seventh Wehrkreis District with headquarters at Munich, and General List, commander of the Fourth Army District with headquarters at Dresden, protested to the Ministry of Defense. Although in view of Blomberg's and Hindenburg's praise of Hitler's intrepid defense of the Reich nothing could possibly come of such protests, one other weak remonstrance was heard. The Schlieffen Society, made up of former army officers and headed by the old field marshal of the world war August von Mackensen, was permitted by Blomberg to state that Schleicher and Bredow had been the victims of "purely political struggles for power" and that their personal honor was unsullied. The pronouncement went on to say: "They had taken ways regarded as hostile to the regime and that had led to the fateful results."[35] The publication of the statement, however, was forbidden by Göring, and the public never heard of it.

Such were the muted repercussions to the executions. Everyone was deeply grateful to Hitler; Blomberg, Gürtner, Hindenburg, and Papen, too. Although Papen did resign his vice chancellorship, he thanked Hitler for telling the Reichstag that any idea that Papen or anyone else in the cabinet was involved in the conspiracy was sharply contradicted by the fact that they themselves had been on the list of those to be murdered. Papen in his letter expressing his gratitude also said he dared hope that Hitler might make a further statement of confidence in Papen's loyalty. He wrote: "I should be thankful if you could sometime find the opportunity to state positively that I have fostered and fought for your leadership and your work on behalf of Germany." In addition he told Hitler he would like to clasp his hand to thank him for the rescue of the country and to congratulate him "for all you have given anew to the German nation by crushing the intended second revolution."[36]

So Papen, too, swallowed the whole bitter dose—the murder of his two associates, his arrest, the SS's search of his papers, the suppression of his speech—and resigned as vice chancellor only to take a new job offered him by Hitler a few weeks later.

3

The Rising in Austria

One man who was saddened by the failure of the Röhm revolt was the chancellor of Austria, Engelbert Dollfuss. Dollfuss had had high hopes of Röhm, which he gained from reports of the Austrian minister to Berlin, Stephan Tauschitz, and quite likely through direct contact with Röhm who never had been reticent in disclosing his ambitions. Dollfuss had believed that the split in the National Socialist movement in the Reich might well unseat Hitler, or at least weaken Nazi influence and diminish the danger of a National Socialist rising in Austria.

The threat to Dollfuss was real enough. The National Socialists in both Austria and Germany were determined to put an end to his rule, and his life was in serious jeopardy. One high official in the Reich propaganda ministry had openly stated that three well-aimed shots were needed: one for Dollfuss and two for his lieutenants, Ernst Starhemberg, chief of the Heimwehr, and the then–vice chancellor Emil Fey. A would-be assassin actually set out from Dresden just before the uprising, but he was arrested in Braunau before he could make his attempt because the Austrian police had been forewarned of his purposes by the German secret police. Another man had succeeded, in October 1933, in firing two shots at Dollfuss, wounding him slightly in the upper arm and chest. The assailant, Rudolf Dertil, was a former Austrian soldier and a member of the Austrian Nazi Party.

The opposition to the rule of the diminutive Austrian chancellor—one of his nicknames was *"Millimetternich"*—had grown steadily from both the Right and the Left since he took office. Dollfuss himself was a prime example of the deep confusion in Austrian politics. A nationalist member of the Christian Socialist Party, he had been a little-known minister of Agriculture before he was elected chancellor as a compromise candidate. His political background was limited to farm areas and problems; an ardent Catholic, he wanted to found a Christian, antimarxist, anticapitalist state, with ideas borrowed from recent papal encyclicals, Mussolini's fascism, and the teachings of Austrian economist and sociologist Othmar Spanns. Dollfuss hoped to create a society based on estates, made up of organized peasants, workers, and industrialists who would renounce materialism and democracy and above all marxism, to form a Christian German state. He had long been one of the "Great Germans" as had so many Austrians, including Hitler and Hitler's father, and though he was anti-Prussian he saw Austria nevertheless as a German state, Catholic and idiosyncratic but indubitably German.[1] Immediately after Hitler became Reichschancellor he sent Dollfuss a telegram with the best wishes of the "German brother people" and in return received an answer in the same vein. Dollfuss had held that the *Anschluss* was merely a matter of time, and in that view he was echoing the sentiments of the overwhelming majority of Austrians. After the defeat of the Central Powers the Austrian constitution was rewritten to include a clause that declared Austria part of the German Reich. In 1921, in two plebiscites, 90 percent of the voters in Salzburg had voted for union with Germany; the pro-*Anschluss* figure in the Tirol was 99 percent. *Anschluss,* union with Germany, had seemed the only hope to the people of the truncated empire deprived of some of its richest farmlands and—with the loss of Bohemia and Moravia to the Czechs—of 70 percent of its industry. Austria was more thoroughly ruined economically and psychologically by the lost war than was the Reich itself. Its economy could be made feebly viable with the help of foreign loans that would only be forthcoming on condition that it remain independent of the Reich. In 1932 a loan of 9 million pounds sterling was made by the League of Nations with the condition that there would be no customs union with Germany for twenty years. Foreign statesmen wished Austria well but only insofar as its politics advantaged their own countries.

France was determined at all costs to prevent an *Anschluss* that would have turned their victory of 1918 to defeat, with the Reich's adding 6 million Austrian Germans to its population. Italy, too, had compelling reasons for opposing the *Anschluss.* In accord with the promises of the Treaty of London, made in 1915 to persuade Italy to join the Allies against the Central Powers, Italy had acquired all the South Tirol—an area of over 5,400 square miles with, in 1910, over 500,000 German-speaking inhabitants as opposed to 16,500 Italians.

But after the war Italy was also anti-French and wanted no part of a French plan to foster a Danubian confederation, with Austria making common cause with the countries of the Little Entente that had emerged with the defeat of the Reich and the collapse of the Austrian Empire. The Little Entente was part of the French system of alliances, and Mussolini was disinclined to do anything to strengthen France.

The Italian dictator was cynical when he talked to foreign diplomats about what the future held. Austria, he said, would inevitably become part of the Reich—it was undeniably German, and he could do little but delay the inevitable *Anschluss*. To this end he provided funds for the pro Dollfuss Heimwehr, and in many speeches and démarches spoke out for the necessity for Austrian independence. But he, like Hitler, had many irons in the fire, and when Hitler assured him at their meeting in Venice, just before the Röhm putsch, that the Austrian problem was not acute, Mussolini was indisposed to press Hitler unduly to stop his anti-Dollfuss campaign.

Hitler had been convinced, since he became chancellor, that the Austrian problem would be resolved inside Austria without need of his direct intervention. The National Socialist movement had begun in Austria.[2] Hitler himself had addressed the Austrian party members in the early days of his membership in the German party; the political use of the swastika and the National Socialist Workers Party had originated in Austria, as had much of the program Hitler formulated for the Munich party.

The political and economic troubles of Austria had paralleled those in the Reich, but after Hitler took power the Reich seemed to be moving out of the deep depression where Austria remained. Twelve percent of its working population was unemployed in 1933, many of them former state officials, one hundred thousand of whom had been dismissed from their posts as a result of the League of Nations' supervision of Austrian finances. Dollfuss could rule only by emergency decrees. His coalition government had had a one-vote majority in the Bundestag and so little popular backing that he had to avoid either convening the Bundestag or holding national elections. The Social Democrats, the dominant postwar party in Vienna, together with the National Socialists, were the bitter enemies of this clerical government-without-majority-support, and every move Dollfuss made seemed calculated to strengthen their implacable resistance to him. His chief support came from Mussolini who agreed to make more funds available to the Heimwehr on condition that Dollfuss suppress the marxist Social Democrats and their armed force, the Schutzbund. Then, in February 1934, Dollfuss had the army turn its guns, including artillery and mine throwers, against the workers' quarters in Vienna, when as a result of the repressive government measures socialist strikes and uprisings threatened civil war. Almost two hundred people, many of them women and children, were killed or wounded, and while Dollfuss and his Christian Democrats could celebrate the victory over godless marxism it was a victory that left him with little moral credit anywhere in Austria or the democratic West. He had been clinging to power mainly through foreign subventions and loans, and his own followers, including even reputedly close associates, were often only weakly attached to him. A number of them were in touch with the Nazis, and many of the recruits for the SS and the SA came from former members of the Heimwehr. Dollfuss was, in fact, ruling by pseudolegal means, making use of an emergency grant of power made during the war, in 1917, that enabled him to forbid elections, invade the independence of the courts, and call a rump parliament to approve the constitution for "a Christian German Federal state based on estates" that he had drawn up in 1934.

Hitler had long been persuaded that, given the weakness of the Dollfuss government, the Austrian Nazis with help from the propaganda and financial resources of the Reich would be sufficient to bring him down. For Dollfuss he had nothing but contempt. The Munich broadcasting station beamed daily messages denouncing Dollfuss as a tool of the church and foreign governments who ruled illegally; large supplies of arms were continually shipped from the Reich to the Austrian SA and to the terrorists whose sporadic bombings increased after the National Socialist Party was declared illegal. Although Hitler ordered the terrorists to stop their activities in August 1933, his order appeared to Austrian Nazi Party leaders as nothing more than a tactical political device intended to placate Mussolini. They were well aware that despite his words he did nothing to stop the export of weapons or to take measures against his chief agent in Austria, Theodor Habicht, under whose direction they were used.[3] Austrian Nazis who had fled to Germany were barracked in Lichfeld as an Austrian Legion awaiting orders. And the anti-Dollfuss campaign continued with speakers dispatched from the Reich to Austria, along with thousands of anti-Dollfuss handbills smuggled across the border that continued the campaign of vilification broadcast by the Munich radio. In May 1933 Hitler sent the Bavarian minister of Justice, Hans Frank, along with his Prussian counterpart, Hanns Kerrl, and State Secretary Roland Freisler to Vienna where, as they landed at the airport, they were told by Austrian officials that their presence was undesirable. They were also told their activities would be limited to one meeting, but Frank unabashedly went on to speak at Nazi demonstrations where he told his audiences he brought greetings from Hitler and then proceeded to excoriate Dollfuss and his "illegal" government.

Dollfuss reacted against the Nazi provocations by forbidding the National Socialist Party in June 1933, ordering the arrest of many of its leaders and the deportation of Habicht. The main result of these measures was that the party went underground with little loss in membership, and Habicht along with a considerable number of Austrian party functionaries took refuge in Munich, where they continued their antigovernment activities with the funds and facilities provided by the Reich untroubled by the Austrian authorities.

Hitler used every political and economic weapon at his disposal. In May 1933 he imposed a tax of one thousand marks on visas from the Reich to Austria, and with this measure and the continuing terrorist attacks on Austrian railways, bridges, and power lines the number of German tourists who had thitherto helped keep the Austrian economy going declined catastrophically. Dollfuss could not do much to counter the German effort to get rid of him. Urged by Mussolini he made halfhearted attempts to placate the Nazis, trying to arrange a meeting with Hitler and offering at one point to give the National Socialists two seats in his cabinet, one of them to go to Habicht.

Negotiations never got very far because each side basically rejected collaboration. Habicht could have said he was willing to retract the demand for holding new elections, but he continued to insist on Dollfuss's legalizing the Nazi Party and granting an amnesty to all the party members in Austrian prisons, neither of which proposals Dollfuss could accept and be likely to survive politically. So with Dollfuss attempting to bypass Habicht and deal with Hitler directly, and with Habicht certain that Dollfuss could not long remain in office, the talks got nowhere.

Even within the Dollfuss government the show of unity was superficial. Starhemberg and Fey were both in touch with the Nazis. Starhemberg, though formally devoted to Dollfuss, promised the future chancellorship to Habicht in the event he himself became president of Austria.

Hitler, with a view to appeasing Mussolini, was ready to give at least lip service to moderating his anti-Dollfuss policy, though Dollfuss with his black clericalism and anti-Nazi measures remained anathema to him. Hitler's solution to the Austrian problem began with the Austrians themselves getting rid of Dollfuss, and Habicht was permitted to make a radio speech from Germany that was an invitation to rebellion. The speech was made on February 12, 1934, at the same time the Dollfuss government forces were shelling the workers' quarters in Vienna, and Habicht, taking quick advantage of the widespread resentment against Dollfuss's measures, declared that while the chancellor and his "regiment" were announcing themselves the great victors over marxism, what they were doing was killing defenseless people, including women and children, with grenades and flame throwers. Until yesterday, he said, the Dollfuss regime had fought only against National Socialism with the marxists as tacit allies, but now it had driven the marxists, too, into illegality and could only subdue them by calling on foreign aid. The Austrian army was shooting at workers it had incited, who had perhaps wrong ideas but were nevertheless good and courageous Germans. The army would have to decide whether tomorrow it would also be shooting at National Socialists and then perhaps on the following day march on the side of the enemies of the Reich against Germany. The chief of the Austrian army, Prince Schönburg-Hartenstein, had called on all nationalist Austrians and old soldiers to rally behind the regime, but the National Socialists would permanently expel any member who responded to his appeal. They witnessed this battle, Habicht said, "with profound bitterness and in deep sorrow bowed their heads before the graves of the dead." They respected all of them: Whichever side they had been on, they had fought heroically for their convictions, and whatever the color of their party, they had demonstrated they were true Germans. The National Socialists themselves had not sacrificed a man or a bullet because any conceivable resolution of the conflict would be directed against Germany and the German people. "But for a German solution," said Habicht, "which the party has sought from the beginning, [National Socialism] is ready at any time to make any sacrifice."[4]

The Socialists were defeated and the Nazis had been declared illegal, but the reaction of the great powers was limited to a joint communiqué issued on February 17 by France and Italy protesting the interference of the Reich in the internal affairs of Austria and repeating their determination to see to it that Austria remained independent. Their pronouncement was meant as a continued guarantee of Austrian independence, but it did nothing to improve the lot of the Austrian people or their support for a government forced to take more and more draconic measures to maintain itself in office. House searches were ordered, hundreds of opposition leaders were arrested—Social Democrats, Communists, National Socialists (including eleven hundred Nazi leaders)—and their party centers were closed. Arrests could be made as a result of denunciations, and alleged Nazis along with genuine ones could be held in jail for an indeterminate period. The proscribed parties were driven underground, but they remained in opposition; the government repressions, far from restoring law and order, only served to increase the number of terrorist acts.

The Austrian National Socialists, like the Dollfuss government, were ridden with factions. One of Habicht's chief rivals in a party without central leadership was Hermann Reschny, an SA Obergruppenführer who had the ten thousand–man Austrian Legion under his control as well as a sizable SA group in Austria itself. Reschny made preparations to order the Austria Legion to march into Austria in October 1933, a date postponed until early 1934 when, with other SA leaders, he considered whether the SA should be summoned home to join the battle then being waged between the government and Social Democratic forces.

Reschny told Habicht nothing of these plans, but Hitler heard of them through the German military attaché in Vienna, and he forbade Reschny to continue with any projects that would involve a rising of the SA. Nevertheless the possibility of a takeover in Vienna remained an alluring prospect, and still another Nazi group, this one in the Vienna police department, separately plotted a strategy for the seizure of power that would be adopted by the actual putschists in July. This group was concentrated for a time in the so-called alarm section of the police, commanded by Leo Gotzmann, but the government became suspicious of the section and reassigned several leaders, including Gotzmann, to other posts. The plotters continued with their preparations for a coup with the help of the SA and dissident army units. They planned to arrest the members of the ministerial council during one of its meetings and at the same time occupy the Vienna police headquarters and barracks along with government buildings and the radio station. The army contingents were to be recruited by a major on active service, Rudolph Selinger, who would also be responsible for any subsequent military operations.

When Selinger failed to enlist sufficient forces from the Bundeswehr he turned to a police official, Konrad Rotter, who was reported to have under his leadership a force of about a thousand men ready to take arms against Dollfuss. They were said to include government officials in the chancellery and in administrative posts, and Rotter would add to them guards of the government buildings and members of the criminal police, with all of whom he had connections.

Plans were made and unmade. They were fragmented, worked up by one group or another. No central authority existed; the only bond that held them together was determination to get rid of Dollfuss. Habicht was in touch with a former member of the Dollfuss cabinet, Anton Rintelin, a man Dollfuss had forced to resign and then sent to Rome as ambassador. Rintelin along with another former member of the cabinet, Franz Winkler, who had been vice chancellor and now was out of both a job and funds, agreed to join the conspiracy, and Rintelin, though like Dollfuss a Christian Socialist, accepted the post of chancellor in the coming National Socialist government. But nothing jelled. No one was in charge of the grand conspiracy, and Hitler refused his approval for any National Socialist attempt to seize power. When Habicht, during one of his optimistic reports on the imminent overthrow of Dollfuss, informed Hitler that the Bundeswehr was on the point of revolting, Hitler told him peremptorily that the party must not take part in the coup—though he added it could participate in a post-Dollfuss government. He also refused to approve Reschny's plans for an SA rising, and he told Otto Wächter, the son of a minister for Defense in a pre-Dollfuss government who journeyed to Berlin on behalf of Habicht, that he forbade any attempt at a coup by the Austrian Nazis. But Wächter, like Habicht and the others, simply did not believe him; they were convinced Hitler was talking only for the record, making no more than a tactical move to dissociate the Reich from any possible embarrassment that might result from the failure of a coup. After all, Hitler's views on the subject of Dollfuss and Austria's becoming part of a great German Reich had not changed; the shipments of arms and ammunition from Germany to Austria continued, and the Austrian Legion now concentrated in a number of German camps remained ready to march. Hitler might be moving overcautiously, but in their view his policy remained the same even though he refused permission for the publication of an inflammatory speech by Habicht. The bellicose man Hitler had named as Landesinspekteur of the Austrian party remained in his job. He also remained at loggerheads with the other aspirants for leading the coming Nazi revolt, and the pressure on each one to act to forestall the others became greater as the length and tension of the waiting period increased.

It was Hitler's desire to placate Mussolini that was affecting Reich foreign and domestic policy and that redirected Hitler's Austrian strategy. In February 1934 Hungary, Italy, and Austria signed the Rome Protocols, designed to offset the French-dominated Little Entente and to take pressure off Austria by increasing her foreign trade and by persuading Hitler to restate his recognition of Austrian domestic and foreign independence. The Rome Protocols also provided for the possibility of Germany's joining the signers, a move that Hitler had no intention of making. Nevertheless, with Austria appealing to the League of Nations to take international measures against German interference in her domestic affairs, it was imperative for Hitler to prevent the isolation of the Reich, and to do this he had to come to an understanding with Mussolini. He imposed silence on Habicht, ordering the attacks on the Dollfuss government to cease along with any references to an *Anschluss*. It was this shift in strategy that made possible his meeting with Mussolini in Venice. It may well be that, as Rosenberg wrote in his diary, Mussolini had agreed with Hitler that Dollfuss should be replaced by a nonparty chancellor and that new elections in Austria should be held, though Mussolini pointed out they could not take place in an atmosphere of terrorism, and the Nazis should be represented in the forthcoming government in proportion to their electoral success.[5] In any event Hitler and Mussolini told one another the Austrian problem should not be an obstacle to their relations. Both were convinced Austria would one day be part of a greater Germany, but Hitler said there was no need for hurry, and Mussolini could readily go along with that view since he shared it.

The agreement to let the Austrian problem cool left Habicht without much backing for his Austrian stratagems. If a putsch were made without him by Reschny, the SA, and the SS, Habicht would be left out of any post-Dollfuss government. He proceeded therefore to patch up an ad hoc alliance with Konrad Rotter, and they—together with Rudolf Weydenhammer (a well-connected German banker), Wächter, and Austrian SS Untersturmführer Fridolin Glass—went ahead with plans for a coup of their own, despite the fact that Rotter reported that the expected help from the police had seriously diminished because so many of them were on leave.[6] Glass claimed he had close connections with a well-disposed Austrian general staff, which proved untrue, but he was in touch with Heinrich Himmler, who was after Röhm's defeat more powerful than before. Himmler was in a position to place Glass in charge of an SS unit, and the conspirators therefore made Glass commander of military operations for the rising, despite his meager qualifications for the job. Glass's military experience had been limited to the three years he had served in the Austrian army, in which he remained a private the whole time. Thanks to Himmler, Glass was the leader of SS Standarte 89 with a theoretical manpower of four hundred, only about half of whom were to appear when the day of the rising came.

The SA was not brought into the action in Vienna at any time, though it had always been counted on as the chief armed support of the coup, and Reschny had agreed just before the start of the rising that the formations under his command would take part. Why this happened, why Reschny not only failed to order out his SA troops in Vienna but also actually warned the police against the plotters he had joined, is part of the crossing and double crossing that characterized the enterprise on both sides. To be sure, Hitler had told Reschny he was to prevent a putsch, but that had happened in May before Reschny had a final meeting with the other conspirators in July at which time he gave no hint of dissent from carrying out the enterprise. He was only one of the ambivalent characters in both the antigovernment and the progovernment forces that clashed in 1934. His rivalry with Habicht had doubtless always been uppermost in his calculations and may well have been the main reason for his becoming an informer and giving the names of Wächter, Glass, and Weydenhammer to the Austrian police, telling them through an intermediary whom to look out for among the conspirators. Nevertheless, it was his SA troops with the arms he had provided from Germany that did march against the government in the provinces.[7]

With or without the SA, Habicht, Wächter, Glass, and the others were determined to go ahead with whatever forces they could muster. The split between the SA and the SS, which had widened considerably since the events of June 30, made it easier for Habicht, who was in Munich, to proceed with his plans without Reschny and the SA. To overturn the Dollfuss government without them could not be displeasing to Habicht, nor would a failure on the part of the SS in Vienna seem a catastrophe to Reschny. Habicht's role in the attempted coup in Vienna ceased with the planning. He remained in Munich during the entire action, poised to fly to Vienna when the time came, which it never did.

The plotters had adopted in its essentials the plan of the dissident Viennese police. They would arrest the members of the ministerial council, occupy the security administration building, the telephone central, Ravag (the Austrian radio center), and the adjoining station in nearby Bisamberg. They dispatched three men to arrest Wilhelm Miklas, president of the republic, who was on vacation in Kärnten, one of the chief centers of Nazi support. Taken into custody Miklas would be forced to name Rintelin to replace Dollfuss as chancellor. For the entire operation the conspirators had some two hundred men at their disposal. The SS Standarte 89 was its only military force, and the SA, which for months had been counted on as the military spearhead, was out of the picture.[8]

Things went wrong even before the start of the rising. The attempted putsch took place on July 25, and on July 24 the plot to kidnap President Miklas had failed. The men sent to seize him had rented an automobile that was spotted as suspicious by the Kärnten police. Two of the would-be kidnappers were taken into custody, while one man managed to get away and escape to Czechoslovakia. Miklas remained free. In Vienna the putschists who were to assemble at noon on the 25th at the gymnasium of the Deutsche Turnbund, to change from civilian clothes into army uniforms, took more time than had been calculated and were late in arriving at the courtyard of the chancellery. That should have given the government forces, the police, and the Bundeswehr time enough to seal off the building, but though the police had known the details of the planned coup from many sources, and even had a man stationed at the gymnasium who saw the cases of guns and ammunition being unloaded and reported all this to his superiors, the countermeasures, too, were late. Both sides, the Nazis and the government forces, were riddled with spies, single and double agents, and spontaneous informers as well. Reschny was not the only one serving two masters—another was Fey who had been deprived of his post as minister of Security, which Dollfuss himself took over, but remained in the cabinet with the resounding title of General State Commissar for Special Security Measures to Combat Undertakings of Enemies of the State. A formidable title, but Fey had no powers that matched it; security was no longer in his hands, and, like Rintelin, he felt himself demoted and left out of the important decisions. Fey was in touch with Wächter, he knew of preparations for the coup, and on the day it took place he was informed of the latest details through a police inspector, Johann Dobler, brought into the plot by his colleague, Rotter, who was greatly in need of police recruits. Dobler had been a member of the Heimwehr but had become a National Socialist while the party was still legal, and he had the confidence of party leaders. He, too, was a double agent, though he remained in the conspiracy and took part in the uprising. He was one of the government's chief sources of information, revealing the details of how the plotters intended to operate. Through him and other agents Fey was kept abreast of the developing crisis.[9]

Fey belatedly acted on the information furnished him, and he moved very slowly. The reports on the progress of the conspirators' activities kept coming in during the course of the morning hours, while Fey busied himself only with having them checked, and it was a little after noon when he went to the chancellery where the ministerial council was in session to whisper to Dollfuss that a coup was in progress. Dollfuss suspended the meeting until four o'clock in the afternoon, and though he told the ministers he was uncertain of the reliability of the reports, he prudently sent them back to their offices to avoid, as he said, their being caught in a mousetrap where they could be captured together. Dollfuss then returned to his own office, together with Fey, State Secretary Karwinsky (who had taken on part of Fey's former security job), and Major General Zehner.

More than half an hour went by, with flurries of activity as government leaders kept in touch with their forces. Karwinsky repeatedly telephoned police authorities to have them check out the reports of armed men in the streets and to step up security in the chancellery. General Zehner gave the alarm to the Vienna garrison but not to the chancellery guards, while Fey ordered the chief of the chancellery defense force, Lieutenant Colonel Pollacek-Wittek to his office, and then sent out the alarm to the guards just as the putschists were entering the building. Not even the main doors of the chancellery were shut when the putschists, dressed as soldiers, arrived in trucks and cars just before one o'clock.

The invaders met no resistance. One section chief, as he saw them enter the courtyard, suspected something must be wrong, because it was the lunch hour and the genuine soldiers assigned to the chancellery were to be depended upon to be eating their midday meal at that time. Another official was suspicious because the "soldiers" he ran into failed to salute him. But on the whole their arrival caused no commotion, and a police officer politely showed the arriving drivers where they could park their cars. A small commando promptly overpowered the military guards who carried only unloaded weapons—the men carbines, the officers revolvers—and the putschists numbering some 150 men stormed into the chancellery. Meanwhile five armed men in civilian clothes forced their way into Ravag, the main Austrian radio station, shooting one policeman who tried to stop them and knocking the other out of the way. They bolted the door of the building, no doubt with their own security in mind, but effectively preventing the main body of reinforcements from reaching them. A small additional group eventually did succeed in gaining entry into Ravag from a neighboring courtyard, but in all only fifteen men managed to get inside the building, and the message they intended to broadcast, proclaiming Rintelin's takeover of the government, was never sent. A loyal employee simply turned off the transmission.

The invaders of the chancellery had fanned out, and one group under the leader of the invading force, a member of the Bundesheer, Franz Holzweber, made its way to the third story where they found Dollfuss. Apparently as the men converged on him he made a move to defend himself—later as he lay dying he explained that after all he had been a soldier—and another former member of the Bundesheer, Otto Planetta, shot him down. Actually two bullets hit Dollfuss—whether or not both were fired by Planetta is not clear. Entering the left side of the neck, one of them was mortal. It went through the spine, paralyzing the chancellor from the waist down, splintering two ribs, and cutting two large blood vessels, before it went out through the right side of the thoracic cavity. The putschists paid no attention to his feeble plea that a priest and a doctor be sent to him; one of them reached under Dollfuss's coat apparently to see whether, as their propaganda claimed, he wore a bulletproof coat, and finding nothing they cut off the sleeve of his coat, exposing the wound. They were ready, one of them said, to provide an Aryan doctor if one could be found inside the chancellery, but no one was to leave the building. All they wanted of Dollfuss was to name Rintelin as his successor. Dollfuss refused.

Two policemen bandaged the wounded chancellor, who spoke lucidly, telling the putschists he had wanted nothing but peace and the best for Austria and asking Fey who had come into the room to please seek Mussolini's help in caring for his wife and children. Soon after that, at 3:45 P.M., he died. When doctors finally arrived at the chancellery to attend him they were told it was too late.

Some 150 government officials—*Beamte*—were in the building and were held as hostages. They were permitted to find chairs and were provided with water, and when Holzweber happily announced that Rintelin was the new chancellor and shouted "Heil Hitler," some of them joined in with their own "Heil Hitler." Later in the afternoon, however, as government forces gathered, the *Beamte* were lined up against the wall and told they would be shot. At this point a putschist in a lieutenant's uniform rushed into the room, ordered the rebels to give up their weapons, and had them led away. The hostages were permitted to resume their seats.

Fey was among those in the chancellery, and he went into action on behalf of the new government. He telephoned police and civil authorities, telling them not to attempt to storm the chancellery. He attempted to send out a broadcast over Ravag and a temporary radio station, saying that Dollfuss was dying and that Rintelin had been authorized to reconstitute a government on a wide basis. He wrote a proclamation declaring that a new cabinet with Rintelin as chancellor had been appointed and calling on the population to maintain calm. As putschists were to testify later, he had been offered the post of minister of Security in the Rintelin cabinet, and Fey did in fact identify himself as head of such when he talked with officials over the telephone. His explanation that he had been forced by the rebels to cooperate seemed unconvincing to many who saw him associating unconstrainedly with them. Despite Fey's announcements it was plain by midafternoon that the coup was not doing well. The invaders in the chancellery and Ravag had lost all touch with the outside leaders. They were barricaded inside both buildings, no reinforcements had reached them, and there never had been enough men to occupy the telephone central or the police barracks. Wächter had at long last persuaded the leader of the Vienna SA, Oskar Turk, to mobilize his men, and at 5:00 P.M. Turk had given them orders to be ready to march. But it was not until seven o'clock that they were in line, and with the police already in the chancellery Turk countermanded the orders he had been reluctant to issue. An ally of Reschny, he had no compelling passion to rescue the SS men.

It was a dismal performance on the part of the rebel leaders. Glass reported later that he had been arrested and held prisoner for a short time at the gymnasium but managed to escape, and dressed in an overcoat he had sought to make identification less easy. He had tried, without success, to gain entry to the chancellery. The story may have been invented to account for the fact that Glass never appeared. Nor did Rintelin, who was waiting impatiently at the Imperial Hotel for the summons to betake himself to the Ballhausplatz where he would assume office. When it came it was in an unpleasant form; in midafternoon Weydenhammer and Wächter told him the police and Heimwehr had surrounded the chancellery, and no one could get in. A last-ditch attempt had to be made to save the day, and they urged Rintelin to go with them to the chancellery and make the attempt.[10] While they were talking, Rintelin received a telephone call from Kurt von Schuschnigg, who President Miklas had just named chancellor, asking him to come to the Ministry of War. Rintelin had no desire whatever to accept Schuschnigg's invitation, but it was followed by the appearance of Schuschnigg's emissary, the newspaper editor Friedrich Funder, who had the mission of bringing Rintelin along. Fearing he might be taken into custody right away if he refused to go, Rintelin accompanied by Funder drove to the Ministry of War where he was arrested.

At six o'clock Holzweber telephoned the German ambassador, Kurt Rieth, to inform him the rising had failed and to ask him to arrange for transportation and a safe-conduct to enable the rebels to reach the German border. Weydenhammer, who had been with Rintelin in the Imperial Hotel, betook himself to the German Embassy and from there managed to make his way over the border to Czechoslovakia and the following day to the Reich. Wächter, dressed as a sailor, went by boat down the Danube to Budapest and then on to Berlin. Rotter and Glass also got away safely: Rotter to the Reich and Glass to Czechoslovakia.

The situation of the putschists inside both the chancellery and Ravag—in the face of hundreds of soldiers, police, and Heimwehr—was hopeless. The government forces had tear gas as well as heavy weapons, but they could not make use of the gas because they had no masks for their own protection. A government spokesman told Fey, who was standing on the courtyard balcony in front of the chancellery, that the putschists would be granted a safe-conduct to the German border if they quit the building within twenty minutes. Eventually more time was granted them while the promise of a safe-conduct was confirmed by Fey, Karwinsky, and Odo Neustädter-Stürmer (a Heimwehr leader and member of the Dollfuss cabinet), as well as by Rieth who, as he explained later, was ready to join with the other guarantors to avoid further bloodshed.[11]

The putschists thereupon surrendered, throwing their arms in a pile in the chancellery courtyard. The ministerial council had meanwhile learned that Dollfuss had been murdered, and the safe-conduct was ignored as Schuschnigg ordered the arrest of all the rebels. The only ones who escaped were those who mingled with the former hostages in the chancellery and, undetected, left the building with them. The rest were taken off to the police barracks they had hoped to capture, and there they were held under strict arrest while they were interrogated by a battery of criminal authorities in hearings that lasted from midnight to early in the morning. The hearings soon disclosed Planetta's and Holzweber's part in the action. They were held on charges of murder and high treason and were hanged on July 30. Most of the others captured at the chancellery, considered minor offenders, were permitted to leave for the German border.

The rising in the countryside, which lasted from July 25 to July 29, had only a tenuous connection with the rebellion in Vienna. Since June, Reschny had been supplying his SA with large quantities of arms smuggled from the Reich, and in the provinces the SA was to provide the chief support for the revolt. The SA leaders outside Vienna had long planned to take to arms at the same time a coup took place in Vienna; they also expected their rising would be joined by the Austrian Legion, which was to cross the border and march on the capital. The SA plan, known as the *Kollerschlag Documents,* fell into the hands of government authorities in the early morning of July 26, the day after the Vienna rising had failed. They were found on the person of an SA courier, Franz Hiebl, traveling on a false German passport, as he was searched near the town of Kollerschlag on the Austrian-Bavarian frontier. It was a wide-angled prospectus, attempting to deal with the broadest possible contingencies beginning with the demission of the Dollfuss government. Its resignation or ousting would result either in the naming of a new chancellor or a battle for the office. In either event the SA would take the field and occupy government buildings in the provincial capitals and district headquarters, where a soothing proclamation would be issued. And though the Kollerschlag Documents were wholly of Nazi origin, the proclamation was to state that Austria would be independent of both the Reich and Italy; the purpose of the revolution, it declared, was to return the country to constitutional government. The SA would ignore the new chancellor, whoever he was, but the documents predicted that when he learned that the SA had seized power in the countryside he must either recognize the Nazis or resist them, and in the latter case the SA would fight him with all its strength. Specific battle plans were lacking. The SA leaders in each locality were to work out their own tactics; only the main strategy was outlined—the SA would occupy public buildings, hoist swastika flags, seize enemy leaders, declare an amnesty for all political crimes, and release political prisoners including Communists and Socialists. As a result the SA believed they could count at least on the neutrality of the Left. Clashes with the police and gendarmerie were to be avoided as long as possible, but if the SA had to fight, the document declared, it was to use its weapons to the utmost, though there was to be no conflict with the army if it could possibly be avoided.

Such was the plan, and as news of the Vienna rising reached the countryside the SA often joined by SS units went into action following the Kollerschlag prescription. In the Steiermark on July 25, swastika flags went up as the National Socialists took over government buildings in towns and villages where they met little or no resistance. But they were joined by no government forces from the police or Heimwehr, gendarmerie or Bundesheer, despite the optimistic predictions of Nazi members of the police and the army. The rising had no more than sporadic and local successes—no central command existed there either— and the scattered units taking part had maintained scanty communications with each other. Many villages were occupied, but they were held with small forces as compared with the mobilized government contingents and not much time elapsed between the pronouncements issued from SA headquarters announcing that the National Socialists had assumed full power in the state and the departure of the outnumbered and outgunned SA from the localities they had occupied. According to plan the SA had captured leaders of the Heimwehr forces and released political prisoners from local jails, but government troops soon made their appearance, and after some sharp engagements the SA and the paramilitary formations that had joined them had to retreat.

It was in Kärnten that the often-predicted popular rising actually took place. There the SA and the SS were joined by farmers' self-defense units of the Landbund, sometimes by so many that crops could not be harvested and prisoners had to be released from jail to work in the fields. In Klagenfurt alone, two thousand prisoners were let out of jail to bring in the harvest, and the provincial government offered the rebels amnesty if they would surrender their arms and return to their farms. But even in the province of Kärnten, once the six thousand men who joined the rising were mobilized, the leadership showed itself uncertain of what to do next.

The rising had its few short-lived successes near the Yugoslavian border where the putschists had the friendly support of Yugoslavian officials, who permitted them to store ammunition and other military supplies in the safe refuge of a foreign country whose authorities in addition would be ready to call on their own troops if Italian forces marched into Austria. Thus it was in Kärnten and Steiermark that the Kollerschlag Documents actually were carried out, and fighting was often bloody, with dozens killed or wounded on both sides.

In most of Austria the government forces had little trouble containing the SA. Upper Austria was quiet, and the lack of rebel forces enabled the government to concentrate its forces against the centers of the rebellion. The rebels fought, but they were vastly outnumbered, and the Austrian Legion as a whole did not march—though a few small units attacked border towns across from the Bavarian frontier before they withdrew.

By July 30 it was all over. The uprising was defeated throughout the country. The Austrian government was hard put to find places to hold those captured, using schools and dance halls as detention centers. The casualties were considerable: over 250 people dead and some 500 wounded. More than one hundred SA men were killed, seven of the SS, three from the Hitler Youth, nine from the Steier Home Defense forces, and eight from the farmers' Landbund. The Austrian army lost twenty-three men, the police four, the gendarmerie ten, and the Heimwehr fifty-six.

After the hasty hangings of Planetta and Holzweber, military courts tried the other chief conspirators, and the sentences were sometimes heavy. Vice Chancellor Starhemberg, who acted as chancellor until Dollfuss was buried, impressed on the council of ministers that any further sign of weakness would make it unlikely that the government would long remain in power, and the official line hardened. Examples had to be made, especially of dissident members of the police or of the armed forces. In Vienna the only member of the Bundesheer on active service who participated in the rising, Ernst Feike, was hanged. Paul Hudle, who had been on the chancellery staff with the rank of major, got life imprisonment. Nine members of the chancellery guard were tried, of whom four received death sentences. Two policemen got life imprisonment. One of the Ravag putschists, Johann Domes, was sentenced to death and hanged; twelve others were given life imprisonment. In the provinces three men were executed for their part in the uprising, and others who were condemned to death later had their sentences commuted to life imprisonment. In addition two men charged with carrying explosives were hanged. The property of everyone condemned by the military courts was confiscated, and personal property was broadly defined—it included family jewels, factories, and businesses. Almost ten thousand prisoners were still in custody in September, but since they could not all be assigned heavy labor, most of them were given odd jobs or, if they were farmers, permitted to go back to their homes.

Despite the display of rigor against many of the putschists and their families, the government had to tread warily to keep what support it had. Thousands of Austrians remained unreconciled, and the semblance of a unified nation had to be maintained as best it could in the still-divided country. Rintelin was sentenced to life imprisonment, and nothing whatever happened to Fey who was even kept on in the Schuschnigg regime. The government could not admit that a minister in the Dollfuss cabinet had taken part in the conspiracy, and it participated in the cover-up. To be sure, Fey's role in the Schuschnigg cabinet was purely administrative, but he was never in danger of being tried for high treason, and until 1936 he remained a leader in the Heimwehr. The whole effort of the government was directed toward securing as wide a support as possible from the portion of the population it could reach with patriotic appeals. Lesser offenders were treated leniently, imprisoned for a few months and then released if they acknowledged their error and assured the authorities they were now dependable citizens. In November of 1935 the first wholesale amnesty was granted, and by 1936 most of those arrested, Rintelin among them, were out of prison and could, if they wished to, emigrate to the Reich.

The failed coup made headlines in the world press but no changes in foreign policy among the powers. Hitler burst into a fury when, while attending the Bayreuth festival, he learned what had happened. He recalled his ambassador, Rieth, for intervening with the Austrian authorities on behalf of the putschists and aiding them to reach the Reich; he had those who had already crossed the border arrested and sent to concentration camps while those who entered the Reich later, after the fighting in provinces, were placed in honorable arrest and sent to the Landsberg prison where Hitler had spent his own easy captivity a decade before. Hitler also angrily summoned Habicht to Bayreuth on July 26 and stripped him of all his functions, abolishing the Landesleitung Habicht had headed that had served as the liaison organization between the Reich and the Austrian Nazis. Papen was appointed ambassador to Vienna with credentials Hitler thought likely to appeal to Schuschnigg and his government. Papen was a practicing Catholic, and the Schuschnigg government, like its predecessor, represented political Catholicism, which in his way Papen did, too. Hitler was conducting a holding operation, and he was certain that time was on his side.

His rage was directed against the ineptitude of those of his followers who had lost a battle and caused him to lose face. He had certainly wanted and expected an uprising in Austria but a successful one that did not involve the Reich or his carefully nurtured relationship with Mussolini. His own ambivalence had appeared plainly when he told Reschny that in the event of a successful coup by the Bundesheer the party might participate in the new government but that it must not take an active part in a rebellion. It was also to be seen in the continuous shipments of arms and explosives, which Hitler then directed the Austrian Nazis not to use.

Mussolini, too, was furious but not quite as furious as he made himself out to be. It is true he sent troops to the Brenner Pass, but they were already on maneuvers not far away. Like Hitler, Mussolini was limited in his Austrian policy by wider considerations. His alternative to coming to some kind of agreement with Hitler was to turn to France, and if Hitler would accept the status quo on the Brenner Pass and pay lip service to an independent Austria, Mussolini was convinced he had more reason to oppose the French hegemonical system than to oppose the Reich's effort to overcome it. Coming to an accommodation with Hitler was more likely to further his aspirations for a greater Italy than strengthening the French network of alliances. Italy had done that in the world war, and then as he and his party saw it had been cynically deprived of the fruits of victory and the territories the Allies had promised. So Austria, for the time being at least, remained independent of the Reich and of Italy, as the Kollerschlag Documents had promised.

4

President and Reichschancellor

Hitler's main concern after the SA and Austrian crises was with Hindenburg's health and what kind of testament addressed to the German people he would leave behind. The president still held fast the loyalties of millions of Germans who had twice voted for him against Hitler, and even in the last days of his life could bar the way to Hitler's total power over the Reich. It was plain to everyone who saw Hindenburg in late spring and early summer that he had not much longer to live. Nearly eighty-seven, he was suffering from a painful bladder infection; he had refused to take to his bed, and in his stolid, uncomplaining fashion he continued his usual routine of receiving visitors and attending to official business. His declining fires made it imperative in June for him to leave Berlin for Neudeck where he would be under less pressure than in the capital.

For years he had had intermittent periods of confusion and forgetfulness and about all that remained intact, ineradicably rooted in his mind, was his faith in the fatherland and in the probity of the German people. He had been deeply disturbed by the killing of the Schleichers and of Bredow and then by the reports that reached him of the involvement of the Austrian Nazis in the murder of Dollfuss. Hitler had been able to reassure him on both occasions: The Führer had promised that the deaths of the Schleichers and of Bredow would be officially investigated, and anyone found guilty of the murders would be legally executed, but the old gentleman was nevertheless troubled by events he could not fully comprehend. In the last weeks of his life he was almost completely dependent on his son and the few selected people who were permitted to see him for the news that reached him and to tell him what it meant.

He remained, as he had been all his life, a monarchist, and his longing for a return of a German Kaiser could only have been intensified by the part he had played in the abdication of Wilhelm II. At the end of his memoirs written in 1919, in the heavy prose of a field marshal addressing a dispirited country in need of counsels of patience and perspective, he wrote: "A high tide of wild political passion and sounding phrases has flooded over our former concept of the state and seemingly destroyed all its sacred traditions. But this flood will run its course. Then out of the eternal heaving sea of the people's life, the cliffs will reappear to which our fathers clung and on which a half century ago the future of the fatherland was founded—the German empire *[das deutsche Kaisertum]* will reappear." As a young lieutenant he had witnessed the ceremony at Versailles where the king of Prussia had been named emperor of Germany, and at the end of a long life the promise of a restoration of a monarch presiding over striving political parties seemed in wonderful contrast to the brawls of the Weimar Republic, the Röhm and Dollfuss murders, the Nazi attacks on the churches, the pogroms against Jews who had served in the front line of the troops he had led. He was aware too of the dismay of many of the conservatives he trusted at the courses the government was pursuing; that was why he had asked Papen to try to bring things in order. But Hitler was Reichschancellor, and Hindenburg wholeheartedly approved much of what he had accomplished. The country was emerging from the depression, some kind of outward consensus of national unity had been restored, and the time of abject helplessness in the face of foreign demands on the Reich was past. Hindenburg was weary, and it was much easier for him to accept what Hitler told him than to make sure that it had some content; in his last months he could only go along and call on an old adviser such as Papen to help make things better.

Papen had a special place in Hindenburg's regard. It was to Papen the president had turned in June, before the Marburg speech, asking him to help set matters right. Although Hindenburg was ready to accept Hitler's explanations of acts of violence he continued to have mixed feelings about him—at least to the extent that he wanted a monarchy, and Papen always retained his confidence. Papen, too, was a monarchist and even before the Marburg speech had talked with both Hitler and Hindenburg about the possibility of restoring a Kaiser to the throne. Although Papen's accounts of what went on at critical times invariably placed himself in an unduly favorable light, he may be believed when he writes in his memoirs that in March 1934 he had a talk with Hitler about a restoration of the monarchy after Hindenburg's death and had found him unexpectedly receptive to the idea.

Hitler's favorable response may be plausibly attributed to his knowledge that Papen was still close to Hindenburg, and every effort must be made to placate the man who was the last obstacle to his assuming ultimate power over the Reich and its armed forces. In any event Papen soon after his conversation with Hitler had a talk with Hindenburg during which he told the president that to avoid the chaos that could well follow on Hindenburg's death or inability to carry out his duties he should, in a political testament, recommend a return to the monarchy.

Hindenburg, according to Meissner, was at first opposed to the idea of a testament, but when Papen later returned to the subject Hindenburg somewhat reluctantly agreed and asked him to make a draft of what he had in mind. Papen did, and when he handed Hindenburg the draft on his next visit early in May it was, Meissner says, taken almost word for word from what Hindenburg had written in 1919 with the addition of some sentences of praise for what Hitler had accomplished. The president read it and then told Papen he would need more time to consider the matter carefully. This he seems to have done, as best he could in the recurrent mists of his advanced years, the pain of his infection, and his failing strength.

But when he summoned Papen to let him know his decision he said he did not consider it proper to recommend a future form of the state to the German people. The time was not ripe for that, and moreover a nation had to decide for itself what form of government it would adopt. He would therefore, instead, prepare an accounting of what he had tried to accomplish on behalf of the Reich and would put his recommendation for a restoration of the monarchy in the form of a personal letter to Hitler. What had changed his mind is unknown. Whether Oskar von Hindenburg or others had dissuaded him from following his first impulse, or whether the decision was wholly his own, is unclear, but he told Papen there would be two documents. He then dictated the testament in two parts signing them on May 14 in the presence of his son and Captain von der Schulenburg.[1] One envelope was addressed to the German people, the other to the Reichschancellor.

For some weeks Hindenburg continued to take daily walks, but his health was deteriorating rapidly. Hitler was kept informed of his condition by Hindenburg's doctor, the eminent Berlin practitioner Ferdinand Sauerbruch, who continued to visit his patient in Neudeck. Papen was never to see him again. Toward the end of July, as the reports on Hindenburg's health became more ominous, Papen suggested to Hitler that they go together to Neudeck, but Hitler put him off, saying it would not be possible to have a useful talk with a man so ill. Nevertheless on July 31 he did fly to Neudeck but without Papen. The president scarcely recognized him when his son told him the chancellor was there, but he falteringly asked him why Hitler had not come earlier. Oskar replied that the chancellor had not been able to make the trip sooner, and Hindenburg said he understood. Oskar then left the two men alone and they talked for some time, with frequent interruptions as Hindenburg's strength ebbed, and then Hitler, visibly moved, took leave and flew back to Berlin. What they talked about is not known. But what is known is that on the same night Hitler made sure no slipup would occur in the naming of a successor to Hindenburg. He called a cabinet meeting for 9:30 P.M., and the Law Concerning the Head of State was immediately approved, providing for the consolidation of the offices of the Reichspresident and the Reichschancellor.

The next morning Hindenburg died. The German radio announced that with the unification of both offices the authority of the Reichspresident had devolved upon the Führer and Reichschancellor and that he would decide who would be his deputy.[2] It was another law that circumvented the constitution Hitler had sworn in January 1933 to uphold, but under the Enabling Act it was legal, as was almost anything else that Hitler might decide to do.[3]

Hindenburg died at nine o'clock in the morning of August 2. As he felt the end approaching he had asked Dr. Sauerbruch to tell him plainly what the state of his health was, saying: "I have the impression Friend Hein [Death] is at the door." Sauerbruch answered that "Friend Hein" was not at the door but was to be seen "suspiciously lurking about the house." Hindenburg then asked to be left alone for an hour or two and to have his New Testament placed within reach on his night table. When Sauerbruch came back to the sickroom, Hindenburg said: "Now you can ask the gentleman to come in. I am ready."[4] He then repeated the wishes he had expressed before; he wanted no great pomp and ceremony at his funeral but to be buried quietly in the cemetery at Neudeck where his wife and ancestors lay. Further, he wanted no hymns of praise or political speeches at the services, only a minister of the gospel who would ask for God's grace. If there was to be a memorial service near the capital he wanted it held in the Garrison Church in Potsdam.

Contrary to Hindenburg's desire for a simple funeral, Hitler had other plans; the occasion presented too auspicious an opportunity for a theatrical display to permit Hindenburg's wishes to be carried out. And the chancellor wasted not a moment in taking over. On the day Hindenburg died, the Reichswehr was ordered by General von Blomberg to take an oath of allegiance to Hitler in person, and the government announced that a plebiscite would be held to confirm the cabinet's decision that the presidential authority would devolve upon the chancellor. The text of the former oath of allegiance was changed. The new version prepared in advance by General von Reichenau, with Majors Foertsch and Röhrecht, read: "I swear under God this holy oath of unconditional obedience to the leader of the German Reich and people, Adolf Hitler, commander-in-chief of the Wehrmacht, and as a brave soldier will be ready at all times to risk my life for this oath."[5]

The former oath had been sworn to the state, the constitution, and the president whoever he might be. The new oath was sworn to Hitler alone, as in the nineteenth century it had been sworn to the person of the king of Prussia and, after the unification of Germany, to the person of the Kaiser. And with full power over the armed forces Hitler modestly separated himself from his august predecessor by refusing to use the title of president. On August 4, Minister of the Interior Frick announced that Hitler had directed that he be referred to only as "Führer and Reichschancellor" within Germany and in his relations with foreign countries as "The German Reichschancellor."

Hitler addressed the Reichstag at a memorial service in Berlin on August 6, telling its members Hindenburg still lived: "One of the deathless of our people." On August 7 came the grandiose ceremony at the Tannenberg National Memorial at Hohenstein. Hindenburg's body together with that of his late wife had been brought from Neudeck the night before; in the presence of the Berlin diplomatic corps and mourners from all over Germany, and under the banners of thousands of troops, sailors, police, the SA and the SS, and to the sound of drums and Beethoven's *Eroica,* Hindenburg was laid to rest in the crypt of the huge monument erected to commemorate the victory he had won in 1914. Only one man followed Hindenburg's wishes for his burial service. The Protestant army bishop Dohmann preached a sermon based on the text from John 2:10: "Be thou faithful unto death and I will give thee the crown of life." The bishop was followed by Hitler who delivered an effusive tribute to the dead war hero that ended with the unprotestant words it was fortunate Hindenburg could not hear: "Enter now, dead commander, into Valhalla."

Hitler had a few more moves to make before the plebiscite, and he was playing a generous role. The day following the burial he proclaimed a general amnesty as well as an amnesty for certain categories of political prisoners. The general amnesty applied to those whose sentences were for no longer than six months or whose fines were for no more than one thousand marks if they had not had a previous jail record. Those sentenced to no more than three months in jail or a fine of five hundred marks were freed even if they had such a record. Included were offenders who had traduced either Hitler or the National Socialist state as well as anyone who had acted overzealously on behalf of the Nazi movement—in effect any of the hoodlums who had physically attacked or otherwise used force against enemies of the party. The amnesty took effect only if the crime had been committed before August 2, the day Hindenburg died. Hitler also ordered that the dossiers of prisoners held in protective custody be reexamined. Nazi sources declared that 414,000 people were released under the general amnesty of the August 7 decree; 6,300 prisoners who had been jailed for various political transgressions were freed by the end of September.[6] They also declared that over eleven hundred of those who had been placed in protective custody at the time of the Röhm revolt had been freed and only thirty-five who had been deeply incriminated remained, for the time being at least, in protective custody. None of this wholesale clemency was extended to old enemies of the party. For the most part the Left, the Social Democrats, and of course the Communists remained where they were: in prisons or concentration camps or underground.

Hitler was concerned with Hindenburg's political testament, and a few days after the Tannenberg ceremony he asked Meissner if there was one, and if there was, who had it. Hitler told Meissner he understood from dependable sources there was such a document and that it was not to be published without his permission. Meissner said he would find out from Oskar von Hindenburg. Hitler then telephoned to Papen who was also uncertain as to what Hindenburg had finally decided to do. He promised Hitler he would immediately question Oskar. When he reported back that Oskar had told him that the documents existed and were in safekeeping in Neudeck, Hitler told him to get hold of them as soon as possible.[7] Papen sent his private secretary, Count Kageneck, to Neudeck where Oskar gave him the two sealed envelopes, including the testament, which Kageneck brought back to Berlin.

A few days later Papen, while on his way to his new ministerial post in Vienna, flew to Berchtesgaden and gave the documents to Hitler who read them carefully. When he came to the part addressed to him in which Hindenburg recommended a restoration of the monarchy, he said, according to Papen: "These recommendations of the dead president are addressed to me personally and I will decide later if and when I approve of their publication."[8] Nothing more was ever to be heard of this letter addressed to Hitler. The so-called letter of accountability addressed to the German people Hitler immediately handed over to his press chief, Otto Dietrich, for publication.

In his letter "To the German people and its chancellor," Hindenburg told them, in what sounds unmistakably like his own words, that only his absolute confidence in Germany's unconquerable sources of strength had given him the courage to be a candidate for the presidency in two elections. "This unshakable faith," he wrote, "gave me the inner strength to carry out unswervingly the burden of my office. The last part of my life has also been the most difficult for me. Many in these troubled times have not understood me, have not comprehended that my sole concern has been to restore a splintered and disheartened Germany to a self-confident unity." From the beginning he had recognized that the basic law of the state and the form of government given the nation in its time of weakness failed to meet the real needs and character of the German people: "The hour had to ripen before this comprehension would become common knowledge. Therefore it seemed to me my duty to lead the country through the valley of its foreign abasement and humiliation, of its inner distress and self-laceration . . . until this hour struck."

The symbol and solid support of this rebuilding had to be the Reichswehr, the protector of the state. In it had to be based the old Prussian tradition of self-understood devotion to duty, simplicity, and comradeliness as the solid fundament of the state.

> The German Reichswehr after the collapse continued to nurture the high tradition of the old army in an exemplary fashion.
>
> The Wehrmacht must always remain, at all times the instrument of the highest state authority, which undisturbed by all inner political developments attempts to hold upright the mission of the defense of the country.
>
> As I return to my comrades above, with whom I have fought so many battles for the greatness and honor of the nation, I call upon the younger generation: Show yourselves worthy of your forefathers, and never forget, if you wish to secure the peace and prosperity of your homeland you must also be ready to make the last sacrifice for this freedom and the honor of the country. To all the men who have built up and developed the Reichswehr go the thanks of the Field Marshal of the World War and its later commander-in-chief . . .
>
> In foreign politics the German people have had to undergo their Calvary. A terrible treaty lay heavy on them and threatened in its cumulative consequences to destroy our nation. For a long time the outside world did not understand that Germany must live not only for itself but as the flagbearer of western culture, for Europe too . . .

Then he came to Hitler: "I thank Providence," he wrote, "that in the evening of my life I have been able to witness the hour of Germany's renewed strength. I thank all those who selflessly, out of love for the Fatherland, cooperated in the task of Germany's revival."

> My chancellor Adolf Hitler and his movement have taken a decisive step of historical importance toward the great goal of uniting the German people in an inner unity over all differences of class and conditions.
>
> I know that much remains to be done and I wish from my heart that behind this act of national awakening and volkisch solidarity there stands an act of reconciliation embracing the entire German Fatherland. I depart from my German people in the firm hope that what I wished for in 1919 and what in slow ripening led to the 30th of January 1933, will ripen to the complete fulfilling and perfecting of the historical mission of our people. In this firm belief in the future of the Fatherland I can close my eyes in peace.[9]

It was about all Hindenburg could say at the end, except for repeating his hope expressed in the letter to Hitler for the restoration of the monarchy. The homilies were the sum of what he had lived for and by: belief in the fatherland, in the Reichswehr above all parties, in the rebuilding of the Reich's spiritual strength after the inexplicably lost war—lost because of divisions within the German people. He had to cling now to the hope he placed in the "Bohemian corporal" to heal the divisions in the Reich and flesh out the old dream of a Germany united in the nurturing of the fatherland, with everyone doing his duty modestly and selflessly. These were the virtues he had been brought up to believe in, and he took them with him to the grave, leaving the Reich to a man he had never comprehended, never could comprehend. Hitler would know how to use his testament.

On August 18 Oskar von Hindenburg addressed the nation over the radio and said that his father had wanted Hitler to succeed him as chief of state. Hindenburg, said his son, called on the German people from his Tannenberg tomb to "rally together, and stand shoulder to shoulder behind Germany's Leader." Stirring words for true believers and acceptable ones for a large majority of the electorate. The next day came the plebiscite: the decision of the German people on whether Hitler was to continue the offices of president and Reichschancellor.

Of the over 45 million voters entitled to ballot, more than 38 million, or about 90 percent, voted "yes." But what brought consternation to the party faithful was the size of the "no" vote. More than 4 million people voted "no," and 872,000 cast ballots declared invalid, some of which represented a more timid way of voting "no." In Berlin almost one quarter of the voters opposed Hitler's takeover, and in parts of Bavaria, too, the nay votes were a surprise and a disappointment to party leaders. The monthly report from the Achbach district declared voters had used the occasion of the plebiscite to express their exasperation with local authorities. At Niederrieden in Swabia, the August report declared: "We all thought it impossible that so many 'no' votes would be cast," and the writer attributed the results to garrulous visitors from Switzerland as well as the number of priests, nuns, and ill-intentioned local louts *(Lumpen)*. The report from the district offices in Heiligenstadt stated that on the whole the vote had been satisfactory but lamented that the "no" vote was up from the last plebiscite in November 1933—from 96 votes to 470. A police record from Munich tabulated over 51,000 "no" votes as opposed to 419,000 "yes" votes and added that, in August, 31 people had been arrested for making derogatory remarks about the country's leaders while many more had been accused of the same crime. In Bauringen officials declared the number of "no" votes (seventy-two) was evidence of how many opponents of the government remained; they believed the priesthood was largely responsible.

The result of the vote, Göring triumphantly announced in an interview with the editor of the *Deutsche Allgemeine Zeitung* on August 21, had come as no surprise. The outside world, if it were honest, would have to concede how deeply Hitler was rooted in the heart of every German. "What statesman," he asked rhetorically, "what head of state can glory in the fact that he knows he has behind him an entire people, unanimous, acting of their own free will?" There was no parallel, he said, for this in world history. As for the 10 percent who had voted "no," he said, "How despondent must be those who, on whatever grounds, have placed themselves outside the volk community?" And he was certain the foreign ill-wishers who had hoped to find allies among the "no" voters were just as disappointed. But they could be assured the government would seek to find out why the 10 percent had voted as they had. First of all they came from circles that felt themselves misunderstood, making a total judgment on the basis of hard but merely transitional measures. But one day they would beat their breasts and perceive their error, convinced by the performance and ultimate success of the National Socialist regime. A small percentage of the "no" votes, as Göring saw it, came from a second group: those who did indeed understand the goals sought by the party but nevertheless, on selfish grounds, themselves sought other ends. But these circles, too, would in time either learn better or they would grow old and disappear from the scene. The third group was a small one composed of the unteachable or the ill-willed. They were not a phenomenon peculiar to National Socialism; they existed throughout the world. They would not be punished for their "no" vote, but they would not be allowed to propagandize their rejection of the National Socialist leadership among the German people and, Göring added, using one of his favorite tropes, "We will strike out with an iron fist if they allow themselves to be drawn into criminal activities that threaten the security of the state."

> Certainly different opinions are possible on one or another of the questions concerning public life. . . . [We want] open and honest criticism of all the difficult problems presented by the reconstruction of our state. But constructive criticism is demanded and can only be made by those who are prepared to do better and have proven their ability to do so. And criticism has to stop at the border where the great questions concerning the nation are all to be taken care of by the Führer.
>
> All criticism must be silent before our Führer Adolf Hitler. When the Führer calls and gives orders, no matter what they are, everyone must obey unconditionally . . .
>
> In a few years the entire German people will stand as one man in devoted allegiance to Adolf Hitler. To achieve this is our greatest and most beautiful task.[10]

So the long climb was finally made, and Hitler stood alone at the summit of the Reich. The army was sworn to his personal allegiance, Hindenburg was dead, and the Leader to whom he had bequeathed his functions was both president and chancellor.

Clearly Hitler was a generous man who amnestied his enemies, who had been chosen by the hero of heroes, Hindenburg, to be his successor, who would suffer criticism and dissent except in cases where they might threaten the well-being of the German people and state. Hitler! Chancellor, chief justice of the highest court and of the other justices as well, president, commander in chief of the armed forces! Where there was power, there was the Leader. The opposition could print and distribute antigovernment leaflets—as the Communist Party and some Catholics did—but those were no more than mutterings among 10 percent of the nation. All the rest that could be publicly heard was a hymn of praise joined in by many prominent foreigners. William Randolph Hearst who was in Munich at the time of the plebiscite declared the vote for Hitler was a new chapter in world history. Hitler, said Hearst, had brought peace and order that a world war had destroyed and had been a boon not only to his people but also to all mankind.[11] The dean of journalism of Washington University in St. Louis declared that Germany's future lay with Hitler. In England the Rothermere press joined in the chorus.

Hitler paid his debts but with promissory notes. On August 20 he repeated to Blomberg that the Wehrmacht remained the sole bearer of arms in the Reich, and at the same time he approved the establishment under Himmler of the SS Verfügungstruppe, the "Ready Formations" that would grow into a full-fledged army complete with tanks and heavy guns, an elite troop training its own officers and men to form a battle group as powerful as anything Röhm and the SA leaders had ever dreamed of!

Hitler was working within the house of cards that Versailles had built. On June 17, the same day Papen talked at Marburg, Hitler had made a speech at Gera that, like so many of his utterances, was designed for everyone he could make use of. It was the closing speech of the Gau Party Day of Thuringia, and from the celebration of this event he turned to the foreign problems of the Reich and Europe.[12] He offered peace and a sword.

> When I am asked the question "what will you do for the pacification of the world" I answer, we have done everything within our power [to this end] . . . not for reasons of self-concern but out of concern for the rights of others. Let other statesmen and leaders manifest the same spirit and learn not only to have consideration for their own rights but also for the right to life of others. . . . We have a great domestic goal before us, a work of reform of our common life, our economy, our culture. . . . This task does not disturb the rest of the world. We have enough to do in our own house and are of the opinion others have enough to do in theirs.

. . . We National Socialists have a gigantic domestic program that requires us to seek peace and friendship with the rest of the world. That also requires us to see to it that the world leaves us in peace and tranquility. For as little as we have the purpose of perpetrating an injustice on anyone in the world, just as little will we in Germany permit ourselves to be ravished. If anyone asks: "What do you propose to contribute to the pacification of the world," we answer: We are a people who love peace and desire peace and above all are unconcerned with the business of other people. We only wish that others take the same path to the pacification of the world. . . . What sense can be made of it when we want peace and understanding with a people and then in this [international] press we have to read that one may not come to an understanding with the German government because that would mean a success for it.

We have only the one desire, that in other nations those who, in remembering the horrors of the last war, also want a genuine reconciliation between peoples, will win through. For we know that if the international clique of warmongers were to achieve their goal then millions of good and decent people, but probably none of the international warmongers, would find themselves on the battlefield. . . .

I can assure the entire world of one thing: As unconditional as is our love of peace, as little as Germany wants war, just so fanatically will we take the necessary steps on behalf of German freedom and the honor of our people.

The world must know: The time for being dictated to is over. As little as we have the intention of bringing other people under our dominance, just so mightily will we defend ourselves against any attempt to continue to keep the German people under lasting dominance.

It had been a speech designed not only for the Hindenburgs and the German electorate but for foreigners as well. Not only Germany but also many foreigners accepted Hitler's aims as conditionally achievable. What he proclaimed was what millions of people wanted to hear and believe. For the Germans his speech was another declaration of independence, another demand for equality, a call for a revitalized Reich: strong, peaceful, and secure from any more invasions of the Ruhr and the Rhineland. It was the kind of speech Hindenburg could thoroughly approve. It was even the kind of speech many Jews could approve, the kind of speech that had brought Hitler to power, and not much of it, as time would disclose, was true.

What Hitler was actually doing to reinvigorate the German spirit seemed undeniable to many highly esteemed observers, at home and abroad. The rectors of the German universities professed themselves enchanted with the transformation of their institutions of higher learning. At a conference in Berlin held in February 1934, they declared:

> National Socialism is the only living and creative force that has freed schol-arship and the German university from the purely specialized, theoretical, and departmentalized splintering, to lead them to the deeper questions of the life and fate of the German people. Sharp criticism of the contemporary universities means not their rejection but springs rather from the radical demand for a new meaning of scholarship and of the university that has never before in all German history been grasped and put into practice.[13]

Rothermere, among other distinguished foreigners, was convinced that the time had come to give back the colonies to the Reich, and he pointed out that "a satisfied Germany will be a peaceful Germany." Jules Romains, the writer and publicist, in an address to a gathering of French and German youth at the University of Berlin in November, spoke of the need for Franco-German collaboration and a European unity that would be conceivable only when a balance of power was reached between the French and German nations.

The chorus of the men of goodwill resounded from all quarters. On the evening before Romains spoke, General Smuts, founder and prime minister of the Union of South Africa, declared that the time had come to make a genuine peace, the kind of peace that had never come to pass at Versailles. Pierre Cot, who until February was French minister of Aviation, along with other members of the Former Front Line Fighters Organization, declared that only a Franco-German understanding would make certain the security of Europe.[14]

It was no wonder that under Hitler's rule German self-esteem was reviving. His repeated declarations of the Reich's fixed purpose to rid itself of the vestiges of special treatment by foreign powers were to most Germans no more than a demand for being treated like the people of any other country and for finally overcoming the crushing imbalances imposed after a heroically fought war that had been incomprehensibly lost. The rough tactics of the Röhm affair and of the concentration camps—in Prussia alone twenty-five or thirty thousand people had been placed in "protective custody" during the two months of March and April after Hitler took power—were relatively minor matters for most of the electorate compared with the successes of the revolution: a drop of two and a half million in unemployment, the continuing upturn in the economy, and the evidences of national unity after the brawling in the streets and in the Reichstag during the Weimar period.

Great works were being built: the network of autobahns, giant shipyards, housing projects. Industrial and agrarian reforms were projected on a grand scale. Almost everyone except Jews and marxists could participate according to their means and abilities. Party speakers repeatedly pointed out that the egocentrism of a failed capitalism was being transformed into the collective purposes of a thriving *volk* community.

Work was provided in the Labor Service for young men from the ages of eighteen to twenty-five. By March 1934 over forty thousand acres of what had been land useless for cultivation had been made arable by battalions of volunteers. Hitler wanted every young man, whether (as he said) the son of a university professor or of a factory worker, to know what it was to work with his hands. Like so much else in the Nazi drive for inspiriting a defeated generation, the appeal was a return to a romanticized past, to a precapitalist, *volkisch* community where no one was unemployed or victimized by profit-seeking predators. The Reich's purposes could readily be dramatized in posters of beaming, happy farmers and workers devoting themselves to immense collective goals, soaring far beyond the individual urge for self-advancement. Everyone was to work, no one was to be permitted a free ride in this new world, no one could go on strike or seek his own advantage at the cost of the *Volk*. In 1934 labor service for young men who, like the members of the armed forces, swore an oath of inviolable fidelity to Hitler, was voluntary, but by 1935 it would be made compulsory.[15] Girls, too, were recruited to aid in households where they would be prepared for the womanly tasks awaiting them after marriage and could meanwhile lighten the burdens of overworked mothers.

All this was the National Socialist answer to the miseries of defeat and the Great Depression. The *volkisch* community would embrace the weal of every man, woman, and child in the Reich, of every worker, as party speakers said, whether of brain or fist, who would use what talents he had on behalf of a mystical fatherland and its Leader. It was an egalitarian society that Hitler was set on building; large landholdings could be retained only if their owners saw to it that their fields were worked efficiently, and if they did not, they would be replaced by land-hungry farmers who would till fewer acres.

A group of farmers meeting in Pomerania was told by Richard Darré, minister of Food Production and leader of the German Farmers Society, that National Socialists would judge the great landowners not by the blood their ancestors had shed in former wars but by whether they had behaved as responsible farmers. The idea of the just price for commodities was paralleled by that of the proper acreage of farm land one family could own. In principle the party was opposed to both large landholdings and large industrial profits. Every enterprise existed only to serve the entire country, not to swell the profits of an individual or corporation. The concept of the entrepreneur was to be replaced by that of the leader of a factory or a business who along with his followers, formerly known as employees, was licensed by the state to fulfill tasks useful to the entire community. No more self-serving decisions of capitalist owners of plants or of trade-union leaders.

Prices of industrial and farm products were fixed, the formerly antagonistic forces of capital and labor reconciled. Strikes and lockouts were abolished, and representatives of the state, called *Treuhändler,* had to approve the levels of salaries and wages.

"A breach of loyalty" on the part of labor or management would be regarded as an attack on the *volkisch* virtue of the aggrieved party, to be dealt with by a court of honor. If a man was dismissed, as it seemed to him unjustly, he had the right of appeal to such a court; the new regulations, Goebbels declared, restored the honor of the worker who was now free of the fetters of international capitalism.

There was much talk of the restoration of honor. Hitler, Goebbels said too, had restored the honor of the German soldier and of the workers as well, as they had both been brought headlong under the dominance of the party.

The same rules applied to business as to agriculture. A law was promulgated, designed to cull inefficient enterprises as well as those that misused their social purposes or affronted the healthy *volkisch* sense as to how needy debtors should be treated.[16] Whereas formerly a creditor could sue for repayment of money due him, the new regulations declared that a judge was to keep in mind the social context of any dispute. On the petition of a debtor who was being forced to vacate his dwelling because of unpaid debts, a ruling calling on him to pay up could be set aside if the creditor's action was thought to have transgressed the healthy *volkisch* notion of how to behave. This healthy sense of the people took precedence over any formal rules. As Hans Frank, president of the Academy for German Law, said, German jurisprudence had to be transformed to provide German laws for the German people.

Strikes were a survival of the disreputable past. The leader of the German Workers Front, Robert Ley, declared that the highest law was discipline; the leader and his followers in any enterprise had a right to demand of the community only in proportion of what they were prepared to give to it. Carl Goerdeler, the mayor of Leipzig and future leader of the 1944 revolt against Hitler, named as Reichskommissar for Price Surveillance, announced that anyone who misused his credit or otherwise willfully failed in his fiscal responsibilities, was subject to imprisonment. In addition Goerdeler promised the punishment of any entrepreneur who sold his goods for prices that did not cover his overhead. He could be jailed and fined an undetermined amount.

The government took account of the foreign reaction to its treatment of the Jews, and it presented what was for Nazi sentiments a reasonable case. Minister of the Interior Frick, in a speech delivered on February 15, 1934, to the diplomatic corps assembled in Berlin, said the core of the Jewish problem in Germany was the need for Germans to be under the leadership of Germans. Other countries, too, Frick pointed out, had demonstrated their desire to protect racially homogeneous populations. The United States Immigration Restriction League had demanded that further immigration of certain races be forbidden, as had the Australian government. A million Greeks and almost 350,000 Turks had been exchanged after the world war to enable them to live in countries of their origins.[17]

The national revolution, he said, had freed the German people from an alien influence that had dominated German politics, culture, economics, finances, the press, political parties, theater, film, and radio. More than half (54 percent) of the lawyers in Germany, 48 percent of the doctors (including 62 percent of those having patients in the health program), and 80 percent of theater directors, were Jews. In Prussia, Jews in leading positions in commerce and industry outnumbered Germans ten to one, and they held twelve of the sixteen places on the executive committee of the Produce Exchange. The German Reich did not want to force Jews to emigrate, but it did want Germans to administer the affairs of the Reich. In a state governed by law, said Frick primly, there was no other way but by the measures the Reich had taken to attain the goal of having Germans govern Germans. The Reich sought only to put a stop to the overgrowth of Jewish influence, as was shown by the fact that the law of April 7, 1933, permitted Jewish officials who had been in office before August 1, 1914, to keep their posts.[18]

The public mood for the first time since the start of the Great Depression was euphoric. In two years, Nazi orators pointed out, unemployment had been cut in half. Housing was up: two hundred thousand new dwellings had been built in 1933, and in March 1934 the government announced that four thousand workers' settlements had been created in East Prussia with about fifty acres (two *Morgen*) of land assigned to each. Marriages and the birthrate showed an increase under the beneficent sun of state subsidies. The city of Berlin made itself the godfather of the third and fourth child of every marriage in the Reich, awarding each of its godchildren thirty marks a month in the child's first year of life and from the second to the fourteenth year twenty marks a month.[19]

Hitler announced in a long speech in March 1934 that taxes would be reduced for all families with children, and no one would be paid income from social security for not working. Everyone, he said, must have the opportunity to earn his bread by honest work and thus contribute to the standard of living of everyone else. Life, he reminded his listeners, grows out of care and trouble, and he wanted the statesmen of other countries to know the German people and its government had no other wish than to live in freedom and peace so as to work for the building of a better world.[20]

Inside the Reich, 2 million Germans went on vacation trips, many of them for the first time in their lives. The People's Theater put on plays at cut prices. Women were encouraged to quit industrial jobs so their places could be taken by married men. Hjalmar Schacht, who had been appointed president of the Reichsbank in March 1933 and was acting minister of Economics in August 1934, set about reactivating the German economy by persuading the Reich's creditors that they had to make sacrifices on behalf of the Reich in their own interests.

The world economic crisis, Schacht told an international agrarian conference in August 1934, stemmed directly from the Versailles treaty, and it could only be resolved by a long-term moratorium on the payment of German debts. Reparations that unhappily, he said, were now owed not to governments but to private creditors could no longer be paid from Germany's resources. Devaluation of the mark would not help. The Reich was heavily dependent on imports of raw materials, which would only be made more expensive if the mark were devalued. That would send up the cost of living, which would mean higher wages and higher prices for German exports and thus sizably diminish any advantages that might otherwise be gained. The Reich's means of transferring funds to its creditors were exhausted. The practical way out of the dilemma was for the creditor countries to import more German goods and to agree to a reduction in the balances owed them. As he had earlier explained, the steady flow of gold and of foreign exchange from the Reich had to stanched.[21] The world could either write off the Reich as a customer and debtor or work with it on the transfer problem and thus pave the way for a general economic recovery.

In one form or another the creditor countries, however reluctantly, came to accept the Schachtian argument that Germany could only pay debts by not paying them for a long time at least and by increasing exports to its creditors. A moratorium (the fourth) on the payment of Germany's debts had been agreed on in mid-February with Britain and the United States. It linked the resumption of payments to an increase in world trade and provided for emergency measures to deal with the transfer problem—all in all a realistic program, Schacht said, for eventual repayment. Agreements following Schacht's spartan formula were concluded in September with Italy, Norway, Sweden, and Belgium and in November with Britain, the latter permitting a ratio of fifty-five to one hundred of British versus German exports in bilateral trade.

The long list of wrongs perpetrated upon the Reich by the treaties that formally ended the world war was still being lengthened in 1934. Hitler was suspect, feared, and derided in all the territories neighboring the Reich, and those with sizeable German minorities saw in them a potential fifth column and an immediate threat to their internal stability. Their measures to keep the local Nazi movements in check were intensified after Hitler came to power.

In the Saar where the administration was in the hands of a League of Nations Commission, whose chairman was an Englishman, Sir Geoffrey Knox—a man the German press regularly indicted for his anti-German bias—pro-Nazi newspapers (twenty of them at one time) were banned for printing what Knox regarded as inflammatory articles as they echoed the propaganda line of the German press across the border. Knox was also accused of appointing anti-Hitler émigré Germans to the police force and of adopting a score of provocative measures, among them the forbidding of Nazi political rallies and the wearing of Nazi uniforms. As the time of the plebiscite drew closer, the National Socialist party was banned in the Saarland and replaced by the German Front, a catchall organization intended to unite all the voters who favored reunion with the Reich. Since that number would turn out to be over 90 percent of the population, the pro-French and separatist parties had a hopeless task.

Even when opposition forces such as the exiled Social Democrats could point to the concentration camps and the repression of religious faiths, free speech, and a free press in the Reich, such accounts could either be dismissed as not much more than the lurid propaganda of the enemies of Germany continuing the atrocity tales of the world war, or if some truth might be conceded to the stories, they could be overbalanced by the Saarlander's experience of the blatant French attempts to dominate a German territory.

In Lithuania, too, German wounds continued to fester. In Memel, for centuries a German city until it became part of Lithuania under the terms of the Versailles treaty, the autonomy promised the German population, which was to be supervised by Britain, France, Italy, and Japan, was whittled to a splinter.[22] German political parties were dissolved by the Lithuanian government, and the Reich press complained that of 228 primary schools in which both the Lithuanian and the German languages were supposed to have equal status, 222 schools taught only in Lithuanian; and the post office refused to deliver mail unless the address was written in Lithuanian. Not only Nazis but also Germans as such were tried for an alleged plot to overthrow the government; more than a thousand German officials were dismissed from their government posts, the German-controlled *Landtag* was forbidden to meet, and protests from the German Foreign Office to the signatory powers went unanswered.

Concerning Poland, where Hitler's new policy was unexpectedly accommodating, criticism in the Reich press was muted, but, despite the Treaty of Understanding and Nonaggression and the trade treaty concluded between the two countries in 1934, German newspapers continued to run accounts of the persecution of the German minority throughout Poland and the Corridor.

All the countries where the post–world war treaties had left a sizeable German population were accused of adopting punitive anti-German measures. In Czechoslovakia where the German minority complained it lived under unrelenting Czech hostility and economic disabilities that put it at a marked disadvantage compared with the Czech and Slovakian populations, evidences of Czech harassment were always apparent. Two Sudeten German youths, aged thirteen and seventeen, after attending a Nuremberg rally were arrested and spent the night in jail when police found parts of Hitler Youth uniforms in their knapsacks. Sudetenlanders, it was alleged in the Reich press, were put in jail and then tried before a military court merely for attempting to join the German work service on the grounds that they were trying to join a premilitary service, a charge that was also made against Knox with regard to the Saarlander youth.[23] And though German and Polish writers exchanged visits and Goebbels journeyed to Warsaw to exchange words of mutual confidence with Polish Foreign Minister Beck, the deep chasms symbolized by the Polish Corridor and the separation of Danzig from the Reich could not be bridged by such pleasantries. The official line, however, continued to move toward a degree of reconciliation: The Polish and German governments agreed to upgrade their legations to embassies and their respective ministers to ambassadors.

In the space of two years Hitler made the German society a projection of his party. All opposition had disappeared—driven underground, or into exile, or concentration camps, or murdered. Big business, which in early 1933 had been wary of Hitler's measures and purposes, under the leadership of the lifelong conservative Krupp had become acclimated to the dictatorship and made its peace with a regime that intended to control it as it did everything else in the Reich. The Reichs Association of German Industry, the chief organization of German industrialists, had at first attempted to influence the Hitler government through the intervention of the conservative Hugenberg, but found, as he did, that he had no power that Hitler did not concede to him. They had also tried to make a common front with labor against the government's high-tariff, profarm measures, which the industrialists believed were hurting the export of German manufactures, but again Hitler had other plans for both labor and capital, and there was no common front. Furthermore the industrialists had within their own ranks men such as Fritz Thyssen who were themselves members of the party. Thyssen urged Krupp to accept the revolution, pointing out that the big industrialists had no choice but to make their peace with the man and movement that could destroy them if they resisted. Thyssen was successful; by early April 1933 Krupp, president of the Reichs Association of German Industry, had agreed on full cooperation with the National Socialist government, and his determination to make the concessions necessary for such cooperation met with only minor pockets of resistance from within the ranks of the industrialists. It was the party, not big business, that called the tune, and it was the party, directly and through the government, that could tell the great concerns what and how much they were to produce and at what costs and under what conditions.

The Reichs Association of German Industry had immediately to purge itself of its Jewish members, a process that may have given less pain to many of its members than some of the other measures they were forced to adopt. The Nazi infiltration of the entire society was very nearly complete by the end of two years of Hitler's rule. His programs were not new. Volunteer work services had begun under private organizations in the early twenties, and public works projects were tried in almost every country suffering under the depression—though Germany with its experience of inflation had been more cautious than most. The demand for equality of arms had been made by every German government that had felt itself free enough from the danger of foreign reprisals to make the claim. What was new was the inquisitional methods of dealing with the crises and the impossibility of resisting. Hitler alone could order the unions dissolved, the entrepreneurs to seek *volkisch* ends rather than profits, the Jews out of public life, and rival parties to disappear, and no opposition was left to say him nay. Sacrifices on behalf of the *Volk* were demanded and made not only out of a conviction that they were justified but because the alternative was a closed enterprise or a concentration camp or both. A controlled profit was better than none, and a job, even one regulated by commissars of the party's choosing, was better than breadlines.

In foreign affairs, too, Hitler was the beneficiary of the consequences of defeat. The Lithuanians, the Czechs, and the Poles, all reacting to Hitler, were in fact taking restrictive measures against all Germans to keep the National Socialists in check. They had a plausible case against Hitler's likely intentions. But the same thing could not be said of the French claim to the Saar or the Polish, Czech, and Lithuanian claims.

They were treating the German minorities within their borders as they were legally bound to, according to the documents they had signed. In their fear of Hitler they were prepared to intensify policies that had helped bring him to power, and as their fears increased they were willing to make concessions to him that they would never have dreamed of making to Stresemann or Brüning or anyone else in the time of the Weimar Republic. By the end of 1934 they were well on the way to being forced to deal with a menacingly great power, one with an impressive industrial apparatus, armed forces, and a population being psychologically prepared to march to the sound of drums.[24]

5

Occupation of the Rhineland

The war machine that Hitler was to build would be, quite simply, the best of its time. It was to combine the latest technical apparatus of the 1930s with the mass manpower that had been the backbone of the world war to create a swift, mobile striking force that had the capacity to overwhelm the Western Allies, despite their long-term advantages in the training of troops and the procurement of weapons. It developed in an incredibly short space of time from a small, professional core with admixtures of short-term volunteers and police formations into a huge, well-trained, and well-equipped army that had no equal among the victors of World War I—though in 1939 France, Britain, Belgium, and the Netherlands had more men, tanks, and guns than the Reich did. Only in planes was the Reich numerically ahead.[1]

This was accomplished despite shortages of all kinds—of raw materials, manpower that was stretched thin to supply the demands of the surging armament industry and of the Wehrmacht—and despite the fierce competition among the armed services for the supplies that could not go around. In addition the incessant internal struggle between the party and those responsible for production and military efficiency was waged from the beginning of rearmament until the end. A man such as Göring was in a unique position among the generals to see to it that the air force, which he headed, got its share and more from the production of the Four-Year Plan, which he also headed. But in the event, no one of the services, not even the navy (which had nothing like the high priority

123

in Hitler's estimation of the army and air force), would be scanted. The navy's manpower increased 500 percent in seven years—from 16,450 in 1933 to over 78,000 at the start of the war, and the amount spent on it in that period from 1932 to 1939 increased twelvefold. It was able to build up a formidable fleet that with its U-boats inflicted enormous damage on its opponents.

In many ways the years of deprivation of the German military had become an advantage. Although it was the British who had invented the tank and British and French strategists such as J. F. C. Fuller, B. II. Liddell Hart, and Charles de Gaulle who saw the need to base warfare on the combination of material, men, planes, and tanks that were high in mobility and fire power, it was Hitler and the German army that put their doctrines into effect.

One of the main reasons for the success of rearming the Reich was a perverse kind of democratic selection in the choices Hitler made for high office. He had a contempt for the traditional officer caste of the aristocracy, and in return it was always suspicious of him. In his choices of men and measures to carry out the National Socialist revolution in the armed forces he was far more flexible than the high command of World War I. The Nazis might make use of the old order—Prince zu Schaumberg Lippe was Goebbels's adjutant, and Prince von Hessen was Göring's secretary—but no one played a part in the leadership, whether political or military, by virtue of royal blood. There would be no crown prince in World War II to lead the armies of the Reich. What was needed to impress Hitler would be a "yes" man such as Keitel or someone with an innovative flair such as Colonel Heinz Guderian who met Hitler's demands for dramatic, high-risk undertakings that would crush the enemy. Guderian was chiefly responsible for the path-breaking German doctrine of tank warfare that met with stiff resistance from a competent but cautious traditionalist such as the army chief of staff, General Beck. The latter told Guderian his tanks were too fast for sound battle procedure when Guderian presented his plan for tank divisions to break through the front in deep penetrations and then encircle the enemy forces. Guderian saw the tanks taking the place of the old cavalry, not on their own but leading in division strength and protecting motorized troops and motorized artillery. When in 1933 he demonstrated to Hitler the use of tanks he had in mind, fast moving and precise in maneuver, Hitler exclaimed: "I can use that! That's what I need!"[2] Guderian was not the only one in the armies of the Western powers who foresaw what the tank could do, but from 1933 he was strongly backed by Hitler, the lance corporal of World War I who had been miles removed from the ways and training of men such as General Beck and who was certain he knew more than they did. Guderian was a colonel when in 1935 he was given command of one of the three tank divisions; in August 1936 he was made a major general and in February 1938 a lieutenant general—a swift rise that reflected Hitler's admiration.

For the air force, too, it was the new strategies that appealed to Hitler, though he appointed a devoted follower rather than an innovative general to lead it. Nevertheless Göring, for all his disabilities, succeeded in recruiting men to serve under him who, like Guderian, were not bound by shibboleths. Göring had been a highly decorated flier in World War I, but he was lazy and a poor administrator. The work of building up the air force had to be done by others, and for the most part Göring was ready to stand aside and let them do it. A civilian, Robert Knauss, who had been a high official of Lufthansa, was one of them; another was General Erhard Milch whose legal father was a Jew, though the son had been Aryanized when his mother swore that his biological father was another; and a third was Colonel Walter Wever, head of the Ministry of Air Command.

Up to the end of 1936 Milch was the chief planner for the Luftwaffe, and he was greatly influenced by Knauss who in 1933 had sent him a persuasive memorandum on the shape of the future air fleet. Knauss, convinced that Germany might well have to fight a two-front war against France and Poland, held that its chief weapon must be a bomber fleet. A considerable number of such planes—Knauss calculated almost four hundred—could be built relatively quickly and would have a decisive effect as nothing else would. Knauss's views were shared by Colonel Wever, who like Knauss believed the bomber—both dive and horizontal—must have a central role in future military operations, though he rejected as greatly overdrawn Giulio Douhet's theory that the air arm alone would win a war. After Wever's death in an airplane accident in 1936, the strategic plans he had developed were continued by General Albert Kesselring who took over his post, soon to be replaced by General Stumpff as the labile Göring shifted around his personnel. The planning continued to be divided along the lines Knauss and Wever had projected, and Colonel Wimmer, who headed the technical section, and Stumpff agreed on the need to move the air force from the modest defensive role of the risk force to that of a decisive offensive weapon to be used against both the battle power of the enemy and the will to resist of the civil population.

The magnitude of the task confronting these leaders may be seen in the scale of increase in Luftwaffe personnel and planes. At the time of Hitler's disclosure of its existence, the air force had twenty-five hundred planes of all types, more than half of which were training and eight hundred of which were ready for battle; personnel numbered nine hundred regular officers, two hundred antiaircraft officers, and seventeen thousand commissioned and enlisted men. By the end of 1937, two and a half years later, their numbers had increased fivefold, with more than 6,000 officers, and by 1939 the officers numbered 15,000, with 370,000 noncommissioned and enlisted men. Thus the officer corps had increased more than thirteen times in four and a half years, and the tiny air force of the clandestine years had grown to more than four thousand front-line planes.[3]

The dizzying pace was set by Hitler. As he saw it, the military men were there to carry out orders and to act as technicians to attain ends that he alone would determine. It was an arm's-length symbiosis of the lance corporal become revolutionist dictator, with the conservative general staff officers, all of whom shared the same goals of rearming the Reich as thoroughly and rapidly as possible consistent with maintaining military quality but many of whom became increasingly mistrustful of Hitler's methods. No general except Göring could be sure of Hitler's lasting favor. Even Blomberg, who more than anyone was responsible for indoctrinating the thitherto apolitical army with National Socialist propaganda, was by 1935 beginning to decline in Hitler's esteem. Blomberg had had his place when his support was needed against Röhm and for commanding the Wehrmacht's oath of allegiance to Hitler, but with Hitler's increasing self-confidence and the emphasis on economic measures to finance the rearmament, he was far less important than he had been in 1933 and 1934. Hitler, it may be to justify his increasing coolness toward Blomberg, began to criticize what he called Blomberg's overhasty Nazification of the army, though he himself wanted that far more than did Blomberg. But none of the military men was indispensable, and any of them who, as time went on, took issue with a Hitler policy or even questioned it was likely to lose his job.

The high command generally accepted the need for the armed forces to become an integral part of the National Socialist state. General von Fritsch, when he was commander in chief of the army, agreed in 1935 that the army had to be National Socialist, and Admiral Raeder agreed that the Wehrmacht and the party must be inseparable.[4] Nevertheless Hitler was always uneasy with the high command and would never fully make his peace with them. Because he trusted Göring the air force could chart its own development in relative independence of the OKW (Oberkommando der Wehrmacht—the general staff of the armed forces; that is, army, navy, and air force) and the OKH (Oberkommando des Heeres—the high command of the army). Milch had left the army at the end of World War I as a captain, and in 1936 he was made general of flyers, and then in 1938 colonel general and general inspector of the Luftwaffe, a meteoric rise shadowed only by Göring's ambivalence toward any possible rival. When the World War I hero Ernst Udet (after Richthofen, the most successful German fighter pilot of World War I) was appointed chief of the technical department of the air force, Milch was not even consulted. Göring, like Hitler, handed out his favors with a lavish hand, but no one was permitted to climb too high for his personal comfort.

Within three years Hitler with Göring's help would get rid of three of the top generals on whom he depended in the first years of his rule. The generals, like the Allies, were to be victims of Hitler's successes in foreign policy.

Hitler for all his new causes was still prospering on the fighting qualities of the army that had fought off the Allies from 1914 to 1918. Despite their declarations deploring Hitler's breach of the Versailles treaty and conferences designed to demonstrate their common front against him, the Allies were in no mood to risk another war, and they were moreover sharply divided among themselves. The Stresa Conference of 1934, attended by Britain, France, and Italy, held a month after Hitler's announcement of the Reich's rearmament, had familiar words of disapproval along with promises of a common front at the forthcoming meeting of the League of Nations in Geneva. Within weeks, however, Italy, with visions of an imperium of its own, would be moving closer to Hitler than to the Stresa Front as it attacked Ethiopia. Nevertheless the Stresa Conference agreement not only promised a common line opposing German rearmament but also reaffirmed the principle of maintaining Austrian independence and the Locarno Treaty of 1925, guaranteeing the common borders of France, Belgium, and Germany as well as the demilitarized zone of the Rhineland. A few weeks later France, seeking to reinsure whatever security the Stresa Conference agreement provided, signed a mutual-assistance pact with the Soviet Union in which both countries agreed to intervene with military forces if the other was attacked. On May 16 this was followed by a similar pact between Russia and Czechoslovakia. The security system created by the Versailles treaty under the League of Nations was crumbling fast, and France was rightly convinced the Rhineland would be Hitler's next objective. No German army of whatever size could operate efficiently without troops in the demilitarized zone, and the occupation of the Rhineland was of prime importance to German military strategy as it was to the French alliance with the Little Entente. For the Reich any defense against France would be enormously complicated if the army had to meet an invasion behind the Rhine with nothing but customs inspectors and the police to defend the territory until troops arrived.

Hitler was working the weaknesses of the opposition. Against the generals he was building up the SS as a separate military force responsible to no one but himself. His personal regiment, the SS Leibstandarte, which had demonstrated its loyalty during the Röhm affair, was to be transformed into a well-armed body independent of the Reichswehr. The transformation was readily accepted by Blomberg who informed the army commanders there would be an SS division consisting of three regiments. To be sure, Hitler declared that in time of war the SS troops would be under the command of the army, but that did not change the fact that the very existence of SS military formations countervened the rooted conviction of every German officer that only one military force—the army—should exist in the Reich. Only the determined efforts of Fritsch and Beck gave the army the right to inspect the SS formations and prevented their being supplied with artillery. Hitler with the pliant Blomberg could go far in remodeling the armed forces, and he could pick off the generals one by one, but he could not afford to impose any measures that would give rise to a common front against him. The result was an intermittent tug of war between Hitler and the OKH and therefore between the OKH and the OKW, the latter of which under General Blomberg was much closer to Hitler's views than was the OKH. In its primary status as the chief defense of the Reich the army felt itself threatened by the OKW, which it thought too subservient to Hitler and too likely to agree with Göring's demands on behalf of the air force and accept almost any decision of Hitler's regardless of its wider consequences.

The conflicts went beyond the internal affairs of the armed forces. Hitler never fully trusted the generals nor they him. And the tension between the armed forces and the party was always perceptible. When conscription was ordered Blomberg declared the army would be the great training school of German youth. But for the party faithful, ideological training in National Socialist Germany was to be accomplished only by the party and for young men by the Hitler Youth. When Blomberg announced the army would crown the work of the Hitler Youth for Hitler and for the party, this meant continuing the indoctrination of army recruits in the National Socialist sense. The older generals, the high command, with few exceptions were always suspicious of the party, and the party leaders heartily reciprocated their mistrust. With the increasing number of young officers and recruits from the ranks of the Hitler Youth, the army was becoming more and more infiltrated with Nazis, which made for further divisions between the leadership and the lower echelons. Also, there were inevitable conflicts of personality and background.

Hitler was ready to take extreme risks for goals that the high command of the army might share but that it considered too dangerous under the circumstances. One of them was the reoccupation of the Rhineland. Beck and Fritsch were as convinced as Hitler of the need for the remilitarization of a territory essential to the defense of the Reich, but they were certain that if France and Czechoslovakia regarded the move as an act of war and decided to fight, Germany could not put up a successful defense. The French air force alone, it was calculated, enjoyed a ten to one superiority over the Luftwaffe, and the other armies were similarly ahead of the Reich's forces in numbers and training—the risk was simply too great.

Hitler had come to power by his repeated willingness to risk everything on one throw of the dice, and there were generals—Blomberg, Keitel, and Reichenau among them—who were ready to go along with his decision. In March 1935 General von Reichenau had prepared a memorandum on the possibility of war with France and Czechoslovakia, and Blomberg on May 2 asked for a study, which he said was purely theoretical, under the cover name of *Schulung*, for a sudden attack on Czechoslovakia while remaining on the defensive against France. Beck, suspecting that the study was not merely theoretical but connected with the immediate political process of the leadership, refuted its findings point by point in the light of the overwhelming French superiority in all arms, and he wrote that if an actual plan for such a war were drawn up he would be forced to resign. He was probably as much in favor of a takeover of the demilitarized zone as was Hitler or Blomberg or Reichenau, but he was always conscious of the traditional responsibility of the high command to maintain the integrity of the Reich above all, and he saw no alternative to opposing what he regarded as likely provocation to an unwinnable war.

As a consequence perhaps of Beck's criticism, Hitler was himself cautious in his Reichstag speech of May 21.[5] He assured the deputies and the world that Germany would maintain its obligations under the Locarno Treaty as long as the other signatories were ready to abide by the pact. "The government of the Reich," he said, "sees in its respecting of the demilitarized zone an unprecedentedly heavy contribution to the pacification of Europe. It must point out however that the continuous increase in the number of troops on the other side can in no way be considered as a complement to such endeavors." He gave himself an additional escape clause by pointing out that France's treaty with the Soviet Union was incompatible with the Locarno Treaty, a view he repeated to the signatory powers in a memorandum he sent to them on May 25.[6]

But the political action was moving in Hitler's direction. Britain's leaders, increasingly concerned with Mussolini's imperial ambitions in the Mediterranean and Africa and the unmistakable drift toward armed conflict, were ready to make considerable concessions to the Reich in their effort to achieve some degree of stabilization in Europe and head off an arms race. On June 18, 1935, Britain and Germany concluded a naval agreement that breached the stipulations of the Versailles treaty and allowed the German fleet to rise to 420,000 tons from 108,000 with a future ratio of thirty-five to one hundred of the British tonnage. The British were desperately trying to work with the methods of the old and the new diplomacy.

The Anglo-German naval agreement was a temporizing move. On the one hand the conservative government of Stanley Baldwin was prepared to offer a deal to Italy and Germany, making concessions to the recalcitrant powers, and on the other hand they were rigidly invoking the Wilsonian principles of collective security as embodied in the League of Nations. It was this espousal of "the rule of law" that had the decisive support in influential circles in the empire, in Europe, and in the United States; if it worked it meant the creation for Britain of a truly grand alliance—the by-then fifty-three nations would vote sanctions against Italy, and it would be a potent preservative of an empire precariously holding together against the shocks of economic and political change. But both Hitler and Mussolini were completely unimpressed by dogmas of collective security, which they thought no more than a pious cover of moral platitudes to enable the satiated nations to keep what they had. In their view the so-called outlaw nation was merely any power that refused to accept the boundaries imposed at the end of World War I.

Then there was dissension between Britain and France. When Mussolini showed himself determined to march against Ethiopia, the British government was the leader of those countries prepared to apply sanctions. France was ready to pay lip service to the precepts of collective security but had added as many bilateral treaties of military alliance or mutual support as possible to the League of Nations moral order. It was a reluctant partner to any design to punish Italy as an aggressor; *aggressor* meant Germany, and the Quai d'Orsay, as the Hoare-Laval agreement of 1935 would indicate, was entirely ready to tolerate Italian expansion in a remote part of Africa if it would mean keeping Italy as a barrier against Hitler's resurgent Reich.

Nor was this all. In the French-Italian Pact of January 6, 1934, the two countries had agreed to prevent the *Anschluss* of Austria with Germany; Italy renounced the aim of annexing the French province of Tunis, and France in return had given Italy a free hand in Ethiopia.

The adherents of collective security seemingly had a textbook example of deliberate aggression in the Italian invasion that began on October 2, 1935, without a declaration of war. Italy had lost a war against Ethiopia in 1896, and Mussolini's design to wipe out the stigma and to evidence the martial prowess of his reborn, fascist Italy seemed to most of the world the chief motive for hostilities rather than disputes over boundaries and water that had led to local clashes where Eritrea, Somalia, and Ethiopia met.

On October 7, five days after the war started, the League of Nations formally declared Italy an aggressor, and on November 18 fifty-three nations voted to apply sanctions—prohibiting Italian imports to their countries and imposing a financial and arms embargo against the miscreant nation—with only two (Hungary and Austria, both Italian clients) voting against. It was, the Italian government declared, "a day of shame and of injustice."

The sanctions, however, were little more than an inconvenience to Rome. While arms and munitions could not be legally delivered to Italy by any of the League of Nations powers with complete control of the air and modern weapons of all calibers, Italy was well enough stockpiled to wage an annihilating war against the antiquated guns and spears of the Ethiopians. Oil sanctions, which might have had an adverse effect on Italy's capacity to wage war, were not voted by the League of Nations precisely because they might have been effective and thus driven Italy further into the embrace of Hitler's Germany. Since the Reich had left the League of Nations in October of 1933, it took no part in the punitive measures; moreover, as Hitler told the officers of the VI Army Corps, the Reich might well find itself any day in the same position as Italy when in pursuit of its rightful claims it in turn would become the object of sanctions.

Mussolini promptly demonstrated his appreciation of Hitler's attitude by letting him know that Italy would not object to satellite status for Austria. In turn, Hitler told the Italian ambassador to Berlin he would greatly regret the downfall of Italian fascism and assured him the Reich would adopt a position of benevolent neutrality toward Italy in its war against Ethiopia.

One unsuccessful attempt was made by Britain and France to conciliate Italy. Foreign Secretary Hoare, who in December 1935 was in Paris on his way to a winter vacation in Switzerland, concluded the pact with Pierre Laval, the French foreign minister, which proposed dividing Ethiopia—half of its territory going to Italy's Eritrea with a port, either Assab or Zeila, to be given Ethiopia in compensation. The pact was wholeheartedly approved by the chief diplomatic adviser to His Majesty's Government, Sir Robert Vansittart, one of the most uncompromising opponents of the Reich, who also happened to be in Paris. But it was a return to the wicked days of realpolitik that the League of Nations powers had presumably given up, and it had to be abandoned; Sir Samuel had to resign from the Baldwin government in the storm of outrage its publication raised in Britain and the House of Commons. The useless sanctions were all that remained.

The climate was becoming more propitious for reoccupying the Rhineland. The risks were greatly diminished with Italy out of the Stresa front; and with the ratification on February 14, 1936, by the chamber of deputies of the Mutual Assistance Pact with the Soviet Union, Hitler had a pretext that would be of use in the sizeable anticommunist camp in both Britain and France to denounce the Locarno Treaty. Mussolini told the German ambassador to Rome that if Germany remilitarized the Rhineland, the Italians would stand at the window and watch the proceedings as interested spectators, nothing more.[7] Thus while reoccupying the Rhineland was still a risk, it was no longer a reckless one, and even Beck joined Blomberg, Keitel, Fritsch, Reichenau, and the others in being willing to go along. The chances of an armed Allied reaction seemed less likely than when Hitler had announced the introduction of conscription.

In addition Hitler had good reason to believe the French would not go to war. Richard von Kühlmann who had been German foreign minister in the latter years of the First World War, has related that during a visit to Paris in March 1936 after a dinner given by the former French premier Caillaux, at which French Minister of Marine Piétri was present, Piétri informed Kühlmann that he had a message from the French cabinet. The French, Piétri said, were ready to be realistic about the Rhineland and realized the Germans would one day remilitarize it. What was essential was that the matter be dealt with through a political understanding rather than a challenge to French diplomacy and the international treaty structure. So France was ready to deal with the problem by negotiation in a way that would also accord with German interests.

Kühlmann was so impressed he broke off his Paris visit to return to Berlin and report to his friend Neurath. Neurath told Kühlmann he would immediately inform Hitler. A few days later Kühlmann was surprised to learn that German troops had marched into the Rhineland. So what was called Hitler's "bold stroke" seems to have been based on a sure thing. When the German troops had begun their march, Hitler told Neurath: "Your friend Kühlmann may have had a good idea or two concerning this matter, but what he does not understand is that when the chains fall, it should be with a loud rattle" (" . . . das wenn die Ketten fallen, es ist mit einem lauten Rasseln").[8] It was a sound he never let his generals forget; whenever they raised any doubt at a risky step he was prepared to take, he reminded them of his prescience and their misgivings in the Rhineland.

In the event on March 7, 1936, only three battalions were ordered to enter Aachen, Trier, and Saarbrücken, while the rest of the troops that were to occupy the Rhineland were quartered in barracks on the right side of the river.[9] The battalions were reinforced by the territorial police who were ordered incorporated into the Wehrmacht.

The modest numbers involved led many observers, then and later, to the conclusion that Hitler would have ordered the troops pulled back had the French marched. Blomberg in fact ordered that if any troops of the signatory powers took countermeasures then the battalions must await his express orders as to what to do.[10]

The evidence that the brigades would have been withdrawn without a fight is flimsy. Hitler was not given to compromise or the admission of error. He had chosen the weekend of March 7 and 8 for the invasion because the French and British would be bound to react slowly over a weekend, which would give the troops time to occupy their positions, and it appears far more likely that rather than suffer the humiliation of having to order a withdrawal without resistance he intended to order the troops to fight if France attacked. Blomberg was to give further orders if the troops were fired on, but in a speech to the Reichstag made the same day as the invasion Hitler assured the deputies that they were all united in two holy commitments.[11] "First in the oath never to retreat before any power or force in reestablishing the honor of our people, and rather to perish in the most abject misery with honor than ever to capitulate." There was no room for retreat in that peroration though his second commitment was accompanied by an olive branch: The Reich, he said, was now for the first time able to pursue a policy of understanding with the peoples of Europe, "especially an understanding with our western peoples and neighbors."[12]

"After three years," he said, "I believe that as of today the German battle for equality can be regarded as ended." The Reich could work with the other European states in collective cooperation, and along with the code word *collective* he added the phrase so many people had long been waiting to hear: "We have no territorial demands to make in Europe." A flood of words and promises were the cover for what he had done. What he said had little truth in it. But he had shifted the power relationship in Europe. He read the deputies the contents of a memorandum Foreign Minister von Neurath had just delivered to the ambassadors of France, Belgium, and Italy.[13] It again informed these signatories of the Locarno Treaty, as had his note of May 25, that the Franco-Russian pact was irreconcilable with the Locarno Treaty. The pact was unmistakably directed solely against Germany; it took no account of French obligations under the Locarno Treaty or under the League of Nations; France had undertaken obligations, in case of a conflict between Russia and Germany, that would compel the use of armed force against Germany without reference to any decision by the League of Nations or anyone else. France alone would decide who the aggressor was and take action accordingly. Therefore, said Hitler, the Locarno Treaty had lost its inner meaning and for practical purposes had ceased to exist. That was the negative side of the speech that accompanied the marching troops. But on the positive side he not only said he had no territorial demands in Europe but also presented a seven-point design for securing the peace that echoed many of the same proposals the Allies had been supporting. He offered to enter into a nonaggression pact with France and Belgium that would include the Netherlands and would last for twenty-five years as well as an air pact with the neighboring states, and he was even willing to evacuate the Rhineland if France and Belgium in their turn would demilitarize a similar zone on their side of the Rhine. He also proposed to make a nonaggression pact with the Reich's eastern neighbors except for Lithuania; Lithuania's inclusion would have to await the settlement of the autonomy problem of the Memel area. And finally came the offer—now that Germany had achieved equality and regained full sovereignty over its own territory. The reasons, Hitler said, that Germany had left the League of Nations had disappeared, and he offered to rejoin. Of course, he added, the Reich would also expect in due course, through friendly negotiations, to discuss the question of colonial equality and separating the League of Nations from its basis in the Versailles treaty.

It was a speech in the classical Hitler pattern; it promised much but contained nothing he had to fulfill. It was designed to ward off any possible attack by France and its allies by accepting in principle the proposals the British and French had been urging to bring the Reich into the system of international agreements they would collectively maintain. It made use of the language the Allies had long been using, though Hitler still had territorial demands to make in Europe;

he had no intention of reentering the despised League of Nations or of again demilitarizing the Rhineland or of stopping his assaults on what remained of the Versailles treaty. But he knew France could not accept the proposal of a demilitarized zone on its side of the Rhine, which was part of the Maginot defense system, and that it could not make a nonaggression pact that excluded its allies.

And that was Hitler's strength. The French and British leaders did not believe in his offers or in his peaceful intentions, but they could not go to war on behalf of maintaining the shreds of a dead treaty. He could make use of the Reich's potential superiority over a France entirely dependent on its alliances for its security. The French and their allies needed time to rearm, time that might even lead to a moderation of Hitler's audacity. The Rhineland was after all German territory. It was the center of German rearmament that would have readily fallen to a swift French attack if no German troops were there to defend it. It was also strategic territory. In German hands it greatly impeded France's ability to come to the aid of allies such as Poland and Czechoslovakia if hostilities with the Reich should ever break out. General Maurice Gamelin and a few members of the French cabinet wanted to take military action, but France could not go to war alone, and the Baldwin government was too concerned with Italy to risk another dose of the bitter medicine Germany had served up during World War I.

The effect of the Rhine invasion in the Reich—the Liberation of the Rhineland, the Germans called it—was electrifying. The Führer had won another bloodless victory over the powers that had long kept the Reich militarily helpless. What the German people, like the French and British, feared most was another war, and not only was there no war as a result of the Rhineland coup, but also there was promise of peace—of German cooperation thitherto impossible, as Hitler said, with the other European powers. Blomberg summed up the feelings in a lyrical outburst on March 8: "Today," he said, "we have the double good fortune not only to shape history but to make this history with the archetype *[Vorbild]* of a Führer whose will, belief and confidence go far beyond the boundaries of human creativity into the realm of superhuman accomplishment *[Wirkung]*. And today this man is not only our archetype and commander-in-chief, but also our comrade to whom we belong with body and soul."[14]

One chapter of revision of the order created by the Versailles treaty was ending. On the Ethiopian battlefield Italian progress had been slow, despite the overwhelming superiority in weapons. World opinion of Italian military prowess was far from meeting Mussolini's proud prognosis. Reports were widespread of the Italian use of poison gas and ruthless bombing of civilian targets, but even with the overwhelming Italian arsenal it was not until May 4, 1936—seven months after the start of hostilities—that the victory was complete. Italian troops entered Addis Ababa and the Negus Haile Selassie fled the country. The king of

Italy was proclaimed emperor of Ethiopia, the Italian Marshal Pietro Badoglio became duke of Addis Ababa, and Mussolini was voted the title of founder of the empire.

Selassie appeared at Geneva to argue his case before the League of Nations against the recognition of the Italian conquest and the partitioning of Ethiopia between Italian Eritrea and Italian Somaliland to form Italian East Africa. But the League of Nations voted instead, forty-four to five, to rescind the sanctions against Italy. The European states returned to the old diplomacy and the very old use of force in place of the Wilsonian rhetoric. The Reich was again a military power, and Hitler could turn his attention to the remaining territories to which he said the Reich had no further claims.

6

The Saar and Rearmament

The first of the dazzling, bloodless triumphs of Hitler's foreign policy came in January 1935. Like most of the others to follow its dimensions would be less a tribute to Hitlerian charisma than to German nationalist sentiment building up in a territory whose administration had been wholly under foreigners since 1918.

The overwhelming vote in the Saar in favor of the Reich was cast under the supervision of the League of Nations and was therefore beyond the reach of the strong-arm tactics described in the foreign press to turn out the "yes" vote in the plebiscites held in the Reich. The Saarlanders could read about such matters, but they had had no direct experience of Nazi repressions, and what they voted for was a return to a resurgent fatherland from which they had been forcibly separated by the unilateral decision of the victorious powers.

France in 1919 had presented its case for the annexation of the entire Saar basin, one of France's major war aims. Premier Georges Clemenceau told Lloyd George that the numerical superiority of Germany with its 65 million inhabitants could only be partially overcome by France with its 40 million people by controlling the Rhine barrier and by possession of the Saar—or if not its possession then at least its detachment from the Reich.[1] In 1915 representatives of French heavy industry had demanded the annexation of the Saar to augment what would be an insufficient coal supply when France recovered the ore of Lorraine after the war. In 1917 Aristide Briand, who was prime minister at the time, had instructed Gaston Doumergue, the French delegate to the St. Petersburg Conference, to obtain the pledge of the czar's support for the French claim to the Saar, and Doumergue in fact succeeded in getting Nicholas's approval only a few weeks before the czar lost his throne.[2] On February 14, 1917, Russian Foreign Minister Sergei Dmitrievich Sazonov wrote to the French ambassador to St. Petersburg to tell him that "on order of his Imperial Majesty, my illustrious master," he had the honor to assure him that Russia would support the French demand that the left bank of the Rhine be separated from Germany and that the entire Saar basin should become part of France.[3]

The French delegation to the Paris Peace Conference, carrying on the same mission as Doumergue, brought along all their heavy artillery. They presented a memorandum declaring the Saar to have been French for many centuries. It had been separated from France, the memorandum said, only by force. The city of Landau had been ceded to France in 1684 and Saarlouis (where, as Clemenceau pointed out, Marshal Ney was born) had been built by Louis XIV. The latter was true, but the city, though held by France until 1815, was certainly German; and as for Landau, the Germans noted, it had no relationship with the Saar but lay eighty kilometers to the east. Petitions in the late eighteenth century from the Saarlanders, the memorandum declared, had expressed "the most ardent wish" to be reunited with France. Among the inhabitants of many other towns the people of Neukirchen had expressed their hope that France would have "the generosity to make them as happy as possible as they expressed their wish for the reunion with the first of the Republics." They wanted France to receive them "in the ranks of her beloved children, to give them the glorious title of Frenchmen which they had borne so long in their hearts and would never cease to deserve."

The people of Saarbrücken had said much the same thing: "May our reunion as pure as it is inviolable place us at the side of France our Fatherland."[4] Today too, in the Saar basin, the memorandum declared, "a sizable number of town and countrymen are passionately devoted to the French tradition; in the region of Saarlouis they are a powerful majority. This city greeted the French troops, as they marched in, with joy and sent an enthusiastic telegram to the President of the Republic." The least, the memorandum declared, the French could demand were the borders of 1814 plus reparations for the destruction carried out by the Germans. Two-thirds of the destruction had been caused deliberately, especially in the coal and industrial area of the north and in the Pas de Calais. The mines had also been flooded at Lens, which produced 8 million tons of coal a year, and in the basin of Gourrières and Dourges, which produced 4 million tons yearly. Finally the general devastation in the Département du Nord had caused the loss of 8 million tons a year. France without the Saar would be economically dependent on Germany; its victory in war transformed to a defeat in peace.

The problem was discussed by Clemenceau, David Lloyd George, and President Wilson on March 28, 1919, and both Lloyd George and Wilson opposed the French demand for the acquisition of the Saar, Lloyd George observing that the same mistake should not be made that the Germans had made in 1871. President Wilson pointed out that the French had never before demanded the borders of 1814; they had wanted to undo the injustice France had suffered in 1871 but not that of 1815. And in fact the French had never made a public statement of their plans for the Saar. It was a region, Wilson said, he had never heard mentioned until after the armistice. Clemenceau's answer, according to Colonel Edward M. House, was that Wilson was opening himself to a charge of pro-Germanism.[5] Wilson said he was ready to grant France the use of the coal mines for a limited period, but the industries of the region must not be deprived of coal. "I regret," Wilson said, "that I must make these objections and ask for your forgiveness . . . it is painful for me to oppose France, but I cannot act otherwise without being derelict in my duty." To this Clemenceau answered:

> You are leaving out sentiments and remembrance. You say you are ready to do justice from the economic point of view and thank you for that. [But] . . . the world is not governed by naked principles, economic necessities are not everything. The history of the United States is a glorious history but it is short. One hundred twenty years for you is a long period, but for us it is short. We have our own concept of history which is not exactly the same as yours. . . . It is not only a question of material reparations, the need for moral reparations is not less important. I know all you have done for the victory. But I think you would lose nothing if in this question you would acknowledge a moment of sentiment that is somewhat other than your principles, but is no less profound.

He then reminded Wilson of the deeds of the Marquis de Lafayette and Comte de Rochambeau who hastened to the aid of the Americans when they were fighting for their independence and who, not motivated by cold reason, had nevertheless forged a memory that linked the two nations forever. He said:

> I am old, in a few months I will have left political life forever. My disinterestedness is absolute. . . . In this region there are at least 150,000 people who are French, who in 1918 sent an address to President Poincaré and have a claim to justice. They want to respect the rights of Germans; I do too. But have regard for the rights of these Frenchmen just as you will need to have regard for the historical rights of Bohemia and Poland. . . . We shall resume our discussion soon again. For the moment I ask you, when you

are alone, to think of what I have just said and conscientiously determine if it doesn't contain a large part of the truth.[6]

André Tardieu, Louis Loucheur, and Clemenceau met the same afternoon and, as Tardieu reported, acknowledged that the case for obtaining the borders of 1814 was hopeless.[7] They however did not give up the attempt easily. They dispatched three more notes on the subject, one of which, that of March 29, Tardieu published. In it was repeated the tenaciously held view that the Saar, one part at least, had been held by France for two hundred years; another part for more than twenty years. Torn from France against the will of its inhabitants it had been Germanized by one hundred years of immigration.[8] The note said,

> we recognize these facts, so that we do not ask for annexation. . . . We do insist on a solution that at least partially recognizes the imprescriptible rights of France to a country dedicated to France by virtue of the will of its inhabitants. This land was French. This fact creates the supposition that it would again gladly be French. The example of Alsace-Lorraine proves this. Even today we know that a majority of the population of Saarlouis is ready to call for a reunion with France.

So the French delegation asked that the League of Nations accord France a double mandate. First the military occupation of the Saar. Second the supervision of, or veto powers over, the local administrations, including education and the naming of mayors and deputy mayors. French citizenship would be granted those who asked for it, and after fifteen years those who had not yet chosen their citizenship would be asked what nationality they wished to adopt. No request for reunion with Germany was to be considered during this period. "After all," the memorandum noted, "Prussia had 100 years to complete its work of coercion." None of this, said the note, was a new claim made by France, nor was it a breach of the principle of self-determination.

Within a few days President Wilson and Lloyd George agreed that the production of the Saar coal mines should go to France, and they also agreed to the creation of an independent Saar under the administration of the League of Nations for a period of fifteen years after which a vote would be held to determine its future. Lloyd George has described how deeply the American president had been wounded by the attacks on him in the French press: "an outrage on international decencies," Lloyd George described them, which had impaired Wilson's health. After Colonel House called on Clemenceau to tell him the president had agreed to the French demands for the Allied occupation of the Rhine and French occupation of the Saar provided the attacks on him stopped, the attacks ceased as if by magic. A wave of Clemenceau's hand had been enough.

The Germans were in a position only to make protests and refute the French claims in memoranda and articles. Count Ulrich von Brockdorff-Rantzau, foreign minister and head of the German delegation to the peace conference, wrote a note on May 29, 1919, accompanying the German counterproposals, in which he said that Germany had come to the conference in the expectation that a united attempt would be made to fashion the peace proposals and then proceeded to enumerate what was being done instead.[9] Although the Reich was ready to supply France with coal from the Saar "until the French mines were back in production," he wrote, the purely German Saar territory was to be taken from the Reich and its later acquisition by France prepared for, although "we owe France not people but coal. For 15 years the Rhineland is to be occupied and the Allies may then refuse to return it, while in the meantime they do all they can to dissolve the economic and moral ties and the Motherland and ultimately falsify the will of the inhabitants." Germany, he said, was prepared to put its entire economic resources in the service of reconstruction of the devastated areas of France and Belgium and to supply 20 million tons to replace the coal from the destroyed mines of northern France. But that was not what France wanted from the Reich or from the Saar.

But whatever the Germans might say of the Saar's history and the desires of its people, they were talking to the hard-of-hearing. And while the French did not succeed in formally annexing the Saar, its coal and other resources became part of the reparations account owed by Germany, and France gained the right to occupy the territory for at least fifteen years. The French hope that the Saar might be separated from the Reich, though it faded, was never relinquished from the time of the armistice to the time of the plebiscite.

In March 1919 careful preparations were made by the French authorities for the reception of a French field marshal—either Ferdinand Foch or Philippe Pétain was to be the visitor—in Saarlouis. Schoolgirls in the city were to assemble in the marketplace, and the daughter of the director of the ironworks, "Fraulautern," whose mother was French, was to present their greetings. They were to sing the "Marseillaise," which few of them knew, with the help of a choir of French soldiers, and the instructions were if they did not know the words they could hum. The note they were to hand the marshal said in French: "We come in the name of all little Saarlouisiennes to present our respects to you and to express our love for France. We want to become good little French girls and we beg you to accept our most tender embraces and to transmit them to our little sisters over there in France. Vive [whichever marshal came]. Vive la France. Vive the country of the Saar." They were also to sing the following verse, which had been written by a French teacher:

The beautiful land of the Saar, is my native land,
I love my country well, I love my pretty valley well.
It is my hearthside that I love, that alone makes me happy.
It is that which leads us to France, to the country of our ancestors.
O, happy day, O time full of joy,
That you see, O fathers, from the high heavens.
May the day of your arrival be blessed,
That returns the past to us,
Sweet France. The Saar to France. Vive la France.[10]

As a German commentator noted, since many if not most of the people in the gathering had lost fathers or brothers who had fought in the German army, the incongruity of the planned occasion was not lost on the Saarlanders.

The French were living in a never-never land. On the one hand they told the Saarlanders how they could depend on a France that, despite all the provocations the Germans had given them, remained the country of humanity and generosity, and they made every formal effort to win over the population. In May 1919 after the terms of the peace treaty were made public, French instructions declared the Saarlanders to be no longer enemies; the use of the word *Boche* was forbidden with regard to them; its use was to be confined to Germans outside the Saar. On the other hand they lost no opportunity to assure the Germans, including the Saarlanders, that they had been beaten. They seemed uncertain that they had really won the war. The sour remarks made by General Garnier-Duplessis about the German soldiers not having fought on German soil were nourished by the fact that France had succeeded in occupying German territory only after the war was over. Alsace-Lorraine, the bridgeheads on the Rhine, and the Saar were only occupied after the last shot was fired, and one French observer remarked that in the Saar it was only the presence of French troops that manifested France's triumph. The French-German imbalances of population remained much the same as they had been before the war, and thus the need, as France saw it, remained to separate as much of Germany as possible from the Reich and to continue to rely on colonial troops to balance the manpower scales.

According to the French budget of 1921 France sent 266 officers and 7,163 troops to garrison the Saar, 3,200 of whom were natives of North Africa.[11] Thus by assigning colonial troops to the duties and privileges of the occupation forces they could experience firsthand the benefits accorded them as they became overlords in a European country that had regarded them as inferiors not as harbingers of a higher civilization.

In February 1920 the League of Nations Council appointed the Saar's governing commission. A Frenchman, Victor Rault, was named president, and the commission, though made up of a representative of the Saar plus two others who were to be neither French nor German, was in the coming years to reflect the views of Rault and of the French government.[12] Rault, a Conseiller d'État, spoke no German, and he referred to himself as a "grand prefet de la République" whose duty was to keep constant watch to ensure the continuation of the advantages accorded France by the Treaty of Versailles and to reconcile this duty with the primary consideration of securing the rights and welfare of the population. He received his directives not from the League of Nations, but from Paris. He was paid for his services the substantial sum of 110,000 francs a year; the other members of the commission were paid 100,000 francs. Rault promptly made his purpose clear: maintaining the French advantages by refusing to permit any kind of official German presence in the territory. The German government had appointed, as a liaison official, a Reichskommissar, Groote, who was president of the Rhine province, to head a Commission for the Transfer of the Saar Territory. Groote asked Rault on February 27 if he might be permitted to establish an office in Saarbrücken to expedite the orderly transfer of the territory, enclosing a list of five people, which included a courier and translator, to accompany him. Rault replied stiffly that no negotiations with the representatives of the German Reich were required; the German commissar had only to turn over his records. Rault was determined to block any representative of the Reich from appearing to have the right to negotiate on behalf of anyone concerned with the administration of a territory France still hoped to sever from the Reich. No point was too trivial for him. On March 8 his commission issued an order saying that from that date personal identity cards could not identify the holder as Prussian, German, Bavarian, or any other kind of Reich German. For all such former identifications was to be substituted "Saarlaender."

The Saar statute provided for the policing of the territory by a peacekeeping force to be recruited from the local population. The French troops sent in to occupy the Saar, however, never left. The German Foreign Office in a series of protest notes pointed out that the continuing presence of the troops violated the terms of the treaty, which made no mention of an occupying soldiery but only of a police force of three thousand men to be raised locally. Rault explained to the League of Nations Council, to which the German government had addressed its protests, that the soldiers (seven thousand in 1921) were not occupation but garrison troops and, until such time as the authorized police force was recruited, performing police functions acting under the orders of the governing commission.

The presence of the soldiers made possible a heavy-handed, unpredictable, and capricious series of arrests and trials before military courts when Rault and the commission declared a state of martial law as a strike was called by the civil servants in the Saar. The governing commission had rejected a protest of these *Beamte* over grievances, including a prohibition of membership in professional organizations they had thitherto belonged to as subjects of the Reich. The governing commission regarded such organizations as nationalistic and therefore subversive, and it had appointed French personnel to replace Germans in such memberships. The strike of the *Beamte* was joined by postal and railroad workers at which point martial law was proclaimed.

When violent incidents occurred as a result of the imposition of martial law the French high command made what seemed to the Saarlanders to be bizarre claims for compensation. During a strike in Saarbrücken, in October 1919, a French officer standing in the window of his hotel was shot and killed by a Vietnamese soldier, a member of one of the colonial contingents among the occupying forces. The French commandant, General Andlauer, thereupon demanded on the officer's behalf restitution of 250,000 francs, on the grounds that the officer had died as a result of the actions of the Saarlanders since the troops had orders to fire on any shadow to prevent sniping from windows. Another soldier was shot and killed, according to the French authorities, as he was pursuing an alleged looter. The soldier had been alone when he was shot, and the circumstances were unclear except for the fact that he was dead, and the Saarlanders were to be held financially responsible for his death. In this case General Andlauer asked for one hundred thousand francs. The same principles applied with regard to property damage suffered by French nationals. When the Saarbrücken warehouse of the Hirsch firm based in Paris, was looted, the French authorities demanded the city pay over two and a half million marks for damages sustained in the course of the riots. Almost a half-million marks' compensation was demanded in the case of an Alsatian, Simon Levy, whose manufactory was plundered during the same riots. The city of Saarbrücken demurred, and the civil courts denied that the damages came under the Prussian law regarding damages arising from public tumult. But the orders of General Andlauer took precedence over any civil courts, and the sums were paid.

Damage done the Saarlanders was written down considerably from such figures. A German girl was raped by a French soldier who also clubbed and stabbed her. She survived for a short time and managed to describe her attacker who nevertheless was never found. The French commandant expressed his profound regret, and the government offered to pay her parents forty thousand marks, or, at the going rate of exchange, eight thousand francs, as compensation.

Local elections were permitted by the governing commission, but the legislators had advisory functions only and the commission could veto the result of any vote, as it could the right of anyone elected to take his seat in the so-called legislature. The French authorities, however, were waging a never-ending battle against a resistant population that gave no evidence of accepting foreign domination. As the *Echo de Paris* wrote on September 2, 1920, the presence of the French troops was the only visible sign of France's victory.

All this said nothing about the less visible signs of reparations paid from the mines and used in part for the support of the occupying troops and administrative apparatus. Saar workers were soon paid in francs instead of marks on the grounds that the mark was a too volatile currency, but one of the most influential French nationalists and a supporter of the Saar's detachment from the Reich, Maurice Barrès, put the matter differently. "How will the incorporation of the Saar be achieved?" he asked. "By way of the introduction of the franc," he explained. "The miners, the smelters, and the administration will be paid in francs. The worker population alone make up more than half of the entire population which will never again want to return to a Germany where the rate of the mark is lower than that of the franc. Moreover, immediate naturalization before the plebiscite will make the plebiscite unnecessary." By June 1923 the franc was the sole legal currency, and the Saar's economic life was wholly oriented toward France. By 1925 there was a full-fledged customs union between the Saar and the French republic.[13]

Political measures accompanied the economic devices. By order of the governing commission, five years of imprisonment and a ten thousand–franc fine was the penalty for casting discredit on the Versailles treaty, on a member of the administration of the Saar, or for insulting or defaming the League of Nations or any of its members.

Even the late allies of France were critical of her policies. In the House of Commons the composition of the membership of the governing commission was questioned in a debate in May 1923; a newspaper article on the qualifications of the individual who had succeeded the Saar entrepreneur Boch on the governing commission was cited, for the man had unduly close ties to connections with French interests, and the Danish commission member, too, was said to be a dubious Dane who lived in France and was merely another tool of the French government. Another speaker declared there were too many French troops in the territory. Former Prime Minister Herbert Henry Asquith called the Saar regime the worst kind of legislative despotism, guilty of the worst oppression of the rights of free citizens, and added that as a critic of the governing commission he would not dare visit the Saar. Sir John Simon, former home secretary, observed that the Saar government could forbid any meetings, processions, or demonstrations that might lead to the making of speeches opposing the administration.[14] The attacks on the governing commission widened in the debate to an attack not only on the whole principle of the League of Nations' administration of the Saar but also as a device in the postwar treatment of Germany. The League of Nations, said Asquith, was regarded by the Germans as a chimera, a posse, a swindle, nothing more than the means for hidden control by France. A member of Parliament from Dundee, Morel, said that France was clearly trying to break up Germany and under the aegis of the

French general staff was raising an army of overwhelming size. Four and a half years after the treaty of peace it numbered six and a half million soldiers with the Little Entente, under control of the French general staff, and Morel added that the allies of France had the right to know what they were to be used for. Such numbers, he said, were not usually recruited to play football.[15] It was impossible, he said, to maintain that Germany was always the aggressor and France always the victim. Another deputy, Charles Burton, pointed out that France had ten thousand armed men to occupy a little place with not even a million inhabitants. Everything the French did was one-sided. They paid the Saar miners sixteen francs a day, whereas in France the same work was paid at the average rate of twenty-six francs. It was for this reason, he said, the German miners were striking. Another member, T. Shaw, assured the House of Commons that even in the heyday of Prussian militarism the Ruhr had not had a military garrison because the German workers would not tolerate one, but now French and British troops were there in droves, and he expressed his admiration for miners who refused to work under the French bayonets. On the one side, he said, was a people of seventy million with a well-organized industry, and on the other a smaller country, less well organized, and with zero population growth: "A catastrophe is unavoidable," he said, prophetically, "if reason doesn't take the place of force." Revenge breeds hate; the Saar is as German as London is British. If German industry is not freed, French cities and villages would not be rebuilt. These were the critics, and though there were no lack of voices defending what the French were doing, it was the critics who were heard.

The foreign attacks on the French administration increased, and one writer, Sidney Osborne, declared the Saarlanders were governed as worthless chattels attached to valuable coal mines and called the League of Nations "a compliant tool of purely French interests." He accused the French of establishing a spy system in the Saar: opening letters, requisitioning private dwellings, and imposing a high court of justice without the consent of the inhabitants. The scholar Michael Florinsky called it a purely artificial state with the highest population density in Europe. The 150,000 French of which Clemenceau had spoken were nowhere to be found. In the first German census taken in 1911, only 339 or 0.05 percent gave their national tongue as French. By February 1925 Prime Minister MacDonald could write to Poincaré that the feeling was widespread in Britain that France, against the provisions of the Versailles treaty, was creating a situation designed to give what it was unable to achieve through her allies during the peace negotiations. "Those of my countrymen who have this impression consider this policy is designed only to perpetuate the dangers and uncertainty of the situation, which means the not-peace-but-war condition, and finally to destroy all the security guarantees which France would temporarily arrange."[16] The *Manchester Guardian* declared that for four years the Saar's inhabitants had been robbed of all civil rights. John Maynard Keynes called the Versailles decision a predatory and unjust act. The former Italian prime minister who had taken part in the peace negotiations at Paris called the Saar administration an "injustice crying to heaven." Newspapers and writers in Sweden, Japan, and even in francophile Belgium and the United States joined in the chorus of condemnation.

The tide of sentiment among neutrals and the late allies of France was running strongly against such policies, and it had its effect. Rault was chosen once more, in 1926, to head the governing commission, but the term was for one year, and he failed to be reappointed despite French pressure on his behalf. His successors— a Canadian, G. W. Stephens, and later an Englishman, Sir Ernest Wilson, a career foreign officer—were much milder in their efforts. Stephens, especially, was well regarded by the Saarlanders as he moved among them, even appearing in the cafés. By 1927 the French troops were ordered out of the Saar by the League of Nations Council, to be replaced by not more than eight hundred "railroad protection troops." In 1930 the council ordered that the protection troops, too, leave the territory within three months and said further that if it was necessary, the Saar had the right to call in German police to maintain law and order.

German attempts to settle the question of the return of the Saar to the Reich were unavailing, but there could be no question of the way the vote would go, despite the hoodlumism of the Nazis and the anti-Catholic measures in the Reich. The Saar Catholics were told by the bishops of Trier and Speyer in a decree of December 3, 1934, that clericals who had appeared at a neutralist rally had acted against the bishops' authority, and two days later the bishop of Trier addressed a letter to the deans of the Saar territory again deploring the appearance of the priests on behalf of the "questionable status quo," calling what they had done "a heavy blow against the Catholic church in Germany."

Until the immediate danger of Hitler's taking power in the Reich became manifest, the decline of anti-German sentiment everywhere in Europe was evident in the utterances of European political leaders and the press. In the Saar the three parties that favored the return of the territory to the Reich— the National Socialists, the Volksparty, and the Center—had the overwhelming backing of the population. Nevertheless, in order to make sure of a large vote, including that of the non-Nazis, the National Socialist Party in the Saar dissolved itself in 1933, and in November 1934 the German Front was established under the leadership of Josef Bürckel, leader of the Palatinate National Socialists, named by Hitler as his plenipotentiary for the Saar. Bürckel replaced Papen who had been sent as ambassador to Vienna.

The Nazis were ready to cooperate with the two parties that hoped for a return to the Reich, their obvious strategy being to paper over any political and philosophical difficulties in favor of a united front that would last until the plebiscite. Even the bitterly anti-Nazi parties favored neutrality only as an interim solution. The Social Democrats favored the status quo under the League of Nations because of Hitler, not because of any desire to remain outside the Reich. They, too, were in favor of the Saar's going back to Germany once a legal state was restored. They were joined in the neutralist decision by the Communists, dissident members of the Center, and other Christian workers groups who believed that rejoining the Reich was one thing and coming under Hitler's domination another. Although members of the non-Nazi parties appeared among the leadership of the German Front, they were there for cosmetic reasons; it was essentially a National Socialist organization. And it had every cooperation from the carefully maneuvering Hitler. In Koblenz, in August 1934, Hitler declared that the Saar was to be the last obstacle dividing France and Germany.[17] Once that question was out of the way, he said, nothing would prevent the establishing of a just peace in Europe. Hitler called on the Saarlanders to put aside all their differences and to unite in voting for a return to Germany. This was the official line. Goebbels, in a similarly conciliatory address in May, had assured the overwhelming Catholic Saarlanders that the Reich was a state devoted to the principles of Christianity in word and deed. He said that men were going around telling of alleged terrorism in the Reich and therefore urging the Saarlanders to vote for a continuation of the League of Nations regime in the territory. These men, he said, were émigrés, Social Democrats seeking to create a domain, and they were guilty of treason. He reminded his listeners that the National Socialists were also a workers party, that the name "worker" was part of the name and purpose of the party. The people of the Saar could vote for return in good conscience, for the Reich was a land of Christian belief and deeds. "You, my men and women of the Saar, can rightfully expect of us that we see in the Saar not a foreign country, but a homeland, eternal Germany."[18]

The propaganda of the German Front was a carbon copy of the same gospel one of its Nazi leaders, Jacob Pirro, told the Saarlanders at a pro-German meeting. The party bickering was over now; they were all German brothers.

Catholics and Protestants, each goes to his own church but both say the same prayer: Our Germany. The worker, the farmer, the entrepreneur, the government official each does his duty in his job and all of them have the same thing in their hearts: Our Germany. . . . The Social Democrat, the Communist, the Centrist, the National Socialist each may have had a different political view but now all have the same thought: Our Germany. From this historical moment on, we are a sworn brotherhood.

There were other voices. A group of émigré Germans—among them well-known names such as Heinrich Mann, Lion Feuchtwanger, Alfred Kerr, Ernst

Toller, Anna Seghers, Theodor Plevier, Prince Max Karl zu Hohenlohe-Langenberg, some of them Communist—called on the Germans in the Saar to vote against the "Fascist barbarism, the loss of freedom, the concentration camps for priests and ministers, and to keep the Saar a bridgehead in the fight for freedom for the Reich." Such a call for a neutral state under the Council of the League had, faute de mieux, an appeal to Social Democrats, Communists, Centrists, and others among the émigrés, but they, too, made clear that they would favor a return to the Reich once it again became a state of law, a *Rechtsstaat*. League of Nations sovereignty provided, at best, an interim solution.

Two roadblocks still had to be dealt with before the plebiscite was held. The Versailles treaty provided that in the event the territory was returned to the Reich, Germany had to buy back the mines, and France demanded that the amount be agreed on in advance of the plebiscite. The League of Nations Council agreed, and the matter was settled by the Reich's undertaking to pay the sum of 900 million gold marks. The second barrier arose because of the aggressive activity of the German Front and the SA along the border. Provocative demonstrations and meetings could overtax the governing commission's police forces, and, as French Foreign Minister Jean Louis Barthou pointed out, the resulting unrest might require the sending of French forces into the Saar to maintain law and order. But this threat, too, was allayed when Hitler's plenipotentiary for the Saar, Bürckel, ordered the SA and the SS to stay away from the Saar border and forbade their holding any meetings or parades there, and a police force without either French or German participation was recruited under the League of Nations Council. Bürckel was a first-class organizer on behalf of the Nazis. He arranged for free railroad tickets to the Saar for those eligible to vote, as well as special trains from German cities to the Saar border. Inside the Saar he organized a door-to-door canvas by German Front adherents.[19]

The plebiscite went off without a hitch, and there could be no doubt, when it was over, of what the Saarlanders wanted. More than 539,000 (90.8 percent) voted for a return to the Reich, 46,500 (8.8 percent) voted for the status quo, and 2,124 (0.4 percent) for France—all that remained of Clemenceau's 150,000.

With the Saar plebiscite safely out of the way, Hitler could turn to the cornerstone of his future foreign policy—the rearmament of the Reich. Contrary to what critics had been saying German rearmament had not gone very far, nor could it before Hitler made his public announcement of the introduction of general conscription. By the autumn of 1934 Germany, by adding the barracks police and short-term volunteers to the Wehrmacht, had increased the size of its army to some 250,000 men, and a year later the number reached 400,000. But it was in important parts a drawing-board army. The two tank divisions that had been formed had only twelve tanks between them in the spring of 1935, and almost everything else was in equally short supply. Without conscription and the allocation of the large sums of money that could not escape public scrutiny not much could be done toward massive rearmament; General von Seeckt's blueprint to make the post-Versailles force of one hundred thousand long-term volunteers a cadre that could be rapidly expanded required manpower on a nationwide scale and major rearmament. Wilhelm Adam, chief of the so-called Troop Office, the Truppenamt, which would become the general staff, estimated in 1934 that in the event of war with Poland the army had sufficient munitions for only two weeks of fighting, and if Poland were to be joined by either Czechoslovakia or France, the Reich would be able to resist with what Adam called "pin pricks." Under such circumstances, he concluded, any risks in the Reich's foreign relations had to be held to a minimum. Nothing should be undertaken that might irritate a foreign enemy or incite the German people. Even the modest goal of raising the peacetime army from twenty-one to twenty-four divisions, the army leadership calculated, could be reached only by the spring of 1938.[20]

The Reich since 1919 had been in a military straitjacket and remained far inferior to its potential antagonists. It is true that the half-militarized SA had a million men, the SS some two hundred thousand, and the workforce armed with spades for which rifles might one day be substituted were at hand, but they were not soldiers and only in a dire emergency could they be used as anything like a serious force to back the Wehrmacht. The air force, according to the provisions of the Treaty of Versailles, was theoretically nonexistent. As a result of the clandestine training in the Soviet Union and the buildup in personnel and planes by way of the civilian air fleet, the Reich in 1933 had 228 air force officers up to the rank of colonel, and by April 1934 the number had risen to 450. At the beginning of 1935 it had 270 bombers, 99 one-seater fighter planes, 303 reconnaissance planes, and the entire aircraft industry employed 4,000 workers. This was what Göring and the German air strategists would call the "risk air force," the umbrella designed to protect the security of the Reich should the enemy—seen as France, Belgium, Poland, and Czechoslovakia—undertake a preventive war while Germany rearmed. It was numerically not an imposing instrument, nor was it nearly a match for the forces of its possible enemies.[21] As Morel pointed out during a House of Commons debate, armies of the Little Entente—Yugoslavia, Romania, and Czechoslovakia—were armed by France and organized by the French general staff. Czechoslovakia had a French general as chief of staff and a peacetime army of 180,000 men, which would expand to 1.3 million in time of war. Romania had a peacetime army of 210,000, which in time of war would number 1.7 million; Yugoslavia's army numbered 140,000 in peacetime and went up to 1.5 million in time of war. Thus, Morel said, the French general staff had under their command, from the Little Entente alone, a force of 6.5 million men who were not there to play football. These were only part of the potential enemy forces; Poland, France, and the Soviet Union were all possible antagonists, and the forces Germany could muster could scarcely balance in numbers those that could be used against her if the preventive war many foreign military men wished to see waged against the Reich would be actually fought. But the political climate in 1935, no matter what general staffs might calculate and no matter how dubious government leaders might be of Hitler's foreign policies, was not made by hard-line French or Czech generals. Hitler's announcement of the introduction of conscription came at a time when British statesmen were prepared to go a long way to adopt conciliatory measures to salvage the peace of Europe. Only a few days before, on March 5, France had announced that recruits must serve two years instead of one to maintain its own security and world peace. A British White Book issued on March 4, while saying the British greeted Hitler's expression of his desire for peace, noted that the spirit in which the German people—and especially their youth—were organized gave rise to a general feeling of uncertainty. When Hitler ordered conscription, and a member of the House of Commons asked whether the planned visit of British Foreign Secretary Sir John Simon and Lord Privy Seal Anthony Eden would nevertheless take place and the answer was "yes," the entire House of Commons applauded. It was a House of Commons intensely aware of the imbalance between the sacrifice of millions of young men in the world war and the subsequent instability of Europe and the British Empire. Lloyd George among others was becoming an outspoken admirer of Adolf Hitler and vigorously defended the policies that were reestablishing the Reich's power. In 1936, when the German army marched in the Rhineland, Lloyd George said a pro-French policy was no longer possible—the whole of England was pro-German.[22] A sharp reaction to the former anti-German policy was evident in many quarters. Harold Nicolson, speaking in the House of Commons in 1938, said what a good many British leaders had long been thinking: "During the war we lied damnably. . . . I think some of our lies have done us tremendous harm and I should not myself like to see such propaganda again."[23]

The British aim in sending Simon and Eden to Berlin was to convince Germany to rejoin the system of collective security as embodied in the League of Nations. It was a difficult if not impossible assignment, since Hitler saw in the League of Nations nothing more than a prayerful representation of the status quo designed to keep the Versailles treaty intact and to declare illegal any change in the map of Europe that lacked the sanction of the victorious powers of World War I. He had nothing but contempt for the League of Nations, but he was wooing Britain in a climate in which many Englishmen were ready to be convinced: that concessions had to be made to bring the Reich back to the European concert of powers. So Britain and the Reich, each for its own reasons, had obvious motives to proceed with friendly conversations that might give each at least a small portion of what it wanted from the other.

The British government had sent a formal note of protest, on March 18, on the announcement of conscription in the Reich as did the other signatories of the Locarno Treaty—France and Italy—on March 21; nevertheless the British visitors came to their meeting with Hitler wreathed in smiles and amiability. Hitler was his most charming self, obviously delighted to welcome his visitors whose very coming belied the seriousness of the formal protests sent him a few days before. And he told them what he had so often told other audiences and what they so ardently wanted to believe, if possible—that he was a man of peace and everything he was doing was aimed at peace. Germany had no territorial demands to make in Europe; it threatened no one. National Socialism was not expansionist. But the Reich was threatened on every side, especially from the east. Germany, and perhaps all of Europe, he said, had been saved from the worst catastrophe of all time.[24] It had experienced bolshevism firsthand, and only when it was armed would it be secure. Hitler completely dominated the meeting. It was he who did most of the talking, with Simon and Eden making rejoinders and politely offering suggestions from time to time. When Eden mildly remarked that there were no signs the Russians planned an attack on the Reich and asked on what grounds Hitler feared one, Hitler replied he had more experience with these matters than did the British generally; he had begun his political career when the bolsheviks were still holding out in their first strike against Germany, and he went on in a long monologue to tell of the Red machinations as he had experienced them. He took the occasion, when Eden mentioned the utility of an east pact that would include not only Germany and Russia but also Czechoslovakia, Poland, and the Baltic states, including Lithuania, to seize with fury on the very mention of such a country. Never, Hitler said, his calm lost, would the Reich deal with or enter into a pact with a country that trod its German minority under foot.[25]

His rage, however, quickly subsided, and he continued on his antibolshevik theme: Never, he said, would there be any cooperation between bolshevism and National Socialism. It was completely out of the question. Hundreds of his party comrades had been murdered by the bolsheviks; German soldiers and civilians had been killed in bolshevik risings, and these victims would block any pact with the communists. And as to collective security, he added, it was not a barrier to war—on the contrary it served to incite and extend it. Much to be preferred were two-power nonaggression pacts, and Germany was ready to make them with the exception, naturally, of Lithuania—at least until the Memel question was settled. He waved aside Eden's attempt to show that a collective pact had room for such two-power agreements. "One cannot," he said, "within the framework of such a general agreement have two separate groups of members."[26] He wanted no part of mutual-aid pacts either, though countries could obligate themselves to lend no aid to an aggressor and "that would localize a war" instead of making it general.

He was reassuring about Austria. He had nothing, he said, against a Danubian pact that would forbid the interference of one of the signatories in the domestic affairs of another, but it was necessary to clarify the precise meaning of "non-interference." As for the return of Germany to the League of Nations, it was possible, but only when the Reich was recognized as a fully equal partner and the Versailles treaty was no longer part of the League of Nations structure. He touched lightly on the system of colonial mandates that, he said, Germany must participate in, but he quickly added the Reich had no demands in the matter at the moment. The talks lasted until seven o'clock in the evening.

The next morning's session was wholly devoted to the subject foremost on everyone's mind—German rearmament. A moment of tension came and went when Simon tried to make clear that in discussing the Reich's rearming, Britain was not departing from its original position that treaties could be changed only by mutual agreement and not unilaterally, but it served only to move Hitler to a torrent of well-rehearsed propaganda. It was not Germany, he said, but the other powers that had disregarded the disarmament provisions of the Versailles treaty; it was they who had failed to fulfill the patent obligation to disarm themselves and asked jocularly if perhaps Wellington, when Blücher had come to his aid at Waterloo, had first inquired of British jurists whether the number of Prussian troops was in accord with the relevant treaties.[27]

The German interpreter at the meeting, Paul Schmidt, a shrewd observer of both Hitler and his British guests, believed both sides to be on their best behavior, each wary not to antagonize the other, and Hitler, he thought, was unusually moderate in tone though unbudgeable on the main points. The decision for conscription, he told his visitors, was unalterable, but he was ready to discuss the size of the coming army. His one condition was parity on land and in the air with the Reich's heavily armed neighbors. Germany could do with thirty-six divisions, or five hundred thousand men, including an SS division and the garrison police, though he denied, as Schmidt noted, that the party formations had any military value. Eden then mildly observed that at least the SS could be regarded as a reserve. As for the air force Hitler said in a response to a question by Simon as to how large he thought it needed to be: "We need parity with Great Britain and France, but if Russia should increase its air strength Germany must have a corresponding increase." Simon asked politely if he might inquire how large the German air force was at present. Hitler, after a moment's hesitation, threw a bomb into the meeting. "We already have achieved parity with England," he said.[28]

For a short time no one spoke, but, Schmidt records, the faces of Simon and Eden plainly showed their surprise, though they said nothing. And when Simon, still pursuing his ardent aim of getting the Reich into some sort of collective security pact, proposed that the Locarno Treaty powers agree to use their air forces immediately to come to the aid of any signatory that was attacked, Hitler said he was ready to join in such an agreement. But, he added, "I can naturally do this only when Germany has the necessary aircraft," and Schmidt observed that against such logic the Englishmen had nothing to oppose. Hitler was ready to make use of the current coin of international dealings—"world peace," "instant help for a country threatened by an aggressor"— and he also prepared the way, too, for future changes in the status quo when he called Czechoslovakia "the extended arm of Soviet Russia."[29] His two major themes, however, remained the same: the danger of the Soviet Union and Germany's right to arms equality. With regard to the latter, he said, of course, that the Reich must have the same arms as other countries, though he was ready to join in a Geneva convention that would bar offensive weapons. Here, too, however, Germany could only undertake such an obligation under conditions of complete equality; that is, when any control over armaments applied to all the powers.

Schmidt was moved to reflect on the different atmosphere of this meeting compared with the disarmament conferences he had attended in Geneva. He thought the heavens would have fallen if two years before such demands had been made as Hitler was now putting forward. But Hitler, Schmidt said, presented his view as though they were the most self-evident in the world, and Schmidt wondered if Hitler's tactic of presenting his opponents with accomplished facts did not get a good deal further than had been possible with the traditional methods of the foreign office.

At eleven o'clock the English visitors left—Simon to return to London, Eden to take the train to Warsaw on his way to Moscow to visit Stalin. An old Nazi confided to Schmidt that he found it "directly tactless" for Eden to make such a visit after he had met with the Führer.

7

The Games of Peace

Everything seemed to be going Hitler's way. It was Germany's turn to be host at the Olympic Games in 1936, and they were made to order for an impresario such as Goebbels to put on an enormous spectacular, confirming in its celebrations and performances how highly the new Reich was esteemed and how it had become a focal point for the entire civilized world. To prepare a favorable climate of international opinion, even Nazi anti-Semitism was muted so that non-Aryan athletes from Jewish organizations were allowed to work out on German sports fields before the games were held so that no effective criticism or boycotts would mar the occasion. Forty-nine nations took part in the games, sending over forty-eight hundred athletes from all the countries of the globe except the Soviet Union. True, there were times when the results of the contests did not follow the National Socialist script, such as when black athletes from the United States made new world records, and one of them, Jesse Owens, won three gold medals against the fleetest runner the Reich and the other Aryan powers could muster. But though Hitler was conspicuously not present when Owens was awarded his medals, the German press had explanations at hand to account for the admittedly magnificent performances of the black athletes. They were closer to nature, German sports writers explained, and the illustrations in the text of the official album depicted amusing little black figures of the kind used in children's comic books of the time, along with photographs of Hitler visiting notables, contests, processions, and the victors, male and female. But, as German writers pointed out, their athletes did very well indeed, winning thirty-eight gold, twenty-six silver, and thirty bronze medals in the huge arena that Goebbels had turned into an amphitheater of National Socialist pomp and ceremony where one hundred thousand people cheered day after day. German athletes won more medals than those of any other country, four times what they had won in 1932 and well ahead of the runner-up, the United States—which won twenty-four gold, twenty silver, and twelve bronze medals—thus confirming the claims of the National Socialist physical and spiritual revolution.

The games were a huge success and National Socialists were on their best behavior to make them so. As *Der Angriff* had written before the games started: "In the next weeks we have to be more charming than the Parisians, more companionable than the Viennese, more amiable than the Romans, more gentlemanly than the Londoners and more practical than the New Yorkers."

German commentators made a great deal of the symbolic significance of the Berlin Olympics: their sportsmanship, their contribution to the peace and understanding among nations so ardently sought by Hitler. And since Hitler was the official *Schirmherr,* the patron of the games, foreign visitors, too, politely paid tribute to the warm hospitality provided by him and the German people. The leitmotiv of the German commentators regularly proclaimed the accomplishments of Hitler and National Socialism. It was National Socialism, one speaker explained, that had made carrying through the Olympic concept possible. "Just imagine," he said, "if the games had had to take place in 1932 . . . think of six million starving, unemployed, living for the day, without hope." They could only have formed an opposition to such a world celebration; marxist propaganda would have incited them toward a kind of counterolympiad as it had already done in Barcelona. Even, he went on, the material provisions for the games would have been lacking and in their place would have been "the palaver of the parties in the tattered Fatherland, in the parliaments of the Reich and of the states and in Berlin. . . . Compare this with the gigantic decisions of our Fuehrer."

Despite the grandiloquence of the rhetoric, no one could quarrel with the brave scene: the brilliant displays of skill, endurance, flags, and music and the palpable evidence of a thriving Germany where the depression was a ghost of the failed past and where people had remade their lives and bodies after the years of despair.

The price tag for the Germans was high but not, seemingly, onerous. The plebiscite held on March 29, between the winter and summer Olympic Games, approved Hitler's courses and his Reichstag with 98.8 percent of the vote, 450,000 voting "no" or marking their ballots incorrectly. Hitler campaigned eloquently on the slate of his unique achievements. "I serve no employer, no class," he told an audience of Krupp workers two days before the plebiscite, beamed to all parts of the Reich at Essen,

I belong exclusively to the German people. What I have undertaken I have done in the conviction: this must be done for our people. . . . I have no inherited estate, no manor, when I stand up for my German farmers it is for the sake of my people because I know they are the fundament of German strength. I do not stand for the arming of the German people because I am a stockholder. I think I am the only statesman in the world who has no bank account. I have no stocks, no part in any kind of enterprise, I get no dividends, but what I want is that my German people be strong and so survive in this world—that is my will.[1]

Hitler and the party turned out the "yes" vote in a landslide. But while such tests of public opinion in a totalitarian country are subject to many questions concerning the methods used to obtain them, there could be no doubt of the overwhelming approval of the German people of the reoccupation of the Rhineland, accompanied as it was by Hitler's repeated assurances of his peaceful purposes. The ballot was headed: "Reichstag for Freedom and Peace"; then in large type was written: "Adolf Hitler"; under it in small letters were the names Hess, Frick, Göring, and Goebbels. Opposite Hitler's name was a space to check—that was all. If a voter checked the only box on the ballot he had voted for the approved list of 741 Reichstag deputies and for the Führer who led them and determined their decisions.

Hitler's plan for securing European peace was contained in a note delivered to the British government by Ambassador von Ribbentrop—not inappropriately from the recipients' point of view, on April 1.[2] It contained nineteen points, including assurances that the Reich would not increase its troops in the Rhineland if France and Belgium did not increase theirs and even an offer to decrease them if France and Belgium did the same. The formulas were broad and sounded much like League of Nations resolutions. The treaties the Reich was proposing would be holy, the note said; they would be made between equal partners, and to ensure the stability of the western borders Hitler offered nonaggression pacts to France and Belgium that would last for twenty-five years and that would be guaranteed by Britain and Italy. In addition he declared the Reich was ready to invite states on its southeast and northeast borders—that is, Poland, Czechoslovakia, and Austria—to conclude similar nonaggression pacts. He repeated his readiness to conclude air pacts on behalf of European security and proposed the establishment of an international court of arbitration whose decisions would be binding on all parties. After the treaties were concluded, Hitler said, the Reich would be ready to return to the League of Nations at which time the question of colonies could be discussed. Germany, he said again, did not seek universal solutions, which would be doomed from the start, but did seek conferences with clearly defined aims. The Reich was ready to ban any kind of inhumane warfare. It was willing to conclude air pacts forbidding the use of gas, firebombs, or poisons; forbidding the bombing of open cities and cities out of range of on-the-ground or naval hostilities; and forbidding the shelling of cities by long-range guns. Submarines would be forbidden to sink merchant ships without warning, and Germany was also ready, the note said, to do away with heavy tanks and heavy artillery if others would also renounce them.

But the plan got nowhere. France, under whatever government, continued to rely on the system of collective security plus alliances, the nonaggression pact with the Soviet Union, and above all Britain with its now-recognized need to balance the rapidly growing power of Germany. Hitler's nineteen points were rejected out of hand by the Quai d'Orsay, despite the mounting evidence that not only Italy but also France's thitherto closest partner, Belgium, was about to redefine its foreign policy. The musical chairs being played in domestic politics by successive French cabinets—Pierre Laval was replaced by Albert Sarraut, who headed the hundredth cabinet of the republic—had no effect on foreign policy, which continued to follow the text handed down with the Versailles treaty. Even when on October 14 the Belgian king told his cabinet that Belgium would thenceforth be independent in its foreign policy, thus declaring his country out of the Franco-Soviet pact and the post–Versailles treaty system, the French government, headed this time by the socialist Léon Blum, had no hesitation in pursuing the same goals that had been sought in 1919. Now the policy became openly a united front against the Reich despite any offers of twenty-five-year anti-aggression pacts. No French government would consider forsaking the widest nonaggression pact of all: collective security for the limited separate treaties Hitler was proposing—in effect, separate Locarno Treaties, but this time without a demilitarized Rhineland and with a vastly more powerful Germany under the leadership of a man for whom all French parties had a deep and abiding mistrust.

Hitler had not expected his plan to be accepted. It was meant to cover the Rhineland operation and to assure the German people that he was leading them to a position of well-merited strength and equality. But despite his incessant assurances of his devotion to peace, every move he made was a step toward war. When civil war erupted in Spain in mid-July—as Generals Francisco Franco in the southwest, Queipo de Llano in Seville, and Mola in the north rose with their troops against the newly elected left-wing government in Madrid—Hitler agreed, within hours of receiving Franco's plea for help, to join the battle. He ordered ten transport planes put at Franco's disposal to fly contingents of Spanish troops, which the Germans estimated to number forty thousand, from Spanish Morocco to the motherland. Hitler from the start of the conflict was convinced a left-wing Spain would be intolerable for the Reich; it would mean an alliance of the Soviet Union, France, and Spain that would encircle Germany, while a Spain under Franco and his rightists would be at the very least friendly if not an outright ally.

Hitler was in Bayreuth attending the Wagnerian festival when on July 25, a week after the rising, a call for help in a letter from Franco was brought by two members of the National Socialist Foreign Organization. Hitler never bothered to call in Ribbentrop until a day after the decision to send the planes, though Ribbentrop was also in Bayreuth, nor did he summon his foreign minister, Neurath. Only Göring, accompanied by Blomberg (later joined by a navy captain), appeared at an ad hoc meeting to learn of Hitler's decision. Both Göring and Ribbentrop at first opposed the intervention, on the grounds that it would lead to serious international complications, but Hitler waved their objections aside. The matter was obviously settled in his mind, and Göring and Ribbentrop quickly withdrew their objections when they saw that Hitler was determined to intervene. Economic considerations played little or no part in Hitler's decision.[3] For him as for Mussolini, the order to send military help was a military and ideological decision—no marxist state would be tolerated in their neighborhood if they could prevent it. The transport planes were only the beginning; hundreds of planes and thousands of men would be sent to Spain from Germany and Italy, matched by thousands of planes and volunteers from the Soviet Union and leftist or antifascist sympathizers in the West.[4]

In every utterance Hitler spoke of peace and in every action of armed force. With Italy as an ally the time was coming for carrying out the *Anschluss* with Austria (whose precarious independence had been sustained mainly by Rome). Now if any coup by the National Socialists in Austria was attempted it was unlikely that Italian troops would be sent to the Brenner Pass to threaten intervention. Papen reported from Vienna in June 1936 that Mussolini had reminded Schuschnigg that Austria was a German state and that its foreign policy must parallel that of the Reich—there could not be a Hapsburg restoration.

With the increasing pressures for a rapprochement with Hitler's Germany, Schuschnigg had little choice but to conclude with the Reich what the official document euphemistically and ungrammatically referred to as a Gentleman or Gentlemen Agreement.[5] It was one-sided: providing for an amnesty for political prisoners, almost all of whom were Austrian Nazis; abolishing the travel restrictions between the two countries; permitting the nationals of each state to organize in the other's country (that is, legalizing the Austrian Nazi Party, as long as they remained within the law); each nation promising to improve the tone of the press coverage of the other country; permitting five newspapers from each country to be imported into the other; and promising to further cultural exchanges through film, radio, and the theater. The agreement also provided that Austria would concert its foreign policy with that of the Reich in the search for peace without violating its commitments under the

Rome Protocols, which called for a common foreign policy of Austria, Italy, and Hungary.

It was obviously a fragile relationship that was being shored up when, in October, Göring journeyed to Budapest to attend the funeral services of Hungarian Prime Minister Gyula Gömbös and took the opportunity to impress Schuschnigg, who was also attending the ceremonies, with his own and the Reich's overwhelming importance. To demonstrate his abounding goodwill he offered to train the Austrian air force and explained that if the Reich had wanted an *Anschluss* with Austria it could have had one long before—it was, after all, Göring said, a matter of interest only to the nearest German division commander. But, he added, Germany did not want an *Anschluss;* the use of the word that meant *union* should be dropped and in its place *Zusammenschluss*— that is, *integration* or *alliance*—should be substituted.

Hitler, too, had nothing but contempt for Schuschnigg and for his native land. When the Austrian state secretary for foreign affairs, Guido Schmidt, visited Berlin in November, Hitler told him in an hour-long meeting that the German peacetime army was in being and the war army would come next. He spoke of the bolshevik danger that threatened Europe and the need for the European states, including Austria, to join in economic cooperation. He had sought in vain, alas, a better understanding with Czechoslovakia, though the oppression of the Sudetenlanders continued; he had tried to effect a general European disarmament, but his proposals unfortunately had been rejected. He did not want war, he assured Schmidt, but he would not permit Germany again to be in the position in which it had found itself in 1914. It was the routine Hitler speech designed for visiting statesmen, and it led to another agreement affirming the opposition to communism of both Germany and Austria and their readiness to work together in the Danubian area and to continue to carry out the measures agreed on in the Gentlemen's Agreement.

On the surface détente had been reached, but it could only be temporary. The harried Schuschnigg, who had his own domestic problems in holding together some kind of consensus among his non-Nazi parties, told an Austrian audience in November that Austria had three enemies: Communism, Nazism, and defeatism. When Neurath pointed out to him that these were provocative words, Schuschnigg explained that his remarks had been made before a small audience and had been blown out of all proportion by the German press. Still, as Neurath and everyone else knew, they represented Schuschnigg's real sentiments much better than did the phrases of the Gentlemen's Agreement.

The agreement produced some results. By early 1937 more than fifteen thousand Nazis, the German ambassador reported from Vienna, had been amnestied, including twelve who had been sentenced to life imprisonment and more than eighty who had been given sentences of ten to twenty years. Not only were thousands of Austrian Nazis amnestied but also the party was certain now of its ultimate triumph. Schuschnigg had forced himself to appoint a pan-German and supporter of National Socialism, Glaise von Horstenau, as minister without portfolio. Moreover, the Austrian chancellor could say or do little that was not immediately reported to Berlin; Papen was provided with confidential papers, copies of internal memoranda of the Austrian Foreign Office that revealed little so much as Schuschnigg's weakness. One of them addressed to the Austrian Embassy in London for transmittal to the British government expressed his wistful hope for a better international climate for Austrian independence, his continued reliance on the League of Nations and collective security, and his helpless wish for military guarantees of Austrian independence by Britain and France, which he said he realized could not be given.

Hitler's Four-Year Plan, announced on November 9, was designed to make the Reich as blockade-proof as possible, to free it from dependence on imported raw materials. Göring, who had already been given the oversight of foreign-exchange dealings and the importation of raw materials, was to head the Four-Year Plan. Hitler was to always be ready to entrust him with tasks of heroic proportions, which Göring with his colossal vanity and capacity for self-indulgence would never be able to master even with the help of men far better qualified. This was to be as true for the build-up of the air force as for the fulfillment of the Four-Year Plan, but Hitler placed far more reliance on loyalty to Göring and their long association during the years of struggle than he did on competence. Hitler stubbornly continued to make use of what he took to be Göring's exceptional abilities even when Göring's limitations became evident to everyone else who had to work with him.

Göring always spoke Hitler's language, and when in a long speech he described the monumental task before him it was in terms that Hitler could readily approve since Hitler had already said the same thing. Germany, Göring repeated, had 136 inhabitants to the square kilometer, Britain 137, but the latter with its colonies controlled one-third of the world and the Reich nothing.[6] Although neither he nor his staff could make the Reich self-sufficient, they could make use of German technology to manufacture such products as synthetic gasoline and rubber, made from domestic materials that would go a long way to increase the war-making capacity of the Reich.

Göring promised he would find substitutes for a wide variety of raw materials —hemp, flax, resins, cotton, silk. And he would manage recovery; wages and prices would not be permitted to rise. To keep them stable he appointed a price commissar, Gauleiter Joseph Wagner. The Gestapo, too, was in the offing. Prison terms and unlimited fines faced those who transgressed Göring's regulations. He issued a series of decrees on the use of manpower and the conduct of trade to fulfill the Four-Year Plan. Firms dealing in iron and metal had to allot places for apprentices, and since it would take all the Reich's manpower to carry out the plan, heads of families over forty years old were to be hired. Construction both private and public had to be approved before it could start. Economic sabotage, defined very broadly, was punishable by death. Any German citizen who willfully and for selfish reasons or other low motives illegally sent German assets to foreign countries or permitted them to remain there, causing heavy damage to the German economy, could be punished by death and his goods confiscated.[7]

It was a program for the realization of National Socialism of the kind Hitler had always promised, and for those who did not like it the alternatives were silence or emigration or a concentration camp. Hitler had decided the German army must be ready for a major war within four years and told German industrialists if they could not do their job within the Four-Year Plan the state would do it for them.[8] In his view, as he told the Austrian foreign minister, the German army up to 1936 had had defensive assignments. In 1937 it would begin to be an offensive weapon. It would be a force capable of not only obliterating the vestiges of the defeat but also carving out a *Lebensraum* without which, as he told his generals, the German *Volk* could not hold its place in the world. The economic means he could give the military in 1933 were 4 percent of the total budget; in 1934, 18 percent; in 1935, 25 percent; in 1936, 39 percent; and in 1938, 50 percent.[9]

Gestapo reports on the state of German morale disclosed a growing fear among the population to say or do anything that might be interpreted as anti-Nazi. One report from Hannover said that people complained about the irresponsibility and high living of lower-echelon party and governmental officials who considered themselves above the law, though they were impressed by the successes of foreign policy: the rearmament, the march into the Rhineland. No serious objections were reported to the harsh Nuremberg laws designed to exclude Jews from German public life, to make intermarriage or sex relations a crime, to compress Jews into a social and economic ghetto where they could live and do business only with one another. The small pockets of resistance to the party and state among former SPD members and Communists were increasingly isolated from supporters in and outside the Reich, and conservatives, such as the former mayor of Leipzig, Carl Goerdeler, who were able to travel abroad could arouse no significant response in London or Washington—where Goerdeler described to influential circles the repressions in the Reich and the danger Hitler represented to European peace. The émigrés, too, gained at best modest support from governments such as that of President Beneš in Czechoslovakia, who permitted for a time a follower of Otto Strasser, Rolf Formis, to broadcast anti-Hitler propaganda from a clandestine radio station near the German border. It was closed down, and Strasser, sentenced to a short term of imprisonment after a Gestapo posse crossed the frontier, killed Formis and then escaped back to the Reich.[10] Few people in the non- or anti-Nazi world were ready to risk inciting Hitler's wrath if his countermeasures could reach them. As in the case of Beneš they might be as revolted by him as were the émigrés, but like the émigrés, including Thomas Mann, they could make protests, however eloquent, only from secure positions.

In the Reich, Hitler was doing so well that his powers under the Enabling Act were unanimously renewed by the Reichstag for another four years. The deputies rose as one man from their chairs to agree with a motion by Frick that Hitler had accomplished what he promised when he was awarded full powers in 1933, and they approved this time without a murmur. Thereupon Hitler, in another gesture they could only approve with similar enthusiasm, formally rescinded the admission Germany had been forced to sign in 1919 of its sole guilt for starting World War I.

Every move Hitler made contrasted with the policies of the men who had led the Reich in the time of fulfillment. When a German pocket battleship, the *Deutschland,* at anchor in the harbor of Ibiza, was bombed by two Red Spanish planes and thirty-one members of its crew killed, the retribution was swift. Two days after the attack Almería was shelled in reprisal by German warships, and the German press reported its harbor installations destroyed.

When the Reichstag voted to extend the Enabling Act, Hitler assured the members of his continued determination to pursue the policies of his revolution based on race—the unique revolution that he compared in its revelation to the discovery that the earth revolved about the sun.[11] Both he and Mussolini placed their revolutions in a cosmic order, though both were convinced, as they told inner circles of their followers, that only war would harden the iron in the souls of their people. They lost no opportunity to explain to mass gatherings that everything they were doing was done on behalf of peace. When in September Hitler introduced Mussolini, who was visiting Germany, to an audience of 1 million people assembled on the Reich sport field in Berlin, they both spoke eloquently of their peaceful intentions, and they paid one another fulsome compliments. Hitler called Mussolini a creative genius and declared that Germany, once again a world power, together with Italy was the strongest guarantee for the maintenance of Europe. Mussolini, speaking in heavily accented German, addressed his German audience as "Comrades" and, echoing Hitler's sentiments, paid tribute to what the Führer had accomplished for the Reich, evidence of which he could now experience firsthand.[12] He himself, he said, had come to Germany and to the Führer on a mission different from most diplomatic visits. He, too, was chief of a national revolution, and his coming to Germany did not mean that tomorrow he would travel somewhere else. The aims of both revolutions were the same—the unity and greatness of their peoples. The Rome-Berlin Axis was not directed against other states.

We National Socialists and Fascists want peace and are always ready to work for it; for a really fruitful peace where the real questions dealing with the mutual relationships of nations are solved instead of being glossed over. The whole world tensely asks what the result of this meeting in Berlin will be—war or peace—and we can both of us, the Führer and I, with a loud voice answer "Peace." . . . The life of a people like that of an individual is not set, given once and for all, but underlies a continuous process of change. Fascism and National Socialism have not only the same enemies who served the same masters—the third international—. . . both believe in the will as the decisive force in the life of a people. We both cherish work as the sign of man's nobility. . . .

The reborn Roman imperium was the product of this spirit as was Germany's rebirth. Fascism, Mussolini said, had its ethic, to which he intended to remain true, and this ethic was also his own: "To speak openly and clearly and when one has a friend to march with him to the end."[13] Elsewhere under the cover of "the inalienable rights of man," politics were dominated by the power of money, capital, and secret societies and by political groups battling with one another. "In Germany and Italy it is completely out of the question for private forces to influence the politics of the state. This community of thinking in Germany and Italy finds its expression in the battle against Bolshevism, the modern form of a sinister Byzantine rule of force." Fascism had fought bolshevism with words and weapons, for when the word had been insufficient and when threatening circumstance demanded, "one has to resort to arms." This is what was done in Spain

> where thousands of Italian fascist volunteers have died for the rescue of European culture. . . . It was twenty years ago when your great Leader hurled his battle cry for the rising of the entire German people: "Germany Awake," Germany is awake, the Third Reich is here. . . . I don't know whether and when Europe will awake . . . secret and yet well-known forces are at work to change a civil war into a world conflagration. What is important is that our two great peoples, the powerful and continually growing mass of 150 million people stand together in a single, unshakable resoluteness.[14]

Like Hitler, Mussolini denied he was a dictator. He was the Leader, the expression of his peoples' yearnings for rescue from fatuous parliamentary debates, the threat of communism, and the corruption of democratic governments.[15] He did not share Hitler's indelible anti-Semitism, but he could adapt himself to it in his references to the power of secret societies and the forces at work to foment another world war. As for marching together to the end, he was about to dump his Austrian friend Schuschnigg, and he would continue to keep his options open for a return to the anti-German alliance if that seemed to promise suitable rewards.

The speeches were a great success. A few weeks later, on November 5, Hitler disclosed in a meeting with the chief military leaders of the Reich—Göring, Blomberg, Fritsch, Raeder, and Foreign Minister von Neurath—what he had in mind for the future. Blomberg, minister of Defense and now a field marshal, had asked Hitler through the Führer's Wehrmacht adjutant, Colonel Hossbach, to call the meeting in order to discuss the armament and raw materials problems confronting the armed forces. Hitler made use of the occasion to make clear to his high command on what assumptions he was making his economic and military plans.

This crucial meeting took place in the *Wintergarden* of the Reichschancellery; it lasted for more than four hours as Hitler, with his usual mixture of wide-ranging worldviews and concrete formulations, explained how he proposed to achieve his goals. The five participants arrived with their adjutants, all of whom were left in an adjoining room with no idea of what was going on. Hossbach was the only adjutant present. He made notes of what Hitler said and five days later expanded them into what was later frequently described as the *Hossbach protocol*, a précis of Hitler's remarks that Hossbach thought of the utmost significance, copies of which he gave to the other military adjutants.[16]

Because it was a long and sometimes rambling discourse, not everyone present grasped its great importance. Admiral Raeder, who had been told by Göring before the meeting that it was designed to advance the rearmament program, thought there was not much new in what Hitler said. Since a good deal of what Hitler told them had already appeared in *Mein Kampf,* this was in that sense true. But Raeder was not thinking of *Mein Kampf,* which he had very likely never read. Hossbach, however, recorded that Blomberg, Fritsch, and Neurath expressed some disagreement with Hitler's analysis of what the Reich must do. A few days later he showed the document to the army chief of staff, General Beck, who was appalled by it.

Hitler started with a down-the-line National Socialist formulation of the German situation. The goal of German politics, he said, was the security, maintenance, and increase of its people. Thus the chief problem was that of space. More than 85 million people, the racial seed of *Germanentum,* was confined to a limited living space unlike that of any other people in Europe, and their numbers could not be maintained within their present territory. The number of Germans in Austria and Czechoslovakia was diminishing, and the present population in Germany could not be sustained. The impossibility of realizing the elementary living claims of the *Volk* was causing tensions. Instead of growth there was sterilization. Thus the German future would be determined solely by a solution of the need for space. For raw materials only partial, not complete, autarky was possible, and in foodstuffs self-sufficiency was out of the question. With a population increasing by 560,000 a year (Hitler had just implied that without more land Germans were sterilized) foodstuffs had to be imported with foreign exchange, and if crops failed a catastrophe would follow. Germany's foreign trade was at the mercy of Britain's control of the seas. The only solution lay in winning more living space, which meant a struggle that had always been at the root of the creation of states and the movements of peoples. That this struggle had evoked no interest in Geneva or in the satisfied nations was explicable.

If the security of the German food supply was a first priority, then the essential space could only be sought in Europe and not, as in the liberal capitalist view, by the exploitation of colonies. It was a question not of gaining more people but of gaining more land—economically usable land. Raw materials, too, would be more expeditiously maintained near the Reich in Europe, not overseas. History had always proved that any extension of a nation's territory could come about only by breaking resistance and taking risks. The British and the Roman Empires were examples. Setbacks were unavoidable. Never had there been land without masters; the attacker always met up with the possessor of the land. For Germany the question was where the greatest profit could be obtained with the least expenditure.

German politics in Europe and overseas had to reckon with the two "hate opponents," Britain and France, for whom a German colossus in the middle of Europe was "a thorn in the eye." Both countries rejected strengthening Germany, and in their view they could count on the support of all their political parties. Following Britain's loss of prestige after Italy gained Ethiopia, the return of West Africa to Germany was unlikely. Britain might approve the award of a colony not in its possession—Angola, for example—to Germany, to assuage German colonial desires, but a really serious discussion of the return of the German colonies could only come about if Britain found itself in an emergency and if Germany was heavily armed. Hitler said he did not share the idea that the British Empire was unshakable. Its lasting qualities were not comparable to Rome's, which had had no powerful opponent after the Punic wars, while Britain faced states superior to it. What existed was an alliance of nations without which the British could not defend colonial possessions and resist nationalist tendencies in Ireland and India. Their weakened position vis-à-vis Japan and the challenge in the Mediterranean, led by a genius, was weakening them. In sum it was clear that 45 million Englishmen could not hold the empire together.

France's position was more favorable. But France had internal troubles. In the lives of peoples parliamentary regimes had been in power only about 10 percent of the time, authoritarian ones about 90 percent. Still, German calculations had to take into consideration as factors of power Britain, France, Russia, and the bordering small nations. The solution of the German problem could only come about through force, and force is never used without risk. The only question was when and how.

In solving Germany's problem there were three possibilities:

Case 1. The time would be 1943 to 1945. After this period the only changes would be to our disadvantage. Rebuilding the army, navy, and air force, as well as the training of the officer corps, was almost complete. The armament is modern, and to wait means it will become obsolescent. The secrecy of the new "special weapons" cannot be maintained forever. German strength will diminish vis-à-vis the rearming of the outside world. Reserves can only be recruited from those currently coming of age; a supplement of older, untrained age groups is no longer available. If we do not move until the period of 1943 to 1945, the lack of reserves can result at any time in a critical food shortage that could not be covered by foreign exchange. In addition the world expects a German attack, and its countermeasures are increasing. Because the rest of the world shuts itself off we are forced on the offensive. What the situation in 1943 to 1945 will actually be, no one can know today. Only one thing is certain: We can wait no longer than that. On the one side will be the great Wehrmacht, and on the other will be the necessity of maintaining it, the aging of the National Socialist movement and its Leader, the prospect of the decline of the standard of living and of the birthrate—leaving no choice but to move. If he still was alive, Hitler said, it would be his unshakable decision to solve the question of living space at the latest by 1945.

Case 2. If social tensions in France lead to a political crisis that absorbs the French army and prevents it from intervening against Germany, that will be the time to move against Czechoslovakia.

Case 3. If France, in a war against another state, is so tied up as mentioned above, it cannot move against Germany. To improve our military and political position, a warlike development must be our first goal, and Czechoslovakia and Austria must be overthrown at the same time to prevent a threat to our flank from the west. If war should occur with France, we must assume that Czechoslovakia will declare war on us on the same day. Our treaties with Poland are valid as long as Germany's strength is unshaken: German checks would result in Poland moving against East Prussia.

It was likely England and presumably France had already written off Czechoslovakia and that that problem would one day be resolved by Germany.[17] The difficulties of the British Empire and the prospect of being involved in a long European war were determining factors in England's nonparticipation in a war against Germany, and England's position would certainly not be without influence on France. France without British support and with the prospect of coming up against German western defenses would be unlikely to march. Without the help of Britain, France would not invade through Holland and Belgium, because that would mean England's hostility. Czechoslovakia's defense forces were growing from year to year, and Austria was consolidating its forces. Adding both states to the Reich, despite the considerable Czech population, would mean gaining foodstuffs for 5 or 6 million people, assuming that 2 million Czechs and 1 million Austrians would be forced to emigrate from the Reich. This would free troops for other purposes and add the possibility of forming twelve new divisions. Italy would not object to Germany getting rid of Czechoslovakia, and while Austria was another matter, what happened there would depend basically on whether Mussolini was still alive. Germany's moving swiftly and with surprise would determine Poland's attitude, but Poland with Russia at its rear would not go to war against a victorious Germany. A speedy victory would also prevent Russia from intervening—that and the attitude of Japan. The year 1938 might be a propitious time with developing tensions in the Mediterranean.

The possibilities were unending. The Spanish civil war, Hitler thought, would not end quickly. It would last perhaps three more years at the rate Franco's offensive was proceeding. Furthermore, Germany did not want a complete Franco victory, but rather a continuation of the war and of tension in the Mediterranean. With Franco in complete possession of the Spanish peninsula, Italy would be kept out of the Balearic Islands, and Germany's interest lay in strengthening Italy so that Italy could stay in the islands. Italy's presence in the islands was supportable for neither France nor England and could lead to a war of both countries against Italy, which would put Franco's Spain on the side of Italy's opponents. Italy probably would not be defeated in such a war— raw materials could be delivered through Germany, which would remain on the defensive on the western borders and attack France from Libya and North Africa. If Germany made use of such a war to solve the Czech and Austrian questions, it was likely England would decide not to move against Germany; without English backing, France would not be expected to go to war against Germany.

The timing of Germany's attack on Czechoslovakia and Austria would depend on the development of the war between Italy, England, and France. Hitler did not want a military arrangement with Italy but wished to move on his own, to begin a blitzkrieg against Czechoslovakia at a propitious moment.

In reply Blomberg and Fritsch were critical. They pointed out that England and France would not inevitably be opponents of Germany; in a war with Italy, France would not be bound to the extent Hitler foresaw, and Germany did not yet have superiority on the western front. Despite the Italian forces in the Alps, which might pin down twenty French divisions, Fritsch said France would still have sufficient troops to invade the Rhineland where German fortifications were of little value. Blomberg also declared the four planned motorized divisions were incapable of moving. And as for an offensive to the southeast, he referred to the strength of the Czech fortifications that resembled, he said, those of the Maginot line and would make serious difficulties for a German offensive. Fritsch said this was the point of a study of the Czech fortifications he had ordered during the coming winter, and he would cancel his planned leave to go abroad on November 10. Hitler rejected this last suggestion, saying the conflict was not as close as that.

Neurath said that an Italian-English-French conflict was not as likely in the immediate future as Hitler believed, and Hitler replied he had been thinking of the summer of 1938. Replying to Blomberg's and Fritsch's remarks on England and France, Hitler repeated that he was convinced England would not fight and therefore did not believe France would go to war against Germany. If a conflict did arise in the Mediterranean leading to a general mobilization in Europe, he was resolved to move immediately against Czechoslovakia. But if the other powers declared their disinterest, Germany would have to go along with them at first.

Göring then declared that in view of Hitler's words Germany should scale down the intervention in Spain. Hitler agreed, insofar as he said he believed he ought to reserve his decision until the proper time.

If Raeder found nothing new in what Hitler had to say it was because he did not doubt that Hitler in due course intended for Austria to become part of the Reich and for Czechoslovakia to disappear. In Hitler's long-held view, both states in their present boundaries were artificial creations of the shameful peace treaties following the world war, and both countries continued to be used by foreign governments as makeweights against a resurgent Reich. Neither Raeder nor anyone else at the meeting was likely to quarrel with Hitler's purpose to change the status of those countries.

But it was the rest of the speech that was disquieting to Blomberg and Fritsch and to Beck when he read it. They could not agree with Hitler's airy writing off of Britain and France, those nations' unreadiness to intervene against Germany in a crisis involving their vital interests. Raeder knew the German fleet was no match for England; as he would say later, all it could do in a war against Britain was to fight and go down with honor.

What was disturbing to the skeptics, which included everyone in the high command except Göring, was that the Reich was headed toward a war it could not win. As they saw it, Germany with or without Italy could not defeat Britain and France and the allies they could muster, which might well include Poland and the Soviet Union.

Hitler was not to be moved by the alleged expertise of the Wehrmacht high command. He had not overcome the innumerable obstacles that had lain in his path to the chancellorship by reasonable objective analyses of the chances for success. The will was what mattered—his will against the indecisiveness and the moral rot investing the leaders of the satisfied powers, men who wanted the peace of the status quo and the easy living their empires provided. On his rise from nowhere he had always been ready and eager to assume risks as unacceptable to his opponents as they were to his foreign minister and to his own generals. His strength had grown from their prudence or weakness or miscalculations.

He and Mussolini along with the Japanese were the very images of those individuals President Roosevelt denounced as aggressors against the world society when he dedicated a Chicago bridge in October 1937, denouncing the reign of terror and international lawlessness. The peace-loving nations, Roosevelt said, must make a concerted effort to oppose those violators of treaties and ignorers of humane instincts that were creating a state of international anarchy and instability. This was the quarantine speech aligning the United States with the peace-loving powers ready to take collective action against Germany, Italy, and Japan—against the men deliberately planning to take over foreign territory by force of arms, a regressive practice that years later would be declared chief among the war crimes or crimes against humanity and therefore for the first time in the history of jurisprudence, or any other kind of history, was declared punishable by death.[18]

But the situation appeared different to Hitler. No one, he said in his speech to the generals, had ever found land without an owner; no empire had ever been founded but from the conquest of territories inhabited by other peoples. In the cases of Austria (whose inhabitants had voted overwhelmingly for union with the Reich in 1919) and Czechoslovakia (with 3.5 million Germans unwillingly ruled by some 6 million Czechs in a state that included 2 million Slovaks as anti-Czech as were the Sudetenlanders, as well as 1.5 million other members of minorities—Ruthenians and Magyars who were also no friends of the Czechs), he would merely be undoing the patent injustices of the dictated treaties if he took over that pseudocountry. It is unlikely that the word *aggression* occurred to him; the word he used in his speech was *Angriff,* or *attack,* which he made clear to the generals he was determined to undertake at the earliest propitious moment.

Mussolini, too, he knew, had old scores to settle. The Italian claims to Ethiopia had been no better and no worse than the claims of the other European powers to many of their African colonies, and there was no lack of local incidents on the ill-defined borders of that part of East Africa to fuel his determination to establish a Roman imperium.

France and Britain, Hitler believed, were caught on the horns of a dilemma. Italy was a member of the anti-Hitler Stresa Front and should be kept from the Führer's embrace. But France and Britain had held to principles of international morality, or said they did, that declared the use of force to settle disputes between nations as inadmissible, though the principles could be less binding on themselves (as when France occupied the Ruhr) than on others. Both were unwilling to risk a major war without overwhelming provocation and military superiority of a kind they had not enjoyed since 1918 with the addition of American forces. The victory of 1918 had been a miracle, but it was a miracle with a very high price that in the opinion of many intellectuals was not worth its cost when it led to the creation of men such as Hitler, Mussolini, and Stalin.

England and France were not alone in their reluctance to risk a major war. The German and Italian peoples, too, were among those who wanted no part of another great war. This was another of the necessary calculations. Hitler and Mussolini always spoke to their mass audiences not of war but of peace and explained everything they were doing as part of a search for peace. Hitler never used the word *war* in such speeches unless to accuse his enemies of wanting it, nor for that matter would he ever declare war on any European power to right the injustices inflicted by war on the Reich.[19]

The third of the powers Roosevelt had in mind among the disturbers of world peace was Japan. Largely dependent on overseas trade to support a rapidly increasing population of 65 million people on a territory smaller than the state of California, where unlike California only 15 percent of the land could be cultivated, Japan was undergoing serious internal disorders that had intensified after the economic crisis of 1929. The population had doubled since 1870, and it was hemmed in by barriers to Asian immigration erected by many nations—including Australia and the United States. A racial-equality clause proposed for the League of Nations Covenant had been voted down by Western leaders aware of the strong anti-Asian sentiments in their countries. High tariffs and the worldwide depression clogged the exports of Japanese goods to Western markets, and the chief trade outlets lay in Asia and Africa.

Japan, like Weimarian Germany, was split into warring factions. Patriotic organizations, incensed at the thwarting of their simplistic nationalist aims by moderates in the parliament and government, went on lethal rampages that led to the killing of high officials, including members of the cabinet. Junior officers of the army and navy were among the nationalist activists—they were well represented among their superior officers, too—and for many of them the need for reform did not stop at Japan's borders.

Like the National Socialist Germans the Japanese were convinced their country required more living space, and Manchuria, a sparsely settled land, claimed but not governed by China, could well provide it. The militarists also believed that the political instability of China, its endemic civil wars, the rise of marxist leaders (Japan in 1928 had created a branch of the police to root out dangerous political thoughts), and the Chinese retaliatory boycotts were justification enough for making certain of Japan's influence on China by the army's occupation of key areas. In this way Japan could exert control over a chaotic and unpredictable country essential to Japan's well-being.

Many of these hypernationalists, unreconciled to the Westernization of Japanese society, turned toward National Socialism as an alternative to what they regarded as the malign influence of capitalism and big business linked to the un-Japanese parliamentary system adopted in the process of Westernization. If the West rejected Japan, they rejected the West. Japanese racism among all segments of the population could easily match that of the West, and Japanese demands for equality did not include the recognition of Chinese or Korean or Manchurian equality.

China and Russia had long been the chief concerns of Tokyo's foreign policy. China's weakness had been a standing invitation to other countries, both Eastern and Western, to demand concessions from whatever government was in power for the benefit of their own economies. China seemed incapable of defending or governing its territories; Russia had easily crushed a Chinese attempt to regain northern Manchuria in 1929 as Chinese forces tried to seize the Soviet-owned Chinese Eastern Railway. When in 1931 Japan occupied Manchuria the chief obstacle to further advance would have been not China but the Soviet Union. Stalin, however, convinced that the main threat to Russia arose from its imperialist capitalist enemies, the United States and Britain, preferred to rely on Japanese promises that they had no intention of occupying all of Manchuria, and the Soviet Union made no attempt to intervene either unilaterally or with the support of the United States and Britain, also alarmed by the Japanese advances.

In 1933 the Soviet Union was ready to open negotiations to sell the Chinese Eastern Railway to Japan, and two years later the deal was finally made. But that was the last sign of the Japanese-Russian rapprochement. The differences between the two countries soon became too broad for any pretext of Russian neutrality with regard to Japan's invasions of Chinese territory, and Moscow's animosity toward Britain and the United States was tempered by the need to confront a threatening power nearer at hand.

Although the Soviet Union had been contemptuous of the League of Nations since its beginning, seeing it as not more than a projection of the power politics of the victorious powers, Moscow soon changed its position. After Japan departed from the Geneva body in 1933 when the Lytton Commission established by the League of Nations had declared Japan should withdraw from Manchuria, Russia took its place in 1934.[20] Even the League of Nations might play a part in Russia's search for a common front against Germany and Japan. Japan's army, overwhelmingly superior to any other in the Far East, had rapidly overrun Manchuria and established the puppet state of Manchukuo in 1932; in 1933 it moved south against the Chinese province of Jehol and then past the Great Wall to establish the outposts of what it called its "co-prosperity sphere."

So by the mid-thirties Japanese militancy was unmistakable even to Stalin's stubbornly marxist reading of international relations. The Soviet Union rapidly proceeded to build up its Far Eastern positions. In March 1936 Moscow made a treaty of mutual assistance with the Mongolian Peoples Republic. Mongolia had been a Soviet satellite since 1921 and the one-sided treaty (Mongolia could hardly be of much military assistance to the Soviet Union) was a signal to Japan that Russia would resist any further advances in that area.[21] Mongolia was in theory part of China, but Stalin waved aside Chinese protests against his concluding a treaty with what he regarded as a paper Chinese province. And while over two hundred Russian-Japanese border clashes took place between 1932 and 1936 no wide-scale invasion of the Soviet Union's client state took place.

Russia's former priorities in the Far East were all reversed. In the autumn of 1936 Chiang Kai-shek was taken prisoner while on a visit to the headquarters of the former warlord of Manchuria, nominally a Kuomintang general, Chang Hsüeh-liang, who unlike Chiang wanted to establish a Chinese government that would include Communists to fight Japan. Moscow vastly confused its well-disciplined Chinese Communist Party by demanding Chiang's release. Chiang had liquidated thousands of his former Communist allies in his purge of the Kuomintang in 1927, but now the Soviet Union suddenly supported the man they had long called "the butcher of China" and "the war lord in the pay of the bankers and big business."[22]

Relations between the Soviet Union and Japan had so far deteriorated that Japan in 1936 joined the Anti-Comintern Pact with Germany and Italy, and by 1937 as Japan invaded China proper the powder train for an ideological war in the Far East like the one in Spain seemed to be laid. In July 1937 Japanese forces had invaded, and six weeks later Russia and China signed a nonaggression pact; Russia was ready to aid China—all of China including the Kuomintang—in its war against Japan. And the Soviet Union was building up its own forces, which expanded to three hundred thousand men in the years between 1936 and 1938. It was the cadre for the well-disciplined forces that would never play much of a role against Japan but would turn the tide against the German invader some years later at Stalingrad.

8

The Tarnished Generals
The Flower War

Werner von Blomberg had served Hitler well. He had been summoned back to Berlin from the disarmament conference in Geneva to be made minister of War in a time of crisis when Hitler needed a pro-Nazi general to replace Schleicher and to smooth the way to Hindenburg's swearing him in as chancellor. Blomberg more than any other Wehrmacht general had helped merge the army with National Socialism. It was he who had ordered the troops to swear a personal oath of allegiance to Adolf Hitler when Hindenburg died; it was he who had ordered party publications into the army barracks and who for the first time in German history had declared that the army was not above politics as far as the National Socialist state was concerned.

Hitler owed him a very considerable debt, of which he was fully aware, but when Blomberg made a spectacularly unacceptable marriage in January 1938 Hitler had no choice but to force him to resign. Blomberg was sixty years old; his first wife, a most respectable lady who had died in May 1932, had borne him three children—two daughters who ran his household after his wife's death and a son who had become an army officer. Wehrmacht regulations required that when an officer planned to marry he get permission—called the *Heirats Consens*—from his immediate superior, and accordingly Blomberg had asked for and received Hitler's consent when Blomberg disclosed his intention to marry a lady he described as "from simple circles." Hitler had nothing whatever against simple circles, on the contrary he preferred them over the aristocracy. Blomberg had similarly informed Göring, who already knew of Blomberg's infatuation, and Blomberg asked him and Hitler to act as witnesses. The marriage duly took place on January 2, in the "great room" of the Ministry of War in the presence of Hitler, Göring, a personal friend of Blomberg's and his former naval adjutant, *Korvetten* Captain Hans Georg von Friedeburg, along with the three current military adjutants, two additional witnesses, and the bride's mother. The Blomberg children, who deplored the marriage, did not attend the ceremony.

The newly married couple were spending their honeymoon at the Golf Hotel in the Thüringen Wood when a police officer in Berlin read a newspaper announcement that Blomberg had married Luise Gruhn. The name seemed familiar to him, and he looked it up in the police files only to discover that a woman by that name had a police record that included arrests as a model for pornographic photographs.

The president of the Berlin police, Count Helldorf, was informed and since Blomberg was not in Berlin, Helldorf unobtrusively, dressed in civilian clothes, went to General Keitel with the police file in hand. Keitel thereupon sent him on to Göring who immediately went to Hitler with the dossier. Hitler was furious and shaken when he read it, the more so since Blomberg was one of the few generals he thought highly of.

There could be no question about what had to be done. Blomberg had made an impossible marriage and must resign. Since Hitler was unmarried, the wife of the Minister of War and commander in chief of the Wehrmacht would become a leading lady of the Reich. The officer corps and especially the wives would never have accepted the new Frau von Blomberg in that role, nor would Blomberg ever have been forgiven for marrying her. Göring, on behalf of Hitler, told Blomberg he had no alternative but to resign.

How much Blomberg knew of his wife's past is unclear. He had not wanted a press release on his forthcoming marriage, though he had permitted one to be issued when his adjutants suggested the marriage could hardly remain secret. He had inaccurately written for the 1939 edition of *Gotha* that the name of his wife was Elsbeth Brunow, and in his talk with Hitler before the marriage he had alluded to her having "a certain past." But Göring said Blomberg was dismayed *(bestürzt)* when shown Luise Gruhn's police record and indicated he was ready to part from her. When, however, Göring made clear he would have to resign whether or not he broke off the marriage, Blomberg declared he would not leave her. He resigned his post and remained married despite the scandal that rocked the entire military establishment. Hitler, his anger abated, consulted Blomberg on a possible successor, told him how sorry he was to lose his services, and promised that if war came he would recall him to duty—but this he never did. The Blombergs, provided by Hitler with fifty thousand marks in foreign exchange, were sent off for a vacation well away from the Reich.

Blomberg, before he departed, had regained Hitler's regard by suggesting that Hitler himself take over the post of Minister of War and commander in chief of the Wehrmacht and providing him with a list of generals he considered most unsympathetic to National Socialism. In return he not only had the travel funds Hitler placed at his disposal but also remained outwardly still in service with full pay. Other members of the armed forces, however, were not as forgiving. General Beck thought Blomberg's name should be struck from the roll of the German army; Admiral Raeder, together with Blomberg's naval adjutant Commander Hubertus von Wangenheim and Hitler's naval adjutant Commander Karl von Putkammer, decided that Blomberg, now in Rome, should be given a last opportunity to act as a Prussian officer should where honor was involved. He would be given the full account of his wife's past and then should either leave her or shoot himself. Wangenheim accordingly proceeded to Rome to deliver the ultimatum, but Blomberg refused to separate himself either from his bride or his life. He complained bitterly in a letter to Keitel about Wangenheim's conduct, and as a result Wangenheim fell into deep trouble with Keitel and Göring for taking on such a task without their knowledge or approval. Göring had talked of having Wangenheim shot, but Raeder arranged for his transfer from the Ministry of War to the naval command.

Four days after Blomberg's marriage Hitler's Wehrmacht adjutant, Colonel Hossbach, was summoned to the Reichschancellery to hear from Hitler not only why Field Marshal von Blomberg had to resign but also why General von Fritsch, commander in chief of the army, had to quit his post too.[1] Fritsch, Hitler told Hossbach, was a homosexual; he had had the proof in his possession for years and now had decided Fritsch could no longer remain in office.

Hossbach had heard rumors of the Blomberg affair, so what Hitler revealed of the circumstances of the marriage came as no surprise, nor did Hossbach question the necessity for Blomberg's resignation. Fritsch's, however, was an entirely different case. Hossbach knew him well, was devoted to him, and was certain the charges against him were trumped up. Hossbach knew that Fritsch, unlike Blomberg, was no friend of the party; he had a good many enemies in the high Nazi circles, among them Himmler and Heydrich who considered him, with his singleminded devotion to the army of the Reich, a danger to the state. In addition Hossbach was certain that Göring himself wanted to be minister of War and had seen in Fritsch the leading rival for the post.

Hossbach's meeting with Hitler lasted from ten o'clock in the morning until late at night, interrupted only by meals and Göring's comings and goings. Göring twice left the room as Hossbach stubbornly continued to declare he did not credit the evidence, in order, as Göring said, to recheck the documents, and each time he returned to announce flatly that Fritsch was guilty, no question about it. But Hossbach remained unimpressed with Göring's bluster or the evidence the Gestapo had assembled.

Hossbach had no hesitation in speaking plainly to Hitler where the Wehrmacht was involved, and he told him bluntly in the course of their discussions that a general must replace Blomberg and that Göring could not be his successor, whereupon Hitler sharply forbade him to bring up the subject. It was a long series of conversations lasting over twelve hours in the course of which Hossbach was shown the dossier, including pictures the Gestapo had collected against Fritsch. Hossbach, who found it all contrived and unconvincing, was contentious. He asked Hitler why he had not pursued further Blomberg's remark about his wife-to-be having a "certain past" and why Hitler had done nothing about the charges against Fritsch that had been in his possession for some years. Hitler had no convincing answer to either question. He said he thought Blomberg was referring to the discrepancy in ages between himself and the bride-to-be, and as to Fritsch he had ordered the Gestapo to burn the evidence (an order that was only partially carried out when the originals were burned but the copies preserved) because at the time he considered Fritsch's services indispensable. Hossbach told Hitler he would have to discuss the matter with Fritsch in person, and this Hitler categorically forbade him to do. Hossbach was placed in a painful dilemma. On the one side was his loyalty to an old and highly esteemed friend whom he was convinced was being framed; on the other side was the direct order of the head of state. Hossbach decided in favor of his loyalty to Fritsch, and on his way home from the Reichschancellery, though it was late at night, he stopped off to see him in his rooms in the Ministry of War.

Fritsch was flabbergasted at the charges, which he declared a shameless lie. He saw in them nothing more than a plot on the part of Himmler and the SS to discredit not only him but also the army. If Hitler, he said, had wanted his resignation at any time he had only to ask for it; the charges were utterly false.

And that in the end was what they turned out to be. They stemmed from the testimony of a professional blackmailer by the name of Otto Schmidt who was serving a six-year prison term and who had been involved in more than a dozen similar cases. One of his victims had been a former cavalry officer, a homosexual by the name of Joachim von Frisch. In 1936 when the Gestapo was making a systematic search of German prisons to discover from convicted homosexuals who their contacts in the Reich at large had been, Schmidt told them of his relations with a Frisch or Fritsch, he couldn't be sure of the name. His testimony, if it implicated Werner von Fritsch, was what Göring, Himmler, Heydrich, and the higher SS wanted to hear, and so the charges had been put together in a dossier prepared by the Gestapo and given to Hitler. Hitler in 1936 had been merely irritated by the report, said he wanted to have nothing to do with such swinishness, and ordered the file burned. In 1938, however, Fritsch was the leading candidate to succeed Blomberg, and at that point Göring and Himmler reminded Hitler of the Gestapo file. Hitler, who had previously waved aside the charges, was now suddenly convinced they were true.

Fritsch had not been Hitler's choice as commander of the army. He had wanted Reichenau, the pro-Nazi general who had written the Wehrmacht's oath of allegiance to the Führer. Hitler had had to give way because Hindenburg, in the last flickering days of his presidency, insisted on appointing Fritsch despite Hitler's and Blomberg's opposition. As time went on, Fritsch's achievement in building up the complex organization of the new mass army from the small volunteer force of the Weimar Republic had been impressive even to Hitler, but Fritsch, though he was loyal to Hitler, had remained critical of some of his cherished projects. Fritsch was convinced the army was growing too rapidly and that quality was being sacrificed to tempo, and he also opposed the formation of the Leibstandarte, Hitler's personal SS regiment, and of the arming of any units of the SS in competition with the army. For his part, Hitler complained that Fritsch was preparing for a defensive war because he wanted to use air power mainly as support for the ground troops and that he had failed to make full use of the new weapons.

In addition trivial but damaging matters came to Hitler's attention. When he had explained to Fritsch about an incident in which officers eating at a restaurant had been overheard referring to Hitler as a house painter, Fritsch had written to their commanding officer advising him to tell them to speak more softly in the future. Fritsch had also returned the gold party badge Hitler sent him, and after clashes between the SS Leibstandarte and army units that had culminated in a battle royal in a camp theater, Fritsch had sent the documents on the occurrence to Blomberg demanding that the Leibstandarte be dissolved. Two weeks later Blomberg had returned the documents with a note saying Fritsch's recommendation should never have been submitted.

So Hitler had become increasingly irritated with Fritsch, and the charges that two years before he had ordered burned became uncontrovertible evidence when Fritsch was the candidate to succeed Blomberg. Whether Fritsch was guilty or not was relatively unimportant to Hitler. He had nothing per se against homosexuals; for years Röhm had been one of his closest collaborators, his sexual habits ignored until he presented a political threat. And in the midst of the Fritsch affair Hitler appointed a notorious homosexual, Walther Funk, to his cabinet as minister of Finance to replace Schacht who had become another undesirable when he opposed Hitler's overspending in his military buildup.

Whether or not Hitler believed the charges to be true, it is clear that he wanted them to be true—wanted a plausible excuse to allow him to be rid of this stiff-necked representative of the old military establishment who too often stood astride his path. And since he wanted to believe the charges, he had accepted more flimsy evidence to bear them out. Fritsch was unmarried, and when Hossbach first talked to him about the accusation of homosexuality Fritsch immediately thought it had to do with a young member of the Hitler Youth he had befriended. Bachelor officers had been urged to take under their wing fatherless members of the Hitler Youth, and Fritsch had asked two such youths to occasional meals and a kind of schoolteaching session on map reading and such where he demanded strict attention to what he was saying, tapping their knuckles with a ruler when they seemed inattentive. And when Hitler had asked him if he knew of any source from which a suspicion of homosexuality might have come, Fritsch repeated to him and Göring what he said to Hossbach— that it could only have been a question of the Hitler Youth. For Hitler and Göring the statement confirmed what they already were determined to believe, and when Schmidt, the blackmailer and jailbird, was actually brought to the Reichschancellery where Fritsch had also been summoned and under Gestapo pressure identified him as the man with whom he had sexual relations, the case for them was closed. No matter that Fritsch gave Hitler his word of honor that he had never seen the man before in his life, the word of the commander in chief of the German army was rejected for the word of the blackmailer.

Fritsch, as his trial would reveal, was unquestionably innocent of the charges against him, but the problem remains as to why he submitted to two Gestapo hearings and the humiliations that he declared in a formal statement, which was made part of the protocol of the trial hearings, had never in all German history been inflicted on the commander in chief of the army.[2]

In the interrogation he was referring to, held in Wannsee where the Gestapo was to grill him in a remote villa secluded behind a brick wall shielding it from the street, his friends were so concerned for his safety that an army tank company was dispatched on maneuvers in the neighborhood to discourage any act of violence against him. Fritsch was interrogated in a small room with a barred window, isolated and bare. Fritsch's friends, including Canaris, the chief of the Abwehr, the Wehrmacht's counterintelligence service, suspected the SD might assassinate him and call his death suicide committed in despair after he had broken under the strain of the accusations.[3]

Ernst Kanter, who accompanied Fritsch to the hearing, was armed with a pistol, and he and an adjutant, Captain von Both, remained in the car to signal the tank company if shots were fired from inside the villa. These precautions may have prevented the SD from carrying out a plan to murder Fritsch.

Fritsch's interrogation was conducted by a Gestapo criminal councilor, Joseph Meisinger, with a well-earned reputation for his crude methods of examination and his browbeating of witnesses. Meisinger's questions covered a wide range of subjects from the Hitler Youths and the stablemen who had served Fritsch to the purely political realm, the latter in an attempt apparently to induce Fritsch to make compromising statements revealing anti-Nazi sentiments.

Although Fritsch made his bitter protest on the treatment he had suffered part of the official protocol of the investigative panel, the mystery remains as to why he submitted to the Gestapo authority at all. To be sure, Hitler had approved the Gestapo hearings and its full participation in the case, but traditionally it had no jurisdiction over the Wehrmacht; if Fritsch had refused to appear before it, the high command of the Wehrmacht might well have backed his refusal. Hitler had wanted Fritsch to be tried before a Gestapo court, but he could not issue such an order without taking the risk of rousing the generals to concerted action against not only the Fritsch proceedings but also the repeated intrusions of the SS and Gestapo into Wehrmacht affairs.

It has been suggested that Fritsch, knowing himself innocent, thought he had nothing to fear from inquiries by the Gestapo or any other Nazi organization. But the fact remains that until he made his formal protest on his own and the army's behalf after the Wannsee interrogation, he gave little help to his friends. He was remarkably passive at the Gestapo hearings and in defending himself in the presence of Hitler, who later told others Fritsch should have thrown his sword at his feet. But Fritsch had long had a high regard for Hitler personally, believing him misled by evil councilors such as Göring and Himmler and utterly incapable of the duplicity Fritsch later came to acknowledge in him. Raised in the rigid tradition of the Prussian officer, with the rigid integrity that had given the tradition its substance and mystique, he could not easily accept the possibility that the head of state could act with the brutalitarian unscrupulousness of the members of the Gestapo and the SD.

In addition, however, there was Fritsch's spontaneous remark about the possibility that a member of the Hitler Youth had testified against him. Although no evidence whatever could be turned up by the assiduous Gestapo interrogations of the two boys themselves, Fritsch obviously thought them capable of bearing false witness against him. They did not, nor did the dozen stablemen and grooms who over the years had served Fritsch, who was a passionate horseman, when they were questioned by Gestapo agents. The most the Gestapo had been able to elicit was the statement of one groom that Fritsch had occasionally, in mock anger, tweaked his ear when he had done something inept. Did Fritsch himself have ambiguous feelings about his relationships with these people? If he did, the Gestapo, for all its zealous efforts, was unable to turn up any testimony that might account for it.

As for Schmidt, he had simply lied as he finally was forced to admit at Fritsch's trial. Schmidt was one of the scores of male prostitutes who made their living in Berlin after World War I turning a trick and blackmailing when he saw the opportunity. On an evening in late November 1933, in the Wannsee suburban railroad station, one of his hangouts, he had observed a homosexual of his acquaintance, Joseph Weingarten, known as Bayern Seppl, leave a men's room followed closely by a well-dressed man carrying a cane. The two of them disappeared behind a link fence separating the station and freight yard, an area of scaffolding and dark corners, where they remained for a short interval. After they reemerged Schmidt had watched the man with the cane board a waiting suburban train. This presented the kind of opportunity made to order for him, and he followed Weingarten to demand pointblank if he had had relations with the man he had just left. When Weingarten acknowledged that he had, Schmidt quickly boarded the train, and after a few stations had thinned the crowd of travelers he sat down beside the victim he had staked out. He told him he was a criminal commissar who knew what had gone on behind the fence but could be silenced by a cash payment.

His prey was a former cavalry captain by the name of Joachim von Frisch who agreed to pay five hundred marks to keep the alleged policeman quiet. A few days later Schmidt came back to where Frisch was living and demanded another two thousand marks to be shared with an alleged superior in the police department. Frisch scraped up the money but demanded a receipt for twenty-five hundred marks, which he was given. Some time later, passing by the house where Frisch lived, Schmidt casually mentioned to a companion by the name of Ganzer that a man lived there whom he had "laid on the cross."[4]

Fritsch's lawyer was Count Rudiger von der Goltz, who oddly enough had also been named by Schmidt (who was given to dropping names of prominent, alleged homosexuals of his acquaintance) as one of his homosexual connections. The man Schmidt had in mind, however, was but another example of his style of upgrading the social or military rank of his victims. This time the man was a lawyer also named Goltz but the only title he had was bestowed upon him by Schmidt. Goltz, unperturbed by the accusation made against him, performed a brilliant job not only of defending Fritsch but also of reconstructing what had actually happened. He successfully prevented the weasel verdict Hitler and Göring had been angling for if they could not get a finding of guilty—"innocent by reason of insufficient evidence." Goltz, with the aid of two other jurists, Dr. Biron, a Luftwaffe judge appointed as investigative judge for the trial, and an army legal councilor, Karl Sack, was able to find in the neighborhood where Schmidt said he had called on Fritsch the retired army captain Frisch, who was now ill and bedridden.[5] Frisch readily admitted, when Biron and Sack visited him, that he had had homosexual relations with Weingarten and had paid Schmidt twenty-five hundred marks, which the receipt and an examination of Frisch's withdrawals from a local branch of the Dresdener Bank bore out. Not only did that evidence come to light but Ganzer, also located by Goltz, confirmed that Schmidt had made the remark about the high officer he had "laid on the cross" as they walked by the house where Frisch lived.

Behind all this was something much more sinister to old-fashioned jurists such as Goltz and his aides than Schmidt and the other street con men. The Gestapo agents, Goltz learned, had also visited Frisch, on January 15, the very time the Gestapo was in the process of compiling the dossier on Fritsch; they too, the local bank confirmed, had investigated Frisch's bank account and found what Goltz had discovered weeks later—that Frisch had indeed withdrawn the sums he had testified he had given Schmidt. In other words, the Gestapo had known right along, before Fritsch was forced by Hitler to resign, that the accusation was a frame-up.

It is not known whether the Gestapo men passed along this information to Hitler and Göring, but it is inconceivable that their bosses, Himmler and Heydrich, did not know of it. And it is clear that the objective of them all was to get rid of Fritsch. It was the Gestapo's job to gather evidence, true or false, to accomplish that end. Hitler, despite his unprecedented ranks, could not do whatever he pleased. Although he was not only the head of state and party, Führer and Reichschancellor, but also the highest judge in the Reich and its highest military authority, in sole command of the armed forces (he had taken Blomberg's advice and made himself minister of War and commander in chief of the Wehrmacht), it would have been imprudent and dangerous for him simply to order a Gestapo court to try Fritsch. Such a court to try the commander in chief of the army could produce a united front in the Wehrmacht to protest against such an unheard-of procedure and thus against Hitler's authority. What Hitler could and did do was to place the Gestapo on an equal footing with the Wehrmacht in the case by giving it the right to have an observer present at all army hearings in the same way the army was permitted to have an observer at Gestapo hearings.

Hitler knew how to handle the generals. At a meeting he called of the chiefs of the Wehrmacht and the field commanders on February 4, he easily led them to accept with only one question, and no dissenting voices, his recital of what had gone on. Few of them had heard of the Fritsch affair, and no one present could possibly deny that Blomberg had had to resign. Hitler's prescription was the same one he had used as a young man explaining to the Austrian authorities why he had not answered the call to be drafted into the army. Again he was a victim. Blomberg had made an impossible marriage at which Hitler himself had been cajoled into acting as a witness, something he would never do again. He had long had to contend with Blomberg's weakness of character—Blomberg had lost his nerve at the time of the Rhineland occupation as he had in every other critical situation, and no one present could deny, after his marriage to Luise Gruhn, that the army was well rid of him. As for Fritsch there was hardly any doubt that he too was guilty of insupportable conduct, and Hitler had been forced to accept his resignation. Fritsch, Hitler said, was the only man who could have been considered as a successor to Blomberg, but he could not be appointed to that office with a serious accusation hanging over him. He had not behaved well; on being confronted with the evidence against him he had mentioned two Hitler Youths who might also implicate him, and Hitler had had no choice but to put the matter before the minister of Justice, Franz Gürtner, who had decided the case must be investigated further. A court-martial would therefore be held in some weeks, and under these circumstances Fritsch could not remain in command of the army, a post that Hitler pledged would never go to a nonprofessional. Thus he allayed the fears of those of the generals who suspected the job might go to Himmler who was anathema to the army. Not only was Himmler no soldier but also many of them were convinced that, as Fritsch wrote on February 1, the SS was spying on them all.[6]

General Göring, Hitler announced, would be raised to the rank of field marshal; he had been rumored to be a leading candidate for the post of minister of War and many of the generals had objected to him almost as violently as to Himmler. The rank of field marshal would make him, now that Blomberg had departed, the ranking officer in the Reich—a post that would provide the opportunity for an array of new uniforms as well as a marshal's baton—and would be almost as satisfying to Göring's wounded vanity as becoming chief of the Wehrmacht. Hitler knew Göring well enough to be sure that would be the result, and he also knew Göring was not up to the job of commander in chief of the Wehrmacht, which he had just taken over himself.

The meeting with the generals lasted an hour and a half. Only one general asked a question—whether, at some future date, an army officer might be named chief of the Wehrmacht—and Hitler replied that indeed might occur at the right time. As the generals filed out one of them whispered to his neighbor, Günther von Kluge: "When you hear all that you could almost believe it."[7] Whether or not they believed it, they seemingly accepted it hook, line, and sinker.

Other changes in the military and civil service were announced on February 4. Neurath was replaced as foreign minister by the former wine salesman Ribbentrop but would become president of the Secret Cabinet Council—a body that as it turned out was never to meet. Three ambassadors in key posts would also be replaced: Ulrich von Hassell in Rome, Herbert von Dirksen in Tokyo, Papen in Vienna. They all, in Hitler's view, were lacking in the enthusiasm that was essential for the bold policies he was pursuing. The Wehrmachtamt in the Ministry of War, the OKW, would now become Hitler's military staff, and headed by General Keitel it would, under Hitler's direction, take over the tasks of the Ministry of War. And finally Schacht, who had objected to the high costs of rearmament, was replaced as minister of Economics by Funk, who approved everything Hitler did.

The generals, even the most critical and perspicacious among them, had no way of knowing what was really happening: that, for example, Gürtner had had only a fleeting glimpse of the Fritsch dossier or that the Gestapo had discovered that Fritsch was not the man the blackmailer had dealt with. As Hitler presented the case, a trial before a military court was certainly required, and if Fritsch had to go, Walther von Brauchitsch was eminently acceptable as a replacement. He was no Reichenau or Göring but was a capable officer with no close party affiliations as far as anyone knew.

On the same day Hitler addressed the generals he wrote letters to both Blomberg and Fritsch that were published in the press, containing all the public was to learn about their retirement. Both men, it appeared, were suffering from overwork and both were going on leave to enable them to regain their health. The note to Blomberg was markedly more friendly than the one to Fritsch. Blomberg had performed unique services for the Reich, Hitler told him; he had labored so ardently that his health had suffered, and Hitler expressed the hope that the holiday on which he was embarking would restore it. Both men, Hitler wrote, had repeatedly asked to be relieved of their heavy burdens. Hitler told Blomberg that now, after five years of rearmament, he could at last allow him to leave his post. Blomberg, he wrote, had resolutely kept his oath of allegiance to the National Socialist government, the military reorganization was completed, and he would go down in German history for his unique achievement for which Hitler thanked him in his own name and in that of the German people. As for Fritsch, Hitler noted that despite Fritsch's leave a short time before (he had gone to Egypt for almost three months, under the watchful eye of the Gestapo) his health had not improved, so Hitler had decided to yield to his wishes and accept his resignation. Hitler thanked him for his "outstanding accomplishments" in rebuilding the army and told Fritsch his name would always be associated with the renewal and restoration of the army "between March '35 and February '38." The letter to Fritsch, who was guilty of nothing whatever, was much cooler than the letter to Blomberg, who in Hitler's and the army's opinion, had brought opprobrium upon them all. Nevertheless Blomberg would travel abroad with his bride for a year at Hitler's expense, while Hitler would see to it that Fritsch's calvary was by no means over.[8]

General Jodl wrote in his diary of January 31: "Führer wants to take the spotlight off the Wehrmacht," and some observers have believed that his next moves to incorporate Austria and then the Sudetenland into the Reich were linked to that end.[9] But what is far more likely is that Hitler, as he always had done in the past and would do in the future, made a most skillful use of events to get on with his grand design that required, as a start, getting rid of Fritsch and a good many others he considered foot draggers or worse, and thereupon taking over the country of his birth, and then mounting the obliterating attack on Beneš and the republic he detested almost as wholeheartedly as he did Austria. Hitler was a man of impulses with a few leading immutable convictions as to what he must accomplish. Hitler the operator was always much more in evidence than Hitler the calculating strategist. Time after time in his rise to power he had made use of circumstances that seemed to indicate he had planned it all the way it actually happened.

The opposition to his courses both inside and outside the Reich was potentially powerful enough to pose a mortal threat to his rule, but it was always divided and never as singleminded and ruthless as Hitler himself. The generals, even Fritsch, who was his most conspicuous victim, were of divided opinions; Fritsch for a long time could not believe that Hitler was determined to get rid of him at any cost, nor would he consider calling on the army to strike a blow on its own behalf for what he considered was primarily a wrong done him as an individual. Only after the Wannsee hearing, when he insisted on making part of the official record his protest against the vicious proceedings, did he for the first time link the attack on him to an attack on the army. General Beck, who within months would became one of the chief opponents of Hitler's policies, felt much the same way. It was contrary to the ethos of the Prussian officer, they both deeply believed, to confound attacks, however unjust, directed at an individual as such, with a threat to the state or the army. It would take Beck, too, a long time to acknowledge Hitler's capacity for perfidy and his danger to the Reich. And even when he did, he still had inhibitions. As he remarked to his eventual successor, General Franz Halder: "Mutiny and revolution are words that do not exist in the lexicon of the German soldier."[10]

Highminded as they were, neither Fritsch nor Beck had a quarrel with the direction of Hitler's main objectives. Fritsch had wanted Seeckt to set up a dictatorship to replace the weak and, as he saw it, treasonous Ebert government, and Beck appeared as a witness for the three young officers who in 1930 were accused of high treason for joining and proselytizing for the National Socialist Party. Both of these intellectual and moral positions were also contrary to the traditional ethos of the officer corps, as Seeckt and Hindenburg repeatedly made clear.

But it was a difficult time for soldiers brought up to serve the legitimate government of the Reich and the German people. The resistance was scattered, and Beck, for one, joined it not because of the treatment accorded Fritsch but because he became convinced that Hitler wanted a war the Reich could not win. Jodl recorded in his diary entry of January 26 that General Max von Viebahn, who had just been posted to the OKW, had said concerning Fritsch's treatment at Wannsee: "If the troops knew [what was going on] there would be a revolution."[11] Few, however, knew in any detail what was going on. The only single issue that united the opposition was the rejection of the party's attempts to infiltrate and control the army. Fritsch was ready to acknowledge the fundamental change in German society with the advent of National Socialism;

he too believed the army should accept it as the political fundament of the state. That did not mean the party could be permitted to place its special interests over those incorporated in the army that was there to defend the fatherland and the entire German people of whatever political persuasion. But that was precisely what Hitler demanded. He saw the National Socialist Party as the expression of the will of the *Germanentum* of the *Volk* overriding any claims on the part of the army or church or any other group to represent the Germanic essence and the deepest aspirations of the German people. It was Hitler, projecting the will of the people through the party, who determined what the political and social goals were to be, and the officer corps had simply to carry out his orders.

In the space of a few weeks after his speech to the generals he relieved from their posts sixteen of them suspected of lukewarm or anti-Nazi sentiments, among them Karl von Rundstedt, Ewald von Kleist, and Ritter von Leeb. Forty-four others were transferred to commands of conspicuously less importance than the ones they had held. Hitler's petty personal rancors were unmistakable to those who were already convinced of his maleficence, but the changes he was making were simply shrugged off by many, perhaps the majority, of the others. Hossbach was summarily dismissed. A telephone call from a junior officer gave him the news, and while he had the temerity to protest to Hitler with unconcealed anger against the manner of his dismissal, his job was gone. Hitler was contrite when Hossbach confronted him; he promised that Hossbach and his family would always have access to the Reichschancellery and predicted that Hossbach himself would have a bright future, but his dismissal held firm. He was succeeded by Gerhard Engel, a man Hitler believed would be a more amenable adjutant.[12]

The rewards for basking in Hitler's favor could be substantial. General von Brauchitsch as he took over his post as commander of the army wanted to divorce his wife of long standing in favor of an attractive new love, a divorcée with whom he was having an affair. Her name was Charlotte Rüffer and among her qualifications to replace Brauchitsch's wife was an extravagant admiration for Hitler. Frau von Brauchitsch had refused to grant her husband a divorce unless she received a considerable capital settlement. To enable him to meet her demand Hitler made a gift to Brauchitsch of eighty thousand marks with which he could pay off his wife. Thus Brauchitsch was set free to remarry but not to join the opposition to Hitler.

On the surface when those who were trying to see that justice was done in the Fritsch affair talked with Brauchitsch, he was friendly enough. In the course of a two-hour conversation with Gisevius in a Berlin hotel, Brauchitsch referred to Hitler as "that fellow" and agreed that the behavior of Hitler and the Gestapo was intolerable.[13] But when Beck gave Brauchitsch a memorandum prepared by Canaris and Hossbach asking whether the army high command should not consider making a démarche to Hitler that would include demands for Fritsch's public rehabilitation and the punishment of those guilty of the procedures used against him, Brauchitsch did nothing. To say he was bought by the eighty thousand marks would be exaggerated, but after he had accepted them how could he be free to turn on his benefactor to whom, as a condition of his appointment, he had promised to bring the army and party closer together and to whom he owed not only his marital freedom but also his eminent post? Neither Brauchitsch nor Keitel forwarded any protests to Hitler. If they had, they would have landed in the same ash can as Fritsch.

The Fritsch case ended as Hitler wanted it to end. In a speech to the same generals he had addressed on February 4, delivered at the Barth airfield in Pomerania on June 13, he gave them no opportunity to protest but only to accept his having carried out a highminded mission on their behalf.[14] This time he spoke emotionally of two victims, himself and Fritsch, both casualties of circumstances and a blackmailer. Again he made use of the Blomberg scandal that, he said, had made him all the more anxious to establish Fritsch's innocence. A court-martial had had to be held—Fritsch himself had demanded one— and owing to a fortunate turn of events it had definitively established Fritsch's complete innocence. In a voice choking with emotion, which very likely was genuine since he was given to self-pity and often spoke as he did now of the rigors of his lonely office, Hitler related how intensely he and Fritsch had suffered during the human tragedy that still engulfed them. He could not now publicly disavow what had been done. To protect the army and Fritsch he had announced that Fritsch's resignation had been necessary because of his ill health, an explanation he would use again in the future in similar cases. The prestige of the army could not again be placed at risk after the terrible events of November 1918. The public had known nothing of the charges against Fritsch, so an official announcement of his rehabilitation could not be made. Privately, however, Hitler said he had written to Fritsch expressing his gratification at the outcome of the trial, the generals themselves now knew of Fritsch's complete innocence in the affair, and the army would be informed that General von Fritsch had been named honorary colonel of his old artillery regiment. Hitler said he had planned, when the Reichstag met, to announce this honor accorded Fritsch together with an appreciation of his accomplishment in building up the Reichswehr, an achievement that by this time had been demonstrated by its performance in marching into Austria. But political developments had made and would continue to make convening the Reichstag momentarily impossible.

Therefore, Hitler told the generals, he must content himself with telling them what had happened. He named none of the chief SS culprits in the persecution of Fritsch, nor of course Göring. He said those responsible were underlings in unimportant positions; the really guilty one was the blackmailer Schmidt, and Hitler said he had ordered that he be shot.[15] He was ostentatiously fair and generous as the case wound up. He could not, he said, expect Fritsch after all that had happened to return to his post and be able to work harmoniously with him.

The Flower War

The Fritsch case had moved to its climax during the mounting excitement of Austria's becoming part of the Reich. Despite the Gentlemen's Agreement, the Austrian Nazis had been increasing their pressure on Schuschnigg. On January 25 the Austrian security police had invaded the offices of an illegal Nazi group and discovered among the papers they impounded the so-called Tavs documents, which were named after the Austrian engineer who was chief of the subversive unit.[16] Tavs was in close touch with party leaders in Germany, and his organization had prepared a blueprint for the overthrow of Schuschnigg that was not far, in its essentials, from the one that was actually used in March 1938. Austrian Nazis were to foment disturbances and riots to force Schuschnigg to call out the police and the army. Then Berlin would send an ultimatum demanding that the Austrian forces retire immediately or the Wehrmacht would march in. If Schuschnigg bowed to the ultimatum the Nazis would take over the Fatherland Front and other pro-Schuschnigg organizations; if he refused, the riots would continue, and German troops would enter Austria to enforce law and order. An attack on the German Embassy in Vienna, spearheaded by Nazis purporting to be pro-Schuschnigg, would unleash the disorders. In either case the country would be rid of Schuschnigg and the Nazis would take over. The Austrian police arrested fifteen people, but they were not in custody for long.

Schuschnigg was in a trap from which no escape was possible without outside help. On February 11, in an effort to appease the National Socialists, he made a pact, the so-called Punktationen, with his pro-Nazi state councilor, Arthur Seyss-Inquart, who had been appointed in 1937 as a gesture toward the Nazis. Seyss-Inquart was a Viennese lawyer who had long been a member of the nationalist wing of the Heimwehr with close ties to the National Socialists. The Punktationen declared Seyss-Inquart the official intermediary—in political matters and aside from the established intergovernmental agencies—between the National Socialists and the Austrian government. They referred to the "closest mutual military relationship" between Austria and the Reich and declared that important principles of National Socialist philosophy not linked to the party could be an integral part of the ideology of the Austrian state. It was a long, windy document that made it even more difficult for Schuschnigg to deal with the ever-mounting demands of the Austrian Nazis since it demonstrated how far he could be forced to make concessions. The Punktationen was immediately made known to Berlin, and when Papen presented Schuschnigg with an invitation to meet with Hitler at Berchtesgaden, promising him, according to Schuschnigg, that no new demands would be made but rather an attempt to improve relations, he could only accept.

Schuschnigg later wrote that when he agreed to go to Berchtesgaden, Papen told him the meeting would be held only to iron out misunderstandings and differences that had arisen since the July 1936 agreement was signed. Papen, though, has denied that he made any promises about limiting what was to be discussed; according to him he told Schuschnigg all outstanding questions between the two countries would be taken up. In any event there was little in the way of discussion. Schuschnigg, accompanied by the Austrian undersecretary, Guido Schmidt, was met at the German border near Salzburg by Papen and an hour and a half later at the Berghof by Hitler wearing a brown shirt with a red swastika armband and black trousers. Hitler greeted him at the entrance, accompanied by an entourage that included three generals: Keitel, Reichenau, who commanded the Bavarian military district, and Hugo Sperrle, head of the Luftwaffe assigned there. They all shook hands, and Hitler was friendly enough until after he led Schuschnigg to his study. Almost from the moment they sat down Hitler the Austrian-born German made clear his contempt for both Austria and Schuschnigg, referring to "your ridiculous defense mechanisms" and accusing him of doing everything in his power to prevent Austria from achieving its destiny as a German state. The harangue lasted two hours and was broken by the call to lunch where the three generals again appeared. They talked politely about what they had been doing—Sperrle of his experience in the Spanish civil war where he had been head of the Condor Legion. None of the generals had any clear idea of why he had been invited, and they remained part of the scenery except for one brief moment after lunch when Schuschnigg was slow to meet Hitler's demand that he sign the one-sided document he had handed him. Hitler thereupon shouted for Keitel to come into the study, telling Schuschnigg curtly he would summon him later.

It was a bleak day for Schuschnigg. After lunch served by SS men in impeccable white jackets, the guests and Hitler moved to an adjoining room where they had their demitasses. Hitler then left the room, and Schuschnigg and Schmidt met with Ribbentrop and Papen. Ribbentrop handed Schuschnigg a two-page document that he said had to be signed as it stood. It provided for the appointment of Seyss-Inquart as minister of Public Security with control over the Austrian police; for an economist, Hans Fischböck, well regarded in National Socialist circles, to be appointed to the Schuschnigg cabinet to oversee German-Austrian commercial relations; for the freeing within three days of all Nazi prisoners, including those serving sentences for the assassination of Dollfuss; for the reinstatement of all Nazi officials and officers who had been relieved of their posts; for the exchange of one hundred German and Austrian officers to be detailed immediately to the other's army; and for the freedom of all Austrians professing the National Socialist creed to be admitted to the Patriotic Front, the only legal political organization in Austria, and to "develop legal activities in accordance with Austrian law," though the party itself remained illegal. And finally the German government reaffirmed the validity of the agreement of July 11, 1936, renewing its full recognition of Austria's sovereignty and independence and declaring it would abstain from any intervention in Austrian domestic political affairs.

The document was a formidable invasion of Austria's sovereignty, but Schuschnigg could do little to modify it. Although it reaffirmed the 1936 agreement and promised that Germany would continue to recognize Austrian sovereignty, the freedom of Austrians to profess the National Socialist creed of itself could provide the intervention in Austrian affairs from which the Reich promised to abstain. Ribbentrop courteously explicated each paragraph for Schuschnigg and Schmidt and noted the objections they made, but nothing of substance was changed, and as Schuschnigg would write later, the first paragraphs spelled the end of Austrian independence.

Schuschnigg was able to extract a few minor concessions—Fischböck instead of becoming a cabinet member was to have the title of federal commissar, and the exchange of Austrian and German officers was modified to two installments of fifty each. In addition, two Austrians Schuschnigg declared particularly objectionable, Gauleiter Leopold and the engineer Tavs, would be deported to Germany. Schuschnigg had to agree, however, that the Austrian chief of staff, the anti-Nazi Field Marshal Jansa, would be replaced by General Böhme who was much more friendly to the Reich.

After what seemed to Schuschnigg a long time, he was again summoned to Hitler's study where he was handed what Hitler told him was the final draft of the protocol that had to be signed without changes. The unhappy Schuschnigg said he could only take cognizance of the document since under Austrian law the president alone was authorized to sign state papers. He himself, he assured Hitler, was ready to sign, but his signature would be of no value. He could not guarantee, for example, that prisoners would be released within three days. Hitler brushed off the refusal, saying curtly: "You have to guarantee that." When Schuschnigg replied, "I could not possibly, Herr Reichschancellor," the infuriated Hitler rushed to the door and shouted for Keitel, who apparently had no idea what was wanted of him. But he promptly appeared at the doorway of the study, which seemed to be all he was meant to do at this point. Hitler dismissed Schuschnigg, informing him that he would be called later.

Keitel had been talking in an amiable fashion with Schmidt, but when Hitler shouted his name his friendliness had dissolved, and Schmidt had the impression that he and Schuschnigg would be arrested at any moment. A half hour went by, and Hitler again summoned Schuschnigg to tell him that for the first time in his life he had changed his mind. This, he said was Schuschnigg's last chance—he would give him three more days before the agreement would go into effect. Papen and Ribbentrop then joined the two men in the study, and the amended protocol was sent out to be typed. Hitler gradually calmed down, telling Schuschnigg the Austrian problem was now solved, and the two countries could abide by the agreement for five years. All four men signed two copies, and Hitler invited Schuschnigg and Schmidt to stay for dinner. But Schuschnigg declined the invitation and was driven back across the border, exhausted and almost certain his country was lost. What he had signed was a document that, as he knew, made it only a question of time before Austria would become part of the Reich, though at the most it also gave him a little breathing space to find out, if he could, who inside or outside Austria might come to his aid to keep the country independent for a little while longer. His decision a few weeks later to try to flesh out the answer to that question was to bring the end.

By June 1938 Hitler was acclaimed by millions of Germans, many of whom had long been opposed to him and his party, as the Reich's most gifted statesman since Bismarck. He had undone much of the apparatus of the reprehensible peace treaties without firing a shot, and the emotions that had brought him to power had spread to engulf thousands of his former enemies. The trial that was to exonerate Fritsch had to be postponed for a week while the court's officers were called to duty, and Austria was deliriously welcoming the German army and her most famous son.

None of the generals objected to Austria becoming part of the Reich. It was German in language and sentiments, even Schuschnigg emphasized its *Germanentum,* and strategically it was of central importance, bordering on Italy, now a quasi-ally, and on Czechoslovakia, which was considered a built-in air base for Soviet or French planes should they be needed against the Reich. As Jodl pointed out, with Austria part of the Reich it was Czechoslovakia, not Germany, that was caught in a strategic vise. Furthermore, Austria would provide the Reich with a dozen armament plants and 400 million shillings' worth of foreign currency as well as badly needed manpower for German industries—as Hitler said, manpower sufficient to field twelve new divisions.

Austria was a prize of unquestionable value; it had been only the inordinate risk involved that Hitler's military critics objected to when the Wehrmacht was divided on whether to implement the theoretical "Special Case Otto," the plan for armed intervention to prevent a Hapsburg restoration.[17] Beck in 1937 had refused to draw up operational plans for "Special Case Otto," and his act of insubordination was known to Keitel. Beck's arguments supported by Fritsch were persuasive, and no plan for invading Austria was drawn up. What Beck had written in May 1937 was that a conflict with Austria could not be localized. German intervention, he wrote, "means a cause of war between Austria and Germany. In case of war France and Czechoslovakia must be reckoned as enemy number 1 with England, Belgium and Russia enemy number 2, and Poland and Lithuania as enemy number 3. . . . Germany is not in a position to risk provoking a Middle European war. Materially it cannot at this time or in the foreseeable future wage a war of any kind."[18]

When, however, ten months later, in March 1938, Schuschnigg ordered a plebiscite to demonstrate Austrian support for him and independence, the situation was dramatically different. Mussolini, the only protector of Austria prepared to use force on her behalf, appeared ready to accept the *Anschluss* with the Reich, and no other statesman in Europe was willing to raise more than an admonitory finger on behalf of her independence. Schuschnigg's appeals for help fell on deaf ears. General Beck could now act conscientiously as the German army's chief of staff to make plans for the military occupation with no second thoughts on possible hostile reaction of the Western powers. Beck had always believed that a primary duty of the chief of the general staff was to use his influence to prevent any government from undertaking military risks that would threaten the existence of the state, and to this end he had not hesitated to oppose risks that were acceptable to both Blomberg and Hitler. But 1938 was not 1937, and the international configurations together with Schuschnigg's call for a plebiscite had made the *Anschluss* an imminent and much less risky goal. When on March 10 Hitler ordered Beck to draw up the operational directive for the occupation, it was to be a plan not for battle but for the march of brothers-in-arms into Austria.[19] And it was unlikely that an armed conflict would erupt either with Austria or with the former protecting powers, despite their repeated assertions that Austria's independence was essential to the stability of Middle Europe. Desirable it undoubtedly remained to Britain and France, but it no longer seemed essential to either of them if it could be maintained only through their military intervention. Moreover, France was without a government during those critical days in March 1938, as Prime Minister Camille Chautemps, whose reconstituted cabinet had been in office only since January 19, resigned on March 10, to be replaced by the government of Léon Blum on the day the German army marched into Austria.

Schuschnigg had presented Hitler with the opportunity he had been waiting for.[20] His plebiscite could easily be construed as a breach of the Berchtesgaden agreement he had signed only a few weeks earlier in which he had declared his readiness to share respectability and power with pro-Nazis such as Seyss-Inquart and those who professed the National Socialist creed. Now he was demanding the country express its determination to unite behind him—for a free, German, independent, social, Christian, and united Austria—to what end if not to break through the Nazi cordon?[21] Even when, under the threat of a German invasion, he called off the plebiscite, the damage was irreversible. Hitler would no longer tolerate Schuschnigg's regime; he ordered Keitel to arrange for army maneuvers between Berchtesgaden and the Austrian border and on March 11 ordered that the strategic and operational plan for invasion be completed by March 12. The OKW, which Keitel headed, had no real general staff with which to carry out a partial mobilization, and it was Beck on whom Hitler had to call to prepare for the march.[22] Schuschnigg for his part could only order Austrian troops not to resist when the Wehrmacht crossed the border.

Beck, with the help of General Fritz von Manstein, had to improvise from scratch in the course of the afternoon and evening of March 10. He performed brilliantly, providing the orders within five hours, and on the whole the operation proceeded smoothly. The troops, supported by planes dropping not bombs but leaflets, were welcomed with rapture by the vast crowds. The photographs of the rejoicing multitudes in the towns and villages of the provinces and in Vienna were not propaganda devices of Goebbels.[23] The Austrians were drunk with the *Anschluss,* overwhelmed by it once it was underway, and in the future they would provide more than their share of enthusiastic activists in the National Socialist Party and government, including the SS, long after the shouts of jubilation had subsided.

The German army marched past dense throngs of men, women, and children with ecstatic faces and outstretched arms, and the invasion with good reason was christened "the flower war" as the festooned soldiers brought Austria "home into the Reich." Despite Hitler's praise of the army's performance, some things went awry. Provisions for the troops were delayed, gasoline failed to arrive on time, and mechanical breakdowns caused some of the tanks to be delivered to Vienna by rail. Meanwhile Himmler's Gestapo and SS rounded up the enemy: Jews, Communists, Socialists, and anti-Nazis of all descriptions. Hundreds of Jews were immediately put to work in as humiliating a fashion as the SS could improvise, such as cleaning streets with toothbrushes. But these were small matters amid the jubilation.

For a short time Hitler seemed to be in no hurry about taking the next steps that would lead to the destruction of the Czechoslovakian state. As Austria was being invaded, General Jodl recorded in his diary: "The Führer says that after the incorporation of Austria there is no hurry about settling the Czech question. Austria must first be digested. Nevertheless the preparations for Case Green [the invasion of Czechoslovakia] will be energetically pursued. They must, with the incorporation of Austria, be worked out anew on the basis of the changed strategic situation."[24]

9

Without Firing a Shot

The annexation of the Sudetenland was to be Hitler's last great bloodless victory, won in the Munich Agreement without firing a shot with the approval (which ranged from resigned to eager) of France, Britain, and Italy. It was a success that, for a few weeks at least, promised to lead to what Neville Chamberlain called "peace in our time," words that millions of Europeans—British, French, Germans, Italians, and others—yearned to hear and believe in but that would only have had substance in a more temperate time and if Chamberlain had been relying on a more reasonable head of the German state. For what Hitler was to bring about in the next few months following the agreement was not a new equilibrium in Europe but the dissolution of the rest of Czechoslovakia. The country was, to be sure, one of the most artificial constructions of the peace treaties, a monstrosity as the Germans saw it and as even its former sponsors had come to regard it. Czechoslovakia had risen out of the ruins of Austria and the Czechs' determination to reverse the former Germanic dominion over them, coupled with the French aim to destroy German power in 1918 and as far into the future as arms and a system of treaties could reach. Czechoslovakia owed its moral sanction to the Wilsonian principle of self-determination that in the summer of 1938 was cited by both friend and foe against the state it had helped create. Nevertheless the dismemberment of the state would be an infallible sign that Hitler could not be trusted even after he had gotten all he had demanded. The destruction of Czechoslovakia was a brutal if bloodless accomplishment of the man whom the British ambassador to Berlin called a remarkable mixture of qualities "fanatical and unbalanced," filled with resentments but also "a constructive genius," as had been evidenced by his rise to power and by the "stupendous" achievements of the first five years of his chancellorship.[1]

The leaders of Britain and France saw the showdown coming. They well knew that after Austria, Czechoslovakia was next on Hitler's list; but they did not know how to prevent the loss of the bastion of the French defense system without war. The more ready Hitler showed himself to use force, the weaker the moral case for maintaining the Czechoslovakian state became in the minds of Chamberlain, Halifax, Henderson, Foreign Minister Georges Bonnet, and Daladier. The best the British, especially, were hoping for was to have the crisis settled in an orderly, "legal" fashion, not by naked force that could well lead to the European war they feared more than almost any kind of peace. The British had weighty reasons for their conclusions. They recognized the military weakness of Britain and France compared with the Reich, they were disillusioned with the highhanded way the Czechs had run the state where Czechs were, at most, a bare majority, and they were increasingly convinced that here again the Allies had gone too far at Versailles and in the Treaty of St. Germain with Austria in turning over millions of people of one nationality to the suzerainty of another people who more resented than tolerated their minority constituents. The complaints of the 3.5 million Germans had been continuous from 1918, though only after Hitler came to power had they been widely perceived as justified. The Sudeten Germans, who for centuries had been part of the Austrian Empire, had never accepted being delivered over to the Slavs of the newly created Czechoslovakia; they had wanted to remain either as part of what was left of Austria in a Danubian confederacy that would maintain some of the advantages of the former Austrian Empire with its tariff-free ethnic borders or as part of the German Reich. The Czechs in the empire had been widely regarded by the ruling Germans as people of secondary status: peasants, hewers of wood, and drawers of water. The founding father of the new state, Thomas Masaryk, was determined to reverse the Austrian-German hierarchy, promising to create another Switzerland, a federated state of nationalities that would include Germans, Slovaks, Poles, Magyars, and Ruthenians, all with equal status with the Czechs. But that is not what happened. From the beginning Czechoslovakia was dominated by the Czechs who were deeply resented by the other nationalities, including the Slovaks who saw them as setting out to rule a Czech national state burdened as Austria had been with minorities.

The Sudeten Germans considered themselves as the prime target of discrimination—socially, economically, and politically. They were forbidden on grounds of national security to work on the fortifications between the Czech borders with the Reich, nor could their enterprises bid on contracts. Thousands of Germans lost their employment in the postal services after the state was founded because examinations were conducted in Czech, which not many of them spoke or wrote. In 1924 a Czech minister, Jiri Stribrny, boasted that forty thousand German postal and railroad workers had been dismissed and replaced by Czechs, and Sudeten Deputy Taub pointed out to the parliamentary budget committee that seven thousand of them had been dismissed even though they had passed the language examination. Moreover the examinations included questions involving details of Czech literary history that were little known to Czechs themselves. As one Sudeten leader, Wenzel Jaksch, wrote, a railway construction foreman might be dismissed for not knowing the birth date or works of a fourth-rate Czech author, and a German employee in a cigar factory (the tobacco industry was state-controlled) was expected to know the difference between the durative and iterative of a Czech verb, while Czech members of parliament often themselves failed to understand the Czech expressions in a bill before them and had to ask for the German or international terminology to be sure of what they were voting for or against. All state employees were required to be proficient in Czech, and the requirement extended to notaries, court interpreters in any language, surveyors, and engineers, as well as district and municipal physicians. Licensed businesses, including taverns, had to display signs in Czech, and German could be used in dealing with the state authorities only when German speakers made up at least 20 percent of the local population. Such requirements were far more severe than those in force in Austria where Czechs had long been protesting any official restrictions on the use of their language.[2]

Half the jobless in Czechoslovakia lived in the Sudetenland. New firms established with the aid of government funds employed Czechs, not Germans. Not only were government contracts for defense purposes awarded exclusively to Czech firms; in order to win any government contract a Sudeten firm had to employ a quota of Czech employees. The center of Czechoslovakian unemployment was fixed in the German-speaking border regions of Bohemia; in 1936 when employment had reached nearly normal levels in the rest of the country, the unemployment figures in the German areas were still over 12 percent.

This was the lot of the Sudeten Germans, while next door Hitler's Reich had succeeded in attaining very nearly full employment. So it was then that many young Sudetenlanders had to go to Germany to find work. Thus on the one side was the German boom and on the other, in central Bohemia and Moravia where the Czechs were in the majority, a relatively high standard of living that the German Sudetenlanders saw no way of attaining.

The Czechs, it seemed to the Sudetenlanders, were determined to assert their authority as the rulers of the region even in the most trivial of matters. Germans asserted that even German-speaking Czech officials, including policemen, made a point of not understanding the German language. In 1938 the British consul in Liberec reported that a Czech policeman complained that a Czech flag flown by a German tavern keeper on Beneš's birthday was too old and flown in too inconspicuous a place, though it was exactly where it had been for three years running. Any German child, the consul reported, wearing white stockings (the customary wear of German children and of the German militants who wore black pants) or a dirndl was likely to be "molested" as he wrote, not only by Czech children but also by adults. The consul also noted that Sudeten German graduates of universities, lawyers, and others were without jobs while Czechs who had a secondary school education were able to go to German towns and be given jobs by Czech firms. The old Czech-German antagonisms were exacerbated as it became evident to both sides that Hitler would not long be content with tolerating the status quo in Czechoslovakia. Only six days after the invasion of Austria, Hitler made a speech to the Reichstag referring to the millions of unredeemed Germans "bitterly mishandled" at the very doorstep of the Reich and asked what great power could long accept such a state of affairs. He was talking, to be sure, about the underlying causes of the *Anschluss,* but the rhetoric applied with equal force to the Sudetenland.

Inside Czechoslovakia the rising anti-Czech sentiment in the Sudetenland was manifest in the career of the former teacher of gymnastics Konrad Henlein who had a Czech mother, which may have led him to emphasize his Germanic zeal. He avoided any mention of his Czech ancestry and germanized the Czech spelling of his mother's maiden name, changing it from Dvoraček to Dworaschek.[3] Henlein was one of the founders of the Sudeten Home Front. It had a modest program of obtaining more home rule for the region within the framework of the Czech state; but two years later Henlein became the leader of the Sudeten German Party that sought to organize all Germans from right to left on the basis of nationality, and three years after that in 1938 he openly demanded *Anschluss* with the Reich. As late as 1937 Henlein had told an English audience at the Royal Institute for International Relations, which he had been invited to address, that he accepted the indivisibility of the Bohemian lands and the possibility of a settlement within the framework of the Czech constitution, but a year later he demanded nothing less than cession of the Sudetenland to the Reich.[4]

Neither side, the Henlein party or the Czech government, would accept the kind of solution the other demanded. Beneš, who had become president of Czechoslovakia after Masaryk's resignation in December 1935, was determined at all costs to keep intact the rickety state he had helped found. In this mission he had powerful allies inside and outside the country. Among the latter were the Sudeten Social Democrats, members of the leading party in Bohemia in 1920 when they polled 43 percent of the vote. Although their strength had diminished to some 10 percent of the Sudeten electorate by 1938, they and the anti-Nazi refugees, including Jews and Communists from the Reich, were passionately anti-Hitler and ready to support any Czech government in preference to him.

Outside the country Masaryk and Beneš had forged a system of alliances that dated back to the founding of the republic. In 1920 and 1922 the Little Entente of Czechoslovakia, Romania, and Yugoslavia was formed as a bulwark against German and Magyar revanchism; in January 1924 came the alliance with France and in 1935 with the Soviet Union, binding Russia to come to the aid of Czechoslovakia if France had already done so. England bore no direct responsibility for the Czechoslovak state, but Prague was convinced that if France became involved in hostilities against Germany, Britain would inevitably be part of the coalition that would support her. Most British leaders, though, were convinced that the imbalances produced by the world war and its turbulent aftermath had to be corrected. From Winston Churchill to Lloyd George to those such as Harold Nicolson who had long rejected the peacemaking of 1918–1919, the preservation of the gerrymandered state of Czechoslovakia no longer seemed politically or morally defensible. In October 1938 Churchill told the House of Commons that Czechoslovakia had suffered from too close an association with France "under whose guidance and policy she has been actuated for so long. . . . I venture to think," he said, "that in future the Czechoslovak state cannot be maintained as an independent entity." Lloyd George declared in 1938 that the British peace delegation at Paris had been "misled by deliberate falsifications" to agree to the Czechoslovakian boundaries. And as for Beneš, Lloyd George wrote: "of the many misfortunes that befell Austria on the eve of her great calamity one of the worst was that Czechoslovakia was not represented at the peace conference by her wise leader, President Masaryk, but an impulsive, clever, much less sagacious and more short sighted politician who did not foresee that the more he grasped, the less he could retain."[5] The reports reaching the foreign minister, Lord Halifax, from the British diplomats in the field were of the same tenor. What had been acceptable in 1919 and the early postwar years had become preposterous in 1938. Why should another generation of Englishmen be asked to die for a country that now appeared to have no real right to exist within its present frontiers designed by peacemakers who had ignored self-determination, one of their own primary principles?

On June 3 the *Times* (London) published a leader that summed up the thinking of influential circles that included the prime minister. The *Times* declared that while rigidly upholding the principle of self-determination was impossible everywhere, the Sudeten Germans unquestionably had a claim on rectifying an injustice grounded in the Versailles treaty. Much could be said, the *Times* went on, for a plebiscite, for it would be a welcome example of peaceful change in the world if the Sudetenlanders wished to be united with Germany. In the past, upholding the status quo had been clung to too rigidly, to such a degree it appeared that only force could change it. Permitting the Sudetenlanders to decide their own future was plainly an opportunity not to be missed on behalf of peace and justice.[6]

For France, too, the prospect of another war on behalf of the state she had been most influential in establishing was appalling. French leaders kept assuring the Czechs and the world press that France would certainly honor its commitments to Czechoslovakia, which meant coming to its aid if it became the victim of unprovoked German aggression. But as the certainty loomed that unless the Czechs made great concessions Frenchmen might have to return to the trenches, the prospect for the Quai d'Orsay or for the French public had little appeal. An eminent French political scientist, Joseph Barthélemy, who taught constitutional law at the University of Paris and was French representative at the League of Nations, asked in *Le Temps* the question French leaders had to answer: "Is it worthwhile setting fire to the world in order to save the Czechoslovak state, a heap of different nationalities? Is it necessary that three million Frenchmen, all the youth of our universities, of our schools, our countryside and our factories would be sacrificed to maintain three million Germans under Czech sovereignty?"

The turning point in the German-Czech crisis came in mid-May. With local Czechoslovakian elections approaching tensions were high, and a series of clashes between Czechs and Sudetenlanders occurred—on May 20 two Sudeten motorcyclists were shot by Czech police near the border town of Eger, and rumors were widespread that the German army had mobilized. Beneš responded on the night of May 20–21 by ordering the partial mobilization of the Czechoslovakian army, and war seemed imminent. But the stories of German mobilization were false; none had been ordered, the borders were quiet, and when the world, especially the Czechoslovakian press and radio, exulted over what they proclaimed as calling Hitler's bluff, asserting that peace had been preserved by the timely Czechoslovakian mobilization, Hitler was furious.

Up to May 21 Hitler had seemed to be in no hurry. On March 28 he had received Henlein in Berlin for a session that lasted three hours. He had assured Henlein that 75 million Germans stood behind the Sudetenlanders and would not tolerate their Czech oppression much longer, but the Reich left it to Henlein to decide what demands they should make to obtain their freedom, and he said the Reich would not act on its own.[7] The Sudetenlanders should put before the Czechoslovakian government maximum demands that the Czechs would find unacceptable; they should ask for so much that their demands could never be satisfied. Henlein agreed, and their common purpose was clear: to keep mounting pressure on Prague that would lead to a period of turmoil that would justify intervention.[8] On April 24 Henlein followed the blueprint. At a meeting of the Sudeten German Party in Karlsbad, he made eight demands on behalf of the German minority. They were vague points, designedly so, for they were intended to lead to protracted negotiations that Henlein knew the Czechs could not readily accept: the Sudetens were to be granted complete equality in rights and status with the Czechs; they were to be recognized as a legal "personality" to guarantee this status; a German territory was to be determined and recognized; an autonomous German administration was to be set up in the Sudeten territory for all departments of public life; legal measures were to be enacted for the protection of Germans outside such a territory; the injustices inflicted since 1918 were to cease and reparations paid for damages done; the government was to recognize and apply the principle of German officials in German territory; and finally, full freedom was to be granted to profess German nationality and the German political philosophy, which was, of course, nazism.[9] The latter was no doubt a demand closest to Hitler's heart, and no democratic government, Czech or otherwise, would be likely to accept it. Nor could the Czechs grant complete autonomy to the Sudetenland without a reorganization of the entire structure of the state. In short the eight points were both nebulous and peremptory, and they would likely lead to long negotiations on their meaning and application. But they were not an ultimatum, and they did not demand outright independence.[10]

Two days before the Karlsbad meeting, on April 22, "The Basis for Case Green," the general plan for an attack on Czechoslovakia, was drawn up by Hitler and Keitel. It prescribed two conditions for a German attack, which it said should not be made out of a clear sky without cause or the possibility of justification. Such measures were justified, the directive said, only for the elimination of the last opponent on the Continent. The German army would march in Case Green only after a series of diplomatic incidents that developed gradually or if a blitzkrieg were ordered as a result of an incident like the murder of a German ambassador in connection with anti-German demonstrations. The directive was updated on May 20, repeating that an attack would be made only as a result of a serious incident that would be an unacceptable provocation and would convince at least a part of world opinion of the moral justification for military force.[11]

The directive was the first signal of Hitler's purpose to deal with Czechoslovakia as he had with Austria. German historians have speculated that Hitler's birthday, April 20, may have given him long thoughts about the ephemerality of human life and the need for haste he had disclaimed earlier. As Jodl had reported when Hitler said Austria must first be digested, Hitler had also ordered that Case Green be pursued energetically, but nothing in the directive of April 22 was a call to immediate action. Czechoslovakia could await the right occasion. Its time would certainly come, but it had not yet arrived.

Until the Czech mobilization and the exultation of the Czech and foreign press over his "defeat," Hitler had seemed willing to wait. On May 20 he had issued a new directive for Case Green in which he said: "It is not my intention to destroy Czechoslovakia by military action in the near future unless an inexorable development of the political relationships inside Czechoslovakia compel it, or political events in Europe create an especially favorable and perhaps never-to-be-repeated opportunity." Again, he said, no sudden attack would be considered without sufficient political justification; it could only take place after a period of increasingly acute diplomatic confrontations that would make it possible to shift war guilt to the opponent or if a "lightning swift action" could be unleashed following an incident that challenged the Reich in such an insupportable fashion to justify to at least a part of world opinion Germany's moral right to take military measures.

Hitler's willingness to wait was not to last long. A few hours after he had issued his new directive for Case Green, on the night of May 20–21, Beneš ordered partial mobilization of the Czechoslovak army. It came as a response to what Beneš believed to be a German mobilization that had, in fact, not taken place. Nothing new had happened, the rumors were unfounded, and Hitler took no immediate countermeasures, but newspapers and radio in the Western nations and in Czechoslovakia acclaimed the success of Czech resolution in confronting the Nazi mailed fist. Hitler was glibly portrayed as the blusterer whose bluff had been called, the traditional bully of fiction, loud and threatening but at bottom a weakling, and he reacted with fury. On May 28 he summoned his leading generals to the Reichschancellery—Göring, Keitel, Brauchitsch, Beck—along with Ribbentrop, Neurath, and party leaders. In a two-hour speech he told them what he would and must do. It was an updated version of his speech of November 5, 1937. He alone would make the far-reaching decisions on whether and when the Reich would attack. But his main decision was made, he said; he would destroy Czechoslovakia. To act was always to take risks, but England and France were not the military equals of the Reich. France was morally weaker than in 1914, and the monolithic Germany of 1938 was stronger than the imperial Germany of 1914. He went on to list his accomplishments on behalf of the Reich since 1933 and declared he could not stop at this point. An overcrowded Germany had to expand to live; it needed space in Europe, and it needed colonies.[12] France would always be the implacable enemy, and England, too, would oppose the Reich's essential expansion that included the coastlines of Belgium and Holland. In the event of war Czechoslovakia stood in the way of a certain German victory in the West. England and France did not want war, Russia was unprepared to attack and would play no part, Poland and Romania would not move for fear of Russia, Yugoslavia and Hungary would stand aside, and Italy was disinterested. The propitious moment had to be grasped. Therefore, Hitler told the gathering, he had ordered the immediate building of the West Wall, "the greatest defense works of all time," and the technical preparations for a breakthrough of the Czech fortifications for a lightning thrust. He summed up his immediate plans in a directive of May 30 in which he said: "It is my irrevocable decision to break up Czechoslovakia by military action in the near future" *(in absehbarer Zeit)*— and he added that when this would occur would be a political and military decision alone; that is, his alone. Czechoslovakia, he then declared, would be defeated not in four but in two to three days by the full onslaught of all German armed strength.[13]

It was not Hitler but the Western allies who were bluffing. They were far behind the Reich in air power. General Vuillemin, chief of the French air force, reported in August it would be destroyed by the Germans in two weeks. France had only old planes, he said, with a top speed of 300–350 kilometers an hour, while the German planes had an average speed of 500 kilometers an hour. The British air force too, Bonnet declared, had only a few hundred modern planes, and its industry was only beginning to turn out 150 planes a month. Poland and Romania flatly refused to join an anti-German coalition over Czechoslovakia, and the wan hope that the Soviet Union would actually join a "peace keeping force" faded too. The United States, though its press and the Roosevelt administration were manifestly anti-Hitler, could promise little or no aid if war came. President Roosevelt told Foreign Minister Bonnet it would be vain to count on the immediate help of American armed forces.[14] And when Bonnet sought to take advantage in the middle of August of the dedication of a war memorial to the American dead of World War I where Ambassador William C. Bullitt was to make a speech, the occasion backfired. Roosevelt had just two weeks before declared the United States would not stand with folded arms if Canada was invaded, and Bonnet wanted the United States representative to say something as comforting with regard to France. But all Bonnet succeeded in obtaining was to have a phrase deleted from Bullitt's speech, which he had read beforehand, in which Bullitt had tamely written of the necessity for putting an end to the secular battles between France and Germany. That sounded as though France might be engaged in merely another struggle for power far removed from the crusade for world peace and order of World War I and a new one of World War II. All Bonnet could succeed in accomplishing was to work out with Bullitt, he says, after many conversations as well as interchanges with Washington, the inclusion in Bullitt's speech of a passage stating that the people of the United States, like the people of France, ardently desired peace and hoped to remain at peace with all nations. "But," Bullitt went on, "as I said on February 22, 1937, if war should break out in Europe no one can say or predict whether or not the United States would be drawn into such a war."[15] That was the best Bonnet could win from a skittish Washington, and what Bullitt said contained neither the words nor the sentiments he was yearning to hear.

Public opinion in the United States was overwhelmingly against any involvement in another European war. Bonnet wrote that Undersecretary of State Sumner Welles estimated the antiwar sentiment in the United States at

80 percent, and the crisis in Czechoslovakia seemed to be a more persuasive argument against America's again attempting to right Europe's wrongs rather than a call to arms. Roosevelt with upcoming congressional elections also had to take into account the widespread belief among American isolationists that he would like to go a good deal further in his support to the Allies than he had gone in the past. On September 9, at a news conference in Hyde Park, the president assured the reporters present that Bullitt's speech did not constitute a moral commitment of the United States to the democracies. The United States, he said, "does not give its support to the anti-Hitler front of the democracies," and those who counted on its aid in the event of war in Europe were completely deceiving themselves—"not a man, not a penny for the war in Europe." Bonnet knew the president would like to do more, but as he regretfully noted there was no chance of seeing the United States go to war until the president was reelected in 1940.[16]

As for the Soviet Union, it was as deeply suspicious as ever of the Western Allies and their aim to involve it in a war with Germany that it would fight alone. The Russian army had been crippled by the Stalin purges. More than half the officers of the army above the rank of colonel had been liquidated, and foreign military attachés in Moscow were certain the Soviet army had lost markedly in efficiency and morale. While Russia might well be able to fight a tenacious defensive war, it was generally agreed in view of the state of the army and the geography that it could not do much for Czechoslovakia even if it wanted to. The countries between the Soviet Union and Czechoslovakia— Poland and Romania—wanted no part of a Russian presence no matter what happened to Czechoslovakia. And while treaties might promise aid in event of "unprovoked aggression," there was no way it could be supplied without the permission of bordering countries to allow their land or airspace to be used. Voices were raised in France declaring that Poland and Romania must be pressed to grant these permissions, and so they were, but France had little leverage. Bonnet tried in vain to persuade both countries of the need to permit Soviet troops and planes to use their territory and airspace to go to the aid of Czechoslovakia. Poland was unmovable in her implacable antagonism to the Soviet Union and would remain so even when, in 1939, the Soviet troops would presumably march in defense of Poland. In 1938 Poland had her own passionate claims on behalf of the Polish minority in Czechoslovakia. The case of Romania was different, but the anti-Sovietism was not. Although the British Foreign Office was informed in September that the Romanian foreign minister, Nicolas Petresco-Comnène, had told his Czechoslovakian counterpart, Emil Krofta, and the Russian commissar for foreign affairs, Maxim Litvinov, that Romania would permit Russian planes to fly over Romania in support of Czechoslovakia, the assurance turned out to be empty. A short time later Lord Halifax was informed the report had been contradicted in Bucharest—no permission had been granted for such flights. The Romanians simply did not trust the Soviet Union. Petresco-Comnène told Bonnet that the Russian desire to march through Romania might well be only a cover for their intention to take over Bessarabia, and, as for permitting Russian planes to use Romanian airspace, that too was out of the question. In any event, he said, from a realistic point of view the Russians could fly over Romanian territory without Romanian consent. Romanian antiaircraft defenses were mediocre, guns could not reach planes flying at high altitudes, and all the Russians needed was to fly high.[17] Furthermore Petresco-Comnène said Romania had no facilities that would permit the large-scale transport of tanks and troops. No railroads ran from the east to the Czechoslovak borders—in fact no roads of any kind could possibly allow the passage of large bodies of Russian troops, equipment, and armor. So neither Poland nor Romania would be of any immediate help to Czechoslovakia even if the transportation had been far more adequate than it was.[18]

The menace of Hitler was clear enough to the governments of Europe, but what to do about the crisis he created was not nearly so plain. For two of the victors of the world war, Italy and Poland, "lost" territories might be regained as a result of French and British weakness. Moreover, as Henderson pointed out, even if France and Britain went to war, the Czech-German problem would remain. And if the war was eventually won, Czechoslovakia would still have to endure a long period of German occupation after which it could not be reconstituted within its present borders. What good would it do to put the German population of the Sudetenland back into the cauldron of racial antagonisms that had produced the present intolerable contradictions? It was a question asked not only by Henderson but also by Halifax and Chamberlain when they were discussing Czechoslovakia with French leaders. The French always had their eyes riveted on Berlin. Bonnet told Polish Ambassador Juliusz Lukasiewicz in Paris in May that it was above all German expansionism that had to be contained.[19] So the Polish demands for equality for the Polish minority in Czechoslovakia were themselves of minor importance compared with the need for a bulwark against Germany.

But the Poles did not agree; like the Germans they were persuaded that they too had irrefutable rights to territory wrongfully awarded to Czechoslovakia. And as the ambassador pointed out, French and Polish policies differed. The entire French press had only recently demonstrated this, indulging in a violent anti-Polish campaign when Poland in mid-March had successfully demanded that Lithuania within twenty-four hours renounce all claims to the city of Vilna.[20] The ambassador complained that all France had wanted to discuss was the march of Soviet troops through Poland. He said he could scarcely bring himself to talk about the French position and preferred to forget the whole matter.

Thus while no one in the Chamberlain or Daladier governments or in British and French embassies in Europe or the United States whose views have been recorded had any doubt of Hitler's intemperance or his readiness to resort to violence, this estimate of him only served to strengthen his bargaining power. The more irresponsible (as Henderson called him) or half-mad (as Chamberlain said) he was seen to be, the more imperative became the need to deal with him by making what suddenly seemed overdue concessions. Attempts at conciliating him that had seldom if ever seemed necessary to their predecessors when they were negotiating with moderate men such as Brüning and Stresemann were taken for granted by Halifax and his colleagues.

Hitler and his rearmed Reich were seen to have a moral case that the worthy statesmen of the Weimar Republic had been lacking. The British ambassador in Berlin in a report to Halifax declared the whole issue a moral one. "I would fight Germany tomorrow for a good cause," Henderson wrote on August 22, "but I refuse to contemplate our doing so for the Sudeten. If they were Hungarians or Poles or Romanians, or the citizens of any small nation all England would be on their side." The whole problem British leaders told one another was one of self-determination, the very foundation on which Czechoslovakia had been built.

Dealing with Hitler was like walking through a minefield that any false or careless move would detonate. The imminent risk doubtless played a significant role in the failure of the Western powers to take advantage of the anti-Hitler sentiment in the Reich. Despite the evidence that high-ranking German generals were ready to take action against Hitler if he should precipitate a European war over Czechoslovakia, how could anyone in Whitehall or the Quai D'Orsay be sure they would indeed act when the time came and that if they did they would be successful? They had as good a cause for their doubts as for giving support to the German opposition to Hitler.

On May 29, the day following Hitler's declaration of his irrevocable intention to destroy Czechoslovakia, General Beck delivered a memorandum to Brauchitsch, refuting point by point what Hitler had just told the generals. He agreed with Hitler only on the Reich's need for more living space and on the strategic danger Czechoslovakia presented, but he did not believe Czechoslovakia could be defeated in four days, and the risk of a British-French intervention was insupportable. The Reich was not, as Hitler said, stronger than in 1914; it was weaker, and a war against the power and resources of the coalition opposing it, which would include the United States, would certainly be lost. Germany might well win the battle against Czechoslovakia, but it would lose the war that would be decided not by arms alone but by the enormous human and material resources of the coalition ranged against Germany that the Reich and its allies could not possibly match. Such a war unleashed by Hitler would lead to a catastrophe not only for Germany but also for Europe.

This was Beck's second salvo in his attack on Hitler's plans and in fact on his dictatorship, for Beck was assailing not only the military but also the political decisions Hitler was making. On May 7 he had submitted to Brauchitsch a similar memorandum that also warned against an attempt to resolve the Czechoslovakian problem by force, citing the coalition, which he predicted would certainly include Russia, that would be arrayed against the Reich. Moreover he pointed out that Britain had no vital concern with Czechoslovakia, and an agreement would be possible if the Reich proposed a tolerable solution.

On June 3 Beck widened his attack in another memorandum to Brauchitsch, writing that the plan for a lightning attack on Czechoslovakia that had been prepared by the OKW (now no more than Hitler's personal staff) would not bear a conscientious scrutiny. The army general staff, he wrote, must decline to assume coresponsibility for the one-sided and inadequate military preconceptions of the directive.[21]

And as the likelihood of war increased—the OKW directive foresaw the invasion taking place at the latest on October 1—Beck stepped up his counterattack. On July 16 he delivered another memorandum to Brauchitsch repeating that the plans for the forthcoming military operation under the unified command of the OKW must be rejected by the army. He even made use of Hitler's own vocabulary to refute him. He wrote that now that the army was again a people's army, a *Volksarmy,* its leaders were the more responsible for refusing to take unacceptable risks. The *Volk,* he wrote, and the army did not want war; they knew instinctively that the planned war afforded no prospect of success. The question of war and peace had become a test of confidence of the people and the army in the OKW. Everyone, he wrote, under his command in the general staff and among the quartermasters general agreed with what he was saying. And on the same day he handed over his memorandum he verbally urged on Brauchitsch what he was convinced must be done. The OKW and the high command of the Wehrmacht must act to force Hitler to stop his preparations for war, including the building of the West Wall. Any attack on Czechoslovakia must be postponed until the military situation had fundamentally changed. If Hitler did not agree, the generals must resign in a body. "Everyone in a responsible position," Beck said, "must feel himself obligated to use every means, to the final consequences, to prevent the war against Czechoslovakia which will lead to a world war that would mean Finis Germaniae." The very existence of the Reich was at stake. "History will burden the responsible leaders with blood guilt if they do not act with their technical and political knowledge and conscience. Their soldierly obedience has its limits there where their knowledge and conscience and their responsibility forbid their carrying out orders.[22] If their counsels and warnings go unheeded then they have the right and duty to resign. If they all resign a war would be impossible to wage. By this deed they would have protected the fatherland from the worst that could happen. Extraordinary times demand extraordinary measures." Beck said further that if the generals did succeed in preventing a war this would give rise to considerable tensions and conflicts between on the one side the Wehrmacht and on the other side the SS and the party bureaucracy, which he contemptuously called the "Bonzocracy." But those risks clearly had to be accepted if Germany was to be preserved.

On July 19 and again on the July 29 Beck went further. He told Brauchitsch a struggle with the SS was unavoidable to restore a state of traditional justice, a *Rechtstaat.* "Indeed," he said, "for the last time fate offers an opportunity to the German people and to the Führer himself to break free from the nightmare of a Cheka and the apparition of a Bonzocracy which is destroying the foundation and well-being *[Bestand und Wohl]* of the Reich." He was careful to include Hitler in what had to be reversed.[23] The watchwords he proposed were "For the Führer—Against the War," "Against the Bonzocracy," "Peace with the Church," "Justice Again in the Reich," "Prussian Integrity *[Sauberkeit]* and Simplicity."

Beck was not the only one in mid-July to come out openly in opposition to what Hitler was doing. The naval chief of staff, Vice Admiral Guse, wrote a memorandum to Admiral Raeder on July 17 saying much the same things that Beck had been telling Brauchitsch. Guse proposed a common declaration by the chiefs of the Wehrmacht, which would include the navy and the air force, to tell Hitler that the war must not be waged. Like Beck he said such a war could not be won and therefore the responsible advisers of the Führer must stop a development that would put at risk the very existence of the Reich. In this view he was joined by Commander Heye who in a situation report pointed out the damage done to the reputation of the Reich by the steamroller tactics of the Nazis in imposing an outward unanimity on the nation. The treatment of the churches and the Jews resembled what the Soviet Union had done and had made the Reich in the eyes of the countries outside Germany appear incalculable *(unberechenbar).* The nations of the world were therefore ready to unite against Germany as they had been against Napoleon.[24]

Neither Beck nor Guse could persuade their superior officers to act. Both Brauchitsch and Raeder agreed fundamentally with what Beck and Guse had written, but they would not risk a confrontation with the head of state. And Beck, as Brauchitsch certainly realized, was putting himself on a collision course with Hitler not only on military but also on political grounds.

What they were proposing, however, was not for but against Hitler, and no one was more aware of that than Hitler himself. The generals were always suspect to Hitler; they had from the start been the one force that could bring him down. The opposition of the chief of the general staff together with the other high-ranking officers and the ambivalent position of General Brauchitsch who, while agreeing with Beck's analysis in general, was noncommittal on what was to be done infuriated Hitler, who accused them of cowardice. "What kind of generals are they," he asked rhetorically, "which I as head of state must, if possible, drive to war?" It was a serious if limited revolt. And he haughtily went on to say: "I don't expect that my generals understand my orders but that they follow them."

Beck's arguments were convincing to those who were prepared to listen to him, but the only tangible response in high quarters in the Reich to what he and Guse were saying was to be seen, ironically, in a directive Hitler issued on June 16. In it he declared that he would attack Czechoslovakia only when, as in the case of the Rhineland and Austria, he was certain England and France would not intervene.

As the preparations for war nevertheless gathered momentum, Beck in late July or early August prepared a final memorandum for Brauchitsch that was intended as the framework for a speech Brauchitsch was to make to the army high command. In it he was to ask the generals to declare that it was their unanimous decision to resign if Hitler insisted on war. The reasons for this unprecedented step were again carefully delineated. Britain was certain to take up arms with the whole world behind her, for she would be fighting not for the state of Czechoslovakia but because the new Germany was a disturber of the peace and a threat to everything England stood for: right, Christianity, and tolerance. A war would not be won by weapons alone, and the huge potential of American industry would be at Britain's service. If the war lasted long enough Britain would be joined by the Soviet Union. On the other side Italy's aid to the Reich would be unsubstantial, and the odds against the Reich were too great to be overcome. In short, Germany could not win a world war.

It was a speech Brauchitsch was never to make, though he did make it possible for Beck to present what he had written at a meeting of the army high command on August 4. In Brauchitsch's private quarters Beck was joined by General Adam who was scheduled to command the west front in the event of war. Adam told the generals the West Wall was not nearly ready, and the German forces available were insufficient for its defense: "I am painting black on black and that is the truth." Brauchitsch in turn said he completely agreed with Adam, and he expected that Adam would repeat his evaluation to Hitler. Of the generals present only Reichenau and Ernst Busch spoke of the need for obedience and submission to the Führer, a position that Beck sharply rejected. Brauchitsch then closed the meeting with the summarizing statement that the higher officers of the army were unanimous in agreeing that they opposed a war that would mean the end of German culture.[25] That was as far as Brauchitsch would ever go.

It was a formidable coalition that was ranged against Hitler. In it were men such as Vice Admiral Canaris (chief of counterintelligence), Franz Halder (deputy chief of staff), Hans Oster (a close associate of Canaris and chief of staff of the Abwehr in the OKW), and General Hermann von Witzleben who commanded the III Army Corps around Berlin. They were prepared to accept any personal risk to prevent Hitler from embarking on a war that could not be won. They were joined by a group of civilians in the foreign office and in industrial and political life who had come to the same conclusion. Some of them, such as Schacht and Goerdeler, had been supporters of Hitler and National Socialism but had come to see them as more dangerous to the Reich than any of its external enemies. Others, such as the socialist leader Ernst Nickisch (who had published a pamphlet in 1932 titled "Hitler: A German Disaster") and his intermediary to the Communist Party, Joseph Roemer, a former free-corps leader, had opposed the Nazi revolution from the start. Niekisch was arrested in 1937 and sentenced to life imprisonment from which he would emerge only at the end of the war.

It was in fact a loose conspiracy with no central organization, united only in its rejection of Hitler and Nazism. The resistance centered around Canaris; and Oster sent emissaries to London, Paris, and other European capitals, as well as to Washington, to warn against Hitler's plans for war and to tell of their determination to thwart them. The emissaries had varied experiences and no success. One of them, the retired lieutenant colonel Hans Boehm-Tettelbach, sent by the army's chief of staff, General Halder, was unable to see anyone of importance in London—no one, in fact, higher than a major in the intelligence service. It was another story in the case of Ewald von Kleist.[26] In mid-August, Henderson informed the foreign office from Berlin that a Herr von Kleist was about to visit London as an "emissary of the moderates in the general staff" to talk with members of the government about the threat of war over Czechoslovakia. Henderson thought it would be unwise for official quarters to see him, but Halifax decided that if Kleist asked to be received "he should not be rebuffed." And when Sir Robert Vansittart, permanent undersecretary of state and well known for his anti-German views, was asked by Kleist for an appointment he agreed to see him, though not, as Vansittart pointed out, in the foreign office. They met on August 18. Kleist told Vansittart that war was a certainty, that policy was being made by Hitler alone; he was the "one real extremist."[27] Hitler had made his decision for war, the date was set (September 27), and Kleist was astonished that the well-informed British did not know it. Hitler was being incited, Kleist said, by his foreign minister, Ribbentrop, but opposed by all the generals—including even Göring, who would rather avoid war but "could not do anything to stop it," and Reichenau, who had "passed for the most extreme and forward of them all."[28] While the generals were without exception, Kleist said, against war, they needed "help and encouragement from the outside"—in effect, an unequivocal statement in which London should make it clear that if Hitler invaded Czechoslovakia, Britain would fight. Kleist saw others in London, including Churchill, who was as impressed by his openness and sincerity as was Vansittart. As he told Churchill, he had been arrested three times on various pretexts and had come to England "with a rope around his neck" to try to prevent the war Hitler was determined to wage. What Kleist had to say impressed Chamberlain too, when Vansittart reported on their conversation, and Chamberlain in his careful fashion wrote to Halifax, "I don't feel sure we ought not to do something." Perhaps he thought of a gesture such as recalling Henderson to London and letting it be known he was being "sent for to consult about the serious position with regard to Czechoslovakia." It would have been a tepid response and not at all what the Germans were urging the British to do. But British leaders, including Churchill, were fighting against the need to fight again and for a cause they thought fundamentally tainted.

In the German foreign ministry, despite its being led by one of Hitler's most slavish courtiers, Ribbentrop, were men who were leaders in the anti-Hitler conspiracy. Career diplomats beginning with the chief officer after Ribbentrop, State Secretary Ernst von Weizsäcker, were as opposed to Hitler's war as were the generals. The counselor of the embassy and chargé d'affaires in London, Theodor Kordt, and his brother Erich, had been assigned by State Secretary Bernhard von Bülow in 1934 to keep track of Ribbentrop who was then the Reich plenipotentiary for disarmament questions and, more important, special deputy of the Führer for foreign questions. The men in the foreign office were well aware that Ribbentrop had aspirations for much higher posts, and Kordt had strict orders not to tamper with his voluble and obtuse memoranda to Hitler, in the hope that they would in time destroy his influence with the Führer. But that was not to be. Hitler's opinion of Ribbentrop's sagacity was confirmed, since what he said was only what Hitler wanted to hear. Erich Kordt had continued as a member of his staff when Ribbentrop was made ambassador to London, and when Ribbentrop was named foreign minister it was mainly due to his influence on Ribbentrop that Weizsäcker, who held the post of chief of the political department of the foreign office, was named state secretary. Kordt told Ribbentrop that not only was Weizsäcker a skillful diplomat but also, as a former naval officer, he "knew how to obey." It was the latter virtue that most impressed Ribbentrop. It was Erich Kordt, too, who was sent by the opposition in August to attempt to persuade Brauchitsch to throw his weight on the side of the generals opposing Hitler. Kordt assured Brauchitsch that Ribbentrop's notion that France and Britain would not intervene was false.

Theodor Kordt took on a parallel mission on September 7 when he arranged to meet secretly with Halifax. To avoid the meeting attracting the attention of reporters at the foreign office, Kordt went to the scarcely less visible Number 10 Downing Street, to Sir Horace Wilson's office. Wilson left the room, returned with Halifax, and then departed again, leaving the two alone. Kordt began by explaining why he had sought a secret meeting with Halifax, saying, "Extraordinary times demand extraordinary means," that he came not as German chargé d'affaires but as the representative of political and military circles in Berlin resolved to prevent a war by force of arms if necessary. To the certain knowledge of Kordt and his friends, Hitler planned an attack on Czechoslovakia, convinced that the war could be localized and that France would not fulfil the terms of its 1924 and later arrangements with Czechoslovakia. The political and military circles for whom Kordt spoke utterly opposed this view, and they believed that the way to a return to concepts of decency and honor among European nations would be finally blocked if Hitler's politics of force were given a free rein. Kordt said he and his friends believed that if Sir Edward Grey in 1914 had made it entirely clear on behalf of the government that Britain could not remain on the sidelines if there were a Franco-German war, the warning, given at the right time, would have had a decisive effect on the Kaiser's government. If now France was ready to fulfil its obligations to its Czechoslovakian ally and if the assertions of the British prime minister were to be taken seriously that the British Empire would not stand aside, Kordt and his friends believed it imperative that the British government state its position unequivocally.

The statement Kordt and his friends proposed could not be unambivalent and firm enough. Hitler and Ribbentrop would probably not dare to begin a war if it was made clear to the German people that a war with Britain would be unavoidable if Czechoslovakia were attacked. But if Hitler did continue on his war policies, Kordt said, with Shakespearian overtones, "I am in a position to assure you that the political and military circles for whom I speak, arming themselves against a sea of troubles, by resistance will end them. With German public opinion," he continued, "and responsibly thinking circles in the army, Hitler's war is unpopular and would be considered a crime against civilization. If the desired statement can be made, the leaders of the army are ready to take up arms against Hitler's policies." A diplomatic defeat would have the most serious political consequences for Hitler in Germany and "would practically mean the end of the National Socialist government."

Kordt ended by saying: "It has not been easy for me to speak in this fashion to the British foreign minister, but the German patriots see no way out of the dilemma other than by a close collaboration with the British government to prevent a war which would be the greatest of crimes."[29] Kordt reported that Halifax had listened with the closest attention, thanked him for his candor, and agreed that a war over the Sudeten question would be a crime and would be unavoidable if Hitler used force against Czechoslovakia. He promised to speak to the prime minister and one or two members of the cabinet and said Kordt could be certain that the matter would be carefully explored and kept confidential.

The British leaders were undoubtedly impressed by what Kordt and the other emissaries of the opposition to Hitler told them, but even if the dissidents were as resolute as Kordt described them, what were their chances of success against the preponderant pro-Hitler forces, the Goebbels-inspired masses, the Luftwaffe formations under the impassioned Nazi Göring, the SS, and generals such as Keitel and Jodl who were convinced of the Führer's genius? How many divisions would march when the dissident generals ordered them into action against the legal head of state and commander in chief of its armed forces? The SS too had its armed forces, and a civil war with it and surely some army units on one side and the anti-Hitler generals on the other would not immediately lead to a peaceful solution of the Czech crisis.

Moreover the case against Czechoslovakia was growing steadily more persuasive in British minds. After only a few weeks in Prague, Lord Runciman, head of the British mission seeking a reasonable solution for the crisis, wrote to Lord Halifax on August 30.[30] Referring to Czechoslovakia as "this accursed country," he went on to report, "Beneš has made his contribution in a long nine page memorandum covered with bolt holes and qualifications. . . . The signs of bad government accumulate from day to day and at any moment H. may find an excuse for crossing the frontier to maintain order . . . if only we could bring Beneš to realize how near he is to a cataclysm we could now make some progress—but he is too clever." And Halifax in turn telegraphed to Runciman on August 31: "If as your telegram seems to suggest Beneš is playing fast and loose, is it not a case for taking drastic steps? His present behaviour will do incalculable harm, and the time at our disposal is too short to permit new tergiversations." Halifax was now convinced that Beneš must be forced to grant major concessions and that he had merely been playing for time. On the same day he suggested to Runciman the need for drastic action he informed the British minister in Prague that Beneš and his government "must, in the interests of their country, clear themselves without delay of the suspicions which are widely prevalent, that, counting on foreign support, they are merely manoeuvring for position and spinning out the negotiations without any sincere intention of facing the immediate and vital issue."[31]

Despite the pleas of the German opposition Hitler had already won his case with British leaders. Even accepting the existence of a powerful resistance to him and Nazism in the Reich, they saw him as firmly in the saddle and certainly capable of waging war.

The closest the British government would come to doing what the resistance was pleading for came when Halifax sent Henderson new instructions in September while Henderson was in Nuremberg awaiting Hitler's speech at the great party rally on September 12. It was then that Halifax sent a message closely following what Kordt and the others had been urging. He instructed Henderson to let Göring and Ribbentrop know that "in the event that France came to the aid of Czechoslovakia as a result of a German attack on that country, the British might well have to become engaged in the ensuing conflict." It was not as bold a statement as the Germans had wanted, but it came close. It was never, however, delivered to Göring or Ribbentrop. Henderson was certain that it would have a devastating result if it ever reached Hitler. The party rally was an incandescent occasion for the celebration of the victories of National Socialism over the maleficence of its enemies, to contrast its strength with the weakness of the past; to challenge its hectic fervors with a cool warning from outside the Reich was very likely to have an effect opposite to what was intended as a call for reflection. It would be catastrophic, Henderson told Halifax, to confront Hitler with another May 21, the day the Czechs had mobilized and Hitler swallowed the bitter pill of his "defeat" without taking action. Henderson was certain this would not happen again, and if it did all their purposes of finding a peaceful solution would be defeated. Halifax was persuaded by Henderson's argument, and the message was not delivered.

Henderson had given sound advice. Hitler's exalted state of mind during the euphoria of the Nuremberg rally that lasted from September 5 to September 12 would have spared no time for naysayers. Nuremberg was a celebration, an occasion for rapturous self-congratulation where the shouts of "Heil" of the assembled faithful bore mass witness to the mana of the Leader who had brought them all to power and Austria "home to the Reich." Hitler in his closing momentous speech to an apprehensive Europe as well as to the gathering of true believers—the SS, the SA, and party comrades from top to bottom—repeatedly reminded them of his and their stupendous achievements. He began with a short address to the Wehrmacht units after they marched past in stiff precision on the Zeppelin Field. "My soldiers," he called them, greeting them, he said, for the first time as soldiers of the great German Reich. He derided again, as he had in the 1920s, the cadavers of the League of Nations and the other international organizations that had helped keep Germany impotent. "No negotiations," he exulted, "no conference and no treaty gave us the natural right to unify the German people. We needed to take this right ourselves and could only take it thanks to you, my soldiers."[32] He worked the soldiers and later the great crowd of the meeting itself with the confident master showmanship that had brought him to power.

In his speech at the final rally closing the party day he was at his peak, celebrating the Reich's—that is, his—achievements and attacking the enemy with biting scorn and sarcasm. The enemies of all of them were still those who had resisted the National Socialist rise to power—the German Nationals, the Centrists, the Social Democrats, the Western democracies, the German

Communists, along with the Soviet Union—capitalism going hand in hand with Moscow's communism. National Socialism had been and remained the target of these forces. The democracies, he said, call themselves the peoples' regiment and call the authoritarian states dictatorships, but only two countries (Germany and Italy) had 99 percent of their people behind them. In most cases the so-called democracies were only societies subtly manipulated and deluded by the power of money and the press. For fifteen years, from 1918 to 1933, this alliance had worked against the most natural interests of the German *Volk*, issued its *Diktats* and compelled their acceptance at gun point, only to protest hypocritically against what they called unilateral breaches of holy laws and still holier treaties, while they themselves without bothering to consult the opinion of the natives had subdued continents using bloody force. If Germany demanded the return of her colonies, they were aghast at the prospective lot of the poor natives who could not possibly be subjected to such a fate. The democracies kept their own colonial peoples in abject submission, sending planes and bombs "to bring the natives to reason"—that is, to compel their dear colored fellow citizens to continue to endure the hated foreign domination.

The democracies complained of the great atrocity of Italy and Germany in trying to get rid of their Jewish elements—these democracies with a couple of inhabitants per square kilometer versus 140 for Germany and Italy. For decades, Hitler said, Germany had taken in hundreds of thousands of Jews; now that it was no longer willing "to be sucked dry by these parasites," the democracies complained. But those hypocritical democracies themselves had no room for Jews; they expected Germany to keep hers, while they themselves would accept no such burden.[33]

Hitler then turned to his main theme: Czechoslovakia was a democracy—that is, a state that had been founded on democratic principles since the majority of its people had been forced, without their opinion being asked, to accept and to submit to this construct of the Versailles treaty. As a true democracy this state set out to oppress a majority of its people, to mishandle and deprive them of their elementary rights. Then gradually the attempt was made to convince the world that this state "had a special political and military mission to fulfill."

> The former French minister of aviation Pierre Cot [he was minister of commerce at the time of the speech], a short time ago told us that Czechoslovakia was there because it is designed to bomb German regions and industries in the event of war, a case apparently of the well known melinite bomb with "civilizing effect."[34]
>
> Its mission, however, is opposed to the vital concepts, interests and desires of a majority of the inhabitants of the state. The majority, therefore, had to remain silent. Any protest against their fate is an attack on the

goals of the state and therefore not in accord with the constitution. This constitution, because it was made by democrats, was tailored, not to fit the rights of those afflicted by it but for the political expediency of the oppressors. This political expediency required finding a design conferring a sovereign hegemony on the Czech people. Anyone who opposed such a pretension is an "enemy of the state" and therefore from a democratic point of view, an outlaw. The so-called state Volk of the Czechs is therefore selected by Providence, which in this case served the purposes of the onetime designers of Versailles, to see to it that nobody can rise against the purposes of the state. Should anyone, however, from the majority of the oppressed peoples of this state, protest, they may then be beaten down by main force or when necessary killed. . . .

Among the majority of the oppressed nationalities in this state are three and a half million Germans as many approximately as there are Danes in Denmark. These Germans are also God's creatures. The Almighty has not created them so the statesmen of Versailles could deliver them over to a hated, foreign power, nor has He created seven million Czechs to watch over and regiment three and a half million people or still less rape and torture them. . . . The conditions in this state as is generally known are unbearable. Politically three and a half million people in the name of self-determination of a certain Herr Wilson were robbed of the right to self-determination. Economically these people were systematically ruined and consigned to slow extermination. . . . If three and a half million members of an almost 80 million people may not sing a song they want to sing, only because it does not please the Czechs, or if they are beaten bloody merely because they wear stockings the Czechs simply do not want to see, or if they are terrorized and mishandled because they greet one another in a way the Czechs do not approve, although they greet one another and not the Czechs in this fashion, if because of any other kind of a desire for a national life they are hunted down and harried like helpless wild beasts— then this may be treated with indifference or even sympathy by the worthy representatives of the democracies because it only concerns three and a half million Germans.

I can assure the representatives of these democracies that we are not indifferent and if these tortured creatures cannot find justice and help of themselves they will get both from us. Depriving these people of their rights must be stopped.

The National Socialist state, Hitler said, had made very heavy sacrifices for European peace. It had not cherished notions of revenge but instead outlawed them in public and private life. In the course of the seventeenth century France, during a period of profound peace, had slowly taken Alsace and Lorraine from the German Reich; Germany had reconquered them in 1870–1871 after a hard war forced upon her and lost them again after the world war. Although the Strasbourg cathedral meant a great deal to her, Germany, for the sake of future European peace, had drawn a final line across the dispute by renouncing the territories. "No one," Hitler said, "could ever have forced us voluntarily to give up our revisionist claims were we not willing to renounce them. We gave them up because we were determined to end out eternal conflict with France once and for all. . . . We have behaved more than loyally."

In the same spirit, he said, he had made other offers to reduce European tensions, and he could not understand why they had not been accepted.

> We have in one important area voluntarily offered to limit our strength in the hope that we would never again have to cross swords with the state in question [Great Britain]. This occurred not because we could not build more than 35% of the ships but as a contribution to the final relaxation of tensions and pacification of Europe. Because a great Polish patriot and statesman was ready to conclude an agreement with Germany, an accord was made that had more meaning for European peace than all the chatter in the League temple in Geneva taken together. Germany has completely satisfactory borders on many sides and she is determined to regard them as henceforth unchangeable and final in order to give Europe a sense of security and peace. This self-limitation and self-restraint is, however, taken by many as evidence only of German weakness.
>
> No European state has done more for peace than Germany, none has made greater sacrifices, but it should be understood that these sacrifices have their limits and this National Socialist state is not to be confused with the Germany of Bethmann Hollweg and of Hertling.[35]

Hitler could assure the statesmen of London and Paris that German vital interests existed "that would be defended" under any circumstances.

Hitler then turned to the partial mobilization of the Czechoslovakian army on May 20–21, an event that was still rankling his self-esteem. The local elections, he said, were to have taken place after the general elections had been endlessly postponed, because the Czechs knew any referendum would show the untenability of the Czech position. They feared this evidence of unity of the German and other nationalities and needed to resort to special measures to influence the results of the local elections.[36] Then the Czechs had come up with the idea that the only practical way to accomplish this would be through "brutal intimidation . . . to demonstrate the sheer power of the Czech state. So Herr Beneš spread the lie that Germany had mobilized and was ready to march into Czechoslovakia."

Such a ruse was not new; about a year before, the press had reported that twenty thousand German troops had landed in Morocco. [The rumor was false; they had landed in Spain.] "The Jewish fabricators of this journalistic lie had hoped to start a war with it. . . ."

As for Czechoslovakia, Hitler said, he could assure his listeners that not a single German soldier had been called up aside from those already in service and that not a regiment had moved to the border. On the contrary the order had been given not to exert the slightest semblance of pressure on the Czechs from the German side. The Reich had no such purpose in mind—on the contrary it was convinced that the local elections would confirm the Sudeten position; the Reich did nothing. This, however, was taken as a pretext to claim that because nothing had happened Germany had been forced to retreat because of the determined behavior of the Czechs and the imminent intervention of England and France.

> You will understand my party comrades, that a great power cannot for the second time accept such a humiliating encroachment. I have therefore taken the necessary precautionary measures. I am a National Socialist and, as such, accustomed to strike back against any attack. I know too, for certain, that yielding to such an unreconcilable enemy as the Czechs fails not only to reconcile him but merely stimulates him to further arrogance. . . . The old German Reich can serve as a warning here. In its love for peace even unto the point of self sacrifice it still at the end could not prevent the outbreak of war.

Hitler said he had therefore taken stern measures on May 28 to strengthen the army and air force and had ordered the immediate completion of the West Wall, "the most gigantic fortification of all time." This task he said he had assigned to the General Inspector of Street Construction of the German Reich Dr. Fritz Todt, who "through the strength of his organizational genius had completed one of the most mighty achievements of all time [the autobahn]."

Hitler loved phrases that compared his accomplishments with those of the benighted past, and what he was saying, as General Adam had told the high command of the army in August, was in large part fantasy. He rolled off the figures on the strength of the West Wall. The West Wall, he said, had been built during the last two years: 287,000 workers from the Todt organization were involved, plus 84,000 others, plus 100,000 from the work service, along with innumerable engineer battalions and infantry divisions. The railroads ran more than eight thousand freight cars daily, carrying over one hundred thousand tons of gravel, and the wall would be finished before the onset of winter; its defensive strength was already fully secured. When finished it would comprise seventeen thousand armored, concrete battlements, and behind this front of steel and concrete would be three and sometimes four lines to a depth of fifty kilometers and behind all this the German people in arms.

In fact the West Wall was begun after the occupation of the Rhineland and was not ready either in September 1938 or when the war started in September 1939. Although German maps showed its dimensions considerably deeper than those of the Maginot line, it proved just as vulnerable when it was breached by advancing Allied forces in 1944.

> I have made these most arduous exertions of all times for the sake of peace. . . . Under no circumstances am I prepared to accept in endless passivity the further oppression of the German volkscomrades in Czechoslovakia. I have not demanded the right of Germany to oppress three and a half million Frenchmen, or that three and a half million Englishmen be delivered to oppression, but I do demand that the oppression of three and a half million Germans in Czechoslovakia stop and its place be taken by the free right to self-determination. In no way am I ready, here in the heart of Germany, to permit a second Palestine to arise because of the prowess of other statesmen. The poor Arabs are defenseless and perhaps forsaken. The Germans in Czechoslovakia are neither defenseless nor are they forsaken. This should be taken into consideration. I think I must express these thoughts on this party day when the representatives of the German Austrian districts are participating for the first time. They know best how painful it is to be separated from the Motherland. They will also be the first to agree most joyously, when I affirm before the entire German people that we would not be worthy of being German were we not ready to take this position and accept its consequences under any and all circumstances.[37]

The speech was skillfully designed for the two nations, Britain and France, in a position to escalate the Czech crisis into a European war. For their benefit Hitler declared he had no further territorial demands in Europe, once the Sudetenland was turned over to him. Alsace-Lorraine he renounced forever, Poland he praised with his encomium for the great "patriot and statesman" Pilsudski who had headed the state when the agreement of 1934 had been made between Poland and the Reich. He made no mention of the Corridor. The Reich's only bleeding border was with Czechoslovakia. One step at a time, and the case he made against Beneš and the Czech government had a far more overwhelming appeal for London and Paris than for the German generals and the others who opposed him in the Reich. But no one he needed was left out of the speech. The German people were told of his deep love for peace and what sacrifices he and they had made on its behalf. Mussolini and fascist Italy were extolled, the hypocrisies of the democracies exposed while Hitler promised them he had no further designs to widen his frontiers; all they had to do on behalf of peace was to right a great wrong they themselves had perpetrated. As for his party comrades, he not only told them what heroes they had been against the forces of darkness but also reminded them that the Jews and their lying international press were still at work putting his peaceful intentions and the peace of Europe at risk.

He ended his speech in a passion of praise for what he had accomplished. Referring again to the Czech mobilization he said that if even a small state thought it could challenge Germany, this could only be explained by the reluctance of the Czechs to see in the Reich more than a peace-ready upstart. He praised his ally, Italy, linking its rebirth in fascism to what he had brought to the Reich. His vision spanned the centuries; he told his audience that as he had stood in Rome in the spring he had inwardly comprehended how the history of humankind is too often in too short periods of time seen and grasped in too small dimensions. A thousand and a half years, he said, span only a few human generations.

> What can grow weary in the course of such a period can also rise again. Today's Italy and today's Germany are a living proof of this. They are regenerated nations and in this sense may be considered new. . . .
>
> The Roman state begins to breathe again. Germany too, although historically far younger, is as a state no new birth. I have had the insignia of the old German Reich [one of the trophies of the *Anschluss* with Austria] brought back to Nuremberg to demonstrate not only to the German people but to the entire world that more than half a thousand years before the discovery of the new world a powerful germanish-German Reich existed.[38]
>
> Dynasties come and go, outer forms have changed, the Volk has become young again but its substance remains eternally the same. The German Reich has slumbered a long time. The German Volk is now awake and is itself the bearer of its thousand-year-old crown. For us who are the historical witnesses of this resurrection there is a proud happiness and a humble thankfulness to the All Powerful. The new Italian Roman Empire and the new germanish-German Reich are actually the oldest of presences. They need not be loved. [But] no power in the world will separate them. . . .
>
> In this hour the first Reichsparty day ends. You are filled with powerful historical impressions of these days. . . . You have the right to raise your German head again with pride, we all, though, have the duty never again to bow it to a foreign will. Let this be our vow. So help us God![39]

It would not have been the day to tell Hitler that Britain might intervene if he used force against Czechoslovakia. Although his speech seemed to leave time before the invasion, it made clear that the time was short. And in the case of the leaders of Britain and France he was preaching to the converted. In August, Chamberlain had dispatched a mediator to Czechoslovakia, Runciman, on an errand that he hoped might lead to a peaceful solution. In the end that could be no other than arranging for the separation of the people of the Sudetenland from Czech domination.

10

Negotiating against the Odds

Viscount Runciman fitted the qualifications Lord Halifax had prescribed for the chief of mission to Prague, "an impartial person of standing and repute," and was a former Liberal member of the House of Commons, who later became minister of Education and then of Commerce. In a telegram Halifax said Runciman was to be an "investigator and mediator acting independently of His Majesty's government," though as head of mission he was as closely, if temporarily, bound to the government as any other emissary. But he was clearly to be allowed to succeed or fail on his own as an additional dimension of British foreign policy, and like the others who had been subjected to the heat of the Czechoslovak cauldron he was soon dispirited by what he found. A few weeks after arrival he was referring to Czechoslovakia as "this accursed country" and to Beneš's proposals as "covered with bolt holes and qualifications," adding in early September that "nothing can excuse his slow movements and dilatory negotiations of the past five months."[1]

Beneš was certainly dragging his feet in the apparent hope that Hitler's intransigence would eventually result in British intervention. His policy was procrastination. If moderate concessions to the Sudetenlanders might earlier have appeased Henlein and his followers, the time had passed. The only alternative open to Beneš in September was to grant, in one form or another, the self-determination that would mean the end of the Czech-dominated state Beneš had always fought for.

Runciman's final proposal, made to him on September 21, was that in districts where the Sudeten population was an important majority "they should be given the full right of self-determination at once."[2] The words summed up what British leaders had come to accept: Beneš had to be bypassed. And Chamberlain two days after Hitler's speech at Nuremberg made the dramatic gesture that was greeted with enthusiasm all over the world. He sent a message to Hitler offering to fly to Germany to meet him the next day, September 15, to try to work out a peaceful solution to the Czech crisis.

Hitler later reported that the message came as a complete surprise—he said he was dumbfounded.[3] He had obviously meant what he said in his Nuremberg speech; he would no longer tolerate the Sudeten Germans remaining under Czech rule and not only the words but also his actions evidenced his intentions. German reserves were called up and sent to their barracks; civilian cars and trucks were taken over by the military; air raid practice sessions with blackouts were continual; horses and carts were requisitioned from farmers and brought to military collection points; troops ready for battle left their barracks for positions designated for an advance into Czechoslovakia.

No signs of the German resistance were evident. General Beck had resigned in August, when Hitler had not only failed to stop his preparations for war but also stepped them up, and no longer was there open talk of forcing the Führer to change his mind. General Halder, appointed army chief of staff to replace Beck, was as opposed to military action against Czechoslovakia as Beck, but either had to remain silent or relinquish the post. The opposition was forced underground, and Chamberlain's offer to meet with Hitler drove it still deeper. Far from the ultimatum the opposition had been asking for, here was the prime minister of Britain offering to visit Hitler, olive branch in hand.

Hitler replied that he would be pleased to meet Chamberlain on September 15 at three o'clock in the afternoon, and he even suggested that Mrs. Chamberlain accompany him, the only sign of hospitality he offered. Otherwise the initiatives and the rigors of travel were left to the sixty-nine-year-old prime minister who had never flown before in his life and would have not only a plane trip to make but also a three-hour train journey from Munich to Berchtesgaden, after which he would confront a rested Führer for hours of crucial negotiation. Hitler was in the driver's seat, and both men knew it.

Nothing like the stage setting that Hitler had prepared for Schuschnigg at Berchtesgaden was set up for Chamberlain. During the trip from Munich to Berchtesgaden, however, troop train after troop train passed the special train carrying Chamberlain, Sir Horace Wilson (Chamberlain's chief adviser on foreign policy), and William Strang who was head of the central department of the foreign office.[4] With them were Ribbentrop and Schmidt (the interpreter), who with Henderson and members of the German Foreign office had met the plane at Munich. The greetings of the population that lined Munich's streets were most cordial, but the atmosphere in the train was heavy as Ribbentrop presided at a luncheon of trout, beef, and Yorkshire pudding, as well as white and red wine and sherry. When they arrived at the Berghof only one general— Keitel—was present, and Hitler went as far as the foot of the stairs to greet them.

It was rainy and foggy, so the view from the great living room where they all sat down to tea was negligible. After twenty minutes, while the conversation ranged stiffly about the weather, the impressiveness of the room, the possibility of Hitler's one day visiting London, Hitler asked Chamberlain if he would like to talk alone or with the advisers present. Chamberlain said he would prefer to talk alone, thus avoiding having Ribbentrop present. Schmidt reports that this had been arranged beforehand, since Göring, Henderson, and Weizsäcker saw Ribbentrop as nothing but a disturbing element in such a meeting, and Hitler had no objection to leaving him out. So Hitler and Chamberlain, accompanied by Schmidt departed for Hitler's spartan study on the second floor, leaving Ribbentrop stranded with Keitel and the British advisers while the momentous meeting took place.

The meeting began on a polite note as Chamberlain said he had long wanted to talk with Hitler to improve Anglo-German relations, and in view of events of the last few weeks a meeting had become imperative.[5] Hitler for his part again expressed pleasure that Chamberlain had been ready to make the journey. Both he and the entire German people, as Chamberlain must have noted from the demonstrations of sympathy of the Munich crowds, welcomed him warmly.

Hitler said he too, since his youth, had wanted to further Anglo-German cooperation. The war had been deeply disturbing to him, and after 1918 he had continued to keep Anglo-German friendship in the forefront of his mind. His racial ideals had led him to seek the collaboration of both peoples, but he had to admit that in these recent years his hopes had suffered heavy blows. But he would be glad if at the last hour it would be possible to return to these ideals on behalf of which he had long struggled.

Chamberlain wholly agreed. He said it was not easy at his age to undertake such a journey, and it was proof for the Führer and the German people of how much Anglo-German rapprochement meant to him as well as evidence of his desire to do everything he could to find a way out of the present difficulties. He then suggested that they make use of this final talk to exchange ideas about the general situation, after which they would know exactly what was in the other's mind and whether or not an agreement was possible. But Hitler said that the Sudeten problem was immediate; the situation was becoming more and more critical by the hour and heading toward a crisis, and they should begin now with the Czech problem, which was decisive for the future of Anglo-German relations. According to the latest reports, three hundred Sudetens had been killed and hundreds more wounded and entire districts had to be abandoned by their inhabitants. Under these circumstances in one way or another a solution had to be found in the shortest possible time. There was no point in continuing diplomatic discussions. The long journey the prime minister had made would be wasted if they kept to mere formalities.[6]

For Chamberlain's better understanding of the situation Hitler said that he could assure him that his entire meaning to the German people rested on the confidence they had in him. He was not a dictator; he had not built his power in Germany on military force but on the trust of the nation whose spokesman and representative he was and whose interests he had to protect. He could not be silent and passive when the entire nation awaited his energetic action and plain words. Other statesmen were subject to the influence of their parliaments; he had to speak directly to the people and especially to the party. Were he to fail to do what was expected of him he would not simply do away with the problem at issue but would destroy his own status. This was the opposite of imperialism. The racist basis of National Socialism precluded imperialism. He knew it was impossible to unite all the Germans in Europe. The Reich had come to an agreement with Poland of its own free will and made the naval agreement with England limiting German sea power. But the preconditions for such a treaty certainly required the mutual determination of each never again to resort to war against the other. Therefore if England repeatedly announced it was ready to intervene against Germany, these preconditions no longer existed, and it would be more just and honorable to denounce the treaty.

Chamberlain broke in at this point to ask whether the denunciation would come on the outbreak of hostilities or before. Hitler replied that if England continually threatened the possibility of intervention while Germany had decided never to go to war with England, this would be a one-sided disadvantage, and it would be more honorable to end the treaty relationship.

Hitler went on to say he had given guarantees to Holland and Belgium; the Saar question had been settled without Alsace-Lorraine even being mentioned, and he had assured France no territorial questions remained between them. One general demand, however, the Reich had made; 10 million Germans had lived in Austria and the Sudetenland, and their urgent demand was to return to the Reich to which they had belonged for a thousand years. The demand of the 7 million Germans in Austria had been fulfilled. The return of the 3 million Germans in Czechoslovakia to the Reich he would make possible at all costs. For this he would take into account any risk of war—even of a world war. At this point, he said, the limit had been reached where the rest of the world could do as it wished, and he would not retreat one single step.

Chamberlain asked if the difficulties with Czechoslovakia would then be resolved with the return to Germany of the 3 million Sudeten Germans. People in England were asking if that was all that Germany demanded or whether in addition it wanted the breakup of the Czechoslovakian state. Hitler answered that aside from the Sudeten question there were naturally similar demands from the Poles, Hungarians, and Ukrainians living in Czechoslovakia, which in the long run could not be ignored, though he naturally could not speak for them. But he reminded Chamberlain that at the time of the *Anschluss* with Austria he had taken into account Italy's opposed interests and guaranteed the German-Italian borders as well as the borders with Yugoslavia and Hungary. So only one problem remained—the Czechoslovakian—and it had to be solved one way or another. He was absolutely determined about this, and he would choose a time that would ensure a solution. He was forty-nine years old, and if Germany should be involved in a world war on account of the Czechoslovakian question he wanted to be sure to be in his full prime to lead his country through it and not to leave the task for his old age or his successor. To be sure, there was the question of Memel, but Germany would be satisfied if Lithuania would strictly abide by the Memel statute. And finally there would always be the question of colonies for Germany to be kept in mind, but this was not a demand that involved war. Someday it had to be fulfilled, and Germany would not retreat from it.

The Czechoslovakian problem in any event was the last great problem that had to be solved. He would, of course, regret it if the Czechoslovakian question led to a world war, but, nevertheless, that danger could not shake him from his decision. In relation to the Czechs he must again emphasize that he had to settle this question in one way or another. He wanted to leave no doubt about his absolute decision to no longer tolerate that a small second-rate country be able to treat the great, thousand-year Reich as something inferior.

Concerning the naval treaty Chamberlain said he could thoroughly understand Hitler's position up to a point. It was a very reasonable treaty made on the assumption that there would be no war between the two countries. If the situation was now so changed that the possibility of war had to be taken into consideration, then the basis for the treaty was in fact gone. But Chamberlain said that the Germans did not seem to understand the difference between a warning and a threat. After 1914 the reproach had been made that England had not made its views plain enough. Critics said the war might perhaps have been avoided if England had made its position plainer. If two peoples believed they were on the verge of a conflict, they had to know in advance exactly what the consequences of such a conflict would be. It was in this sense that England had acted and made no threats but only given a warning. England could not be blamed for the warning; on the contrary she could have been criticized for not giving it.

Hitler replied that he could follow the prime minister's train of thought in part, but often things had gone so far that they could not be changed very much after a certain point was reached. In 1914, too, in his view, England's warning had come too late, the difficulties had progressed too far. He had to stand by his major position: that the naval treaty required both parties to refrain under any circumstances from war against the other. If therefore England let it be known from time to time that under certain circumstances it must, nevertheless, consider the possibility of a conflict with Germany, the logical foundation of the treaty disappeared. When one party voluntarily limited the strength of its fleet and the other party kept all possibilities open, it was precisely at this point that a warning made the disadvantages of the first party strikingly apparent.

Chamberlain thanked the Führer for his clear and open explanation of the German position. He thought he had understood the Führer correctly: that on racial grounds he wanted the return of 10 million Germans. Seven million Austrian Germans had returned to the Reich; 3 million Sudeten Germans must under any circumstances return to the Reich. But Hitler had given the assurance that there would be no territorial demands elsewhere that would lead to a conflict between Germany and other countries. Chamberlain said he had also understood the Führer to be ready to risk a world war to make certain the 3 million Sudetens would return to the Reich. At the moment he merely wished to say that it must be possible for the Führer and him to prevent a world war because of the 3 million. He also thought he had understood Hitler to say that Czechoslovakia could not remain a spearhead in Germany's flank.

If the Sudeten Germans were again to become part of the German Reich, Chamberlain asked, would Hitler still regard the rest of Czechoslovakia as a spearhead in Germany's side? Hitler replied that that would be true as long as Czechoslovakia had an alliance with other countries that made it a threat to Germany. She had already caused the Reich to build an air force twice the size of what had been foreseen. Chamberlain then asked if this threat would be alleviated if, on the one hand, Czechoslovakia's relations with the Soviet Union changed so that Russia would be relieved of its obligations if Czechoslovakia were attacked, and on the other hand, if Czechoslovakia, like Belgium, would not have to rely on aid from Russia or any other country. Hitler answered that Czechoslovakia in any case would not long continue to exist, because the nationalities, including the Slovaks, wanted to be completely free of her. Chamberlain said Great Britain had no interest in the Sudeten question in itself; that was a question between the Germans, or the Sudetens, and the Czechs. Britain was interested only in the maintenance of peace. Hitler replied that peace in any event had ceased to exist in Czechoslovakia. The Germans had been oppressed for decades, and with the growth of the power and prestige of the Reich the oppression had gradually led to revolt. The rule of force in Czechoslovakia, the shooting of Sudetens, and the posture of the Czechs that daily became more threatening—all were designed not to resolve the difficulties but on the contrary to increase hatred.

Chamberlain said that as a practical man he asked himself how the Sudetens would return to the Reich. They lived not in a compact area but instead were pretty well scattered, and even if 80 percent of the Sudeten population was German and would go to Germany, a considerable number lived outside in the rest of Czechoslovakia. So the question was not only of borders but also of resettlement. Hitler answered that, of course, only the Sudeten area as a whole came into consideration, and only the areas where a majority was German should go to the Reich. An exchange of the minority populations would have to take place. But he feared this discussion was theoretical; events were moving forward rapidly. Entire villages had been evacuated. Ten thousand refugees were already on German soil. Localities with three thousand inhabitants had been attacked with gas.[7] He could no longer merely observe such events. He had made his intentions clear at Nuremberg, and it was a mistake to regard what he said as empty phrases. He could under no circumstances continue to watch the persecution of Germans and was determined to act quickly. Chamberlain suggested they could make a common appeal to both sides. Hitler said he could not possibly appeal to the Sudetens who were the victims of persecution. The nervous tension of the population in the border areas had to be taken into account, and it had reached the breaking point. The sound of artillery fire directed against defenseless Sudeten districts could be heard in German territory. At the same time, on the German side, whole divisions had been assembled with air support, which meant a monstrous nervous tension; in the midst of all these preparations Germany had to look on while old German cities such as Eger were attacked by Czechs. Furthermore, this had to be taken into consideration: Germany had been led to take a false step before in 1918. Yet in its two thousand years of history the Reich had always conducted itself courageously and heroically, and, if the English were just, they had to admit this had been true in the last war, too. The Germans believed for better or worse that the Czechs were brutal and inwardly cowardly, and it was easy to imagine their feelings as they saw fellow countrymen oppressed by an inferior people. If the prime minister could imagine England being enslaved by an inferior race, his blood too would rise, just as did the Germans' in the case of Czechoslovakia.

Hitler repeated he would not participate in an appeal to Czechoslovakia, and Chamberlain for the first time showing signs of impatience replied that he asked himself why Hitler had let him come to Germany if he had already determined to proceed in a certain direction without considering the possibility of an armistice. Hitler replied that he had thought it necessary to find out immediately if perhaps a peaceful solution of the question might not be possible, though he had to emphasize that the question had to be settled in the shortest possible time. Moreover, he pointed out, Czechoslovakia had used the prime minister's journey to mobilize. Chamberlain again emphasized that he was acting to save lives and therefore made his suggestion that a kind of armistice be brought about for a short period. Hitler replied that an immediate pacification in the Sudetenland could be brought about if the Czech state police were withdrawn and confined to barracks. Did England, he asked, agree to the detachment of the region and the changes in the present constitution? If she did and was ready to announce it as a fundamental decision, then there would be an enormous relaxation in the area. It was essential to know whether England agreed to the detachment of the Sudetenland on the basis of the right of self-determination of peoples, not as something discovered by him for Czechoslovakia in 1938 but as something already existing in 1918 for creation of a moral foundation for changes in the Versailles treaty. On this basis the talks could proceed, but the prime minister had first to say whether he recognized the necessity for detachment of the Sudeten area on the basis of the right of self-determination.

Chamberlain agreed that self-determination was the heart of the matter. He was not in a position to give a categorical answer on behalf of the British government—he also naturally had to consult France and Lord Runciman—but he could declare his personal point of view after hearing what Hitler had to say, and he had come to see the whole situation in a clear light. He was now ready to find out if his view was shared by his ministerial colleagues. He himself was ready to recognize the principle of self-determination and the detachment of the Sudetenland. Under these circumstances he wished to return to England to report to the government and obtain approval of his personal position. Meanwhile he proposed that both sides consider the practical methods of working out basic procedures for solving the problem.

Hitler said he would gladly spare the prime minister another trip to Germany; he was much younger and could undertake a trip to England, but he feared if he went there the unfriendly demonstrations would make the situation more complicated rather than simpler. To shorten the prime minister's journey, he suggested the next meeting take place on the lower Rhine in Cologne or Bad Godesberg.

Chamberlain asked if it would not be possible in the meantime to see to it that the situation did not become more acute. Hitler answered that the possibility of the situation's becoming more acute was there, for if the great military apparatus Germany had built up were set in motion, once started it could not be stopped. If there were major incidents—border violations and the like—the danger would be greatly increased. But even at the risk of appearing weak, as the British press might represent it, he was ready to give an assurance that, in the course of the next few days, if at all possible he would not give the order to set the apparatus in motion. It was clear that everyone in Germany would be happy if the return of the Sudeten Germans under the previously discussed conditions could be accomplished by peaceful means. He himself would be especially pleased if the return of the Sudetenland would lead to an improvement of Anglo-German relations.

Hitler could not understand the position of France. On the one hand France had permitted the Saar to vote, while on the other hand it was ready to go to war if the Sudetenland voted. Chamberlain replied that England had never taken such a position and had only wanted a peaceful and just solution.

He asked Hitler again how the political peace might be kept while the cabinet was consulting during the next few days. Hitler said that England should make the Czechs stop their mobilization—such measures might easily lead to another incident like the one on May 21, and that would develop into a most serious situation. Chamberlain said he took it Hitler would do all in his power to keep things as peaceful as possible the next few days. Hitler replied that under the circumstances he could do little, but he would do what he could, though he could not make any public proclamation. The two men issued a combined communiqué saying they had had an open and wide-ranging discussion, that Chamberlain was leaving the next day to consult with the British cabinet, and that a new meeting would be held in a few days.

The meeting was a partial success for both sides. Chamberlain had wanted above all to preserve the peace and succeeded in accomplishing that for the time at least. Hitler wanted to undo what was left of the Versailles treaty and put the detested Czechs in their humble place; he not only had the divisions and the air force ready at the border but also had a moral argument that the British and French, now that he had the military strength to enforce it, found most persuasive. When Chamberlain accepted the transfer of the Sudetenland to the Reich, Hitler had what he wanted, with the important exception of the humiliation of Beneš and the Czechs. He was ready if not anxious to inflict a violent solution on the Czechs no matter what the risk but had to keep the other considerations in mind. At the point in the meeting where Chamberlain asked why if no peaceful solution was possible he had let him come to Germany and seemed ready to break off the talks, Hitler in the opinion of his interpreter seemed shaken; his tone softened markedly as he declared the crisis could be settled if the Sudetenland went to the Reich. But essentially he was ready to go to war while Chamberlain was not. That made the difference between the bargaining power of the two men, and it gave Hitler all the edge he needed.[8]

He dealt skillfully with Chamberlain, and he offered peace. He had no further territorial demands in Europe—he did not mention Danzig or the Corridor; in fact, he pointed out he had made his peace with Poland as he had with France. And Alsace-Lorraine presented no more of a problem than the Tirol when he conceded the latter to Italy. What Chamberlain and many of his countrymen saw as a chief brutality of his regime—his blatant racism—Hitler turned into a guerdon of peace. He wanted no Czechs or Poles or any other Slavs. National Socialist racism was a limitation on any territorial demands.

So the word *peace* hung in the air, and it was to be had if only justice was done and the Sudetenland returned to the Reich. This had to be accomplished without delay; no time remained for bargaining or for counting noses and examining birth certificates and town records. The sense of urgency was such that Chamberlain assured Hitler it would be only a matter of days before he met with his cabinet and the French and Runciman. It appeared that all that remained for the next meeting, if the sessions Chamberlain had with his advisers and allies ran as he meant them to, was to work out details and technicalities of transfer of land and population.

When Chamberlain returned to Germany five days later he was in high spirits. His mission in effect seemed to him and to the British delegation mainly accomplished, with approval of the British and French governments as well as formal consent of the Czechoslovaks to the terms Hitler had laid down at Berchtesgaden. Chamberlain was housed in the palatial splendor of the Hotel Petersberg on the right bank of the Rhine across from where Hitler was staying at the far more modest Hotel Dreesen frequented by villagers and Rhine tourists.[9]

But in fact the negotiations beforehand had been deceptively easy. More than the Rhine separated the two men. The whole picture had changed now dramatically.

Again Hitler was friendly and courteous as the two groups met at the Hotel Dreesen after the British had crossed the Rhine in ferryboats accompanied by two police launches.[10] After the Berchtesgaden meeting Chamberlain had not been able to get a copy of the German interpreter's minutes, due to Ribbentrop's churlish insistence that this was an internal German document and therefore not to be made available to the man who had contributed a large section of it. This time Chamberlain had brought along his own interpreter, Ivone Kirkpatrick, who had been chief of chancery at the embassy in Berlin, spoke fluent German, and knew all the personages present. The four men preceded by an SS guard went up a flight of stairs to the hotel's conference room on the second floor. It was furnished sparely with chairs and a long table at which Hitler sat down at the head with Chamberlain to his right and the interpreters on either side surrounded by empty chairs.

At a sign from Hitler, Chamberlain began by cheerfully announcing he had secured the consent not only of his cabinet and of the French government but also of the Czechs for the acceptance of the basic principle of self-determination for the Sudetens.[11] All Germans in Czechoslovakia would therefore have the opportunity to decide for Germany, and the question was only in what form the decision would be made. He suggested the simplest method would be for large sections of Sudeten territory where inhabitants were more than 50 percent

German to go to Germany without a plebiscite, with the provision that people who would be affected could be transferred, if they wished, from one area to another. Overwhelmingly German areas would present no problem, but where the inhabitants were mixed, a commission of three—a Czech, a German, and a neutral member as chairman—would decide the border, taking into consideration political, geographical, and military aspects. Since the proposed cession of territory would leave the Czech border fortifications in Germany and since Hitler had said he wanted no further Czech territory, Chamberlain suggested a British guarantee of Czech security to replace the existing Czechoslovakian alliances, thus making the country a neutral state with no military obligations. The Czech border would not be guaranteed in perpetuity but could be altered as in the present instance, by negotiation.

Hitler thanked Chamberlain for his efforts on behalf of a peaceful solution of the Czechoslovakian question and asked whether the proposals had been submitted to the Czechoslovak government. When Chamberlain said they had been, Hitler replied that he was sorry, but he regretted they could no longer be maintained. The situation, he said, was perfectly clear. It was not a question of wronging Czechoslovakia but of undoing an injustice perpetrated on the Germans and other minorities for twenty years.

Basically a man who had committed an injustice had no right to complain when his misdeeds were righted. Czechoslovakia was a completely artificial construction created for political reasons, and he went on to recite the wrongs also done the Hungarians and Poles who would no longer tolerate being part of the state. It was a state without history or tradition or conditions of existence, he said. In twenty years the Czechs had been unable to win the sympathy of the component nations. Although he was speaking for the Germans, it was his duty to say that the demands of the other minorities had his full sympathy. The problem was at a critical stage in his view, and no delay was possible. With military preparations on both sides a solution had to be found in a few days either by agreement or by force—by October 1 at the latest. The Germans had no confidence in the Czechs (particularly none in Beneš), the Czech army was being mobilized, and the bolsheviks threatened to take over. He realized Chamberlain and the British government had done their best to perform the necessary surgical operation on Czechoslovakia, and he was ready to cooperate with them. Since 1918, 480,000 Sudeten Germans had emigrated from Czechoslovakia. The latest statistics showed 103,780 refugees had fled since the start of the crisis. Whole villages were empty; from some, men had fled, in others they had been conscripted or arrested; women had stayed in some, in others children had been left wandering in the streets or fields. These people could not view the problem with the same equanimity as those in the conference room. A series of armed clashes had occurred—Germans, Poles, and Hungarians were deserting from the

Czech army, crossing over into the Reich. The Czechs were trying to cut them off. In three or four days there would be a real frontier war. Fundamentally neither the Sudetens, the Slovaks, the Poles, nor the Hungarians wanted to remain in Czechoslovakia, and the Czechs wanted to thwart them by force.

Chamberlain was aghast. Here he was back in Germany with everything Hitler had asked for, and Hitler coolly told him he had changed his mind. That this was characteristic of Hitler's tactics when he saw an opening Chamberlain may have known in theory, but confronted with the reality it was baffling. At Berchtesgaden, Hitler had been left victorious but unfulfilled; he had wanted much more than the principle of self-determination by the Allies who had once denied it to the Germans. He thirsted for revenge on Beneš, and he wanted to make use of the superb army he had created to show the Czechs their humble place. Nourished by long-smoldering rancors he now had upped his demands to this likable but, as he said, calcified old fool with the umbrella who represented a decadent England.

The lives of millions of people were at stake, and Chamberlain could only say he was disappointed and puzzled. He had taken his political life in his hands, he told Hitler, to obtain what the Führer had asked for. When he had first flown to Germany he had been applauded; now he was being accused in England of yielding to dictators and capitulating. Even many people in his own party were resisting what he had done. What he had hoped for was to show the world that treaty revision could be accomplished by peaceful means, and he obviously was not yet ready to abandon his search.

If Hitler, he said, had any proposals to make he would of course be pleased to hear them. Hitler replied that there was only one possibility. A frontier line must be drawn at once from which the Czechs must withdraw their army, police, and state organs, to be replaced by German forces. The frontier would be the language frontier based on existing reliable maps. If the Czechs claimed this did not represent the real minority situation, a plebiscite would be held; he did not want to steal territory that did not belong to Germany. Germans who had left the territory in 1918 would be entitled to vote, and the Czechs who had been planted there would not. The plebiscite would be carried out by an international commission. Where there was a Czech majority Hitler said he was prepared to surrender the territory and withdraw his troops. Arrangements would have to be made for Germans who had left to vote, and he repeated that planted Czechs would not vote. Czechs were entitled to no indemnification because Sudetens had paid more in taxes in proportion to numbers than had Czechs, and Czech property had been inherited from the Austro-Hungarian monarchy, which was the fruit of German money. As for a guarantee of the Czech borders England could do as it wished, but Germany could undertake such a guarantee only if other neighbors and Italy did so.

Chamberlain said he had not had in mind a German guarantee but rather a nonaggression pact between Czechoslovakia and the Reich. Hitler said that would be possible only after Hungary and Poland worked out their problems with the Czechs. He said again the situation was clear: Either a peaceful solution with borders following the lines of nationalities or a military solution that would set strategic boundaries. That was to be the leitmotiv of his demands at the Bad Godesberg meeting: Either do it my way and right now, or I order my troops to march.

Chamberlain had his own chalk line drawn firmly in his own mind. Hitler insisted on immediate occupation of the Sudetenland. Chamberlain was determined that this would not happen. The Sudetenland would go to Germany, well and good, but not by force or appearance of force in the shape of an occupying army.

He pointed out that Germany could get what it wanted by force, but that would involve an element of hazard and he could not understand why, if Hitler could get what he wanted by peaceful means, he should take a course that involved loss of German lives and a certain element of risk. Hitler, mollified, said he preferred a good understanding with England to a good military frontier with Czechoslovakia. The decisive element was speed; they were at the mercy of events, and an irreparable incident could occur at any moment. His solution followed by a plebiscite would prevent that.

The meeting was interrupted by two messages—one to Chamberlain reporting that Sudeten bands, supported by military forces, had entered Eger. Hitler commented that whatever the report, he could categorically declare that no German troops had crossed the border. The other interruption came when Hitler received a message that twelve German hostages had been shot in Eger, but this had no effect on the deliberations except to send Hitler off on an ever-ready tirade against the Czechs and the difficulties he was experiencing in refraining from military measures.

The talk continued in a more subdued tone on the question of plebiscites, the imminent danger of incidents, and a bolshevik takeover of Prague—any of which could lead, Hitler said, to military intervention. Then it was readily agreed the two men would meet again the next day, and Hitler at Chamberlain's urging said he would do his best to prevent any incident but in return demanded of Chamberlain that the Czechs be spoken to sharply to the same end.

The meeting ended a little before eight o'clock. It was scheduled to resume at noon the following day, September 23, but on reflection Chamberlain was not disposed to meet Hitler again without putting in writing his cautious displeasure over Hitler's performance of the day before. So instead of crossing the Rhine he dispatched a letter explaining that he was ready to present Hitler's proposals to the Czech government, but the difficulty lay in the provision that the territory be occupied by German troops in the immediate future.

I do not think you have recognized the impossibility of my putting forth any plan unless it will be considered by public opinion in my country, in France and indeed in the world generally as carrying out the principles agreed upon in an orderly fashion and free from threat of force. I am sure that an attempt to occupy forthwith by German troops the areas which will become part of the Reich at once in principle and very shortly afterwards by delimitation would be condemned as an unnecessary display of force.

He added that there was no doubt if German troops did move, then the Czechoslovakian government would have no option but to order its army to resist.[12]

He repeated that everyone was agreed the Sudetenland was to go to the Reich, and the immediate question was how to maintain peace and order pending final arrangements for transfer. He was ready to ask the Czechoslovak government whether this might not be accomplished by the Sudeten Germans themselves by creation of a suitable force or by forces already at hand under supervision of neutral observers. The Czechoslovak government, he said, could not be expected to withdraw their armed forces and police with an invasion threatening. But if his plan seemed acceptable he would urge them to withdraw from areas where Sudeten Germans were in a position to maintain order. It was a polite, sensible, and wholly ineffectual letter made to order for the man who had made his career blasting the Versailles treaty and the virtuous pretensions of the democracies.

Hitler's reply was prompt and uncompromising. It followed a few hours after he received Chamberlain's letter; Hitler reminded him that once before, in 1918, Germany had accepted promises in the form of President Wilson's Fourteen Points and then had been shamefully betrayed.

What interests me is not the recognition of the principle that this territory is to go to Germany, but solely the realization of this principle, and the realization that puts an end in the shortest possible time of the sufferings of the unhappy victims of Czech tyranny and at the same time corresponds to the dignity of a great power. I can only emphasize to Your Excellency that these Sudeten Germans are not going back to the German Reich in virtue of the gracious or benevolent sympathy of other nations, but on the ground of their own will based on the right to self-determination of the nation, and of the irrevocable decision of the German Reich to give effect to this will.

The Czechs had no justifiable cause for complaint. He had declared himself ready to allow plebiscites in the whole territory and corrections of the border under control of an international or Czech-German commission, and he would withdraw German troops from frontier areas provided the Czechs did the same. But he would not leave territory that must be considered as belonging to Germany without the Reich's protection. The Sudeten Germans could not maintain order alone because of obstacles the Czechs had put in the way of their political organizations. It was impossible for the Reich to refrain from giving immediate protection to this territory. Hitler wrote, "Your Excellency assures me it is now impossible for you to propose such a plan to your own government. May I assure you for my part that it is impossible for me to justify any other attitude to the German people."[13]

Hitler referred to his profound mistrust of the Czechs, a mistrust, he wrote, that "leads me to believe that the acceptance of the principle of the transfer of the Sudeten Germans to the Reich by the Czech government is only given in the hope to gain time so as to bring about a contradiction to that principle. . . . The German Reich is however determined by one means or another to end these attempts which have lasted for decades to deny by dilatory methods the legal claims of oppressed people."[14]

He closed with a convoluted but to Chamberlain's ears chilling statement that translated "either my way or war." He wrote: "Germany in any case has decided that if, as now appears to be the case, she cannot gain the recognition of the clear rights of the Germans in Czechoslovakia by way of negotiations, to exhaust the other possibilities which then alone remain open to her."

No time was wasted on a written translation, and the letter was delivered by Schmidt who translated it for the prime minister at the Hotel Petersberg directly from the German text. Chamberlain in his reply retreated, which was all he could do if the negotiations were to continue. His brief note brought to Hitler by Sir Horace Wilson and Ambassador Henderson at 6:00 P.M. assured Hitler that Chamberlain was ready to present Hitler's proposals to the Czechoslovak government. He asked that Hitler therefore provide him with a memorandum that he would immediately forward to Prague asking the Czechs to answer as soon as possible. He said that in the meantime he would be grateful for Hitler's assurance that no action would take place on the part of the German army, and he added that since acceptance of the proposals would be a matter for the Czechoslovak government he could be of no further use in Germany and would return to England.

It took some hours to draft the German memorandum that followed, and it was not until after dinner that Ribbentrop telephoned to say it would be available at the Hotel Dreesen at 10:30 P.M. The British delegation—Chamberlain, Horace Wilson, Nevile Henderson, and Ivone Kirkpatrick—meanwhile crossed the Rhine again to meet with Hitler, Ribbentrop, Weizsäcker, and Schmidt in a banquet room at the now nearly empty Hotel Dreesen. Hitler was friendly and courteous; he thanked Chamberlain for his efforts to find a peaceful solution, which Hitler said he knew had involved great physical effort as well as political courage. The Führer said he still hoped for a peaceful outcome, and if it occurred it would be largely due to the prime minister's efforts. Chamberlain replied that he was grateful for Hitler's words, and he had listened with hope to what Hitler had said of the possibility of a peaceful solution, but perhaps Hitler could tell him more about it together with the memorandum he had agreed to produce. Ribbentrop thereupon handed over the memorandum that belied all the friendly words. It conceded nothing whatever.

It was now after eleven o'clock on September 23, and the German memorandum demanded the Czechs evacuate some areas of the Sudetenland by 8:00 A.M. on September 26, with occupation by German troops of most of the rest by September 28. It was accompanied by maps in color showing areas to be taken over immediately marked in red, those where plebiscites were to be held marked in green. The plebiscites would take place under the control of an international commission before November 25. All installations—including rolling stock and military, economic, and transport equipment—were to go undamaged to the Reich.

Schmidt translated the memorandum sentence by sentence, and Chamberlain did not attempt to disguise his consternation. "With great disappointment and deep regret," he said, "I see Herr Reichsminister, that you have not in the least supported my efforts to preserve the peace."[15] The proposals he said were nothing but an ultimatum, and Henderson interjected "Diktat," the same epithet Hitler had used for years to characterize the Versailles treaty.

Hitler, apparently taken aback by Chamberlain's reaction, replied that the document was not an ultimatum and pointed to the heading, "Memorandum." But Chamberlain, Wilson, and Henderson now waded in and declared that the timetable alone was impossible; the time was too short, allowing hardly forty-eight hours for the Czechoslovak government to give the necessary orders and only four days to evacuate the area. The danger of shooting incidents out of which a European war was certain to develop was enormous. The whole document, said Chamberlain, was written in terms of dictation and not of negotiation.

At this point a note was brought in to Hitler by an adjutant. Hitler read it and handed it without comment to Schmidt for translation. It read: "Beneš has just announced over the radio that he has ordered general mobilization of the Czechoslovakian army."[16]

For Hitler the news could not have come at a better moment. His promise to Chamberlain that the German army would not be sent into action had included the escape clause "unless some extraordinary measures on the part of the Czechs force me to move." Here were the extraordinary measures. But he responded with the only show of magnanimity he would evidence during the entire talks. "My agreement that I would undertake no steps against Czechoslovakia while these negotiations were in progress I shall keep to despite the outrageous *[unerhörte]* provocation as long as you, Herr Chamberlain, are on German soil." The tension was broken. Not only would Hitler not respond immediately to the Czech challenge with the order to march, but also he told Chamberlain that for his sake he would make a concession. "You are one of the few men," he said, "for whom I have ever done that. The first of October will suit me for the evacuation to begin," and he crossed out the September 28 date in the memorandum and inserted the change. Then with a few minor corrections the memorandum was handed over for retyping.

As the negotiations awaited the final text Hitler remarked that the borders were very different from what they would have been had they been imposed by force, and Chamberlain said he was ready to forward the memorandum to the Prague government. It was 2:00 A.M. when the two principals said farewell, and Hitler again thanked Chamberlain most cordially for his efforts on behalf of peace, adding that the solution of the Sudeten question was the last great problem that remained open. "There need be no contention between us," he told Chamberlain. "I will not stand in the way of your pursuing your non-European interests and you can without danger give us a free hand in Middle and Southeast Europe." At some point the colonial question would have to be solved, but there was time enough for that and certainly no cause for war. It was an offer that stemmed from Hitler's convictions about how to conduct foreign affairs, though it had no appeal for Chamberlain. The official communiqué, issued September 24, declared the meetings had taken place in friendly spirit and that the prime minister had undertaken to present the German memorandum to the Czechoslovak government.[17]

From this point on the situation deteriorated rapidly. The only thing that had been agreed on was that Chamberlain would deliver Hitler's memorandum to the Czech government. The two sides were as far apart as ever, and the next move had to come from Chamberlain, who flew back to London on Saturday, September 24, as a British colonel, Mason-MacFarlane, flew to Berlin, bringing with him the map showing areas to be evacuated and the text of Hitler's terms. After landing in Berlin he motored to the Czechoslovakian frontier, arriving in the dark to walk ten kilometers through the barbed wire and other border entanglements the Czechs had erected to deliver the documents it took the Czech government only a few hours to decide to reject. Opinion had hardened as the Bad Godesberg conference went on, as was evident when the British and French governments told the Czechs "they cannot continue to take the responsibility of advising them not to mobilize," and the British minister in Prague informed the Czech minister of foreign affairs only that he was instructed to deliver the German terms.[18] Chamberlain, in transmitting the terms, included no advice as to whether to accept or reject them, expressing the hope that the Czech reply would be transmitted through him.

Whatever was to be done had to be done quickly. Chamberlain met with members of his cabinet and called a meeting in London the following day, Sunday, the 25th, with the French ministers. The barometer read *storm* and was falling. On the day he returned the French called up half a million troops, and a few days later the British ordered mobilization of their fleet, while SS and SA formations moved from the Reich into Sudeten villages as forerunners of the army's occupation.

On Sunday as the British and French cabinet ministers met in London the Czech ambassador, Jan Masaryk, son of the late Czechoslovakian president, informed Lord Halifax in a note that his government "absolutely and unconditionally" found the German terms unacceptable, adding: "We rely on the two great western democracies whose wishes we have followed much against our own judgement to stand by us in our hour of trial."

But the proceedings of the meeting of the British and French ministers at Number 10 Downing Street that began at 9:25 P.M. would have given him little comfort.[19] Including Chamberlain and Daladier, ten British and eight French ministers or advisers were present, among them sophisticated anti-Hitler if not anti-German observers such as Vansittart and, from the French Foreign Office, Alexis Léger. Chamberlain began with a concise account of the Bad Godesberg meetings, and Daladier said that though the copy of Hitler's memorandum had reached him only at 11:30 that morning the council of ministers had already unanimously rejected it. They had considered its terms in the course of the afternoon, and they could not accept the idea of suppressing the international commission favored by the British and French ministers, nor could they agree to Hitler's right to take the territory by force. The Czechoslovak army would resist, and a European war would result. Second, the French ministers had also unanimously refused to agree to a plebiscite in the green area of Hitler's map where the majority was Czech. This would result, Daladier said, in destroying Czechoslovakia, enslaving her and then realizing the domination of Europe, which was Hitler's object.

Chamberlain pointed out that the Germans were not proposing to take those areas by force, but only to take territory handed over by agreement. The troops would only be admitted to preserve law and order, which the German government maintained could not be preserved in any other way. The area marked in red would not necessarily be the final frontier, which would be determined later under a plebiscite under international control. In green areas where a plebiscite showed a majority not wishing to go to the Reich, they would remain Czech. Hitler had also agreed that in the red areas, where a majority would subsequently be found not to wish to go to Germany, he would not want them in the Reich. Hitler had even indicated, said Chamberlain, that in one large area shaded green he did not expect a plebiscite would give a German majority. He did not want that area but only wanted to show that the proportion of the German population was larger than supposed in order to obtain more considerate treatment for the German minority later.

Daladier pointed out that many democrats lived in areas to be left to the ax and executioners of Herr Hitler. It was essential to safeguard Allied honor by ensuring departure of those democrats and also of Czechs who wished to withdraw. The green areas where plebiscites were to be held coincided with the most important districts in Moravia, and if they were occupied Czechoslovakia would be at Germany's mercy. His understanding of the document subject to correction was that Hitler should immediately take over the red areas without an international commission, and if the democrats there wished to leave for Czechoslovakia, Hitler could reply that they were in his territory; as for the plebiscite in Moravia Hitler's demand amounted to dismemberment of Czechoslovakia and German domination of Europe. So the council of ministers had concluded.

Chamberlain replied that there was some misunderstanding; the areas marked red were not to be considered as permanently German. The areas to be ceded and the definitive frontier would be decided only after the plebiscite. Hitler had said he would agree to the plebiscite under the control of an international commission, and he would withdraw his troops from any area found to be racially mixed. The Anglo-French proposals had laid down that areas to be transferred should include those over half Sudeten, and this was the same proposal made by Hitler. The main difference was that the Anglo-French proposal had not contemplated immediate occupation of the red areas by German troops but had thought that would take place only after the frontier had been determined. Hitler thought that if matters were delayed in this fashion, disorder and conflict would result. The question of Czechs or German democrats wishing to leave the ceded areas and Germans wishing to leave Czechoslovak territory was to be settled later and arrangements made for an exchange of populations. The German military occupation would be confined to areas shaded red, and even if the eventual frontier had to be drawn inside the territory at present shaded red Hitler had said he would abide by such a result if the international commission so decided and would withdraw his troops. But, affirmed Chamberlain, he did not wish to spend too much time in this connection. Even accepting the objection raised by Daladier, what did he propose to do next? Daladier proposed that they should ask Hitler to return to the Anglo-French proposals agreed on Sunday, September 18.[20]

And if Hitler refused? This was the key question, and Chamberlain asked it. Daladier could only answer with a shrug of the shoulders. In that case, he said, each of the Allies would have to do his duty. Chamberlain pressed: What should be done in the hypothesis of a refusal? Daladier said he had no further proposal to make.[21] Chamberlain pointed out that Hitler had said the memorandum was his last word; if Britain and France refused, he would take military measures and be guided by statistical and military considerations. The conference therefore had to consider the probability that if the reply to the memorandum followed lines being suggested, Hitler would take it as a rejection and march into Czechoslovakia. What would be the French attitude in such an event? Would France declare war? Daladier answered that France would fulfill her obligations; it was because of the news from Germany that she had asked 1 million Frenchmen to go to the frontier. Chamberlain asked if the French general staff had a plan, and, if so, what was it? He assumed it was impossible to give direct assistance to the Czechoslovaks, so the French government would plan to carry on hostilities against Germany in some other area. Daladier agreed that direct aid could not be given but said France could assist Czechoslovakia by drawing the greater part of the German army against France.

Chamberlain expressed hope that Daladier would not think he was bringing pressure upon him, but it was essential to know the conditions before making any decisions. He would therefore like further information and would ask Sir John Simon to put certain points to Daladier. Simon said that the British ministers would like to be informed whether French land forces would invade Germany, and Daladier replied that General Gamelin would later give the conference a full technical explanation of the plans he had already drawn up. Simon asked whether the French troops called up to man the Maginot line would remain there without a declaration of war, or was it the intention of the French government to declare war and take active measures with their land forces?[22] Daladier said that would depend on many things.

Simon assured Daladier he was asking these questions not with the object of creating difficulties but because the British as close friends were primarily interested in what would take place. He asked a second question: Was use of the French air force over Germany contemplated? That would mean active hostilities with Germany. Daladier said he had considered the possibility of an air attack, and in all countries where fighting had recently taken place there had been air attacks. In Spain they had been violent, and though Franco had had air superiority for months and property and lives had been destroyed, it had not won the war. Daladier had not answered the question, and Simon tried again. He had merely asked, he said, what France contemplated might be the use of land forces and then in what way the air force might be used. Now Daladier answered both questions in a fashion. He said it would be ridiculous to mobilize land forces and do nothing with them in their fortifications and equally ridiculous to do nothing in the air.

The West Wall, the so-called Siegfried Line, was incomplete, and a land offensive should be attempted against Germany; through the air it should be possible to attack important military and industrial centers in spite of certain legends that had been spread abroad. But Daladier said he wished to speak more of France's moral obligations. He had agreed only a week before to dismember a friendly country bound to France. This, he said, was France's sacrifice to the peace of Europe, and like a barbarian he had been ready to cut up this country without even consulting it. The task had been hard, he said, and perhaps a little dishonoring, but this was better than beginning again where they had left off twenty years before. At what point, he asked, would the Allies be prepared to stop? He, too, was seeking peace, and if means could be found for Hitler to take over the areas the French had agreed to abandon, even if this added to French sacrifice, he would agree.[23] The Czechs were human beings and must be asked what they thought, and one concession he would not make, a concession, marked on the map (in Moravia), which had as its object the destruction of a country and Hitler's domination of the world.

Simon explained politely that his question had not been asked on the assumption that everyone agreed with Hitler's map, but as a practical matter—what, if Hitler's proposals were not accepted the French government proposed to do. If the answer were that France proposed to fight, they must have decided by what broad methods they proposed to open the struggle. Daladier thought a commission might be set to work with a time limit of a week to ten days, at the end of which German troops would occupy areas where the Sudeten inhabitants were a definite majority; or an international commission would permit the Czechs to return from their fortifications avoiding retirement before a German invasion. This would be a progressive invasion as a result of a decision by an international commission, as had been done after the last war. He, too, hated war, and the commission should be set up with a time limit so districts would be evacuated within a week and peacefully occupied by German troops.

In the present circumstance the Czechoslovak troops would not evacuate those districts without fighting. The principle of granting autonomy to the Sudeten population was painful to the French government, but it could be accepted. He could not accept, however, Hitler's proposals for the green areas, particularly those relating to Moravia. The red areas might be turned over to the Germans under an international commission within a week.

Chamberlain merely said that though the proposal sounded extremely reasonable, he was sure Hitler would turn it down. He did not think an international commission could be assembled and carry out its assignment within a few days. Hitler had said he had no satisfaction for twenty years and was determined to reach a solution at once. He had postponed action as a result of Chamberlain's efforts but only for a few days and would not accept further delay in Chamberlain's opinion.

The prime minister asked what France and Britain would do, faced with a German invasion as they well might be within two or three days? The Germans with their usual thoroughness had taken every step to effect a rapid conquest, and their advance might go at a more rapid pace than had been contemplated, past Prague and to the frontier they had laid down for themselves. The Reich must know what attitude the French government intended to take. They could mobilize and await events, but Daladier had indicated the French plan was to undertake offensive operations against the Siegfried Line and bomb German factories and military centers. Chamberlain wished to speak quite frankly and say the British government had received a disturbing account of the condition of the French air force and the capacity of French factories to maintain supplies for it after likely heavy losses in the early days of a war. What would happen if war had been declared and a rain of bombs descended on Paris, French industrial centers, and airdromes? Could France defend itself and make an effective reply? What assurances had she received from Russia? The British government had received disturbing news about the probable Russian attitude. The tone of the French press did not sound bellicose and gave the impression France was not prepared for war in a few days. It would be poor consolation if in fulfillment of all obligations France attempted to come to the assistance of its friend and found herself unable to keep up resistance and collapsed.

Daladier was glad to reply to these questions, he said, and in return asked questions of his own. Was the British government ready to give in and accept Hitler's proposals? Was it ready to bring pressure on Prague that would lead to the disappearance of Czechoslovakia? It was not in certain newspapers where real public opinion was to be sought but in the attitude of those who, despite a first reaction of surprise, had well understood why the Sudeten region had to be sacrificed to peace, but who would not understand why a weak people should be delivered to an adversary superior in numbers. A million Frenchmen had manned the borders and the barracks without hesitation—that was the real exposition of the French national statement. If Hitler put forward demands, must we agree to them? He would then be master of Europe and after Czechoslovakia would come Romania and Turkey. He might land in Ireland. He was ready to agree to measures of conciliation that were in accord with moral sentiment, but a moment came to call a halt and that moment, in his opinion, had come.

The question of French aviation, Daladier said, had been raised many times before. One visitor who had been a general in the British army had declared the French air force did not exist and cited figures. Daladier admitted the French air force was inferior to its German counterpart in pilots and material, but France was perfectly capable of mobilizing an air force and attacking Germany. As for Russia he understood it had five thousand planes, at least eight hundred of which had been sent to Spain, and wherever they arrived they had put German and Italian planes out of action. Two hundred Russian planes had been sent to Czechoslovakia, flown by Czech pilots, and French observers thought them good. Russian production was roughly equivalent to that of Germany.[24]

The Allies, the premier averred, were too modest. Britain did not talk of its navy, and the German fleet was inferior to the French, but the main question was whether the British government intended to accept Hitler's demands. If so, they should at least send for a representative of the Czech government.

Sir Samuel Hoare, secretary of state, said carefully that he did not disagree with much of what Daladier said, but asked if war broke out tomorrow what steps could be taken by Britain and France to prevent Czechoslovakia from being overrun? Naval action was slow; Russia might have many planes, but was it certain what it would do? Would it come in with the full force of its aviation? At this point Daladier indicated it would. Whatever action would be taken, Hoare nonetheless figured, would be slow in its effect, and within a few weeks the greater part of Czechoslovakia would be destroyed. Therefore in his view the action of His Majesty's Government would greatly depend on the answer to the question of how the overrunning and destruction of Czechoslovakia could be prevented.

Daladier asked three more questions: Did Britain accept Hitler's plan? Did Britain expect to bring pressure on the Czechoslovak government to accept Hitler's plan when Daladier knew Britain would certainly not do so? Did His Majesty's Government think France should do nothing?

Chamberlain replied that as to the first question, it was not for the British or French governments to accept Hitler's proposals; that was a matter for the Czechoslovak government. As for the second questions, he had received the preliminary reply from the Czechoslovak government but understood it did not wish any action until sent a more detailed document. The Allies could not exert pressure on the Czechoslovak government since they had no means to compel it to reverse its decision. Britain was concerned with what would happen when that decision was transmitted to Hitler. As for the third question, that was a matter for the French government to decide. What it decided would entail serious consequences for Britain. He asked if it would be possible for Gamelin to come to London the next day, and Daladier said it would. Chamberlain said he had asked his cabinet to return for consultation after the present meeting and asked the French minister if he would object to withdrawing for half an hour while the British cabinet met. This it did, and the decision was made to adjourn until the following day, September 26, when Gamelin would be asked to attend.[25] It was on the evening of that day that Hitler was to deliver a speech to the Reichstag, and to prevent, if possible, his taking an irretrievable step toward war Chamberlain again dispatched a note with Sir Horace Wilson. Chamberlain knew the Czechoslovak government would turn down what Hitler had repeatedly made clear was his last word, and he also knew Hitler would be bound to react violently; the problem was somehow to keep the reaction short of military action.

September 26, 1938, was to be a long day for Chamberlain. He first met with Daladier and Gamelin, telling them of the Wilson mission to Hitler of which Daladier expressed approval. Then he met in late morning with the French and British ministers to sum up their deliberations in anticipation of Hitler's speech that evening. The Czechoslovak government, he said, was determined to resist; the French had said they would fulfill their treaty obligations, and the British would not see France overrun or defeated by Germany. But on the slender chance that peace could be preserved he had sent his confidential advisor, Sir Horace Wilson, to Hitler with a personal conciliatory message; he hoped Wilson would see Hitler in the course of the afternoon, and Chamberlain would ensure that moderate elements in Germany would be informed of Wilson's mission.[26] Daladier declared himself in full agreement with the prime minister and added that many Germans felt the same way.

Halifax spoke briefly on the situation of Poland and the possibility of the Czechs coming to an agreement with Poland over Teschen. Bonnet said Beneš had agreed in principle to renounce Teschen, but Polish ambitions might rise, and the British and French should jointly tell the Poles not to refuse so genuine an offer. Daladier added that the head of the Polish army, Marshal Smigly-Rydz, had promised in writing two years before and also given his personal word of honor that he would never permit the Polish army to attack Czechoslovakia.

Chamberlain and Daladier agreed that a notice could be given the press on Wilson's flight to Berlin, scheduled to start within a few minutes. Daladier's only objection was that the Czechoslovak government might feel itself neglected, and perhaps without divulging the terms of the Chamberlain letter to Hitler they should be told it contained nothing disagreeable. He therefore proposed they send for Masaryk and inform Prague that its position was in no way prejudiced.

With approval of a telegram prepared by Halifax, to be sent to the embassy in Warsaw affirming Anglo-French support for a peaceful solution of the Teschen problem, the session was at an end. The French could go home and all could await what Hitler would have to say.

Hitler viewing the new Reichschancellery. Left to right: Bormann, Hitler, Speer, Morell, and Hoffmann. (photo courtesy Bildarchiv Preussischer Kulturbesitz)

Hitler and Röhm in 1932. (photo courtesy Süddeutscher Verlag)

Hitler greeting President von Hindenburg; behind Hindenburg, his son Oskar, 1933. (photo courtesy Süddeutscher Verlag)

Hitler, Blomberg, and Goebbels, January 1933. (photo courtesy Süddeutscher Verlag)

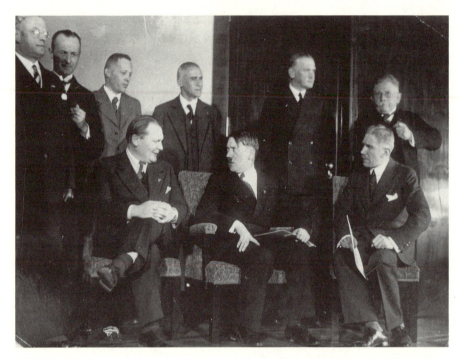

Hitler and his cabinet, January 30, 1933. Seated: Göring, Hitler, and Papen; standing: Seldte, Gericke, Schwerin-Krosigk, Frick, Blomberg, and Hugenberg. (photo courtesy Süddeutscher Verlag)

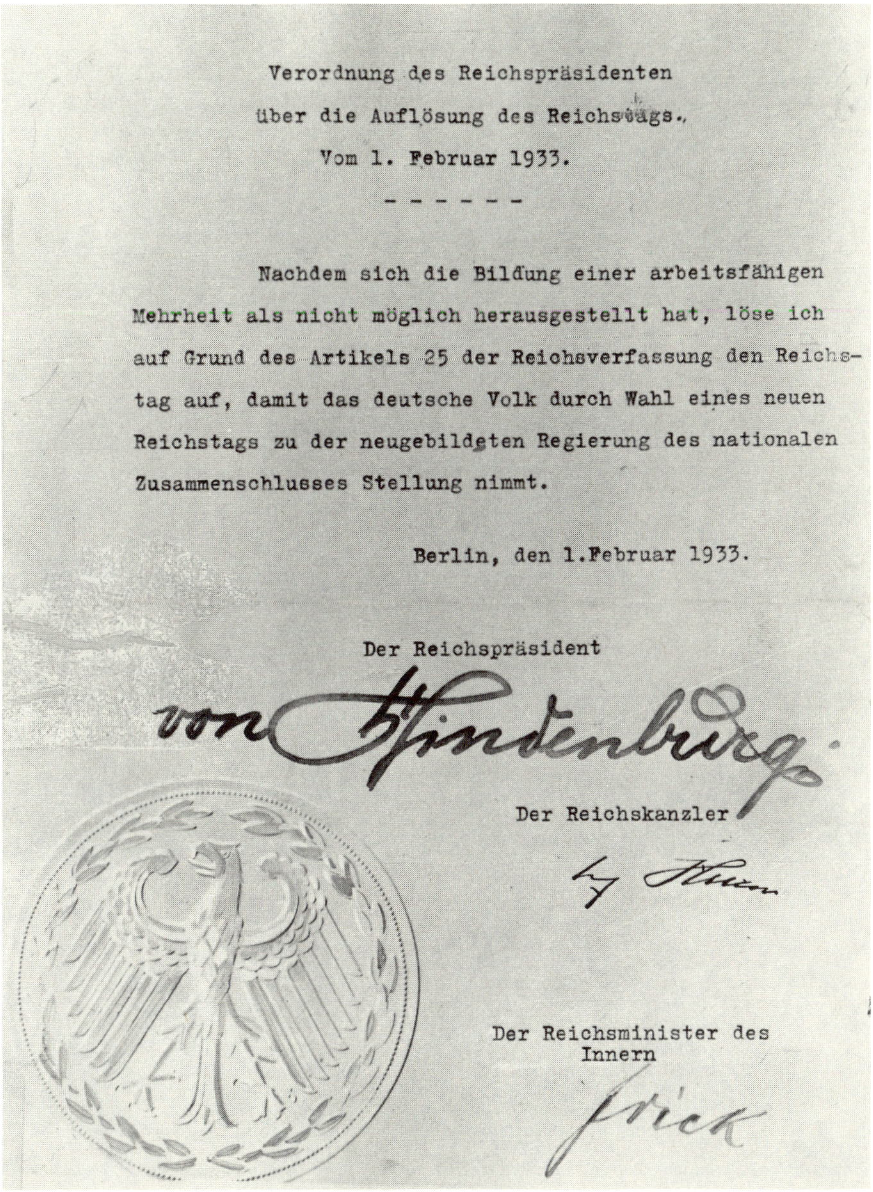

Verordnung des Reichspräsidenten
über die Auflösung des Reichstags.
Vom 1. Februar 1933.

- - - - - -

Nachdem sich die Bildung einer arbeitsfähigen
Mehrheit als nicht möglich herausgestellt hat, löse ich
auf Grund des Artikels 25 der Reichsverfassung den Reichs-
tag auf, damit das deutsche Volk durch Wahl eines neuen
Reichstags zu der neugebildeten Regierung des nationalen
Zusammenschlusses Stellung nimmt.

Berlin, den 1.Februar 1933.

Der Reichspräsident

von Hindenburg

Der Reichskanzler

Der Reichsminister des
Innern

Frick

Hindenburg's order, countersigned by Hitler, for the dissolution of the Reichstag, February 1, 1933. (photo courtesy Süddeutscher Verlag)

The burning Reichstag on the night of February 27, 1933. (photo courtesy Süddeutscher Verlag)

Van der Lubbe testifying at his trial, 1933. (photo courtesy Süddeutscher Verlag)

Hitler taking leave of Hindenburg at the memorial services for the dead of World War I, 1934. Left to right: Generals von Blomberg and von Fritsch, Foreign Minister von Neurath, Goebbels, Göring, Sepp Dietrich, Admiral Raeder, and Colonel Oskar von Hindenburg. (photo courtesy Süddeutscher Verlag)

Hitler speaking at the funeral services of President von Hindenburg, 1934. (photo courtesy Süddeutscher Verlag)

Opening of the Olympic Games, Berlin, 1936. (photo courtesy Ullstein Bilderdienst)

Mussolini's arrival in Munich, September 25, 1937. (photo courtesy Süddeutscher Verlag)

Hitler during his speech on March 15, 1938, in Vienna. (photo courtesy Ullstein Bilderdienst)

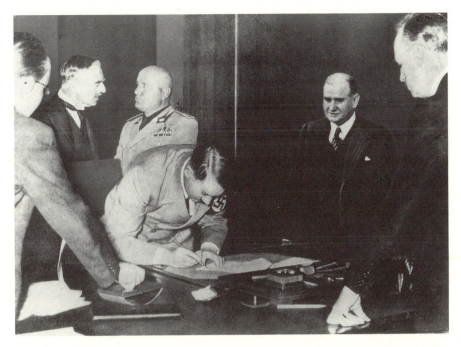

Hitler signing the Munich Agreement. Left to right: Chamberlain, Mussolini, Hitler, Daladier, and Ribbentrop, 1938. (photo courtesy Süddeutscher Verlag)

General Ludwig Beck in 1938. (photo courtesy Süddeutscher Verlag)

Kristallnacht: the night of the broken glass, November 10, 1938. (photo courtesy Ullstein Bilderdienst)

The signing of the German-Soviet Nonaggression Pact, August 23, 1939. Left to right: Ribbentrop, Hencke, Stalin, Hilger, and Molotov. (photo courtesy Ullstein Bilderdienst)

Hitler as he heard the report of the French surrender in 1940. (photos courtesy Süddeutscher Verlag)

Soviet Foreign Minister Molotov during his visit to Berlin, 1940, with Gustav Hilger of the German Embassy in Moscow and Hitler. (photo courtesy Süddeutscher Verlag)

Hitler in front of the Eiffel Tower, June 1940. (photo courtesy Süddeutscher Verlag)

Signing of the Three-Power Pact, September 27, 1940. Left to right: Japanese Ambassador Kurusu, Ciano, Hitler, and Ribbentrop. (photo courtesy Süddeutscher Verlag)

Left to right: Keitel, Brauchitsch, Hitler, and Halder at Hitler's headquarters, July 21, 1941, four weeks after the beginning of the Russian campaign. (photo courtesy Süddeutscher Verlag)

Slovakian President Tiso with Hitler, October 1941. (photo courtesy Süddeutscher Verlag)

Hitler with Ciano accompanied by Hitler's adjutant, Colonel Schmidt, Ribbentrop, and SS Captain Schulze at the Wolfschanze, October 27, 1941. (photo courtesy Süddeutscher Verlag)

Generals Paulus and Seydlitz in Stalingrad, summer 1942. (photo courtesy Ullstein Bilderdienst)

Hitler and Field Marshal von Manstein, July 1942. (photo courtesy Süddeutscher Verlag)

Hitler greeting just-named Field Marshal Rommel in the Berlin Sportpalast, September 1942. (photo courtesy Süddeutscher Verlag)

Hitler and Speer, December 10, 1942. (photo courtesy Süddeutscher Verlag)

German soldiers just prior to surrender at Stalingrad, February 1943. (photo courtesy Ullstein Bilderdienst)

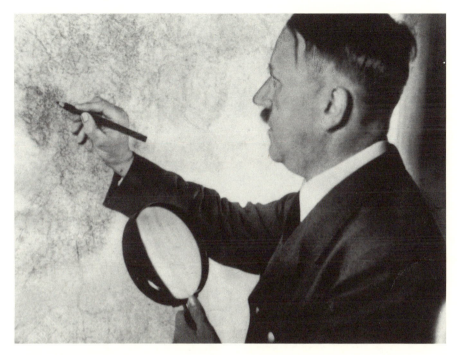

Hitler at the Wolfschanze a few days before the Stalingrad surrender. (photo courtesy
Süddeutscher Verlag)

Hitler, accompanied by a doctor, greeting wounded soldiers ten weeks after the Stalingrad defeat, March 21, 1943. (photo courtesy Süddeutscher Verlag)

Hitler greeting Heinrich Himmler in the Wolfschanze, East Prussia, October 1943. (photo courtesy Süddeutscher Verlag)

Hitler and Göring in Berchtesgaden on the day of the Allied invasion, June 6, 1944. (photo courtesy Süddeutscher Verlag)

Hitler at the Wolfschanze, July 15, 1944 with (left to right) Stauffenberg, Admiral von Putkammer, and Field Marshal Keitel. (photo courtesy Süddeutscher Verlag)

Hitler after the attempt on his life, July 20, 1944, with Mussolini, Bormann, Dönitz, Göring, and others. (photo courtesy Süddeutscher Verlag)

Hitler's barracks after the attempt on his life, July 20, 1944. (photo courtesy Süddeutscher Verlag)

Field Marshal Edwin von Witzleben appearing before the court in Berlin after the July 20, 1944, attempt on Hitler's life. (photo courtesy Ullstein Bilderdienst)

Hitler at a ceremony awarding Iron Crosses to Hitler Youths, Berlin, April 20, 1945. (photo courtesy Süddeutscher Verlag)

One of the last photographs taken of Hitler, Berlin, spring 1945. (photo courtesy Süddeutscher Verlag)

Purportedly the last photograph of Hitler, viewing the ruins with his adjutant Julius Schaub, April 1945. (photo courtesy Süddeutscher Verlag)

A German prisoner of war reads the headlines announcing Hitler's death in *Stars and Stripes*, May 3, 1945. (photo courtesy Süddeutscher Verlag)

11

The Agreement

After the meeting in Bad Godesberg and the awkward sessions with the French in London, Chamberlain was determined to do more than wait. It was to ward off the worst that he wrote his letter to Hitler. As tactfully as possible he informed the Führer that the Czechoslovak government, while adhering to acceptance of the proposals for transfer of Sudeten German areas, regarded as unacceptable the proposal for immediate evacuation of those areas and immediate occupation by German troops before terms of cession had been negotiated or even discussed. He reminded Hitler that he had thought this would be condemned as an unnecessary display of force, that the Czechoslovak government had pointed out that Hitler's proposals went far beyond what had been agreed to in the Anglo-French plan, and the country would be deprived of its national existence, yielding large portions of its carefully prepared defense positions and without time to prepare new ones. The whole process of moving the population would be reduced to panic-stricken flight.

He reminded Hitler that the Czech government still accepted the proposals for transfer of Sudeten areas. A settlement by negotiation remained possible, and he suggested that German and Czechoslovakian representatives meet to discuss the way in which territory was to be handed over. Such discussions could be completed in a short time, and he was ready for the British government to be represented if the two principal parties wished it. He ended with a personal appeal: "Convinced that your passionate wish to see the Sudeten question promptly and satisfactorily settled without incurring the human misery and suffering that would inevitably follow on a conflict, I most earnestly urge you to accept my proposal."

Chamberlain did not stop there. Through Halifax he sent a telephone message for Sir Horace Wilson that since Wilson left, the French had definitely stated they would support Czechoslovakia by effective measures if that country was attacked and that Britain would be brought in. This was the alternative to a peaceful solution and should be made clear to Hitler. Halifax authorized a communiqué saying the German claim to a transfer of Sudeten areas had been conceded, but if despite all the prime minister's efforts Germany attacked Czechoslovakia, France would come to its assistance and Britain and Russia would stand by France.[1]

At five o'clock, three hours before Hitler was to deliver his speech, Wilson, accompanied by Henderson and Kirkpatrick, delivered Chamberlain's letter to Hitler at the Reichschancellery. With Hitler were Ribbentrop and the interpreter Schmidt. The Führer had already met with Sir Frederic Maurice, head of the British Legion, the organization of former British front-line fighters representing a group for which Hitler always professed admiration. It was the same bond he talked about between him and Daladier who had also been a front-line soldier in the world war. Maurice had offered to provide through the legion a nonpolitical group to oversee the plebiscites that were to take place, and Hitler had accepted.

The meeting with Hitler was extraordinary. As Schmidt ended the translation of Chamberlain's letter, Hitler sprang to his feet, shouting, "It makes no sense at all to continue to negotiate," and moved swiftly to the door, seemingly on the point of leaving the rest of them. But he returned to his chair, saying it was a question of giving Germany something in theory but of delaying the moment, of giving it in practice. "On the first of October I shall have Czechoslovakia where I want her," he said. "If France and England decide to strike, let them." He did not care.[2]

Wilson said the prime minister was appealing to Hitler, to which Hitler responded it would be better to appeal to Beneš who had not the slightest intention of giving up an inch of territory. Henderson added that the British government would see to it the Czechs did hand over the territory, and Hitler gestured his dissent. Henderson repeated that His Majesty's Government would see to it and could put pressure on the Czechs and surely Herr Hitler trusted Mr. Chamberlain. Hitler replied that unfortunately Mr. Chamberlain might be out of office any day, and he wanted action, not words. Soon he would have four hundred thousand refugees from Czechoslovakia in Germany.

At this point Wilson asked if Herr Schmidt, who had stopped translating the letter as Hitler's fury exploded, could not continue his translation, and Hitler reluctantly gave his assent. When Schmidt had finished, Hitler, somewhat subdued after his outbursts, said he had already mentioned the sending of a Czech representative in his memorandum, but it must be clear that the representative would discuss not modifications but merely means of executing the terms. If, Hitler said, he could not be given the territory he would take it. Wilson assured him the British and French governments would ensure that the Czechs did hand over the area, and it was quite clear the Germans could achieve what they wanted by peaceful means. The conversation continued in a slightly more relaxed fashion as Wilson said the British hoped to influence the Czechs in the direction of a settlement, and he hoped Hitler in his speech would not slam the door. In return Hitler said he hoped Wilson would be present during the speech so he could sense the feeling of the German people. As the crisis had deepened and he had become more certain he would resolve it his way, he saw his role in a mystical light; it was no longer a Leader or a man who would be talking, it was the German people themselves.[3] What he heard was the echo of the old Nazi battle cry that had brought them all to where they were: "Hitler is Germany, Germany is Hitler," an immanent truth for the Austrian-born pan-German that duly elected democratic statesmen could not possibly match.

On their way to the door Hitler informed the British representatives that the text of telephone conversations between Prague and London had been intercepted and that Bcncš had told Masaryk, the Czech ambassador in London, not to cede an inch but to play for time. The remark was hotly denied by the Czechs, but Göring had told the same story to François-Poncet, and Hitler certainly believed it to be true.

That evening at ten o'clock Goebbels spoke the same language to the thousands of keyed-up party faithful assembled at the Sportpalast. Turning to Hitler he invoked the formulas that had brought them all to this peak of exaltation and communion:

> You can rely on your Volk, just as your Volk can rely on you. As one man they stand solidly behind you. We know that no threat and no pressure no matter where they come from can ever turn you from your and our implacable demand for justice . . . the German people with rock-bound conviction are one with you. Now in the hour of solemn decision we repeat before you with full and strong hearts: "Führer order: we follow. We greet you, my Führer, with the old battle greeting: Adolf Hitler, Sieg Heil," The Führer speaks.

And Hitler had every reason to be in top form. The audience that included foreign diplomats and journalists from all over the world was ready to hang on every word that would either send another generation back to the slaughter that had ended twenty years before or bring in a time of peace.

From his opening sentences Hitler made plain the time had come to take over the Sudetenland. He began by reminding his audience that on February 20, before the invasion of Austria, when talking to the Reichstag deputies he had made unconditional demands on behalf of the 10 million Germans still outside the Reich. The German nation, he said, had heard and understood him. One man, Schuschnigg, had not understood and had been swept away. A second time at the Nuremberg party day he had made this same demand, and again the nation had heard him. "Today," he said, "I come before you and for the first time speak before the German Volk itself. . . . The world should have no room left for doubt; now not a Führer or a man speaks, now the entire German Volk speaks. . . . If I am now the speaker for this German Volk then I know: At this very moment a millionfold Volk joins in my every word."

The question, he said, was not so much Czechoslovakia, it was Herr Beneš, and Hitler launched into his familiar attack on what had produced this man who incarnated the complex of troubles. It was the Versailles treaty and the rejection of Hitler's innumerable offers for European peace that had forced him to build up the Wehrmacht. He had repeatedly proposed disarmament, and when those offers were refused Germany too had to be armed. The Reich could be proud of its Wehrmacht. He had seen to it that the new army was equipped with the most modern weapons, he had ordered his friend Göring to build for him an air force to protect Germany against any possible attack so the Reich had the best air and tank defense on the face of the earth. Nor, he said, had he neglected his efforts for peace. His pact with Poland was worth more than all the drivel of the Geneva peace palace [home of the League of Nations], and it had been made possible because Poland was governed not by a democracy but by a man. He and this man, Pilsudski, in one short year had reached an agreement that banished the threat of war for at least a decade. Hitler had also, he said, tried to establish good and lasting relations with other nations and given guarantees to Western countries and bordering states. He had voluntarily renounced a naval competition with Britain to give her a feeling of security. He had not done that because he could not build up a fleet, but only to ensure a lasting peace between both peoples. But a prediction was part of this agreement. "It is not a matter for one side to say: 'I don't ever want to wage war again and to this end I voluntarily limit my weapons to 35%,' and for the other to declare: 'If it pleases me I will make war from time to time.' That won't do." Such a treaty was only morally justified when both peoples promised one another never to wage war. "Germany has the will to do this. We all hope that those in England who gain the upper hand will have the same determination."

Hitler said he had gone further. After the return of the Saarland he had said there remained no more differences with France. "The question of Alsace-Lorraine no longer exists for us. It is a borderland, the people in this land have never in the last decades been asked their opinion. We have the feeling that the inhabitants of this province would be happiest if it was not again fought over. We all want no war with France. We want nothing from France—nothing."

These were adroit ploys to neutralize public opinion in the only countries that might decide to defend Czechoslovakia. The reminder to France that it had never permitted a plebiscite in Alsace-Lorraine, to Britain that he had been ready to accept naval inferiority, to both that he promised to make no further territorial demands—all this left Beneš naked and alone in the sentiment of millions of the compatriots of Daladier and Chamberlain.

Thus having established the case for his generosity and readiness to sacrifice for peace he could turn to the main target of his rancor. Two problems remained. Ten million Germans had been left outside the Reich—no small number he pointed out; in fact it was equal to one quarter the population of France. And if France for forty years had never surrendered its claim for the few million French in Alsace-Lorraine, then the Reich had a claim on behalf of the 10 million. "There is a limit," he said, "where indulgence *[nachgiebigkeit]* must stop before it becomes weakness."

"I would have had no right to justify myself before German history if I had simply been willing to surrender the ten million. I would have no moral right to be the leader of this people. I have taken enough sacrifices upon myself. Here was the limit beyond which I could not go. How right this is was evidenced by the Austrian vote."[4] Now the final problem that had to and would be solved remained. "It is the last territorial demand that I have to make in Europe but it is a demand that I will not renounce and that I will, so help me God, fulfill."

He went into the familiar history of what had happened when in 1918 the insane, so-called statesmen of Europe tore apart the traditions, national will, and economic necessities of Middle Europe and arbitrarily created new states. To this Czechoslovakia owed its existence. "The state began with a lie and the father of the lie was Beneš." At Versailles, Beneš had assured those present there was such a thing as a Czecho-Slovak nation, and the Anglo-Saxon statesmen had not found it necessary to verify what he claimed.

> If they had, they would have been able to discover no Czecho-Slovak nation existed and that the Slovaks wanted to have nothing to do with Czechs. So the Czechs through Herr Beneš annexed Slovakia and to make the state viable took three and one-half million Germans against their right and will to be accorded self-determination, and as if that wasn't enough they had to take a million Magyars, Carpathian Romanians, and several hundred thousand Poles.... As Herr Beneš lied this state together he solemnly promised to divide it on the pattern of the Swiss cantonal system.... We all know how he dissolved this cantonal system: He began a regime of terror....[5]

The state was needed, Hitler went on, against Germany; a French minister of Aviation, Pierre Cot, had made this clear: "We need this state," Cot had said, "because from it the German economy, German industry, will be most easily destroyed by bombs." And this state now serves Russia as a port of entry.

Beneš, said Hitler, had ruined the Sudetens economically, and even the democratic world apostles could not lie that fact away. The Sudetens had the highest death rate of any Germanic group, their birthrate was the lowest, and their unemployment was the worst. This had gone on for twenty years while the Germans in the Reich had looked on helplessly. If somewhere a traitor was locked up and another who was cursing out the regime from the pulpit was arrested, then there was excitement in England and outrage in America.[6] But if hundreds of thousands were driven from their homes and thousands slaughtered that did not bother those elegant democracies in the least.

After praising Mussolini as the chief of the only great power in Europe with sympathy for the distress of the Reich, he promised that if ever Italy were to find itself in the same difficulties, he and the German people would come to its rescue so that not two states but a bloc would be defending themselves.

Hitler said he had told the Reichstag on February 20 that it was an impudent lie that Germany had mobilized, and it served to cloak the Czech mobilization, though Germany had not called up a single man.

> I had no thought of solving this problem by military means. I still had hoped that the Czechs at the last minute would see that their tyranny could not be maintained any longer. But Herr Beneš thought that with the support of France and England everything was permitted and nothing could happen to him. And above all: if everything else failed there was the Soviet Union.
>
> So his answer was shootings, arrest, imprisonment for anyone who failed to please him. In this way came my demand at Nuremberg. For the first time I spoke out on behalf of the self-determination for these three and one half million—almost twenty years after President Wilson's declaration—that must finally take place.

Beneš's answer, he said, had been new killings, new imprisonments, new arrests. The Germans had to flee.

Hitler turned to his dealings with Chamberlain. After he had made plain German patience was at an end, England and France had agreed that the only solution for Czechoslovakia was to free the German territory and return it to the Reich. Beneš, however, had found another way to circumvent the cession. He agreed the territory must go to Germany, but what had he done? Nothing at all except to drive the Germans out. And at this point the game was over.

Beneš, Hitler said, had hardly spoken when he began his new military subjugation, which was worse this time than it had been before. Ten thousand refugees fled one day, the next day 20,000, then 37,000, on and on until the very day in which he spoke 214,000 refugees crossed the Reich's border. Whole districts had been emptied, villages burned down as the Czechs sought with grenades and gas to smoke out the Germans. "But," said Hitler, "Beneš sits in Prague and is convinced 'nothing can happen to me because in the end England and France are behind me.' "[7]

Hitler said he had delivered in his memorandum the last and final German proposal to the British government. It contained nothing but what Beneš had already promised and was very simple. The areas that were and wished to be German would go to Germany, not when Beneš had succeeded in driving out 1 or 2 million Germans but immediately, and he went on to tell of the linguistic and ethnic basis on which the cession would be made through records existing for decades.

> Herr Beneš now says this memorandum introduces a new situation. In what way? Only because what Herr Beneš has promised, this time, for a change, must be adhered to! That is the new situation for Herr Beneš. What has he not promised in his lifetime! And he has kept nothing! Now for the first time something will be kept. . . .
>
> I have demanded that now after twenty years Herr Beneš be forced to face the truth. On October 1 he will have to give over this territory.[8]
>
> Herr Beneš sets his hopes on the world and he and his diplomats make no secret of it. They say: "It is our hope that Chamberlain will be overthrown, Daladier set aside and that turmoil will appear everywhere." They set their hope on Soviet Russia. . . .
>
> And here I can now say only one thing: Two men stand up to one another: There is Herr Beneš: and here am I. We are two men of different kinds. When Herr Beneš was creeping around the great peoples' struggles, I was doing my duty as a decent German soldier. And today I stand opposite this man as the soldier of my people.

Hitler thanked Chamberlain and assured his listeners that after the solution of the Sudeten German problem he had no thought of absorbing the rest of the Czech state. "We don't want any Czechs," he shouted.

> I have only a few things to make plain; I am thankful to Herr Chamberlain for all his efforts. I have assured him that the German people want nothing but peace, only I have told him that I cannot overstep the limits of our patience. I have further assured him and repeat it here: when this problem is solved there exist no further territorial problems for Germany in Europe. And I have further assured him that the moment when

Czechoslovakia solves its problems, that is, when they have accommodated themselves with their minorities, peacefully and without oppression, then I no longer have any interest in the Czech state. And that will be guaranteed him. We want no Czechs. But I declare, as well, before the German people that my patience is exhausted in the matter of the Sudeten problem. I have made an offer to Herr Beneš that is nothing but the realization of what he has already agreed to. Now the decision is in his hands: Peace or War!

I go before my people as its first soldier, and behind me, as the world may know, an entire people marches and one different from the year 1918! If then a wandering scholar [President Wilson] succeeded in injecting our people with the poison of democratic phrases—the people of today are no longer the people of that time. Such phrases act like wasp stings on us and we are immune to them.

In this hour the entire German people are bound to me: my will is theirs precisely as I see their future and their fate as the source of what I do.

And we wish to strengthen this common will as we did in the time of struggle, in the time when I as a simple unknown soldier appeared to conquer a state and never doubted of success and the final victory. Then around me closed a band of brave men and brave women. And they went with me.

And so I ask you, my German people: March now behind me, man for man, woman for woman.

In this hour we are all of one will. It is stronger than any anguish and any danger and if this will is stronger than anguish and danger it will defeat anguish and danger. We are resolved: Herr Beneš must now choose.

Looking up rapturously to the heavens, Hitler ended to the frenzied shouts of the twenty thousand party brethren present, chanting Goebbels's words: "Führer order: We follow."

And Goebbels rose again from his seat, turning to Hitler, saying: "My Führer: In this historic hour I speak for the entire German people when I solemnly declare: The German nation stands as one man behind you to carry out your orders; true, obedient and enthusiastic. Never again will there be a November, 1918, if you call upon us our people will go forth to battle firm and resolute and defend the life and honor of our nation to their last breath. That we swear unto you; so help us God."

As Goebbels finished Hitler got up from his seat raising his arm in an arch and then letting it fall slowly to the table as he said, "Yes."9 That was in fact what the handpicked crowd had declared to him at every pause in his speech. Goebbels had seen to that, and Hitler had given his audience his full repertoire of eloquence and venom. But the roars of approval he heard, as he would discover the next day, were not the voice of the German people; it was Chamberlain who had heard that, when he drove through Cologne to Bad Godesberg.

The hubris of his Sportpalast performance carried over to the letter Hitler wrote to Chamberlain, which he gave to Sir Horace Wilson the next morning when Wilson came to the Reichschancellery. The letter was an elaboration of points Hitler made in his speech of the night before, written in the same belligerent tone.[10] The Prague government, he wrote, asserted that the proposals in his memorandum of September 23 went far beyond the concessions made by the British and French and would deprive Czechoslovakia of any guarantee of its national existence. "This assertion is based on the Czechs' surrender of the greater part of their prepared defense system before they have been able to provide new measures of their military protection. In this fashion the military and economic independence of the country would be done away with. And the plebiscite I proposed would result in a panicky exodus. I must say plainly that I can make no sense of this entire argument and can't even see it as being seriously meant."

He went on to say that Prague simply ignored the fact that his proposals in no way involved one-sided German measures or the use of force but instead relied on the one hand on a free and uninfluenced vote and on the other hand on the results of deliberations of a German-Czech commission. In the same way, the exact demarcation of the border of the area where the voting would take place, as well as the voting itself, would be removed from any one-sided German control. Other details, too, would be reserved for the German-Czech commission. The Czechs had already agreed to the separation of the area, and the immediate occupation by German contingents was a security measure to make sure the final determinations would be made quietly and smoothly. These measures were indispensable. If the German government removed them and subsequent negotiations were to continue as had the usual dealings with the Czechs, the present disastrous conditions in the Sudetenland would continue for an incalculable length of time.

> After all that has happened, you will understand my not having the slightest confidence in contrary assurances of the Prague government nor would the British government be in a position to obviate this danger through possible diplomatic pressure.
>
> That Czechoslovakia would lose part of its defensive positions is an unavoidable result of the separation of the Sudeten area, to which the Prague government has already agreed. If we were to wait for the implementation of the final accord when the Czechoslovak government would have completed its defense system for its remaining territory, it would undoubtedly take months or years, which is the sole point of Czech objections.

But the country, Hitler continued, was not threatened in its political and military independence. His memorandum made clear the German occupation would go only to the indicated lines, and the final determination of the borders would follow in the manner described. Prague had no reason to doubt that the German military measures would be held to within their limits. And if they did, the British and eventually the French guarantees would be an additional guarantee of the strict adherence to his proposals. Moreover, he wrote, he could point to his speech of the day before in which he had declared that he rejected any acquisition of Czech territory, and he was even ready to give a formal guarantee for the territorial integrity of the rest of Czechoslovakia.

There could be not the slightest question of a threat to the independence or economy of Czechoslovakia. On the contrary, after the separation of the Sudetenland, Czechoslovakia would be more healthy and more unified than it had been. If, finally, the Prague government worried about the fate of Czechs in the occupied territory, Hitler could only express his astonishment. It could be sure that nothing whatever would happen from the German side that would resemble the measures the Czechs had taken with regard to the Sudeten Germans. Therefore, he said, he could only take it that the Prague government was using his proposals for occupying the territory with German troops to distort the sense and goal of what he was seeking to do in order to work up public sentiment in third countries, especially England and France, for unconditional support of Prague's purpose and the possibility of a general military conflagration. "I even leave it to your judgment whether you see this state of affairs as called for."

In conclusion, he wrote, he would like to take the opportunity to thank Chamberlain most heartily for the confirmation of his efforts "to impede such machinations and to attempt to bring the Prague government to reason at the last moment."[11]

Hitler was ready to explain to President Roosevelt, too, why he had to take the measures he proposed. They exchanged letters, Roosevelt citing among other reasons against a recourse to arms the Kellogg-Briand Pact of 1928 to which sixty-three countries of the world, including Germany, had subscribed. It was something of a routine citation for Roosevelt on behalf of a pact that would often be referred to but would never have much efficacy since it permitted every country to resort to arms in its own defense, the only reason ever given for going to war. Hitler's reply to Roosevelt reminded the president of Wilson's promises in 1918, which had been solemnly accepted by the warring nations, the subsequent shameful betrayal at Versailles, and their connection with the founding of the Czechoslovak state.

He went on to remind the president of the insupportable conditions of the Germans in Czechoslovakia, of the flight of 21,400 of them from the Czech terror, and declared he was certain that Roosevelt would recognize the patience of the German government and its desire for peaceful understanding of the possibilities to this end had been exhausted with the proposals in the German memorandum and that the keeping of war and peace lay with Czechoslovakia. Roosevelt replied that the question was not so much errors of the past but the fate of the world, and he renewed his plea for a peaceful solution of the crisis.[12]

What Roosevelt was doing was intended to strengthen the position of Chamberlain as well as to demonstrate American concern for maintaining peace, but it had no discernible effect on Hitler. What affected Hitler was something else. It was the response of the Berliners outside the selected audience of the Sportpalast.

In the late afternoon of September 27 long columns of the Second Motorized Division of the Wehrmacht coming from Stettin rumbled through Berlin on their way to Saxony and the Czech frontier—trucks filled with soldiers, motorized cannon, dispatch riders on motorcycles. The mechanized, fast-moving units of the Reich's armed might moving southward from Stettin toward Saxony and the Czech frontier drove for hours past the Reichschancellery. But the crowds on the Berlin streets were silent as the divisions went by hour after hour. Hitler had ordered the movement in the morning with the expectation that the patriotic fervor of August 1914 would be rearoused by their appearance, but the troops drove past silent crowds, some of them holding out their arms in the Hitler greeting. Nothing like the exaltation of 1914 was to be seen or heard. No patriotic songs, no shouts of "Heil." Even the deputy to the press chief, Alfred Berndt, reported: "The people on the streets raised their arms in greeting to the troops but they were solemn and silent. What was going on in their heads?" For a short time as they rode past the chancellery balcony, officers rose from their seats on the vehicles, stood at attention, and saluted Hitler; then the balcony was empty, and the salutes stopped. Hitler had the lights turned out and watched from behind the curtains of his chancellery window. Suddenly he turned away, saying much the same thing he had said a few weeks before of his generals: "With people like this, I can't make war."[13]

The euphoria of the Sportpalast was over, replaced by anger. It could only be the Jews who were responsible for this incredible apathy of the Berliners, and Jews would pay for it. The unshakable bond between the German *Volk* and the Leader who was proclaimed its voice only a few hours before had withered away on this gray, misty autumn day.

The international preparations for war similarly came from the top down: The British fleet was mobilized, the French reserves were called up, the Polish ambassador to Berlin was handed a map with the demarcation line between Polish and German troops on the invasion of Czechoslovakia, which had been prepared by the Wehrmacht. But nowhere in Europe were there huge demonstrations for war as there had been in 1914.

The only sound resembling a mass call to battle had been heard a week before in Czechoslovakia, when angry crowds in Prague that included Sudeten German Social Democrats had demonstrated against the decision of the Czechoslovak government to cede the Sudetenland and to demand that Beneš replace his prime minister, Milan Hodža, and his cabinet. Beneš had chosen for the job of leading a nonparliamentary government a general, Jan Syrový, who continued to make the crucial decisions. But he was working with brittle tools, as his state was crumbling. At a cabinet meeting of the Syrový government held September 26, two newly appointed Slovak members, Matúš Černák and Imrich Karvaš, agreed that while there was no resistance among the Slovaks, there was no prowar sentiment either, and the government had to make concessions to Slovak nationalism to win popular support. The Czech minister of Justice, Waldemar Fajuor, expressed agreement with them.[14]

Hitler had seemingly made up his mind to go to war. At the Reichschancellery tables had been laid for luncheon for the Wehrmacht commanders, and word went around that mobilization would be ordered for three o'clock. Everyone with the faintest excuse to be there, invited or uninvited, had come to the chancellery. Göring who, like the generals, wanted to avoid war, along with Neurath who was out of office but after all was president of the Secret Cabinet Council, though it had never been called on for advice, was ready to gird for war convinced that was what Hitler wanted; SS and Wehrmacht officers and the anxious foreign diplomats appeared one after the other to appeal for the last time for a peaceful settlement.

Mobilization was imminent, but the pressures on Hitler to accept the Sudetenland without war were building up. Göring, Neurath, and Weizsäcker were all against a war. François-Poncet, requesting an urgent interview with Hitler, explained to Weizsäcker over the telephone that the French government had instructed him to make new proposals that went far beyond anything yet suggested. The Italian ambassador, Bernardo Attolico, arrived at the Reichschancellery bearing messages of support and a plea for negotiations from Hitler's revered friend, Mussolini.

Chamberlain's message delivered through Henderson assured Hitler that the prime minister was convinced Hitler would do all he could to avoid war, that Chamberlain was ready to fly again to Germany, and if a meeting with representatives of France and Italy were held then all the remaining problems would be resolved within a week.[15] The British position was succinctly summed up by Wilson who told the German press adviser of the London embassy, Fritz Hesse, that the British government was ready to guarantee the Czechs would carry out Hitler's proposals, but their form made it impossible for a democratic country, especially France, to tell the Czechs to accept them. The plan was an expression of sheer power; the British government accepted it up to the point where military occupation began. Any other terms of occupation, whether by German police or English troops, were possible.[16] Nothing, said Wilson, would please the British more than to have the Czechs surrender of their own free will, but he saw no way to force them to do that.

At 11:00 A.M., François-Poncet arrived at the chancellery with a military map showing the districts to be ceded to Germany in bright red.[17] Ribbentrop was at Hitler's side and seemed to François-Poncet to be intent on diminishing anything the latter was saying that might lead to a peaceful solution. Hitler was well disposed to the ambassador; he considered him the ablest diplomat he had ever met, and he was impressed with his map, which had been drawn up by the French general staff. François-Poncet reminded him of how together they had saved the peace at a critical moment during the Spanish revolution, but he assured Hitler a conflict with Czechoslovakia could not be localized and that all of Europe would burst into flames. Did Hitler want to accept the opprobrium of a European war when his demands had been three-quarters met?

It was at this point that an SS man interrupted to tell Hitler that Attolico had arrived with an urgent message. Hitler left the room to return fifteen minutes later, saying to François-Poncet, "Mussolini, too, wants me to delay."[18]

The talk continued, with Hitler nervous and distracted. François-Poncet asked him if he, the ambassador, should report to Paris that Hitler remained inflexible, and Hitler replied he would give his answer in the course of the afternoon. Hitler's adjutant, Captain Fritz Wiedemann, later described the scene as Ribbentrop and Göring met in an anteroom before joining Hitler where he was talking with Attolico. Göring went up to Ribbentrop and said, "If there's war I'll tell the German people that you made it." The two men shouted at one another, and Göring told Ribbentrop he was ready to march if Hitler ordered him to and was ready to fly the first plane against the enemy, only he would see to it that Ribbentrop was in the seat next to him. "You criminal fool," Göring called him.[19]

Göring and the uninvited Neurath did their best to convince Hitler that he had already won his major objective, and Hitler slowly came to agree. Neurath pointed out that in any event Hitler could not occupy the Sudetenland in one day; he had to do it in stages. Chamberlain's and Mussolini's proposal for a conference could accomplish everything Hitler wanted.

Chamberlain had not only declared in his radio address that he was ready to go to Germany a third time but also sent the same messages to Hitler and Mussolini. At 10:00 A.M. on the twenty-eighth, on his instructions, the British ambassador to Rome, Lord Pugh, appeared at the Palazzo Venetia to ask Mussolini to support Chamberlain's effort to call for a conference. Mussolini telephoned Attolico to go immediately to the Reichschancellery, and it was there that at noon he delivered what was to be the final appeal to Hitler to stop his war machines. This time it would. Hitler said to Attolico: "Tell the Duce I accept his proposal."[20]

The peace was saved but not without last-minute skirmishes. Göring, Neurath, and Weizsäcker had drawn up a plan for the German occupation army to move by stages into the areas held by the Czechs. Hitler had glanced at the document and approved it. Ribbentrop had known nothing of this and completed a document of his own that was designed, purposely or not, to antagonize the European powers as much as possible with timetables and restrictions that could only lead to conflict. Weizsäcker told him tersely that Hitler had already approved the procedures to be followed and that nothing could be added. Ribbentrop was enraged and seemed to one observer obviously ready to try to reopen with Hitler the whole question of war or peace. But Weizsäcker instructed Schmidt to translate the document Hitler had already approved to be given to Attolico. Ribbentrop could only rage: Hitler had already given his assent to a practical timetable in contrast to Ribbentrop's impossible schedules and conditions that could have sabotaged the proposed conference before it started.

Henderson recorded the exact sequence of events on September 28. Hitler saw Göring and Neurath between 10:15 and 11:15. He then met with François-Poncet and was interrupted by Attolico's visit with the message from Mussolini, and when Henderson met with him a little after noon he told him he had postponed mobilization for twenty-four hours. After Henderson gave him Chamberlain's message they were interrupted by another visit from Attolico, who told Hitler that Mussolini was prepared to accept the British proposals for a four-power meeting and would be present. It was Mussolini who, at Hitler's request, chose the site of Munich, and it was to begin the next day, September 29, at noon, though it actually was 12:40 before it began.

Hitler met Mussolini in Austria, boarding Mussolini's train in Kufstein across the former Austrian border. Ribbentrop met Daladier at the Munich airport. Chamberlain, after landing at noon, went directly to the Führerhaus.

The meeting at the newly built Führerhaus on the Königsplatz opened officially with Hitler thanking his guests for accepting his invitation. This pleasantry was followed by a denunciation of Czechoslovakia, whose existence in its present form, he told them, threatened the peace of Europe. The need for immediate action was to become the drumbeat of the conference.[21] The number of Sudeten refugees, he said, had risen to 240,000; the flight continued, and the problem, he warned, had to be solved within the next days. At Mussolini's urging, he said, he had delayed mobilization twenty-four hours, and a longer delay would be criminal. The powers actually were not widely divided, he said; the main decisions had been made. It should be possible to evacuate areas to be ceded in seven days and settle all territorial problems in ten. In deference to public opinion in England and France he was ready to leave open the question of whether German troops should occupy areas where plebiscites were to be held if the Czechs did the same. But the conference had to act.

Chamberlain, in turn, thanked Hitler for his invitation and Mussolini for his initiative and agreed they must act. He said he was especially pleased with Hitler's statement not to resort to force. He was sure they would arrive at concrete results.

The first order of business was provided by Mussolini who presented the program given him by Attolico, prepared by Weizsäcker, Neurath, and Göring. The occupation would begin on October 1, and the guaranteeing powers—England, France, and Italy—would see to it that it would be complete by October 10 without damage to any installations. How this would be accomplished would be determined by a commission composed of representatives of the four powers together with Czechoslovakia. Areas in dispute would be occupied by international forces until plebiscites were held, and the occupation would take place in stages beginning October 1.

The atmosphere was charged but friendly. Daladier, too, thanked Mussolini, agreed with the need to act quickly, and accepted Mussolini's proposal as a basis for discussion. Chamberlain added that representatives of Czechoslovakia should be present since England could not give the guarantees required without assurances from Czechoslovakia. Hitler replied that the Czechoslovak government was already destroying installations, and the real question was how to get them to accept the proposals. What they wanted to do was delay until new fortifications were built and favorable economic decisions taken.

Daladier assured Hitler the French government would not permit that but agreed with Chamberlain that, as he cautiously put it, a Czech representative should eventually be consulted.

But Hitler would not tolerate a Czech presence at the conference and was seconded by Mussolini. Hitler said no Czech was at hand with authority to speak, and the real question was what would happen if the Czechs rejected the proposals of the great powers. *Great* was a word Hitler relished using to qualify his Germany since the acquisition of Austria and to emphasize the gulf between it and the Czechoslovakia of Beneš. Chamberlain pointed out that he could not give a guarantee before he knew whether it would be fulfilled and said other minor questions remained. For example, cattle were not to be taken from the area the Germans were to occupy. Did that mean that farmers were to be sent off but the cattle remain? Hitler's answer was that German law would, of course, be authoritative, but at present it was the Czechs who were driving out German cattle and not the other way around. The four powers must execute their authority with the Czechs and see to it that the terms of the agreement were held to. Daladier noted that in London he had already approved the loss of German territory without consulting the Czechs, and he was ready, if it made difficulties, to withdraw his proposal for a Czech presence in the interest of a quick solution. Hitler remarked that the Czechs only respected force.

In the event, the Czech representatives appeared but only to receive the finished agreement and to comment on it as they read the provisions; they were not permitted to change a word.[22] They were a forlorn group. Hubert Masařik, an official of the Czechoslovak Foreign Office, flew from Prague on the afternoon of September 29 and was met at the Munich airport by police and Gestapo who treated him, as he said, as though he was under police suspicion. He was brought to the Hotel Regina where the British delegation was staying, but the British were at the conference table a half-mile away, and it was not until some hours later that he could meet with a member of the British delegation, Ashton Gwatkin. Gwatkin told him little in detail of what was being decided, though Masařik had the impression the conditions would be much more severe than the earlier English and French proposals. Again the need for haste was emphasized; matters had to be concluded, he was informed, at the latest by the next day. At 10:00 P.M. Masařik and the Czechoslovak minister to Berlin, Votech Mastny, were brought to the Führerhaus where Wilson handed them the map with the demarcation lines and areas to be immediately occupied by Germany. Masařik attempted to protest, but Wilson twice told him peremptorily that no objections would be heard. The two Czechs were then left with Gwatkin while Wilson returned to the conference table, and, though Masařik and Mastny argued with Gwatkin for some revision of the treaty, Gwatkin told Mastny the British had already approved it and, no doubt covering his peremptory mission, went on to explain how difficult it had been to deal with Hitler. The Czechs, he made clear, either had to accept the treaty as it stood or deal with the Germans alone, and Gwatkin assured them the French were of the same opinion.

At 1:30 A.M. Masařik and Mastny were ushered into the conference room to sit down with Chamberlain, Daladier, Wilson, Léger, and Gwatkin. Neither Mussolini nor Hitler was present. The Czechs were given an opportunity to read each article and make comments, but that was all. In response to a question by Mastny about the status of the Czechoslovak members of the boundary commission Chamberlain said they would have the same rights as other members, and in response to another question the Czechs were told that perhaps British or international troops would enter the plebiscite zones.

But Masařik and Mastny had not been invited to discuss or remonstrate. They were informed again that no statement or answer was required of them, and Léger repeated that the four statesmen had little time at their disposal. On this same day at 5:00 P.M. Czech representatives on the international commission were expected in Berlin where details of evacuation of the first zone, which would take place the following day, would be spelled out. Chamberlain was visibly weary, and Masařik complained that he yawned continually. One of the

French delegates informed the Czechs there could be no appeal, no possibility of changing anything in the document they had just read. Everyone, including the late allies of the Prague government, was tired of the Czechs. Their reputation for procrastination was well established. In the minds of those at the conference they had lost any title to their national state, and no possible reason occurred to anyone to listen to their explanations of why they disliked what had happened to them.

The agreement provided for everything Hitler demanded: occupation of the Sudetenland in four stages, to be concluded by October 10; areas of predominantly German character to be occupied by German troops; the commission to arrange for plebiscites where necessary to determine final boundaries. Inhabitants of the region were to exercise their option of domicile for either Czech or German areas within six months. Britain and France guaranteed the reduced territory of Czechoslovakia against unprovoked aggression, to be joined by Germany and Italy after Polish and Hungarian claims were settled. The claims were settled, but neither the Germans nor Italians ever guaranteed the Czechoslovak borders for which Hitler certainly had other designs.

François-Poncet later wrote that Hitler failed to get everything he wanted at Munich, that instead of the brutal unilateral solution he had demanded at Bad Godesberg an international agreement had been worked out. François-Poncet and many others have also remarked on Hitler's surly reaction to the great triumph he had won. He was impatient and abstracted, cool to Chamberlain, unfriendly to Daladier, animated only when he talked with Mussolini. The humiliation of the Beneš government he had achieved, but the ultimate satisfaction of conquest was denied him, and the "Bolshevik aircraft carrier," which he said was Czechoslovakia, remained anchored outside the Reich. He was signing the kind of document he had often denounced, an international agreement in place of a surrender he alone imposed.

Months later, in August 1939, talking about Poland, he would say he hoped some swine would not again intervene for a negotiated settlement, which may well be an insight into the way he felt about Munich, though *swine* would not have been the word he would have used for Mussolini. Yet he said much the same to Schacht: "This fellow Chamberlain spoiled my march into Prague." Clearly he was unappeased by Munich.

Nevertheless peace for the time was saved. Chamberlain used the occasion to take advantage of Hitler's remark about wanting above all a lasting peace with England to persuade him to sign a joint statement in which both men declared that the Munich Agreement and the naval treaty Britain and Germany had signed were symbolic of the wish of both peoples never again to wage war against one another. It seemed to be as Chamberlain said when he returned to London waving the document at the rejoicing crowds that greeted him: "Peace in our time." And so it might have been, had he been dealing with anyone but Hitler. For it was Chamberlain who was the hero of the thousands of Germans who spontaneously greeted him after the conference as the man of peace and reconciliation. And outside Daladier's hotel, the Vier Jahreszeiten, more crowds gathered to shout, "Vive Daladier, Vive la paix," until Himmler ordered the police to disperse them.[23]

Although Hitler was the obvious victor at Munich, it was the opposition to him that the crowds represented, and the opposition was suddenly as helpless as the Czechs. Witzleben, Halder, General von Brockdorf-Ahlefeld (the commander of the Potsdam 23rd Division), and the rest had been ready to place Hitler under arrest if he ordered the attack on Czechoslovakia. A "flying squad" under a former member of the Erhardt Free Corps, Friedrich Wilhelm Heinz, had been formed to kill or take him captive in the chancellery, and the head of the Berlin police, Count Helldorf, who had lately joined the conspiracy, was to guarantee at least their neutrality. Even Brauchitsch thought that perhaps the time had come for action. But the Munich meeting put an end to such possibilities, even if Brauchitsch had ever issued the order for a coup. The plans had nothing of the precision of a general staff operation. No one knew exactly what would happen after Hitler was arrested or killed. Some kind of military dictatorship for a short period had general support—Göring seemed a possible candidate as a successor to Hitler—but the planning, such as it was, did not go beyond making Hitler harmless.

The meeting of the international commission held in Berlin on the evening of September 30 was the first of a series that was to cut Czechoslovakia to the provisional size Hitler had in mind. Meetings went on for almost two weeks; the last one that approved the final borders the Reich had insisted on was held on November 21, and by that time the chargés d'affaires had replaced the ambassadors and Czechoslovak sovereignty was a shadow of its former self with an uncertain future.

Czechoslovak representatives did not have an ethnographical map of the Sudetenland, so an Austrian linguistic map of 1910 had to be used, and despite François-Poncet's effort to persuade the commission to declare that a preponderance of nationality meant 75 or 80 percent, Henderson and Attolico, confirmed by Paris and London, declared it meant only a majority. In fact, no one really wanted plebiscites, which would likely lead to clashes, and the Czechs agreed to demarcation lines without plebiscites, and the lines were for the most part what the Germans insisted on.

The occupation as Hitler demanded at Bad Godesberg began October 1, and neither in those areas nor in the rest of the Sudetenland was any untoward incident reported. The army was welcomed by the Sudetenlanders with flowers and shouts of joy, as had been the case in Austria, and as in Austria the Gestapo came along and arrested thousands of former Social Democrats and Communists to complete Hitler's triumph. The Führer himself opened the former border at Wildenau near Asch as Zone 3 (Eger-Karlsbad) was occupied. Crowds of Sudetenlanders shouted their welcome to their deliverer from a long captivity while thousands of fellow Sudeten Germans began theirs.[24] A plebiscite held in December voted over 98 percent to be incorporated into the Reich.

The Czechoslovak government, though headed by a general, showed no desire to fight the Wehrmacht. At a cabinet meeting on September 30 Syrový said the choice was either to commit suicide or to be murdered, and no voices were raised in favor of another possibility—war. The Czechs, whether in the government or the army, saw their military situation as hopeless. Their strategic doctrine was based on alliances, and no allies remained. By accepting the Munich Agreement they would at least stay alive, if in a truncated state. Beneš resigned as president on October 5 and pointed out in a farewell broadcast that the Czechs and Slovaks would survive in a more homogeneous state, a hint that he, too, like the statesmen of Britain and France, had come to recognize that mistakes had been made. He went into voluntary exile in the United States to await further historical developments. The Slovaks and the Carpatho-Ukrainians demanded and were conceded autonomy by Prague; the Poles marched into Teschen, and Hungary was awarded Magyar districts in Slovakia and the Carpatho-Ukraine by a German-Italian commission whose decision was immediately accepted by the Czechoslovak government. In all, one-third of the population of Czechoslovakia had to be surrendered to the neighboring areas from which they had been unwillingly depatriated in 1919.

The Czechoslovak government could not do much else but accept the loss. The general staff agreed they could not fight the Germans alone, and a combined German-Polish attack was facing them. No fortifications existed opposite the Polish border—despite the dispute over Teschen the Poles since 1919 had been considered an ally and, like Czechoslovakia, bound to France. As for the Soviet Union it would give the Czechs no encouragement. Stalin was not about to go to war with the Reich, and while treaties were always a very minor consideration in his calculations he was not even obliged to fight for Czechoslovakia unless France took up arms. So the Czechs could only accept the diminution of their state and ascribe it not to mistakes of their own leaders but to brutal decisions of the great powers who sold them out.

Although voices of protest over the agreement were heard, it was greeted with jubilation in Britain, France, and Germany. Churchill was one of the dissenters; in a speech to the House of Commons on October 5 he called it "the first sip, the first foretaste of a bitter cup. . . ."

A crowd of over half a million welcomed Daladier back to Paris. He and Bonnet, who met him at Le Bourget, could scarcely make their way past the frenzied multitudes. Chamberlain, too, was ecstatically greeted in London. In a dispatch to the French Foreign Office the ambassador to the Soviet Union, Robert Coulondre, warned that Munich could result in a Russian-German rapprochement.[25]

Bringing the Sudetenlanders into the Reich marked Hitler's third great achievement in the work of reordering the map of Europe. Already he had taken back the Saar, annexed Austria, and now it was the turn of the Sudetenlanders who thitherto had been forced to live in the jerry-built structure blueprinted in Paris in 1919. Beneš had tried to delay the inevitable, and Hitler brushed him aside once the new balance of European forces reasserted itself.

Hitler was on a different wavelength from that of men such as Chamberlain and Daladier. He lived more spaciously in the past and future then he did in the present. The present was a continuous challenge, a confrontation, a trial of strength, and mainly an obstacle to be overcome, whereas the future was all his, a spectacular his will could shape. It was the thousand-year Reich, the greater Germany that would train Slavs and other lesser races as helots, with a many-domed Berlin eclipsing Paris and Rome, a shining mirage that reflected light on all his purposes. The Czechs were important only as an instrument in the hands of his enemies or as far as they were capable of being Germanized.

12

The Crumbling of Munich

The peace of Munich was hailed throughout the world but not by its chief beneficiary, Adolf Hitler. His displeasure with it was noted by people who, like his interpreter, Schmidt, were present at the signing and in the days immediately thereafter, and it was particularly evident in the speeches he made following what was regarded by almost everyone else as his greatest triumph since he became Reichschancellor. Not only did he get what he ostensibly wanted but also the Sudetenland was handed over with the full approval and obvious relief of the British, French, and Italian governments. Even the Czechs tried to put on a good face for what they had had to accept. Syrový formed a new government with a complete turnabout in Czechoslovak foreign policy. Beneš resigned and went into his exile, first in England and then in the United States. The former Czechoslovak ambassador to Rome, Frantisek Chvalkovský, met with Hitler on October 13 to assure him Czechoslovak policy would thenceforth be based on close collaboration with Germany. The fortifications had been surrendered to the German army intact. The Communist Party was proscribed, and the Czechs promised that no anti-German organizations would be tolerated in the post–Munich Agreement state. But none of this impressed Hitler. The aircraft-carrier mother ship was still afloat in the midst of what he thought of as the focus of German influence in Central Europe. The rancors still festering since his pan-German youth had not been assuaged by mere acquisition of the populations and territory he had demanded and been awarded.

For a few days the meaning of the Munich Agreement was rapturously mis-read as rejoicing crowds of citizens, certain they had been spared another great war, welcomed home their leaders. Daladier, who had profound doubts about the agreement, was greeted by the immense crowd shouting "Paix, La Paix!" when he landed at Le Bourget. Mussolini was enthusiastically acclaimed as his train crossed the Brenner Pass, welcomed by the king when he reached Florence and by cheering thousands in Rome. In London, Chamberlain worn out by his labors and close to physical collapse, responded to happy shouts of thousands of welcomers by waving a copy of the agreement he and Hitler had signed, declaring it meant "Peace in our time!" The House of Commons approved what he had done by a vote of 366–144, despite abstentions, which included thirty or so Conservatives—among them Churchill, Leopold Amery, Harold Macmillan, and Harold Nicolson. They were certain the Munich Agreement was a catastrophe. The first lord of the Admiralty and one of Hitler's symbols of British anti-Germanism resigned, and Churchill denounced the pact in a speech to the Commons:

> I do not grudge our loyal, brave people, who were ready to do their duty no matter what the cost, who never flinched under the strain of last week, the natural, spontaneous outburst of joy and relief when they learned that the hard ordeal would no longer be required of them at the moment; but they should know the truth. They should know that there has been gross neglect and deficiency in our defenses; they should know that we have sustained a defeat without a war, the consequences of which will travel far with us along our road; they should know that we have passed an awful milestone in our history, when the whole equilibrium of Europe had been deranged. . . . And do not suppose this will be the end. This is only the beginning of the reckoning. This is only the first sip, the first foretaste of a bitter cup which will be proffered to us year by year unless, by a supreme recovery of moral health and martial vigour, we rise again and take our stand for freedom as in the olden time.[1]

The Soviet deputy commissar for foreign affairs, Vladimir Potemkin, summed up the Russian view to the French ambassador to Moscow, Robert Coulondre: "My dear friend," he said, "what have you contrived here? I see no other possibility for us but a fourth partition of Poland."[2]

But Sumner Welles, the U.S. undersecretary of state, saw in the Munich agreement the promise of a new world order "based on justice and law," and President Roosevelt said he "rejoiced at the signing of the Agreement." A former British prime minister, Baldwin, said: "It was just as though the finger of God had drawn the rainbow once more across the sky. . . ."[3]

It can scarcely be doubted that Hitler wanted to thrash the Czechs. In mid-August he had told Ribbentrop he had firmly decided to use arms against them, and instead he had been maneuvered into accepting an international settlement by circumstances he could not control. The pleas of Chamberlain and Mussolini that he accept peacefully what he had threatened to take by arms and the revulsion of the Berliners to the display of motorized might on its way to the front forced him to agree to an international solution he had wanted no part of and the significance of which he proceeded immediately to play down.

Hitler's rejection of the agreement was immediately made manifest in his decree for the administration of the Sudetenland. It was issued October 1, the day he returned to Berlin, only hours after the conference, naming Henlein to the post of Reichskommissar for the newly acquired area. It made Henlein directly responsible to Hitler and completely ignored the accord Hitler had just signed with representatives of Britain, France, and Italy.

On October 9 Hitler's spleen burst forth in a direct denunciation of the individuals and democratic system he deplored in Britain. He spoke in Saarbrücken to an audience of workers on the West Wall and to Saarlanders who had lived for years under the French occupation.[4] He told the gathering he was talking to them "in these days of great events" because he was convinced no one could have a better understanding of what had happened than the men and women of the Saarland who themselves had known what it was like to be separated from the Reich and then be joyously reunited with it. For almost two decades the Saarlanders, too, had suffered a painful separation and then been overjoyed when, at last, the hour of freedom had struck that permitted them to return to their common greater Germany. Millions of Sudeten Germans had just gone through the same trials of separation and experienced the same exaltation. He said it was at the beginning of this year, twenty years after the collapse, that he had determined that the 10 million Germans outside the Reich's borders would return to the Reich. "I was fully aware that this return could only be enforced through our own strength; the other world had neither seen nor did it want to see that, contrary to the so-called right of self-determination, ten million people were separated from the German Reich and oppressed because of their Germanism, and it neither understood nor wanted to understand that these oppressed people had only one great yearning: Back to the Reich!"

He went on to make plain that the Reich was to be thankful only to itself—that is, to him—that the Sudetenlanders were indeed back in the Reich. "These international world citizens," he said, "who, of course, sympathize with every criminal brought to justice in Germany were deaf to the sufferings of ten million Germans. And today their world is still filled with the spirit of Versailles. Don't tell us that these people have freed themselves of it. No: Germany has freed itself of it!"

Several preconditions had been essential to bring about this solution:

One: The inner solidarity of the nation. I was convinced when I made my decision that I was the leader of a manly people.

I know that many in the rest of the world and some, too, in Germany do not understand that the Volk of 1938 are not the Volk of 1918. No one can overlook the great work of education that our philosophy has brought about. Today a peoples' community has developed from a strength and vigor that Germany has never known before.

[The second precondition for the success of the struggle was] the national rearmament to which I fanatically dedicated myself just six years ago. I am of the opinion that it is cheaper to arm before the event than it is, unarmed, to fall prey to events and then to pay tribute.

The third precondition was the security of the Reich. You yourselves are witnesses to a mighty construction that is being completed in this very place. I don't have to tell you about it individually. I need express only the conviction that no power on earth will ever succeed in breaking through this Wall!

In his fourth point Hitler paid tribute to his gaining the Italian ally:

We have also won foreign political friends. The Axis which people in foreign countries sometimes thought they could ridicule has proved itself not only lasting in these past two and a half years but it has demonstrated its staying power even in the most trying hours. We are happy that this work of 1938, the reincorporation of ten million Germans and some 110,000 square kilometers of land into the Reich could be consummated without bloodshed, despite the hopes of so many international mischief makers and profiteers. When I mention the collaboration of the other world in this peaceful solution I must, again and again, speak of the one true friend we have: Benito Mussolini. We all know what we have to thank this man for.

Hitler gave a cool salute to Chamberlain and Daladier without naming them. "I should also like to mention," he said, "the two other statesmen who troubled themselves to find a way to peace and who concluded the treaty with us that assured the rights and the peaceful world of many millions of Germans."

The democracies, he pointed out, had a built-in weakness. "The statesmen," he said, "on the other side want peace, we must believe them. But they rule in lands whose inner framework makes it possible for them to be replaced at any time to make room for others who do not have peace so much in mind. All that is needed in England instead of Chamberlain is for Mr. Duff Cooper, or

Mr. Eden, or Mr. Churchill to come to power, we know exactly what the goal of these men would be: to begin a new world war immediately. They make no secret of that, they say it openly."

Having duly referred to his cosigners Hitler returned to his theme that it was only the power of the Reich that brought the Sudetenlanders home and that basically nothing had changed. "The experience of the last eight months strengthens us in the resolve to be watchful and to neglect nothing that must be done for the protection of the Reich."

Nor were the Jews to be forgotten in their unholy alliance with communism. "We know, too," he told his audience, "that the Jewish international enemy that has found a political base and imprint in Bolshevism, now as before lurks threateningly in the background. And we know further the power of a certain international press that lives only by lies and calumny. That enjoins on us the duty of being watchful and aware in the defense of the Reich. At all times the will for peace but at any hour ready for defense!" Thus, while he wanted peace it could only come about through increasing the Reich's military might. "As I announced in my Nuremberg speech, I have therefore decided to continue to build up our fortifications in the west with even greater energy. Henceforth I will also include in the fortifications the two great areas that up to now have lain outside our defenses, the Aachen and Saar areas."

Rewards for the faithful Germans were already at hand:

> In addition I am happy to be able to cancel in the very next days measures that we had to adopt during critical months and weeks. I am glad that all the hundreds of thousands of our men can again return home and our reserves be again released and I thank them for the way in which they fulfilled their service and did their duty. I especially thank the hundreds of thousands of German workers, engineers and so on who have worked on these fortifications, ten thousand of whom today stand in your midst. You have helped, my comrades, to assure the peace of Germany! My special thanks, however, goes to the entire German people who have borne themselves so manfully.
>
> As a strong state we are ready at any time for a politics of understanding with our neighbors. We have no demands to make on them.

But he warned the neighbors against making any criticism of the Reich's internal policies. "We want nothing but peace," he said solemnly.

> We want only one thing and that holds especially for our relationship with England. It would be well if people in Great Britain would gradually put aside certain allurements of the Versailles epoch. We will no longer tolerate

the tutelage of governesses. Inquiries by British politicians about the fate of Germans or members of the Reich inside its boundaries are not in order. We do not concern ourselves with similar matters in England. The rest of the world would have sometimes grounds enough to be distressed by their own national practices or for that matter by events in Palestine.

Having told off his foreign critics he could again hold out his olive branch. "We ourselves have great tasks ahead of us, enormous cultural and economic problems remain to be solved. No people can need peace more than we but no people knows better than we what it means to be weak and delivered over to the mercilessness of others."

And now he could end in a paean of praise for what he had accomplished.

> You yourselves have had to endure so much suffering that you can under-
> stand that I am anxious about the future of this Reich. And I call upon
> the entire German people, too, to be always concerned and ready. It is a
> miracle that we have been able to experience a German resurrection in so
> short a time. It could have turned out differently! We should always remind
> ourselves of that and strengthen our resolve to serve this Germany! Man for
> man and woman for woman to put aside all personal interests the moment
> the overriding interest of our people and the Reich demand it.
>
> Today, for the second time I stand in your midst. Then the jubilation
> was an expression of your joy over your own return home. Today you know
> the jubilation of millions of other Germans who too have again come home
> to the Reich. With them we can join in devout witness to our beautiful,
> united German Reich. Germany, Sieg Heil!

Hitler had in fact accomplished a prodigious feat of statesmanship. He had reduced a bastion of French revanchism without bloodshed with the approval of onetime victors such as Daladier, short-sighted Poles, and even Czechs who, after the signing at Munich, were replacing the Beneš hard-liners. It was an achievement Bismarck himself could not match. But ten days after Munich and the radiant hope of peace in our time, Hitler had taken it all back. The Reich must be stronger than ever.

He received a succession of foreigners: the Czech Foreign Minister Chval-kovský, in Munich; the departing Japanese Ambassador Togo, at Berchtesgaden (where Hitler was presented with a decorative Japanese table as a gift from the mikado and in return gave Togo an autographed photo of himself); François-Poncet, who paid a farewell visit (he was leaving for Rome and looking forward to what he was sure would be a more agreeable climate, an illusion he would not long sustain). Hitler received the departing French ambassador on October 18, at the mile-high Eagle's Nest, in the so-called tearoom that Martin Bormann, Hitler's reverential secretary with plenipotentiary powers, had just completed for the Führer on the Kehlstein.[5] It was the most dramatic of Hitler's showplaces; it could only be reached by an elevator that rose through the massive cliffs to a summit where, when the weather was clear, the sweep of the Bavarian Alps as far away as Salzburg lay at the feet of an observer looking out of the glassed-in aerie. François-Poncet called the view "hallucinating," but Hitler did not much care for the tea house; his own visions were even more intoxicating.

Hitler, who had a mild fondness for François-Poncet, received him graciously, telling him how much he regretted the ambassador's departure but how little he thought the Munich Agreement was doing for world peace. He said he had hoped the Munich meeting would begin a new era of rapprochement, but this had not occurred; the crisis had not ended and, in fact, threatened to reappear. England resounded with menacing words and calls to arms, and he repeated the thesis of his recent speeches that the English considered themselves to have rights superior to those of the rest of the world. When François-Poncet pointed out that Hitler's talk at Saarbrücken had given the impression the sacrifices made at Munich had been in vain and had only served to whet the appetite of the Third Reich and to reinforce the arguments of the opponents of the treaty, Hitler replied that it was the British who were at fault. He had not uttered a word against France nor had he maltreated the Czechs. He had only asserted the rights of the German people that had been trodden underfoot. The ambassador told him the statesmen of Europe had to ask themselves whether the Munich Agreement would prove to be a dead end or whether it meant the democracies and the authoritarian states could collaborate on making a general peace and eventually restore Europe to a normal and lasting life. Hitler declared himself ready to sign a formal, written document with France guaranteeing their mutual frontiers and to make no difficulties about the Franco-Soviet pact already in force. But concerning arms limitation: While he had no objection to it in principle, he reminded François-Poncet that given Germany's central and exposed position in Europe where a coalition could readily move against the Reich, the latter needed armed superiority over each separate state among the possible attackers. Furthermore, if he entered into arms limitation talks, the English opposition would claim he was doing so in response to their anti-German agitation. His mind was not made up. He was ready at any time to consider taking up the problem of how war could be humanized. As for economic and monetary affairs, which he left to the experts, he was ready to further their efforts.

The two men made a friendly tour d'horizon of Hungary where Hitler said he had done Europe a favor by preventing the Hungarians from proposing a four-power conference to deal with their territorial claims. Such a conference would only have led to needless conflict between the sides in the dispute. Concerning

Spain, Hitler said he had never considered using her as a permanent threat to France. Spain needed good relations with France, as Franco had demonstrated during the September crisis.

This was mainly chitchat, but Hitler was also suggesting to an experienced diplomat that he, the Führer, might be more pro-French than pro-British and that he relied more on the goodwill of France than on that of Britain to forestall another European collision.

At the end of a meeting that lasted almost two hours, Hitler presented François-Poncet with a decoration that, as time went on, he bestowed on many representatives of the Axis satellites—the Grand Cross for Distinguished Service of the German Eagle.

Hitler, the onetime vendor of his own postcards, had become the uncontested strong man of Europe. Although the agreement at Munich determined that the four signatories would together define the final boundaries of Czechoslovakia, Hitler at this point could rid himself of such encumbrances without meeting the slightest resistance from Britain and France. No British Legion would patrol the streets of Czech towns when plebiscites were held because no plebiscites were held; no one wanted them, they could only lead to disputes and disputes to complications that it had been hoped the agreement would push aside. The Munich Agreement provided that the Hungarian and Ruthenian demands on Czechoslovakia would be settled by the four powers, but Hitler did not want that either. Southeastern and central Europe was his domain. The Reich, in the presence of Italy, would decide on Hungarian and Ruthenian claims against Prague and Bratislava.

The Czechoslovak state itself was threatening to fall apart. As Henderson wrote Halifax, none of its minority peoples wanted to remain under Czech dominance. The democracy so lavishly praised in the Western world had been operational far more for the Czechs than for their non-Czech countrymen. Slovakia was granted autonomy early in October, but, as often happens with such late concessions, this act for which the Slovaks had long been clamoring only served to incite demands for complete independence. Ruthenia, too, had been granted autonomy, but there too a surge of sentiment for complete independence swept through the province.[6]

No one in the Allied camp had had much good to say for the Czechs for a long time, and they fared no better after Munich. The British ambassador to Poland, Sir Howard Kennard, though increasingly critical of Foreign Minister Josef Beck for his demands on Czechoslovakia, nevertheless referred to Czechoslovakia as "the spoilt child of the Allies and of Geneva" and described Prague's seizure of Teschen in 1921 while Poland was fighting against the Soviet army as "short sighted . . . to use no stronger term."[7]

Hitler had undone much of the network of post–world war treaties, and what remained in the autumn of 1938 was the determination of both former victors and vanquished who had felt themselves shortchanged to make the most of the opportunities he had provided. Poland, under Beck's maneuvering, aimed to detach both Slovakia and Ruthenia from the Czech state. Hungary, which had lost more than 3 million ethnic Hungarians, more than one-third of the Magyar people, to its neighbors in 1920 (there was no plebiscite), now sought a cession of Slovakian border territory where 330,000 Magyars lived, and these demands included what a British observer called "all the important Slovakian towns and vital lines of communication."[8]

Even with the best of intentions it would have been impossible to define borders acceptable to all the countries concerned. They had former nationals in adjoining territories—the Hungarian government claimed that almost a million Hungarians lived in Czechoslovakia and more than one hundred thousand Slovaks in Hungary.[9] As a result of Munich, 750,000 Czechs became German citizens. They had the choice of keeping their land under German rule or moving to Czech territory without compensation from the Reich if they did decide to move, and few of them did; those who stayed had no minority rights whatever.

Every Balkan country had long-standing grievances against a neighbor's mistreatment of its fellow countrymen, and they all feared the emerging of new alliances directed against them. Poland, with 4 million Ukrainians, felt itself threatened by Ukrainian nationalism as well as by German and Russian designs and, despite its mixture of peoples and bucolic backwardness, liked to regard itself as a great power capable of dealing with the Soviet Union and the Reich on equal terms.

The Western powers at Munich had left Czechoslovakia and, with it, East Central Europe to German domination. Hungary had no choice, after direct negotiations with Czechoslovakia failed, but to turn to the Reich to obtain satisfaction of its demands on Czechoslovakia. Munich provided for the four signatory powers to arbitrate the problems of borders and minorities if Hungary and Czechoslovakia had not settled them within three months of signing the agreement. But the new balance of power was far more compelling than the paragraphs of the Munich accord, and when it became clear a few weeks after the signing that Hitler rejected the four-power conference, no one else wanted it.

What Hungary and Poland actually were seeking was a common border that would strengthen both countries against Soviet and German designs. Although Hungary proposed plebiscites in disputed areas, Prague was certain that what it was demanding would only mean the end of Czechoslovakia. The result was the breaking off of direct negotiations. Confronted by the threat of Hungarian military action, Czechoslovakia asked the German government to arbitrate in the hope that its acknowledged dependence on the Reich would help. And this time the Czechoslovak government was at least partially right. Neither Hitler nor the German high command wanted a common border between Poland and Hungary, nor did they want a Slovakia or a Ruthenia with ties to Hungary. They wanted the assertion of German dominance in the Balkans, and by acting with Italy as judge and jury in a case involving the Reich's strategic interests they could vastly improve that prospect.[10]

The two Axis nations were not in agreement over what to do. Hitler was not disposed to be generous to Hungary in the new situation. He never outgrew the deep Austrian-German prejudices of his youth. Although he detested the Czechs, he was not much fonder of the Hungarians and told the former Hungarian prime minister, Daranyi, when they met in Munich in mid-October, that Hungary had done nothing to evidence its solidarity with the Reich during the crises leading up to the meeting at Munich. It was Mussolini who was ready to help Hungary's cause in the Vienna decision; for years he had promised Hungary support in its revisionist claims, as Ciano reminded Ribbentrop when they met in Rome in late October, and the time had come for the Axis to deliver something tangible. Moreover, Ciano pointed out, the arbitration itself would have a favorable psychological effect on the Balkan countries, demonstrating that Britain and France no longer played a significant role in the region.[11]

But Mussolini's wishes could only be realized through Hitler, who late in 1938 was in the driver's seat of the Axis command car. Mussolini could only sit admiringly or sullenly by, depending on what Hitler decided, though only a few months before, at the time of the *Anschluss,* Hitler had been the anxious supplicant for Mussolini's forbearance.

It was the Reich that would have the last word on the Hungarian demands, and a German Foreign Office memorandum summed up the possibilities. An independent Slovakia, the memorandum declared, would be weak and economically unstable, and close ties to Poland and Hungary would be politically undesirable. The best solution would be for it to remain part of a Czechoslovakia that had close ties to Germany, and its later separation from the Czechs would always be possible. Similarly Carpatho-Ukraine or Ruthenia would not be an independent state, though as such it would have the advantage of establishing a claim on behalf of a future Ukraine state that would include fellow nationals now living in Poland, the Soviet Union, and Romania. An independent Ruthenia with a frontier with Hungary and close relations with that country desired by Hungary and Poland would facilitate, the foreign office said, anti-German bloc-building and was therefore opposed on military grounds by the German high command. So here too the best solution was an autonomous Carpatho-Ukraine linked to Slovakia or Czechoslovakia. The catchword *(Stichwort) self-determination* would be applicable in the case of both Slovakia and the Carpatho-Ukraine as a counter to Polish-Hungarian aims.

This was the content of the memorandum prepared by the head of the political section of the foreign office, Ernst Woermann, and it was well tailored to what Hitler had in mind. His fantasy of a Europe under domination of a conquering *Germanentum* had been temporarily thwarted, not appeased, by Munich, and on October 21 he issued a directive to the Wehrmacht to prepare for dealing with what remained of Czechoslovakia.

A week before Hitler issued his directive, Field Marshal Göring told a meeting at the Air Ministry in Berlin that the mobilization of the Reich's resources for war would begin, and he outlined the crash program for the coming months.[12] It was a swaggering Göring speech designed to impress his audience with his indispensability to Hitler and therefore to the Reich, and it was also a chilling portent for German workers and employers. They would either perform what the plan demanded or face the most dismal consequences. He kept using the word *brutal* to emphasize his implacable determination. It tended to be blunted by his addiction to any form of self-indulgence—from opéra bouffe uniforms to morphine. Still, the speech was an unmistakable call to arms, far removed from any notion of peace in our time. The economy was to be entirely reoriented toward military production. The blueprint was Hitler's answer to the loud demands for rearmament in Britain and France. Let the democracies rearm! Nazi Germany would outproduce them manyfold.[13]

The Führer, Göring said, had given him the task of increasing armament, especially plane production. The latter must expand fivefold, the navy must quickly increase battle strength, as must the army especially in heavy artillery and tanks—in other words, with weapons designed for attack. Everything that would advance rearmament must be produced in enormous quantities: fuel, rubber, powder, and after them canals, roads, railroad building. It all had to be done at high speed, and Göring said he wanted no memoranda, only action. The economy had to be turned around, if necessary with "brutal" methods. This was the time for the private sector to show what it could do, and if it failed, Göring said, he would not hesitate to change everything "ruthlessly" to a state economy. No washing machines, printing presses, or the like were to be manufactured; machines had to produce machines. Three shifts were to be taken for granted: apprentices trained, women recruited. The eight-hour day was a thing of the past; if workers resisted he promised to introduce forced labor and construct labor camps. The Sudetenland must be exploited, Slovakia and Czechia would be German dominions. Jews had to be driven from the economy, but he wanted, he said, no "wild commissar economy" such as had developed in Austria where twenty-five thousand commissars had been appointed in the early days of the *Anschluss,* thirty-five hundred of whom still remained at their posts—most of them of no use whatever, Göring declared.

Emphasizing his own eminence over men such as Bormann and other mere party functionaries, Göring said Aryanization was not a matter for the party but for the state. Göring would see to it that no foreign currency would be made available to Jews, and if necessary he would set up ghettos in the large cities.

To reinforce what he was promising he called on an assistant in the Four-Year Plan, State Councillor Rudolf Schmeer, who declared the battle against the Jews had to be waged much more ruthlessly; Jewish work detachments should be formed, and then the Jews would decide to leave the country. But at this point Göring, who was apparently getting weary, abruptly ended the meeting without any concrete decisions being made.[14]

A month later Göring revealed more of the plan to a meeting of the Reich Defense Council. This was an outwardly impressive gathering of Reichministers, the commanders of the army and navy, and the chiefs of staff of the Wehrmacht, along with Heydrich (who was representing the SS) and other high members of the party and state. Göring's speech lasted three hours as he described the great task the Führer had entrusted to him. He reminded his audience that the Reich Defense Council had been established in 1933 but had never met until it was revived in September 1938. Its chairman was Hitler himself who had named Göring his permanent deputy. Its task, he told them, would be to bring together all the force of the nation to increase German armament production by 300 percent. The council was made much of in Göring's speech, but he would testify later, at the postwar Nuremberg trial, that it was merely a paper organization, apparently too unwieldy, and was superseded a year later, after the start of the war.[15]

The arms program went ahead but without help of the council, which never did much more than permit Göring to make his long speech in which he promised not only to restructure the economy but also to reshape foreign policy so arms would be delivered only to countries that paid cash and only by exception for political reasons. If that seemed an invasion of Ribbentrop's domain, so much the better. Göring was always looking for an opportunity to remind the foreign minister of his subordinate place to the number-two man of the Reich. But the need for foreign currency was real; as he pointed out, the chief jobs of Germany's industries were to provide for the armed forces and to produce goods for export that would be paid for in cash. Exports were high on Göring's list.

On November 2 a four-power conference, different from that foreseen in Munich, met in Vienna at the Belvedere Castle. Present were the foreign ministers of Germany, Italy, Slovakia, and Hungary and their staffs. Ribbentrop and Ciano were to hand down verdicts as the lawgivers. Koloman von Kanya, foreign minister of Hungary, and Frantisek Chvalkovský, foreign minister of Czechoslovakia, were humble petitioners awaiting their decisions. Since this was a meeting of the foreign ministers of authoritarian states with no representatives of democracies present, it was a pattern of National Socialist and Fascist no-nonsense procedures.[16] It lasted two hours.

Ribbentrop welcomed them all and reminded them that they were meeting in the castle that had belonged to Prince Eugene, a German statesman and field marshal of Italian ancestry, who two hundred years before had brought peace and justice to Southeast Europe.[17] He introduced Ciano, who also had words of praise for Prince Eugene and for the Axis and said he was sure a new era was dawning in Middle Europe. The Italian was followed by members of the Hungarian and Czechoslovakian delegations, Hungarian Foreign Minister von Kanya, Minister of Culture Count Teleki, Czechoslovak Foreign Minister Chvalkovský, and his deputy Ivan Kvno, all of whom expressed their gratitude to Germany and Italy for acting as arbitrators and recapitulated their nations' claims on one another. A pause for lunch permitted them all to eat and sit stiffly together, after which the German and Italian peacemakers withdrew to make and record their decisions.

The meeting resumed at 5:00 P.M. when the verdict was rendered. That the official document had been prepared in haste was indicated by the listing of the name of the Czechoslovak foreign minister, which appeared as Franz instead of Frantisek Chvalkovský.

The awards pleased neither of the petitioning states. While Hungary was given substantial territory—twelve thousand kilometers with a population of more than 1 million, mainly Magyars, it did not get Bratislava and much else it wanted. In this tangle of nationalities its gains included, with the Magyars, 20,000 Germans as well as 140,000 Slovaks and a scattering of 40,000 Ruthenes, Poles, Romanians, and Jews. Bratislava, the capital of Hungary for two hundred years until 1774, was to remain the capital of Slovakia.[18] Hungary was awarded five cities it had claimed, including Neuhäusel and Karchan and the capital of Ruthenia, Ungvár, which it had surrendered in the former redistributions. Chvalkovský, representing the state that had suffered only losses of territory and people, could solace himself with having managed to keep a Czechoslovakian state patched together, but this was all Hitler was ready to grant him, and the grant was an indeterminate lease.

Hungarian nationalists, after years of malnutrition, could not bear to accept as final what they regarded as the meager awards just made in Vienna, and the Budapest government stubbornly continued to misread Hitler's mind. Daranyi, after his October 14 visit to Hitler, was convinced the Führer had told him the Carpatho-Ukraine had no interest for the Reich, a report the Hungarian government desperately wanted to believe, even though the Vienna award had failed to restore the lost provinces to Hungary. But after the Hungarian Regent, Miklos Horthy, on November 6 led the triumphal march of his troops to reoccupy the liberated areas of Slovakia and Ruthenia, Hungarian rejoicing was muted. From Budapest's point of view, Hungary had been given a mere token restitution for old wrongs—the next step was occupation of all Ruthenia. For this reckless venture they believed they had the backing of Mussolini and hoped Hitler would accept a military coup that transferred a Czechoslovakian province to Hungary, even if he did not support it.

The gamble failed. No Balkan border could change without Hitler's approval. That Budapest had some notion of the risk may be seen from the roundabout way news of Hungarian intentions reached Hitler. On November 20 the Hungarian military attaché in Rome informed Mussolini that the situation in Carpatho-Ukraine was becoming increasingly intolerable and that despite the fact the Reich had warned Hungary such a move would be "inopportune" and would lend no assistance if complications developed, the Hungarian army planned to invade Ruthenia within twenty-four hours. Budapest preferred to believe Hitler did not really disapprove of Hungary's acquiring Ruthenia but was chiefly concerned with the unfavorable consequences for Hungary—a wild misreading of the German Leader's attitude. In fact Hitler was furious, denouncing the Hungarian plan as a repudiation of the Vienna decision Hungary had just agreed to. Mussolini promptly declared he was of the same opinion. Hungary had no choice but to give up any immediate plan of taking over the Carpatho-Ukraine. Military units that had crossed the border were quickly withdrawn.

Hungary's aspirations were of negligible consequence to Hitler. Increasingly confident, with no visible threat at home or abroad, he needed to get rid of the stain of Munich and of the truncated Czechoslovakia that had survived it.

On November 8 Hitler delivered his traditional speech in the Munich Bürgerbräukeller in memory of the party "martyrs" who had died during the 1923 uprising.[19] At the outset he turned that failed attempt at a coup into a victory; he had foiled the Bavarian separatists, he told his audience, and prepared the way for overthrow of the incompetent republican government. He thereupon told off the British who, he said, had declared in 1918 that they were fighting not the German people but Prussian militarism and the Hohenzollerns. The German people, the British had promised, could live in freedom after the defeat of their masters, within the framework of an international democracy. "This freedom," he said acidly, "we then came to know. The German people have learned that lesson. The collapse that Germany then experienced thanks to its credulity will not be repeated in the next thousand years." He could admit that today in Britain and France men were in charge who wanted peace. But other men, he said, made no secret that they wanted to make war on Germany, and Churchill could become prime minister tomorrow.

> And if the British opposition don't want to destroy the German people but only its regime, that is precisely the same thing, because the regime destroys no one unless they seek to destroy the German people. If anyone declares they want to free the German people from the regime, I say to them, you are not competent to represent the German people. If anyone is competent to speak for the German people, my dear British parliamentarians, I am

that one. The German regime is an inner affair of the German people and we forbid any kind of schoolmasterish supervision.

In this connection I can also assure you of this: The German people will not be frightened by any bombs, falling let us say, from Mars or from the moon. Here too, in the German fashion, we will maintain our self-control.[20]

If these British advocates or attorneys for world democracy now complain that we have destroyed two democracies this very year, I can only ask: What is a democracy? Who has the right to speak in its name? Has the dear Lord handed over the keys of democracy to Churchill and Duff Cooper? . . . Democracy, as we see it, is a regime supported by the will of the people. I once became Chancellor of Germany following the rules of parliamentary democracy and, in fact, as the leader of the by far largest party. Following the rules of parliamentary democracy I then obtained an absolute majority and although Mr. Churchill may doubt it I now have the unanimous support of the German people. I have removed this year not two democracies, but I can almost say, as an arch-democrat, two dictatorships, namely, the dictatorship of Herr Schuschnigg and the dictatorship of Herr Beneš. . . .

I am only the representative of my people. As such I will do everything I believe necessary and if Mr. Churchill asks me: How can a head of state possibly cross swords with a British parliamentarian? I answer him: Mr. Churchill, you should only feel yourself honored. You can see that when in Germany even the head of state does not hesitate to cross swords with a British parliamentarian how highly the German people esteem British parliamentarians. Moreover I am not a head of state in the sense of a dictator or of a monarch, but I am the leader of the German people. I could have assumed, you may be sure of that, any other kind of title. But I stayed with my old one, and will stay with it as long as I live because I don't want to be anything else and will never consider being anything else. That satisfied me. Mr. Churchill and these gentlemen are deputies of the English people and I am the deputy of the German people. The only difference is that Mr. Churchill has received a fraction of the British vote while I represent the entire German people. . . .

It was a grandiloquent speech perfectly designed for its beefy, "old fighter" audience with its heavy sarcasm when he spoke of the effete British and the tributes to everyone present for the mighty deeds they had performed with him in righting old wrongs. It was a litany of mutual praise for himself and the party leaders. The message was not new, but it would always be titillating. To be reminded of the collapse, through perfidy, of the Kaiser's Reich, of the meretricious promises of the Allies, the years of struggle, and then the glorious triumph of their cause was endlessly invigorating no matter how many times the recital was repeated.

But as for the regime's capacity for destruction—within hours of the speech Nazi hoodlums were racing through the streets of German cities burning synagogues, smashing property, strewing sidewalks with broken glass of store windows. All the synagogues in the Reich were burned down or partially destroyed—even chapels in cemeteries, as Heydrich complacently reported. Destruction of property was enormous: houses, warehouses, anything Jewish that could be hacked or burned.

Although the numbers of Jews killed during the "action" was relatively small—thirty-six—it was accompanied by the rounding up of twenty thousand Jews throughout Germany, to be jailed either in "protective custody" of the police or the concentration camps of the SS. Laws, orders, and decrees followed one another, designed to separate Jews from the rest of the population and to make it impossible for them to make a living in the Reich. It was the first large sign of the Final Solution.

The occasion for the extraordinary pogrom was the shooting in Paris on November 7 of a German diplomat, Ernst vom Rath, by a seventeen-year-old German Jew, Herschel Gruenspan (Grynszpan), whose family was being deported from Germany as a result of a Polish law depriving anyone with a Polish passport the right to return to Poland if he had been out of the country for more than four years without interruption and had no contact with the Polish state.[21]

After the *Anschluss* the chronically anti-Semitic Warsaw government had wanted to prevent the return of twenty thousand Polish Jews who had migrated to Austria in the pre-Nazi decades. Warsaw had delayed putting the law, passed on March 31, 1938, into effect because of the urgency of Polish claims militantly advanced during the Czechoslovak crisis, but after Munich the law became operative as of October 30. Meanwhile anyone living abroad with a Polish passport had to present it at a Polish consulate and have it approved for reentry into Poland. If this was refused the holder of the passport lost his Polish citizenship.

With the prospect of having fifty thousand Polish Jews as stateless residents, the Reich ordered the Polish Jews out of the country, and by the end of October, seventeen thousand had been transported over the border by the Gestapo.[22] Among them were the Polish-born Gruenspans: Herschel's father, a tailor by trade, mother née Silberberg, and a brother and a sister who still lived with their parents. Herschel, who had been born in Hannover, had been living with an uncle, Abraham, in Paris in meager circumstances. He had no job; in fact he had never had one since he left elementary school from which he had not graduated. He and his uncle did not get along, and he had left Abraham's apartment to live in a rooming house, the Suez, where he had to pay for his room in advance. His situation was precarious; he had 320 francs, and from that he had to pay 22.50 francs a day for room and breakfast at the Suez. Both his German visa permitting him to enter the Reich and his Polish passport had expired, and the French government's permission to reside in France had expired two months before, in August. When he received a postcard from his deported sister telling him of his family's plight, he bought a gun with the intention of avenging his and his family's troubles by killing the German ambassador. He shot and mortally wounded the wrong man. The ambassador, Count Welczek, was not on call to anyone who came to the embassy, so a young member of his staff, Ernst Eduard vom Rath, who had reception duty that day, was assigned to talk to the visitor. Herschel had no experience whatever with firearms; three of his shots missed his target completely at a range of six feet, but two bullets hit Rath who died of his wounds two days later.

It was ironic that Rath, of all members of the embassy, would be Gruenspan's victim. Although he had joined the Nazi Party in 1932 and the SA in 1933, he was a devout Christian and, disillusioned with the party's godlessness and relentless anti-Semitism, had turned against it. He was even reported to have referred to Hitler as "anti-Christ."

The shooting precipitated the devastations of the Kristallnacht and the long list of penalizing laws and regulations separating Jews from the rest of German society. The pogrom starkly revealed the purpose of the leaders of the German state not only to destroy the livelihood of German Jews but also to get rid of them as a presence, forcing them to emigrate or disappear by any means that would eliminate them from the Reich. It tore the last veil from the stubbornly held notions of many Jews that the anti-Semitic measures thitherto adopted were the rash of a disease that would disappear with time. The shooting of Rath was seized upon by rabid ideologues led by Goebbels as an opportunity to demonstrate to the world the loathing the German people had for Jews and their eagerness to rise against their Jewish oppressors and scour them out of Germany. The SA were called on for their first big assignment since the Röhm massacre. The Brownshirts, rather than the SS for whom the task was considered too menial, were to be the agents provocateurs to incite the *Volk* to a spontaneous display of righteous wrath.[23] For Hitler and the political leaders, the murder was one more piece of evidence of the machinations of people far more important than the Gruenspans. These were the Jewish wire-pullers who ruled the world outside the Reich, who had been foiled in their attempt to ignite a world war by the Munich Agreement, but who continued to lurk in every country awaiting another opportunity to destroy Germany.

Hitler had not mentioned the wounding of Rath in his Buergerbräu speech to the old fighters on November 8. Despite his unwavering hatred of Jews, he would never be directly involved with an anti-Semitic pogrom or later with the exterminations. But he never made a secret of his intention to destroy the Jews "in one way or another." In *Mein Kampf,* in speeches, in private conversations, and finally in his Last Will and Testament his passionate hatred of Jews outlasted all other emotions. It may be that he saw himself as the *Feldherr* of the war against Jewry, issuing the directives but not the battle orders that he knew revolted a good many even of his devoted followers.[24] In the case of the Rath murder, the SA agents provocateurs themselves had to burn down the synagogues and smash the windows. The German people did not rise; they looked at the senseless destruction, "the political revival of the gutter" as Speer called it, like him shaking their heads or like Göring welcoming the penalties against the Jews as a just punishment of undesirables but regarding the damage as a wicked waste of scarce materials. A few people, like Rath himself perhaps, the anti-anti-Semites, identified themselves with the Jews or felt they should. Few did anything further, and aside from performing individual acts of kindness there was nothing much they could do.

Rath died November 8, elevated by Hitler before his death to the rank of Legation Councilor, First Class. Hitler sent a telegram of condolence to Rath's parents, but he never mentioned him in any speech, in contrast to what he had done in similar circumstances two years earlier. His wrath was selective: It could be assuaged or stimulated by the political climate. In 1938 he could teach the Jews and foreign critics a lesson, and he doted on teaching lessons. The penalties inflicted on the Jews were enormous: Göring ordered that all damage done to Jewish homes and workplaces be cleaned up immediately by the Jews who had suffered the damage. A fine of 1 billion marks, later increased by another quarter of a billion, was levied and was followed by a series of restrictive laws. All this bore no resemblance to what had happened in 1936 when the leader of the German Foreign Organization in Switzerland, Wilhelm Gustloff, had been killed in Davos by a Jewish emigrant, David Frankfurter. Gustloff had been shot down on February 4, 1936, just before reoccupation of the Rhineland, and no riots erupted, no indemnities were imposed. Hitler duly opened the Winter Olympics in Garmisch-Partenkirchen. Six days later Hitler delivered a graveside address at Gustloff's burial in Schwerin, but aside from expressing his condolences to Gustloff's widow that was all.

In the graveside address he had pulled out the bathetic stops of his oratory, praising the heroism of a simple man and the patriots and National Socialists like Gustloff who were the victims of international Jews, the same behind-the-scenes plotters who had lived in his head and served him all his life and who he could summon again to explain why Rath was killed. But at Schwerin his avenging sword was unsheathed only at the graveside, though circumstances were much the same as in the case of Rath's murder.

Rath was killed in a different political climate. The penalties were vastly different, too—none when Gustloff was killed, but in Rath's case death and destruction and extension of the Aryan paragraph, decreed in 1933, to long pages of exclusions. Jewish children still in German schools had to leave. No German could teach them; they had to attend Jewish schools taught by Jews. They were forbidden to attend theaters, including moving-picture theaters, concerts, museums, lectures, circuses, anything of a "cultural" nature, as well as public baths and sport places. They were forbidden to use hotels, such as the Vier Jahreszeiten in Munich, frequented by Aryans. They were prohibited from driving cars, and their licenses were rescinded. Pensions of former government officials continued to be paid, but Hitler ordered that they be scrutinized to see if they could not be reduced. Jewish physicians, apothecaries, and veterinarians were forbidden to practice their professions; they were not to be awarded diplomas after January 31, 1939. Tradesmen could not run independent shops; retailers were forbidden to make use of marketplaces, fairs, or exhibitions; Jews could no longer be managers of enterprises; and if a Jew had a job as section head of a business, he was to be dismissed with six weeks' notice.

The list of proscriptions was long. Jews could not be members of cooperatives and had to quit those they had joined. If Jews had been insured against any of the damage done to their property during the riots, insurance payments went not to them but to the state. Jews could be forbidden to make use of such public places as parks or could use them only at specified times. Jewish enterprises were either to be alienated to Aryan ownership or liquidated within a given period; meanwhile Aryan conservators were appointed as managers. Jews could be forced to sell land or forest preserves within a specified time, and their property rights could not be inherited. Within a week of the decree coming into effect, they had to deposit all stocks, shares, and securities in a designated bank. Jewelry made of gold, platinum, or silver could not be pawned, inherited, or sold on the open market, nor could precious stones, pearls, or other such articles of value, which could only be disposed of along with art objects worth more than one thousand marks through government agencies.[25] This was the semifinal solution, in the shadow of the Final Solution. What it made clear was that Jews were simply not to be tolerated in the *volk* community.

And what were the Jews to do? They were not permitted to earn a living or do business, nor could they easily emigrate because of penalties against taking out of the Reich funds or objects of value, and because, as National Socialist propaganda gleefully pointed out, no country wanted them. Foreign newspapers printed true horror stories of mistreatment of German Jews; humanitarian committees especially in the United States called sternly for action, but where governments were concerned it was mainly outcry and moral outrage with no change in immigration policy. Even before the murder of Rath, President Roosevelt called a conference that took place at Évian on Lake Geneva in July 1938. Attended by representatives of thirty-two nations, its only visible result was the establishment of the Intergovernmental Committee on Refugees with a seat in London, which would continue to seek a solution for Jewish emigration. Australia announced it had no real racial problem and wanted none; no commonwealth country—so a British spokesman, Sir John Suckburgh, reported—had territory suitable for large-scale immigration. How right he was may be seen in the decision reported in the Nazi press that Rhodesia had declared it was ready to admit twenty-five Jews as settlers. They would be under observation for five years, at the end of which time they could be banished if they had not been found suitable. If they were found suitable, Rhodesia would be ready to accept 150 additional Jews. Canada declared it would admit agricultural workers but no others. France already had two hundred thousand refugees and would accept no more. The United States agreed only to fill its quota of 27,370 annual immigrants from Germany and the former Austria, which had thitherto not been fully utilized.

This was more or less the same story worldwide. The Jews had no way to emigrate, and that did not change after the Kristallnacht, despite widespread indignant protests, furious denunciations of the Reich, and journalistic uproar. President Roosevelt held a news conference on November 12 to tell the press that news of the Kristallnacht had deeply shocked public opinion in the United States. To get a clearer picture of what had happened he had asked the secretary of state to order the ambassador in Berlin to return to the United States for consultation. The Intergovernmental Committee on Refugees, he said, would be widening its scope. He too did not know where the refugees might go but said he had given a great deal of thought to the subject and would make a later announcement. In response to a question he said he did not plan to ask Congress to modify the immigration laws.

Economic consequences due to individual or corporate action were something else. Organized boycotts of German goods had been attempted before but now became much more effective. One German toy company lost all its outlets in England, another all in the United States. In Holland one of the largest trading companies that had represented Krupp as well as German automobile manufacturers gave up its German contracts in favor of English firms. Even exports of armaments were affected, with a loss of 20 to 30 percent of business.[26]

A memorandum of the German Foreign Office, distributed to all embassies and consulates, declared the aim of the government to be the emigration of all Jews living in Germany. Measures taken up to 1938, the memorandum declared, had not succeeded, but the new laws would result in widespread emigration to which would be added Jews from nations such as Hungary, Poland, and Romania that also wanted to rid themselves of Jews. The exodus had to be controlled, and it was in the German interest that Jews be divided and not permitted to settle in any single state that would inevitably be anti-German. Jewish immigration to

Palestine, which the Reich had once favored in the so-called Haavara Agreement, had been reduced to a trickle by Arab resistance and British measures, and in any case the agreement permitted only emigration of a few wealthy Jews.[27] The Reich did not want a Jewish state that would always represent a danger, and German policy was to prevent strengthening the Jewish position. Furthermore, the flooding of Jews to countries all over the world would result in an increase of anti-Semitism, the best propaganda for the Reich's Jewish policy.

It was a sober summary of the Reich's Jewish policy. The doors were shutting on German Jews; not only was life to be made unbearable in Germany but those who emigrated were to be scattered throughout the world in countries that did not want them. Only temporary refuge was possible for them, anywhere but Germany. And how long would the new provisional solution last? The foreign office did not say, nor did Hitler, nor would any official document ever say. The Jews simply had to disappear; they were a danger to Germany wherever they lived.

On the evening of November 10, less than twenty-four hours after the events of the Kristallnacht, Hitler addressed a group of journalists in Munich in a secret talk that was never printed while he was in power. The only surviving text comes from a phonograph recording. In his almost hour-long speech he did not make mention of the events of the preceding night, though everyone present had either witnessed or heard of the burnings and destruction that had swept Munich and the rest of the Reich's cities just a few hours before. The speech was ostensibly a thank-you address to the journalists. Why he was silent on a subject that obsessed him can only be surmised, but obviously he wanted to avoid any direct connection with an event that he knew many of his listeners deplored. If Göring and Himmler objected to the waste and destruction, the journalists, who included members of the nonparty press, would not be likely to take a more sympathetic view of a pogrom Goebbels unconvincingly explained as arising from the spontaneous wrath of the *Volk*.

Hitler never placed himself on public record explaining or approving the Kristallnacht. His speech to the journalists was unrelated to the subject uppermost on the minds of everyone present. Like many obsessed people, he was well aware that he must not always disclose the depths of his resentments or the measures he was ready to adopt to appease them. When Hess in 1941 reported to Himmler to receive orders concerning the concentration camp to be constructed at Auschwitz, Himmler told him the extermination of the Jews had been ordered by Hitler himself. In fact, no one else could have given the orders. But no written Führer order for the exterminations has ever been found, nor has one been found for the Kristallnacht.

The speech of November 10 was a tribute to the art of propaganda as practiced by the German Reich since his coming to power.[28] One of his fixed ideas had always been that Germany had been defeated and betrayed in 1918 by propaganda, not by force of arms, and he was convinced that propaganda had been a crucial force in bringing him to the chancellorship. Now he congratulated the newspapermen and himself fulsomely on what they had accomplished. It was propaganda that had been decisive; if the German people had behaved differently from other people and from their own proclivities in the past, it was because of the propaganda for which he and the press were responsible. He had had to conceal his real purposes.

> Circumstances compelled me to speak for a decade of almost nothing but peace. Only by the continuing emphasis on the German will to peace was it possible for me to win the German people little by little to gain their freedom and to give them the armament that was always essential for the next step. It is obvious that such propaganda for peace, repeated year after year, has its questionable aspects; it can only too easily lead in the minds of many people to the fixed notion that the present regime is basically identical with the decision and will to keep the peace under all circumstances.

But peace had its limits. "That however would not only lead to a false estimate of the goals of this system but to the German nation, instead of being armed against events, being filled with a defeatist spirit that in the long run would deprive it of the successes of today's regime." It had been necessary to reverse the psychology of the German people gradually so as to bring them slowly to understand that when certain things cannot be gained by peaceful means, then they must be gained by force. To this end he had had to shed light on certain events so that the inner voice of the German people would cry out for the use of force. That meant to "illustrate certain events so that in the minds of broad masses of the Volk the conviction would gradually grow that when something can't be remedied peacefully it must be remedied by force—in any event that things can't continue as they are."

In the end, only success is decisive. "At the moment of the last decisive test it had been the nerves of the others that had broken without our actually having to resort to arms. That was one of the most essential tasks of our press campaign which was also not understood by many. They said 'that is all exaggerated; moreover it is not fair, after all Czechoslovakia is a small state.'" The propaganda had worked magnificently, he said, both on the German people and on "the gentlemen in Prague" who knew German, read all the German newspapers, and whose nerves had been broken by the barrage of the German press. The dimensions of the success had only become clear to him when he stood in the midst of the Czech fortifications. "There," he said, "I understood what it meant to occupy a front of almost 2,000 kilometers without firing a shot. Gentlemen, this time with propaganda in the service of an idea, we have really won ten million people and more than 100,000 square kilometers of land without firing a shot. That is something prodigious."

He then went on to deride the French press, its indiscipline and divided opinions. One paper, he said, had a few years back written that to accept the German offer of a three hundred thousand–man army would be a crime and then three years later demanded to know why the offer had not been accepted. He said he had come to power with the people behind him, and in place of a press that attempted to make history and policy on its own account he had tried to forge the press into a useful arm. At the end of that year, 1938, he was more than satisfied with the result. Great tasks lay ahead; above all the self-confidence of the German people had to be strengthened. Doubters among the hysterical intellectuals remained; at the end of February of that very year they had talked of catastrophes ahead, of catastrophic policies, and then in mid-March of an unprecedented victory. "Everything won, thanks to our courage and resolve, everything in order, Germany unconquerable, a world power."[29]

Finally Hitler listed statistics to show that Germany, from a racial point of view, was in numbers as well as worth beyond any competing power. "America," he said, "has 126 or 127 million people and if Germans, Italians, Negroes and Jews are subtracted, that leaves no more than 60 million people who call themselves Anglo-Saxons." Russia had no more than 55 or 56 million Great Russians, the British Empire not even 46 million English in the mother country, France less than 37 million "real Frenchmen," Poland only 17 million Poles. But in Germany from 1940 on there would be 80 million people "who really racially belong to us." And the meaning of such statistics? "Who doubts the future of this human block is himself nothing but a weakling. I believe unconditionally in its future."

It was not only a swaggering, boastful speech but also Hitler demanded of his listeners the kind of obedience and trust only the true believers, the old fighters, had been willing to accord him in the past. He was talking about another world war when he spoke of great events to come. No wonder the speech was secret— he had deliberately misled the German people, he told the journalists; he had designedly spoken of nothing but peace until he was ready to risk another great war. Now he demanded of the intellectuals he had been deriding that they march in lockstep behind him without questioning his aims or purposes. It was a speech he would not have dared make before the signing of the Munich Agreement; he had reversed the treaties of Germany's conquerors, and he had done it without firing a shot.

13

The March into Prague

Hitler evidently had no precise plan for his next moves. This is apparent in his keeping his options with Poland wide open, though Danzig and the Corridor had long been recognized as inevitable targets of German revisionism. But in dealing with Poland he rattled no sword after Munich and instead proposed what seemed to be peaceful, even generous, solutions that the Poles could conceivably accept and live with. As early as May 1935 the German ambassador to Poland, Hans von Moltke, had suggested to Foreign Minister Beck the possibility of an autobahn crossing the Corridor to connect East Prussia with the rest of Germany. Beck had been noncommittal, and he remained so when Hitler three years later, in 1938, raised the possibility again.

Józef Lipski, the Polish ambassador to Berlin, told Ribbentrop in November 1938 that in his opinion the German proposals for an autobahn and double-track railroad across the Corridor would not fail to interest his government, but Beck would only say the matter was complicated and required study. He never went much further than that, and it is uncertain how far he could have gone. Moltke reported that Polish army officers were critical of Beck as too pro-German; the hard-liners in Poland were convinced no such concessions would be made to Hitler without endangering Poland's security. They had little cause to worry. Hitler's powers of persuasion had no perceptible effect in causing Beck to discuss details of any solution for an autobahn and railroad, not to mention Danzig and the Corridor.

On January 5, 1939, Beck journeyed to Berchtesgaden where he met with Hitler in the still-deceptive glow of their anti-Czech collaboration.[1] Beck opened the discussion by saying that German-Polish relations had withstood the test in September, and if they had cooled since then both countries should try to get at the causes and remove them. One of the difficulties was Danzig, which Beck said cautiously, concerned not only Poland and Germany but also third parties such as the League of Nations (the very mention of which could not fail to irritate Hitler). What, asked Beck, with no doubt the explosive fervor of the National Socialist majority of the city in mind, if the League of Nations should pull out of the administration of Danzig? And what about the promised guarantees of the Czech borders? These were questions that needed attention.

But Hitler, ignoring the League of Nations and the Czech guarantee, plunged into matters that he thought really merited attention. His aim was quite simply to bind Poland to the Reich's side, and he wasted no time in preliminaries. The Polish-German nonaggression pact of 1934, he said, remained the basis of the relationship. Germany wanted a strong national Poland. It did not matter whether Russia was czarist or bolshevik—she would always be a dangerous neighbor. So Poland's position, from the Reich's point of view, had to be maintained. The Polish army greatly eased Germany's burden; Polish divisions on the Russian border relieved the pressure on German divisions. Rumors in the world press about German designs on the Ukraine had no foundation, he said. Poland had nothing whatever to fear in this regard. Germany had no interests and did not care what other countries were doing there. As for the Hungarian arbitration, he went on, it had perhaps led to misunderstanding in Poland. He did not mention the common frontier that Poland wanted with Hungary but limited himself to reproaching the Hungarians for their tepid behavior during the Czech crisis. They had only joined in the Czech affair when it was no longer dangerous. The Reich had not wanted to arbitrate the Hungarian-Czech dispute, but he had had to act when both Hungary and Czechoslovakia asked for German adjudication. A few weeks after the Vienna award, when Hungary made new demands on Czechoslovakia, the Reich could not revise what had just been decided, nor if Hungary resorted to arms could it permit the Czechs to march into Budapest. The Reich had to prevent an international conflict; that was what had determined its actions.

Poland and Germany, he said, should move forward to a new relationship; they should make a final agreement resolving the difficult but not insoluble problems that separated them. The question of Memel, he said confidently, would soon be solved in Germany's favor, but there remained the emotionally difficult question of the Corridor and Danzig. Poland and Germany must be ready to seek entirely new ways to deal with them. As he saw it, Danzig, following the will of its inhabitants, would again be part of the German community but with Polish interests, especially economic interests, fully protected. This would also be in the interest of Danzig because the city would not be economically viable without Poland. Therefore, he said, he was thinking of a formula in which Danzig would become part of the German community and at the same time remain economically a part of Poland. "Danzig," he declared, "is German, will always be German and will sooner or later come to Germany." He could assure Beck that Poland would not be confronted with a fait accompli. He was suggesting a reasonable solution tailored, he was convinced, to Polish sensibilities.

The Corridor, Hitler went on, presented a difficult psychological problem for Germany. It would be nonsensical to deprive Poland of access to the sea; its right to that had to be acknowledged absolutely. Equally, Germany's need for a connection with East Prussia had to be acknowledged, and here too the interests of both countries might be served by adopting new methods. If this was done the Polish-German agreement of 1934 could be expanded into a treaty that would guarantee their mutual borders including the Corridor. It wasn't easy, he said, to give such a guarantee, and it would be criticized especially by the bourgeoisie, but he was a realpolitiker and just as no one in Germany took exception to the South Tirol or to Alsace-Lorraine the Corridor would become a dead issue once the guarantee was given.

Another problem for them both, Hitler said, was the Jewish question. He was determined to drive the Jews from Germany. They would be able to take part of their possessions, certainly more than they had brought in when they had emigrated to the Reich, but the longer the process took the less they would take out. Had the Western powers shown more understanding for German colonial demands, he might have proposed African territory for the settlement of not only German but also Polish Jews. The Western powers had shown no such understanding, and Germany had to stand firm in its demands for colonies to sustain its own population. Sooner or later the Reich would get back its colonies, he was convinced of that. But the costs of the unresolved colonial question and the resulting tensions had led to the considerable armaments on both sides. If one day the Western powers struck a balance they might see that the rights to which Germany was entitled had cost them billions. It would have been much cheaper to concede Germany's claims in the first place.

Beck thanked Hitler for his comprehensive explanation of the German position and said that Poland too held steadfastly to its relationship with the Reich. The tensions, he said, with the Soviet Union during the September crisis had been acute, more so than appeared on the surface. Russia had brought up army corps to the Polish frontier, and Poland had taken countermeasures. Poland wanted to find a supportable modus vivendi with the Soviet Union but would never be dependent on Russia and would resist, as in the past, closer relations by way of an Eastern pact. Poland was not as nervous as France with regard to security and thought nothing of the so-called security system that had been swept away with the September crisis. This had been a turning point in history. Concerning the Ukraine, Beck said, he was reminded of the words of Pilsudski about the Balkanization of Middle Europe. In the Carpatho-Ukraine agitators were at work, and it could develop into such a center of unrest that it would threaten further complications for Poland. That had been the chief reason for Poland's desire for a common frontier with Hungary.

As for German-Polish relations, Beck said cautiously, he took note of Hitler's desires. The Danzig problem seemed to him extraordinarily difficult, and he had to take Polish public opinion into consideration. He was not speaking, he said, of the "coffee house opposition," of the chauvinistic hypernationalists, but of the real views of the people, and therein lay the greatest difficulty for a solution of the Danzig question. But he would gladly ponder the problem in tranquility. He went no further, made no mention of the Corridor, merely renewed his assurance that Poland would abide by the 1934 pact.[2]

It was an inconclusive meeting. What Hitler was offering had its attractions. No German government had been willing to accept, much less guarantee, the Polish border dividing German territory, and only the ultranational Führer, Hitler, could offer that, as he reminded Beck he had done when he renounced the Reich's claims to the South Tirol and to Alsace-Lorraine.

But neither Beck nor anyone else in the ruling Warsaw hierarchy would ever bring themselves to accept Hitler's offer. A German autobahn and railroad across the Corridor would compromise Polish sovereignty, and Danzig restored to the Reich even with the most solemn guarantees of Polish economic rights in the city would only be seen by the ardently nationalist inheritors of Pilsudski's authoritarian state as an unthinkable retreat. A surrender to the Ur enemy, or to Soviet Russia, was an unrelenting threat to Poland's independence. As every Pole knew, Poland had a precarious strategic position. If Russia was strong, she dominated Poland; if the German states were strong, they dominated; and if both Russia and the Germans were strong, they partitioned. The time of the signing of the Treaty of Versailles had been a moment in history when Russia and Germany, on opposite sides, had both been weakened by a lost war, and the victorious Allies wanted to keep them that way as long as possible.

Poles saw the offer as a foot in the Polish door that would only lead to a demand for space in the living room, and they were unwilling to make any concession that might conceivably diminish the power or prestige of the hard-won state awarded them at Versailles. The German ambassador to Poland, Moltke, told Beck in early March 1939 during a conversation about the endemic anti-German sentiment in Poland, that aside from the foreign minister himself and a half-dozen others, none of the leading Poles had any interest in a policy of understanding with Germany.

An alliance with either Germany or the Soviet Union was unthinkable. It would compromise independence, expose Poland to retaliation by the excluded power, and upset the delicate balance of Warsaw's foreign policy. Any hint of concession to the territorial claims of either Russia or Germany seemed, to Polish leaders, to point inexorably to dissolution of the state. Both Germany and the Soviet Union had claims on Poland's Germanic, White Russian, and Ukrainian minorities. No matter how strongly pressed by well-wishers in England and France, Poland would never permit Soviet armies to march into its territory, even armies of alleged succor, in the well-founded fear that they would never leave. And as for Hitler's offer, Beck told the Romanian foreign minister, Grigore Gafencu, Poland would never permit Danzig to be restored to the Reich, and if Beck himself had been ready to make the trade Hitler was offering, Polish public opinion would make it impossible to carry out.[3] Beck told Gafencu how ill he was—he was suffering from tuberculosis—but his own fate was of small consequence compared with the magnitude of the issues he felt he alone could adequately deal with. So what may have seemed a reasonable offer to neutral observers such as the League of Nations high commissioner in Danzig, Carl Burckhardt, and the British ambassador to Berlin, Henderson, was a booby trap to Beck and his critics alike. Poland's security, in Beck's view, lay in the might of its army and the need of Germany and Russia to maintain tolerable relations with a Polish state that separated their hostile camps. Hitler, he was convinced, would never weaken the Polish bastion against Soviet Russia for the sake of Danzig—which was, he conceded, overwhelmingly German but essential to Poland's economic survival. Danzig could be independent and German in administration but not part of the Reich.

Admittedly, influential Poles were likely to be more anti-Soviet than anti-German. The Polish ambassador to the United States, Count Jerzy Potocki, in mid-January 1939, sent a report to Warsaw declaring that the American press, radio, films, and magazines were almost completely in the hands of Jews who portrayed the Reich as badly as possible and knew nothing of the situation in Europe, regarding Hitler and National Socialism as the great evil and danger confronting the world.[4] President Roosevelt, Potocki wrote in another report, was under the influence of his Jewish friends such as Secretary of the Treasury Henry Morgenthau; the newly appointed justice of the Supreme Court, Felix Frankfurter; the governor of New York, Herbert Lehman; and Bernard M. Baruch. Roosevelt was trying to divert Americans from their domestic troubles by crying up the specter of fascism and made no mention of the Soviet Union.

Beck, like Potocki, had no intention of being saddled with either Hitler or Stalin. He wished a plague on both their houses. He vastly overestimated the impregnability of Poland's political position and the strength of its army.

Hitler, for his part, was convinced he was offering the Poles a golden opportunity to settle their differences with the Reich and link their fortunes with it. They would need little instruction in the dangers to Poland of the Soviet Union and world Jewry, and their authoritarian government would readily share his low opinion of the functioning of the democracies. Up to the time when it became clear that neither Beck nor any other Polish leader would accept his offer, Hitler was following his blueprint sketched in *Mein Kampf.*[5] The Reich would only be freed from the threat of a blockade at the expense or with the help of the Soviet Union. It was the Soviet Ukraine, not Tanzania, that could provide the breadbasket and living space the thousand-year Reich must have to survive and prosper, and the numerically superior Soviet armed forces would always threaten to join those of the West as they had done in 1914. Hitler could not fight the West and the East at the same time, and Poland must be either a subservient ally or a victim.

How resolutely Hitler determined to bind Poland to the Reich may be seen in his wooing of Beck despite the coolness he encountered. On October 24 Lipski had been invited to Berchtesgaden where Ribbentrop presented Hitler's grand plan. Lipski forwarded it to Warsaw, and a week later Beck sent detailed instructions to politely but firmly reject it. The instructions, praising the rapprochement with the Reich, were intended to remind Ribbentrop and Hitler that Poland's existence remained rooted in the Versailles treaty. Poland, the Reich had to be told unequivocally, required four indispensable conditions: unrestricted access to the sea, possession of railroads serving Danzig harbor, inclusion of the city in the Polish customs area, and safeguarding rights of the Polish minority in the city. The instructions contained soothing words for the Reich. They acknowledged the city's German character and the right of its German inhabitants to "a national and cultural life" and reaffirmed Beck's readiness to engage in discussions. But they intended to make plain that Poland's survival rested on the hard rock of those four conditions, and any attempt to incorporate Danzig in the Reich would mean war.

It took until November 19, two and a half weeks, for Lipski to deliver Beck's reply to Ribbentrop.[6] The atmosphere of their meeting was markedly friendly, doubtless to soften Beck's refusal and sustain Ribbentrop's hope that Beck might change his mind. This possibility, dim as it might be, was strengthened in the course of the conversation as Lipski told Ribbentrop he believed Hitler's proposal of a corridor through the Corridor might eventually be acceptable in Warsaw.

November 22, three days after the Polish "no" was delivered, Moltke in a meeting with Beck tried to brush it aside. He told Beck all over again that

Ribbentrop viewed Polish-German relations in the context of high policy *(ein Problem der grossen Politik)*. The German foreign minister had told Lipski that a high policy that had demonstrated its value and preserved peace should not be brought into question by this or that dispute. Moltke informed Beck that Ribbentrop continued to place utmost significance on good German-Polish relations and that Ribbentrop, after listening with close attention to what Lipski had to say about Danzig, concluded that a solution of the city's problem had to be sought in a new way. Ribbentrop always understood that Danzig was a critical problem for Poland and that Poland would never agree to its radical solution.

Beck, too, was conciliatory. He told Moltke it was due to passions aroused by the Danzig problem that Lipski wished to make Poland's position clear, and an open dialogue was the only way to proceed.

Moltke replied that their talk had been very satisfactory, and the German government, despite strong popular feelings aroused by Danzig, was determined to negotiate with due consideration for the general principles of German-Polish politics. Two days after Moltke's meeting, on November 24, Hitler issued a directive to his armed forces stating that Danzig would return to Germany by way of a military coup but not, the directive said, "by a war with Poland."[7] He apparently accepted the fact that Beck could not simply yield Danzig without arousing furious popular resentment in Poland, but a coup to be carried out "at a politically favorable time" would present the Warsaw government with a fait accompli that would save face and leave it free to accept Hitler's generous inducements as a quid pro quo. Hitler also intended to clear up an outstanding Lithuanian problem at the same time. German occupying troops coming from East Prussia for the Danzig mission were not to be divided between Danzig and Memel; the latter, however, was to be taken over simultaneously in a separate operation.[8] Naval and air support were to be provided as necessary.

As late as January 26, 1939, Ribbentrop meeting with Beck in Warsaw continued to urge Hitler's proposal, promising backing for Poland's aspiration for a greater Ukraine, but while Beck again declared he would give his most careful consideration to Hitler's offer it was plain to Ribbentrop that the answer would again be "no." As he left Warsaw he turned to the German ambassador to say: "The Poles are stubborn, we shall have to find another kind of solution." For once Ribbentrop was right. If Hitler could not gain Poland as an ally he would destroy it. Destruction demanded a lightning attack before any outside help could reach Poland, and for this he needed the strategic base of all Czechoslovakia as he had needed Austria to subdue Czechoslovakia.

January 30, 1939, was the sixth anniversary of Hitler's "seizure of power." The day began with a morning serenade by the Wehrmacht in front of the Reichschancellery in honor of its commander in chief, followed by rituals of awards and promotions handed out by Hitler, and ended with his two-and-a-

half-hour speech delivered in the evening. On this day of National Socialist jubilation Hitler bestowed awards on winners of the German national prize for 1938,
three of whom—Ferdinand Porsche, Ernst Heinkel, and Willy Messerschmidt—
were designers of air or land vehicles for the Wehrmacht, while the fourth,
Fritz Todt, was constructor of the autobahn and West Wall and the Reich's
munitions minister-to-be. After these ceremonies Hitler awarded promotions in
the Wehrmacht and bestowed titles of professor and councillor of building and of
justice. All this was a low-keyed preparation for the "government speech" at the
Kroll Opera House that began at 8:15 before an audience of Reichstag deputies,
the first meeting of that body since elections nine months before on April 10,
1938. The Reichstag had swollen to 855 deputies, including 41 representatives
from the Sudetenland, and Hitler could proudly call it the "Reichstag of Greater
Germany" and in his speech promised an even greater Germany to come.

Hitler spoke from a podium in front of the just-elected officers of the
chamber, chosen by acclamation: as president, Göring, with three vice presidents,
Hanns Kerrl, Hermann Esser, and Dr. h. c. Emil von Stauss.[9] Behind them,
replacing a swastika banner, was a huge, plastic Reich eagle.

The orator began with his ritual tirade against internal enemies of National
Socialism, describing the chaos of the Weimar period with its 35 parties (in
a speech in 1936 he had put the number at 47) united, he said, only by their
hatred of the National Socialism that had brought unity to the torn country.[10]
How much blood had been shed to win this German unity! Hundreds of
thousands, millions had given everything they had, enduring scorn, mockery,
defamation, and hardly-to-be-borne terror. The battle had been won, he made
plain, by himself, by an enormous effort of will, by decisions fanatically held to.
The accomplishments of 1938 had demanded iron nerves that were completely
lacking in the pessimists, skeptics, and indifferent intellectuals who had opposed
National Socialism and who now, after victory, appeared as "annointed experts"
on the national awakening.

Hitler turned, as he had on so many occasions, to a denunciation of President
Wilson, his Fourteen Points, and the promise of self-determination, altogether
repudiated for Germany and Austria after Germany was left defenseless.

He went on to tell his audience how on March 11, 1938, he had had to order
German troops into an Austria in complete disorder and with what wild acclaim
the Austrians had welcomed them.

As for Czechoslovakia, he stated plainly he had decided to attack that country
on May 28, the invasion to take place by October 2. It was Beneš, he told his
audience, who had been responsible for this development. Goaded by what
Hitler called "certain foreign circles," Beneš had ordered Czech mobilization in
order to provoke the Reich and then humiliate it. Despite the fact that Beneš had
been twice assured that Germany had not called up a single man, the fiction

was maintained and spread that German mobilization had forced the Czechs to act and that it was Czech determination that forced Hitler to cancel his orders. Since Germany had neither mobilized nor had any intention of attacking Czechoslovakia the situation could only lead to a heavy loss of German prestige. Hitler had thereupon given orders to prepare the attack with a force of ninety-six divisions and to speed construction of the West Wall.

The narrative of triumphs past led to assertion of a kind of German Monroe Doctrine for Middle Europe, an area, he said, where Germany would tolerate no outside meddling. "If certain newspapers and politicians now maintain that Germany by military blackmail threatens other peoples, this rests on a gross distortion of the facts. Germany, in this territory where neither England nor any other Western nation has any business, has brought self-determination to ten million VolksGermans." No one had been threatened by this; the Reich was only defending itself against the attempt of third parties to intrude.

> I don't have to assure you, my Deputies, men of the German Reichstag, that we will not tolerate in the future any attempt of the Western states to meddle there and thus prevent natural and reasonable solutions. We were therefore all pleased that, thanks to the initiative of our friend Benito Mussolini and thanks, too, to the praiseworthy readiness of Chamberlain and Daladier, it was possible not only to arrive at a peaceful settlement but to set an example for a reasonable solution of other vital problems.

Indeed, he continued, "without the resolve to deal with this problem one way or another, the European great powers would never have reached such an agreement." Hence, it had been Hitler who was the deus ex machina of the Munich Agreement. It had been his readiness to go to war to solve the problem, come what may, "one way or another," that had rescued the Sudetenland. Standard Hitler braggadocio, but undoubtedly true.

And now he demanded the unconditional assent of the German Reichstag and the German people to whatever he might have in mind for the future. It was nonsense, he said, to believe that obedience and discipline were necessary only for soldiers. On the contrary the *Volkscommunity* was brought up in discipline and obedience; it mobilized forces serving the interests of everyone in contrast to the politically and socially disorganized Germany of preceding decades.

New strata of leadership had to be formed, where character was more important than any so-called intellectual or alleged spiritual qualities: "What is decisive is not abstract knowledge but the innate capacity to lead and with it responsibility and decisiveness, courage and steadfastness. . . . The German Volkstate of today knows no social prejudices . . . it knows only the laws of life and necessity that people have arrived at through reason and knowledge." Clearly the Reichstag deputies, leaders in the party and state, must strive to resemble him, the mirror image of the born leader he had described, who in 1938 had decoded if not the laws of life at least the laws of power politics in Central Europe.

Hitler then turned to economics. Here the source of the Reich's trouble, he told his men of the Reichstag, lay in overpopulation of living space, 135 people to every square kilometer.

No other way was open to Germany than to maximize production in the living space it had. The effort to achieve the Four-Year Plan must be stepped up and more and more workers mobilized. In the first six years of National Socialism's coming to power the task had been to get all unemployed to work in productive jobs; in coming years the task was to make better use of workers, improve working conditions, and at the same time increase the working force and production.

Referring to the anti-German press campaign in Britain, he said: "We have no right to believe that if Germany in the future should be weakened its fate would take another form." On the contrary, the same men who had been responsible for the assault on Germany were preparing a new war. These "war apostles," men such as Duff Cooper, Eden, Churchill, and the American Harold L. Ickes, who was Roosevelt's secretary of the Interior, believed they had the right to calumniate other peoples and their leaders but that no one had the right to defend themselves against them. In itself the notion that Germany planned an attack on the United States would be turned away with a laugh and the continuous British hate campaign of the war apostles ignored, but the political structure of the democracies made it possible that the worst warmongers might come to power in the course of a few months. The security of the Reich made it imperative that the German people be informed about the machinations of these men. The German people had no hate for England, the United States, or France; Germany wanted only peace and quiet, but these other nations were being constantly incited by Jewish and non-Jewish warmongers. It was necessary for German propaganda to reply; the German people had to be informed who these warmongers were who wanted war at any price, and the Jewish "world enemy" would be overcome, as it had been inside Germany.

As for the lamentations over the plight of the Jews, he said:

> It is a shameful spectacle to see the whole democratic world weeping for the poor, tortured Jews and do nothing to help them. They say they are not in a position to help although they have ten people to the square kilometer and Germany 131. They say they can only accept them if they get a capital payment from Germany for their immigration. In any case Germany for centuries had been good enough to take in these elements although aside

from political and sanitary infections they brought nothing. . . . What these people possess today they obtained by the worst kind of manipulation at the cost of the German people who are not as crafty as they.

It was the Jews who had been responsible for the German postwar inflation, and the rest of the world had appropriated Germany's foreign capital and all its colonial possessions. At the end of the war eight hundred thousand German children had died of hunger and malnutrition, and nearly a million milk cows had been driven off by the Allies. Over a million German prisoners of war had remained in captivity for a year after the war ended; a million and a half Germans were driven from their homes with nothing but the clothes on their backs. Millions of *Volkcomrades* had been torn from the Reich without a hearing or the slightest possibility of going on with their lives.[11]

We are determined to stop this nesting of a foreign people that knew how to grab for itself any number of leading positions and to get rid of them, because we want these leading positions for the benefit of our own people. . . . Above all, German *Kultur,* as its name declares, is German, not Jewish, and its administration and care belong in the hands of our Volk. If the rest of the world hypocritically cries out against the barbarous exiling from Germany of such an irreplaceable, culturally most valuable element, we can only be astonished at the implications. These countries should be thankful to us for making these glorious culture-bearers available to them and to the rest of the world. According to their own explanations they have no grounds whatever to excuse their refusal to admit these valuable people to their own countries. . . .

For Europe will know no peace until the Jewish problem is cleared away. . . . The world had space enough for settlements; only the idea must be finally abandoned that God has chosen a certain percentage of the Jewish people to live as beneficiaries on the body and productive work of others. Jewry must be made to conform, as other people do, to solid constructive practices or sooner or later it will suffer a crisis of unimaginable proportions. And I should also like to add something else on this day that is perhaps not only memorable to Germans. I have often been a prophet in my lifetime and for the most part been laughed at. During the years of my battle for power it was mainly the Jews who laughed at my prophecy that I would one day take over the leadership of the German state and with it of the entire German people, and then find a solution for the Jewish problem among many others. I believe that the resounding laughter of Jewry in Germany has since stuck in their throats. I will be a prophet again today. If international, finance-Jewry in and outside Europe should again succeed in plunging the nations into a world war, the result will be not the bolshevization of the earth, and with it the victory of Jewry, but the destruction of the Jewish race in Europe.

The non-Jewish peoples, he said, were no longer defenseless against propaganda; they had National Socialist Germany and Fascist Italy to enlighten them. The Jews could continue their campaign of calumny in states where they were protected with their control of the press, films, radio, the theater, and literature, but woe unto them if they again succeeded in driving the masses into a completely senseless war that would serve only Jewish interests. The masses no longer wanted to die so this rootless, international race could make money out of war and satisfy its Old Testament lust for revenge. The Jewish watchword, "proletarians of the world unite," would be conquered by a higher one, "Workers of all the nations, know your common enemy."

Hitler's confident prediction that the Jewish race in Europe would be destroyed if war came would be borne out the more readily because it was he who was both prophet and executioner. The very word *Jew* triggered a litany of stored invective, repeating not only his own lifelong anti-Semitic fervor but also similar convictions held by generations in Germany and Austria, in Poland and the Baltic countries, and among the nationalities of the Soviet Union. Even the great democracies of the West were not exempt, and Hitler did not exaggerate their reluctance to admit Jews.

Still he was never able to unite the anti-Semites of the world. His vision went no further than the latitudes of a mighty empire ruled by National Socialist Germany, which had a limited appeal even to the most rabid anti-Semites outside the Reich.

Hitler refuted the charge made in "the so-called democracies" that National Socialism was an enemy of religion. No one in Germany, he declared, was persecuted because of his religious beliefs. The Reich year by year had increased the millions of marks it granted to both the Protestant and Catholic churches, from 130 million in 1933 to 500 million in 1939, plus considerable amounts to local community organizations. He asked how much England, France, and the United States had given their churches. Furthermore, not one church had been closed nor any service forbidden in the Reich, though he conceded that pastors could certainly be imprisoned for illegal political activities.[12]

He praised the lofty moral character of National Socialism with its purpose of maintaining the biological integrity of the German people. Five years before, he said, leading members of the National Socialist Party had been shot because of homosexual practices (a statement that must have surprised anyone who had swallowed his explanations of the killings in 1934; he had accused the leaders of the Röhm revolt of mutiny and high treason in his speech to the

Reichstag on July 13 and uttered not a word about homosexuality). If foreigners, he now said, and certain democratic statesmen protested the fate of a few German priests, they could only be acting for political reasons, because they had been silent when hundreds of thousands of priests were killed in Russia and tens of thousands of priests and nuns slaughtered like animals in Spain. And now, after Barcelona had finally fallen, he openly admitted what he had steadily denied during the course of the Spanish civil war—the presence of thousands of German and Italian "volunteers." Those forces had been placed, he said, at General Franco's disposition to stem the bolshevik tide in Europe. It had been National Socialism's concern for the culture and civilization of Europe that demanded the intervention.[13]

Fortunately the Reich had found allies inside and outside Europe. Italy and Japan, like Germany, had to struggle to maintain their existence. The Italians, heritors of ancient Rome together with descendants of the *Germanen* who had long been in contact with one another, had finally, after years of conflict, won their way to a united confrontation of the threat of bolshevism. He spoke of Italy's heroic battle for "vital rights" in Ethiopia, and with oblique reference to the unglamorous historical record of Italian military forces in Africa said the army of Fascist Italy was in no way to be compared with Italy's armed forces at the time of disunity. Germany was a staunch friend. Any attempt on the part of any international coalition to bring down Fascist Italy would cause Germany to spring to Italy's side. It was men, he said, who made history, and great men were only the strongest, most concentrated representatives of a people. National Socialist Germany and Fascist Italy were strong enough to guarantee peace and end any conflict that irresponsible forces might unleash.

That did not mean that Germany wanted war but only that Germany well understood that other countries, too, were by virtue of their strength and courage entitled to their share of the world's goods. Germany and Italy were brought together by common interests and joined by a heroic Japan in the Anti-Comintern Pact against the threat of bolshevism. Germany had no territorial claims against England and France, aside from the return of colonies. If there were tensions in Europe they were due to the conscienceless foreign press and radio and anti-Nazi—that is, anti-German—films made in America. If this did not stop, it would be countered by anti-Semitic films produced in the Reich. With the Jewish international press and propaganda curbed, mutual understanding of peoples of the world would be restored.

He again extended his hand to Britain with the same appeals he had made to Chamberlain. What conflict of interest existed between England and Germany? he asked. No German and especially no National Socialist wanted to cause the British Empire any difficulties. It would be a great good fortune for the whole world if these two peoples could arrive at a relationship of trust. The same thing was true for France. Obviously all Britain and France had to do was to give him a free hand in matters that did not concern them.

He riffled through a list of countries with which he foresaw good relations—"friends of peace" he called them. He praised the nonaggression pact with Poland as well as the "great Polish Marshal and patriot Pilsudski" who served his country in the same way as National Socialist leaders served theirs. The Polish-German pact of friendship had been one of the stabilizing factors during the uneasy months of the past year.

To the west, north, and south, he said, Germany had peaceful borders, and he expressed hope that Czechoslovakia would not fall back into the ways of Beneš. He welcomed the addition of Hungary and Manchukuo to the Anti Comintern Pact as a happy sign of consolidation of worldwide resistance to the Jewish-bolshevik menace.[14] Germany's relations with the United States suffered under the campaign of calumny leveled at Germany on the pretext that the Reich threatened American independence, but he was convinced this view was not shared by millions of Americans. Despite the gigantic Jewish-capitalist, anti-German propaganda campaign, the Americans did not believe a single word of what they were told. Germany, like every other country, including America, wanted peace and friendship; it would not mix in American affairs, and America must not mix in Germany's. "We have succeeded without bloodshed in finally creating the Greater Reich of the German people." This process required almost two thousand years and the labors of dukes, generals, kings, and Kaisers, and he thanked God for blessing this generation "with the boon of living in this time and this hour."

That was the benediction, and Göring rose to promise limitless obedience of Hitler's grateful people. "Here we sit," he told Hitler, "your first coworkers, my Führer, all of us united in the will to hold fast to our liege loyalty and to stride into the future, suffused with the will to follow you blindly to the highest ends, to the victory of our great German Volk. You have led us to unimaginable successes. You have made life great again, worthy of living and glorious. . . . You have created Greater Germany. How weak are all our words of thanks!"

Hitler had ranged himself amid the heroes of German mythology and history, and Göring's version improved on that. All that dukes, kings, generals, and Kaisers had accomplished culminated in Hitler, and in return the German people could only follow him rapturously, in blind obedience, to ever-greater heights.

As for the speech itself, part of it might have appeared naïve. How could Hitler believe Britain and France would sit by, accepting his professions of desire for peace as he acquired domain over strategic, non-German territories? In the late 1930s, however, in both Britain and especially France, a violent antiwar sentiment had arisen among tens of thousands of people who were ready to grant Hitler almost any concession rather than wage another war. Peace at almost any price seemed a better alternative to sober citizens who preferred any peaceful solution to the mass slaughter of the world war and the bleak disillusion that had followed the victory. Chamberlain and Daladier headed the governments of countries that could only put all their material and spiritual possessions at risk in another war. For the German people the bloodless victories Hitler celebrated were theirs too, and for both sides it was he who would decide on the next card to be played.

It was a long speech, and the most important part of it lay in what Hitler did not say. He had referred several times to the menace of bolshevism, Jewish bolshevism, but for the first time in a speech on foreign policy he had made no mention of Soviet Russia whose foreign minister, Maxim Litvinov, had been born Wallach-Finkelstein and most of whose founders Hitler had repeatedly and erroneously identified as Jews. It was an omission immediately noted by many attentive observers, including Stalin.

Hitler had not made up his mind whether to move east or west. The decision did not depend on him. He could offer inducements to Beck, but Beck in turn could not, even if he wanted, force a quasi alliance with the Reich on the president, Ignacy Moscicki, or the commander of the Polish army, Marshal Edward Smigly-Rydz, both of whom had rejected Hitler's proposals when Beck consulted them. Nor could he have had much more success with Polish public opinion, which, as the German ambassador to Warsaw observed to Beck, was almost unanimously anti-German. Poland had been founded on the defeat of the two Germanic powers, and any rapprochement with Berlin could only go so far without shaking the base of the Polish state.

One easy conquest and an important step toward those to come lay at Hitler's doorstep—he could close his accounts with the Czechs. In his speech he had warned them against returning to the ways of Beneš, and though the Prague government showed no signs whatever of doing that, Hitler was certain that in any future crisis Czechoslovakia would inevitably be on the side of his enemies. He would not need to order a shot fired to destroy the Czech state; its leaders were too demoralized after the Munich meeting to offer serious opposition to any German demands, and they had no foreign support. Their state remained vulnerable to its built-in conflicts; it still had bitterly divided, warring minorities within its borders, many of whom wanted to be completely free of Prague. In addition, since 1933, Czechoslovakia harbored increasing numbers of anti-Hitler refugees—German Jews, Social Democrats, and Communists—who were a constant irritant to the Führer with their articles in the Czech press denouncing his rule.

Hitler very likely never had any serious intention of carrying out his promise to guarantee Czechoslovak borders once problems of the Polish and Hungarian minorities were resolved. In Hitler's view, the guarantee would be forthcoming only when the other powers were ready to do the same thing. That time would only arrive when he gave the signal. The signal would never be given. On February 8 Britain and France wrote separate notes to Berlin suggesting it was time to give Czechoslovakia the guarantees promised at Munich. Hitler's reply was indirect; it went not to London and Paris but to a leader of the Slovakian independence movement, Voytěch Tuka.

Four days after the British and French notes were sent, Hitler received Tuka in the new Reichschancellery in the presence of Ribbentrop and the leader of the German minority in Slovakia, Franz Karmasin. Tuka, a university professor turned politician, was a well-known crusader for Slovakian independence. Basil Newton, the British minister to Czechoslovakia, said he was regarded in Slovakia as "a national hero." In 1928 he had been convicted by the Prague government of high treason and sentenced to prison where he had remained until a short time before his meeting with Hitler. On release he was made head of the Hlinka Guard, an SA-like nationalist Slovak formation.

Addressing Hitler as "Mein Führer," Tuka thanked him for granting the audience and assured him he was entitled to speak in the name of the Slovakian people.[15] Czech courts and prisons, he said, legitimized this claim. The Führer not only had raised the question of Slovakia: He was also the first to recognize the worthiness of the Slovak people, and the Slovaks wanted to join in the fight to preserve European civilization under his leadership.

It was clear to the Slovaks, Tuka said, that spiritually as well as economically their living together with the Czechs had become impossible. That they were still a part of the Czech state was possible only because the present government was believed to be transitional, but he and his comrades in arms were determined to yield to the urgent demand of the Slovak people to create an independent Slovakia. Its fate lay in the hands of the Führer. Tuka said that just as he had suffered in prison for his convictions he was also ready to sacrifice his life for his ideals.

If an insurrection broke out the Czechs would immediately seek to beat it down in blood, Tuka said, but a mere word from Hitler would suffice to bring such an attempt to a halt. The same thing was true of the aspirations of the Hungarians and the Poles; a word from the Führer would put a stop to them too. "I lay the fate of my people in your hands, my Führer," he said, "my people await their complete liberation from you."

Hitler in reply made clear that he was a man of generous goodwill toward the Slovaks, but with his many other cares during the Czech crisis he had been misled. He had been unaware of the true yearnings of the Slovak people; up to now he had no idea of the Slovak independence movement. He had given too much credence to Hungarian claims and had been so concerned with the German problem that he had been unable to study Czechoslovak problems. Even six months before, he had thought Slovakia wished to return to Hungary.[16]

Hitler said that he had been assured of the need for Slovak independence from all sides. Only since his talk with Béla Imredy in September had he been aware that Slovakia on no account wanted to be part of Hungary. At the time people were thinking entirely in *volkisch* terms, and he would never have considered sacrificing a single person for goals the Slovaks did not themselves seek. He was as objective toward the Czech people as toward any other, as long as they did not threaten the German people's right to existence. But now the situation was such that the Czechs in the depths of their hearts still had the wish to join in any anti-German action. They saw the sole reason for their existence as taking part in any European conflict that might erupt against Germany and joining any group with anti-German politics. This in short, he said, was what he called the Beneš mentality. The problem of Czechoslovakia had first been approached as purely ethnographic, and now Hungary proposed to disregard ethnographic principles. That could not be done, and he had so warned Hungary. A German reckoning with Czechia was not in order as long as the Czechs remained loyal; in that case they had nothing to fear. But it seemed as though the Czech government regarded the situation as a temporary embarrassment, and Hitler said he saw with discomfort the old hope of retaining the former borders, the old tendencies coming to life again, beginning to reassert themselves. He saw these manifestations in newspapers, in speeches, in utterances of responsible personalities, and in all kinds of sources. Chvalkovský himself, Hitler believed, had the best of intentions, but events did not stop with the goodwill of individuals. He had left Chvalkovský in no doubt that the moment he saw that this anti-German development was not to be arrested he would strike quickly and ruthlessly. No one would hold him back, and no one would help the Czechs, he was convinced of that.

Furthermore, if a major solution were to come about, Poland and Hungary would certainly want to participate. The ethnographic principle would be overrun, and Slovakia would be threatened. Under the present circumstances no distinction would be made between Czechia and Slovakia. A German saying went, "Caught together, hanged together," and in such circumstances where sheer force dominated, individual rights commanded no support. If the Slovaks in time of crisis had declared themselves independent, the situation would have been simple for Germany. Slovakia was in no danger; it had done the Reich no injury. Germany had no interest in its disappearance and would have immediately guaranteed its borders.

The logic of Czech ill will was forcing a solution. How insane it was for leading Czechs to continue to see in other evidences of European tension a flicker of hope for their nonsensical dreams of revenge. That, he said, was an incurable, major delusion. Even the Führer of greater Germany would never have such dreams. For example, he could never think of taking back Alsace-Lorraine.

The Slovakian people wished to be a free and happy people who determined their own fate, and he now understood that. Hitler said he could recognize an independent Slovakia at any time—even that day. He could not guarantee Czechoslovakia, because he certainly could not guarantee anything that would give the Czechs an open invitation to mobilize against Germany. He had hoped to arrive at a good relationship with Czechoslovakia, but others had predicted that Czech mentality would not permit it, and the predictions seemed to be realized. The Czech politicians in their megalomania were a Slavic outpost of Asia against Europe instead of what they ought to be—the outpost of Europe against bolshevism.

Summing up, Hitler repeated that he was sorry he had not known earlier of the Slovaks' desire for independence; he regretted that the situation had not been as clear when the solution would have been simple. If the Czechs were not ready to come to him with their national lot he saw the future darkly for Slovakia, too.

Tuka humbly replied that he knew the Czechs' future was dark, and that was why the Slovaks wanted to be free of them. Hitler said again that he feared Beneš's followers were raising their heads, strengthened by foreign support.[17] The Czechs were pouring oil on fire, so it could well be that things would get out of hand for them. After holding forth on Germany's strength and the strength of its army, he ended with the pregnant remark that it would be reassuring to know that Slovakia was independent.

Tuka took leave in an exalted mood. He told a councillor of the Reich's foreign office, Walter Hewel, who had been present and recorded the conversation, how enormously Hitler had impressed him. He could call this day, he said, the greatest of his life. He had never before had an opportunity to comprehend the unprecedented development of Germany during the last six years. Now, after he had listened to the Führer, he could understand it.[18]

So Hitler's mind was made up. Czechoslovakia had to disappear, and the Slovaks were to be the instruments of its dissolution.

What he told Tuka was all the Slovak secessionists needed to know. Their grievances, despite the grant of autonomy, remained unassuaged and would only fester until Slovakia was independent. Although the nationalists had gained considerable ground—nine thousand Czechs, state employees, and teachers employed in Slovakia had been forced to return to their Czech homeland— Slovak leaders nursed their rancors. Peter Pares, British counsel in Bratislava, recited reasons for their unhappiness in a report written February 3, 1939:

> It seems to be indisputable that the Slovaks were promised and therefore expected to receive a certain degree of autonomy within the Czech-Slovak state. But the Czech statesmen who made these promises failed to keep

them, and the Prague government began a policy of centralization which was the very reverse of these undertakings. In addition to the Slovaks' natural exasperation caused by the feeling that they had been duped, there was a further source of disagreement between Czechs and Slovaks in the former's violent anticlericalism which they endeavoured to introduce even into Slovakia. The majority of the Slovaks, who are a very pious and Catholic people, were extremely displeased and shocked.

Unfortunately, tactlessness in religious matters persisted and the narrow-minded selfishness of the Czech political parties, which were transplanted to Slovakia, led them to make a practice of filling even such insignificant posts as that of a janitor or railway porter with Czechs on the ground that no suitable Slovaks were available. After twenty years of great progress in education it was unwise to continue to employ this old pretext and to pay no heed to the growth of general dissatisfaction, which only increased the strength of the opposition headed by Father Hlinka.[19]

Catholic Slovaks and anticlerical Czechs had remained spiritually alienated, and Czech officials had made no secret of their contempt for Slovak cultural backwardness. The Prague government used a big stick and a small carrot to keep the Slovaks within the confederation. Alarmed by demonstrations for Slovak independence, they now withheld subsidies they had been providing Bratislava, and Pares reported in late February that funds were on hand for only one month's pay for officials while claims for travel expenses and allowances had gone unpaid for four months.[20] So the Slovaks had their autonomy and an empty treasury. It was their empty treasury that reminded them of their grievances.

The autonomy granted them had been promised before and long ago. In May 1918 Masaryk, in search of President Wilson's support for the new state he envisioned, had met with American, Czech, and Slovak leaders in Pittsburgh where they signed a joint statement in favor of the union of the two peoples in a future state in which Slovakia would have a separate parliament, administration, and law courts. With the defeat of Austria, the state was proclaimed in October 1918 by the Czechoslovak National Committee meeting in Prague. The United States and the Allies had recognized Czechoslovakia as an Allied nation, and its boundaries were confirmed in the treaties of Versailles and St. Germain.

But it was a Prague-centered state that developed, and Slovakian autonomy was never to become a reality until twenty years later. This time the Slovaks were granted their own administration and parliament within the Czechoslovak state, with another cleric, Monsignor Joseph Tiso, who with the death of Hlinka had become head of the Peoples' Party and minister-president of Slovakia.

Tiso was in favor of continuance of a Czechoslovakian state in which Slovaks would play an equal role with Czechs, but he had no way to put a stop to demonstrations for Slovak independence without alienating many of his most fervent followers. Prague could not continue to supply funds to a province clamoring for the disappearance of Czechoslovakia.

What Prague needed above all was Hitler's willingness to tolerate the continued existence of a state he had detested since it was founded. The Prague government was well aware of the minefields in its path and on February 22 addressed an aide-mémoire to the four Munich powers assuring them that to facilitate the guarantees Czechoslovakia was prepared to solemnly declare its strict neutrality and absolute nonintervention in any eventual European dispute.

What Hitler wanted had little to do with Czechoslovak neutrality: He wanted sole control of Prague's foreign and domestic policies. He ignored Czechoslovakia's aide-mémoire, and Weizsäcker disapprovingly pointed out to the Czechoslovak chargé d'affaires that the note had been addressed to the four Munich powers without having been discussed with the German Foreign Office.

Hitler's answer to British and French inquiries of February 8 about the German guarantee came only on February 28 and was addressed to London and Paris. It was blunt; it proclaimed an East European Monroe Doctrine, asserting Germany's paramount interest in that region. Germany, it said, was the country most deeply concerned with pacification of Eastern Europe; the Czechs theretofore had made use of intervention of other powers to create disturbances. A guarantee by the Reich of Czechoslovakia's borders would only heighten tensions that had led to the Munich Agreement.

The Prague government then went further in its acts of submission. On March 1 it made a dramatic concession; it stated it was ready to accept a German minister, to be named by Berlin, in the Czechoslovak cabinet. That would mean, the government representative said, that no decision would be taken by the cabinet that was incompatible with friendly relations with the Reich. Furthermore, the Czechoslovak government was ready to reorganize and reduce its army in accord with German wishes, and German military attachés in Prague could be increased as needed to oversee that this was being done.

These proposals were unprecedented in European politics. The invitation for a representative of a foreign government to take part as a full-fledged member in the decisions of a vital governing body, with the writ to police its military strength, was a deep incursion into Czechoslovak sovereignty. The proposals included three minor provisions: expansion of a German-Czech commission for protection of minorities, a quick adjustment of the remaining German-Czech border disputes, and a plan for economic and monetary cooperation. They were all moves of humble submission. No response whatever came from Berlin.

On March 9 the Czechoslovak foreign minister, Chvalkovský, made another despairing attempt to find out what Czechoslovakia could possibly do that might win any sign of tolerance from Hitler. He asked the German chargé d'affaires in Prague, Andor Hencke, with whom he felt he had good relations, to tell him confidentially, on a personal basis, what Hitler wanted of the Czech government. Would the Reich be ready to lend economic aid only on condition that Slovakia be independent? Two leading Slovaks, Ferdinand Ďurčanský and Mikulas Pruzinsky, had just visited Field Marshal Göring and had the impression the Reich would only lend aid if Slovakia declared its independence. Hencke replied, in accord with standing instructions from Ribbentrop to give no explicit answer to such requests, that he had no information on the subject but that no doubt there was some kind of misunderstanding. Chvalkovský asked bluntly if the German government wanted Slovakia to be independent, as Hencke must have some knowledge of such plans if they existed. Hencke replied stiffly he had no such knowledge, that Czechoslovak relations with the Reich were governed by the Munich Agreement and subsequent treaties. Chvalkovský begged Hencke to make inquiries in Berlin, not in a pressing fashion, he said, but "with a light hand" to find out if Slovakian independence was really a precondition to economic aid and if that was what the Reich wanted. As the responsible foreign minister of the central regime he had the right and duty, he said, to ask for confidential information, and if Berlin really wanted an independent Slovakia, Prague would have to consent to that solution. As foreign minister of the central government it would be senseless to represent a policy that Berlin did not approve, and he would rather give up his thankless job today than tomorrow. Hencke could only limply reply that Chvalkovský would do best to direct his inquiries to Pressburg (Bratislava), which would, however, be difficult in the absence of Göring from Berlin. Chvalkovský could only repeat his plea to Hencke to help him get a clearer view of the situation—perhaps, he suggested, this might even be possible by telephone? Hencke said this would be technically impossible, though he did not say what the difficulty was. Chvalkovský again asked Hencke to regard this request as purely personal and confidential, "from man to man," while Hencke was awaiting his instructions from Berlin. Hencke duly made his report of the conversation to Berlin, and on its margin a note was written: "Answer, on the verbal instructions of the Foreign Minister, will not be given."[21]

That was the situation when on March 10, 1939, the day following Hencke's report, Stalin made a fateful speech in which he made clear his unwillingness to go to war for the warmongering, hypocritical, and moralizing West—to pull, as he said, anyone else's chestnuts out of the fire. If Hitler needed final assurance that he need not fear Russian intervention if he were to confront the Western Allies with another bloodless coup, Stalin gave him reason. Coming after other hints noted by attentive observers of the possibility of a German-Russian rapprochement emanating from both Berlin and Moscow, the speech was a flickering green light. Above all else Stalin wanted to avoid war with Hitler's Germany. He agreed with those who saw Munich, from which the Soviet Union was conspicuously absent, as an attempt on the part of the West to turn Hitler to the East, to the vista of the conquests written of in *Mein Kampf.*

In a speech on the occasion of the Eighteenth Party Day, Stalin drew up a balance sheet of international affairs since he had spoken five years before at the Seventeenth Party Day. It was a vintage Stalin speech. Like Hitler, Stalin wrote his own speeches. (Who would dare speak for either of these two?) And his words were written so the common man would have little trouble with their meaning.

Stalin spoke as a marxist; he called a plague on both houses of the non-aggressor capitalist nations and their mirror image, the aggressor fascist nations.[22] The capitalists were timid hypocrites, unwilling to stand up to fascist aggressors, headed for economic collapse, and they richly deserved their unhappy lot. Many changes, he said, had taken place since the meeting five years before. For capitalist countries it had been a time of deep disturbances, economically and politically. Economically it had been a time of depression with industries collapsing in the United States, Britain, and France. Politically it had been a time of serious conflicts and disturbances. An imperialist war had been waged for almost two years, ranging from Shanghai to Gibraltar, affecting 500 million people. The entire postwar system, the so-called regime of peace, had been shaken to its foundations. The economic crisis that erupted in the capitalist countries in the second half of 1929 had lasted until the end of 1933, followed by an upswing, which usually develops in a period of recovery, but not by prosperity. On the contrary, a new economic crisis had appeared, affecting first the United States and then spreading to England, France, and other countries. This current crisis would be harder to overcome than former ones. It had erupted not in a time of peace but while an imperialist war was already in progress, in a time when Japan in the second year of its war against China had disorganized the enormous Chinese market and made it almost inaccessible to other powers, in a time when Germany and Italy had shifted their economies to a war basis and squandered their reserves of raw materials and foreign currencies, in a time when all the great capitalist powers had shifted to a war basis. As a result, Stalin said, capitalism had far fewer means at its disposal to recover by normal means. Ultimately the present crisis, in contrast to former ones, was not a general one but had mostly affected the economically powerful states that had not yet shifted to a war basis. As for the aggressor states—such as Japan, Germany, and Italy—that had organized prodigious economies on a war basis, the huge growth of postwar industries had yet to suffer a crisis of overproduction, though it was close. In their war fever the aggressor states had wasted gold reserves and raw materials and would have to face a severe crisis at the very moment when the economically powerful nonaggressor nations were beginning to emerge from their own crisis. Stalin continued:

> There can be no doubt that German industry, if nothing unforeseen happened, would experience the same downward trend that Japan and Italy had just gone through. What did it mean to organize an economy on a war basis? It meant pointing it in one direction—war. It meant producing goods for war, not consumption, shrinking to the uttermost, production, especially production of goods for general use, throttling popular consumption and ultimately thrusting the country into an economic crisis. That was the picture of economic crisis in the capitalist countries.
>
> ... such an unfavorable economic development can only exacerbate relations among the powers. The latest crisis has already mixed the cards and intensified the struggle for markets and raw materials. All this reflects the intensity of the battle among the powers. The new economic crisis must lead to an intensification of the imperialist struggle and has already done so.
>
> Germany had suffered heavily as a result of the First Imperialist War and the Versailles Treaty and now demanded an expansion of its territories in Europe and the return of its colonies taken from her by the victors of the First Imperialist War. That is how the bloc of the aggressor nations came about. A new division of the world by means of war lies ahead. . . .

The reason the nonaggressive powers were systematically making concessions to the attackers was because of fear of a revolution. Britain and France had rejected collective security and "every country may defend itself against the aggressors as it wishes and as it best can."

> . . . Thus Germany is goaded to march further east, she is promised plentiful and easy pickings and she is urged on: "Just begin a war against the Bolsheviks and everything will go well!" It must be admitted that it looks very much as though they wanted to encourage the attacker.
>
> The uproar in the English, French and American press over the Soviet Ukraine is characteristic. The gentlemen of this press shouted themselves hoarse telling how the Germans, now that they had the so-called Carpatho-Ukraine with about seven hundred thousand inhabitants in hand, were about to march against the Soviet Ukraine, and that no later than the spring of this year the Germans would annex the Soviet Ukraine with its more than thirty million inhabitants to the so-called Carpatho-Ukraine. It

appears that the purpose of this suspicious uproar was to incite the Soviet Union against Germany, to poison the atmosphere and provoke a conflict with Germany without any visible reason for it.

It is naturally possible that there are crazy people in Germany who dream that an elephant—the Soviet Ukraine—will affiliate itself with a mosquito—the so-called Carpatho-Ukraine. If there are really such insane people at hand in Germany, there can be no doubt that a sufficient quantity of strait jackets can be found for them in our country. But let us leave the crazy people to one side and turn to normal people. Is it not clear that it would be patently absurd and silly to speak seriously of the annexation of the Soviet Ukraine to the so-called Carpatho Ukraine?

. . . Even more characteristically certain European and American politicians and journalists have lost patience and no longer want to wait for the march on the Soviet Ukraine. They now begin to reveal what really lies behind the noninterventionist policy. They say quite openly, putting it black on white, that they are sorely disappointed in the Germans. Instead of moving further East to the Soviet Union—just think of that!—the Germans have turned against the West and demanded colonies. One might think that the Czechoslovakian territory delivered to Germany was the price of beginning a war against the Soviet Union but that the Germans now refuse to pay the bill.

Far be it from me to moralize over the nonintervention policy, to speak of betrayal, treason and such, for it would be naive to preach morality to people who have none.

. . . The tasks of the Party in the field of foreign policy are the following: (1) To continue the policy of peace and to strengthen economic relations with every country. (2) To be prudent and not permit our country to become involved in conflicts by war-mongers who are accustomed to allow others to pull their chestnuts out of the fire. . . .

The most important part of this speech concentrated on economics, suggesting a spectacularly new course in Soviet foreign policy. As Stalin would later confess, he gave a signal, a wink he called it, to Hitler, who understood. Along with the already-stigmatized aggressors—Germany, Italy, and Japan—Stalin referred to warmongers in general and to unnamed but identifiable powers that expected others to fight their battles. He mentioned the desire of those "nonaggressive" powers to deflect the German lightning eastward. He paid cautious tribute to Hitler's acumen in declining to pay his debt for being allowed by the peace-loving powers to take over the Sudetenland.

Observers in both camps noted the wink. Among them was the German military attaché in Moscow, General Koestring. Writing to a member of the army general staff, Colonel Kurt von Tippelskirch, Koestring referred to the matter-of-fact, ironic tone of the speech as contrasted with Stalin's customary inflammatory style and pointed out that if the Reich saw its chief antagonists in the West, Stalin could hope for a period of tranquility for the Soviet Union vis-à-vis Germany.[23] "A conflict in Europe," Koestring wrote, "would be the best deal for the Soviet Union." The able German ambassador to Moscow, Count von der Schulenburg, noted that Stalin's irony was much more sharply directed against Britain than against the "so-called aggressor states."

But regardless of Stalin's speech, Hitler's plans for the destruction of Czechoslovakia were proceeding rapidly. On March 11 the general staff, on Hitler's order, drew up the military demands for an ultimatum to be presented to Prague. It was a program for the occupation of a vassal state. The Czechs were to agree to no resistance by the army or police; troops would remain in barracks and lay down arms; no military or private planes were to take off; public life would continue; government officials, railroad, and postal employees would stay on their jobs at the disposal of the new authorities; economic life would continue; "complete restraint" was required of press, radio, theater, and of all public gatherings. Four days later the order was signed in Berlin by the president of Czechoslovakia, Emil Hacha, and Foreign Minister Chvalkovský.

In a last-ditch attempt to keep Slovakia, the Prague government on March 11 dismissed the Slovakian prime minister, Tiso, along with two members of his government regarded as too conciliatory toward the independence movement.[24] Two days later Tiso and Ferdinand Durčansky, a minister deposed with him, were flown to Berlin where they were received at the Reichschancellery.

Hitler held all the cards and played them skillfully. He informed the Hungarian Regent, Horthy, that at long last Hungary would be permitted to acquire the Carpatho-Ukraine, thus throwing a small but tasty morsel to both Hungary and Poland who would now have their common frontier. It was a meager but welcome compensation for surrendering hope of acquiring Slovakia. Horthy professed himself "endlessly grateful" in a handwritten letter sent to Hitler on March 13. He confided that a border incident would take place on Thursday, March 16, that would precipitate the Hungarian occupation of Ruthenia. It was, he wrote, a sign of friendship he would never forget and his gratitude would remain rock-ribbed *(Felsenfest)*.

Tiso too had cause to be grateful. Although deprived of his prime ministership by the Prague government, he had a special plane placed at his disposal in Bratislava, and while other prominent Slovak ministers fled to Vienna he met Hitler in the Reichschancellery on March 13 in the presence of Keitel, chief of staff of the high command of the armed forces, and Brauchitsch, commander in chief of the army, along with the secretary of state, Ribbentrop. It was a reception committee not unlike the one with which Hitler had received the Austrian chancellor in 1938.

But Tiso was a willing guest and a good listener as Hitler recited his new list of grievances against the Czechs.[25] It was, the Führer said, the Reich that had prevented the breakup of Czechoslovakia at Munich, and far from being grateful the Czechs had turned violently on the Germans remaining in the country. The Czech government had continued to publish attacks on Germany, its inflammatory leaflet propaganda contrasting with German forbearance. The Czechs had "thrown oil on fire" and, as Hitler had told Chvalkovský, this occurred in an area economically interdependent and in need of tranquility. Germans had been dismissed from their jobs and bloody incidents had taken place in Bruenn and Iglau; in short the German population was worse off than ever.[26] All this while not a hair of the Czechs living in Germany had been touched. Hitler explained again, as he had to Tuka, that he had been deceived when he had thought the Slovaks wanted to be part of Hungary and had learned only later that they wanted to be masters of their own lives.

Now, Hitler said, he had summoned Tiso to obtain a clear view of the Slovak situation. The Reich had no interests beyond the Carpathians; the question was whether Slovakia wished to live its own life. He did not want to be reproached by Hungary for conserving a state that did not want to be conserved. The Slovaks had to make their decision within hours, not days. If Slovakia wanted independence he would back independence, even guarantee it. If it delayed or did not want to be free of Prague, he would leave Slovakia to its fate, for which he would no longer be responsible. Slovakia had never belonged to Germany.

Hitler asked Ribbentrop if he had anything to add, and Ribbentrop dutifully repeated what Hitler had just said—the decision must be made within hours, not days. He passed over to Hitler a report he said had just arrived that described Hungarian troop movements on the Slovak border. Hitler handed the report to Tiso, who thanked him for his words and declared he had long yearned to hear from the Führer's own mouth how he felt about the Slovaks. He assured Hitler he could rely on them and asked to be forgiven if, under the impress of Hitler's words, he could not express himself clearly at the moment or even make a decision. He wished to discuss the matter with his friends and quietly consider the whole question. But, he assured Hitler, the Slovaks would demonstrate that they were worthy of his concern.

Tiso was as good as his word. The Wilhelmstrasse had thoughtfully provided him with the text, in Slovakian, of an appeal to Hitler to act as protector of the independent state of Slovakia. It declared the sovereign Slovak people had freed themselves from the unbearable Czech yoke and, following the will of the overwhelming majority of the population, proclaimed independence of the

Slovak state. The country was determined to live in peace and friendship with its neighbors but needed powerful protection and asked the Führer of the "mighty German Reich" that "under his rule had always stood for freedom and self-determination" to be guarantor of the state and protector of its borders. The appeal to Hitler was not submitted to the Landtag; it became evident in Bratislava that deputies who favored asking the protection of Hungary instead of Germany might vote against asking for Hitler's protection. Two days later, on March 16, Tiso sent a telegram to Hitler that followed the Reich's prescription; it read: "In deep faith in you, Führer and Reichschancellor of the Great German Reich, the Slovak state places itself under your protection. The Slovak state asks you to undertake this protection." A day later Hitler answered that he therewith undertook the protection.[27]

Even before the happy exchange of telegrams, Czechoslovakia had ceased to exist. The isolated Czech leaders had no choice, save to beg for an audience with Hitler who would reveal what they had to do. Hacha and Chvalkovský were to be rendered incapable of discovering, through diplomatic channels, what Hitler demanded of them. Ribbentrop instructed the German diplomats in Prague to seal themselves off from any attempts by Czech officials to obtain interviews. The answer to that riddle could only come from the mouth of Hitler. As for the Carpatho-Ukraine, its prime minister, Monsignore Voloshin, was not even summoned to Berlin. On March 14 Voloshin sent a telegram to Hitler seeking to place Ruthenia too under Hitler's protection, but Hitler had already awarded Ruthenia to Hungary. Voloshin was coolly advised that in the Reich's view the Carpatho-Ukraine should not attempt to resist the Hungarian invasion.

Chvalkovský did what he had to do. He asked the German chargé d'affaires in Prague, Andor Hencke, to have the kindness to arrange a meeting for President Hacha with Hitler. Hacha and Chvalkovský had to ask for an audience; they had to go to Berlin as petitioners not as emissaries; they had to listen, not to negotiate. They arrived in Berlin in the late evening of March 14. Because Hacha was sixty-six years old and had heart trouble his doctors had ruled out air travel, so he and Chvalkovský arrived by special train. Traveling with them was a forlorn entourage made up, as Paul Schmidt the foreign office translator observed, of routine bureaucrats left over from the Masaryk-Beneš days of Czech pride and presumption.

The Czechs were met at the Anhalter station by State Secretary Meissner and an SS honor guard and driven to the Hotel Adlon where they awaited instructions. An hour later Ribbentrop arrived for short ceremonial talks. It was one o'clock in the morning of March 15 when the president of Czechoslovakia and his foreign minister were driven to the chancellery where an honor guard of Hitler's SS Leibstandarte and a military band were drawn up. So Hacha was received as a head of state and dutifully inspected the guard while the band played the *Präsentiermarsch*. Then Hitler received the Czech visitors in his huge study with its gilded panels over the doors depicting the four virtues: wisdom, prudence, fortitude, and justice.[28]

Hacha obviously had no inkling of what to expect, and he naïvely began by thanking Hitler for receiving him, saying he had long wanted to meet the man whose "wonderful ideas" he had often read and followed. Everyone sat down, and Hacha went on, distancing himself as far as he could from the country's former presidents, Beneš and Masaryk. He was a jurist, he said, and had never been concerned with politics or politicians—"politicasters" he called them, with whom he seldom came in contact.[29] He had as little as possible to do with members of the government. He had seen Masaryk once a year at a formal supper for judges and seen Beneš even less frequently. He had never had anything to do with the Czech political establishment. The entire regime was foreign to him, so much so that after the great change, at Munich, he had asked himself if Czechoslovakia had been fortunate in becoming independent. He had accepted the presidency only as a patriotic duty.

Being president was the most difficult task of his life. He had the impression, he said vacuously, that the fate of Czechoslovakia lay in the hands of the Führer. He did not complain over what had happened in Slovakia; he had long been convinced that the different peoples in the body of the state could not live together. Although their languages were similar, they had developed differently. Czechoslovakia was closer to Germany than was Slovakia, which had much in common with the Magyars. So he was pleased that developments had taken this course, an attitude shared by four-fifths of the population. He thought the Führer would not have a very good experience with the Slovaks. Hitler, he said, had undoubtedly heard the rumors that Prague had breached the constitution. That must be charged to his account. He was a jurist, however, and knew there had been no breach when the Slovak government had been dissolved. He deplored some of the measures taken, but they had to do with maintenance of order. He shed no tears over the loss of Slovakia.

At last he came to what he said concerned him most—the fate of his country. He thought the Führer, of all men, would understand his view that Czechoslovakia had the right to aspire to a national life. Its geographical position, of course, demanded a special relationship to Germany. That was the foundation of Czech national life, and most Czechs agreed with this. Naturally there were exceptions, but it must be remembered that the new Czechoslovakia had existed for only six months. People reproached the country for still harboring many followers of the Beneš system. But those named were really not its friends; they existed only in journalistic circles, and the government was attempting with all its means to silence them. This was about all he had to say.

Hacha had misread all the portents. It was not merely a lifelong hatred of Czech aspirations he was confronting, but he was about to witness a violent Hitlerian outbreak of wrath, by a man with a nightmare vision of a Europe dominated by a millenarian Reich for which the Czechs were one contemptible obstacle.

Hitler began in a low key, accompanied by a Viennese *Höflichkeit* rarely at hand for his helpless victims.[30] He expressed to Hacha his regret that he had to require this long journey. But just this morning, after long reflection, he had become convinced that the journey, despite the advanced age of the president, would be of great use to his country since it was only a matter of hours before Germany would strike.

Basically, Hitler said, the German Reich had no enmity for any nation. "Nations that do us no injury are either dear to us or at least uninteresting; the German people have no hatred of Czechoslovakia, though Czechoslovakia has a different attitude." At the time of the Rhineland occupation, the Czech government had sent a note to France saying that if France wanted military action against Germany, Czechoslovakia was ready to go along. Czechoslovakia had done this though the question concerned ancient German territory. Czechoslovakia had done the same thing with regard to Italy at the time of the Ethiopian war, and by 1938 the situation had become insupportable. It was the well-rehearsed recital of old woes and of his own high purposes. He had no enmity, he said, for any nation, but he was a front-line soldier, a ruthless warrior on behalf of the rights of his own people, resolved to take any step necessary in this struggle. Czechoslovakia's very existence after Munich was due solely to his loyal attitude. At risk of arousing enmity of a friendly country he had forced Hungary to renounce its political ambitions and accept ethnographic principles in resolving its border problems, though this had the most ridiculous consequences for the Hungarian economy and customs services. For other countries Czechoslovakia had been merely a means to their own ends. London and Paris had made no attempt to help Czechoslovakia. For his part, Hitler said, he was completely indifferent to Slovakia and was glad that Germany had no obligations to her. He had no interests east of the Carpathians. He had told Chvalkovský explicitly that if the Beneš tendencies did not disappear he would strike ruthlessly. Chvalkovský had understood and had asked for patience.

But the months had gone by without any change. The new regime had not succeeded in causing the old psychology to disappear, as could be seen in the press, word-of-mouth propaganda, and the firing of German employees. At first he had not understood the situation, but as matters became clear he had come to see that if these developments continued the relationship with Czechoslovakia would be the same as it had been six months before. Why hadn't Czechoslovakia reduced its army to a reasonable level? The present army was a monstrous burden for such a state because it only made sense as a support of its state's foreign mission. Since Czechoslovakia no longer had a foreign mission such an army was senseless. The spirit of the army had not changed, and he gave examples. From these symptoms he had become convinced that the army too was a heavy political burden for the future.

So on Sunday he had made his decision. He had summoned the Hungarian ambassador and told him he had withdrawn his support from Czechoslovakia. He had given the order for German troops to march in, for incorporation of Czechoslovakia in the German Reich. He wanted Czechoslovakia to enjoy the most complete autonomy and its own way of life, more than it had in the Austrian period. The attitude of Germany toward the subdued Czechoslovakia would be decided tomorrow and the day following and would be dependent on the attitude of the Czech people and army toward German troops.

"At the moment," Hitler said, "we are experiencing a great historical turning point." He did not want to oppress or denationalize the Czechs; he was doing all this not out of hatred but to protect Germany. If Czechoslovakia last autumn had not yielded, the Czech people would have been eradicated. No one would have prevented him from doing that. It was his will that the Czech people have a full national life, and he firmly believed that a formula could be found in which Czech wishes would be widely met. If, though, it came to battle, force would be met by counterforce. They would rub one another out, and it would no longer be possible for him to make the promised alleviations. In two days the Czech army would cease to exist. Germans of course would die, too, and hate would be engendered that would compel him to rescind autonomy. The world would not bat an eye. He pitied the Czech people when he read the foreign press. It reminded him of the Germans saying: "The Moor has served; the Moor can go."

This was the way things were. Two courses were open to Germany: a hard one where no concessions would be granted, and with the past in mind Czechoslovakia would be brought down in blood, and another whose conditions he had described. That was why he had invited Hacha to come. The invitation was the last good deed he could render the Czech people. If it came to battle, the gushing blood would necessarily carry hate with it. Perhaps Hacha's visit could prevent the worst from happening. Perhaps it would lead the way to a construction that would be more ample for Czechoslovakia than any hoped for in the old Austria.

The hours were passing. At 6:00 A.M. the next morning troops would march in. Hitler said he was almost ashamed to say that opposite every Czech battalion stood a German division. Military action would certainly not be minor but undertaken with full force. He suggested that Hacha withdraw, with Chvalkovský, to discuss what could be done. "If you want to prevent bloodshed, it would be best if you telephoned Prague immediately and advise your war minister that no resistance is to be made by the Czech troops."

Hacha replied that the situation was now very clear to him; resistance would be senseless. He asked how he could arrange in four hours to prevent the entire population from resisting. Hitler said Hacha could discuss that with his entourage. The German military machine was rolling and could not be stopped. Hacha should talk with his office in Prague. It was a major decision, but Hitler said he foresaw the possibility of a long period of peace for both peoples. If the decision was different he foresaw the destruction of Czechoslovakia.

Hacha asked if the entire goal of the march-in was to disarm the Czech army, and if so perhaps that could be accomplished in another way. Hitler said his decision was irrevocable, and everyone knew what a Führer decision meant. He saw no other possibility and turned to the others present to ask if they did. They agreed with him. The only possibility of disarming the Czech army was through the German army. It was the worst day of Hacha's life, Hitler said, but in a few years the decision would be understandable and in fifty years it would be blessed. The two Czechoslovaks left the room together with Göring, Ribbentrop, and all the other Germans present except Hitler.

Hacha and Chvalkovský had sat like two stone statues while Hitler denounced their predecessors, and Hacha was close to the end of his physical and psychic resources as he came to realize what Hitler demanded. He retained his outward composure until they had left Hitler's study and Göring took over. Göring threatened to obliterate Prague with his Luftwaffe if Hacha did not sign the paper prepared for him that yielded Czech sovereignty. Hacha fainted. Schmidt heard Göring call loudly for Hitler's personal physician, Dr. Morell, who appeared and was able to revive the president with a hypodermic injection—a frequently used weapon in Morell's meager medical arsenal.

Lurid stories later went around describing macabre scenes of the meeting. According to one account Hacha had the impression Hitler was pursuing him around the table, flourishing the piece of paper he would have to sign to turn his country over to Hitler. But Schmidt, the translator, present almost the entire time, saw no such scenes. Schmidt would write after the war that, though Hitler could not talk in moderate tones about Beneš and the Czechs, he had seen the Führer far more exercised during the Munich crisis. Hitler had spoken with fervor, he reported, as he always did when the subject of Czech malefactions arose, but in this meeting there were no outbursts, only the long list of impassioned complaints and the stricken faces of the two Czechs.

A clear telephone line with Prague seemed impossible to obtain. A voice would be heard indistinctly, followed by silence. Ribbentrop excitedly ordered Schmidt to get hold of the Reich minister in charge of the Post—lives were at stake, he roared. Minutes went by, and when the telephone line seemed again to be working Hacha was summoned from conversation with Göring in the next room. The line promptly went dead again, and Ribbentrop exploded to Schmidt over the base incompetence of the minister of Post who was asleep while "we here are all hard at work." It was then that Hacha fainted and that Göring called for help. "I think he'll be all right," Göring said. "For an old man it's been a pretty strenuous day." Ribbentrop shouted that the telephone staff at the foreign office would be fired on the spot if the line was not in order in an hour. The connection with Prague was made, and the recovered Hacha and Chvalkovský talked with their people at the foreign office, though with difficulty, as was evident from Chvalkovský's loud voice and slow speech.

An hour and a half after the telephone calls, Hacha and Chvalkovský returned to the Führer's study to sign the papers. Hitler was much more relaxed. He said that in one place or another confrontations might take place, but in general they could count on a frictionless invasion. Furthermore, he thought, the bitterness the occupation might cause would slowly diminish as recognition dawned that a century-long coexistence of the two nations would be useful. The presumption that the two peoples must do battle would disappear. Czechoslovakia was rooted in the German Reich, and reason itself must make clear to everyone that only the closest coexistence of both peoples had to be the order of the day. Denationalization would play no role; that was far from National Socialist ideology. "We do not want denationalization, the one side should live as Czechs and we want to live happily as Germans. The German Reich could be generous in this matter."

Hacha assured Hitler that what he had said was of utmost importance. Hitler continued to say that Germany could not endure economic, military, and political opposition. Czechoslovakia should keep its own head of state and its principles that he would put into practice, and that would provide the basis for pacification of the region for centuries to come. Hacha threw in that there should be no soul-selling, as in the Austrian period, and asked if a customs union was planned. Hitler laughingly waved off the first part of Hacha's remark, about soul-selling, and Göring answered the second in the affirmative, because, he said, Germany and Czechoslovakia were one economic area. In addition, Czechoslovakia would be given orders for goods that would double its production. Hitler added that the Czechoslovakian people would gain economically through the union with Germany. It would take its part in the greater Germany economic sphere. He did not want to destroy the Czech economy but to revive it enormously. Hacha asked if guidelines for this were already at hand. Hitler answered that this would be a subject for an economic commission, since the whole problem had come up for him so unexpectedly. A couple of weeks ago he would have known nothing of the matter. He returned again to the Beneš tactics and to the circle supporting him and of his own May 28 decision to act, which he had confided only to a small circle. He ended with the remark that the measure that had been taken was final, bearable, and had to be unambiguous. In any event, the Czechs would have more rights than they had ever given the Germans in their territory. Then the agreement was signed.

14

The End of Appeasement

On March 15 a German army of tanks and infantry commanded by Generals Blaskowitz and List moved into Prague and the rest of Bohemia and Moravia. It was a raw, snowy day, and the troops marching into Prague in ranks of six clumped past a silent, hostile population vastly different from the rejoicing masses that had deliriously welcomed their "liberators" in Vienna and the Sudetenland. Many of the Czechs in Prague, a British journalist reported, kept to the side streets to avoid having to look at the invaders.

Hitler and his entourage arrived at Hradčany Castle, the sprawling gothic seat of the Bohemian kings overlooking the city, in the early evening of the fifteenth, and it was there that they spent the night.

It was an ides of March that would prove as fateful for him as for the Czechs. Up to then Chamberlain and many others might well, however guardedly, have tried to accept his repeated assertions that he was essentially undoing injustices imposed on the Reich, that he wanted no Czechs in his Germanic state, and that he had no further claims in Europe once the last of the intolerable wrongs inflicted on a betrayed Germany were righted. Over and over he had repeated that he sought only to restore a *Volks-German* state united by blood and history.

Despite the searing news of the invasion, it seemed for a little while that Chamberlain still clung to a hope that Hitler might be brought to ways of peace and reason. Chamberlain sourly told the House of Commons on March 15 that German troops had crossed borders that the Reich had accepted in Munich without, as far as he knew, consulting any of the powers that signed

360

the agreement.[1] While this, he said, had occurred with consent of the Czech government, it had to be regarded as a violation of the spirit of the Munich Agreement. "It is natural," he told the House, "that I should bitterly regret what has now occurred, but do not let us, on that account, be deflected from our course. Let us remember that the desire of all the peoples of the world still remains concentrated on the hopes of peace." Setbacks and disappointments had to be endured, he said, but the goal of peace was of too great importance for the welfare of mankind to be lightly set aside.

Permanent Under Secretary of State for Foreign Affairs Sir Alexander Cadogan, noting in his diary that Chamberlain was continuing a policy of appeasement, wrote: "Fatal!" Two days later, however, in a speech on March 17, the eve of his seventieth birthday, in his native city of Birmingham, Chamberlain reversed himself, joining the ranks of those who had long held that Hitler could not be trusted and that he could only be stopped by a force that matched his own, by as many powers as might be recruited against him. Not only the Reich's neighbors, Chamberlain said, were deeply concerned but others too, perhaps even countries beyond the borders of Europe. Britain would consult France and its partners in the commonwealth, and every aspect of British life would be scrutinized; nothing that would buttress national security could be overlooked. Was this invasion, he asked, the last attack on a small state, or would others follow? Was it perhaps even a step in the direction of an attempt to dominate the world by force? The end of an old adventure or the beginning of a new one? Chamberlain said he hoped that it would be unthinkable for such a challenge to be made, but should it be made he was certain of support of nations that cherished peace, but even over peace—*freedom*.[2]

To his longtime critics, of course, it was ludicrous to hear this old gentleman continue to recite the beatitudes of peace lovers. He was dealing with Hitler, the man many people including Chamberlain himself at times thought possibly insane.

And Hitler was certain he knew his man, this scion of the bloodless, gutless inheritors of British power. Hitler was on a roll. His next stop was Memel, and it did not take him long to get there. On March 22 Germany and Lithuania signed the treaty Hitler demanded, returning Memel to the Reich. Again, there was nothing and nobody to hinder him, not even a moral case, should he have been interested in one, against return of a German city that had only been handed over to foreign sovereignty when the Reich could not prevent its loss. Lithuania, under this new treaty, was to be awarded a free zone in Memel's harbor, and both Lithuania and Germany bound themselves not to use force against one another or to assist any third power against the other.

Mussolini was completely unprepared for Hitler's invasion of what remained of the Czechoslovak state. Hitler had given him no indication whatever of his plans, and the irate Duce refused to let the Italian press publish the news that the German ambassador, Prince von Hessen, called on him to deliver. "The Italian press," Mussolini told Ciano, "would make a laughing stock of me; every time Hitler occupies a country he sends me a message." Ciano scornfully noted the propagandistic reasons Hitler had given Mussolini for the invasion—the Czechs had failed to demobilize, they continued to maintain contact with the Soviet Union, and they mistreated their German minority. That might do, Ciano said, for Goebbels's propaganda but should not be fed to Mussolini.

Many observers thought that the Italian invasion of Albania on April 7, about which the Germans were not warned either, was a result of Mussolini's pique. But the plan to take over Albania and confirm *Mare Nostrum* and the new Roman imperium had been prepared months before; it had awaited what Mussolini considered a propitious political moment. Thus on April 12 the crown of Albania, thitherto resting on the uneasy head of King Zog, was conferred upon the king of Italy by unanimous vote of the Albanian assembly. Zog and his queen, Geraldine, a former Hungarian countess, took refuge in Greece and a few months later in Britain.

The end of Czechoslovakia's independence provided Hitler with the last base he needed if he was to attack Poland. As he had secured the Rhineland before moving into Vienna and occupied Austria before moving into the Sudetenland, he again established a greatly improved strategic position: the increment of the Czech stockpile of munitions produced by the Skoda works and the freedom to deploy his armies against a Polish adversary without regard to a Czech border. He could invade Poland without looking over his shoulder. Until the latter part of March he still had not given up hope of making Poland an ally, but by the end of the month he was ready, as he had promised his general staff he would be at the right political moment, to obliterate Poland for decades to come.

He had been a persistent wooer, and the Poles had waited too long. On March 21 Ribbentrop received the ambassador to Berlin, Lipski, to present Hitler's urgent proposal to bring Poland into the German orbit. Again Ribbentrop sketched the well-rehearsed relationship the Reich foresaw; Danzig and the Corridor would be of insignificant concern in the vaster perspective of the Reich and Poland, working together, in their common interests. He did not spell out what the rewards would be but hinted that Slovakia, whose protection, to the consternation of the Poles, the Reich had just guaranteed, would have a place in Poland's future and so would the Ukraine.

He offered nothing precise, just the glittering prospect of compensations to come once Poland accepted the return of Danzig to Germany, the corridor through the Corridor, and a joint anti-Soviet policy; then everything would fall into place and minor dissensions fade. He reminded Lipski of common historical interests, how Germany in fact had made a Polish state possible following the world war, and how Hitler had prevented General Schleicher from making an alliance with Russia that could have led to the fall of Poland. But Danzig was a German city and must return to the Reich, though with due regard for Poland's special interests, and the autobahn connecting a severed Prussia had to be built. The Poles would be richly rewarded for making such minor sacrifices.

Although he was proposing nothing new, Ribbentrop was so carried away by his own eloquence that he urged Lipski to return to Warsaw immediately, that very day, to place Hitler's prospectus before Beck. Lipski, he said, should not put the journey off because of the danger that Hitler might regard any delay as a sign Poland might reject his invitation. Although the conversation took place at the very time the return of Memel was being arranged with Lithuania, and Lipski asked Ribbentrop directly whether he might wish to tell him something of his conversations with the Lithuanian foreign minister, Ribbentrop divulged nothing whatever of the negotiations with Lithuania. He merely urged Lipski to arrange for Beck to come to Berlin for new talks with Hitler because, he explained, Hitler had now decided on his Eastern program, which would have to be quickly realized, and the Reich must now know definitively where Poland stood.

The Polish answer came four days later, March 26, delivered by Lipski when he returned from Warsaw. Couched in friendly terms and referring to the many evidences of Polish goodwill toward the Reich it was nevertheless an unmistakable "no."

Poland, the note said, would indeed cooperate with the Reich, it would do everything to make communication between the two Prussias easier; the fullest autonomy would continue to be granted German citizens of Danzig, but Polish sovereignty would be maintained in the Corridor, and Danzig would remain a free city. Further evidence of resistance to Hitler's offer was provided by the German ambassador to Warsaw, Moltke, who reported that three to four classes of reservists, from 1911 through 1914, had been called up for duty. Still, Beck was evenhanded: The British were asking Warsaw to join in a statement with Britain, France, and the Soviet Union warning against an attack on any of them, and Beck had refused. Polish policy remained to stay aloof from a commitment to either the Russian or German camp. In Beck's view, as in Pilsudski's view in earlier years, only in neutrality between its two powerful neighbors could Poland's future be assured. In place of the British proposal for a joint declaration by Britain, France, the Soviet Union, and Poland, Beck had suggested to London a British-Polish agreement to coordinate their policies, pointing out that Poland already had an alliance with France as did Britain. His proposal made no mention of the Soviet Union, which, from the Polish point of view, would be almost as great a threat as an ally as she would be as an enemy. In any event Beck could well feel himself strengthened in any negotiations with

Hitler by the clear call for Poland to participate in the movement to stop Hitler. His instructions to Lipski, as Lipski returned to Berlin, were a continuation of Beck's former line but with a more belligerent edge; there would be no change in the status quo of Danzig or in Polish sovereignty in the Corridor. An agreement could readily be reached with the Reich on all the lesser differences, but on crucial points there would be no accommodation.

By the time the German ambassador to Warsaw met with Beck, on March 28, Beck's position had stiffened.[3] Referring to Ribbentrop's statement that any attack on Danzig would be regarded as an attack on the Reich, Beck told Moltke that any attempt on the part of Germany to change the status quo in Danzig would be regarded as an attack on Poland. Any similar attempt on the part of the Danzig senate would produce an immediate Polish reaction. The Polish government, Beck continued, had no intention of committing any act of violence and looked toward an understanding with the Reich. But when Moltke said, "You want to negotiate on the points of bayonets," Beck did not deny it; he simply replied: "Following your system."

And when England agreed to adopt Poland into its cordon sanitaire without reference to the Soviet Union, all the long-suppressed Polish ardors to put the Reich in its place were released. For the first time since 1919, Poland got what it had been looking for and had always been denied—the guarantee of its post–world war frontier by Great Britain.

It was an ad hoc alliance Britain was attempting, and its prospect was not greeted enthusiastically by all the intended beneficiaries. The Polish ambassador to Paris, Juliusz Lukasiewicz, for one, was critical of Britain and France and the invitation to the Soviet Union to participate in the anti-Hitler coalition, complaining to the American ambassador, William C. Bullitt, that it was "childish, naive and unfair" for Britain and France to push Poland toward hostilities with its powerful neighbor mainly to satisfy British public sentiment and pointing out that within the last twenty years Britain and France themselves had been pursuing a policy of weakness. But for most Poles the British guarantee was precisely what Poland needed and deserved, and it made no mention whatever of the Soviet Union.

On March 31 Chamberlain went further in a speech to the House of Commons.[4] He extended the British guarantee to Danzig. He did not mention the city, but there was no mistaking that Britain was aligning itself with the Polish position in Danzig.

> As the House is aware, certain consultations are now proceeding with other Governments. In order to make perfectly clear the position of His Majesty's Government in the meantime before those consultations are concluded, I now have to inform the House that during that period in the event of any

action which clearly threatened Polish independence, and which the Polish Government accordingly considered it vital to resist with their national forces, His Majesty's Government would feel themselves bound at once to lend the Polish Government all support in their power. They have given the Polish Government an assurance to this effect.

I may add that the French Government have authorized me to make it plain that they stand in the same position in this matter as to His Majesty's Government.

Now there was no possibility that Hitler could persuade Beck to accept the German offer. Up to this point it had seemed possible that Beck would manage to continue a semblance of neutrality between Russia and Germany; from here on Poland became part of what Hitler called the encirclement of the Reich.

For Beck as for Pilsudski, Russia, especially bolshevik Russia, was anathema, more damnable even than Hitler's Reich. Their revulsion was perhaps understandable in light of Polish and Russian history, for it took little account of geography. No major military aid could be provided for Poland by any Western ally; only the Soviet Union could provide that. The guarantee of Poland's borders with the Reich was well-nigh worthless in short range—at least, unless the Soviet Union was cooperating with Poland and the West. So the British guarantee did much to strengthen the ardor of the most belligerent and patriotic Poles, though it promised support neither Britain nor France could supply unless the Soviet Union was a party to the alliance.

Stalin had already made it clear that the Soviet Union was not prepared to pull anyone else's chestnuts out of the fire. On March 28 Stalin again indicated that the only chestnuts that interested him were his own. The Soviet Union, through its foreign minister, Litvinov, informed the Estonian and Latvian governments in similar notes that they were not quite the sovereign states they pretended to be. The notes came out of the blue, no event precipitated them, their origin and purposes were Moscovian. The note to Estonia stated that maintaining Estonia's independence was a matter of interest not only to itself but also to the Soviet state. Therefore, the note went on, any treaty Estonia might make voluntarily or under pressure that might have the effect of diminishing its independence and sovereignty would be regarded by the Soviet Union as unacceptable. The note was sent, Moscow said, in the spirit of genuine goodwill for the Estonian people, with the goal of strengthening their sense of security and maintaining Estonia's sovereignty and its political and economic independence against any attempt, open or clandestine, that might seek to diminish them.

Estonia replied promptly and stiffly that it alone could decide whether its foreign obligations were being fulfilled, and it alone had responsibility to watch over its neutrality and independence. The Baltic coast with its approaches to

Leningrad was a neuralgic point for the Soviet Union. Moscow's notes have usually been interpreted as directed against possible German demands for naval bases that would threaten Leningrad. Coming a day after the British guarantee to Poland, the Russian notes could be read as an invitation to the British to keep their hands away from the Baltic states. Up to this point, the only threat in that region had been manifested in the German demand on Lithuania to agree to return the Memelland to the Reich. Berlin had made no demands involving the other two Baltic countries. But the British-French invitation to Poland and Romania to join in the anti-Hitler bloc was pressing, and Stalin was making plain that he would tolerate no similar strategy in the Baltic unless it had his approval.

On April 17 Stalin gave another indication that the Soviet's foreign policy was not as fixedly anti-German as the West would like.[5] The newly appointed Russian ambassador to Berlin, Alexej Merekalov, met for the first time with the German secretary of state, Weizsäcker, to discuss among other things the fulfillment of the Soviet arms contract through the Skoda works now under German control. Toward the end of the discussion, which was to be continued in other quarters, Weizsäcker remarked that the atmosphere for such talks was not exactly improved by reports of a Russian-English-French air agreement and similar evidences of Russia's cooperation with the West. Merekalov, Weizsäcker noted, took this as an opportunity to turn to politics and asked about German views of the situation in Middle Europe. Weizsäcker replied that as far as he knew Germany was the only country not taking part in the present saber-rattling. Merekalov asked about the German relationship with Poland and reported military brushes sporadically occurring on the German-Polish border. After Weizsäcker denied any such had taken place, Merekalov asked him bluntly how he regarded German-Russian relations. Weizsäcker replied that the Reich had always had the desire to live with the Soviet Union in a mutually beneficial economic exchange. The Russian press, it seemed to him in recent days, had adopted a somewhat different tone from that of the anti-German American and English presses. As for the German press, Merekalov (who certainly kept track of it), Weizsäcker said, could draw his own conclusions. The ambassador said Russian policy had always been straightforward. Ideological differences had hardly damaged Russian-Italian relationships and need not disturb German-Russian relations. Soviet Russia had made no use of the friction between Germany and the Western democracies and did not want to do so. There was no reason, as far as Russia was concerned, why it should not live in normal circumstances with Germany, and out of normal relations better ones could grow. With this remark, Weizsäcker reported, Merekalov took his leave. He intended, he said, shortly to make a trip to Moscow.

The conversation in Berlin was one more sign that Stalin was coming closer. From time to time, since Hitler first took power in 1933, the Kremlin had given signs that Russia would welcome better relations with the Reich.[6] In July 1935 the leader of a trade delegation, Bessonov, asked Schacht in the course of their discussions whether political relations between the two countries might not be improved. Schacht had merely replied that this was a matter for the foreign office. The possibility of improvement was again brought up by Bessonov at the German Embassy in Moscow at the end of November 1935, when he reminded Werner von Tippelskirch, a member of the Russian section of the German Foreign Office, of "the natural common interest of their two countries." On July 3, 1936, in Berlin, Bessonov returned to the theme, outlining possibilities of a bilateral Russian-German nonaggression pact.

In 1935–1936 no German replies followed. The Kremlin's cautious approaches had shattered on Hitler's adamant refusal to listen to them.

But other times required other strategies, and it now appeared to Stalin that Hitler might be listening. The indications required moderately sensitive detection devices. And the note Litvinov delivered to Count von der Schulenburg on March 18, 1939, while sternly disapproving of annexation of Czechoslovakia, made no formal protest as was immediately noted by both Schulenburg and Tippelskirch. The latter pointed out that Stalin was more critical of the method of annexation than of the result and had not found it necessary to recall his ambassador from Berlin. The Soviet note, Schulenburg observed in transmitting it to Berlin, merely declared it was not possible for Moscow to be silent and give the false impression the Soviet regime was indifferent to events that could not be regarded as legitimate. Schulenburg noted that Litvinov, in answering questions of foreign journalists at his press conference, made no answer when asked what practical result he believed the Soviet note would have. The note, in short, confined itself to comfortable observations: praising the peaceful historical record of the former Czechoslovak republic, rejecting the German claim that Hacha had trustfully turned over his country to the Reich, and declaring it was difficult to admit that any people would willingly assent to destruction of their independence and absorption in another state. In view of these circumstances, the note stated limply, assimilation of the Czech and Slovak state could not be regarded as legal under recognized norms of international law and self-determination.

If Stalin, like Hitler, was keeping his options open, this was no longer true of Beck. Poland's acceptance of the British guarantee of its borders in the event of a German attack reversed what he and Pilsudski had been striving to accomplish— that is, to keep Poland a neutral between the great powers, Germany and Russia. On the one hand the British guarantee of Polish borders on the Reich was a recurrent dream come true; on the other hand Poland's acceptance of it was a fateful decision that aligned Warsaw, in Hitler's view, with the enemy camp.

As for the British they too had taken an extraordinary risk. To recruit their *posse comitatus* they had given Poland power to declare war on their behalf. And the grounds for Britain's going to war were quickly extended when Chamberlain on March 31 announced to the House of Commons that a permanent agreement between the two countries "would be designed to assure Great Britain and Poland of mutual assistance in the event of any threat, direct or indirect, to the independence of the other." In other words, if Poland decided to fight for Danzig, Britain would join.

Moscow remained aloof and tentative, clearly a potential part of the anti-Hitler coalition but not easy to pin down with any hard-and-fast commitments. Early in April an article in Tass denied a report that Russia had agreed to supply the Poles in the event of war, and while Britain in mid-April extended its guarantees to Greece and Romania if they considered themselves threatened, Moscow declared the Soviet Union would not go to war on behalf of Romania, though the Western powers regarded Romania, on whose oil supplies the Reich must depend, as indispensable in the anti-Hitler alliance.

Stalin would simply not be nailed down. On April 18 the Soviet Union submitted the draft of a treaty for an alliance with the Western powers, but its terms were Moscovian. It provided for a treaty to last for five to ten years in which the participants agreed on mutual assistance, including military assistance, in case of "an aggression in Europe against any one of the signatories." It embraced "all east European states between the Baltic and the Black Sea and which border on the Soviet Union." Britain was to declare the assistance that she had just promised Poland was limited to assistance against aggression on the part of Germany, and the pact between Poland and Romania that had been signed in 1921 and had been directed solely against the Soviet Union now would include any aggression by other nations against the Soviet Union. It was a proposal that Halifax reluctantly admitted was unacceptable to Poland—a country, he said, that would not be publicly associated with the Soviet Union—and the attitude of Romania was much the same. Britain had to walk a chalk line; Poland was a fighting nation, perhaps the only one in Europe, spoiling for a fight with the Reich. So the Russian proposal could not be readily accepted.[7] Some two weeks later it was followed by news that Litvinov had lost his post as foreign minister. In the announcement as it appeared in the *Frankfurter Allgemeine Zeitung* his name appeared as Litvinov-Finkelstein.[8] Litvinov had left office, the announcement said, voluntarily.

Indications that the Soviet position might be shifting were noted by attentive observers in the foreign offices, but this had no visible effect on the campaign of the French and British governments to bring Russia into the collective security they were seeking against Hitler. The so-called antifascist forces were so powerful throughout the West that motives of realpolitik were seldom mentioned in the minutes of higher councils.

On April 15 President Roosevelt addressed a cable to Hitler with a copy to Mussolini that called on them to mend their ways or else.[9] The cable has been called a moral declaration of war against the dictators, or at least against these two dictators. It merely enabled Hitler to display his talent of sarcasm and ridicule without leaving much ammunition for the proponents of the collective security system. Roosevelt's was a preposterous telegram. Mussolini first refused to read it, then, according to Ciano, he called it a result of progressive paralysis—referring to Roosevelt's well-known infirmity. After reciting the anxieties of the peace-loving countries the president had asked Hitler whether he had any intention of attacking thirty countries, which he named: among them were Finland, the Baltic countries, Sweden, Norway, Denmark, Ireland, France, Portugal, Spain, Switzerland, Poland, Hungary, Russia, Bulgaria, Turkey, Iraq, the Arab states, Syria, Palestine, Egypt, and Iran. "Such an assurance," he said, "clearly must apply not only to the present day but also to a future sufficiently long to give every opportunity to work by peaceful methods for a more permanent peace. I therefore suggest that you construe the word 'future' to apply to a minimum period of assured nonaggression, ten years at the least, a quarter of a century if we dare to look that far ahead." He would immediately transmit such an assurance to the governments of the nations he named and ask that they in turn give like assurances for him to transmit to Hitler.

"Reciprocal assurances," Roosevelt said, "such as I have outlined will bring to the world an immediate measure of relief." Important problems could be dealt with in a peaceful atmosphere. The United States would be glad to take part in these discussions. Three days later the German information service announced that Hitler regarded the communication as so important that he would answer it in the name of the German people before the Reichstag, which he convened on the 28th of April for this purpose alone.

It was an occasion made to order for Hitler's style of oratory and invective.[10] It enabled him to recall days when the so-called peace-loving nations chopped off large sections of German territory and had one law for Germany and another for themselves. It was the old tirade that he knew by heart, but he also had some pertinent and important things to say about the Roosevelt telegram, and he abrogated two treaties—the one he had made with Pilsudski in 1934 and the naval agreement he made with England in 1935—treaties he said that had been made valueless by the actions of the other parties. He left open the possibility of negotiations with Poland should the Polish government wish to resume them and give up its alliance with Britain. Before he received Roosevelt's telegram, he said, the world radio and press was aware of its contents and regarded the telegram as a very able tactical paper designed to place on the "people-ruled states" the responsibility for the warlike measures of the plutocracy. He had decided to convene the German Reichstag to hear his reply and would then confirm or reject his policies. It was a very long speech, lasting over two hours. The telegram had provided Hitler with easy targets that he could not fail to knock down. Again he presented himself as a man of peace. The return of the Saar had removed all territorial problems between France and Germany, and this he had accomplished not out of fear of France but as an expression of his belief that Europe had somehow to be brought to peace and freed from pressures of revisionism. He had made binding statements to a number of states, and not one of them could complain that any demand of Germany had been in conflict with them.

He was happy, he said, that Holland, Belgium, Switzerland, Denmark, and others had seized upon these expressions of the German Reich as an opportunity to declare their own unconditional neutrality. As for the three countries in Europe that Roosevelt complained had lost their independence, he proceeded to give historical reasons for their change in status. Austria, Bohemia, and Moravia were all part of the German cultural community. What the democratic peacemakers at Versailles had done was to award the Czechs the role of an anti-German satellite that was of itself incapable of survival. Roosevelt had referred to three European countries and one in Africa that had fallen victim to dictators, but Hitler did not mention Ethiopia, in which he had not even a polemical interest. It was he, Hitler said, with the aid of responsible men, who had succeeded at the last minute in preventing an explosion that would have affected many millions of people and who had found a solution that got rid of the Central European danger zone. The Munich solution, however, could never have been a final one, and Czechoslovakia collapsed of its inner contradictions.

Whether the solution was right or wrong, he said, it certainly had nothing to do with Britain or the Munich Agreement. As little, he went on, as for example English measures in Ireland, whether right or wrong, are subservient to German control or criticism. If Britain holds that Germany must be resisted under all circumstances by means of the policy of encirclement, then there was no point in the naval agreement. Here, as in the case of Poland, he left the door to reconciliation slightly ajar and suggested that if the British government should still wish to avoid an armament race and again enter into negotiations with Germany, no one would be more pleased than he. As for the Baltic states, they were important German trading partners, and he was happy that the point of friction with Lithuania had been eliminated and friendly relations could be fostered that resulted not in political compliments but practical, economic work. The democratic world in this case, too, deeply regretted that no blood flowed as 175,000 Germans returned to their beloved homeland without a few hundred thousand being shot. That this deeply pained the world apostles of humanitarianism, Hitler said, was not to be wondered at. As in the case of Czechoslovakia, they conjured up the notion that military measures—that is, German mobilization—was directed against Poland.

The Corridor, Hitler said, had been intended by the Versailles peacemakers to prevent forever any understanding between Poland and Germany. He had recognized unflinchingly the necessity for Poland's access to the sea, and above all that the lives of peoples that Providence had destined or damned to live next door to one another should not be artificially or unnecessarily embittered. The late marshal Pilsudski had been of the same opinion, and to decontaminate Polish-German relations the marshal and he had concluded the treaty in 1934 in which Poland and Germany finally renounced war with one another. Germany had left Poland's mutual assistance pact with France untouched; but this did not mean Poland was free to enter into any such new pacts.

One question had been left open that sooner or later had to be settled—the question of the German city of Danzig. Although Danzig was a German city and wished to be part of Germany, Hitler said, the city had treaties with Poland imposed by the Versailles peace dictators. While the League of Nations, once a major cause of unrest, was now represented by an extraordinarily tactful high commissioner, the problem of Danzig in one way or another had to be resolved, as the League of Nations, "this monstrous institution," gradually faded away. In the peaceful solution of the Danzig problem he had seen another opportunity for a definitive relaxation of tensions.

He had made a concrete offer that he would now share with the deputies of the Reichstag, so they could judge whether he had not served European peace in making the most extraordinary concession imaginable when he recognized Poland's right of access to the sea. He was not, he pointed out, a democratic statesman; he was a realistic National Socialist, and it had to be made clear to the Warsaw government that just as it wanted Poland to have access to the sea, Germany needed access to its province in the east. The problems were difficult, but Germany was not responsible for them; those responsible were "the prestigitators of Versailles" who in their malice and recklessness had set up a hundred powder kegs, each provided with an almost inextinguishable fuse. These problems could not be solved by formulas. A road to the sea and a German road through the Corridor would have no possible military significance; their meaning would lie solely in psychological and economic areas. Hitler listed again the proposals he had offered the Polish government: Danzig would return as a free state within the framework of the German Reich; Germany would obtain a road and a railroad line under its own control, which would have the same extraterritorial character for Germany as the Corridor had for Poland. In return, Germany was ready to recognize Polish economic rights in Danzig with a sizable free port and complete security of access to it. The Reich would recognize as final its borders with Poland and would conclude a twenty-five-year nonaggression pact that would last long beyond Hitler's own lifetime. The independence of the Slovak state would be guaranteed jointly by Poland and Hungary, which would preclude German hegemony in that area.

Poland, however, had been ready only to discuss the replacement of the League of Nations' commissar and easing traffic regulations in the Corridor and had turned down this offer. Hitler said he greatly regretted this incomprehensible attitude and added ominously that it was not the worst aspect; like Czechoslovakia a year before, Poland too, under pressure of a worldwide, lying, demagogic campaign, had mobilized troops, though Germany had not called up a single man and had no thought of attacking Poland. What he had tried to do had been for the benefit of both countries, and Poland would have surrendered nothing since Danzig would never be Polish. But instead of accepting his offer, Poland had entered into its mutual assistance pact that could compel Poland, under certain circumstances, to take part in a war against Germany. These obligations contravened the treaty he had made with Marshal Pilsudski and the German-Polish nonaggression pact that he would never have concluded under present circumstances. What is the point of a nonaggression pact, he asked, when one partner leaves open a host of exceptions? Either you have collective security—that is, collective insecurity—and the eternal danger of war, or a clear treaty that basically precludes any possible use of weapons between the parties. Therefore, the treaty he had made with Pilsudski was no longer valid. He had so informed the Polish government, though he could only repeat that this did not mean any change in his fundamental attitude. If Poland wished to enter into new negotiations, he could only welcome that, if such an arrangement would be based on clear and equal obligations for both parties. Germany, in any event, would be glad to undertake such obligations and fulfill them. If a new wave of anxiety had appeared in Europe in these last weeks those responsible were in the service of propaganda of international warmongers who, through fabrication of persistent rumors in the democratic states, attempted to ready Europe for a catastrophe that would lead to a bolshevik destruction of European culture.

There was not much sign of a German-Soviet rapprochement in these words, which ended Hitler's usual summary of selected events past; now he could turn his full attention to Roosevelt who, he said, had sent him a telegram in which he told how millions of people live in continual fear of a new war or even a series of wars. To this Hitler replied that fear of war disturbed mankind for a long time and rightfully so. From the Treaty of Versailles in 1919 until 1938, fourteen wars had been waged and in none was Germany involved, unlike states of the Western world in whose name President Roosevelt spoke. In addition, twenty-six "interventions" had taken place with bloody force in which Germany again had taken no part. The United States had been involved in six of these interventions, and the Soviet Union had waged ten wars or armed military actions, so Hitler said it would be a mistake to take it that the fear of war on the part of European or non-European peoples could really be ascribed to anything for which Germany might be held responsible.[11]

> Mr. Roosevelt says in his telegram that every great war, even if confined to other continents, would, while it lasted and for generations to come, be a

heavy burden. Nobody knows this better than the German people for it was they who bore the burdens of the Versailles Peace Treaty that could not have been liquidated in a hundred years although it has been precisely American teachers of international law, historians and professors of history who have proven that Germany was as guiltless as any other people of the outbreak of the World War. Of itself I don't think that every war must be catastrophic for the entire world unless a system of obscure treaty obligations is designed to involve the entire earth. For centuries, including as I said before, the last decades, the world has witnessed continuing wars and if Roosevelt's notions were correct the combined sum total of these wars would have resulted in a burden on mankind for millions of years.

Hitler went on: "Mr. Roosevelt also believes that in case of war the victors, the conquered and neutral nations would all suffer." He had been of this opinion for twenty years, but, unfortunately, responsible American statesmen had not been of the same opinion when they took part in the world war and its outcome. Roosevelt declared, Hitler said, that three independent nations in Europe and one in Africa had to sacrifice their independence. "I don't know what nations he has in mind under the three in Europe," but if he was talking about the provinces that had returned to the German Reich, Hitler had to tell the president that he was making a historical error. They surrendered their independent existence not recently but in 1918 when they were torn, despite solemn promises, from their communities and fashioned into nations that they had never wished to be and which they were not. As for Africa, he said, Roosevelt had made a mistake there for "not one nation in Africa had lost its freedom although almost all the former inhabitants of the continent had been handed over with bloody force to the sovereignty of other peoples: Moroccans, Berbers, Arabs, Negroes. . . . The swords and bombs used by these conquerors had certainly not been stamped 'Made in Germany' but 'Made in democracies.'" He made no mention of Ethiopia.

"Mr. Roosevelt," Hitler went on, "says that all international problems should be decided at the conference table." His answer: "Theoretically one must believe this is possible for reason tells us that in many cases the justified demands of one side and the need for conciliation on the other are manifest. For example, in all reason, logic and according to all principles of human and higher justice including God's laws, all the peoples of the world have the same right to its goods. . . ." But while some countries, he said, have a ratio of 15 inhabitants to a square kilometer, others had to find nourishment for their population at a ratio of 140 or even 200 people to a square kilometer, and even then their colonies were taken from them. Hitler said he would be pleased if problems like that could be solved at the conference table, but he was skeptical because the greatest conference of all time was undoubtedly the League of Nations, which was supposed to settle all the problems of the world. The first state, however, to hold back from this work was the American union, and the League of Nations in almost twenty years of activity had been unable to solve one really decisive international problem.

> In addition, in these last years a good many problems have been brought before world conferences without a single one being resolved. If your notion, Mr. Roosevelt, that all problems can be solved at the conference table were correct, then the peoples of the world, including the American union, in the course of seven or eight thousand years must have been led either by the blind or by criminals. For they have all, including the statesmen of the American union and indeed its greatest ones, formed its history essentially not at the conference table but by means of the strength of its people. The freedom of North America had been as little won at the conference table as was the conflict between the northern and southern states.

"Mr. Roosevelt," Hitler continued, "believes that it is necessary to go into a conference room as before a court and that both parties should enter and leave it in good faith having been accorded equal justice." Hitler's answer: "The German representatives will never again enter a conference which is a tribunal for them. For who will be the judges? At a conference there are no accused or accusers and no judges but only two contenders. And if no reasonable outcome resulted they would never submit their claims to foreign powers. . . . Mr. Roosevelt declared further that he understood that some nations fear the direction of German policy." His answer was a question:

> Through what process has Mr. Roosevelt determined which nations feel threatened by Germany and which do not? Or is Mr. Roosevelt, despite what must be the overwhelming burdens of his labor on behalf of his own country, able to determine the inner psychic and spiritual frame of mind of other peoples and their governments? Mr. Roosevelt, finally, wants to receive assurances that German armed forces will not attack the states or possessions of the following independent nations and above all would not march into them. . . .

Hitler then proceeded to name thirty-odd countries.

> My answer: I have taken the trouble to inquire of those states, first, whether they feel themselves threatened and, second, whether Mr. Roosevelt's question emanates from them or at least has their approval. The answers were

completely negative, sometimes harshly so. Some countries, for example, Syria, could not be addressed because at the moment they are not in possession of their freedom, but are occupied under the military power of a democratic state and are therefore without rights. Aside from that, all the states bordering on Germany have received more binding assurances, and—more important—proposals than Mr. Roosevelt asked of me in his strange telegram. . . . Further, Mr. Roosevelt is guilty of some historical errors. He mentions, for example, Ireland and asks that Germany not attack Ireland. I have just read a speech by the Prime Minister of Ireland, De Valera, who, strangely enough, contrary to President Roosevelt, blames not Germany for the continued domination of Ireland, but England. . . . Similarly, it has escaped Mr. Roosevelt that Palestine at the moment is not occupied by Germans but by the British and it was through the most brutal of force that its freedom has been limited and its independence lost, for the benefit of Jewish interlopers. The Arabs living in this country are not complaining about German aggression but continually appeal to world opinion against the barbaric methods with which Britain tries to subdue this freedom-loving country that is only defending its freedom.

Hitler brought his long two-and-a-half-hour speech to an end with customary praise of his own achievements and recital of his attempts to persuade other countries to reduce their armaments when the Reich itself was completely disarmed. He contemptuously dismissed Roosevelt's accomplishments, his easy task of administering the richest country in the world, a country rejoicing in all possible earthly resources, leaving the president free to concern himself with global problems. "You have," Hitler said, "135 million people on 9½ million square kilometers, with enormous riches, all the treasures of the earth, fruitful enough to feed a half billion people and provide them with all necessities," while Germany had not 15 inhabitants to a square kilometer as the Americans did, but 140. Germany lacked all the mineral and other treasures of which the United States was disposed. Yet he, Hitler, who twenty-one years ago was an unknown worker and soldier, had restored Germany's strength. And while Roosevelt, Hitler said, could readily concern himself with much larger issues than he, Hitler's interests were concentrated on those of his own people for whom he desired justice and peace, as indeed he did for the entire human community.

Thus at the same time as he instructed his ambassadors in London and Warsaw to deliver notes abrogating the naval agreement of 1935 with Britain and the 1934 treaty with Poland, he wished everyone on earth peace and prosperity.

If Hitler had hoped to intimidate Britain and Poland with his speech, no immediate signs of nervousness appeared. On the contrary Polish newspaper distributors in Posen spontaneously boycotted German newspapers, and the

British ambassador in Warsaw reported "a tendency to boycott German books." The Russian ambassador to London remarked to Halifax, as he pointed to passages in Hitler's speech, that the man was simply not to be trusted, and Halifax, who fully agreed, recorded no reply. On the whole, neither Roosevelt's questions nor Hitler's answers had any unpredictable results. Governments and presses held fast to their entrenched positions—those who considered Roosevelt a warmonger disparaged the speech, those who regarded him as a possible savior of the civilized world hailed it, and Hitler continued to be either a gangster or a Siegfriedian hero depending on the previous bias of the paper.

But on May 3, 1939, came an ominous sign of a major earthquake impending in European relations. On the last page of Russian newspapers the presidium of the Supreme Soviet announced in a four-line paragraph that Litvinov had asked to be relieved of his post as foreign minister, and on the front pages it was reported that Molotov had been named to the post. Molotov was chairman of the Council of People's Commissars and, more important, unlike Litvinov-Finkelstein, as the German papers always referred to Litvinov, was not a Jew. The shift was totally unexpected. Tippelskirch, counselor of the embassy in Moscow, noted that Litvinov on May 2 received the English ambassador and the day before had been named guest of honor and stood near Stalin on the tribune in Red Square for celebration of May Day. The momentous meaning of the change was missed by people who should have known better. Even the well-informed Schulenburg thought it of no great importance, as did the British ambassador to Moscow, Sir William Seeds, who believed Litvinov's crusade for collective security would continue under Molotov. But one envoy knew better. The British ambassador in Rome, Sir Eric Drummond, reported to the foreign office the "astonishing theory" of his French colleague François-Poncet that Litvinov had been fired so Stalin could come to an agreement with Germany; the Reich could attack Poland and take back the Corridor unpunished.

The possibility of a German-Russian rapprochement had occurred to some observers. At a meeting in Rome on April 6, Göring had met with Mussolini and Ciano when they approvingly discussed the evidences of Russia's desire for a better relationship with Berlin. Mussolini, like Hitler, had made a career of his implacable anticommunism, but unlike Hitler he wanted to postpone any military action and declared he welcomed the new evidences of Soviet friendliness that Ciano said he had also observed in recent dealings with Soviet diplomats.

Hitler's speech contained hostile references to communism but no unfavorable mention of the Soviet Union. In his talks with visiting diplomats his anti-Soviet line seemed as solid as ever. To the Romanian foreign minister, Gafencu, who shared his anticommunist sentiments and his at least lip service to maintaining peace, Hitler said a major war would end with both victor and vanquished lying under the same ruins, to the profit of only one man, Stalin.

Stalin was playing his cards even closer to his chest than was his suspicious habit. Marshal Voroshilov, people's commissar for Defense, was unaware of any change in policy. When Colonel Firebrace, the British military attaché, met with Voroshilov on May 8 he reported him eager to join the anti-German coalition. Firebrace reported that Voroshilov said, "it was necessary to close the front against Germany and that it depended on us whether it was to be closed or not," a statement he repeated toward the end of their conversation. Firebrace commented, "allowing for the bellicose tendencies of a Red General it was evident to me that this member of the Kremlin Inner Circle would not have spoken thus if the highest authority had determined to change Soviet policy."[12]

Nevertheless Stalin had decided to sound Berlin, to discover if there was any possible way of avoiding the mortal clash with the Reich he dreaded more than anything in the world. Hitler's Germany was a force that could destroy him, and despite the decades of mutual recrimination both he and Hitler beheld common enemies in the major "plutocratic" powers. Hitler so far had made no reply to the veiled but unmistakable Soviet overtures. Apparently neither he nor Ribbentrop, whose diplomatic purpose was to say what he thought Hitler wanted to hear, had read, much less digested, Stalin's refusal to pull Britain's chestnuts out of the fire. But the dismissal of the despised Litvinov made an immediate impression, and Hitler summoned Schulenburg to report on the significance. Schulenburg at the moment was in Teheran, so Gustav Hilger, a talented specialist on Russian affairs, was dispatched to Berchtesgaden. Commercial counselor of the embassy, he was an engineer by profession and spoke fluent Russian. Born in Moscow of German parentage, he had been employed in the Soviet Union before the world war, during which he was interned. Following hostilities he served on a German committee in Moscow concerned with the welfare of prisoners of war and then had joined the staff of the German Embassy as a counselor for economic affairs. He arrived in Berchtesgaden on May 10 and accompanied Ribbentrop to the Berghof, appearing before Hitler in the presence of General Keitel and two members of the foreign office: Julius Schnurre, an expert on the economies of Eastern Europe, and Hewel, the foreign ministry's representative at Hitler's headquarters, and like Schnurre, a legation counselor.

Hitler asked Hilger why Litvinov had been fired and whether Hilger believed the Soviet Union was prepared to come to an understanding with Germany.[13] Like other members of the embassy staff including Schulenburg, Hilger warmly favored German-Russian rapprochement and spoke at some length while Hitler listened without interruption. Although a detailed report of Stalin's March speech had been sent by the Moscow Embassy, neither Hitler nor Ribbentrop had paid any attention, and Hilger had to read the chestnut passage to them twice. Listening to Hilger's sober estimate of Soviet strength, Hitler suspected he was a victim of Soviet propaganda, but behind the cautious analysis were intimations of dazzling possibilities, and he listened attentively. Hitler did not, as Hilger hoped he would, give him any instructions to sound Moscow's intentions, but ten days later Legation Counselor Schnurre went to Moscow to resume the economic negotiations that had been languishing.

The trade talks were a useful cover for the desire of both sides to enter into political negotiations. Both had kept their options open; demands the Russians were making were essentially the same for east and west—the Baltic states were to be brought into the Soviet defensive glacis; Romania and Poland were to be made harmless and more vulnerable to territorial claims of the Soviet Union. Before Hitler and Stalin made their final decisions the Russians could continue to meet in formal sessions with representatives of France and Britain to discuss terms of an anti-Hitler alliance, and Hitler could assure Beck and Chamberlain that the way to a peaceful—that is, anti-Soviet—understanding remained open. Hitler's short-term goal was to prevent Russia from joining the encirclement being formed in London, while Stalin's was to ensure the Soviet Union against having to confront the Reich alone, which he was convinced was what the Western powers would like to see. A European conflict—Western powers against Hitler, with Russia on the outside—would give the Soviet Union an opportunity to rebuild its forces after the devastating purges. Stalin had a far better chance of achieving this respite through accommodation with Hitler than by joining the alliance against him.

Hitler and Stalin were circling one another like two stiff-legged, bristling pit bulls undecided whether to go for the other's throat or wag their tails. Any wrong move could bring catastrophe. For Molotov to invite Schnurre to Moscow to revive economic negotiations, as Schnurre suggested, would considerably dampen negotiations with Britain and France, just as Russia was pressing for help in acquiring bases in the Baltic countries as part of the price for joining the anti-Hitler alliance. Molotov was aware that the Reich's immediate goal was to keep the Russians out of the anti-German encirclement but needed to keep open the likelihood of joining it to strengthen his hand with Hitler. Hitler in turn could not be sure of the substance behind the Russian advances. They could be intended only to strengthen Stalin's bargaining power with the Allies, and when that became clear in a British-French-Soviet pact, Hitler would be humiliated by the bolshevik state that was a primal, historic enemy of National Socialism. Hitler and Stalin had their worlds at risk by a measure of cooperation with the other, and they were both aware of the allures and perils.

Meanwhile each ostensibly continued his previous courses. Ribbentrop and Ciano on behalf of the Reich and Italy concluded their Pact of Steel in the Reichschancellery on May 23, symbolizing what Hitler referred to in a telegram to Mussolini as their "inseparable partnership to protect the inheritance of civilization and secure a peace based on justice." While the British and French could sweeten their promise of support of the Soviet Union to include the case of a direct German attack on that country, they could not budge the Poles from their refusal to accept the promise of Russian troops on Polish soil.

For his part Hitler had made up his mind on only one point: He would rid himself of the Polish state. On May 23, when he addressed the generals and admirals of the Wehrmacht in the Reichschancellery to brief them on his intentions, his decision to invade Poland was the only revelation in the speech.[14] On the whole he delivered a rambling discourse sounding a good deal like one of his impromptu table talks. He touched vaguely on a variety of topics without going into any, remarking that the British feared economic dangers more than power of arms, that economic problems had to be solved for Germany too, and that for this, great courage was required. The real solution had to come through acquiring foreign territory; he had accomplished the unification of Germany but further successes could not be achieved without bloodshed. Danzig, he said, was not what he was aiming at; the problem was to round out Germany's living space in the East and to secure the Reich's food supply. The speech contained the single sentence that left no doubt of his intentions: Poland was to be attacked at the first opportunity. As to Russia, he merely repeated what Molotov had been telling German negotiators: that closer economic relations would be possible only if political conditions improved, though Hitler added it was not out of the question that Russia might be "disinterested" if Poland was destroyed. His own decisions, he said, were found to be correct; if Russia should take an anti-German course, Germany's relationship with Japan would become that much closer. What he was telling the generals was to allay any doubt of his all-encompassing political vision. He was well aware of the presence of skeptics, but Poland, Danzig, and the Corridor were not debatable even among his harshest critics in the Wehrmacht. Their fear was his recklessness in fomenting a conflict against a coalition the Reich could not defeat.

As for Russia, it had been Stalin who made the advances toward rapprochement, but the Russian way in negotiation was to be elaborately cautious, often beyond the endurance of people across the table. Soviet diplomacy on propitious occasions could move with lightning swiftness but was well known for interminability, endless discussion, hair-splitting, awaiting instructions. German negotiators dealing with Moscow, like their British and French counterparts, seemed to spend more time trying to read what lay behind Russian tactics than on business at hand. But Stalin was playing on a vast chessboard; Russia was a major Far Eastern as well as European power and in the East confronted a powerful and bellicose Japan. If Japan joined the Axis in a military alliance, Stalin was facing the possibility of a two-front war and was determined to avoid even fighting a one-front war not of his choosing if he possibly could. Stalin had no more confidence in the moral principles of the so-called peace-loving nations than he had in those of the Axis and Japan. So his negotiations with Britain and France on the one side and Germany on the other often stagnated as he probed and sounded and calculated. His best case would be to stand by while Hitler and the West fought it out—the longer the better. His worst case would be to find himself alone in a war to the death with Hitler.

From Hitler's point of view, Russia was not a significant military factor. In his directive to the Wehrmacht on April 11 he merely noted contemptuously that an intervention of the Red Army "so far as it is capable of such" in a German-Polish conflict would result only in bolshevizing Poland.[15] But a Russia cooperating with the Reich was an enormous potential asset. Soviet presence on the Reich's side might well prevent Britain and France from even going to war over Poland, and availability of their raw materials promised to make any Allied blockade illusory. Hitler would have to pay a stiff price to Moscow, but he could use the assets of others to finance it. The major obstacle was psychological; a decision to make common cause with Russia would reverse almost everything he and his party had stood and bled for, though with Litvinov gone their implacable anti-Semitism need not be compromised.

Negotiations between the Soviet Union and Britain and France seemed for some weeks to hover on the verge of completion. On April 18 Litvinov had submitted the draft of the Russian proposal for an alliance with the West that on the face of it seemed almost ready for signature. It proposed an agreement for a period of five to ten years. The three countries pledged to provide one another with all manner of assistance including "that of a military nature" in case of aggression in Europe against any one of them and in addition aid in the event of aggression to any East European state "lying between the Baltic and the Black Sea and bordering on the USSR." Britain, France, and Russia were to settle within a short period of time the extent and forms of their military assistance. The Litvinov draft also provided for a formal declaration by the British government affirming that the help they had promised Poland would be available solely in the case of an aggression by Germany, thus spelling out that whatever the Poles might think the Soviet Union would not possibly be the aggressor. Further, the agreement would provide: "That the treaty alliance which exists between Poland and Romania is to be declared operative in case of aggression of any nature against Poland and Romania or else to be revoked altogether as one directed against the USSR." It was contorted language, but Litvinov explained that this clause was necessary because the original Polish-Romanian treaty had been aimed solely at the Soviet Union. Litvinov felt he had to define the aggressor by name to avoid any possibility of stigmatizing the Soviet Union. He suggested that since the recent British declaration of assistance to Poland might leave open the possibility of aggression by the Soviet Union, a clause should explain that it "concerned exclusively aggression on the part of Germany."

On April 21 Halifax sent a telegram to the ambassador in Paris, Sir Eric Phipps, explaining that the main British criticism of the Soviet proposal, though they found it "logically complete," was that it took too little account of practical difficulties and would require a very long time for its negotiation. His objection to the Russian offer, however, actually had to do with Polish sensibilities, for as he said, "It is undesirable to do anything to disturb Polish confidence at the present time and it is important that Polish self-reliance should be maintained. To enter into an arrangement with the Soviet government at this stage by which Soviet assistance would be afforded, whether Poland likes it or not, would have a most disturbing influence in Warsaw." The difficulty was that the governments of those countries, such as Poland and Romania, were reluctant even to engage themselves in a treaty of mutual assistance with the Soviet Union or even publicly to admit that Soviet assistance would be welcome to them. So, Halifax said, "His Majesty's government have proposed that the Soviet government should of their own volition make a declaration which would steady the situation by showing the willingness of the Soviet government to collaborate and at the same time would not disturb the possible beneficiaries of Soviet assistance by requiring them to accede to any arrangement to which the Soviet government was a party." Therefore, said Halifax, "we are doubtful whether the time is yet ripe for the comprehensive proposal which the Soviet government have made to us. . . ."[16] The conflict was never to be resolved. The countries that had formerly been under Russian domination wanted no part whatever of Russian occupation even with the threat of Nazi occupation hanging over them. Britain saw their point and put all its weight behind the alliance with Poland; Russia was a secondary consideration.

Russia was also a threat as a neutral country. A British Foreign Office memorandum of May 22 pointed out the danger of Russia's not joining the anti-Hitler coalition and sitting out a European war while England and Germany destroyed one another. That was one of the reasons, the memorandum stated, why Russia should be brought into the anti-German front. Molotov was well aware of such considerations in British policy, but instead of conciliating them he upped the Soviet price for joining the West. On June 2 he stated that the Baltic states would be included in the security system. Just as the Western powers had declared that any attack on the Netherlands and Belgium would be the equivalent of an attack on them, the Soviets declared that the Baltic states were a matter of life and death for them, so any direct or indirect aggression against one of them would be a cause for Russian intervention; any change of government in a Baltic state could signal a foreign influence that would justify Soviet countermeasures. When the Western Allies evinced a disinclination to accept the Russian proposal, Molotov announced that they did not want a pact with the Soviet Union.

It was the British and French now who were the suppliants; London agreed to dispatch William Strang, chief of the Middle European section of the foreign office, to negotiate with Molotov. And while the political discussions dragged on, the Allies sent a military mission to Moscow to work out the practical measures the anti-Hitler coalition would undertake when it included the Soviets.

Such were the public appearances, but accompanying them, with no publicity but only rumors, were ominous signs of a potential Russian-German rapprochement. On May 30 the Russian chargé d'affaires in Berlin, Georgi Astakov, told Weizsäcker that the Kremlin wanted no wall of separation between it and Germany, and on May 31 Molotov told the Supreme Soviet that Hitler was harmless and not to be feared, a message that reflected the new thinking of Stalin.[17]

The negotiations between the Soviet Union, Britain, and France proceeded slowly. As Strang pointed out, the pattern seemed fixed; the Russians would make a demand that the British declared unacceptable but would nevertheless soon, if reluctantly, come around to adopting in the form the Kremlin proposed. By then the Soviets would have thought of something else, and the Russian price was up. On June 29 the British accepted the demand that the Baltic states be included among the guaranteed powers, but by this time the Russians proposed that the guarantee include "indirect aggression," a shapeless concept that would enable the Soviet Union to intervene in the internal affairs of the Baltic states allegedly for their own protection. "Indirect aggression," Molotov said, was to be defined in a secret clause of the treaty as "an inner coup d'état or reversal of policy in favor of the aggressor."

Stalin was always suspicious of the West, though some observers thought the Allies simply acted too slowly, caviling over minor points. But essentially Stalin was being invited to join a war he did not want; the chestnuts were not his. Other weaknesses in the British position were apparent to many who wished them well, such as the League of Nations high commissioner at Danzig who was convinced Britain and France were making a mistake in wooing a Soviet Union that would welcome a division of both Poland and India, or the British ambassador in Berlin who, though strongly anti-Hitler, was convinced the Germans still had a good moral and political case in Danzig and the Corridor and that Britain was making a mistake to allow the romantic Poles to make decisions that could involve Britain in a war that could result as much from Polish intransigence as from Hitler's. But for Chamberlain the die was cast. Hitler with the march into Prague had demonstrated his unreliability, and Poland had to be supported as a nation willing to fight to stop him. Despite all their shortcomings, the Poles were the one anti-Hitler nation in Europe ready and eager for battle, and on the whole, delighted to have Britain's guarantee. Even the peace-seeking Chamberlain and Halifax felt they could not seriously temper Britain's commitment. Thus the stage was set for war; the Poles were ready for it—psychologically ready—the Allies dreaded but were resigned to it, and Hitler was convinced he could isolate and defeat Poland in a matter of weeks. But even by mid-August, he was undecided as to procedure; his propaganda buildup was the same as it had been in the recent past. The inevitable conflicts between Poles and Danzigers and between Poles and Germans followed the prescription that had been well set in the Sudetenland, in Austria, in the Saarland, and in the Rhineland; peaceful Germans were being attacked by bands of terrorists. For their part, Polish newspapers ran stories on German martial inferiority compared with the valiant Poles and predicted an easy Polish victory in the coming conflict. The high commissioner of Danzig, Professor Carl Jacob Burckhardt, no admirer of Hitler's, who was invited to Berchtesgaden and flown there in Hitler's own plane, even complimented the Führer on German forbearance in the tense situation that demonstrated, he said, the Reich's inner strength. Hitler was so impressed by Burckhardt's praise that he asked Albert Forster, the Gauleiter of Danzig, who was present at the meeting, to be sure to bring Burckhardt's observation to Ribbentrop's attention. But Hitler and Burckhardt had more to talk about than Hitler's self-restraint. In the course of their conversation, two weeks before he would make his pact with Stalin, Hitler told Burckhardt what he really had in mind if forced to act by the obtuse Allies.[18] He would, he said, if Britain and France persisted in their stupidity, make an alliance with the Soviet Union, attack and crush the Allies, and then turn with his massed power against the Soviet Union, which had always been his target.

Negotiations between the Western powers and the Soviet Union dragged along; agreement always seemed just around the corner. Three weeks after political negotiations had begun, Strang declared the pact more or less in final form, and Tass on August 12 reported at the head of its foreign news column the arrival of the British-French military mission, cordially received by Molotov along with top military leaders: Budenny, commander of the Moscow defense district, Timoshenko, commander of the Kiev military district, Kovalev, commander of the White Russian defense district, the air and naval chiefs, the army chief of staff, and others. They were all present that night at a gala dinner at which Voroshilov, commissar of War and member of the Politburo, presided. Toasts were exchanged, and the atmosphere was friendly.

But this was from beginning to end a charade. Behind the scenes Germany and Russia were moving toward an embrace. On the same day that the Russian press announced the arrival in Moscow of the Western military mission, Count Schulenburg sent a telegram to Hitler saying Stalin would be pleased to receive the political emissary the Reich had been urgently proposing. Schulenburg's telegram arrived at Berchtesgaden during Hitler's talk with Ciano, but Hitler told his guest nothing of its contents. A few days later, on August 19, Stalin disclosed to a secret meeting of the Politburo his reasons for the revolution in Soviet policy. He said he was absolutely convinced that Germany would not go to war if the Soviet Union joined the Western alliance, but if Russia accepted the German offer of a nonaggression pact, war would be inevitable. Under these circumstances, he said, the Soviet Union would have many opportunities to remain outside the conflict and could, with profit, await its turn.

> We must accept the German offer and send the French-British mission, with a courteous rejection, back home. I repeat that it is in your interest that if war breaks out between the Reich and the Anglo-French bloc, it is essential for us that the war should last as long as possible, so both sides exhaust one another. On these grounds we must accept the pact offered by Germany and once war is declared work for its lasting as long as possible. In the meantime, we must continue our political work in the warring countries so that we will be well prepared when the war comes to an end.[19]

Up to late in the afternoon of August 20 Stalin had not been in a hurry to conclude the nonaggression pact. At 2:00 P.M. Schulenburg met with Molotov at the Kremlin, and while the meeting was cordial it was Schulenburg who kept pressing for haste in arranging the Ribbentrop visit and Molotov who kept explaining why more time was needed. Schulenburg spent a frustrating hour with a friendly but unshakable Molotov, stolidly resisting repeated pleas for speed; the Soviets could not move up their timetable; they had to have the text of the nonaggression pact in hand, and the German proposal they had received was by no means conclusive.[20] The Soviet Union had nonaggression pacts with other countries that might serve as a pattern—such as those with Poland, Latvia, and Estonia—and Molotov left it to the German government to choose the most appropriate one as a basis for its draft.

Schulenburg was dispirited as he departed from the Kremlin, and then, within a half hour of his return to the embassy, the skies cleared. A transformed Molotov, obviously just talked to by Stalin, telephoned to apologize and make an immediate appointment.[21] He regretted the trouble he was causing but asked Schulenburg to return at 4:30 P.M. to receive the text of the Russian draft of the treaty he was now authorized to present. When Schulenburg reappeared at the Kremlin, Molotov handed over the text of the nonaggression pact and told him Ribbentrop would be welcome to come on August 26 or 27.

The text of the Russian draft bound each signatory to refrain from any act of violence or aggression on its own part or together with other powers and not to lend support to any third power engaged in an aggression against the other. Any dispute or conflict between Germany and the Soviet Union was to be settled by peaceful means and by consultation or a commission of arbitration. The treaty was to last for twenty-five years and if not terminated would automatically be renewed for another twenty-five years.

August 20 was a crowded day. By way of the foreign office in Berlin, Hitler addressed a telegram to Stalin that arrived at the embassy in Moscow shortly after midnight. He expressed pleasure at the signing of the German-Soviet trade agreement, the conclusion of the nonaggression pact, he said with his usual sweeping grandeur, would be useful for centuries. He declared the tensions with Poland were becoming insupportable and asked that Ribbentrop, who would have full negotiating powers, be received on August 22 or, at latest, August 23.[22] As soon as Hitler's telegram was translated into Russian, Schulenburg repaired again to the Kremlin where at 3:00 P.M. he handed it to Molotov who, reading it through, Schulenburg reported, was enormously impressed. Schulenburg still was urging all haste and asked if Stalin's reply might not be given him the same day. That too was now possible, and Schulenburg and Molotov met again at 5:00 P.M. when Molotov handed Schulenburg a terse, friendly reply. Stalin thanked Hitler for his "letter" and expressed hope that the pact would lead to important improvement in the political relations of the two countries whose peoples had need of peaceful relations. The pact, he said, laid the basis for relaxation of political tensions and establishment of peace and cooperation. The Soviet government would be pleased to receive Herr von Ribbentrop on August 23.

Meanwhile the conference of the British, French, and Soviet military missions had deadlocked on the simple but vital issue raised again and again by Voroshilov: Would the Poles and Romanians permit the forces of the Soviet Union on their territory to fight against the common enemy? Admiral Drax, chief of the British mission, and the French general Doumenc, who headed the French representatives, tried day after day, from the time the conference first met on August 14, to define what the military assignments of each power would be, but progress slowed and then stopped when Voroshilov insisted on being told first whether the forces of the Soviet Union would be permitted to cross Polish and Romanian territory to do battle. French and British representatives tried to explain that, once hostilities began, Poland would, of course, be prepared to welcome the Russian ally on its territory to fight the common foe. Voroshilov hammered away to expose the hollowness of such optimism in the face of immediate Polish refusal to agree. How, he asked, with no common border with the Reich, could the Soviets come to grips with the enemy except by way of Poland?

The British and French were sympathetic to the Soviet position; they too wanted Soviet soldiers at hand by any available route, but the Poles said "no" and refused to budge. The chief of the Polish general staff, General Stachiewicz, said the issue was not even debatable—no Russians on Polish soil.[23] The Polish ambassador in Paris asked Foreign Minister Bonnet if he, as a Frenchman, would permit Germans to defend Alsace-Lorraine, and Beck told the British ambassador to Warsaw that Voroshilov was trying by peaceful means to gain territory that the Soviets had failed in 1921 to gain by force.[24] The Poles, even with their national existence at stake, would tolerate no Soviet troops crossing their borders any more than they would Germans. Drax and Doumenc explained at length to Voroshilov how simple it all really was. Of course the Poles would welcome Soviet assistance once the Germans invaded; the details were insignificant—they all had a common enemy that had to be defeated. Voroshilov remained unimpressed and returned to his question: Could the Russians engage the enemy by way of Poland and Romania? The French especially were desperate. Here was a key military conference, and no high-flown rhetoric about the common enemy and common purposes could cover the fact vitally affecting French security that the Poles would not permit themselves to be succored by Soviet troops deployed through their borders. At no point would the Poles, despite French and British pressure, go further than to refer to the "technical" possibility of accepting Russian aid. On August 23 Beck told the French and British ambassadors to Warsaw that Doumenc could go so far as to state: "We have received assurances that in the event of a common action against German aggression, cooperation between Poland and the Soviet Union, under technical conditions that will be later determined, is not out of the question. The French and British general staffs are of the opinion that all hypotheses of such cooperation should be immediately examined."[25] That was the limit of Polish concessions.

But nothing in Voroshilov's carefully chosen words or courteous demeanor suggested the feverish activity in Berlin and Moscow that was turning the military conference into an empty *tableau vivant*. On the contrary, Voroshilov was bland but insistent. He patiently explained that while he had full powers to conclude an agreement, there could be none unless the Poles agreed that he could engage the invader through Poland. He was never to get what he wanted or, at least, what he said he wanted.

The French, in exasperation, turned up the heat on their Polish ally. They unilaterally accepted, without Polish approval, the Russian demand for dispatching Soviet troops through Poland. The meeting between Voroshilov and Doumenc on August 22 exposed the disarray of the Allies. Doumenc announced that the French answer to the Russian demand was "yes," that he had been instructed by Paris to agree. But Voroshilov was unenthusiastic over the news. He wanted to see the document Doumenc had received and to know whether the British agreed and whether this held for the Poles and the Romanians. Doumenc had no document; he had to take flimsy refuge in reciting his instructions. The French government agreed to the Russian demands, he kept repeating, while Voroshilov kept inquiring about the others: the British, Poles, Romanians? Had they agreed? None had, Doumenc was forced to acknowledge.

Ribbentrop by now was on his way to Moscow. Voroshilov and Doumenc, of course, knew this and even referred to it without mentioning him by name; Doumenc spoke only of "someone who is to arrive shortly." Over and over again Doumenc tried to get Voroshilov to reconvene the conference on the basis of his instructions from Paris, but it was no use. Voroshilov declared politely that nothing would be accomplished by another meeting; talking would be an utter waste of time unless the Allies were of one mind on the deployment of troops by way of Poland. With Ribbentrop winging his way, the question was moot. The military missions met only once more, on August 25. Voroshilov apologized for not having been available the day before, but, he explained, he had been away on a duck hunt. He now declared what the British and French already suspected: that in view of the changed political situation there was no point in further meetings.

Each side blamed collapse of the conference on the other. Voroshilov told the Allies their governments had delayed, procrastinated, and made impossible conditions, and as the conferees departed he made plain, in an unusual outburst, his dislike and mistrust of the Poles. "During the whole time of our conversations," he said, "the Polish press and Polish people were continuously saying that they did not want the help of the Soviets, and from Romania there was no answer at all. Were we to have to conquer Poland in order to offer her our help, or were we to go on our knees and offer our help to Poland? The position was impossible for us."[26] Admiral Drax said the Russians were as duplicitous as they had been in 1918, merely attempting to use the conference through the Western Allies to gain harbors and island concessions from the Baltic states.

In Berlin, Henderson told Hitler the Allies were in fact lucky not to have the Soviets on their side, a view shared by Drax. Each side was convinced of its rectitude and the guile of the other. The German ambassador to London, Dirksen, had written weeks before the military missions met that the proposed British delegation was unimpressive. Drax, he pointed out in his report to Berlin on August 1, was in command of the Plymouth (he actually wrote Portsmouth) naval base and had never been a member of the strategic planners groups, and General Heywood was a front-line army commander, not a strategist. He and Drax were competent but not the choice that might be expected for such weighty decisions. Actually none of these criticisms had much weight. The conference collapsed not because of personnel but because Hitler and Stalin came to embrace what each believed was a transitory yet invaluable alliance for his own purposes.

Explaining to the Supreme Council of the Soviets on August 31 why the negotiations with the Allies failed, Molotov said Britain and France had tried to isolate the Soviet Union, encouraged Poland in its intransigence, and sent second-rate people without proper credentials to the military meetings.

It was a grotesque wedding of National Socialism with communism. Ribbentrop with his party of twenty landed at the Moscow airport to be greeted not by Molotov but by the deputy people's commissar for foreign affairs with the resonant name of Potemkin, along with the German and Italian ambassadors and their entourages. For the first time in history the German swastika flag, flanked by flags with the hammer and sickle, flew at the airport. So hurriedly had the National Socialist flag been stitched together that the swastika was in correct position only on one side and was reversed on the other.

But the meetings with Stalin and Molotov left nothing to be desired. Ribbentrop reported when he returned to Berlin that he felt completely at home in his Soviet surroundings, and among the many toasts drunk during his two-day visit was one proposed by Stalin: "to the Führer and Reichs Chancellor of Germany so deeply beloved by his people." Ribbentrop had been armed with plenipotentiary powers by Hitler but felt it necessary to get Hitler's explicit approval for Stalin's conditions regarding the Baltic states, which Stalin wanted completely within the Soviet orbit. This caused no difficulty. Hitler's immediate telegraphed reply read simply: "Yes, agreed."

Nothing could delay or cast a shadow on this marriage of enormous convenience to both dictators. Their respective spheres of influence were quickly affirmed in a secret protocol attached to the nonaggression pact, and any doubts either side may have had as to the other's enthusiasm were dissipated. If suspicion of Ribbentrop's intentions had led Stalin to dispatch Potemkin in place of Molotov, it vanished. Ribbentrop said "yes" to everything. Neither side made any demands the other found indigestible. As Ribbentrop's plenipotentiary powers indicated, Hitler was ready to be generous. The Russians could have almost anything they wanted if they left him free to deal with the Western powers on his own terms. The Soviet Union got what it could not get from the Western Allies: a large piece of Poland, hegemony over the Baltic states, and, above all, no war.[27] The pact was also a signal triumph for Hitler, bearing with it the possibility that Britain and France would not after all come to the defense of Poland and the prospect of a quick, historic victory.

On the very day Ribbentrop flew to Moscow, August 22, Hitler made two speeches at Berchtesgaden to the chiefs of the Wehrmacht. With the Soviet pact about to be concluded he spoke in a mood of self-congratulation more fervent than usual, reminding the generals and admirals, especially those he knew wanted a political accommodation with the West, of his unique political genius.[28] It was he, he told them, who had been right in taking great risks when so many others had opposed them. It was now or never for Germany; a war now was the only solution. The Four-Year Plan had been pronounced a failure by Göring, Japan was a dubious ally, and Mussolini was endangered by a "nitwit King" and the "treacherous scoundrel of a Crown Prince." He, the Führer, had tried to work out a supportable relationship with Poland, but it had become clear that in any conflict with the West the Poles would attack the Reich, and this was the propitious moment to prevent that from happening. First of all it was propitious, Hitler said, because of his personality and his political capabilities. "No one in the future will be likely ever to have the confidence of the entire German people . . . there will never be a man with more authority than I. My existence is therefore a great asset *[Wertfaktor]* and I could be laid low at any time by a criminal or an idiot." Next to him as a unique personality was Mussolini, and without Mussolini the Italian alliance was uncertain. "After all," Hitler was quoted as saying: "there are only three great statesmen in the world: Stalin, I and Mussolini." He had met the statesmen of the West, Daladier and Chamberlain and the others, and they were worms.

Politically, too, the situation was ripe for action, though Hitler said he expected no more than friendly neutrality from Franco, since Spain did not yet possess a fascist party with the determination of the German party. On the favorable side, too, was Italy's rivalry with France and England in the Mediterranean, the tension in East Asia between Japan and England, and the unrest in the Muhammedan world. Romania was vulnerable and threatened by Hungary and Bulgaria; Turkey was ruled by small, weak men. All this would not be true in two or three years, and no one could say how long he would still be alive, so this, he repeated, was the time to strike.

The relationship to Poland had become insupportable. His offers to Poland had been fruitless because of England. An attempt on his or Mussolini's life could change the situation for the worse. "We have," he said, "to accept risks with ruthless determination. We stand before hard alternatives to strike or sooner or later be destroyed." He had taken risks before, the most dangerous of which was when he ordered the march into the Rhineland, though he had been warned by François-Poncet that France would go to war if he gave the order. And now too there was great risk. Iron nerves were needed and iron determination. Britain was not much of a threat, its rearmament trivial. Nor was France with its low birthrate. A blockade would not work because of Germany's autarky and the assurance of supplies from the East. Hitler said that he had been convinced that Stalin would not accept the English offer, and now with the forthcoming Russian pact Poland was on the spot where he wanted it. When the speech was over Göring rose to his feet—according to one account, he jumped on a table, but that, taking his corpulence into consideration, seems unlikely—and thanked Hitler, assuring him that the Wehrmacht would do its duty.[29]

A luncheon followed, and it may be that in its course it became clear to Hitler that all the generals were not persuaded that Britain would stay out of a war or be of negligible effect if it came in. In any event, after lunch Hitler addressed the high command for a second time in a further attempt to convince those he would never convince.[30] In his second short speech he said he thought there would be a stoppage of imports but no blockade. A long period of peace would not be good for Germany. What was decisive was spirit; machines did not fight, men did, and qualitatively the Germans were better. Hitler said he would use a propagandist pretext to start the war; whether it was true did not matter. "What counts in war," he said, "has nothing to do with justice but only with victory. Close your heart against pity, proceed brutally, eighty million people must gain their rights. It is the stronger who is right." He was sure, he said in closing, that the German Wehrmacht would be up to the demands on it.

A flurry of activity to save the peace that raised false hopes in the days before outbreak of war on September 1 had little to do with Hitler himself. He wanted war; he would keep peace only on his terms. Göring, unlike Hitler and Ribbentrop, would have been glad to postpone or even avoid war. Although he basked in his military titles and the luxuries of high office, he had grown fat and self-indulgent since his remote days as a war hero, and he did not lust for battle. He would loyally carry out Hitler's decisions but unlike Ribbentrop preferred parades over bullets. He thus eagerly participated in the peripheral attempts of the Swedish industrialist Birger Dahlerus to bring the two sides together.[31] Since early in July, Dahlerus had commuted back and forth from London to Berlin interviewing, cajoling, and pleading for direct negotiations between Britain, Poland, and the Reich. He talked with Chamberlain, Hitler, Henderson, Halifax, Cadogan, and, seconded by Göring, with anyone else in authority in London who would listen to him. He never spoke to Ribbentrop, arch rival of Göring and of anyone else who had the Führer's ear. Ribbentrop wanted, with no intervention of third parties, whatever he was convinced Hitler wanted. What Hitler wanted in these last days of peace was a Polish plenipotentiary, someone on whom he could impose his terms without any delay, and the Poles, armed with their own inflexibility as well as with memories of Schuschnigg's and Hacha's disastrous visits to Berchtesgaden and Berlin, were ready to send no one but the Polish ambassador to Berlin with no negotiating powers. Dahlerus was unable to accomplish anything more than could the accredited diplomat operating through official channels. Britain and Germany had no need of a third party, and Dahlerus found Poland intractable.

And so the lines of battle were drawn. Hitler was determined either to bring Poland into the German orbit on his terms or to destroy it as a military power. The British, with their centuries-old tradition of opposing any power that dominated the Continent or sought to dominate it, had given the Poles the backing they had always sought that could only strengthen their resolve to resist Hitler by force of arms. With the Soviet Union on the sidelines, Hitler was convinced the Western powers would not intervene if the Reich attacked Poland. France and Britain had no real way of preventing a swift German victory. And in any case, from Hitler's point of view, whether or not the Western Allies immediately joined the conflict was of secondary importance. As he told the Wehrmacht officers, this was the time to strike, and as for Britain and France the Reich would eventually have to deal with them. The only concessions he was ready to make were designed for purposes of propaganda. He would, he told the high command, always be able to contrive a plausible cause of war.[32] He ordered 150 Polish uniforms to be provided by German counterintelligence so he could always produce, with corpses of concentration-camp inmates dressed in those uniforms, the evidence that Polish soldiers had invaded German territory. In his efforts to appear as a victim of Polish irresponsibility, he also made a far-reaching, generous offer to resolve the major Polish-German conflicts and, in a naïve attempt to appease Britain, expressed his readiness to guarantee the security of the British Empire. But the offer was never more than a ploy. When on August 30 the British ambassador went to the Reichschancellery to meet with Ribbentrop, it was the echo of such proposals Henderson heard, not the substance. They met at midnight, after the deadline Berlin had given the Poles for appearance of a plenipotentiary. Ribbentrop was at his worst—haughty, loud, striking Mussoliniesque poses with arms folded across his chest—every inch, as Henderson saw him, the former wine salesman acting the statesman. Henderson understood German pretty well, but he reported that when Ribbentrop read to him the Hitler proposal that would immediately return Danzig to the Reich, guarantee the Polish borders and access to Gdynia, and calling for a plebiscite of the Polish and German populations in the Corridor, Ribbentrop had read at such speed that Henderson could only partly understand him.[33] Contrary to normal diplomatic usage, Henderson was never given a copy of the text. Ribbentrop, on express orders from Hitler, as he testified in March 1946, refused to turn the document over, though Henderson twice asked for it; the offer to Poland was made for the record only. Ribbentrop, after his reading, merely threw the document on the table, declaring it was no longer valid.

All this occurred only hours before German troops were ordered into Poland.[34] A few days before, Hitler had countermanded his orders to begin the attack, and he had done this in time to reach all but a handful of troops. On August 30–31, as Ribbentrop and Henderson met, less than twenty-four hours remained during which the advance might be stopped, but with no Polish plenipotentiary at hand and both sides unwavering, war was certain.

Hitler had one more device prepared for the great occasion; a trumped-up attack by "Polish invaders" on Reich soil.[35] At Gleiwitz in Silesia on the night of August 31, six armed men dressed in civilian clothing, not Polish uniforms, invaded the radio station. Gleiwitz lay only three miles from the Polish border in a lightly populated area with little cover of woodland. Thus it would have been difficult to move any soldiers wearing Polish uniforms without them being detected. But that presented a minor problem for the German Security Service of the German SS, the SD. The men held the radio station only a short time, broadcasting a message in German and Polish that the station was occupied, and drove off, leaving a corpse behind. Hitler referred to Polish border violations in his proclamation to the Wehrmacht on September 1 but never mentioned Gleiwitz either then or when he addressed the Reichstag later in the day or at any other time. In the euphoria of setting his mighty Wehrmacht in action, he felt no need to make use of this justification of the attack.

The word *war* was not used either in the army communiqué of September 1 or in Hitler's speech to the Reichstag in the midmorning of that day. The high command announced that the Wehrmacht was undertaking "the active protection of the Reich on orders of the Führer" and that since early morning the troops had begun a "counterattack" at all the German-Polish borders. Driving from East Prussia, Pomerania, Silesia, and Slovakia, five armies of the German army went into action following bombardment from air and sea as the Luftwaffe and the ship of the line, the cruiser *Schleswig-Holstein,* which was visiting Danzig harbor, attacked Polish installations. The Polish army that a few years before had been many times the size of the German army was to be smashed in a few weeks.

The decision to go to war was Hitler's alone; none of his advisers, civilian or military, was called on for advice. On the fateful day he wore the field gray tunic of the Wehrmacht that bore little resemblance, except in color, to the uniform he had worn as a corporal in World War I. This time the well-tailored coat had gold buttons with the gold "sovereignty eagle" of his Third Reich on the left sleeve. It was the uniform of the commander in chief of the armed forces, different from that of an army general who wore the eagle on the right side of his chest or of an SS general who wore the eagle in silver on his left sleeve.

15

The War

Shortly before ten o'clock in the morning of September 1, Hitler left the Reichschancellery to make his way to the Kroll Opera House where the Reichstag had been meeting since the great fire. The crowds along the way were sparse; observers at the British Embassy, which included neutrals such as Birger Dahlerus and the Berlin correspondent of the *Neue Zürcher Zeitung,* noted how few spectators stood behind the lines of SA men on both sides of the street and how subdued the onlookers were. Berliners had plainly shown during the Czech crisis how little enthusiasm they had for war—their apathy had aroused Hitler's wrath—and the gloom was again manifest in the size of the crowds, the thinly scattered applause, and the muted cheering that accompanied Hitler's progress. The Reichstag, too, summoned for that morning, was diminished in numbers—more than one hundred of the deputies were missing, either called up for service in the armed forces, delayed by failure to receive their notice of the meeting, or for some other reason. But no seats could be left vacant on this historic occasion; Göring had quickly arranged for party functionaries to sit where deputies were missing, and the substitutes could vote too if need be.

The fervor of Hitler's call to arms was muted by his desire to keep Britain and France from joining the war, so while he could and did revile the Poles, he said nothing defamatory of the British or French or even the Jews.[1] The Reich, he said, had been forced to resort to arms against Poland, and he had no demands to make on the Western states; the border between France and Germany was final, and he recounted his offer of friendship to England. Germany had no interests in the West; the West Wall was its boundary for all time. Other European states, he said, understood the Reich's position, and he thanked Italy, which had long supported the Reich but would not be called on for help in a task that was the Reich's alone. Soviet Russia and Germany had no quarrel between them, any conflict would only benefit others. So the two countries had concluded a pact that barred for all time any use of force between them, that bound them to consultation on certain European problems, that made economic cooperation possible, and above all would prevent both countries from wasting their strength against one another. This meant a mighty change for the future and was final. The Reich's goals were merely to solve the problems of Danzig and the Corridor and to ensure a peaceful common life with Poland. To attain these ends Hitler said he was prepared to fight on until another Polish regime was ready for the peace that existed on the other borders of the Reich.

Poland had attacked Germany, he said, since 5:45 that morning (actually the German attack began at 4:45 A.M.), and from now on the Reich would retaliate bomb for bomb. Whoever used poison gas would be met with poison gas, and whoever violated the rules of humane warfare would be met with the same measures.

He said he had again put on his field gray uniform, and he would take it off only after victory was achieved, or he would not survive. If anything should happen to him, Göring would be his successor and next in line would be party comrade Hess. "As a National Socialist and German soldier," he said, "I go into this battle with a strong heart. My whole life has been nothing but a single battle for my people, for their rebirth, for Germany, and above this battle stands one avowal only: belief in this Volk. One word I have never learned—that is capitulation." The applause of the deputies was characterized by the chief of staff, General Halder, as "according to command, but thin."

The German attack was successful beyond all expectations. On the very first day of the war the Luftwaffe, making spectacular use of dive bombers, achieved complete control of the air, destroying most of the Polish air force on the ground, on the airfields of west Poland, and before Warsaw and knocking out the Polish railroad system and supply lines. And so massive were the tank attacks, slicing deep into Polish territory, that forty Polish divisions, including eleven cavalry brigades, never reached their battle stations. Minor setbacks occurred: conquest of the Westerplatte, site of the Polish arsenal in Danzig harbor, was held up until September 7 by what the high command regarded as insufficient preparation of landing forces from the *Schleswig-Holstein*, despite the heavy support of the ship's guns. But the entire Polish campaign was over in little more than three weeks, and when the Soviet armies joined the war on September 17 they barely had time to engage the Poles before German troops entered Warsaw.

The promised Anglo-French aid to Poland never materialized. The French military convention with Poland concluded on May 19 provided for massive French help to go into action, at the latest, two weeks after mobilization of French forces, but no French offensive was unleashed—only minor sorties. Troops remained behind the Maginot line, and the British air force bombed German coastal installations on the North Sea. The Poles were on their own, and, though units fought bravely, neither their strategy that called for defense of every foot of territory nor their forces that included cavalry armed with lances was a match for the Wehrmacht.[2]

The German fighting machine brought with it grim, anonymous contingents that had never been used before in European warfare, ostensibly assigned to keep the rear of the German armies secure from sabotage and partisans. Part of neither the regular police nor the army formations, they were the so-called Einsatz Groups of the Security Police under command not of the army but of Heydrich and Himmler of the SD and SS and operated with all the brutality Hitler had promised in his speech of August 22.[3] They were formed to liquidate the born enemies of National Socialism, men and women and children, not for crimes of any kind but on National Socialist principles. Thousands of Jews were flogged and massacred by these commandos; their depredations were such that General Johannes Blaskowitz, commander in chief of the invading Eighth Army, sharply protested to Hitler against the "illegal shootings, arrests and confiscations." He was concerned, Blaskowitz wrote, for the discipline of the troops who saw this happening and could not intervene. On-the-spot attempts with the SD and Gestapo had no success, he wrote, and their chiefs should be ordered to restore legal conditions, above all to put a stop to executions without due process *(rechtmässigen Urteilen)*. The only result of Blaskowitz's protest was a sharp rejection by Hitler who railed against such "childish notions" in army leaders, adding that wars were not waged by Salvation Army methods, and that he had never trusted Blaskowitz.[4]

Another German general, the former commander in chief of the army, Werner von Fritsch, who had been forced out in the trumped-up scandal of 1938, was killed on September 22, just before German troops entered Warsaw. He had returned to active service as honorary chief of his old command, the Twelfth Artillery Regiment, and he was severely wounded as he joined a reconnaissance on the front line. As an officer tried to help him, Fritsch merely waved him off, saying "Oh let it go." He had been formally rehabilitated after the collapse of the false charges, but Hitler never reinstated him as commander in chief, and Fritsch died as he wished to—in battle. General Jodl, in a formal tribute, called him "one of the best soldiers the German Army has ever had." Hitler ordered the flags of the Twelfth Artillery Regiment to fly at half-mast and said to Jodl, with perfect hypocrisy, "If only I had prevented this assignment."[5]

The swift conquest of Poland was a notable victory, another in Hitler's series of spectacular triumphs, though this one cost blood and left powerful enemies in the field. Contrary to Hitler's and Ribbentrop's confident predictions, Britain and then France declared war on September 3 after Hitler refused to withdraw his troops from Poland as London and Paris demanded. When news of Britain's declaration came, Hitler seemed to have a moment of foreboding, staring into space, then turned morosely to ask Ribbentrop: "What now?"

As Hitler well understood after September 3, this was not to be merely a short, dazzling campaign; it was the beginning of a long war. Nevertheless he could enter a scarred, bombed-out Warsaw in a triumph that was in large part of his own making. It was he, the ex-corporal, who had determined the victorious strategy. Revolutionary use of tanks had been mainly the creation of a gifted, innovative former infantry officer, Heinz Guderian, who had early, when the Reich was still using pasteboard tanks because real ones were forbidden under the Versailles treaty, planned a blasting, mobile, far-ranging, armored attack that would demolish the static defense tactics characteristic of World War I. Older, more conservative staff officers opposed Guderian's unconventional doctrines. But his revolutionary vision was precisely what Hitler was seeking, and it was Guderian's tank strategy that was imposed by Hitler on the general staff. Thus Hitler determined not only when the war started but to a large degree how it was fought. The Polish campaign ended in an inspiriting victory, and while its success could not subdue the doubts and hostility of the hard-core military and civilian opposition Hitler could walk securely among his victorious troops with the self-assurance of a conquering hero.

Stalin had cautiously waited until mid-September before ordering his troops into Poland. Despite German pressure to begin the invasion promptly he had no intention of finding the Soviet Union fighting France and Britain and waited until their nonintervention was certain before giving orders to cross the frontier. The intervention, Moscow declared piously, was made necessary by the disappearance of the Polish state. This nullified all Soviet-Polish treaties and threatened the security of Soviet Russia as well as Ukrainian and White Russian minorities in Poland.

The Russian invasion began September 17, and while it had completely different ideological goals it brought with it much the same social devastation as did the German onslaught. Soviet police formations with the mission of destroying Poland's national life and traditional class structure operated as the Russian version of the SS Einsatz Groups. Well over a million Polish citizens, officials, people from all walks of life, among them entire families, were summarily arrested and deported to the Soviet Union, and thousands of Polish prisoners of war, if they were officers, were executed without trial or mercy. In the course of the Soviet occupation more than eight thousand Polish officers disappeared, never to be heard from again; like those murdered in the Katyn forest they were simply taken out of prisoner-of-war camps and shot as class enemies on Stalin's orders.

The Poles, too, contributed their share of atrocities. At the start of the war large segments of the ethnic German population in Poland were indiscriminately attacked, and seven thousand were killed by police, soldiers, and inflamed civilians who considered them all spies and traitors, though thousands of *volks Germans* had loyally responded to Polish mobilization orders and were ready to fight for Poland.

On September 19, two days after Russian troops invaded, Hitler made a triumphal speech in Danzig, declaring the war over and offering peace to Britain and France. The war was not over; Warsaw capitulated only on September 27, but a week earlier he felt he had to make clear to the world that it was Germany that had won the war, without any help from the Soviet Union. Another small dissembling appeared in the course of his speech: He said this was his first visit to Danzig, though he had actually been there in 1932 when he reviewed SA formations at the airport and was welcomed by a delegation from the Free City's police. Now he said he had long resolved to enter Danzig only when it was again part of the German Reich, an assertion that elevated this visit to a far more heroic occasion than he would have depicted by reminding his audience of his 1932 review of the SA at the airport. Nevertheless, remnants of the Polish army would fight on until early October, and the British and French would have none of his offers to end hostilities and acknowledge his new conquest.

September 1939 was a high point of ostentatious Soviet-German collaboration. On September 27 Ribbentrop again flew to Moscow, and this time he not only felt at home, he was feted, even lionized, under the benign gaze of Stalin himself. On this second visit he was banqueted in the dazzling dining room of the former czar, in the jovial presence of Stalin, Molotov, and high dignitaries, and the toasts were many. Molotov went around the table clinking glasses with every German guest, including the ambassador and senior members of the embassy staff as well as Ribbentrop and his entourage who had flown in two planes from Berlin by way of Königsberg. Molotov stopped at the place of each German in turn and was followed by Stalin, the latter in the mellowest of humors, informing guests waggishly at one point that it was understandable that Molotov might want a drink now and then, but he should not use a toast to Stalin as a pretext on every such occasion.

The visit went splendidly. With the war with Poland ended, Hitler was ready to make generous concessions to his new friends, and Ribbentrop said the Führer had agreed with the Soviet view that Lithuania, which in August had been declared a German sphere of influence, would now be part of the Soviet zone. This would be accomplished with minor Soviet territorial concessions.[6]

Ribbentrop thought it would be fair and equitable if the Germans were to get a little more space for East Prussia from Lithuania but did not press the matter when Stalin seemed unenthusiastic. Stalin also declined to relinquish the Polish oil fields allotted him in the secret agreement with Germany, though Ribbentrop pointed out that the Russians had oil enough in their domain, and the Germans had little. The Ukrainian people, Stalin explained, had expressed urgent claims to the area. He said, however, he was ready to raise annual Russian exports of oil to Germany to five hundred thousand tons from the agreed-upon three hundred thousand. It was to be exchanged for German coal and steel tubing.

The Soviet Union and German Reich on September 28 presented the façade of a united front. A Border and Friendship Treaty with secret protocols defined their spheres in Poland and the Baltic states, with Lithuania part of the Russian sphere. An official declaration signed by Molotov and Ribbentrop announced to the Allies that, with the fall of Poland, a sure basis of lasting peace was at hand in Eastern Europe. The joint statement declared in the interest of every nation the war between Germany and Britain and France should be ended. If the efforts of the Soviet Union and Germany were unsuccessful, "it would be clear that England and France are responsible for the continuation of the war and in such a case the governments of Germany and the USSR will mutually consult on the necessary measures."

With Poland agreeably partitioned, the Soviet Union and Germany continued to proclaim cooperation. In a speech to the Reichstag on October 6 Hitler had harsh judgments only of the defeated Poles.[7] Despite vainglorious promises of its leaders, he said, the Polish army had been destroyed in two weeks. Its commanding general fled, surrendering Warsaw without resistance. This Hitler contrasted with the heroism of other nationalities such as the Spaniards, who tenaciously defended the Alcazar in 1936, and the Germans who broke through a numerically superior czarist Russian encirclement early in World War I. As for Soviet Russia, he said, it was organized on political principles that differed from Germany's, to be sure, but presented no cause for enmity. And why, he asked rhetorically, should there be a war in the West? For the rebuilding of Poland? Germany had no demands to make on Britain or France. War could only be waged now in order to destroy present-day Germany, to create a new Versailles treaty that would only lead to a new conflict. Never in world history had there been two victors, but often there had been only one conquered, which had, it seemed to him, been the case in the last war.

In a speech to the Supreme Soviet on October 31 Molotov echoed Hitler's sentiments.[8] The former Polish state he called "the 'unlovely' product of the Treaty of Versailles," and he too expressed his firm belief in coexistence of two politically different but cooperating states. Soviet troops, he repeated, had only entered Polish territory when the Polish state had broken apart, and they had been greeted with jubilation by the Ukrainian and White Russian populations. The Soviet Union's pacts with the Baltic countries took full account of their sovereignty, and the Soviet Union was ready to work with Germany in its effort on behalf of peace. Molotov was optimistic—Soviet negotiations with Finland, Turkey, and Japan were in progress, and it was possible, he said, to talk of the beginning of better relations with Japan.

The Soviet relationship with Finland, however, was becoming strained. Along with the Baltic states, Finland was part of the new order in Soviet-German relations. It had been delivered into the Soviet sphere with the Soviet-German agreement of August 23, and Stalin, after defeat of Poland, wasted no time in making this clear to the Finns. When Finland, in contrast to the Baltic states, refused to join in a mutual-assistance pact with the Soviet Union, Moscow sent a memorandum to Helsinki on October 14 demanding cession of Finnish territory to increase the area of protection for Leningrad: lease of the Finnish port of Hangö for a naval base as well as a strategic zone on the Karelian Isthmus and islands in the Gulf of Finland, against compensation in eastern Karelia. Finland was ready to move its border thirteen kilometers to the west of Leningrad and cede islands in the Finnish gulf for the preferred Soviet territory but not to yield territory on the Karelian Isthmus or permit a Soviet base at Hangö. In the opinion of both the government and the overwhelming majority of Finns, Hangö as a Russian naval base would be a standing threat to Finland's very existence.

Finland had owed its independence from Russia not only to the Russian Revolution but also to German military forces in driving out Red troops remaining in Finland in 1918.[9] In 1939, a country of 3.5 million people, it had to rely on its own small, ill-equipped army. As the world looked on with admiration, astonishment, and folded arms, Finland chose to challenge the Russian Goliath. For the time being at least, it was left to Stalin's mercy while the Reich and the Soviet Union worked over the Poles and conducted their separate wars before confronting one another.

Moscow made use of a device it had successfully employed in the Far East when in 1922 pro-Soviet apparatchiks in Tannu Tuva proclaimed its independence from Outer Mongolia and placed it under Russian protection. In 1939 the Soviet Union invited a handpicked Finnish "People's Government" headed by Otto Villem Kuusinen, a leader of the Comintern who had lived in Russia for more than two decades, to "liberate" Finland.[10] Kuusinen's government called for military assistance against the Helsinki government, which is what Stalin provided. In line with marxist dogma the Finnish Communists may actually have expected widespread support among the Finnish proletariat, but if so they were disappointed. The Finnish Right, Left, and Center united behind the Helsinki government. Even Stalin's ally Hitler never recognized the newly proclaimed

"People's State"; following the terms of the pact he had just signed with Stalin, Germany remained neutral throughout the Russian-Finnish conflict, leaving its resolution to direct negotiations between Finland and the Soviet Union.

The future for the Poles was grim. Both the Reich and the Soviet Union wanted to rid themselves of any Polish state that could present a threat, and the occupation policy of each followed its ideological pattern: the German— racist and National Socialist; the Soviet—Communist, as in every other part of the Soviet Union, and anti-Polish. During World War I, Germany's rule over Poland had been strict, but German propaganda could plausibly proclaim that the Kaiser's army invaded as liberators of Poles and Jews and all other nationalities from czarist oppression. In 1939 a line from Dante's *Inferno* could have been engraved over both German- and Soviet-controlled areas: "Abandon all hope, Ye who enter."

German Poland was divided into two parts: the one assimilated into Reich territory; the other, the "General Gouvernement" with 14 million Polish inhabitants, had its administrative center in Kraków—Warsaw was not to be rebuilt.[11] Although Hitler publicly spoke of the desirability of reestablishing an independent Poland, the unpublicized instructions by and to the bureaucracy were different. The General Gouvernement was to be a staging zone providing workers and raw materials for the German war effort; otherwise it had no defined future. No powerful Polish state was to rise again; the only purpose of the General Gouvernement was to serve the Reich. Hitler appointed as governor-general Hans Frank, a single-tracked party lawyer whose sole ambition was to realize the programs of his Führer. Announcing that forced labor would be required of all Poles in the General Gouvernement between the ages of eighteen and sixty, Frank said succinctly: "The duty to work applies to everyone who is capable of working."

It was Himmler, on whom Hitler bestowed the title of Reich commissar for the strengthening of Germanization, who expressed the guiding spirit of the plans for Poland. Starting with the schools, Himmler said Polish children should be taught to count (at the most up to five hundred) and be able to write their names and should learn that it was a heavenly commandment to obey the Germans, to work energetically, and to be well-behaved; it was not necessary that they be able to read. Children who might be Germanized because of ethnic background or even appearance could be sent to Germany, given German names and, in due course, become Germans. The population of the General Gouvernement, an inferior people, was to exist without leaders, a working folk who could provide itinerant helpers and hands for special tasks such as paving streets, breaking stones, and construction.[12] They would live better than they had under Polish governance, and since they were people without culture some of the Germans' superiority might rub off on them. The success of the measures to be taken, he said, would depend on the chiefs of the enterprises to which they were assigned who would be, if possible, old party comrades chosen by the SS and police officials. Those Poles deemed capable of being Germanized were in no way to be defamed or called derisory names, but the casual worker moving from one job to another was not a candidate for Germanization, and such workers were not to have the same pay or living conditions as Germans. They were to have no close contact with Germans, they would carry foreign passports, and it was hoped they would be provided in time with good leadership and adequate subsistance.

Frank saw his mission more narrowly—the Poles living in the General Gouvernement, he said, were to follow the orders given them and forever renounce their short-lived dream of sovereignty; sovereignty would be exercised by the Führer of the German Reich.[13]

Jews were dealt with separately. On November 23 Frank ordered that all Jews from the age of ten were to wear armbands with the Star of David on the right arm. SS Gruppenführer Heydrich had issued precise instructions in late September—Jews in the occupied territory were to be concentrated in collecting centers near railroad facilities, at junctions if possible. These centers would serve a purpose Heydrich did not spell out; he merely referred to a final goal that, he said, would require some time to attain. Final goal *(Endziel)*—final solution *(Endlösung)*. Adoption of the code word *Endlösung* for the gas chambers for all Jews would come a few years later, though Heydrich came close to it in 1939.

The fate of the Poles in the territory acquired by the Soviet Union differed mainly in the glossary associated with measures taken against them. Stalin, like Hitler, was determined to get rid of the people who had governed Poland and might govern it again and ordered these class enemies destroyed. Many of the fifteen thousand Polish officers executed on Stalin's orders at Katyn and elsewhere were reserve officers—lawyers, doctors, engineers, and other members of the professional classes, and they and the two to three hundred thousand Poles who died in Soviet labor camps or exile were guilty of nothing more than their class origins.

Hitler wasted no time after the defeat of Poland in starting the mechanism for his next campaign—this, the decisive one, against France. Three days after he made the speech with his offer of peace to Britain he ordered the high command of the Wehrmacht to prepare the offensive, despite the winter coming up, to be undertaken as soon as possible. It was a campaign strongly opposed by all the senior army generals, who expressed both military and political misgivings as they took account of the risks against a German success. General von Leeb, commander of Army Group C, cited the antiwar sentiment of the German people and the unfavorable reaction in neutral countries, especially the United States, to another breach of Belgian neutrality. He believed a German victory impossible, he wrote to Brauchitsch, because it could only be won by complete defeat of Britain and France, for which he saw no chance whatever. Rundstedt, commander of Army Group A, predicted losses would be enormous, weather uncertain, and victory dubious. The commander in chief of the army, Brauchitsch, was against the campaign, as was his chief of staff, Halder, and they worked on plans they were convinced could only end in disaster for the Reich. The risks were simply too great, chances of victory too slim. But Hitler had a long record that he often recited of his being right and the generals wrong: the march into the Rhineland, the occupation of Austria and Czechoslovakia, the hectic pace of German rearmament—all had been boldly accomplished against advice of the generals. It was he, Hitler, who had infallibly known what to do and had made the right decisions despite the generals' stubborn opposition. So orders went out to prepare for campaign "Yellow" against France, and the generals, reluctantly but dutifully, drew up the plans.

But since the generals' overriding loyalty was to the fatherland, they resumed the structuring of a plot to get rid of Hitler if he persisted in a course they were certain would mean defeat of Germany. Some of their planning resulted in stratagems far removed from the standards of the general staff. While the Polish campaign was in progress, General von Hammerstein, commanding Army Detachment A near Frankfurt, invited Hitler to visit his headquarters where Hitler would be placed under arrest. Although Hitler considered accepting the invitation, he never came, and the plan simply fell through.[14]

Another plot, this one nonmilitary, came close to killing Hitler on November 8, as he was making a speech at the Bürgerbräukeller in Munich. A cabinetmaker by the name of Georg Elser, with infinite patience and many weeks' work, managed to build and install a bomb in a hollowed-out pillar of the room in which Hitler was to give his speech in memory of the party's "old fighters." The bomb exploded at the precise time for which Elser set it, but Hitler had begun his speech earlier than planned and had left for Berlin when the bomb exploded, so while it killed six and wounded sixty in the Bürgerbräukeller audience, it did no harm to Hitler. Elser was picked up by German customs officers at the Swiss border, interrogated, and then delivered without any kind of trial to successive concentration camps in Sachsenhausen and Dachau where he was executed just before the end of the war. Nazi propaganda declared he was recruited and paid by British intelligence, but while circumstances remain unclear it seems likely he was working on his own and on his anti-Hitler convictions. All sorts of explanations have been given for Elser's action—among them that the bomb was a Gestapo plot to feign an attack on Hitler's life and thus shore up German enthusiasm for the Führer and the war. Himmler announced in the *Völkischer Beobachter* that British intelligence and the renegade Otto Strasser, who had fled the Reich for refuge in Switzerland, were responsible, but no evidence linked either to the plot.[15]

At best, it became evident, any anti-Hitler conspirators would be making their way through formidable minefields. Ranged against them would be the party apparatus, the Gestapo, the SS, and the considerable support Hitler would find in the army itself. Most younger Wehrmacht officers were pro-Nazi, and many older ones were either apolitical or deeply impressed by Hitler's achievements. But those who joined in the plot, the military men as well as the civilian members of the Resistance, were ready to accept the risks of committing high treason against the head of state, and thus the plans for battle against the West as well as the plot to get rid of Hitler went forward simultaneously.

There were unforeseen interruptions: a former Norwegian minister of War, founder and leader of the tiny (2 percent) Norwegian anti-Semitic Nassonal Samling (National Assembly Party), Vidkun Quisling, in December 1939 informed Alfred Rosenberg, head of the foreign office of the National Socialist Party, of something the German navy had long feared—an alleged British plot to occupy, with Norwegian approval, Norway and part of Sweden to prevent shipments of Swedish iron ore from reaching the Reich along the long Norwegian coastline. This would not only imperil Germany's war production but also multiply the hazards confronting German raiders and U-boats operating on their way to the North Atlantic.

Admiral Raeder, commander in chief of the navy, since the beginning of the war had been urging on Hitler the need for control of Norwegian harbors. It was true that if Norway remained neutral, Germany could continue to use the long neutral zone running the length of the Norwegian coast that in theory was off limits to Allied attack. Raeder hoped that with Russian pressure on Norway, Norwegian harbors might come under German control, because he foresaw mortal danger if the British took them. In mid-February 1940 his fears were fanned when an unarmed German supply ship, the *Altmark,* carrying three hundred British prisoners of war transferred from ships sunk by the raider *Graf Spee,* was captured in Norwegian waters by three British destroyers. The *Altmark* was being convoyed by two Norwegian torpedo boats that made no resistance to the British attack. Seven German sailors were killed during the action as the destroyer *Cossack*'s crew boarded and searched the *Altmark,* and there was no doubt that the seizure was a flagrant breach of Norway's neutrality. What was in doubt from Raeder's point of view was the ability or willingness of the Norwegians to maintain their neutrality. With the approaching offensive against France it was difficult for Raeder to persuade Hitler to act, and only on March 1 did Hitler order preparations for occupation of Norway and Denmark—known as *Weserübung.*

The stubborn neutrality of the Scandinavian states had delayed a widening of the war. The League of Nations had urged its members to aid the Finns, and both Britain and France declared readiness to send forces in support of Finland.

But Sweden and Norway refused transit across their territory, and Finland was forced to end its hopeless struggle in February 1940 when it made a tolerable peace with the Soviet Union.[16]

The Allies' strategy of relying on naval blockade nevertheless made the creation of a northern sea front an irresistible temptation. The British cabinet approved the mining of Norwegian waters, to be followed by landings in Narvik, Stavanger, Bergen, and Trondheim. The mining operation was code-named *Wilfred* by Churchill, who was by then head of the Admiralty, and the plan of occupying Norwegian waters included, if all went well, taking the Swedish ore fields.[17]

Weserübung was only hours ahead of the Allied invasion. Parallel with the Norwegian landings, German detachments occupied all of Denmark, which would provide an essential air and supply base for a Norwegian campaign. The invasion of Denmark was met with protests from the king and the Danish government but little military resistance. But while Denmark was swiftly occupied, German forces—sea, land, and air—had to fight a stiff Norwegian campaign against overwhelmingly superior British sea power as well as tenacious Norwegian resistance.

Under command of General von Falkenhorst, who had fought on the Finnish front against the Russians in World War I, the German invasion forces won a brilliant but costly victory. A Norwegian campaign had not been high among the priorities of the army general staff—one commander had to make use of a tourist map to plan his Norwegian landing the night before it occurred. The German navy lost about a third of its strength, including one heavy and two light cruisers, ten destroyers, six submarines, and twelve transports. The destroyers were able to land troops in the battle for Narvik, but their supply ships were torpedoed by British submarines, and the destroyers, unable to escape, were sunk. The German land, sea, and air operation was a bold stroke on a far larger scale than the Allies had looked for and in the end was aided by the still greater success of the German army in France, which put an end to the possibility of any successful Allied campaign in Norway. The strategic position after occupation of Denmark and Norway was greatly improved, but the advantage could never be fully exploited because of the irreplaceable losses of warships. The most evident gain lay in assurance of the iron ore delivery by way of Narvik. A smaller advantage lay in cutting off Scandinavian ore and wood destined for Britain. In addition, U-boats on their way to battle stations in the Atlantic could operate more freely without danger of having to navigate shallow coastal waters that could be mined.[18]

An unforeseen consequence of the invasion of Denmark and Norway was noted by the astute ambassador to Moscow, Schulenburg. In a report to State Secretary von Weizsäcker on April 11, he observed that relations with the Russians had lately become cooler—this was evident in even trivial matters such as the Soviet delays in issuing visas to *volks* Germans returning from Polish imprisonment.[19] Other signs were more significant. The Soviets, Schulenburg wrote, had failed to carry out their promise to provide a German naval base near Murmansk, they had stopped deliveries of oil and grain to the Reich, and a high Soviet official, People's Commissar Anastas Mikoyan, had become pointedly unfriendly. The Russians had gone out of their way to be unpleasant. With German occupation of Norway and Denmark all this had changed. Molotov was again at his old, cheerful, helpful best, "amiability itself," Schulenburg noted, promising all possible assistance with any difficulties. He ascribed this dramatic shift to the Soviets' enormous relief at not being forced into the war by Allied operations in Scandinavia. A stone, he wrote, had fallen from the Soviets' breasts. He pointed out that the Soviet government, always well informed, had known of the British-French plans for an invasion of Norway and wanted to avoid measures that might serve the Allies as a pretext for involving the Soviet Union in the war. Molotov belatedly ascribed the stopping of oil and grain deliveries to the Reich as "overzealousness on the part of a lesser state authority," though, as Schulenburg noted, the "lesser authority" was Mikoyan himself—the highest authority after Molotov in the Soviet hierarchy.

Hitler had had one of his acute anxiety crises during the Norwegian campaign. A similar one had occurred after his risky order to the German army to march into the Rhineland in March 1936. In 1940 the German destroyers had landed a mountain regiment, mainly Austrian, in Narvik, after a harrowing voyage for mountaineers—packed together, as a German staff officer noted, like "oil sardines" and wretchedly seasick. The landings had been made, but the destroyers had been sunk and the troops left exposed, without hope of land or sea reinforcement, to the vastly superior firepower of the British navy and the Anglo-French troops. General Dietl had no apparent way out. In the deep snow he had to rely on drops by the German air force; everything—munitions, provisions, equipment, and all other supplies—had to come by air. Göring's proposal to send an additional division on a transatlantic passenger ship could not possibly be carried out, and Hitler's notion that Dietl and his men might be rescued by way of seaplanes was not much more realistic than Göring's fantasy. Hitler had thereupon issued the order on April 17 for Dietl to evacuate Narvik and lead his troops into Sweden where they would be interned. The order, written by Keitel and signed by Hitler, was received in Berlin by a young staff officer, Lieutenant Colonel Bernhard von Lossberg, who upon reading the order was beside himself with indignation.[20] The whole Norwegian operation, he said, had been centered around capturing and holding Narvik; almost all Germany's modern destroyers had been sacrificed in the action, and now Hitler had decided to surrender the all-important harbor without a battle. Lossberg rushed to the Reichschancellery where he appeared before Jodl and Keitel, declaring he had received an impossible order for General Dietl that he had not forwarded and would not forward. The military situation, Lossberg said, gave no grounds for such an order; the decision was only the result of a crisis of nerves of the high leadership, like the one that occurred during the worst days of the battle of the Marne in 1914. Lossberg wrote in his memoirs that Keitel was speechless, apparently at the effrontery of a lieutenant colonel faulting his superiors, but Jodl unpredictably agreed with Lossberg that Hitler's decision was basically wrong, though, he added, there was no way of changing it. Lossberg repeated that he would not deliver Hitler's order; Narvik, center of the battle, could not be surrendered without dire necessity. As Jodl still maintained he could not change Hitler's decision, Lossberg asked if the order could not at least be delayed until evening, by which time Lossberg hoped to get it rescinded. Jodl approved, and Lossberg brought his protest to Brauchitsch who agreed with him but, like Jodl, said he would not intervene. Falkenhorst and Dietl, he said, were not under his command but under the Führer's. Lossberg, however, had thoughtfully prepared a radio message for Brauchitsch to sign, which he now handed over. Hitler had just made Dietl a lieutenant general, and the message read: "Congratulations on your promotion, I am convinced that you will defend your decisively important post till the last man." Brauchitsch agreed to sign the message, and Lossberg went back to Jodl in the Reichschancellery, showed him the message, and told him he would substitute it for the one the Führer and Keitel had signed, at the same time tearing up Hitler's version. Jodl warmly shook Lossberg's hand, saying he would bring everything into order the next day, and this, incredibly, is what happened. It was Lossberg's, not Hitler's, order that reached Dietl.[21]

Hitler permitted Dietl to remain in Narvik where, with his force of two thousand mountain troops plus twenty-five hundred survivors from the sunken destroyers, he held out until Allied capture of the city on May 18. The Allies did not stay long, however, evacuating Narvik on June 9, departing because the French front was in dire need of reinforcement. Dietl and his mountain troops remained to fight another day.[22]

Hitler was far better when he planned on the grand scale, as well as when devising coups de théâtre. The high command of the armed forces, the OKW, had devoted the entire winter to planning an attack against France that was essentially a replay of the Schlieffen Plan of 1914.[23] General von Manstein, chief of staff of Army Group A, was the principal critic of this strategy, not only because it was what the Allies expected but also because he foresaw a blitzkrieg like the one in Poland moving with such speed and destructive power that it would annihilate enemy resistance and the possibility of bogging down in the trench warfare that had characterized World War I. Against stubborn opposition of the high command of the army, the OKH, Manstein wanted to move the weight of the offensive from the right wing to the center, driving through Holland, Luxembourg, Belgium, and the Ardennes, mounting a massive tank attack through a wooded area where tanks were not expected, splitting the French forces at the prolongation of the Maginot line. What Manstein was proposing was stiffly resisted by Brauchitsch, Halder, and Jodl but was precisely the strategy to appeal to Hitler—bold, breaking with tradition, bearing promise of deadly, overwhelming blows and the swift annihilation of the enemy.

An accident aided the neo-Schlieffen plan. Two German air force officers early in January 1940 had flown in foggy weather over German territory and become lost over Belgium. Inexplicably they carried with them the then-current plan for the offensive on a major front sector. And though after their emergency landing they tried to burn their papers, they were not completely successful, and Belgian military intelligence got hold of enough legible material to piece together German intentions. The accident could have dealt a lethal blow to the Schlieffen strategy. But it seemed so unlikely to the Dutch high command—especially that the Germans could have been so idiotic as to make the plan readily available— that they believed the whole incident a plant, a ruse de guerre.[24]

The misreading made no difference. Hitler, partly because of the breach of security, finally decided in favor of Manstein's plan and plunged himself into every detail of its development.[25] He himself devised the unprecedented attack on the key strong point, Eben Emael, defending Liège, by manned gliders landing silently and literally "out of the blue" in the middle of the fortifications and busied himself as well with preparations for similar stratagems for capture of bridgeheads and frontier fortifications. Manstein readily persuaded not only Hitler but also the gifted tank commander Guderian, who welcomed a plan based on surprise and massive tank attacks moving forward at all cost.

It was the Manstein Plan that propelled the German attack on May 10, an attack that Hitler grandiloquently proclaimed to the troops would determine the fate of Germany for a thousand years. That prediction turned out to be a considerable exaggeration, but the attack itself was overwhelmingly successful. Belgium and Holland fell according to plan—Holland in five, Belgium in eighteen days—and the French army together with the British Expeditionary Force was defeated in less than three weeks. Seventy-five enemy divisions had been destroyed and 1.2 million prisoners taken. The opposing armies at the start of the offensive had been numerically approximately equal—the Western Allies in fact had an edge in tanks and the Germans in planes.[26] But there the balance ended. German planes cooperated brilliantly with ground forces, serving as hit-and-run artillery, dive bombers with screaming motors ratcheting up the sense of disarray and hopelessness of defending troops. A counterattack by tanks commanded by Colonel Charles de Gaulle had no success, nor did any other counterattack. The Germans encountered only minor checks and minor delays in their timetable.

The Allies were outfought and outgeneraled. When in mid-May, only a little more than a week after the attack began, Churchill, prime minister since May 10, at an emergency meeting in Paris asked the Allied commander in chief, General Gamelin, where his strategic reserves were, the laconic answer was: "None." The German army was driving to the coast to corner the left wing of Allied forces against the sea; the entire British Expeditionary Force had to be embarked, if it could be embarked, in any kind of craft available, from the harbor and beach at Dunkirk back to Britain.

The Allies seemingly had little hope of preventing the destruction of their stranded army. But it was at that point that both Rundstedt and Hitler decided to halt the advance of the tanks before they made the final drive to complete the encirclement and destroy the troops on the beach. The order to stop was incomprehensible to Brauchitsch and Halder, as well as to Guderian and other tank commanders who saw no reason why they should stop at the very point of victory. For two days, time enough to strengthen the defenses, the tanks did not move. It would later be conjectured that Hitler, who was now again making overtures of peace to the British, wanted to spare them this ultimate humiliation, but Hitler was not given to chivalrous gestures, and the more likely explanation is the one that he and Rundstedt gave at the time: Rundstedt wanted a respite for his hard-driven tanks before the final assault, and Hitler, seconded by Keitel and Jodl, believed operations on the low-lying, marshy plains of Flanders and the dunes on the French coast would be precarious for tanks whose full strength would still be needed for the defeat of remaining French forces. Moreover Göring, delighted by the heroic challenge, promised that the Luftwaffe alone would prevent evacuation on the beachhead; tanks would only be a hindrance to saturation bombing by his Luftwaffe. Another consideration may be as an astute observer has pointed out that Hitler did not have the same killer impulse that he had with the Poles and was more readily distracted.[27]

The German miscalculation was large. Not for the first or last time were Göring's promises empty. From May 27 till June 4 the British succeeded in evacuating 98,671 men from the beach at Dunkirk and 239,555 from what was left of the harbor itself, making use of anything that would float: excursion steamers, motorboats, fishing boats, barges, hundreds of small craft—altogether more than eight hundred–odd vessels, mainly British but also French and Dutch—plus assorted navy ships, including destroyers and a cruiser. Almost all British troops were regulars, the irreplaceable nucleus of any future army. Losses of material were enormous—Churchill wrote that "we had lost the whole equipment of the army to which all the first fruits of our factories had hitherto been given: 7,000 tons of ammunition, 90,000 rifles, 2,300 guns, 120,000 vehicles, 8,000 Bren guns and 400 anti-tank rifles."[28] A heavy loss but nothing like the loss of men of the expeditionary army. The German air force did its utmost to carry out

Göring's boast, but bomber loads were less effective, exploding on the marshes and sand dunes bordering the Channel along the coast, than they would have been on more solid terrain. The Luftwaffe, which was operating from distant home bases, was up against British fighter planes that included the new, deadly Spitfires, which were flying from nearby airfields. German plane losses were high, their success this time only moderate. German air superiority over the battle lines remained, but German air dominance began to fade. No war could be won by heroic embarkations, but the British had managed to salvage an army that seemed doomed, and German control of the air over the battlefield had been challenged in the dogfights.

When the attack on remaining French forces began and broke through the defenses on a wide front, General Vuillemin, chief of the French air force, called desperately for more air support. He wanted British planes stationed in France under his command, and his pleas were joined by a government facing loss not only of Paris but also of the war. Churchill and the cabinet felt they had no choice but to refuse. The planes were needed for defense of a Britain almost stripped of armament. This decision was no solace to the French high command who saw their troops torn to ribbons as a result of inadequate air support as well as lack of almost everything needed on the ground.

Defeat, as has been long observed, has many fathers, and the list of those responsible for the lost battles is very long. The Maginot line where Gamelin had spent much of his time had not only cost billions of francs, it had proved worthless. French military leaders blamed everyone who had been in power, including the British ally for what many regarded as hoarding its air force for Britain's defense. Paris was captured by the Germans without having to be bombarded from the ground or air. Gamelin had been relieved on May 18, replaced by the Belgian-born, seventy-three year old Maxime Weygand who had been Foch's chief of staff in World War I. A towering hero of that war, "the savior of Verdun," Marshal Pétain, was named vice president of the cabinet. Reynaud himself took over the ministry of National Defense and War.

As German columns drove ever more deeply into remaining French defenses, Reynaud called for help from President Roosevelt—civilization, that is to say France, was again in mortal danger. Roosevelt was ready to do anything in his power to help but could not declare war or produce troops nor could anyone else in all the world. The American president promised to provide ever-increasing war supplies, double and more than had been sent, but had to add, however reluctantly, that only Congress could declare war, and it was an instant, armored ally France needed. As defenses crumbled, a desperate Reynaud turned again, at Churchill's urging, to Roosevelt. But again all Roosevelt could do was urge France to battle and promise even more help. Churchill pointed out that Roosevelt had committed himself; the United States would surely enter the war and Allied victory in the end was certain. Reynaud begged Roosevelt for permission to publicize the president's hearty promises of almost all-out aid. But Roosevelt, with an eye on Congress and public opinion that heavily opposed American intervention, knew he had to refuse, and Reynaud was left with the consolation of the note itself. What use it was to the thousands of refugees and dispersed troops clogging French roads is unclear.

Nothing, it seemed to Reynaud, Weygand, and Pétain, could save France from chaos but the cessation of hostilities. Not all Churchill's considerable talents of persuasion and his dogged conviction that with the assured help of America the Allies would win in the end could affect the harsh reality of overwhelming military defeat. Churchill refused to release France from its commitment never to seek a separate peace with the enemy, but French leaders saw no other way to preserve the core of their country. The high command including Weygand and Pétain, unable to organize a defense and faced with a new enemy as Mussolini decided Italy had to participate in the Axis triumph, saw no alternative than to ask for an armistice.

When news came to Hitler in his field headquarters he did an awkward little dance, with arms outstretched as if to conduct an invisible orchestra, then lifting one bent leg stiffly, with his hands limply at his side in a solemn victory prance. "The greatest battle of destruction in history," the usually terse bulletin of the high command declared of the success in Flanders and Artois, and so it seemed. "The greatest field commander of all time," Keitel called Hitler, and the defeated Gamelin called him "a demonic genius." Göring could only insert his own impressive bulk under the halo of glory surrounding Hitler by telling representatives of the press that no German was better qualified than he to describe accomplishments of the incomparable statesman and military genius, Adolf Hitler.

The lance corporal of World War I who had lacked the martial bearing, according to his superior officers, to warrant promotion to become a noncommissioned officer had led a triumph not only over the Allied commanders but over the high command of the army too, and while a few hundred thousand enemy troops escaped his net the Continent was at his mercy.

The armistice was concluded in the same converted dining car where the German armistice commission had been confronted by an implacable Foch in 1918. The scene was an updated version of the 1918 meeting in the forest in Compiègne, replayed in the very spot and wooden car where the chief of the German delegation, the Centrist leader Matthias Erzberger, had been required by Marshal Foch to state explicitly that the Germans were asking for an armistice. "What brings you gentlemen here?" Foch had demanded of the commission. When Erzberger replied that they awaited proposals for an armistice, Foch had said curtly: "I have no proposals to make." The Germans had to appear not as negotiators but as supplicants.

Hitler was present this time, together with Göring, Hess, Keitel, Ribbentrop, Raeder, and Brauchitsch. On the French side of the narrow wagon-lit table were General Huntziger, the French ambassador Noël, Vice Admiral Le Luc, and General Bergeret of the air force. Hitler and his retinue rose as the French came in, and both sides bowed. Keitel read the preamble to the armistice, which Schmidt translated into French:

> France has been conquered after a heroic resistance. . . . Germany therefore does not intend the conditions of the armistice or the negotiations to have the characteristic features of calumniating such a courageous opponent. . . . The aim of the German demands is to prevent a resumption of the battle, to provide Germany all security for the continuation of the war forced upon her against England, as well as to create the preconditions for the shaping of a new peace.

But Hitler was still under the indelible impression of the armistice signed in 1918, and the terms of 1940 often repeated terms of 1918. France was to be permitted an army of one hundred thousand men, stripped of its air force; its fleet was to be interned in French harbors, under German and Italian supervision; a large part of the country, including Paris, was to be occupied by the Germans, its remaining sovereignty confined to a third of the country and the colonies. Still, as Huntziger told Weygand over the telephone when communications were established between the armistice car and temporary headquarters of the French government in Bordeaux, the conditions were hard but did not impugn French honor.

Hitler's immediate aim was to keep the French fleet out of British harbors, to be free to concentrate German military power against Britain without having to deal with any French resistance on the Continent or in North Africa; otherwise France no longer presented any military problem. Britain was the only remaining enemy, and in the euphoria of his victory Hitler was warmly disposed. If he could make peace with Britain, not only would the war be over but also a new Europe under German hegemony would change the face of history as Britain acknowledged what it had never before accepted—domination of the Continent by a single power. Italy, whose leader still had wan hopes of replacing French control over Nice, Corsica, Tunis, and the other territories he considered important to his Roman imperium, was not to be permitted representation at the armistice table with France; the Italians would meet separately and demand only minor concessions. As Huntziger said, Italy had declared war but not waged it. Huntziger also said as the armistice talks began that France would not accept an Italian occupation and if necessary would fight on. "We have been defeated by Germany," he said.[29]

From Hitler's point of view, Britain should recognize that it had little to gain by continuing the war. Churchill, to be sure, could rely on help from the United States and even eventual American intervention, but Britain's world position would be fundamentally altered. He was prepared to make a generous peace, helping to support Britain with its burdens of an empire he considered a stabilizing factor in a world with many threatening, inferior races. All Britain had to do was recognize his generosity and German superiority on the Continent. He had no inkling of the depth of fear, contempt, and revulsion that would prevent such a shift in British policy. In his aura of military victory the German Leader could even speak of the possibility of the Jews being shipped off to a part of the world where they could live and do no harm—Madagascar.

Among conditions of the armistice was a clause obligating France to turn over anyone who had been arrested for aiding Germany and to deliver to German authorities anyone demanded by the Reich. Since Hitler's coming to power thousands of refugees from National Socialist Germany had fled to France where their intense anti-Hitler campaign deeply irritated the Führer. Huntziger protested inclusion of the clause as an infringement to the right of asylum but Keitel refused to alter it, as he did most of the other clauses Huntziger wanted amended. All the conquered countries surrounding Germany in their time— Austria, Czechoslovakia, and now France—had been a continuing irritant to Hitler when they permitted publication of anti-Nazi articles by émigrés, and when Huntziger spoke of the right of asylum, Keitel cut him short, referring to the major warmongers who were rightful objects of the clause. The clause was not negotiable, and though Huntziger had no way of predicting its consequences it would condemn a great number of the refugees living in France and its colonies to Auschwitz, not Madagascar.

French reports in the summer of 1940 agreed in describing the behavior of German troops occupying French territory as "correct." In contrast to their atrocity propaganda of World War I, Frenchmen, if heartbroken, were unfailingly polite. To Churchill's despair, following strictly the terms of the armistice, the French government turned over to German authorities more than four hundred German pilots, most of whom, as Churchill glumly remarked, had been shot down by British planes over French territory.

It was the French and British who now conducted large-scale hostilities, not against the Germans but with one another. Survival for Britain depended on continuing control of the sea lanes, and Churchill again and again urged the French to bring their warships either to British or to neutral harbors where they would be interned and disarmed until the war was over when they would be returned to France. The alternative, British Admiral Somerville told the commandant of the French fleet at Oran, if he did not comply within six hours, was an all-out assault that would sink his fleet. The ultimatum was carried out. A British squadron that included the aircraft carrier *Ark Royal* attacked the ships lying at anchor, sinking a battleship, two destroyers, and an aircraft carrier supply ship. More than 1,200 French sailors were killed on July 3 and 154 more in a second attack on July 6. The French government now headed by Pétain broke diplomatic relations. These attacks and others against warships in British, Egyptian, and African ports resulted, as Churchill said, in "removing the French navy from major German calculations." They did not lead to full-scale war between France and Britain but incited French Foreign Minister Paul Baudoin to say that the British had stained their honor, that it was their foreign policy that had lost France's one-time ally, Italy, led France into a war it did not want, and then had reserved the British air force for defense of Britain.

Hitler was at his zenith when on July 19 he addressed the Reichstag where, while excoriating Churchill, he again spoke of the desirability of peace. He also announced, while promoting his generals to higher ranks, that Göring was now a Reichsmarshal and recipient of the Great Cross of the Iron Cross, neither of which awards had ever previously existed in the Reich.[30]

Hitler now busied himself with preparations for the campaign against Britain. On July 16 he ordered preparations for a surprise attack "on a broad front from Ramsgate to the neighborhood westward of the isle of Wight" in which the Luftwaffe would act as artillery and elements of the navy as engineers. He was well aware of the risk of landing large bodies of troops and their artillery support on a shore defended by a vastly superior sea power and depended on the Luftwaffe to break enemy resistance. The Luftwaffe and navy would clear the way for crossing the Channel, and the invading army would follow, seaborne as well as airborne, with parachute troops and airborne infantry. He was convinced he had to move quickly so as not to lose the political and military initiative the Wehrmacht had won on the Continent. The British position, he told Halder, was hopeless—the war had been won by Germany. The question was how long it would take to bring essential shipping together and how artillery support of the flotilla could be guaranteed. The transport itself, he said, presented the greatest risk, and the crossing should, therefore, be undertaken only if no other way was open.

All the while he was thinking about Russia, Stalin, he noted, was coquetting with England—the Russian leader did not want Germany too strong, though no sign of Soviet activity against Germany had been detected. Nevertheless, the Russian problem had to be taken into account and contingencies weighed. Assembling forces for an attack against the Soviet Union, Halder informed Hitler, would take from four to six weeks. Their aim would be to defeat the Soviet army or at least occupy enough Russian territory to prevent an air attack against Berlin and vital German industries. The political goals of a campaign against the Soviet Union in the army's view would be to establish a Ukrainian state and a Baltic confederation, with White Russia going to Finland.

Hitler's long-range plans for Europe were nebulous only in their details. Western Europe was to develop a wide-ranging economic structure under

German leadership, with parts of France and Belgium incorporated in the German state. The "greater Germany" economic area would include the Polish General Gouvernement, the protectorate of Bohemia and Moravia, Slovakia, Alsace-Lorraine, Luxembourg, Holland, and Belgium, along with the African colonies that would soon be annexed; that is, a German-dominated European economy would be created ranging from the Iberian Peninsula to the Urals.

The notion of founding a Jewish settlement in Madagascar soon disappeared, but a lively competition over who ran what promptly developed between Ribbentrop's foreign office, Göring's Ministry of Economics, Himmler's SS, and the Wehrmacht.[31] Goebbels with his propaganda ministry represented a hard line against France, which was to be no more, in his view, than an enlarged Switzerland—an agrarian country that, deprived of its western Pas de Calais and northern, industrial Briey-Longwy areas, which would become part of the Reich, would serve as a vacation land for German tourists. In Goebbels's view, the reappearance of France as a great power did not lie in the German interest, and with the same end in mind some circles, including Göring's ministry, favored an independent Brittany. In the new National Socialist order the Netherlands would become part of the Reich; Belgium would be divided into French-speaking and Flemish-speaking zones—that is, between a Walloon and Flemish district at least ideologically assimilated into the Reich, though the Walloons too were to be targets of a pro-Reich, Germanic movement under the fascist leader, Léon Degrelle. No final decisions could be made, but Hitler's aims were clear enough: Europe would develop its economy under German hegemony. German domination over French industrial and strategic areas was to be secured with an eventual outright acquisition of French territory, and no potential as a great military or economic power lay in the French future. Only Britain and the Soviet Union remained to be dealt with. In sum, Hitler was preparing to create a vastly more unbalanced arrangement of states, in reverse, than the one ordained at Versailles, which had left Germany defenseless and France overwhelmingly dominant. Hitler's new order made Versailles seem quaint.

Until the defeat of France, Hitler had never planned an invasion of England. He now hoped that Britain would see the impossibility of victory, and if Churchill could not be persuaded to make peace, then other more sensible men would take his place. Among them were the foreign secretary, Lord Halifax, the ambassador to Spain, Hoare, the duke of Windsor, and Lloyd George. Moreover, he did not want to see the empire destroyed; that, he said, would benefit the Soviet Union and the United States, not Germany, and reasonable Englishmen must come to see that the war instigated against Germany was irrevocably lost and that essential British interests would best be served by accepting that fact and thus retain, with the help of the Reich, its world empire. The late nineteenth-century and early twentieth-century British strategy of keeping Germany off balance with an all-powerful British fleet and a mighty French army, with its allies, had failed. Whitehall must come to accept this and make an invasion of Britain unnecessary. Hitler saw this plainly; the trouble was that the British did not. They did not understand that they were beaten, that their strategy had failed, and that they must accommodate themselves to the new order. If they did not, he would reluctantly invade. But he had no comprehensive plan for the invasion. The only possible reason, he thought, for continuation of the war was Churchill's reliance on the Soviet Union and the United States. After the defeat of France the British had little left to fight with. The United States could not yet intervene with large forces, only Russia could do that, and therefore the British must be relying on Soviet intervention on their behalf. The appointment of a man widely regarded as friendly to the Soviet Union, a socialist, Sir Stafford Cripps, as ambassador to Moscow in May 1940, increased Hitler's suspicions of a British-Soviet understanding.

Only when it became clear to Hitler that Britain, under all circumstances, would continue to fight, did he reluctantly order preparations for the invasion. On July 2, 1940, the Wehrmacht was officially informed of his decision, and on July 12 he ordered actual preparations. He believed British superiority at sea would be largely overcome by the German air force, with an initial landing force of one hundred thousand men, tanks, and motorized vehicles. A successful invasion could be developed from southern England.

The primary necessity everyone—including Hitler and the high commands of the army, navy, and air force—agreed, was attainment of indisputable air superiority over the Channel and the south of Britain. The Reich had 2,355 planes: almost 1,000 two-engine bombers, 316 dive bombers, 702 fighters, 261 destroyers, and 78 reconnaissance planes. It had no four-motor bombers, few planes carrying torpedoes, and lacked long-range fighters, though the two-engine bombers could only carry out their missions with fighter escort.

On the British side were considerable advantages, some of which were not known to Hitler. Perhaps most important was that when a plane was shot down the pilots and crews were lost to the Reich, while the British could parachute into their own territory. Another weighty factor was the radar system Britain had developed, unknown to the Germans. A network of fifty-two stations in August 1940, from Pembrokeshire to the Falklands, warned the defense well ahead of time of distance, direction, numbers, and flight levels of the advancing air armadas, giving the defense time to concentrate against them. Radar and "Enigma," the cipher that from April 1940 enabled the British to decipher German radio transmissions with their directives for targeting, were inventions the Germans could neither match nor master. None of the preconditions that had made German air attacks in France so devastating was present in the attack on Britain. In France the German planes had flown in support of the swiftly moving land forces of tanks and motorized infantry, and the combination had been enormously successful. In Britain the planes were on their own, attacking scattered targets with slow two-engine bombers escorted by fighter planes whose range did not permit them to stay long over British territory or even to operate over outermost targets. The Luftwaffe was opposed by well-trained fighter pilots, the new, innovatively designed Spitfires and Hurricanes, and a communications system the Reich could not counter.[32] No amount of strategic shifting of targets and tactics could change those intractable facts.

And then there was the specter of Soviet Russia. In early July, too, at the same time the Wehrmacht was apprised of Hitler's decision to invade Britain, the OKH began the planning of operations against the Soviet Union. At a meeting of the Berghof on July 31, Hitler told Halder that if Russia was defeated, England's last hope would be blasted.

Although he continued to reiterate to his staff and foreign visitors that England was, in fact, defeated—a conviction shared by many in the high command, including Jodl—the Russian dagger, as he called it, never ceased to prick him during all the fury of the bombing of Britain. Russia had to be disposed of, the sooner the better, and between late July and early September he decided to attack. May 1941 was the date he had in mind for the attack. He sketched the major offensives: one toward Kiev, another toward Moscow with 120 available divisions plus 20 on leave.

Plans for the invasion of Britain, though never abandoned, became more and more theoretical, while those for invasion of Soviet Russia took shape. By August 5 Major General Marcks, commander of the Sixteenth Army, had prepared a detailed outline of attack to be mounted from the Reich, Poland, Hungary, and Romania. Like campaigns in the West, it was to be based on surprise and speed.

The air attack on Britain continued. As time went on and stormy autumn weather approached, weather that would make landings impossible, air dominance (except for brief periods over Sussex and Kent) continued to elude the Luftwaffe. On one day, August 15, of 520 German bombers and 1,270 fighters dispatched over Britain, 57 were shot down. The stepped-up attacks cost the Luftwaffe eight hundred planes, while British production in dispersed plants not only continued but actually rose.

The invasion, originally scheduled for September, had to be postponed; the German air force hammered at one strategic target after another: the ports of London, Liverpool, Southampton, and vital manufacturing centers. For eighty-six days and nights, from September 1940 to January 1941, industrial areas were bombed—Birmingham, Leeds, Sheffield, and Coventry. Terror bombings of civilians were sporadic—Hitler alone, he announced, would order them. When carried out, as against Coventry (the code name of which was *Moonlight*

Sonata), they were called reprisals against British raids, and if Hitler was reluctant to order systematic, full-scale terror attacks it was not because of any humanitarian sentiments but because he doubted their efficacy in bringing Britain to the bargaining table. The bombings inflicted immense damage, but Britain, with its dispersed targets and main manufacturing centers for the air force beyond operational range of German fighters, was able to replace its lost planes. Although the Royal Air Force was sorely tried, sufficient pilots and planes were always on hand to inflict heavy and finally insupportable losses on the Luftwaffe. The invasion was postponed for weeks, then vaguely until perhaps the next spring. But early in December, Hitler told Halder that "Sea Lion" was no longer under consideration, which meant that nothing was left of the invasion but the empty landing barges collected on the French coast.

Hitler could never order the landings; Britain could not be knocked out of the war by land assault, and the great coalition he dreamed of, consisting of Italy, Japan, Spain, and even France added to the Reich, attacking the wide-flung British perimeter, fell apart before it could be organized. If Britain could be shut out of the Mediterranean, and the submarine attack on British shipping took sufficient toll, Britain, cut off from Middle Eastern oil and the main artery linking its Asian commonwealth, would be in dire straits. Gibraltar was a key to the Mediterranean and Spain's joining the war a key to conquest of Gibraltar.

Up to their meeting on October 23 at the French frontier town of Hendaye, Franco had retained friendly but arms-length relations. He had repeatedly informed Hitler of his fervently hoped-for success of the German war effort, but he had remained effectively neutral, and after the Allies were defeated in France he announced a policy of nonintervention, of "not taking part in the war," by which he meant he was pro-Axis at heart but nonbelligerent in practice. At Hendaye, Hitler relied on his much-acclaimed persuasive power with leaders of countries he was wooing. England, he told Franco, was defeated, the United States could not bring much help for months to come, and Russia if it joined the war would come in on the German side. But Franco was unconvinced—he had little love for England and a warm desire to retrieve Gibraltar, which had been in British possession since 1704, but he was far from certain that Britain had been defeated. Moreover, when Admiral Canaris, chief of the Abwehr, who had cordial relations with Franco, was sent by Hitler to help persuade Franco to enter the war, Hitler had chosen the wrong man for the mission. Canaris, the antibolshevik, had a warm sympathy for the Spanish people and for Franco himself, and he did not believe Spain's entry into the war would benefit either Spain or any other country—including Germany. His advice to Franco did nothing to further the latter's desire to enter the war.[33]

The talks took place in Hitler's sumptuous parlor car alongside Franco's train on its wide-gauged track. Hitler and Ribbentrop waited for an hour on the station platform for the arrival of Franco, who appeared with a retinue that included his brother-in-law and foreign minister Ramón Serrano Suñer. Suñer was a sharp-witted, sharp-tongued diplomat, contemptuous of Ribbentrop's manner, which he thought was a cover for his ignorance. Franco was deeply grateful, he told Hitler, for Germany's and Italy's indispensable help in his battle against the Spanish Republic, but the battle had been enormously costly, and Spain needed time to recuperate—he would sign a secret treaty of alliance with Germany and Italy and agree to join the war on their side but would set no date, and the promises were dead on arrival. Franco could not cooperate at this juncture, he regretfully explained to Hitler, with an attack on Gibraltar, for which Hitler promised aid of the specialists who had captured Eben Emael. The best he was in a position to offer was continued benevolent nonparticipation and his fervent wishes for success of the Axis. He was ready to join the anticommunist pact with the Reich and Italy and the Three-Power Pact they had made with Japan, but he could not allow his joining to be published because, he said, Spain needed everything from food to weapons and was unable to fight at this juncture, even for the prize of Gibraltar and the promise of French-African colonies.

Nor was the Pétain government, despite its resentment of bombings of French ships and loss of lives, ever ready to take its place on the side of Germany against its ally of World War I and the beginning of World War II. The resistance forces under de Gaulle would be considerably strengthened by such a move.

Mussolini, though convinced of Hitler's historical mission, was much more anxious to win laurels for Italian arms than to subordinate his policies to Hitler's purposes. The targets he chose after conquest of Albania all proved beyond Italian competence to reduce, and almost everywhere he marched, on the French border or in Africa or in Greece, he would disclose not strength but weakness. In all the theaters of war he chose his armies were soon checked, and in Africa, though his troops outnumbered the British force three- and fourfold, he soon stood in need of German reinforcements to prevent an outright disaster.[34]

Japan was ready to join a three-power pact with the Reich and Italy, but the alliance concluded at the end of September 1940 was, in Tokyo's view, limited to Japanese aims. It provided, as a condition of "a lasting peace in the world," recognition of the leadership of Germany and Italy in Europe and of Japan in Asia, with due regard for the interests of the Soviet Union. As for Hitler, like Napoleon before him, he could not rest on having won hegemony over Europe unless Russia was once and for all eliminated from carrying out its potentially lethal role as Britain's dagger on the Continent.

On October 24, the day after Hitler met with Franco, his special train moved to another French railroad station—at Montoire—where accompanied by Ribbentrop he greeted Pétain and the French premier, Pierre Laval. Hitler immediately announced to these visitors, too, that the war had been won by

Germany, that England was defeated and sooner or later would be forced to admit it. But Pétain was no more convinced than Franco, and on the day he met with Hitler in the chancellor's parlor car an unofficial Vichy emissary, Professor Rougier, met with Churchill in London.[35] A former professor of philosophy at the University of Besançon, Rougier assured Churchill on behalf of Pétain that the French would never deliver their fleet to the Germans, would provide no bases in North Africa, and in short would do nothing dishonorable to damage Britain. Pétain was deeply suspicious of Britain but implacably hostile to German dominance, and Hitler had no better luck with him than with Franco. Pétain, who appeared at Montoire in full uniform before the former corporal of the German army, was courteous but aloof and manifested no enthusiasm whatever for joining Hitler's coalition against Britain. Laval, though well disposed to the Reich, showed no sign of having an opinion different from Pétain's.

October 24 was no happy day for Hitler as it became clear that Pétain would not join in any kind of military alliance with the Reich, and the unsettling news arrived from the German Embassy in Rome that Mussolini was preparing an immediate invasion of Greece. Hitler had had no warning of Mussolini's intentions, and he was beside himself when he learned of them. Among other unpromising considerations, he wrathfully pointed out to his entourage, it was too late in the year to mount an invasion over Greek mountain passes that would be covered by autumn mists and then winter snows.

He promptly set out to change Mussolini's mind. That would not be easy. Mussolini in his turn had been equally furious when he learned that Hitler, without saying a word to him, on October 12 had ordered a military mission, including planes and German troops that were ostensibly to act as instructors to Romania. Mussolini bitterly complained to his son-in-law and Foreign Minister Count Ciano that Hitler was always confronting him with accomplished facts, and this time he would pay him in the same coin: Hitler would learn of the Italian invasion of Greece in the newspapers.

Hitler's train proceeded not back to Berlin but to Florence, but by the time he arrived, October 28, it was too late.[36] An exultant Mussolini greeted him with news that Italian troops had crossed the Greek frontier. It was a decision Hitler deplored, but since he had just ordered German troops into Romania and before that into country after country without consulting Mussolini, he was in no position to express his irritation. The notable difference, however, as Hitler would have been pleased to point out, lay in the fact that Hitler's operations were patently successful, and he had no need to call on the Italian ally, whereas the Italians no sooner moved into action of any sort when they were in need of German help.

Neither the Italian alliance nor the Three-Power Pact alone could bring Britain to the peace table. Time was pressing: Britain and the United States were building up their armaments at a furious rate; the Soviet Union was an uncertain factor. Thus, when Molotov arrived on his fateful visit to Berlin the morning of November 12, he came at a time when Hitler was convinced he had to make a final decision to deal with the Soviets once and for all as an ally or as an enemy.

16

The Last Bunker

Molotov appeared at the Anhalter with a suite of sixty people, including sixteen security men, a physician, and three personal aides—a retinue befitting an emissary of Stalin. The German ambassador to the Soviet Union, Schulenburg, and Hilger, both strong supporters of German-Russian collaboration, traveled with Molotov. It was a cold, drizzly November day, and they were greeted at a station decorated with flowers, green branches, and Soviet flags with hammers and sickles, by an honor guard from Hitler's SS Leibstandarte, Field Marshal Keitel, Ribbentrop, and members of the foreign office staff. A band played the "Internationale," which, as a member of the Soviet Embassy noted, would have landed the musicians in a Gestapo death camp a short time before. Now the high party functionaries, generals, and any Gestapo men present stood at stiff attention until the notes of the music faded in the damp air. The music of the Soviet national anthem was identical with that of the "Internationale," and it had been pointed out, at a preparatory meeting at the foreign office, that it might be a dubious choice in Berlin. Half the population of the city had once voted Social Democratic or Communist, and a good many Berliners, it was observed, might be tempted to join in the chorus, singing the German text they had known by heart before Hitler came to power. But the "Internationale," along with "Deutschland, Deutschland über Alles," and the Nazi battle song, the "Horst Wessel Lied," had been played by a Soviet band when Ribbentrop flew to Moscow in August 1939, and it was solemnly played again on Molotov's arrival in Berlin.

Molotov and his delegation were driven in black, open Mercedes limousines to the guest house, Bellevue Castle in the Tiergarten. They drove past crowds more curious than enthusiastic; the National Socialist Party had not turned out its cheering sections, and Berliners were accustomed to motorcades of state visitors.

The pourparlers opened inauspiciously. From the time of his arrival, Molotov, who had been warmly welcoming in Moscow, was cordial but businesslike. In Moscow he had been not only the diplomat but also the solicitous host; in Berlin he was a diplomat and a gimlet-eyed lawyer who insisted on reading all the fine print.[1] Ribbentrop was less pointedly austere than usual—friendlier, Schmidt noted, by far than during meetings with Ciano. Hitler, for his part, was effusively cordial when he received Molotov at the new Reichschancellery. He was obviously determined, Hilger thought, to win Stalin over to his purposes— something he had been unable to accomplish with Franco and Pétain.

Relations lately had not been smooth between Moscow and Berlin. Stalin, making good use of German involvement in the West, had forced Romania to cede Bessarabia, which had once been part of czarist Russia, and northern Bukovina, which had a large Ukrainian population that had never been part of Russia. Hitler, in dire need of a continuous flow of Romanian oil, had counseled acceptance of the Soviet demand. The Hungarians and Bulgarians, too, had claims on Romanian territory, and again any armed conflict would threaten production of the Romanian oil fields, and so for the second time the Axis intervened, and another Vienna award by Italy and Germany handed down on August 20 forced Romania to give in to the Hungarian-Bulgarian demands. As a placebo the Axis powers announced their guarantee of the diminished Romanian borders. Stalin had sharply protested; the Balkans were a place of Soviet interest, and he had instructed Molotov to make that interest unmistakable while the Reich was in need of Soviet cooperation. The Italian-German guarantee was a challenge to further Soviet demands on Romania. Axis arbitration of the Hungarian-Romanian dispute, without Soviet participation, was a breach, as Molotov would not fail to point out, of the consultative clause of the German-Soviet Treaty of Friendship. Other manifestations of strained relations were apparent: The Russian press noted that Stalin, up to the time of Molotov's visit, had not received the German ambassador for six months. German deliveries of finished goods to the Soviet Union were far behind schedule; German troops had been moving through Finland ostensibly on their way to Norway; a German military mission had visited Bucharest.

Hitler, however, for his part, kept the Russian door ajar. On October 13 Ribbentrop dispatched a nineteen-page letter to Stalin telling him how much both countries had benefited by cooperating, laboriously describing development of the present unstable European situation, and inviting Molotov to visit Berlin. He recounted Britain's perfidious designs on the peace of Europe; Germany's continuing military triumphs; its repeated efforts to end the war and prevent Britain from extending to Romania, the Balkans, and Scandinavia; the pacific goals of Germany, Italy, and Japan acting in concert; and the opportunity for the Soviet Union to seize a historical moment by joining in the common purposes of the Three-Power Pact. The Reich, he assured Stalin, would be pleased to act as a friendly intermediary to help settle any outstanding Japanese-Soviet divergences, so that Moscow could adjust its long-term policies in the right direction. Stalin, not without a touch of irony, thanked Ribbentrop for his "instructive letter" and agreed to Molotov's visit.

Hitler, when he received Molotov in the Reichschancellery, began by assuring him that he saw no important conflicts of interest between the Reich and the Soviet Union.[2] Each had only to recognize that the other had basic needs, and they could readily come to an understanding and continue their peaceful cooperation. But the Reich was at war, the Soviet Union was not, and therefore the Reich was forced to take measures that were really for benefit of both countries. Molotov agreed wholeheartedly with all the expressions of friendship and the rewards of togetherness, and Hitler went on: Britain no longer had a dagger at its disposal on the Continent; Germany had only to strike the final blow and deal with political questions following the last battle. The Reich, he assured Molotov, sought no military help from the Soviet Union; it wanted to meet Russia's requirements as it had in the case, for example, of Lithuania. He spoke in vague terms of the desirability of Germany's colonial expansion in central Africa, of the Reich's need for raw materials and keeping enemy powers with their naval bases from establishing themselves there. But in no case would the interests of the Soviet Union be infringed.

Hitler then set out the global evidences of good intentions. Germany had no concerns in Asia, aside from those arising from economics and trade, nor any colonial aspirations there. In Europe: Germany, Russia, and Italy all required access to the sea, but these needs did not conflict. In the Balkans the Reich was acting only under necessity of making certain that essential raw materials were made available. Hitler mentioned Romania and Greece and the necessity of preventing Britain from obtaining air and naval bases in those countries. He said, and Molotov heartily agreed, that achieving such goals would be vastly less expensive by peaceful than by military means. The United States, in Hitler's view, was pursuing an imperialistic policy, and the European nations had to prevent the Anglo-Saxon powers from securing bases on the Continent. A kind of Monroe Doctrine had to be devised along with a common European colonial policy. Russia's drive for ice-free harbors and assured access to the open sea had his full support, and any attempt of Britain to gain a foothold in Greece had to be resisted. When Molotov asked why Salonika represented a danger to

Germany, Hitler pointed out that it was close to the Romanian oil fields that Germany must protect but promised as soon as peace was restored that German troops would immediately leave Romania. He would also seek to aid Russia in its search for security in the straits.

Molotov readily went along with Hitler's tour d'horizon but observed that Hitler's statements were of a general nature. And while he was in agreement with them Stalin had given precise instructions that he was deputed to carry out. He joined Hitler in the conviction that both parties had gained a great deal from their treaty of friendship, but difficulties remained—such as the question of Finland. The Finnish problem was unresolved, and he asked if the German-Soviet treaty, as far as it concerned Finland, was still controlling? From the point of view of the Soviet government, he said, no changes had occurred; Finland belonged firmly in the Soviet orbit. As for the Three-Power Pact, what did the "new order in Europe and Asia" mean and in what way did it include the Soviet Union? Then, too, there were questions that had to do with other Soviet interests in the Balkans, the Black Sea, Romania, and Turkey. What was the new order in Europe and what form would it take?

Hitler without answering any of the questions assured Molotov that none of those problems would be dealt with under the Three-Power Pact without Soviet participation, and this was true not only in Europe but in Asia too where the Reich, he repeated, would be pleased to aid Moscow's cause as a go-between. Under no circumstances would the Soviet Union be confronted with accomplished facts. Concluding the session, Hitler said, the problem of Western Europe had to be solved by Germany, Italy, and France, just as questions in the East essentially concerned the Soviet Union and Japan, though Germany would act as an intermediary if Moscow wished. In any event it was necessary to oppose what Hitler called the American attempt to "earn a profit out of Europe," adding that the United States had nothing to look for, either in Europe or in Asia.

Molotov said he completely shared Hitler's assessment of the role of the United States and Britain. Soviet participation in the Three-Power Pact seemed to him basically acceptable on the condition that the Soviet Union was regarded as a partner and not as a mere object, but goals and the meaning of the pact, especially in the greater Asian sphere, had to be more precisely defined.

At this point, with an air-raid alarm in the offing, the meeting adjourned until the next day. The talks had gotten nowhere. The two men stalked one another warily, each holding fast to his wallet. Stalin had no intention whatever of going to war on Germany's side; the guarantees he sought were aimed at increasing Soviet security against the designs of Germany and Japan and of Britain as well. He aimed, as he told the Politburo, to stay out of the war until both sides were exhausted.

On the second day Hitler and Molotov met again with the same people present—Ribbentrop, Molotov's deputy Dekanosov, and the interpreters.[3] Hitler was less ingratiating this time. He pointed out that regarding Soviet territorial claims on Romania, Germany had expressed disinterest only in Bessarabia's becoming part of the Soviet Union; Bukovina, he said, had not been included, and there, as in the case of Lithuania, the Soviet Union had departed from the German-Soviet agreement. As for Finland, Hitler repeated sanctimoniously, it had no political interest for the Reich, as had been demonstrated in Germany's benevolent neutrality during the Russian-Finnish war. But the Reich was dependent on Finnish deliveries of nickel and lumber and wanted no new war in the Baltic Sea. A psychological factor, moreover, weighed heavily: The Finns had defended themselves courageously and won sympathy from the world, including Scandinavia and Germany. The Reich had economic interests in Finland as important as those in Romania, and, he said, he expected the Soviet Union to recognize this just as he had recognized the Soviets' interests in Lithuania and Bukovina.

Molotov had complaints of his own. While Germany, for its part, should have an understanding for the Russian requirements, Hitler not only had paid no attention to Moscow's proposal that southern Bukovina be ceded to the Soviets but also had proceeded to guarantee all of Romania.

Hitler replied that the Reich's measures were taken for security reasons only and in no way contravened its agreements with the Soviets. Nor was his desire to avoid the unforeseeable consequences of a Baltic war a breach of the German-Russian agreement placing Finland in the Russian sphere of influence. The guarantee of Romania, given, as he kept emphasizing, at the request of the Romanian government, in no way impaired the Soviet-Romanian treaty ceding Bessarabia. The Soviet Union must understand that Germany was fighting a war of life and death, and that battle had to be successfully concluded. Future successes would be all the greater as Germany and Russia were enabled to fight back-to-back against a common foe and so much the less if they confronted one another breast-to-breast. In the first case there was no power in the world that could oppose both of them.

Molotov agreed and emphasized that Stalin, especially, wanted relations between the two countries deepened and activated. Still, questions had to be clarified that might well be of secondary importance but nevertheless disturbed the atmosphere of German-Russian relations. One of them, Molotov said all over again, was Finland, where there should be neither German troops nor anti-Soviet political demonstrations.

Hitler denied that Germany had played any part whatever in such demonstrations, which, he added, were easy to stage. And as for German troops, he could assure Molotov that as soon as a general settlement was arranged none would reappear in Finland.

Molotov plodded stubbornly on. He said Finnish delegations had also been sent to Germany, and they, along with "Finnish personalities," had been received by the Reich. All this plus the presence of German troops on its soil had led to an ambiguous attitude on Finland's part. For example, the word had gotten around "that no Finn accepted the Russian-Finnish peace treaty." The Soviet Union had to put an end to the Finnish question once and for all.

Hitler, too, relied heavily on repetition to make his points. Germany wanted no war in the Baltic area because it needed Finland's nickel and lumber; it had no political interest there and, unlike Russia, had occupied no Finnish territory. In any case, transport of German troops through Finland would end "in a few days" and no further transport would take place. The decisive question for Germany was whether Russia would again go to war with Finland.

Molotov, an expert at avoiding direct answers, repeated that Russia had to clear up the Finnish problem. Finland lay in its sphere of interest.

The two men bickered on, Hitler expressing fear that if another war broke out between Russia and Finland, Sweden and Britain might become involved, Molotov remarking that while both Germany and Russia were interested in peace in the Baltic, only a Soviet-German agreement could secure it. Hitler said that if either England or the United States sought air bases in the area, Germany would be forced to intervene and suggested that the Soviet Union would do well to postpone further demands on Finland for six months or a year. Molotov said again that peace in the area could be assured if Russia and Germany were in complete agreement, but he could see no reason for Russia to put off demands on Finland. Hitler could only repeat that there should be no war in the Baltic— a war would greatly impede future Russian and German cooperation. Molotov said it was not a question of war in the Baltic, it was the Finnish question and abiding by the Soviet-German treaty of last year.

Neither budged. Molotov declared he could not understand Germany's fear of a war in the Baltic and pointed out how greatly the military situation had improved with conquest of Denmark, Norway, Holland, Belgium, and France. Hitler said he knew something about military matters and thought the United States might well become involved in the war. He asked bluntly whether Russia would declare war on the United States if America intervened in a Finnish conflict. Molotov avoided a direct answer, saying the question was not immediate, and Hitler replied it would be too late when it was. To close this part of the discussion Hitler said both sides agreed that Finland belonged in the Russian sphere, and he and Molotov should turn their theoretical considerations to more important matters.

He then brought up a subject always congenial to him—the breakup of Britain's world empire. He said it was there, in an empire in dissolution where a minority of 45 million people had ruled 600 million, that Russia could find its way to ice-free and really open world seas. The United States, too, was expecting to gain from the fall of Britain, but Germany was intent on avoiding any detour toward its aims; it intended to strike directly at the heart of Britain and its empire. That was why he had opposed Italy's war against Greece, waged on the mere periphery just as a war in the Baltic would be. Still, the conquest of Britain would put an end to the empire that could not be governed from Canada. A worldwide perspective lay before the Soviet Union and the Reich. In the course of the next weeks the negotiations between the two countries must define the Soviets' part in dealing with the British collapse; lesser matters must be put aside, and this was true for all states affected: Germany, France, Italy, Russia, and Japan.

Molotov said politely he had followed Hitler's train of thought with interest and agreed with it, but what was decisive was to clarify the nature of German-Soviet cooperation after which Italy and Japan could be consulted. What had been begun would not be altered but simply taken as a starting point for the future.

Hitler admitted the perspectives presented difficulties but asserted that Germany did not wish to annex France as the Russians seemed to think; what the Reich wanted was a world coalition of concerned powers—Spain, France, Italy, Germany, the Soviet Union, and Japan—a community of interest from North Africa to East Asia that would be funded by the British bankruptcy. So any differences had to be put aside. Not only the relation between the Soviet Union and Turkey had to be considered but also those in greater Asia that Germany had recognized as a Soviet sphere of interest. He was talking, he said grandly, of fifty to a hundred years in the future and of an area where the nations involved would have space enough for their fields of activity.

Molotov observed that Hitler had raised a large number of issues in Europe and elsewhere. First, though, he wanted to discuss questions in Europe. The Soviet Union's position as a Black Sea power linked with the Danube explained its dissatisfaction with the guarantee Romania had accepted from Germany and Italy without consultation with Russia. As he had twice pointed out, the guarantee patently seemed directed against the Soviet Union's interests, "if one may express it so grossly." So the question arose, Molotov said boldly, of rescinding it. To this unveiled challenge Hitler replied stiffly that the guarantee was necessary for a certain time and could not be rescinded.

Molotov diplomatically turned back to the straits and said the situation would be more threatening for the Soviet Union if the British were entrenched in Greece. He referred to matters that could not possibly raise Hitler's ire, such as the Crimean war in the mid-nineteenth century and the Allied expeditions against Russia in 1918–1919, and asked Hitler how Germany would respond if the Soviet Union gave the same guarantee to Bulgaria as the Reich and Italy had given Romania. Russia, he said virtuously, would first discuss such a matter with Germany and, if possible, Italy. Hitler replied that as to the straits, Ribbentrop would soon be discussing a revision of the Montreux Treaty in favor of the Soviet Union, and Ribbentrop, who had had little opportunity to say anything, was quick to agree.[4]

Molotov, returning to the necessity for a Soviet guarantee of Bulgaria, assured Hitler that the Soviet Union would not "by a hair's breadth" intervene in Bulgaria's internal affairs. Hitler said Germany's and Italy's guarantee of Romania had been the only way to persuade Romania to cede Bessarabia to the Soviet Union without hostilities. In addition Romania's oil wells represented an absolute German-Italian requirement, and the Romanian government itself had asked that Germany protect the wells "in the air and on the land," since Romania did not feel secure against a British attack. The Reich would not permit a British landing in Salonika or an attack on the oil fields. Nevertheless, he assured Molotov, at the end of the war any German troops would be withdrawn. As for Bulgaria, he asked Molotov whether Bulgaria itself had asked for a Soviet guarantee; he had no information that it had. The decisive question was, nevertheless, Hitler went on flatly, whether Moscow thought it possible to obtain security in the straits by a revision of the Montreux Treaty. He recognized that Molotov would have to discuss this matter with Stalin.

Molotov replied that Russia had only one goal in this connection: to be secure against any attack through the Dardanelles. The Soviet Union would like to settle this problem with Turkey, and that would be easier with a guarantee to Bulgaria. Hitler replied that this just about corresponded with Germany's thinking in the matter, according to which the Dardanelles would be open in time of war only to Russian warships passing through the straits but closed to everyone else.

Returning to Bulgaria, Molotov again promised Hitler that Russia would not interfere in Bulgaria's internal affairs and was ready to assure Sofia of an outlet to the Aegean Sea. Then he repeated his question about Germany's attitude to a Soviet guarantee of Bulgaria. Hitler again wanted to know whether Bulgaria had asked for such a guarantee and added he would have to talk the matter over with the Duce.

The talk returned to Hitler's main topic of their meeting: strategies leading to and following the collapse of the British Empire. Hitler said that while he was uncertain whether plans for dealing with the collapse could be carried out, a historical opportunity would be missed if they were not. In any case the foreign ministers of Germany, Italy, Japan, and the Soviet Union should consider the matter anew in Moscow. He noted how late it was that day and with the possibility of a British air attack in mind thought it best to break the talks off since the chief points had been discussed. Reduced to formal generalization he said he thought Russia's efforts to secure its place as a Black Sea power needed study as did its wishes with regard to its future place in the world. Molotov in closing said many new problems had been raised in the meetings, and then he made a remark far more agreeable to Stalin's ears than to Hitler's: "the Soviet Union, as a great power, could not remain on the sidelines with regard to the major questions of Europe and Asia." He expressed Moscow's gratitude to the Reich for aiding in improvement in Soviet relations with Japan.

The meetings stagnated—no open break appeared—but differences remained wide and clear from beginning to end. When Hitler pointed toward the Indian Ocean for the site of ice-free harbors, Molotov replied that the Soviet Union was more concerned with peace and security of territory bordering on the Soviet Union. And when Molotov and Ribbentrop met on the evening following the session with Hitler and had to retire to Ribbentrop's private air-raid shelter, Molotov pointedly asked him: "Why, if England is already defeated, are we sitting in this air raid bunker?"[5] And whose bombs had they heard exploding nearby? The questions did not sound like the inquiry of a well-disposed ally.

On the surface they all remained polite, Molotov saying he was almost grateful to the British for sending him to an air-raid shelter because it gave him such a good opportunity to discuss matters with his host. But when Ribbentrop took from his coat pocket a closely typed page that sketched German proposals for dividing the bounty of the coming British collapse, and Molotov asked if he might not have a copy, Ribbentrop said he had only his own text and was unable to provide a copy.[6] And when Ribbentrop spoke of an ice-free harbor for the Soviet Union "in the south," Molotov asked him what body of water he had in mind, to which Ribbentrop had no precise answer, saying only that he thought of the Persian Gulf or the Gulf of Arabia. Molotov remained friendly, cool, and uncommitted. When Hitler declared the war already won and in the same breath announced Germany was fighting a war of life and death against Britain, Molotov said it looked to him as though Germany was fighting for life and England for death. Over and over again Hitler spoke of the splendid vistas of the future, and Molotov did his best to bring him back to statements of how precisely German-Soviet differences might be ironed out. Hitler evidenced his frustration. He never appeared at the formal reception Ribbentrop gave the Soviet visitors at the Hotel Kaiserhof or at the gala reception at the Russian Embassy.

The meeting, in fact, was a disaster. November 15, one day after Molotov left, Hitler told a small circle of his military entourage that he had never expected much to come of Molotov's visit. What the talking revealed was the direction of the Russian plans. "Molotov let the cat out of the bag," he said and expressed relief that the Soviet-German pact "won't even remain a marriage of convenience."[7] To let the Russians into Europe would mean the end of Middle Europe. In short the Soviet Union would not simply turn control of Europe over to Germany, would not join the war against Britain, expected to be included in any new settlements in Europe and Asia, and could serve as the British dagger at Stalin's convenience.

It was the dagger that kept pricking Hitler. In his speech to the Reichstag of July 19, 1940, in the euphoria of his historic victory in the West, he had offered Britain what he called a "generous peace," an offer that an hour later British radio announced was rejected.[8] He could only account for Britain's stubbornness by ascribing it to reliance on Russia. July 31 he told his generals assembled at the Berghof that if Russia was defeated, England's last hope would be gone. Therefore he said flatly, Russia must be destroyed by the spring of 1941.[9] Still he delayed any final decision. A two-front war, as he well knew, was always dangerous, and friendship with Russia had advantages; he could point that out one day but return the next to plans for all-out attack. Meanwhile his air force pounded Britain with intermittent terror attacks such as the one on Coventry that was a retaliation against the British attack on Berlin during Molotov's visit. Hitler's nondescript Channel armada assembled in ports up and down the European coast included two thousand barges, as had Napoleon's invasion fleet assembled in 1805, and lay idle as losses of German planes and pilots forced him to halt daylight air raids and indefinitely postpone the invasion.[10] The signing in Berlin on September 27 of the Three-Power Pact— the alliance of Japan, Italy, and Germany—could not conceal the defeat of the air force.

The military deployment against the Soviet Union took shape slowly. The plans Hitler placed almost entirely in the hands of the OKH, the high command of the army; the OKW, General Walter Warlimont complained, was bypassed as Hitler concentrated on grand political strategies while he supervised the air war on Britain and development of the army's preparations for what he intended to be a lightning invasion of the Soviet Union. It was he alone who was warlord, statesman, global strategist, and tactician. On August 5 Major General Marcks, chief of staff of the Eighteenth Army, presented a fairly detailed plan that he promised, though Moscow was again a chief target, would not repeat Napoleon's ill-fated campaign of 1812 and would bring the Russian army to decisive battle. Halder on December 5 spoke of the danger of merely pushing the Russians back; their army had to be broken and throttled. Everyone seemed to agree. The invitation to Molotov to come to Berlin was part of Hitler's strategy of at least temporary alliance to carve up the British Empire, but Molotov's unenthusiastic response was evidence not only of Stalin's wariness but also of outright hostility and resulted, on December 18, in Hitler's issuing the long-pondered order, "Case Barbarossa," which had previously been called "Otto."[11]

Case Barbarossa still dealt, though in more precise terms than the plans that preceded, with strategy of a possible attack; it did not yet represent a final decision. A few weeks after it was issued, early in January 1941, Hitler told a meeting at which Mussolini, Ciano, Keitel, and Jodl, among others, were present that as long as Stalin lived, no danger of war was likely.[12] Stalin, he said, was "intelligent and cautious but when he is no longer there, the Jews who now are relegated to the second and third row will again move to the first row. One must also be careful—the Russians are always making new demands" and said that while the Reich had useful treaties with the Soviet Union, "I prefer to rely on my military strength," much of which he pointed out had to be concentrated on the Russian border.

It is worth noting that Hitler was talking to a mixed audience of friendly admirers but not to intimates, and what he was saying was designed to impress his listeners, not gird them for a final struggle. He was aware that his army had to be sent into action not only in the Balkans but also for major objectives or it would lose its edge, and a Russian campaign he believed could be swift and successful, leaving Britain and the United States no alternative to accepting his unassailable overlordship of the Continent. The Soviet Union, he was convinced, was a booming giant waiting to be toppled; its performance in the Finnish war had been mediocre; it had never recovered from Stalin's purges of the high command. Case Barbarossa called for another blitzkrieg "to defeat Soviet Russia before the end of the war against Britain in a quick campaign."[13]

Hitler after his triumph in the West was no longer impressed with the need for avoiding a two-front war. He had waged an incipient two-front war against Poland and the Western Allies with great victories on both fronts. Besides, Providence, one of the rare transcendental factors he acknowledged, might take a hand; Stalin could change his mind on joining the Reich's crusade, or Britain, with impetus from U-boats and the Luftwaffe and counselors less implacably anti-German than Churchill, such as the duke of Windsor, could come to reason and talk peace.[14]

But Göring, Ribbentrop, and other party leaders showed no enthusiasm for opening another front, nor did most of the generals. Many of the army high command had long favored German-Soviet collaboration. Some had been assigned to duty in the Soviet Union in the days of the Weimar Republic when Moscow took a hospitable view of the need for German rearmament and the training of German troops with tanks and weapons forbidden by the Versailles treaty. And while the generals agreed that the Russian army evidenced glaring deficiencies in battle-readiness, they had no fervor whatever for a second front. But war against the Soviet Empire remained alluring to Hitler. It had long been tied to his dreamland of a Germanic National Socialist Empire, and it promised an outlet for the deepest sentiments he lived by and for: destruction of communism and of the Jewish conspiracy ruling the powers that kept him from colonizing with a superior race the central realm of bolshevism and Jewry. Moreover, in the decision to rearm on an unprecedented scale, to reoccupy the Rhineland, to risk war over Austria and Czechoslovakia, and then to mount the massive attack on France, Hitler had overridden the doubts and hesitations of the generals, and it was he who had been proved right and they wrong. Now he was in an unassailable position, where no one—from the German Resistance to his own party comrades and to chiefs of the armed forces—could plausibly say him nay. When a man such as Admiral Raeder attempted it, Hitler could brush him aside as a sailor limited by obsession with British sea power and lack of firsthand experience with the all-powerful German land forces. After the war General Halder testified at Nuremberg that he had regarded Case Barbarossa, when the order was issued, as "madness," but there is no record of his saying that to Hitler at the time, though it would doubtless have expressed his convictions and those of most of the high command. Warlimont, along with others in the Wehrmacht's top echelon, said Case Barbarossa hit them like a cold shower, but he did not say that to Hitler.

General Jodl was one of those convinced from the time "Barbarossa" was decided on that Hitler was right, that Stalin intended to attack the Reich at a propitious moment.[15] Believing as he did in Hitler's military and political genius, he was persuaded Hitler would go to war with the Soviet Union only when every other alternative had been exhausted. He also believed that the Soviet Union would be a tough opponent, and that was one of the reasons Hitler would attack only as a last resort. Similar opinions were voiced even by foreign nonadmirers of Hitler such as the son of the former president of Czechoslovakia and ambassador to Britain, Jan Masaryk, who believed when war erupted that Hitler had intuitively divined Stalin's intentions and preempted a Soviet attack. One former Soviet intelligence officer born after World War II wrote a book intended to be the first of three volumes to show that Hitler had anticipated a long-planned Russian attack by only a few days. The contrary evidence, however, has continued to be overwhelmingly convincing to most critical observers.[16]

Stalin, as he had made plain to the Politburo in 1939, always had in mind going to war with Hitler's Reich, but the armed conflict would best come when the present combatants were exhausted. He feared, with good reason, the might of the Wehrmacht at the peak of its strength, and he was in no hurry; on the contrary, he had also told the Politburo the present war should last as long as possible. The Soviet Union could "wait until it is our turn." His actual anti-German moves were few, but these unmistakably showed his claw marks. Moscow addressed a telegram of friendship to the new anti-German Yugoslav government that had overthrown its pro-German predecessor, received a Yugoslav military mission, and swiftly signed a pact of friendship and nonaggression with the Yugoslav minister to the Soviet Union who had also become a member of the new Yugoslav cabinet.[17] The pact concluded on the night of April 5–6, 1941, guaranteed the independence of both countries and their territorial inviolability.

This was about as far as Stalin's overtly anti-German courses ever went. It was enough to confirm Hitler in his designs for both Yugoslavia and the

Soviet Union. Yugoslavia, the poorly armed, rickety construct of Versailles and St. Germain, was immediately scheduled for invasion along with Greece and was defeated after eleven days of fighting.[18] Italian troops occupied the Adriatic coast opposite Italy, and the Hungarians, the Batschka, south of their border. Belgrade, though declared an open city by the new Yugoslav government, had been mercilessly bombed by the Luftwaffe despite pleas of the German ambassador, Victor von Heeren, who informed Berlin that the anti-German coup had been carried out by a small clique against the majority of the population. Hitler was determined to punish the Belgrade government that had changed sides. Croatia was spared air strikes because of its anti-Serbian population, unscathed by the Luftwaffe that, on Hitler's orders, confined itself to support of invading ground troops.

A German army under General List moved on both Greece and Yugoslavia from Bulgaria on the morning of April 6, meeting tough Greek resistance as it attacked the so-called Metaxas line.[19] Greek troops fought tenaciously, causing the commander of one German division to say: "It looks as though the Greeks are ready to fight to the last Greek for England." The mountainous terrain, too, made for slow progress, and British units sent into the country when the Italians first attacked, mainly made up of New Zealanders and Australians, put up strong resistance. The Luftwaffe controlled the air, and the seasoned German divisions slowly, with heavy casualties, defeated Greek and British forces. Again British command of the seas enabled most British troops to be rescued, this time for another campaign in Africa.

By the end of April, Greece too, except for Crete, was forced to lay down arms, and the concentrated German attack moved on to capture the island stronghold. There, though with heavy losses, German airborne troops under General Student and General von Richthofen were able to occupy a large, heavily defended island against hard-fighting ground troops and a vastly superior sea power. Invading forces lost more than half the parachute and glider-conveyed troops—the German Eleventh Flight Corps lost six thousand men and more than half its planes. British losses, too, were high—in men and warships; nine of the ships were sunk, and seven were heavily damaged. The invasion began May 20 and was completed in eight days, a spectacular performance but was so costly that the planned attack on Malta was never ordered.

Victories in Yugoslavia and Greece had useful side effects for the Reich—they made it unlikely that Turkey would join the war on the British side and made it easier to hamper British supply lines moving through the Mediterranean to Suez. Above all they deprived the British of air and naval bases on the flank of German armies invading the Soviet Union. But the war in the Balkans and perhaps the prospect of a rainy season resulted in a delay in the attack on the Soviet Empire. The vast offensive scheduled for mid-May was postponed one critical month.

Meanwhile Stalin fawned upon Hitler. Stalin was a communist but was always guided by realpolitik far more than marxist dogma, which he felt capable of improvising on his own. For him, Hitler was a renegade tool of high finance, a loose cannon, but no more an ideological enemy than Churchill, though a more immediate threat.

In the shadow of his disastrous attempt to bolster an anti-German Yugoslavia, Stalin was eager to make concessions. On April 13 he suddenly concluded a neutrality pact with Japan that had appeared hopelessly sidetracked up to that very day. But as German troops were storming into Belgrade, Stalin decided to cut his risks and secure his eastern borders. The moribund neutrality pact was revived and concluded in a matter of hours. And as the Japanese foreign minister, Yosuke Matsuoka, was departing Moscow, Stalin, who seldom appeared on such ceremonial occasions, arrived at the station platform and ostentatiously, before the assembled diplomatic corps, embraced the German ambassador, Schulenburg, and the military attaché, Colonel Krebs, assuring Schulenburg heartily: "We must always remain friends."[20] Soviet deliveries to Germany, markedly slow since the first of the year, rose in the course of the month of April. A treaty for fuel-oil deliveries to the Reich was signed on April 12, and special deliveries of rubber were rushed from the Far East to Germany. On May 9 the Kremlin broke diplomatic ties with enemies of the Reich, informing the representatives of Belgium, Norway, Greece, and Yugoslavia that since their countries had lost their sovereignty, a diplomatic presence was no longer required in the Soviet Union. A Soviet ambassador was accredited to the pro-Reich Vichy regime in France.

For Hitler the ideological struggle with the Soviet Union, which had smoldered (it had only been damped down for a period of wary collaboration), now broke out in full fury; he declared privately that the coming conflict would be no ordinary war between two states; it was to be a war of extermination against a subhuman enemy. March 30, 1941, three months before the start of the campaign, he informed Halder and other members of the high command that "One must forget any concept of comradeship between soldiers in this war."[21] It was to be fought, he said, with any means, and the generals had to overcome personal scruples; for harshness today meant leniency in the future. Any Communist Party official or any commissar or *Politruk* captured in battle was to be separated from other prisoners of war and shot immediately without court-martial or any legal procedure. Leningrad, because of its name and association with the chief hero of the Russian Revolution, was to be razed—obliterated from the map and from history. Some of the generals said the Case Barbarossa order was a bluff, another attempt to put pressure on Stalin, but such wishful thinking withered with the venom and all-out weaponry Hitler was preparing to destroy the communist state.

What he was preparing was extermination of Soviet power, of bolshevism. It was also an opportunity to carry out the pledge to the Reichstag that the war would lead to extermination of the Jews in Europe. Up to now he had dealt with them harshly in the Reich, and the solution to the problem was to be sought in emigration or deportation to a faraway place such as Madagascar. With the attack on Russia began the plans for the Final Solution—the *Endlösung:* mass extermination. Orders that would lead to "special treatment" of Jews and large numbers of Poles and Slavs went out in the same period.[22]

Not only was Leningrad to be destroyed but no surrender of it or Moscow would be accepted. Inhabitants were to be driven out or killed. It was to be a war of extermination, he said: "If we don't understand that, in thirty years we'll have to do it all over again." No Soviet intelligentsia was to survive. The German army would destroy the armed forces, and behind the lines would be the SS, the Gestapo, and the occupying cadres under Rosenberg, Göring, and Himmler with orders to deal implacably with the population. State Secretary Backe instructed party leaders slated for duty in the occupied territories: "Do not be afraid to make decisions that may be wrong."[23] The final purposes were what they must keep in mind, and the harshest and most ruthless methods must be the stock in trade of party satraps who were, Backe said, to conduct themselves with dignity while they made use of them.

Hitler proved mainly right in his estimate of the Soviet army when German forces numbering 3.6 million men, including six hundred thousand Romanian and Finnish troops, attacked in the early morning hours of June 22. Troops totaling 6.25 million faced one another across a border stretching from Petsamo, in the far north of Finland, to Galati, in Romania. In numbers the sides were fairly even, though Soviet forces had three times as many planes and tanks and more troops assigned to rear areas. The numerical superiority, however, was illusory, as Hitler and his high command knew; it was more than compensated for by the far higher quality of the Wehrmacht. Tanks and planes were, with the unexpected exception of one tank series, no match for German forces, and this was true too of the decimated Soviet leadership. The purges had taken a huge toll on numbers, quality, and morale of top echelons of the Soviet army. After the war and Stalin's death, Russian field marshals and generals testified to "monstrous damage" done the army as tens of thousands of commanders and political leaders had been liquidated.[24] The Frunze Military Academy had been virtually forced to replace almost all its highly regarded teaching staff with untrained officers. In the field a spot check in 1940 revealed that of 225 regimental commanders not one had completed academy training, only 25 had finished military school, and the remainder had merely completed a lieutenant's course. Defense forces seemed to have no coordinated plan: German air superiority was won on the first day, the Luftwaffe destroyed large numbers of Soviet planes on the ground, border positions were quickly and easily cut through, and bridges were captured intact.

The German armies slashed through the Soviet armies on all three fronts—Army Group North against the Baltic states and Leningrad, Army Group Center moving against Moscow, and Army Group South against the Ukraine—their armor encircling the positions they overran, taking tens of thousands of prisoners for which not nearly enough camps or supplies were prepared. In addition the army not only had no orders to follow the international conventions on treatment of prisoners, as they had for the British, French, and other nationalities taken prisoner in the West but from Hitler himself they had the grim reminder that Russians were subhuman. Admiral Canaris was one of the high command who attempted to improve treatment of the Russian prisoners to comply with the Hague and Geneva conventions.[25] His memorandum addressed to Keitel had no success; Keitel would never have dared try to persuade Hitler to change a decision. Soviet soldiers, Hitler had declared just before hostilities, were of a different order; Russians were not comrades who had lost a battle but, like Jews, an inferior species deserving extermination.

The massive attack of the armies was not another blitzkrieg, because lightning actions were impossible on the bad roads and in the enormous distances. Nevertheless the armies made uneven but dramatic progress, often moving so rapidly that overrun units could escape an uncompleted encirclement and thus become part of the partisan forces operating in the rear. Despite German victories and high Soviet losses, Soviet troops and tanks kept coming, among the latter, though few in number, the T-34, unpredicted by German intelligence and superior to German tanks. On the whole, though there were checks in the advances in the north against Leningrad and Murmansk and slow progress in the south where the Soviets had numerically superior concentrations of troops and more than half their tanks, apparently expecting the main onslaught in the Ukraine, the German victories were spectacular. In early July troops advancing on Moscow encircled and destroyed no less than forty Soviet divisions under Marshal Timoshenko and on July 16 captured Smolensk, five hundred kilometers west of Moscow.

The Wehrmacht simply did not have the forces needed for the long battle line. Fifteen hundred planes had to be concentrated against Britain; factories were producing 227 tanks a month, not the 600 planned; the infantry was only partly motorized, and many field pieces had to be horse-drawn. Again Hitler overrode the advice of his generals, among them Halder, Brauchitsch, and Guderian, who wanted to capture Moscow as the primary target, taking precedence over the Ukraine. He decided to throw the weight of the attack south against the economically vital Ukraine and there in mid-September achieved one of his greatest victories: encircling and destroying seven Soviet armies, capturing the capital, Kiev, and over 450,000 men with nine hundred tanks and unscathed trainloads of building materials for Soviet factories. But Moscow and Leningrad remained in Soviet hands. Tanks, too few for the long front, had had to be diverted from the middle sector and Moscow to the south, while armies advancing on Leningrad and the strategically important, because it was ice free, harbor of Murmansk failed to reach targets.

Stalin was silent for twelve days after the attack exploded on June 22, apparently numbed by the attack and its success. He had been warned of the assault from many sources, which included Churchill, Roosevelt, Soviet intelligence, and his own generals such as Marshal S. K. Timoshenko, but chose not to believe them. Hitler would never attack, he was convinced, until Britain was out of the war.[26] Generals had pleaded with him to order full-scale defensive measures, but he shied away from them because he believed such actions would be provocative to a trigger-happy Hitler. The most the importunities of the Soviet generals obtained was an order to mobilize Soviet rear forces; front lines were left vulnerable. But after his silence and stupefaction, he moved ruthlessly to stem the damage—by removing generals (shooting some of them), taking over the post of minister of Defense, rallying the demoralized forces that had seemed unable to contain the German onslaught—with a stirring summons to the whole population to wage all-out war in defense of the Soviet fatherland.

It had seemed that nothing could stop the German army. Within weeks Hitler was convinced the victory was won. In mid-July he told Ambassador Ōshima Hiroshi that it would be Stalin who would suffer Napoleon's fate; Germany would not lose a single soldier to hunger or cold. Everything had been foreseen and prepared for—entire barracks were ready for transport to the Eastern front.[27] In the early autumn, with capture of Kiev, he announced another "greatest victory of all time," and the German generals agreed with him. The Russian army, they thought, could not recover; all that remained were coups de grâce.[28]

And then came the rains and mud and the clogged lines of communication bringing up supplies. Tanks, armored troop carriers, and big guns were slowed. The Russian spaces began to take their toll.

This was only a start of what it would be like. The wet period slowing the advance was followed by a mud period that bogged it down, and that was followed by a precocious freeze that began in early November, forecasting a winter in which wood fires were needed to get frozen engines started; the ground turned to cement in which no trenches and no shelters could be dug. Worse, the troops froze in their summer clothing because neither Hitler nor the high command expected they would be fighting when the cold struck. And here the Russians were superior—they had winter clothing and equipment designed to function in arctic weather.

As to psychological warfare, neither the Soviet nor the National Socialist propagandists scored great successes until loss of a German army at Stalingrad reinforced the Soviet anti-Hitler rhetoric, and on the German side Hitler, in 1944, finally permitted captured Soviet troops to be recruited under the SS. In 1941 propaganda distributed by the Luftwaffe—400 million leaflets dropped over Soviet lines—repeated German tactics of World War I, promising that the German arms would deliver Russians from their tyranny.[29] When German troops entered the Ukraine, a major victim of Stalin's terror, they were often met by hopeful village delegations offering salt and bread as a sign of welcoming submission. Neither the leaflets nor the welcoming had any effect on high policy. The Ukrainians, too, like all Slavs, were an inferior people, to be kept in line by the Reich's police forces, the SD, and the Einsatz commandos.

Soviet prisoners had no luck at all—branded by Soviet military doctrine as deserters, traitors, and criminals whose families were deprived of all government assistance. Russian soldiers, the Soviet troops were told during the Finnish war, do not surrender; they fight until they die, saving the last bullets for themselves.

Stalin regarded every prisoner of war, every encircled commander forced to surrender to the Germans as a deserter subject to the death penalty. He exacted the same penalty for defeat without surrender. The commander in chief of the west front, Army General Pavlov, his chief of staff, General Klimovskich, Chief of Operations General Semenev, Commander of Intelligence Troops General Grigorev, and Commander of Artillery General Klic were all executed in early July and their fates shared by dozens more as the Red Army lost battles.

Not only defeated generals were Stalin's victims. In the spring of 1940, a year before the German attack on the Soviet Union, more than fifteen thousand Polish soldiers, who were mainly officers in Russian prisoner-of-war camps, were executed on Stalin's orders. Between four and five thousand were shot, most of them in the back of the head, and buried in the Katyn forest ten miles west of Smolensk. Although Moscow and later the Nuremberg prosecution blamed the massacre on the Germans, Soviet responsibility was finally admitted by Russian authorities in 1992. Stalin's enemies were everywhere and of every nationality. The Polish officers were class enemies who should not be left alive to fight another day against a Red Army.

Despite the capital punishment promised on return to the homeland to anyone who had surrendered, the Germans captured 3.8 million Soviet soldiers in the first months of the war.[30] Not many survived, partly because large numbers were already half-dead when taken after ferocious fighting, partly because food often was not available, and partly because they were widely considered subhuman.

It was a merciless war. Hitler and the German high command had not expected the large-scale partisan operations, and no matter how much territory the German armies gained, behind the front in the conquered steppes and forests the partisan war raged with a ferocity rare on other fronts. No holds were barred, few if any prisoners taken, and when they were it was only to elicit information from them, often under torture. Partisan warfare developed into a major front the German forces would never obliterate, though they sent specially trained units against forest strong points with orders that matched the brutality of their opponents. The German rear was never secure, the hemorrhage of lost men and supplies on their way to eastern battle lines never stanched.

All in all it was warfare that paid no attention whatever to humanitarian, prewar conventions, to which neither the Soviet Union nor the Reich ever felt bound. Although individual commanders might attempt to conform to customary rules of warfare, neither Hitler nor Stalin made the slightest pretense of observing them in their struggle. Between 90 and 95 percent of German soldiers made prisoners of war in the period 1941–1942 died in Soviet prison camps; in the entire course of the war, between 1.1 and 1.2 million German prisoners died, most of them captured after the end of the war, while 2.1 million Soviet prisoners perished in German camps, a fate they deserved, in Stalin's view.[31]

Hitler was fanatically anti-Slav. One Soviet general, Andrei Vlasov, who had fought heroically and successfully in defense of Moscow in the winter of 1941, was captured in July 1942, after his Second Assault Army was decimated on the Volkhov Front. Convinced, like other Russian generals, that Stalin's brutality directed against his own people coupled with his military blunders would be the ruination of the fatherland, Vlasov founded, in captivity, a Committee for the Liberation of the Russian People, attempting to organize Soviet units in German prison camps for battle against the partisans, offering to recruit a million anti-Stalin liberation troops to fight on the German side. But Hitler would not tolerate any kind of organized Soviet force that could become the nucleus of future Russian military power. It was only toward the end of the war in 1944, when German armies everywhere were retreating, that Vlasov could make a beginning at forming an army to fight on the German side, and only through the SS, not the Wehrmacht, that he could gain Hitler's consent for it to fight at all.

What Hitler could win were short-term objectives—spectacular enough to be celebrated, like the conquest of the Crimea, Sevastopol, and the Kerch Peninsula, the latter lost in the winter of 1941 but regained in ten days by Manstein's army in the spring of 1942. Hitler's grand strategy for 1942–1943 was to strangle what he was convinced was the last resistance by conquest of the remaining great wheat and coal fields of European Russia, blocking all traffic along the Volga with capture of Stalingrad, depriving the Soviet war machine of fuel with capture of the Caucasian oil fields.

The strategy failed because he could never amass sufficient power to overcome the attrition of the spaces and the enormous reserves of manpower at Stalin's disposal. Much of the Caucasian oil was set on fire by retreating Russian troops; the remainder could not be held long enough to be used by the Reich. Army Group South had only sixty divisions plus those of its poorly armed allies—half of the forces needed. Numbers were to be compensated for by quality, willpower, and wishful thinking.

Hitler added a fresh, now-open enemy with incalculable resources to his list when he declared war on the United States after the Japanese attacked Pearl Harbor.[32] In his speech to the Reichstag on December 11 he recited the list of hostile acts against National Socialist Germans by President Roosevelt and felt elated by his freedom to retaliate against American indignities. The Soviet Union was the immediate threat. The new enemy was as yet only a cloud on the horizon, though it would grow rapidly.

The battle for Stalingrad began in October 1942 when the Sixth Army of General Friedrich Paulus succeeded in reaching the Volga and could go no farther, though in the city of Stalingrad itself the infantry fought forward from house to house, factory to factory, against desperate resistance from the Red Army. Eventually Paulus's army was not only stopped in the city on the Volga but lacking reserves it could not ward off a massive counterattack that first broke through the Romanian divisions and then those of the Italian ally. Now it was the Germans' turn to be encircled; the Russian high command had learned how a modern war could be fought; Paulus's exhausted forces were surrounded by fresh, well-equipped troops brought in from the Far East. Stalin could be certain that the Japanese would not attack his Far Eastern army because a redoubtable agent, a German journalist and press attaché of the embassy in Tokyo, Richard Sorge, had informed Stalin of the date of the German attack in 1941. Sorge learned that the Japanese were going to move south against French Indochina, were withdrawing troops from China, and would not attack the Soviet Union.[33]

As the autumn froze into winter Paulus's army at Stalingrad had no shelter but the skeletonized, bombed-out buildings they had captured. Göring's promise that the Luftwaffe could supply food and munitions to the encircled Sixth Army proved, like earlier promises, empty. The Luftwaffe could bring in only a fraction of what was needed, and the Sixth Army froze and starved. For the first time in German history an army of what had been 250,000 men was forced to surrender in the field; they had run out of hope of relief. They did not fare well as prisoners of war, no better than Soviet prisoners in German hands; of Paulus's army that surrendered at Stalingrad five thousand men returned from captivity.[34]

Blame for the loss of the Sixth Army was Hitler's alone, and there was no disguising it, though he, like Stalin, preferred to meet the tidings of defeat by replacing generals: Guderian, one of the war's most brilliant commanders, had been dismissed in December 1941 when the offensive against Moscow failed; Brauchitsch was replaced by Hitler himself; Army Chief of Staff Halder had been dismissed in September 1942 for a faltering campaign in southern Russia and was replaced by Kurt Zeitzler who was far more admiring of Hitler than was Halder. For the defeat at Stalingrad all the potential scapegoats were dead or prisoners of the Soviets.

Hitler had run out of luck. His overriding of the advice of his generals in the winter of 1941–1942 had again proved to be a correct decision when he ordered the advanced lines to hold, even while the generals on the Moscow front pleaded for a retreat and a shorter line. It was he who avoided a debacle. But later, at Stalingrad, despite importunities of his generals, he demanded that the army hold. He refused to permit Paulus to retreat, to break out of the Russian encirclement. This time he was proved wrong. Paulus could not be rescued by relieving tank divisions under General Hoch, sent too late to break through, though Hoch got within thirty miles of Stalingrad. Iron will was what counted in Hitler's estimation: Once Stalingrad was lost it would not be regained; Paulus and his men had to stand and fight even though at the end there was nothing left with which they could load their guns.

The commander of a German air squadron, Major Thiel, was ordered to fly into the Stalingrad *Kessel* a few days before the surrender to determine whether air landings were still possible. Thiel reported to Field Marshal Milch that he had met with Paulus and a number of officers, including General von Seydlitz, and their situation was beyond repair. Paulus told him that this was the fourth day the army had nothing to eat; heavy weapons landed by parachute could not be moved because there was no fuel. The last emaciated horses had been killed and eaten—starving soldiers had thrown themselves on one of them to break open the head and devour the brains raw.[35]

Hitler was sorely disappointed in Paulus. He had just made him a field marshal and expected him, he said, to shoot himself rather than become a prisoner. Presciently, Hitler declared the Soviets would use Paulus for their own purposes, parade him as a trophy, and the prediction turned out to be accurate. In captivity Paulus became one of the leading members of the Free Germany National Committee, founded in the Soviet Union of prisoners of war and German émigrés to reinforce the anti-Hitler resistance in the Reich, and in 1946 was produced by the Soviets as a witness for the prosecution at the Nuremberg trials.[36]

From Stalingrad the road only went down in every sector. In Africa where Rommel with three German divisions was fighting a remarkable campaign against superior British forces, Hitler could not summon up either the guns or the men required to achieve a victory that would have enabled him to link up with the Japanese and mortally wound the British Empire. He could reward Rommel by making him, like Paulus, a field marshal. But it was Rommel who said he would rather have been awarded a fresh division instead of the promotion. Rommel could produce memorable tactical victories, but with shiploads of fuel, tanks, and essential supplies routinely sunk by the combination of the Ultra intelligence and superior British naval and air forces in the Mediterranean, neither he nor any other German general could produce a winning strategy. And in 1943, in Tunisia, General Hans-Jürgen von Arnim, like Paulus, was forced to surrender to a far more powerful Anglo-American force in a defeat that compared at least numerically with the debacle at Stalingrad. In North Africa 275,000 prisoners fell into Allied hands, half of them Germans, the rest of what was left of an Italian army under Colonel General Messe that had fought well but vainly against the well-supplied British forces under General Bernard L. Montgomery. Mussolini awarded Messe the rank of field marshal as Messe went into captivity. Hitler sent Arnim a radio message of appreciation for his valorous exploits.

Hitler had one rousing piece of news in the midst of his mounting troubles, though it was mainly Goebbels who appreciated it. That was the decision of Roosevelt, meeting with Churchill at Casablanca on January 27, 1943, to announce the war aim of the Allies to be unconditional surrender of Germany, Italy, and Japan. The phrase "unconditional surrender" dated back to the American Civil War when General Ulysses S. Grant had demanded unconditional surrender of Fort Donelson, and the initials of Grant's name, U. S., were delightedly proclaimed by stalwart Northern patriots as standing for the terms the South must accept. The demand, though it was originally applied to only one fort, was acceptable to many, including probably most Americans and Britons, as befitting Hitler's Germany, but it was considered dubious by others, including Secretary of State Cordell Hull and the future commander in chief of the Allied invasion, General Eisenhower, who thought it would likely stiffen German resistance. At any rate, the announcement of the Allied war aim provided a sharp propaganda tool for Goebbels and Hitler who cited it to confirm their repeated assertions that the Reich was in fact fighting a battle for its very existence.

"Unconditional surrender" undoubtedly made it more difficult for the German Resistance, though the Resistance would soon include Field Marshal Rommel, to recruit waverers who were anti-Hitler but traditional German patriots. Whether or not it cost as many lives, both Allied and German, as its critics charged, it certainly played at least a minor role in prolonging the war to the bitter end. A leading member of the German Resistance, Adam von Trott zum Solz, met in January 1943 with the American OSS resident in Bern, Allen Dulles, to try to explain to him how important it was for the German opposition that the Allies distinguish between Germans and Nazis. But Dulles told him that the United States could not stop short of total military victory, and to allow Germany any doubt of its defeat would be unthinkable. Similar incidents occurred when other members of the German Resistance met with American and British officials; the answer was always the same based on the received wisdom that no Germans were to be trusted even if they called themselves anti-Nazis.

Nevertheless the attempt on Hitler's life made by highly respected members of the Wehrmacht high command on July 20, 1944, most of whom had been conspirators to get rid of him since 1938, was not deterred by the prospect of unconditional surrender.[37] Nor was Germany's minister of War Production, Albert Speer, long an admirer of Hitler and member of his inner circle, eventually deterred from planning to kill him. Carl Goerdeler, the former mayor of Leipzig, and Max Habermann, a former union leader, agreed that removal of Hitler must be accomplished without regard to unconditional surrender. The former commander in chief of the army, General Ludwig Beck, even believed that a coup must be attempted without regard to the likelihood of success. The only point now, Beck said, was that action against this criminal regime should come from within the German people; Germany must suffer the consequences of all that had been done and not been done. The total rejection of Hitler became the overriding dynamic of the German opposition; his overthrow was the vital target—unconditional surrender could be dealt with after that.

Stalin was not present at Casablanca. He had been invited but was fully occupied, he explained, by the battle at Stalingrad and could not travel. It was also true that he had little interest in participating in any Allied conference unless preparatory to opening a second front. Always suspicious of the democracies, he was convinced that Churchill especially was delaying any plan to invade Europe in the hope that the Soviet Union and Germany, continuing the battle alone, would fatally weaken one another.

The leader of the Soviet Union had a plan for Germany different from Roosevelt's unconditional surrender. His aim was a communist Germany bound to the Soviet Union, and all Soviet propaganda was devoted to that end. The manifesto of the Free Germany National Committee made the distinction the Western Allies were unwilling to concede. It told the German people that they were not the enemy; the enemy was Hitler, Nazism, and fascism. Luftwaffe Lieutenant Heinrich von Einsiedel, shot down by the Soviets in 1942, was reminded by his Soviet interrogators that his great-grandfather, Bismarck, had it right—Germany and the Soviet Union should cooperate. They assured him that Stalin wanted a strong Germany once Hitler was gotten rid of. It was the Hitlerites that had to be destroyed, not Germany. That was the official line used for recruiting of all the prisoners of war on behalf of the Free Germany National Committee and the similar Alliance of German Officers *(Bund Deutscher Offiziere)* founded in Moscow in September 1943. They, as German leaders who had seen the light, were to broadcast the message by radio from Moscow and by loudspeakers at the front to troops across the lines, telling them the war was being fought by the Soviet Union not against the German people but against Hitler, against Nazism. Goebbels was incensed to hear at the end of November 1943 a broadcast from Moscow by one of the most highly regarded field commanders, Walter von Seydlitz, calling on the German people to rise against Hitler. General von Seydlitz had been forced to surrender at Stalingrad; he had sent Paulus a sober, irrefutable analysis of the situation of the Sixth Army and the necessity for ordering an attempt to break out of the encirclement. He was now president of the Alliance of German Officers.[38]

The distinction between the fate of Hitler and that of the German people was made again, two and a half years after Casablanca, when the Soviet army entered Berlin accompanied by slogans that appeared on placards on the city's shattered streets: "Hitlers come and go but the German people, the German state, lives on." The grim realities of Soviet occupation never remotely resembled the propaganda slogans, but they were in promising contrast to the policy of unconditional surrender.

After Stalingrad the net was closing inextricably on Hitler. The Wehrmacht could still achieve significant local victories, but the war in Russia was essentially a slow retreat. Despite numerical inferiority, the disaster at Stalingrad and the blandishments of the Free Germany National Committee, the German armies continued to fight in the most demanding of military operations—strategic retreat. They were forced to move back day after day, with little or no hope of final victory, toward German bases and cities that were being systematically destroyed by Allied planes that took severe losses but were never stopped.

As the armies retreated on all fronts, more than territory was liberated; the Soviet armies and the Western Allies, which had invaded in June 1944, overran the death camps. The concentration camps were mainly in Poland, long rumored to be the killing centers of millions of alleged enemies of the Third Reich. Now the rumors, which had been widely disbelieved in foreign countries as well as in the Reich itself, were discovered to be all too true. As Auschwitz, Treblinka, and in the West the other extermination centers were captured, no Allied propaganda could have exaggerated what had gone on in those camps where millions had worked and starved and were executed. "Arbeit Macht Frei" engraved on the gateposts of Auschwitz was an irony that no propaganda of the Allies could exaggerate.[39]

Precisely when the decision was made to exterminate the Jews is not known. Hitler had hinted at it a few months before the start of the war in a speech to the Reichstag on January 30, 1939, when he said: " . . . if the international Jewish financiers in and outside Europe should succeed in plunging the nations once more into a world war, then the result will not be the Bolshevizing of the earth, and thus the victory of Jewry, but the annihilation of the Jewish race in Europe!" Not until July 31, 1941, however, just after the invasion of the Soviet Union, was an explicit order given by Göring to Heydrich to make "all necessary preparation with regard to organizational and financial matters for bringing about a complete solution of the Jewish question in the German sphere of influence in Europe." And on January 20, 1942, at the Wannsee Conference held at the edge of Berlin, Heydrich told the gathering of SS leaders and officials of various ministries—Foreign Affairs, Eastern Territories, Four-Year Plan, Interior, and Justice—that Göring had made him "responsible for the preparation of the final solution of the European Jewish question" and that the meeting was being held to achieve clarity in basic questions.[40] It was the Wannsee meeting that set in motion the apparatus of slaughter. The word "extermination" was never used, but everyone present knew what the "final solution" was, and no one but Hitler could have ordered it.

What remained unshaken, from beginning to end of the war, was Hitler's vindictiveness. When the acting Reichsprotector of Bohemia and Moravia, Obergruppenführer Reinhard Heydrich, was mortally wounded in May 1942 by two Czechs, who had dropped by parachute from a British plane and ambushed him as he drove to his office, Hitler's reprisal was characteristically overscale: more than five thousand people were killed in retaliation.[41] The village of Lidice, though it had no direct connection with the *Attentat,* was ordered obliterated. All the adult male population was shot, the women were deported to Ravensbrück, children worthy of Germanization were sent to Germany to be raised by SS families, and the village was burned and plowed under. Another Czech community, Ležáky, suffered a similar fate—there the entire population, including the women, was shot because a secret radio station had been discovered. It was a pattern Hitler always had ready to hand. Leningrad he had ordered leveled, its name and living space obliterated, and he planned an identical fate for Moscow where the city would be replaced by an artificial lake. In the case of the Heydrich assassination the reprisals were so devastating that many Czechs were convinced Beneš had gone too far by urging the assassination.[42] Heydrich's death, they believed, was hardly balanced by so many casualties among Czech resistance forces. It was a reasonable conclusion that Hitler wanted the Czechs to keep in mind.

Hitler's war aims continued to elude him, and the mounting strain was evident to many who talked with him. He was his own prisoner living for most of the Soviet campaign in a grim, efficient, well-camouflaged East Prussian bunker—the Wolf's Lair. He called it "the most swampy, mosquito-ridden, climatically unpropitious climate" that could be found for him under artificial light and ventilation secure only against enemy bombs. Count Ciano noted before Stalingrad, when he and Mussolini met with Hitler at Salzburg, how exhausted he seemed. Guderian, who had not seen Hitler for more than a year, remarked in February 1943 how greatly he had aged—he was bent, his speech labored, his left hand trembled, his eyes were dull and protruded slightly, and his gaze was fixed. He kept going on drugs prescribed by his physician, Morell, whom he had met through his friend and photographer, Heinrich Hoffmann. Morell had been a ship's doctor and specialist in skin and venereal diseases. He was a generous dispenser of pop stimulants; Göring called him "Reich's Spritzmeister" because of his use of revivifying shots to improve his patients' health and spirits. Sulfanilamides, strychnine, phosphorus, hormones, and stimulants to step up circulation along with antigas tablets and pastilles taken by the dozen were a regular ration for Hitler. Dr. Karl Brandt, who headed the Nazi euthanasia program and had also acted as Hitler's personal physician, declared that Morell's treatment aged Hitler four or five years annually.[43]

What Morell could not accomplish, the assassination attempt of 1944 hurried along. The attempt on Hitler's life on July 20 left him deeply shaken with more marked Parkinsonian symptoms—a bent figure with tremors involving his left hand, his left leg, and all his left side.

Hitler never could bring himself to visit the twin scenes of destruction that were bringing him and his country down: the Russian front or the ruined German cities. Goebbels told the public of the "wonder weapons" to come, but as Allied advances, both East and West, closed in, he ordered a scorched earth policy in the Reich that Speer did his best to prevent from being carried out. Appalled by the commanded destruction of essential structures, Speer told Hitler bluntly that "no one has the right to take the viewpoint that the fate of the German people is tied to his personal fate."[44] In those last months of the war Hitler was fighting on behalf of nothing but his own survival, summoning expended armies to defend Berlin, recruiting old men and boys—*Volkssturmmänner*—some as young as twelve years, to blow up the Russian tanks.

Hitler liked to ascribe his rise to power to a triumph of will, and his will to survive remained indomitable. In the autumn of 1944 he ordered a massive, surprise offensive in the Ardennes directed against the American forces advancing on Germany, in the irrational hope that its success could turn the tide of battle in the West and lead to a final victory against his ill-assorted tormentors. Taking advantage of overcast skies that prevented the overwhelming Allied air superiority from asserting itself, the offensive that began in mid-December initially had striking success, splitting the American and British forces, but began to sputter after the fifth day and was finally defeated after two weeks of hard fighting.[45]

Unbowed, on December 28 the physically broken Hitler, in a speech to division commanders delivered as the attack ground to a halt, reminded them of the Roman experience after the catastrophic defeat by the Carthaginians at Cannae when, deserted by friends and betrayed by allies, given no chance of rescue by any sensible military calculation, Rome was saved by the intrepidity of its remaining defenders.

The man who rose to thank Hitler for his speech was Field Marshal von Rundstedt who had many years before given Hitler the advice, which Hitler had disregarded, not to attack France. Now when the situation was really hopeless,

Rundstedt assured him in the name of all present that the officer corps would do everything possible for victory of the 1944 offensive.

Nor was Rundstedt the only one to be inspired by last-ditch oratory. General von Greim, a career soldier and fighter pilot since the end of World War I, was another. In the war's last days Hitler summoned Greim to Berlin to appoint him field marshal and commander in chief of the Luftwaffe to replace the disgraced Göring. Greim managed with the aid of his dauntless friend Hanna Reitsch to land their small plane at the Brandenburger Gate, despite heavy ground fire from Russian troops that badly wounded Greim in the foot.[46] Even as the Russians were closing in on the Führer bunker, and in the midst of the moonscape of the shelled-out city teeming with Soviet troops, Greim as he lay in a hospital, was convinced by Hitler that final victory was in sight. "Just don't give up your faith," Greim told the chief of staff of the Luftwaffe, General Koller, "it will all come to a good end. My meeting with the Führer and his strength have enormously strengthened me. It has been like a fountain of youth. The Führer sat at my bedside and explained everything."[47]

For the Ardennes, Hitler had scraped together a quarter of a million men including battle-wise Waffen SS contingents as well as battle-worn Volksgrenadiers and former members of the Luftwaffe who had little experience as infantrymen. German forces possessed 970 tanks and 1,500 fighter planes, but the latter included no jets and had insufficient gasoline. With the return of clear weather, the air was again overwhelmingly dominated by the Allies, and the Wehrmacht had no reserves to match those available to the Allies.[48] The offensive was shattered.

In his speech Hitler declared himself still confident of victory if every German did his duty. But doing one's duty was not nearly enough; generals had to work miracles holding on to territory they could no longer defend, providing reserves they did not have. Guderian, who, though once before dismissed, had become Hitler's chief of staff, was peremptorily fired in February 1945 because Hitler found him a defeatist. He had told Hitler that the SS chief, Himmler, appointed by Hitler to command the Home Army and then the Army Group Vistula, after the attempted army coup of July 1944, was in need of a general staff officer to advise him, as indeed he was. Hitler could not tolerate such an affront, and though he reluctantly approved the appointment of the staff officer, Guderian was soon dismissed from his post. Himmler, as a Wehrmacht general, did not long remain in favor. He had no success whatever as an army commander and soon resigned his command of Army Group Vistula because of "ill health." When Hitler learned that he was trying to make a deal with the Allies, Himmler, the man he had long called "der treue Heinrich," was added to his growing list of traitors.

At the last military conferences in the Berlin bunker Hitler and his remaining generals were going through stylized motions, ordering fragments of divisions to move from one hopeless position to another, not on wide-flung battlefields but in the rubble of the streets of Berlin. He was lucid but disoriented. He had always been given to angry tirades—the "carpet chewer," the irreverent called him; now Guderian, for one, had the impression that Hitler, in a hysterical rage, would have attacked him physically had Göring not intervened and guided Guderian to another room.[49] He refused to leave Berlin. On April 25, rejecting the entreaties of advisers to fly south for a last stand, he said: "I can only achieve a success here in Berlin; it may be only a moral success but at least it has the possibility of saving face and winning time. It's perfectly useless for me to go south where I have no army." On April 27, two days before he wrote his Last Will and Testament, with Soviet tanks a few blocks away, he could still talk grandly of remote strategic objectives, telling his bunker conferees about them. "We have no oilfields left," he said. Both Austrian oil fields were lost, and that was catastrophic because it made wide-scale operations impossible. Once the situation in Berlin was cleared up, he said, "We have to see to it that we regain the oilfields. The enemy wages war with oil from overseas, we have it at our gates."[50]

Goebbels, following the text of Hitler's previous recitals, reminded the remaining staff in the Berlin bunker of the rescue of Frederick the Great in the Seven Years' War when the coalition of Britain, Austria, and Russia ranged against him was miraculously dissolved with the death of the czarina, Elizabeth, and the accession to the Russian throne of a devout admirer of Frederick, Czar Peter III. Hitler, too, saw the parallel in the death of Roosevelt and that of the eighteenth-century czarina, with the West turning at long last to the Reich against the Soviet hordes taking over Europe. Meanwhile he ordered any general shot who moved his command post without permission and any straggling *Landser* hanged who could not find his regiment in the vast confusion.[51] Corpses with placards around their necks were hanged along roadsides by squads who had been seeking deserters, the inscriptions announcing that the culprits hung there "because I was a coward" or "I had no confidence in the Führer."

The cost of fighting to the last was enormous. When, in mid-February 1945, waves of British and American planes bombed Dresden to the ground, some twenty-five thousand people were killed and tens of thousands wounded in an undefended city whose antiaircraft batteries had been moved to the front because the city had never theretofore been attacked and the guns had been sorely needed by the hard-pressed fighting troops.[52] Nothing whatever was gained by the destruction of Dresden. The terror attack, which combined fire, fragmentation, and phosphorus bombs, was ordered by Allied strategists to break German civilian morale, and it no more succeeded than did Hitler's attempt to gain time until the Allies fought one another.

What remained intact for Hitler were his tattered copybook maxims: Hold out at any cost, no matter how hopeless the military situation may seem; never admit defeat; never compromise on essential articles of faith, like the need for the targeting of Jews as the ultimate enemy. This last sentiment would be inscribed in his Last Will and Testament.[53]

Nor would Hitler again pursue the possibility of negotiations with that key member of the coalition ranged against him—Joseph Stalin. Between December 1942 and June 1943—that is, in the time when the battle of Stalingrad was nearing its end and until just after Paulus and his army had surrendered—two talks in Stockholm between a German diplomat, Peter Kleist, and a conceivable Soviet emissary named Edgar Claus did take place. Claus was of uncertain nationality but unquestionably had a privileged entrée to the Soviet Embassy in Stockholm. Kleist, a former member of Ribbentrop's foreign affairs bureau was head of the Central Office East Europe, which oversaw the repatriation of Germans to the Eastern territories, and was in Stockholm on official business. He met Claus through a German acquaintance living in Stockholm who had been impressed with Claus's intimate knowledge of Soviet affairs and his connections with high officials in the Soviet Embassy, including the ambassadress, Mme. Kollontai.[54] Claus, who spoke both Russian and German with a heavy accent, identified himself only as a businessman with no interest in politics but informed Kleist that he was certain that the Soviets were ready to seek an end to the war as soon as possible. He said he could arrange meetings with interested parties in the Soviet Embassy; if the Reich would accept the borders of 1939, peace, he assured Kleist, would be arranged within a week. Count von der Schulenburg, with whom Kleist discussed the matter on return to Berlin, took Claus very seriously, telling Kleist that Stalin might have two possible goals in mind—he either could end the war with Germany and return to the former status quo and the rebuilding of the Soviet Union or could threaten the Allies with a separate German-Russian peace.

Kleist's assignments soon called him back to Stockholm. He had barely reached his hotel when Claus, to his considerable surprise, turned up. Claus resumed the explanations of Stalin's enigmatic purposes and in answer to Kleist's question of why, especially at this time of calamitous German defeats at Stalingrad and in North Africa, Stalin was ready to enter into negotiations with the Reich, Claus took a handful of papers from his pocket, repeating that he was no politician and would quote his Soviet sources directly. Notes in hand he proceeded to say that the Soviets were determined not to fight a minute longer than necessary in the interests of Britain and America. Hitler, blinded by his ideology, had been taken in by the intrigues of the capitalist countries and entered the war. The Soviet Union, by using its last resources and with American help, could very possibly defeat the Reich after a murderous battle, but Russia, hemorrhaging from its many wounds would then be unable to resist the Western powers.

No second front was in sight; the whole weight of the war lay on Russia. What the Allies wanted, and Russia emphatically did not, was a second front in the Balkans (this was a reference to the Anglo-American campaign in Italy that, if Churchill had had his way, might have been extended into Yugoslavia and from there spread to the other Balkan countries). Russia needed time to recover; Germany was in possession of large sections of Russian territory that would only be reconquered with enormous Soviet losses. An agreement with Germany would be something entirely different from continuing the war. One guarantee of maintaining a peace agreement would lie in the need for the Soviet Union to heal its wounds, repair war damages, and proceed with industrial construction. A second guarantee would be economic assistance that Germany could furnish the Soviet Union. Furthermore, if Germany were destroyed, the Soviet Union would be entirely dependent on American help that could be denied at any time.

Then Claus returned to his recital of Stalin's worldview that he said aimed at revolutionizing the Far East, especially China, far more than Europe. He wanted Kleist to meet again with a minor Russian diplomat by the name of Alexandrov, a man Claus called Kleist's friend but whom Kleist vaguely remembered having once fleetingly encountered. At the moment, Claus said, Alexandrov was in Stockholm and in a position to continue the discussions Claus had initiated.

The meeting would never take place. As he stepped off the plane on return to Berlin, Kleist was seized by the SD and placed under house arrest. Although the chief of the security service, Ernst Kaltenbrunner, was interested in his account of talks with Claus, Hitler when he heard the story was incensed. Hitler called both Claus and Alexandrov "impudent Jewish provocateurs," and while Kleist after two weeks was released from house arrest he was never to see Claus again.[55]

Whether Stalin was actually instigating moves toward a German-Soviet separate peace remains unclear. He was doing all he could to needle the Allies to hasten their landing in the West, and with his deep distrust of Churchill and Roosevelt it was not impossible that he would again make an approach to Hitler.[56] Even though Stalin had been the victim of Hitler's latest onslaught, in Stalin's murderous world such an event was always a contingent move on the part of any power he did not control. All that is certain is that Hitler, even in the extremity of losing an army at Stalingrad, would have nothing to do with him.

Hitler's world shrank gradually to the space of his last bunker headquarters where he was in charge of the scene. Speer noted that when Hitler visited Munich as the air bombardments were creating vast devastation, Hitler refused to look at ruins. Although on drives back from conferences in the nearby neighborhood of the Königsplatz he had been accustomed to take circuitous sightseeing routes in the city he had basked in, he now made a beeline to Prinz Regentenstrasse. Speer also noted that what Hitler talked of rebuilding after the devastating air raids was not living space for the bombed-out inhabitants but a state theater that he said people needed to maintain their morale. The sight of Germans in their rubble he avoided whenever he could, and finally he would disown even the German people. Toward the last days of the war he declared they had shown themselves weaker than people in the East, that only the inferior were left, and, still the social Darwinist, it didn't matter much what happened to them.[57]

Hitler never had a friend, an unconditionally trusted confidant; Speer thought that if Hitler had been capable of friendship he, Speer, might have filled that role. But Hitler had known only enemies, or useful, manipulable neutrals, or party comrades in the best of times, and then in defeat had come the bitter revelation, as he learned that Göring and then Himmler were seeking to make peace with the Allies, that even the most ardent of party comrades could desert.[58] His worshipful female companion, Eva Braun, chose to die with him, and he accepted her sacrifice without much show of emotion. He married her the day before he decided they would die together, referring to her in his Will as "meine Gattin" instead of "meine Frau," which is the usual expression for one's own wife—"Gattin" is the honorific title for someone else's wife.

Until the end some of his extraordinary ability to reduce complicated matters to their essentials remained with him; he foresaw clearly that the alliance between Stalin, Churchill, and Roosevelt would be very short-lived and would soon shift to cutthroat hostility. It was he who had created the alliance, and once he was removed it crumbled.

Hitler's explanation of what had gone wrong was concise: He had been betrayed. How could the Leader, he asked rhetorically, carry out the task assigned him by Providence when betrayal—by the Wehrmacht, the SS, the reactionaries, and his closest associates—was all around him? Betrayal could take the form of simple ineptitude—a failure to follow orders. During his last staff conferences he returned again and again to this latter outrage. He had ordered the Ninth Army to move northwest to defend Berlin, and incomprehensibly, he said, it had moved west—a fatal mistake. How could he lead, he demanded, "If every troop commander does what he wants to?"[59] But these were lamentations; what he at long last saw unmistakably was that no relieving army would arrive at the bunker but that a Russian tank might appear at any moment.

He had been living from day to day sustained by occasional intimations of a miraculous rescue. But if they proved to be only illusory he always had the ultimate weapon at his command—suicide. He had often explained how easy that was, a split second, he said, and everything was over. That was why he so roundly condemned Paulus for surrender at Stalingrad. All Paulus had to do to prevent that ignominy was to pull the trigger of his service revolver. Hitler was prepared to pull the trigger with the muzzle at his own head. When the time came he would make his preparations unflinchingly, dictating his Will with its conventional as well as paranoid instructions, ordering the poisoning of his shepherd bitch before he and Eva died—he by a pistol shot, she by a cyanide pill.[60]

Hitler's death released a mighty flood of consequences unforeseen by him or by most of his enemies. One was the successful founding of a Jewish state in the midst of a hostile Arab world. To be sure, "a national home for the Jewish people" had been promised by the British government as early as 1917 in the Balfour Declaration, but without the Holocaust and Auschwitz the Zionist drive for a Jewish state at the end of World War II would have lacked the numbers and intensity that powered it as well as the outpouring of sympathy and admiration much of the Western world expressed for survivors of the Nazi killings.

A far more disturbing consequence of Hitler's defeat for the postwar balance of power and moral equilibrium was the spectacular rise of Soviet power to dominate half of Europe, and, together with a communist China, much of Asia after World War II. From 1945 on the Soviet Union set the boundaries, the form of government, and the foreign and domestic policies of Poland on whose account the war had started, subjecting the Poles to a totalitarian domination rivaling that of Hitler. Millions of people in Czechoslovakia, Romania, Bulgaria, Hungary, and East Germany lost whatever independence they had and became part of the army of unfree labor toiling on behalf of the Soviet Union. Stalin took Hitler's place as the chief enemy of the Western world, and only a few years after unconditional surrender the Western Allies were asking the Bonn government for West German military contingents to help contain him. The work of the gas chambers, where millions of innocent noncombatants had been suffocated, was over, but hundreds of thousands of other equally innocent people would be sacrificed in the name of another totalitarian ideology. West Germany and Japan moved on to unprecedented heights of prosperity and well-being, both freed of internal thought police and defended against external assault by powers that had defeated them.[61]

As a war to end wars in a world to be kept in order by the Four Policemen that Roosevelt enumerated—China, Britain, the Soviet Union, and the United States—World War II had limited success; it was followed by war after war, hundreds of them, large and small, two recruiting the Four Policemen on opposite sides and one splitting the West.[62]

What dominated the post–World War II era, however, was mobilization of the West against what it came to believe was the most widespread tyranny since— some said including—Hitler's, until it unpredictably collapsed of its own weight. What had kept the precarious peace from a shooting war between the Soviet Union and the West was the threat of mutual nuclear destruction far more than any consensus of peace-loving nations.

Britain and France were victors, it seemed to many of their inhabitants, only in a theoretical sense. Both emerged from the war impoverished, greatly weakened, and both lost their empires, not to Hitler but to successor, indigenous states. It had become impossible in terms of power politics and in the pervading climate of public opinion for Western proconsuls of any nationality to rule comfortably over an empire of alien colonies. It also became morally unacceptable to protect what many people believed to be the ethnic or racial integrity of the country they lived in against the rising tide of immigration arising from overpopulation and economic misery in the Third World. If there was a difference in readiness for assimilation among immigrants, Hitler made it impossible to cite problems of assimilation as a barrier to settlement in any Western country. A new all-inclusive ethos emerged—antiracist, antiwhite, even antimale—almost all of it professing true democracy and often imposing its own immutable rigidities called by its critics "political correctness" in the place of free discussion. These were all part of Hitler's bequest; Hitler, who had to be defeated, had been defeated, but his bequest lived on.

Appendix

Hitler dictated his political testament on April 29. In it he turned again to his theme of how he had tried to keep the peace in 1939 and how he had suffered the betrayal of July 1944 and repeated his determination not to fall alive into the hands of his enemies. He would not become a spectacle for the "Jewish-incited masses" but would die in Berlin. In a second part of the testament he cast both Göring and Himmler out of the party for their secret dealing with the enemy without his knowledge. He named Dönitz as Reichschancellor with Goebbels as minister of the party, Bormann as foreign minister, Seyss-Inquart as minister of War, filling the remaining posts with other still-true believers. He closed the political testament by admonishing the new leaders of the nation to hold fast to the racial laws and to continue "merciless opposition to the world poisoner of all peoples, international Jewry." In addition to the political testament he dictated a private testament to record his decision "to take the girl as wife" who after long years of friendship had made her way to the beleaguered city to share his fate and to die with him. That, he said, would compensate them for what they both had been robbed of by his long labors in the service of his people. As for his possessions, such as they were, they belonged, he wrote, to the party. If the party no longer existed, then they were left to the state, and if the state was destroyed, he needed to make no further decisions. The paintings he had bought in the course of the years had never been intended for private use, always for a gallery to be built in his birthplace, Linz, on the Danube. He earnestly hoped it would be possible for this to be done. He gave Bormann final authority to distribute any personal belongings that would serve as mementos or "for the maintenance of a simple, domestic existence" to his siblings, his wife's mother, and his coworkers, especially his secretaries, Frau Winter and the others "who sustained me with their work over the years." He himself and his wife chose death, he said, to avoid the shame of dismissal or surrender. It was their will to be cremated immediately in the place where he had done the greatest part of his daily work in the course of his twelve years of service to his people.[63]

Notes

Chapter 1: The Grasp for Power

1. So-called a "front" because of a short-lived statement of unity by the national parties made at Bad Harzburg in October 1931.

2. It was a widely held view. The *New York Times* correspondent in Berlin, Guido Enderis, wrote in a front-page article published on January 31, 1933, "Herr Hitler was maneuvered into heading a coalition of Nazis and Nationalists by Lt. Col. Franz von Papen. The new cabinet is a compromise . . . [it] leaves Herr Hitler no scope for gratification of any dictatorial ambitions. He accepted the chancellorship on less sweeping terms than he laid down in his audiences with the President in August and November of last year."

3. Herbert Michaelis and Ernst Schraepler, eds., *Ursachen und Folgen,* 9:9–13.

4. Hindenburg had little choice as to whether to dissolve the Reichstag until new elections could be held. He had just sworn in a nationalist, minority government, and only another general referendum would give it an opportunity to win a majority and overcome the parliamentary handicaps of the unstable coalitions that had preceded it. Even Hugenberg, who had been ready to refuse to join the cabinet on the issue of new elections, which he rightly feared would result in a further accretion of Nazi strength, had come to see that an election was imperative if the present government was to have any more staying power than its predecessors in a fragmented Reichstag.

5. *Münchner Neueste Nachrichten.*

6. *Augsburger Post Zeitung.*

7. Joseph Wulf, *Presse und Funk im Dritten Reich,* 20.

8. Michaelis and Schraepler, *Ursachen und Folgen,* 9:33.

9. Allied Control Authority for Germany, *Trial of the Major War Criminals before the International Military Tribunal, Nuremberg, 14 November 1945–1 October 1946,* vol. 35, doc. 203D, 42–48.

10. The limitations on German armament in the treaty, part 5, were imposed "in order to render possible the initiation of a general limitation of the armaments of all nations."

11. In 1928 two Polish-born brothers, Julius and Henri Barmat, who were in the textile business, were sentenced respectively to eleven and six months' imprisonment for bribery after a trial involving their dealings with highly placed Social Democratic politicians in Berlin. In 1929 Max, Leo, and Willy Skarlek, clothing suppliers, were accused of having defrauded the city of Berlin of more than ten million marks. Their operations, too, involved a considerable number of political figures. In 1932, after a long trial, Leo and Willy Skarlek were sentenced to four years' imprisonment, their business and political accomplices to lesser terms. Although the Barmats and Skarleks were Jews, most of

the others involved with them were not. The national crime rate of Jews was, in fact, about that of the rest of the population: slightly higher than that of Protestants, lower than that of Catholics (Bernt Engelmann, *Deutschland ohne Juden,* 117). See also E. L. Woodward and Rohan Butler, eds., *Documents on British Foreign Policy 1919–1939,* 2d series, 5:3–6.

12. Martin Broszat, "Zum Streit um den Reichstagsbrand," 275–79.

13. Michaelis and Schraepler, *Ursachen und Folgen,* 9:66; Fritz Tobias, *Der Reichstagsbrand,* 213.

14. Among the pictures was a drawing of the hanging of four revolutionaries in Chicago in 1886 for a bomb explosion in which many people were killed. The caption declared the bombing was prearranged by the police themselves as a pretext to suppress the workers' movement. Tobias, *Der Reichstagsbrand,* 208.

15. Oberfohren had been the author of a number of anonymous letters attacking Hugenberg; when his identity was revealed, in May 1933, he committed suicide.

16. *Weissbuch über die Erschiessungen des 30. Juni 1934.* Ernst and Heines were two of the dozens of SA leaders killed during the June 30–July 1, 1934, purge.

17. Internationaler Militärgerichtshof, *Der Prozess gegen die Hauptkriegsverbrecher vor dem Internationalen Militärgerichtshof. Nürnberg, 14. November 1945–1. Oktober 1946,* 9:483.

18. Michaelis and Schraepler, *Ursachen und Folgen,* 9:64; Walter Wagner, *Die deutsche Justiz und der Nationalsozialismus,* 3:14.

19. What follows is a transcript from the tape:

Göring: It was a political crime and I was also convinced the crime had to be looked for in your party. Your party is a party of criminals which must be destroyed.

Dimitrov: Is it known to the Prime Minister that the party which has to be destroyed rules over one sixth of the globe, namely the Soviet Union, and that this Soviet Union maintains diplomatic, political and economic relations with Germany and hundreds of thousands of German workers benefit from its economic orders?

President of the Court: I forbid you to make Communist propaganda here.

Dimitrov: Herr Göring is making National Socialist propaganda here. [Turning to Göring] The Communist outlook on life prevails in the Soviet Union, the largest and best country in the world and here in Germany it has millions of followers among the best sons of the German people. Is this known?

Göring: [In loud voice] I'll tell you what is known to the German people. The German people know that you are behaving insolently. That you have come here to set fire to the German Reichstag. But I am not here to allow you to question me like a judge. . . . In my eyes you are a scoundrel who should be hanged.

President: [To Dimitrov] I have already told you not to make Communist propaganda here. That is why you should not be surprised if the witness is so agitated.

Dimitrov: I am greatly pleased with the reply of the Prime Minister.

President: Whether or not you are pleased is quite immaterial. Now I deprive you of the right to speak

(Georg Dimitroff, *Georg Dimitroff, Leipzig 1933 Speeches, Letters, Documents*).

20. Michaelis and Schraepler, *Ursachen und Folgen,* 9:68.

21. Broszat, "Zum Streit," 275–79; Alfred Berndt, "Zur entstehung des Reichstagsbrands," 76–90.

22. Tobias's book *Der Reichstagsbrand,* which gives the evidence for van der Lubbe's having set the fire on his own, appeared in 1962. In 1972 another book, with the same title, appeared under the auspices of the *International Committee for the Scientific Investigation of the Causes and Consequences of World War II.* Historians, politicians, and writers of international repute were members of the committee and the book appeared under the editorship of four "scientific co-workers." They attempted to refute in detail the thesis that van der Lubbe alone could have had sufficient time and means to have set the widespread fire and violently attacked Tobias and Hans Mommsen, another proponent of the sole van der Lubbe incendiarism. However, a subsequent article in the *Vierteljahreshefte für Zeitgeschichte* by Alfred Berndt, appearing in 1975, has demonstrated that contrary to former calculations van der Lubbe had a minimum of twenty-three minutes—time enough to set the widespread fire—and suggested that the whole matter requires a good deal of further investigation.

But the case is far from ended. Walther Hofer and Christoph Graf published an article in the February 1976 issue of *Geschichte in Wissenschaft und Unterricht* based again on the research of the International Committee for the Scientific Investigation of the Causes and Consequences of World War II. The authors tell of new documents that have come to light and that are in the possession of the committee which they say proves conclusively the National Socialist guilt. The new material includes a detailed report by Hans von Kessel, who with his brother and close relations to SA leaders, and Richard Breiting, the then-editor of the *Leipziger Neuesten Nachrichten,* is said to fully corroborate the accounts of the Nazi responsibility for the fire. But a former collaborator of Breiting's on the Leipzig paper, Alfred Detig, has seriously impugned Breiting's alleged testimony, and other "new" evidence for the conspiracy has been markedly unimpressive.

Along with Communist propagandists, serious scholars have been ranged on the side of the proponents of the Nazi conspiracy theory, though a number of them have distanced themselves from the International Committee as its promised revelations have come under critical fire. The weight of the evidence still seems to corroborate substantially what Tobias wrote in 1962.

23. No party outside the nationalist coalition increased the percentage of its vote. It would have been difficult for them to do so with so many newspapers suspended, meetings forbidden, and speakers and voters intimidated. Scheringer was one of the three officers tried in 1930 on charges of high treason because they belonged to the National Socialist Party for which they had tried to recruit other officers. He was condemned to eighteen months of fortress arrest during which he announced he had converted to the Communist Party and renounced Hitler (Eugene Davidson, *The Making of Adolf Hitler,* 290–91).

24. Hans Roos, "Die 'Präventivkriegspläne' Pilsudskis von 1933," 344–63.

25. The Polish action was not mentioned in the cabinet meeting on the afternoon of March 7.

26. Hitler told Goebbels at Berchtesgaden, on March 26, that he had decided to order the boycott after thorough consideration in the loneliness of his mountain retreat (Michaelis and Schraepler, *Ursachen und Folgen,* 9:387).

27. Neurath testified at Nuremberg that one of Hindenburg's conditions for appointing Hitler chancellor was that Neurath stay on as foreign minister.

28. Allied Control Authority for Germany, *Trial of the Major War Criminals*, 19:447; Eugene Davidson, *The Trial of the Germans*, 171–72.

29. The book presented to Hindenburg, *The Jewish Fallen of the German Army, Navy and Colonial Forces 1914–1918, A Memorial Volume,* cited figures: of the 550,000 Jews of German citizenship, 100,000 had served with the German armies during World War I, and it listed the names of 12,000 who were killed.

30. Leon Poliakov and Josef Wulf, *Das Dritte Reich und seine Diener*, 532.

31. Michaelis and Schraepler, *Ursachen und Folgen*, 9:282.

32. Hindenburg used the phrase when he met with Hitler in 1931 and was deeply irritated by Hitler's pretentions to explain to him what was truly German. Hindenburg told his state secretary, Otto Meissner, that he would never appoint Hitler Reichschancellor; at the most, he said, Hitler might aspire to become Postmaster General where he could lick the backside of Hindenburg's picture on German stamps. Hitler was not a Bohemian; he was born in Austria, in a little town near the Bavarian frontier. Hindenburg had fought against the Austrian army in the war of 1866 and apparently thought Hitler's birthplace to be in another Braunau in Bohemia (Hans Otto Meissner and Harry Wilde, *Die Machtergreifung: Ein Bericht über die Technik des nationalsozialistischen Staatsstreichs,* 48, 49, 273).

33. Michaelis and Schraepler, *Ursachen und Folgen*, 9:133.

34. Ibid., 134–35.

35. Hans Schneider, "Das Ermächtigungsgesetz vom 24. März 1933," 197–221.

36. Michaelis and Schraepler, *Ursachen und Folgen*, 9:6.

37. The "cultural struggle" or *Kulturkampf* was so named by Rudolf Virchow in the Prussian Diet in January 1873. The *Kulturkampf* was a bitter and protracted battle between orthodox Catholics led by the German bishops and the Center Party against the mainly nationalist and Protestant followers of Bismarck who believed all aspects of German life should be subordinated to the sovereign power of the state. Linked to the ancient conflict between church and state, the *Kulturkampf* was set off by the decree of papal infallibility of the Vatican Council of 1870 and the demand of the church hierarchy in the Reich that a group calling themselves Old Catholics, opposed to the Vatican decree, be dismissed as teachers in German schools. The secular authorities refused and the stage was set for a much wider battle, including the recognition of the validity of civil marriage, over the respective rights of church and state where each made claims intolerable to the other. Anticlerical legislation was enacted in Prussia and the Reich, the number of religious orders was restricted, and the Jesuits were expelled. The Church resisted, and in the course of sixteen years the tumult subsided and most of the legislation was repealed. The Jesuits were not permitted to return to the Reich until 1917.

38. Dietrich Geyer, "Sowjetrussland und die deutsche Arbeiterbewegung 1918–1932," 2–37.

39. Michaelis and Schraepler, *Ursachen und Folgen*, 9:164.

40. The *New York Times* reported that Göring went through the formal agenda in ten minutes instead of the four to six hours formerly taken up by interruptions and the heckling of opposition parties (March 22, 1933).

41. F. A. Sir, ed., *Dokumente der Deutschen Politik*, 1:25; Michaelis and Schraepler, *Ursachen und Folgen*, 9:82.

42. Schneider, "Das Ermächtigungsgesetz," 197–221.

43. Heinrich Brüning, *Memoiren 1918–1934,* 659–60.

44. Rudolf Absolon, *Die Wehrmacht im Dritten Reich,* 43; Walter Görlitz, *Der Deutsche Generalstab,* 398.

45. Görlitz, *Der Deutsche Generalstab,* 399; Karl Dietrich Bracher, Wolfgang Sauer, and Gerhard Schultz, *Die nationalsozialistische Machtergreifung,* 735.

46. *Schulthess' Europäischer Geschichtskalender,* 120; Absolon, *Die Wehrmacht im Dritten Reich,* 78.

47. Absolon, *Die Wehrmacht im Dritten Reich,* 78–79.

48. It is an exaggeration that Blomberg was the only Nazi army general. General Beck was in 1930 commander of the First Cavalry Division. He celebrated the National Socialist election victory of 1930 and was sympathetic toward the two officers who were being tried in Leipzig for high treason for proselytizing on behalf of National Socialism. Beck soon, however, became disenchanted with Hitler and by 1938, when he resigned, was ready to initiate a coup d'état against Hitler if he precipitated a war over Czechoslovakia (Davidson, *Making of Adolf Hitler,* 361).

49. *New York Times,* March 22, 1933.

50. Maria Zelzer, *Weg und Schicksal der Stuttgarter Juden,* 160.

51. Ibid., 167–68.

52. Jakow Trachtenberg, *Die Greuelpropaganda ist eine Lügenpropaganda sagen die deutschen Juden selbst;* Eric H. Bochm, *We Survived.*

53. The ceremony held on the Wartburg in Thüringia was hailed by the German liberal press and denounced by arch-conservatives such as Metternich (Franz Schnabel, *Deutsche Geschichte im 19 Jahrhundert,* 2:246).

54. Hans-Wolfgang Stratz, "Die Studentische 'Aktion wider den undeutschen Geist' im Frühjar 1933," 347–72.

55. Rain forced the postponement of the ceremonies in Cologne, though in nearby Bonn they took place as scheduled.

56. Joseph Wulf, *Literatur und Dichtung im Dritten Reich,* 45.

57. Michaelis and Schraepler, *Ursachen und Folgen,* 9:460–61.

58. Wulf, *Literatur und Dichtung,* 9.

59. *Schulthess' Europäischer Geschichtskalender,* 169.

60. Anton Ritthaler, "Eine Etappe auf Hitlers Weg zur ungeteilten Macht/Hugenbergs Rücktritt als Reichsminister," 193–219.

61. On March 16 British Prime Minister MacDonald submitted to the disarmament conference at Geneva a British draft plan providing for eventual general disarmament under international control after a five-year transitional period. The European powers were to each adopt a militia system that required eight months of service. During this five-year period Germany would be allowed an army of 200,000 men, as opposed to 400,000 for France, 200,000 for Poland, 250,000 for Italy, and 100,000 for Czechoslovakia. France, Italy, Japan, Russia, England, and the United States would each retain five hundred planes, whereas Germany would not be allowed any planes until the five years of transition were up.

On May 16 President Roosevelt sent a telegram to the king of England and the heads of state of all the nations participating in the disarmament conference expressing his hope that all offensive weapons might be reduced immediately before being eliminated. Roosevelt proposed that no nation increase its armament over the limitations imposed by treaty, that nonaggression pacts be concluded, and that the signatory powers agree to send no armed forces of "whatever nature across their frontiers" (Woodward and Butler, *Documents*, 2d series, 5:240–42).

62. *Schulthess' Europäischer Geschichtskalender*, 138.

63. Leaving the League of Nations was to take effect two years later, in 1935. The Reich, however, withdrew its delegation from the disarmament conference immediately. The chief of the delegation, Rudolf Nadolny, had been called back to Berlin, but he was not told of Hitler's decisions until after they were officially announced (Rudolf Nadolny, *Mein Beitrag*).

64. Hitler's protestations to the contrary, the SA was a quasi-military formation, and its chief of staff, a former army captain, Ernst Röhm, wanted it incorporated into the Reichswehr. The army was unalterably opposed to such a move, and until the problem of the rivalry between it and the SA was resolved Hitler could not move rapidly with expansion. What he could do was to authorize the establishment of a number of departments to prepare the way for expansion—for example, in April he opened an office of air defense in the Defense Ministry—as a cover for an embryonic army and navy air force staff; he also ordered army and navy military attachés to be assigned to foreign embassies and legations and blueprints prepared for increased armament production. In May he reestablished military courts, which were forbidden under the Versailles treaty. In August, the volunteer farm work programs that had been organized by the Stahlhelm and the Nazis, and since 1931 by the state, to alleviate the unemployment of youths under twenty-five years old, were consolidated under a state secretary with the goal of providing not only work but also premilitary training. In September the so-called garrison police who lived in military barracks were separated from the regular police forces and given military training. In the event of mobilization they would be under army orders. In October the new offices created for an expanding army were multiplied, though no significant increase in the personnel of the armed forces took place.

Göring, former Luftwaffe captain and the last leader of the famed Richthofen fighter squadron, began preparations for the re-creation of German airpower as soon as he took office in Hitler's cabinet as Reichskommissar for Air Travel. Flying clubs paralleling those of the SA and SS were founded with the aid of government funds. Two sections of the Air Defense staff that had been created in April were transferred to Göring's ministry in mid-May. At the end of August, Hindenburg, in an unprecedented act, awarded the former Captain Göring, "in recognition of his outstanding services in war as in peace," the rank of infantry general, with the right to wear the army uniform (Absolon, *Die Wehrmacht im Dritten Reich*, 64).

65. Woodward and Butler, *Documents*, 2d series, 6:39.

66. Ibid., 40.

67. *Schulthess' Europäischer Geschichtskalender*, 238.

68. In all, 7.8 percent of the ballots were declared invalid; Woodward and Butler, *Documents*, 2d series, 6:38.

Chapter 2: Röhm: The Early Disenchanted

1. Ernst Röhm, *Die Geschichte eines Hochverräters*, 9.

2. The formation of the *Kampfbund* in September 1923 was announced by Hitler on behalf of the SA, and by the chiefs of two other paramilitary groups, Oberland and

Reichsflagge. It was from the latter that Röhm had recruited his Reichskriegsflagge when its former leader broke with Hitler a few weeks after they had agreed to join forces. "What," Röhm asked rhetorically, "was the moment we yearned for? Should we not take the King in our midst to call out to him: 'Fate has bestowed on you the duty to be the Leader in our battle. Be our Duke and lead us—we will not rest until Germany is again free and happy.'" Heinrich Bennecke, "Die Memoiren des Ernst Röhm," 179–88.

3. Hitler's language is an echo of what Lenin once wrote when he named a man who had recently stolen party funds as delegate to the Fifth Congress of the Russian Social Democratic Workers Party in 1907. Lenin said he regarded the man as an "intelligent scoundrel" and added: "You can't make a revolution with gloves or manicured fingernails. A party is not a girls' boarding school. Party members can't be measured with the rules of narrow bourgeois morality. Sometimes a blackguard is useful to the party precisely because he is a blackguard" (Günther Wagenlehner, *Staat oder Kommunismus*, 42).

4. Michaelis and Schraepler, *Ursachen und Folgen*, 10:130.

5. Ibid., 9:539–40.

6. The arrests were offensive to so many people that even Mueller protested them to Frick.

7. Michaelis and Schraepler, *Ursachen und Folgen*, 9:543.

8. Ibid., 298.

9. Ibid., 549–50.

10. In the Concordat the Reich promised to respect the confessional and administrative freedom of the church, and to exchange diplomatic representatives with the Vatican. Catholic organizations existing solely for religious, cultural, or charitable purposes would be protected by the state; in return the Vatican agreed that all priests serving in Germany should be German citizens and that bishops were to take an oath of allegiance to the Reich.

11. Ibid., 10:157–63. Papen's career up to the time of the speech had been erratic. Born in Westphalia of an old Catholic family, his military career, including his clumsy attempts to sabotage the Allies' war machines three times during World War I, had been marred by a series of spectacular gaffes. When he was military attaché in Washington, he was declared persona non grata by the American government after an Allied agent found purloined documents in the briefcase of one of the staff of the German embassy, including Papen's plans to sabotage factories manufacturing munitions for the Allies in the United States. On his way back to Germany under a British safe-conduct his luggage was searched when the Dutch ship on which he was sailing arrived at Falmouth and the British discovered more of Papen's documents, including checks given to German agents to blow up Canadian bridges.

After his return to active service in the German forces operating in Palestine, Papen went on leave from Nazareth. There the British, when they captured the city again, found a cache of Papen's papers having to do with fomenting rebellions in India and Ireland and sabotage in the United States. The discovery of the papers eventually led to the execution of a number of German agents.

After the war Papen formally became a member of the Center Party and for twelve years was one of its deputies in the Prussian Landtag. Having married the daughter of a rich industrialist he was able to buy a controlling interest in the Centrist newspaper

Germania and became chairman of its board, wherein he promptly fired the old editor and imposed his own idiocyncratic line on the paper's policy.

This and similar deviations eventually led to the party's disavowing him shortly before he was unexpectedly named chancellor. Papen's appointment in June 1932 was greeted, according to François-Poncet, the French ambassador to Berlin, with incredulity when it was announced at an economic conference in Paris. Even the German ambassador who was present had never heard of him. It was a commentary on the state of German politics in 1932 that Papen could be seriously considered for such a post. General Schleicher, who thought Papen would be sure to follow his own reasonable instructions, had urged the appointment on Hindenburg, who was old and weary and had been ready to appoint a one-time soldier that Schleicher assured him with some reason was apolitical.

It was Papen who fatuously announced, when Hindenburg reluctantly named Hitler chancellor, that the conservatives, with a large majority in the cabinet, now had Hitler in their power. It had been largely on Papen's urging that Hindenburg had changed his mind and made the appointment of the "Bohemian corporal" he had repeatedly said he would never name chancellor. Characteristically, Papen considered Hitler's appointment a personal triumph.

12. Bracher, Sauer, and Schultz, *Die nationalsozialistische Machtergreifung,* 944.

13. It was a theoretical claim. In fact, the Reichswehr provided arms for the SA and welcomed its presence as an armed force on the eastern border.

14. Otto Meissner, *Staatssekretär unter Ebert-Hindenburg-Hitler,* 362–65.

15. Röhm in his antireaction crusade agreed with Gregor Strasser who had broken with Hitler when the Führer threw out the socialist plank on which, along with nationalism, the party had been founded. Strasser would later be accused by Hitler as having taken part in the Röhm conspiracy, but the evidence points the other way. Strasser was actually attempting a reconciliation with Hitler, a move that may have led to him being included among those to be liquidated by Göring and Goebbels, both of whom feared him as a rival. In any event Röhm had little interest in either economics or socialism except as a battle cry recalling Hitler to the people's state and army (Bracher, Sauer, and Schultz, *Die nationalsozialistische Machtergreifung,* 921).

16. After the SA was disarmed in the summer of 1934, 177,000 rifles and 650 heavy and 1,250 light machine guns were counted—arms enough for ten divisions (ibid., 947).

17. Max Domarus, *Hitler Reden und Proklamationen 1932–1945,* 1:379–81.

18. Ibid., 410–25.

19. Ibid., 385.

20. He was referring to the dissidents of 1925, who had then included Goebbels, before Hitler won them back to their former devotion.

21. Michaelis and Schraepler, *Ursachen und Folgen,* 10:166–67.

22. Hindenburg could still act contrary to his advisers' wishes where the army was concerned. In January he had appointed General Fritsch as chief of the army high command, though both Hitler and Bromberg had wanted Reichenau for the post.

23. Papen, it was reported, was trying to persuade Hindenburg to declare a state of emergency that would be a prelude to a restoration of the monarchy but was unable, he said, to get Hindenburg's son Oskar to present the idea to his father.

24. Reichenau, like Schleicher before him, had the reputation in the army of being a political soldier. Soon after Hitler took power he excused the SA transgressions, noting "recognition necessary that we are in a revolution. Decay in state must be extirpated

[muss fallen], that can only be done with terror. The party will move ruthlessly against Marxism. Task of the Wehrmacht, 'Order Arms' *[Gewehr zu Fuss]*. No support, in case the persecuted try to seek refuge with the troops" (Militärgeschichtliches Forschungsamt, ed., *Handbuch zur deutschen Militärgeschichte 1648–1939*, 43).

Reichenau had considerable influence on the far-less-dynamic Blomberg. Both shifted from wanting the army neutral in politics, in a posture of "order arms," to becoming staunch supporters of Hitler and National Socialist indoctrination of the Reichswehr.

25. Meissner, *Staatssekretär*, 365.

26. Bracher, Sauer, and Schultz, *Die nationalsozialistische Machtergreifung*, 944, 954; Hermann Foertsch, *Schuld und Verhängnis*, 43.

27. Hitler's chauffeur, Erich Kempa, reported that Schneidhuber, "a typical old World War I officer," had been delighted to learn that Hitler was in Munich when he greeted Kempa at the ministry that morning. The SD leader, Werner Best, was one of those who thought Schneidhuber "loyal and decent" and opposed his being shot. But Schneidhuber, Heydrich believed, was "just as dangerous as the others," and Hitler was obviously convinced of his guilt (Bracher, Sauer, and Schultz, *Die nationalsozialistische Machtergreifung*, 954).

28. Franz von Papen, *Der Warhheit eine Gasse*, 135.

29. Hitler proposed General Ludendorff, who later denounced Hindenburg for making Hitler chancellor.

30. Uhl was commandant of Röhm's Stabswache, and no one knows what he told his captors before he died. His confession was cited for the first time in Hitler's speech and was never mentioned to the cabinet.

31. Domarus, *Hitler Reden*, 1:421.

32. Michaelis and Schraepler, *Ursachen und Folgen*, 10:219.

33. The reference to acts of violence was to other SS men in Silesia who had murdered imprisoned communist leaders, Jews, both men and women, and a Centrist state councillor.

34. Along with Hitler and Frick, Gürtner signed the law adopted by the cabinet on July 8, retroactively legalizing the measures taken between June 30 and July 2 as having been necessary in an emergency of state. One anonymous Bavarian jurist attacked the law as illegal and invalid but his protest was published only in 1957 ("Promemoria eines Bayerischen Richters zu den Juni-Morden 1934," 102–4); Michaelis and Schraepler, *Ursachen und Folgen*, 10:221.

35. The chief of the army high command, General von Fritsch, and the chief of staff, General Beck, asked Defense Minister von Blomberg to convene a military court of honor to judge the charges against Schleicher and Bredow and in the event of their being found without merit to rehabilitate both men. Blomberg, however, refused. Militärgeschichtliches Forschungsamt, *Handbuch*, 78.

36. Michaelis and Schraepler, *Ursachen und Folgen*, 10:220; Davidson, *Trial of the Germans*, 213.

Chapter 3: The Rising in Austria

1. Gerhard Jagschitz, *Der Putsch*, 45.

2. The German Workers Party, nationalist, anticlerical and anti-Semitic, was founded in Aussig, Austria, in 1903. In May 1918 the name was changed to German National

Socialist Workers Party, though it had a more liberal, democratic program than its predecessor. In 1920 the party had close connections with the German Workers Party to which Hitler belonged and they exchanged speakers, Hitler among them. The Austrian party, however, because of forthcoming elections, declined to aid Hitler's 1923 Munich putsch, as he had demanded it should, and after the failure of the uprising many German Nazis, among them Göring and Gregor Strasser, fled to Austria where they continued their full-time political activity as best they could. In 1926, following a split in the Austrian party, it was refounded as the National Socialist Workers Association—or the Hitler Movement—placing itself directly under Hitler.

The Nazi movement in Austria took on a new life when Hitler became chancellor of Germany. Between one-fifth and one-fourth of the population voted National Socialist at the beginning of 1933. By 1934 the government estimated Nazi adherents at 30 percent of the population and in border areas as high as 60–70 percent. Membership in the illegal SS rose from just under five thousand in January 1934, to almost ten thousand in July. As in Germany an intense rivalry had developed between the SA and the SS, a rivalry that grew considerably after the killings among the SA in the Reich.

3. Habicht was born in Wiesbaden and had served in the German army in World War I. A man of passionately radical sentiments, he had belonged to the Communist Party before becoming a National Socialist. He fled to Austria after a communist was murdered in Wiesbaden, a crime in which the German authorities suspected he had played a part. In 1931 Habicht had been elected to the Reichstag from Hessen-Nassau, though he was living at the time in Linz. As anti-Dollfuss as Hitler, he kept his job as Hitler's man of confidence mainly because he kept telling his leader what Hitler wanted to hear, that the Dollfuss regime was nearing its end and only needed a push to send it into the abyss. Papen believed that Hitler had promised him the post of *Reichsstatthalter*, or governor, after the fall of Dollfuss.

4. Michaelis and Schraepler, *Ursachen und Folgen,* 10:239–40.

5. Ibid., 246–47.

6. Weydenhammer was born in Germany and served as a captain in the Bavarian army during the world war. He was a director of the Deutsche Bank and had influential connections with German and Austrian industrialists.

7. One Austrian historian, Gerhard Jagschitz, has suggested that Reschny wanted the putsch to fail in Vienna so he could lead his victorious SA from the countryside to the capital (*Der Putsch,* 82).

8. The SS group was made up mainly of young men, some of them former soldiers, who had been dismissed because they were known to be National Socialists. A company of the Austrian Bundeswehr was supposed to capture the Bisamberg radio sender. Twenty-five uniformed security guards and ten officials of the criminal police were also to make arrests, while twenty of the latter held the police headquarters for the arrival of Otto Steinhaus, named by the conspirators as the new police president.

9. Dobler, after the failure of the putsch, was arrested. Regarded as a traitor by both sides, he committed suicide.

10. Michaelis and Schraepler, *Ursachen und Folgen,* 10:257.

11. Rieth reported to the foreign office that he thought the men would be murdered if he was not a witness to the safe-conduct.

Chapter 4: President and Reichschancellor

1. Meissner, *Staatssekretär*, 381.

2. Hitler as Führer and Reichschancellor never got around to naming a deputy, though Hess had the title of "Deputy of the Führer" in party affairs and, with the start of the war, Göring had been chosen to be Hitler's successor as head of state in the event of his death.

3. Article 51 of the Weimar Constitution had provided that the succession of power in the event of the death or incompetence of the president should temporarily fall to the chancellor, but an amendment passed by a two-thirds majority of the Reichstag, while Schleicher was chancellor, substituted the president of the Reichs Court for the chancellor. However, as Papen pointed out in his memoirs, the Enabling Act permitted Hitler and his cabinet to set aside constitutional provisions if they did not affect the Reichstag and Reichsrat as institutions. It also declared that the rights of the president remained undisturbed.

4. Meissner, *Staatssekretär*, 376.

5. Michaelis and Schraepler, *Ursachen und Folgen*, 10:270.

6. Gerd Rühle, *Das Dritte Reich*, 2:274.

7. Papen himself wondered why Oskar had not delivered the envelopes to Hitler and suggests, probably correctly, that Hindenburg had told his son to deliver them only to Papen.

8. Papen, *Der Wahrheit eine Gasse*, 374.

9. Michaelis and Schraepler, *Ursachen und Folgen*, 10:272–74.

10. Ibid., 283–84.

11. Rühle, *Das Dritte Reich*, 2:279.

12. Ibid., 208.

13. Ibid., 222.

14. Ibid., 398.

15. Ibid., 332. By June 1933 work service was compulsory for applicants for jobs in specific government agencies and for any student who, having passed his Abitur examination, wanted to attend a university or technical school. Those born before January 1, 1915, were to serve a half year, all others a full year.

The work service was not originated by Hitler. In June 1931 Hindenburg sought to combat the staggeringly high unemployment among young people by ordering that young volunteers be recruited to work for land improvement and similar purposes, and in 1932 the Papen government had appointed a Reichskommissar to administer the voluntary labor service. Private organizations, too, had their labor service camps; the Stahlhelm, before it was merged with the National Socialists, had more than one thousand camps with seventy thousand men (Absolon, *Die Wehrmacht im Dritten Reich*, 128).

16. Rühle, *Das Dritte Reich*, 2:374.

17. Sir, *Dokumente der Deutsche Politik*, 2:176–81.

18. The April 7, 1933, law was called the Law for the Restoration of German Official-dom.

19. Rühle, *Das Dritte Reich*, 2:334.

20. Ibid., 339.

21. Every discoverable leak was plugged. In April the amount of money a German was permitted to take out of the country was reduced from 200 to 50 marks, and in September the value of goods he could bring back with him from abroad was reduced from 50 to 10 marks.

22. Britain, France, Italy, and Japan were the "Signatory Powers" responsible for ensuring that the terms of the Memel Statute were carried out.

23. Ibid., 99.

24. The Wehrmacht, before Hitler came to power, had taken steps toward expansion with a rearmament program designed in 1932 based on the Allies recognizing Germany's right to equality. The pace was accelerated soon after Hitler took office. On May 4, 1933, Minister of Defense Blomberg noted in an interview that the victorious powers after the world war had forced Germany to adopt the British system of long-term enlistments, but they now wanted to change to the short enlistment period of a militia favored by the French. But, Blomberg said, the time when the Reich could be dictated to was over, and Germany would make its own military decisions (Absolon, *Die Wehrmacht im Dritten Reich*, 46).

Chapter 5: Occupation of the Rhineland

1. Militärgeschichtliches Forschungsamt, *Das Deutsche Reich und der zweite Weltkrieg*, 2:282.

2. Heinz Guderian, *Erinnerungen eines Soldaten*, 23–24.

3. Militärgeschichtliches Forschungsamt, *Das Deutsche Reich*, 1:479, 484–96.

4. Ibid., 515.

5. Domarus, *Hitler Reden*, 1:505.

6. Militärgeschichtliches Forschungsamt, *Handbuch*, 160.

7. Ibid., 163.

8. Kühlmann gave this detailed account to the American historian the late Harold C. Deutsch in an interview in 1945 and though Professor Deutsch was not able to find corroborating evidence in the French archives, Kühlmann's chronicle is no doubt accurate. But it is also true that Hitler did not hesitate to take *va banque* risks, and he wanted the Rhineland occupied at almost any cost, as he would Austria and Czechoslovakia when their turns came.

9. Militärgeschichtliches Forschungsamt, *Das Deutsche Reich*, 1:425.

10. Militärgeschichtliches Forschungsamt, *Handbuch*, 164.

11. Militärgeschichtliches Forschungsamt, *Das Deutsche Reich*, 1:425.

12. Domarus, *Hitler Reden*, 1:596.

13. Ibid., 592.

14. Militärgeschichtliches Forschungsamt, *Handbuch*, 166.

Chapter 6: The Saar and Rearmament

1. David Lloyd George, *Memoirs of the Peace Conference*, 265.

2. Ibid., 252.

3. Also on February 14, 1917, a treaty was concluded between Britain, France, and Russia that provided for the French occupation of the Saar until all the conditions and guarantees of the eventual peace treaty were fulfilled (Adam Buckreis, *Politik des 20.*

Jahrhunderts, 273). Friedrich Stieve, ed., *Der Diplomatische Schriftwechsel Iswolskis aus den Jahren 1914–1917,* 213.

4. Reichstag, *Das Saargebiet unter der Herrschaft des Waffenstillstandsabkommens und des Vertrags von Versailles,* 2.

5. Charles Seymour, ed., *The Intimate Papers of Colonel House,* 396.

6. In the German census of 1910, 339 people, or 0.05 percent of the population, reported French as their native tongue (Michael T. Florinsky, *The Saar Struggle,* 14).

In 1935 2,000 votes were cast in favor of joining France as opposed to 450,000 for Germany.

7. Loucheur was a French economist and deputy minister for liberated territories.

8. Reichstag, *Das Saargebiet,* 10–11.

9. Michaelis and Schraepler, *Ursachen und Folgen,* 3:357.

10. Reichstag, *Das Saargebiet,* 37.

11. Vietnamese troops were also sent to the Saar in the early days of the occupation.

12. The other members of the commission were a Dane who lived in Paris, a Belgian, and a Canadian.

13. Friedrich Grimm, *Frankreich am Rhein,* 167 (citing Maurice Barrès); Florinsky, *Saar Struggle,* 42.

14. Wolfgang Scheidewin, ed., *Die Saar und Ruhr-Frage im Englischen Unterhaus.*

15. Heinrich Schneider, *Das Wunder an der Saar.*

16. Sidney Osborne, *The Saar Question,* 165; Alcide Ebray, *La Paix malpropre,* 271.

17. Domarus, *Hitler Reden,* 1:446.

18. Michaelis and Schraepler, *Ursachen und Folgen,* 10:287–88.

19. Peter Hüttenberger, *Die Gauleiter,* 140.

20. Militärgeschichtliches Forschungsamt, *Das Deutsche Reich,* 1:400, 419.

21. In 1935, the German air force calculated France would have a ten to one advantage in war planes by April 1936 (Militärgeschichtliches Forchungsamt, *Handbuch,* 528).

22. Aus dem Archiv des Deutschen Auswärtiges Amt, *Akten zur Deutschen Auswärtigen Politik 1918–1945,* series C, 5:1:221.

23. James Morgan Read, *Atrocity Propaganda 1914–1919,* 187.

24. Aus dem Archiv des Deutschen Auswärtiges Amt, *Akten,* series C, 3:2:1024; Michaelis and Schraepler, *Ursachen und Folgen,* 10:324.

25. He was referring to the trial of 126 Memel Germans before a military court for alleged acts of treason.

26. Michaelis and Schraepler, *Ursachen und Folgen,* 10:327.

27. Ibid., 328.

28. Ibid., 329. Hitler was bluffing. The Reich, in 1935, could equal Britain neither in planes nor men (Militärgeschichtliches Forschungsamt, *Handbuch,* 526). Although Göring, in an interview on March 11 with G. Ward Price, special correspondent of the *Daily Mail,* had disclosed that the Reich already had an air force, he had given no figures. Göring had the title of "General of Fliers" because civil as well as military aviation came under the command of the minister for air travel, a cover post also held by Göring. He had told Price that the Reich had an air force designed not to attack any country, but strong enough to defend Germany. The Reich, he said, had been asked by the British government to join in an air pact providing for collective action against an aggressor—to place its air force at the disposal of any threatened country—and the Reich had agreed.

Germany, too, Göring explained, was ready to defend world peace, and her willingness to hasten to the aid of any endangered country made the raising of a military air force essential. It was the first time any high-ranking Nazi had declared the Reich prepared to join in any form of the collective security so ardently sought by many political leaders in Britain, and it would be the last anyone would hear of it, though Hitler confirmed the Reich's adherence to the principle of mutual aid against any disturber of the peace to Simon and Eden.

29. Ibid., 330.

Chapter 7: The Games of Peace

1. Domarus, *Hitler Reden*, 1:612–13.

2. Michaelis and Schraepler, *Ursachen und Folgen*, 10:460–67.

3. Spain was the third largest exporter of iron ore to Germany, after Sweden and France. Its supplies of pyrites, wool, hides, and resin were also considerable, and their shipments would help foot the bill for German military aid. None of these factors, however, seems to have influenced Hitler's decision to send help; the dispatch of five thousand men in the Condor legion and eighteen thousand volunteers came later (Militägeschichtliches Forschungsamt, *Handbuch*, 179).

4. Hans-Henning Abendroth, "Die Deutsche Intervention im Spanischen Bürger-krieg," 117–29.

5. Aus dem Archiv des Deutschen Auswärtiges Amt, *Akten*, series D, 1:238.

6. Rühle, *Das Dritte Reich*, 4:253.

7. Ibid., 263, 264.

8. Militärgeschichtliches Forschungsamt, *Handbuch*, 151.

9. Ibid., 148.

10. Michaelis and Schraepler, *Ursachen und Folgen*, 11:314.

11. Rühle, *Das Dritte Reich*, 5:19.

12. Ibid., 287, 288–90.

13. Ibid., 289.

14. Ibid., 288–90.

15. A leader's notion that he was in some mystical fashion the projection of a people's will was not new. Andrew Jackson had believed that, as did the communist hierarchy in the Soviet Union.

16. Domarus, *Hitler Reden*, 1:748.

17. Ibid., 752. (The case scenarios are paraphrased by the author.)

18. Charles A. Beard, *American Foreign Policy in the Making 1932–1940*, 187.

19. The only country on which he declared war was the United States, after the Japanese attack on Pearl Harbor.

20. The United States had a member on the Lytton Commission, but the Soviet Union declined to send a representative. In 1931 the Soviet Union saw itself more threatened by the governments represented on the Lytton Commission than by the Japanese.

21. David J. Dallin, *Soviet Russia and the Far East*, 66.

22. Ibid., 61.

Chapter 8: The Tarnished Generals: The Flower War

1. Friedrich Hossbach, *Zwischen Wehrmacht und Hitler 1934–1938*, 105–23.

2. These hearings were held by the investigative panel of which Karl Sack, chief justice of the army, and Ernst Kanter, Reichs war councilor, were members.

3. The security service, the SD, and the Gestapo were branches of the SS, all of them under the command of Himmler.

4. A German writer has suggested that Schmidt may have been a police informer. He had often been sentenced to prison but did not serve his full sentences (Johann Adolf Kielmansegg, *Der Fritsch Prozess*, 55).

5. Foertsch, *Schuld und Verhängnis*, 136–37.

6. Ibid., 148.

7. Hans Bernd Gisevius, *Bis zum bitteren Ende*, 296; Harold C. Deutsch, *Hitler and His Generals*, 208.

8. Foertsch, *Schuld und Verhängnis*, 107–8.

9. Michaelis and Schraepler, *Ursachen und Folgen*, 11:564.

10. Deutsch, *Hitler and His Generals*, 196.

11. Gert Buchheit, *Ludwig Beck*, 113.

12. This did not prove to be the case. Engel was as critical of Hitler as Hossbach had been, though he was more tactful, and he held his job until 1942.

13. Gisevius, *Bis zum bitteren Ende*, 323.

14. Foertsch, *Schuld und Verhängnis*, 129–30; Deutsch, *Hitler and His Generals*, 403–5.

15. This, like so much else in the speech, was untrue. Schmidt, in fact, was sent to a concentration camp—Sachsenhausen—where he remained until July 1942 when he was actually shot.

16. Michaelis and Schraepler, *Ursachen und Folgen*, 11:617.

17. In fact, the pretender to the Austrian throne, Otto von Hapsburg, as the crisis peaked, urged Schuschnigg to allow him to become chancellor though such a step would have invited not only German intervention but also a hostile reaction from Czechoslovakia among others.

18. Militärgeschichtliches Forschungsamt, *Handbuch*, 175.

19. Directive No. 1 read: "The conduct of the troops must take into consideration . . . that we do not wish to wage a war against a brother people. It lies in our interest that the entire undertaking should proceed with no use of force, in the form of a peaceful march welcomed by the population. Any provocation therefore is to be avoided. If however there should be resistance it is to be ruthlessly broken by force of arms" (Militärgeschichtliches Forschungsamt, *Handbuch*, 217).

20. Close advisers and well-wishers warned him against ordering the plebiscite. Michael Skubl, police president of Vienna, whom Schuschnigg planned to name to his cabinet as a balance to Seyss-Inquart, pointed out how vulnerable to criticism the vote promised to be. For example, he told Schuschnigg, government employees, including the police, were to vote not in secret as in the case of regular elections but in the presence of officials of the Fatherland Front in improvised polling places. Mussolini told the Austrian military attaché in Rome, who informed him of the decision to hold the plebiscite, that Schuschnigg was holding a bomb that would explode in his hand (Michaelis and Schraepler, *Ursachen und Folgen*, 11:654). The British ambassador in Berlin, Nevile Henderson, spoke of "Schuschnigg's ill-conceived and ill-prepared folly," sentiments shared by many Austrians and foreigners who opposed the *Anschluss* but regarded Schuschnigg's tactic as certain to lead to disaster. Moreover, the Austrian constitution required that a plebiscite be approved by the entire government and then

ordered by the president, neither of which had been done. Only four days separated Schuschnigg's announcement and the actual voting, so little time for debate or even printing leaflets would be left.

21. Ibid., 635.

22. Brauchitsch was absent from Berlin on army affairs.

23. Buchheit, *Ludwig Beck*, 127. On March 14 the British minister in Vienna, Sir Michael Palairet, telegraphed to the secretary of state for foreign affairs, Viscount Halifax: "It is impossible to deny the enthusiasm which both the new regime and last night's announcement of incorporation in the Reich have been received here. Herr Hitler is certainly justified in claiming that his action has been welcomed by the Austrian people" (Woodward and Butler, *Documents*, 3d series, 1:43).

24. Militärgeschichtliches Forschungsamt, *Handbuch*, 222.

Chapter 9: Without Firing a Shot

1. Halifax wrote to Henderson in Berlin on March 11, 1938, after the *Anschluss:* "What we were witnessing was an exhibition of naked force, and the public opinion of Europe would inevitably ask when the facts were known what there was to prevent the German government from seeking to apply in similar fashion naked force to the solution of their problems in Czechoslovakia or to any other in which they thought it might be useful. The conclusion must be that German leaders were people who had no use for negotiation, but relied solely on the strong hand" (Militärgeschichtliches Forschungsamt, *Das Deutsche Reich*, 1:639). Woodward and Butler, *Documents*, 3d series, 1:98.

2. Wenzel Jaksch, *Europe's Road to Potsdam*, 216, 254ff. As the Czech crisis became more acute, authorities sometimes took small steps to improve relations with the Sudetenlanders. The British consul at Liberec reported that a local policeman who refused to answer inquiries in German, though he was able to do so, was fined 100 crowns by the police chief—half his monthly salary.

3. Ronald M. Smelser, *The Sudeten Problem 1933–1938*, 66.

4. Martin Gilbert and Richard Gott, *The Appeasers*, 106.

5. Jaksch, *Europe's Road to Potsdam*, 277.

6. Michaelis and Schraepler, *Ursachen und Folgen*, 12:194.

7. Domarus, *Hitler Reden*, 1:838.

8. Michaelis and Schraepler, *Ursachen und Folgen*, 12:115.

9. Jaksch, *Europe's Road to Potsdam*, 287.

10. On May 13, while visiting England, Henlein met with Churchill and told him a central parliament in Prague, representing all parties, should have control of foreign policy, defense, finance, and communications. Frontier fortresses should be manned by Czechs, but the Sudetens should have local autonomy; that is, town councils and a diet for matters of their common regional concern. Henlein said he was ready to submit boundary questions to an impartial tribunal. All the political parties would be free to organize, and impartial courts of justice would function in the autonomous districts. Officials in the postal services, railways, and police would be German-speaking in German-speaking districts.

11. Michaelis and Schraepler, *Ursachen und Folgen*, 12:154.

12. Gert Buchheit, *Soldatentum und Rebellion*, 152–53.

13. Militärgeschichtliches Forschungsamt, *Handbuch,* 229.

14. Georges Bonnet, *De Washington au quai D'Orsay,* 227, 205.

15. Ibid., 207. Bullitt's speech in 1937 had actually used somewhat stronger words. He had said: "We hope to remain outside a war; but we well know that it is always possible that a nation will be foolish enough to drag us in."

16. Ibid., 305, 212.

17. The Soviet Union had never accepted Romania's acquisition of Bessarabia, which had been recognized by the Treaty of Trianon in 1920. Russia had administered the territory from 1812 to 1917 and only lost it during the tumult and weakness of the revolution in 1918 (ibid., 202).

18. Churchill has argued that this was not true; two railroads, he has written, ran from the Soviet Union to Czechoslovakia over the Carpathian mountains and might have transported thirty divisions. It was an overly optimistic estimate in the Romanian view; the railroads were notoriously inefficient, and in any event the Romanians were unwilling to test the capacity of whatever railroads they had with Russian soldiers aboard (Winston S. Churchill, *The Gathering Storm,* 305).

19. Michaelis and Schraepler, *Ursachen und Folgen,* 12:175.

20. Vilna after the world war was claimed by both Lithuania and Poland, and the frontier between the two countries had been closed from 1927 to 1938. When Germany occupied Austria in 1938 Poland, using the closed frontier as a pretext, took the opportunity to force Lithuania to acknowledge Polish sovereignty over the city (ibid., 180).

21. Buchheit, *Ludwig Beck,* 145, 146.

22. Ibid., 161.

23. Ibid., 165–66.

24. Ibid., 159, 160.

25. Ibid., 167, 168.

26. Ewald von Kleist-Schmenzien was a conservative landowner from East Prussia and editor of a newspaper Hitler had banned in 1933. He was also a friend of Niekisch. Despite their political differences the two men had a powerful bond in their rejection of Hitler, and Niekisch had hidden Kleist in his Berlin apartment during the 1934 slaughter when Kleist was on the list of those to be liquidated.

27. Woodward and Butler, *Documents,* 3d series, 2:683.

28. Joachim von Ribbentrop had been named foreign minister by Hitler to succeed Neurath in February. By training and temperament he was conspicuously ill-equipped for the job. A devoted Nazi, he had impressed Hitler, for whom he had a boundless admiration, by his fluent French and English and by reverently echoing whatever Hitler said about foreign policy. Ibid., 684.

29. Erich Kordt, *Nicht aus den Akten . . . ,* 280–81.

30. He arrived in Prague on August 3.

31. Woodward and Butler, *Documents,* 3d series, 2:192, 193, 195.

32. Domarus, *Hitler Reden,* 1:900.

33. Ibid., 899.

34. Ibid., 900.

35. Bethmann Hollweg was chancellor from 1909 to 1917, Count Hertling from 1917 to 1918.

36. Actually, 92 percent of the Sudeten voters had gone to the polls to vote for the Unity Party (Domarus, *Hitler Reden,* 1:903).

37. Ibid., 905.

38. No germanish-German Reich had, in fact, existed. Hitler is referring to "The Holy Roman Empire of the German Nation," a complex of lands ruled for ten centuries by Frankish and German kings. The insignia consisting of the crown, scepter, and jewels of the Holy Roman Empire had just been brought back from Vienna to Nuremberg after an absence of 150 years and installed on Hitler's order in the Meistersinger church.

39. Ibid., 906.

Chapter 10: Negotiating against the Odds

1. Woodward and Butler, *Documents,* 3d series, 2:192, 248.

2. Ibid., 675–79.

3. Domarus, *Hitler Reden,* 1:907.

4. Paul Schmidt, *Statist aufdiplomatischer Bühne 1923–1945,* 394–99.

5. Aus dem Archiv des Deutschen Auswärtigen Amts, *Akten,* series D, 2:627–36.

6. Henderson, who had remained with the others in the living room, wrote that while they were awaiting the return of Chamberlain and Hitler, reports kept coming in of more and more killings. A British investigator, however, later said only one person had actually been killed.

7. The phrase appears only in the German text of Schmidt's note and may have been erroneously transcribed. Gas was not used, and if Hitler had made the charge seriously more would have been made of the accusation.

8. But he was also aware that Chamberlain's mission of peace, as he had told Chamberlain, was enormously appealing to the German people, and he could not merely present them with another war.

9. The Petersberg Hotel was owned by the well-known Cologne manufacturer of "4711" cosmetic products, and the British were provided with enough soap, hair dressing, bath salts, and perfume to enable Ivone Kirkpatrick to share his lavish samples with his wife when he went back to England.

10. Ivone Kirkpatrick, *The Inner Circle, Memoirs of Ivone Kirkpatrick,* 113–18.

11. Aus dem Archiv des Deutschen Auswärtiges Amt, *Akten,* series D, 2:694–701.

12. Schmidt, *Statist,* 402.

13. Ibid.

14. Woodward and Butler, *Documents,* 3d series, 2:487.

15. Domarus, *Hitler Reden,* 1:920.

16. Schmidt, *Statist,* 405.

17. Ibid., 407.

18. Domarus, *Hitler Reden,* 1:921; Woodward and Butler, *Documents,* 3d series, 2:517.

19. Woodward and Butler, *Documents,* 3d series, 2:520–35.

20. The two governments had agreed that some Sudeten territory, when over half the populace was German, must go to the Reich by direct transfer or following a plebiscite. The frontier would be adjusted by an international body including a Czech. Britain would join in an international guarantee on the new boundaries against unprovoked aggression (ibid., 526).

21. Ibid.
22. Simon then was chancellor of the Exchequer (ibid., 527).
23. Ibid., 529.
24. It was not true that Russian planes had done better than those of the German Condor Legion. Likewise, Daladier's other figures were not entirely accurate (Michaelis and Schraepler, *Ursachen und Folgen*, 12:404).
25. Woodward and Butler, *Documents*, 3d series, 2:520–35.
26. Ibid., 537.

Chapter 11: The Agreement

1. Woodward and Butler, *Documents*, 3d series, 2:550.
2. Ibid., 555.
3. Domarus, *Hitler Reden*, 1:923.
4. Ibid., 927.
5. Ibid. Hitler was greatly exaggerating what had gone on. It was certainly true, however, that Czechoslovakia was no Switzerland, and Beneš had never intended it to be.
6. Hitler was referring to the hue and cry in the foreign press when Pastor Niemöller was arrested by the Gestapo in July 1937. Niemöller was one of the scores of pastors and priests sent to concentration camps for their criticism of National Socialist policies.
7. The Czechoslovak government had imposed martial law *(Standrecht)* in many Sudeten localities, and shootings had sporadically occurred. Runciman reported, however, in mid-September, before he left the country, that he had been credibly informed that the number of killed on both sides was not more than seventy. Hitler was greatly exaggerating the violence and the universal yearning of the Sudetens to join the Reich. Thousands of young men who could have fled across the border joined their Czechoslovakian units when the call came for mobilization. No more than forty thousand Sudeten Germans joined the Henlein "Free Corps" (Sudeten Legion) that assembled in the Reich (Jaksch, *Europe's Road to Potsdam*, 309).
8. Domarus, *Hitler Reden*, 1:931.
9. Ibid., 933.
10. Ibid.
11. Ibid., 934.
12. Ibid., 936; Michaelis and Schraepler, *Ursachen und Folgen*, 12:427–31.
13. Gisevius, *Bis zum bitteren Ende*, 376.
14. Beneš had assured his fellow countrymen in a radio speech on September 22 that he saw the situation clearly and steadily and was unafraid. "I have my plan," he said. But when it turned out that it was no plan of his but the decisions of others that would determine what happened, he became an object of derision and the Czechs made a play of words on his "plan" to become, "I have my plane"—the one that would take him to exile in London.
15. Michaelis and Schraepler, *Ursachen und Folgen*, 12:426.
16. It apparently did not occur to him that occupation by the German police, which would inevitably include the Gestapo, would not be much more face-saving for British policy than the appearance of the Wehrmacht.
17. André François-Poncet, *Souvenirs d'une Ambassade à Berlin, Septembre 1931–Octobre 1938*, 327–29.

18. Ibid., 328.

19. Neville Henderson, *Failure of a Mission: Berlin 1937–1938,* 168.

20. Domarus, *Hitler Reden,* 1:940.

21. Michaelis and Schraepler, *Ursachen und Folgen,* 12:443–47. The entire conference, from beginning to end, lasted less than fourteen hours.

22. Ibid., 455–57.

23. The joint statement came as a complete surprise to the French. The government knew nothing of it until it was published; Bonnet considered it additional evidence of France's secondary role at Munich.

It was calculated that the consumption of beer at the Munich Oktoberfest trebled after announcement of the agreement.

24. Twenty thousand Social Democrats were seized, most of whom were deported to Germany. Seven thousand anti-Nazi Sudeten Germans went to concentration camps. The Prague regime forbade the Communist Party and any propaganda of the German immigration and was to do nothing to oppose anti-Semitic threats or demonstrations (ibid., 472).

25. On October 4 People's Commissar of Foreign Affairs Vladimir Potemkin, told Coulondre that with Russia excluded from deliberations of the Western powers, the only course left was a fourth partition of Poland (ibid., 490).

Chapter 12: The Crumbling of Munich

1. Churchill, *Gathering Storm,* 328.

2. Michaelis and Schraepler, *Ursachen und Folgen,* 12:490.

3. Jaksch, *Europe's Road to Potsdam,* 326–27; Keith Eubank, *Munich,* 233.

4. Domarus, *Hitler Reden,* 1:954–56.

5. François-Poncet, *Souvenirs,* 341–49.

6. Self-government had been promised Ruthenia by the Treaty of St. Germain and the Czechoslovak constitution, but in fact the province had been ruled from Prague.

7. Woodward and Butler, *Documents,* 3d series, 3:101.

8. In 1920 the Treaty of Trianon deprived Hungary of more than half its population—ten million of its eighteen million inhabitants—together with seventy-four thousand square miles of territory that became part of the victorious Czechoslovakia, Romania, and Yugoslavia.

9. Slovak communists a few years later declared the figure as high as 450,000.

10. Aus dem Archiv des Deutschen Auswärtigen Amts, *Akten,* series D, 4:106.

11. Michaelis and Schraepler, *Ursachen und Folgen,* 12:537–38.

12. Ibid., 522–25; Internationaler Militärgerichtshof, *Der Prozess,* 27:160–64.

13. One aftermath of Munich was general agreement in Britain and France that the two countries had to undertake arms programs. In September 1938, as Churchill later wrote, Britain was phasing out its old biplane Gladiator fighters, to be replaced by the greatly superior Hurricanes and Spitfires. At the time of Munich, Britain had only five squadrons of Hurricanes; by July 1939 it had equipped twenty-six squadrons of formidable fighters (Churchill, *Gathering Storm,* 338).

14. Michaelis and Schraepler, *Ursachen und Folgen,* 12:525.

15. Internationaler Militärgerichtshof, *Der Prozess,* 9:322; Michaelis and Schraepler, *Ursachen und Folgen,* 12:525.

16. The new prime ministers of Slovakia and Ruthenia, Joseph Tiso and Augustin Volovsin, both clerics, accompanied Chvalkovský. Their presence in Vienna was evidence of the decentralization of the formerly Prague-run state as well as of the need to appease the Slovaks and Ruthenians for their inevitable loss of territory.

After Munich Czechoslovakia had become a one-party state overnight. In the span of a few weeks the former political parties, with the exception of the communists, who were now outlawed, were brought together under the leadership of Rudolf Beran, head of the Agrarian Party, into a single Unity Party.

17. Prince Eugene of Savoy was of French birth; his mother, Olympia Mancini, was a niece of Cardinal Mazarin. The prince had left Paris in 1683 to serve as a volunteer in the Austrian army and had risen to its chief command. In 1687 the army he commanded defeated the Turks at Zenta in Hungary. Eugene was long celebrated for his military prowess, valor, and chivalry.

18. The Hapsburg emperors had been crowned in Pressburg as kings of Hungary, and the Hungarian parliament met there as late as the mid-nineteenth century. It became the capital of Slovakia in the present century.

19. Domarus, *Hitler Reden*, 1:966–69.

20. Hitler was referring to the panicky reaction reported in the American press when a radio broadcast of a science-fiction drama, "War of the Worlds," was taken to be real by many listeners who tuned in late and rushed to their telephones to find out if the Martians had really landed.

21. Helmut Heiber, "Der Fall Grünspan," 134–72.

22. The Polish government had twice refused the German request to admit deportees from the Reich without the reentry notation on their passports.

23. Himmler, chief of the SS, disliked Goebbels, and when he heard of the disorders complained of their likely effect on foreign countries. He dispatched SS formations to arrest Jews and to prevent unauthorized looting. Heydrich, head of the security service, the SD, reported that 174 plunderers had been taken into custody (Michaelis and Schraepler, *Ursachen und Folgen*, 12:587).

24. In October 1941, at his headquarters, he told guests that included Himmler and Heydrich, that he had prophesied to the Reichstag on January 30, 1939, that the Jews would disappear from Europe if war was not avoided. "This criminal race," he said, "has two million war dead of the World War on its conscience, now hundreds of thousands more. Let no one say to me: we can't send them into the swamps! Who is going to worry about our people? It's a good thing when the alarm is sounded that we will extirpate Jewry. The attempt to found a Jewish state would be a grave error" (Werner Jochmann, *Adolf Hitler—Monologe im Führer Hauptquartier 1941–1944*, 106).

25. Michaelis and Schraepler, *Ursachen und Folgen*, 12:605–7.

26. Raul Hilberg, *The Destruction of the European Jews*, 25.

27. The Haavara Agreement between the Reich and the Jewish Agency for Palestine permitted German Jews to emigrate and to make contracts with German exporters to transfer funds to Palestine. The exporters were paid in marks from the Jews' blocked German funds, and immigrants received Palestine currency from the agency on arrival in Palestine.

28. Domarus, *Hitler Reden*, 1:974–77.

29. Wilhelm Treve, "Rede Hitlers vor der Deutschen Presse."

Chapter 13: The March into Prague

1. Aus dem Archive des Deutschen Auswärtiges Amt, *Akten,* series D, 5:127–32.

2. Ibid., 132.

3. Grigore Gafencu, *Last Days of Europe,* 41, 46.

4. Michaelis and Schraepler, *Ursachen und Folgen,* 13:10–12.

5. Beck told Eden in early April 1939 that four men controlled the Polish government. They made up an inner cabinet determined that Poland would not come under German influence and would rather see "half the country devastated than submit to German rule" (Woodward and Butler, *Documents,* 3d series, 5:37).

6. The delay may have been deliberate on Warsaw's part to downplay any sense of crisis.

7. Michael Freund, ed., *Geschichte des Zweiten Weltkrieges in Dokumenten,* 1:328, 329–30.

8. Memel, on the northeast tip of East Prussia, had, like Danzig, been detached from Germany after the world war. Both Poland and Lithuania claimed the city but the Allies placed it and its surrounding territory, called the Memelland, under the League of Nations with a French garrison. The Memelland with 140,000 inhabitants became part of Lithuania as a result of a coup carried out in 1923 against the small French contingent by Lithuanian troops wearing civilian clothes. The coup was well timed: it occurred the day before the French marched into the Ruhr where French energy and resources would be absorbed for months to come. Lithuanian forces were not only securing an outlet to the sea, they were retaliating against seizure in 1920 by Polish troops of Vilna which the Allied high command had three times awarded to Lithuania. After Hitler came to power some indication of the sympathies of the Memellanders became evident in the Lithuanian election of October 1935, when 81 percent of Memellanders eligible to vote elected 24 deputies from the German unity list and 18 percent chose 5 deputies from the Lithuanian lists. By December 1938, 87.3 percent had voted for the Memel German list and 12.7 percent for the Lithuanian.

9. Kerrl was minister for Church Affairs in Hitler's cabinet; Esser was the longtime editor of the *Völkischer Beobachter;* Stauss, a banker, was a former member of the German National Peoples Party (DVP) before joining the National Socialists in 1933.

10. Domarus, *Hitler Reden,* 2:1047–68.

11. The actual number of cows driven off by the Allies, a German historian has noted, was 140,000 (ibid., 1057).

12. What he said was technically true up to the start of World War II, although many clergymen were imprisoned on a catch-all charge of anti-government activities. After the opening of the war thousands of German and foreign clergymen would be sent to concentration camps for alleged crimes against the state which included any hint of criticism of the National Socialist leadership or state.

13. Domarus, *Hitler Reden,* 2:1061.

14. Manchukuo was created in 1932 by Japan from areas its armies conquered.

15. Aus dem Archiv des Deutschen Auswärtiges Amt, *Akten,* series D, 4:183–85.

16. Slovakia had been part of the Hungarian kingdom from the eleventh century until 1918, and Hungary laid claim to Ruthenia and Slovakia.

17. Michaelis and Schraepler, *Ursachen und Folgen,* 13:27–30; Freund, *Geschichte,* 1:426.

18. Freund, *Geschichte*, 1:427.

19. Andreas Hlinka, until his death in August 1938, had been chairman of the Slovak Peoples' Party and a leading supporter of autonomy. Woodward and Butler, *Documents*, 3d series, 4:94.

20. Ibid., 157.

21. Freund, *Geschichte*, 1:435.

22. Michaelis and Schraepler, *Ursachen und Folgen*, 13:38–45.

23. Ibid., 45–46.

24. Durčansky broadcast from Vienna a call for an independent Slovakia under German protection.

25. Aus dem Archiv des Deutschen Auswärtiges Amt, *Akten*, series D, 4:212–13.

26. The German Embassy in Prague was reporting a very different story. The Czech population, it said, was remarkably passive, even forthcoming, not because of affection for the Germans but because of popular opposition to the Prague government. The violence that would call for the Reich's intervention was lacking. Only minor clashes and anti-German incidents were reported from scattered localities.

27. Aus dem Archiv des Deutschen Auswärtiges Amt, *Akten*, series D, 6:8.

28. Albert Speer, *Inside the Third Reich*, 114.

29. Aus dem Archiv des Deutschen Auswärtiges Amt, *Akten*, series D, 4:229–34; Schmidt, *Statist*, 427–32. Before becoming president Hacha had been chief justice of the Supreme Administrative Court.

30. Aus dem Archiv des Deutschen Auswärtiges Amt, *Akten*, series D, 4:231.

Chapter 14: The End of Appeasement

1. *Parliamentary Debates, House of Commons*, fifth series, vol. 345, cols. 435–38 (as cited by Eubank, *Munich*, 263); Michaelis and Schraepler, *Ursachen und Folgen*, 13:90.

2. Freund, *Geschichte*, 2:14–20.

3. Michaelis and Schraepler, *Ursachen und Folgen*, 13:197.

4. Ibid., 206; Domarus, *Hitler Reden*, 2:1117.

5. Michaelis and Schraepler, *Ursachen und Folgen*, 13:344.

6. J. W. Brügel, *Stalin und Hitler*, 35f.

7. Michaelis and Schraepler, *Ursachen und Folgen*, 13:347–48.

8. Litvinov was born Meier Moiseevich Wallakh (Maxim Litvinov, *Notes for a Journal*, intro by E. H. Carr).

9. Aus dem Archiv des Deutschen Auswärtigen Amts, *Akten*, series D, 6:202–4.

10. Domarus, *Hitler Reden*, 2:1148–79.

11. Hitler exaggerated the military actions, but the following did take place: the Polish-Russian War (1920–1921), Greece-Turkish War (1920–1922), Chinese Civil War (1922–1928), war between Bolivia and Paraguay (1932–1935), Italy and Ethiopia (1935–1936), Spanish civil war (1936–1939), Japanese-Chinese wars (1932, 1937), Finnish-Russian border war (1918), Polish-Lithuania border wars (1920, etc.) (ibid., 1166–1967).

Hitler was apparently thinking not of post–World War I interventions but of the war with Mexico (1846–1848), the Spanish-American War (1898), and the coup against Colombia in Panama (1903). In addition, the occupation of Nicaragua (1912), and of Haiti (1915) and the Dominican Republic (1916).

12. Woodward and Butler, *Documents,* 3d series, 5:471.

13. Gustav Hilger, *Wir und der Kreml,* 280–82.

14. Domarus, *Hitler Reden,* 2:1196–201.

15. Ibid., 1131.

16. Woodward and Butler, *Documents,* 3d series, 5:268–69.

17. Brügel, *Stalin und Hitler,* 46–47.

18. Carl J. Burckhardt, *Meine Danziger Mission 1937–1939,* 272; Michaelis and Schraepler, *Ursachen und Folgen,* 13:394–400.

19. On August 19, the same day as Stalin's disclosure, a trade and credit agreement was signed in Moscow for 200 million marks' worth of German goods to be bought by Russia and 180 million marks' worth of Russian goods for Germany. Freund, *Geschichte,* 3:159–60.

20. The proposal had been made verbally by Schulenburg to Molotov on August 18. Ribbentrop instructed Schulenburg to say merely that Germany and the Soviet Union could readily reach an agreement not to go to war or otherwise use force against the other, with a duration of twenty-five years (Aus dem Archiv des Deutschen Auswärtiges Amt, *Akten,* series D, 7:101).

21. Ibid., 126.

22. Freund, *Geschichte,* 3:160–61.

23. Woodward and Butler, *Documents,* 3d series, 7:211.

24. Michaelis and Schraepler, *Ursachen und Folgen,* 13:431.

25. Woodward and Butler, *Documents,* 3d series, 7:150.

26. Ibid., 614.

27. The secret protocol declared that in event of "territorial-political reorganization of the Baltic states (Finland, Estonia, Latvia, Lithuania)," the northern boundary of Lithuania would mark the boundary of spheres of influence of Germany and the Soviet Union. It also provided "in the case of a territorial-political reorganization of Poland" for a demarcation line marking the Soviet and German "spheres of influence" "approximately" along the Narev, Vistula, and San Rivers (Michaelis and Schraepler, *Ursachen und Folgen,* 13:457–58).

28. No complete text of the two speeches of August 22 has survived. Members of the high command made notes including Admirals Boehm and Canaris and Generals Liebmann, Halder, and Greiner. The following text is a compilation from those sources (Winfried Baumgart, "Zur ansprache Hitlers vor den Führern der Wehrmacht am 22. August 1939," 120–49; Hermann Boehm, "Zur ansprache Hitlers vor den Führern der Wehrmacht am 22. August 1939," 294–304; Helmuth Groscurth, *Tagebücher eines Abwehroffiziers 1938–1940,* 180). Aus dem Archiv des Deutschen Auswärtiges Amt, *Akten,* series D, 7:167–70.

29. Domarus, *Hitler Reden,* 2:1237.

30. Ibid., 1237–38; Aus dem Archiv des Deutschen Auswärtiges Amt, *Akten,* series D, 7:171–72.

31. Birger Dahlerus, *Der letzte Versuch.*

32. Internationaler Militärgerichtshof, *Der Prozess,* 41:17 and 26:523. In his August 22 speech he said: "I will give propagandistic grounds for the outbreak of war regardless of whether or not they are credible. The victor will not be asked whether or not he spoke the truth. How a war begins or how it is waged is not a question of right but of victory."

33. Hitler's proposal included the right to vote of all Germans who had lived in the Corridor in January 1918 (Michaelis and Schraepler, *Ursachen und Folgen*, 13:582).

Schmidt, the Reich's astute interpreter who was present at the meeting, denied that Ribbentrop read the text of Hitler's proposal at an unusual speed. He described Henderson's German as only fair and said Ribbentrop read at a normal rate (Schmidt, *Statist*, 459; Internationaler Militärgerichtshof, *Der Prozess*, 10:311).

34. The attack actually began at 4:45 A.M. on September 1.

35. Jürgen Runzheimer, "Der Überfall auf den sender Gleiwitz im Jahre 1939," 408–26.

Chapter 15: The War

1. Domarus, *Hitler Reden*, 2:1312–17.

2. John Strawson, *Hitler's Battles for Europe*, 91.

3. Robert M. W. Kempner, *SS im Kreuzverhör*, 18.

4. Groscurth, *Tagebücher eines Abwehr-offiziers*, 426; Major Engel, *Heeresadjutant bei Hitler 1938–1943*, 67–68.

5. Groscurth, *Tagebücher eines Abwehr-offiziers*, 366; Domarus, *Hitler Reden*, 2:1367.

6. Ingeborg Fleischhauer, "Der Deutsche-Sowjetische Grenz- und Freundschaftsvertrag vom 28. September 1939," 457.

7. Domarus, *Hitler Reden*, 2:1377–93.

8. Michaelis and Schraepler, *Ursachen und Folgen*, 14:55–63.

9. In the Treaty of Brest-Litovsk, signed March 3, 1918, between Germany and the Soviet Union, Russia renounced control over Finland, Latvia, Lithuania, and Estonia.

10. David J. Dallin, *Soviet Russia's Foreign Policy 1939–1942*, 133.

11. Michaelis and Schraepler, *Ursachen und Folgen*, 14:143.

12. Ibid., 131.

13. Ibid., 135.

14. Peter Hoffmann, *The History of the German Resistance 1933–1945*, 114.

15. Otto Strasser, a former Social Democrat, joined the National Socialist Party in 1925 and left it in 1930 because of differences with Hitler. He was a founder of the Schwarze Front and fled Germany in 1933. His brother Gregor was killed during the so-called Röhm putsch in 1934. Michaelis and Schraepler, *Ursachen und Folgen*, 14:404–15; Anton Hoch, "Das Attentat auf Hitler im Münchner Bürgerbräukeller 1939," 383–413.

16. Finland retained independence but was forced to cede territory in the southeast and lease Hangö as a naval base.

17. *Wilfred* was the well-known name of a bumbling, cartoon character given to chronic misfortune. Churchill said he chose the name because it was "by itself so small and innocent."

18. Karl Dönitz, *Zehn Jahre und Zwanzig Tage*, 111.

19. Michaelis and Schraepler, *Ursachen und Folgen*, 15:71.

20. Bernhard von Lossberg, *Im Wehrmacht Führungs Stab*, 65–69.

21. Dietl was killed in an airplane accident in 1944.

22. Militärgeschichtliches Forschungsamt, *Das Deutsche Reich*, 2:219; Gerda-Luise Dietl and D. Kurt Herrmann, *General Dietl*.

23. OKW was the general staff of the armed forces, Army, Navy and Air, headed by the subservient Keitel who agreed with Hitler on everything, and Jodl who considered

Hitler a military genius but did not hesitate to disagree with him. OKW became in effect Hitler's personal staff.

24. Jean Vanwelkenhuyzen, "Die Niederlande und der 'Alarm' im Januar 1940," 17–36; Erich von Manstein, *Verlorene Siege*, 116.

25. Although at first only Generals von Rundstedt and Guderian had enthusiastically pushed the Manstein plan, by the end of January the skeptics in the army high command had been persuaded of its merits and on January 30 Brauchitsch issued a new directive embodying its strategy.

26. At the start of the war in the West the Germans had four thousand planes available, about a thousand more than the Allies. The Allies had 3,383 tanks, the Germans 2,445 (Militärgeschichtliches Forschungsamt, *Das Deutsche Reich*, 2:282).

27. The observer was Harold C. Deutsch.

28. Ibid., 296; Winston S. Churchill, *Their Finest Hour*, 141–42.

29. Aus dem Archiv des Deutschen Auswärtiges Amt, *Akten*, series D, 9:549–54.

30. Domarus, *Hitler Reden*, 2:1540–59.

31. The question of a Jewish settlement was to be resolved in the eventual Franco-German peace treaty. A memorandum in the files of the foreign office, written in July 1940, spelled out the proposed settlement of Jews in Madagascar where twenty-five thousand inhabitants would be evacuated and recompensed. The island would be mandated by the French to the Reich, the Jews, self-governing, would be citizens of the mandate, not of the Reich. The foreign office memorandum, written by Legation Secretary Fritz Rademacher, pointed out "in addition" that the Jews would be a pledge in German hands for good behavior of their co-religionists in the United States and the decision would have significant propagandistic advantages, giving the Jews, after thousands of years, an independent state with their own cultural, economic, administrative and juridicial institutions. The Madagascar plan appeared again in foreign office records in mid-August when Rademacher reported that SS Gruppenführer Heydrich, who was to play a leading role in the Holocaust, was discussing the plan with Ribbentrop, and on August 30 when Rademacher noted only that the plan was under discussion by government authorities. The plan was still alive in October 1940 when the German ambassador in Paris, Otto Abetz, noted that Madagascar was to be considered in relation to a Jewish settlement and a German naval base rather than among colonial-political demands of the Reich.

The foreign office memorandum, however, looks like the product of bureaucratic musing. Removing twenty thousand Madagascan inhabitants would have created little space for the millions of Jews in Europe and it is unlikely that Hitler ever seriously intended to establish a Jewish state which, in his view, would only be a Pandora's box waiting to be opened. In his offhand comments to luncheon and dinner guests he often spoke of the need of ridding Europe of Jews, on one occasion saying they would best be shipped off to Russia but that they must be gotten rid of was the theme (Aus dem Archiv des Deutschen Auswärtiges Amt, *Akten*, series D, 10:92–94; Jochmann, *Adolf Hitler—Monologe*).

32. Prototypes of Spitfires flew in November 1935, those of the Hurricanes in March 1936.

33. Michaelis and Schraepler, *Ursachen und Folgen*, 16:46ff; K. H. Abshagen, *Canaris*, 321–24.

34. In East Africa the Italian troops numbered 90,000 plus 182,000 native troops, against 22,000 British; in North Africa, Marshal Balbo commanded 160,000, opposed by 36,000.

35. Michaelis and Schraepler, *Ursachen und Folgen*, 16:127–34; Elmar Krautkrämer, "Der Sturz Lavals im Dezember 1940," 79–112.

36. Schmidt, *Statist*, 506–7.

Chapter 16: The Last Bunker

1. Schmidt, *Statist*, 515ff. Molotov had never had any previous diplomatic experience nor was he a lawyer; he had risen through the ranks of the party apparatus. A convinced Communist, he lived well in state-provided housing, including dachas, but at his death it is reported his estate, left in an envelope, consisted of only five hundred rubles to cover his burial costs (Felix Chuev, *Molotov Remembers: Inside Kremlin Politics;* Vladimir Yerofeyev, "Ten Years in PCFA Secretariat").

2. Aus dem Archiv des Deutschen Auswärtigen Amts, *Akten*, series D, 11:1:455–61.

3. Ibid., 462–72.

4. The Montreux Convention, signed in July 1936, provided for freedom of transit for the ships of all nations through the Straits in time of peace and war, if Turkey was not a belligerent. If she was a belligerent only ships of countries not at war with Turkey had this freedom.

5. Michaelis and Schraepler, *Ursachen und Folgen*, 16:249.

6. Ibid., 248.

7. Engel, *Heeresadjutant*, 91.

8. Domarus, *Hitler Reden*, 2:1560.

9. Walter Warlimont, *Im Hauptquartier der deutschen Wehrmacht 1939–1945*, 129; Domarus, *Hitler Reden*, 2:1564.

10. The center of the city of Coventry along with the fourteenth-century cathedral was destroyed: in the mass attack of almost 500 German aircraft, 380 people were killed (Churchill, *Their Finest Hour*, 376–77; Militärgeschichtliches Forschungsamt, *Das Deutsche Reich*, 2:1396). Domarus, *Hitler Reden*, 2:1580.

11. On November 25, Molotov handed the German ambassador in Moscow the Soviet conditions for joining the Three-Power Pact: German troops were to withdraw immediately from Finland, the Soviet Union would strengthen its strategic positions in Bulgaria, the Dardanelles, and the Persian Gulf, while Japan would renounce all rights in northern Sakhalin where it had mining concessions.

Hitler changed the cover name from the utilitarian "Otto" to the name of "Red Beard" with its rousing implications of a crusade.

12. Michaelis and Schraepler, *Ursachen und Folgen*, 16:395–98.

13. Guderian during the Polish campaign had dealt directly with the Russian ally, and confirmed Hitler's view (Engel, *Heeresadjutant*, 86). He told Hitler the Red Army was badly armed, the tanks old, Soviet intelligence poor. Other competent generals said much the same thing. Halder, echoed by General Köstring, who had been military attaché in Moscow in 1931–1933 and 1935–1941, considered the Red Army weak. Halder reported armaments as second-rate like the French, old material and poor tanks, troops inferior, leadership inept (Generaloberst Halder, *Kriegstagebuch*, 215). Contrary opinions

Hitler listened to but ignored. Raeder warned him against the two-front war Hitler had condemned the Kaiser for waging. In September 1940, well before "Barbarossa," the admiral raised strong objections to a Russian campaign before England was defeated and repeated his arguments after Barbarossa was ordered (Hans-Adolf Jacobsen, *1939–1945 Der Zweite Weltkrieg in Chronik und Dokumenten*, 246–47; Erich Raeder, *Mein Leben*, 246–50). Michaelis and Schraepler, *Ursachen und Folgen*, 17:41.

14. The former king, not unfriendly to Hitler, had declared in July that the continued heavy bombardment of Britain would lead it to talk peace (Paul R. Sweet, "Der Versuch amtlicher Einflussnahme auf die Edition der 'Documents on Foreign Policy, 1933–1941,'" 265–303).

15. Kesselring agreed with Jodl. He later wrote he thought Hitler was "indisputably correct" in believing the Russians would attack at a favorable moment (Albert Kesselring, *Soldat bis zum letzten Tag*, 113–14). Davidson, *Trial of the Germans*, 352.

16. Viktor Suworow, *Der Eisbrecher: Hitler in Stalins Kalkül;* Gabriel Gorodetsky, "Stalin und Hitlers Angriff auf die Sowjetunion," 645–72.

17. Freund, *Geschichte*, 3:159. It was only on March 25 that Hitler persuaded the Belgrade government to join the Three-Power Pact.

18. Yugoslavia was a nation made up largely of mutually disdainful Serbs, Croats, and Slovenes and was dominated by the Serbs. Considerable numbers of Slovenes, Croats, and Macedonians called up for military service in March and April 1941 refused to report (Michaelis and Schraepler, *Ursachen und Folgen*, 16:406).

19. Named after the former prime minister and dictator, Joannis Metaxas.

20. Philipp W. Fabry, *Der Hitler-Stalin-Pakt 1939–1941: Ein Beitrag zur Methode sowjetischer Aussenpolitik*, 379.

21. Davidson, *Trial of the Germans*, 335; Domarus, *Hitler Reden*, 2:1681–83.

22. Poles and Jews in territories assimilated to Germany after the defeat of Poland were subject to the same penal codes. They could be executed for any act of violence against a German by reason of his being a member of the German *Volk*, or if the Jew or Pole failed to obey orders of a German official, or if they were in possession of a gun or other lethal weapon. Poles and Jews were to be tried by special courts and could not testify under oath (Michaelis and Schraepler, *Ursachen und Folgen*, 19:435–38).

23. Ibid., 17:129–30.

24. German intelligence had, however, disastrously underestimated Soviet reserves. Although its tactical intelligence was generally accurate, its strategic intelligence failed to detect large Red Army formations (David M. Glantz, *Soviet Military Deception in the Second World War*, 23). Militärgeschichtliches Forschungsamt, *Das Deutsche Reich*, 4:55.

25. Joachim Hoffmann, *Die Geschichte der Wlassow-Armee*, 141; August von Knieriem, *The Nuremberg Trials*, 336–37.

26. Churchill, unlike Stalin, was not silent on June 22. He announced in an improvised radio address that Russia's danger was Britain's danger and the danger of the United States, "just as the cause of any Russian fighting for his hearth and home is the cause of free men and free peoples in every quarter of the globe" (Franklin Watts, ed., *Voices of History*, 324).

Another possibility strengthening Stalin's worst suspicions of a possible separate peace between Britain and Germany, leaving Russia to fight alone, was suggested by Rudolf

Hess's flight to Britain in May 1941. The Churchill government did what it could to fuel Stalin's uncertainties, and he in turn was the more resolved to give Hitler no pretext to strike (Rainer F. Schmidt, "Der Hess-Flug und das Kabinett Churchill," 1–38).

27. Michaelis and Schraepler, *Ursachen und Folgen,* 17:569.

28. A former Soviet general estimates that in the first eighteen months of the war about 3 million men, or 65 percent of the Soviet armed forces, were taken prisoner (Dimitri Volkogonov, *Stalin: Triumph and Tragedy,* 439).

29. Alexander Dallin, *German Rule in Russia 1941–1945: A Study of Occupation Policies,* 66. On the day the war started, Hitler told the German people and the world that the enemy was Judeo-Bolshevism; the German people had never held hostile sentiments against the peoples of Russia. That was as far as he went to win the people of Russia (Michaelis and Schraepler, *Ursachen und Folgen,* 17:231).

30. Hoffmann, *Die Geschichte der Wlassow-Armee,* 131.

31. Ibid., 137.

32. Roosevelt had made little pretense of neutrality, and Hitler remarked that American participation in the war would make little difference—the United States was already doing everything possible to aid Britain. In his speech on December 11 announcing a state of war he cited a long list of violations of neutrality and acts of war against the Reich (Domarus, *Hitler Reden,* 2:1804–8).

33. Guderian reported in mid-November the arrival from Siberia of the first of the Far Eastern troops in European Russia.

Sorge had fought as a volunteer in the German army in World War I. He became a communist and Soviet agent, operating with great success until the Japanese arrested him in October 1941. A. G. Ploetz, *Geschichte des Zweiten Weltkrieges,* 817.

34. Some ninety-one thousand men went into Soviet prison camps. The rest had been killed in action or died of other causes. Some thirty-five thousand wounded and a handful of specialists were flown out of the encirclement.

Long before Stalingrad, only six months after the Soviet campaign started, the German Eastern Army had already suffered heavy casualties. By December 1, 1941, it had lost a quarter of its strength, and its successes, though dramatic, fell far short of breaking Soviet resistance. When the tables turned at Stalingrad, not much would be left of the Hitlerian nimbus of "the Greatest Field Commander of All Time" *(Der grösste Feldherr Allerzeiten).* In its place, though whispered, that accolade became, for a rapidly growing number of skeptics, the derisory acronym *Gröfaz.* It was a transformation that would lead to open, if prudently disguised, revulsion when later in the war Allied air bombardment destroyed German cities and many thousands of their inhabitants. In the thousand-year Reich a survivor lettered a sign on top of a ruined house: "We thank our Leader, the Greatest Field Commander of All Time." It also led to something unprecedented in German history—the attempted assassination of the commander in chief by some of the leading members of the high command of the German Wehrmacht on July 20, 1944.

35. Walter Kempowski, *Das Echolot,* 2:180.

36. Paulus was freed from Soviet confinement in 1953, after which he lived in East Germany.

37. The number of those executed as a result of the failed attempt on Hitler's life is estimated at over 150. Among them were Field Marshal Edwin von Witzleben

and Admiral Canaris, who had been opposed to Hitler from the early months of his chancellorship, and latecomers to the Resistance such as Field Marshal Rommel, who became part of the conspiracy only in 1944. Rommel was forced to take poison to prevent a trial that Hitler preferred to avoid because of the evidence of a war hero's rejection of him. The powerful bomb, carried in a briefcase by a foremost member of the conspiracy, Colonel von Stauffenberg, to the Wolfschanze (Wolf's Lair) near Rastenberg in East Prussia, failed to kill Hitler. The device had to be exploded in a relatively flimsy wooden barracks instead of the concrete bunker where Führer briefings usually took place. The conspirators, aware that the Gestapo was closing in on the plot, were convinced they had to go ahead with the assassination attempt even though neither Göring nor Himmler, Hitler's most likely and dangerous successors, was present. Stauffenberg, who had flown to Berlin after he had armed the bomb and witnessed the explosion, was one of those immediately shot following a summary court martial as was Hitler's old enemy General Beck, who had unsuccessfully attempted suicide.

A widespread cover operation, Valkyrie, ranging from Paris and Vienna to Berlin and Danzig was set in motion by the explosion. Believing Hitler dead, the conspirators who planned to replace Hitler with General Beck proceeded to order the dismantling of the entire Nazi governing apparatus: the arrest of all Gauleiter, senior SS, SD, Gestapo and police officials, the heads of propaganda offices, and the "rapid" occupation of concentration camps (Hoffmann, *History of the German Resistance,* 420). But with Hitler still alive, Valkyrie succeeded only in disclosing the far-flung anti-Hitler network of army officers and the civilian resistance that was mobilized to hold off a counterattack by the SS and by pro-Hitler forces in the army and to enable the conspirators to restore the Reich to a traditional state of law. The National Socialist state remained in full control, and most of the conspirators were quickly dealt with. Many of those hanged died especially slowly as they hung from meat hooks with thin ropes or piano wire around their necks; they were photographed by moving picture cameras for Hitler's later viewing. The Gestapo arrested hundreds of people, including members of the families of the accused, Goerdeler, Count von Helldorf (the president of the Berlin police), and, in late August, thousands more regarded as politically suspect. Show trials presided over by a people's court by the shouting hanging judge, Roland Freisler, until his death during an air raid in February 1945, continued until a few weeks before the end of the war. Despite the refined tortures by the Gestapo, the accused bore themselves well. The unbowed Field Marshal von Witzleben told Freisler at the first trial: "You can hand us over to the executioner but in three months time this outraged and suffering people will call you to account and drag you alive through the mud of the streets." The main beneficiary of the failed coup was the policeman Himmler who, with so many of the former high command in disgrace, became the second most important man in the Reich. Four of those in the briefing room died, and nine were injured, but Hitler survived the blast with light wounds that did not prevent him from greeting Mussolini who arrived later in the day (Hoffmann, *History of the German Resistance,* 397–503; Michaelis and Schraepler, *Ursachen und Folgen,* 21:408–16). Harold C. Deutsch, *The Conspiracy against Hitler.*

38. Michaelis and Schraepler, *Ursachen und Folgen,* 18:65.

39. The threatened camps presented a military problem to the ever-vigilant Himmler. Early in 1943 he ordered two of his adjutants, Richard Gluecks and Oswald Pohl, to take drastic measures against an Allied bombing raid. The camps were to be protected by

additional high walls inside barbed wire fences that were to be placed so as to leave a lane in which SS police dogs could roam. Beyond this barbed wire would be an outer lane surrounded by more barbed wire where mines would be laid in case the wall was breached by a bomb and thus enabling the inmates to break out. The dogs must be trained like the hunting dogs of Africa to tear to pieces anybody but their keepers; they were to be loosed only as darkness fell and returned to their kennels at dawn (Kempowski, *Das Echolot*, 3:453–54).

40. Jeremy Noakes and Geoffrey Pridham, eds., *Documents on Nazism 1919–1945*, 485–89.

41. Hitler appointed Heydrich to the post of Reichsprotector after ordering the too lenient Neurath on sick leave. Michaelis and Schraepler, *Ursachen und Folgen*, 18:244.

42. In all, 199 men were shot, 198 women sent to Ravensbrück, 98 children were transported; 143 women and 16 children survived (Michaelis and Schraepler, *Ursachen und Folgen*, 17:380, 18:213).

The reprisals included 477 Czechs who allegedly had expressed their approval of the attack on Heydrich and five priests who had given the parachutists asylum in their church (ibid., 18:243). The Gestapo cast a wide net: Entire families of anyone aiding the escape of the attackers were ordered executed (MacDonald, *Killing*, 197).

43. Kempowski, *Das Echolot*, 3:165–70; Michaelis and Schraepler, *Ursachen und Folgen*, 18:158. Hitler's judgment was showing evident signs of strain. In a long letter to his friend Mussolini, written on February 25, 1943, some six weeks after the surrender of Paulus at Stalingrad, Hitler told the Duce how proud and happy he was to bear the heavy burden that had been thrust upon him. He even detected bright spots in the crumbling fronts and cited examples: The entire Caucasus army had been extricated from that region without serious loss of equipment; the SS Totenkopf division that in June 1941 had numbered twenty thousand men and subsequently fought continuously on the Soviet front until reduced to 370 men had been disbanded and then brought up to strength with new recruits to rejoin the battle. In other words, Hitler expected Mussolini to share his satisfaction that a party-led division that had been cut to pieces and survived in name only with the remnants of less than 2 percent of its original strength was fighting again. In the same vein he confided to Mussolini that a recently captured Russian general placed Soviet losses at 11.3 million men while Hitler said German losses amounted to only 1.4 million men. "I shall fight in the East," he assured Mussolini, "until this colossus finally falls and indeed with or without allies because the existence of this danger alone is so monstrous that Europe can have no rest if it, in fathomless frivolity, continues to exist at the edge of a volcano." Like the ghostly Totenkopf division, he would continue the heroic struggle, and, to manifest his ineluctable resolve, he was calling up sixteen-year-old boys for military duty (Kempowski, *Das Echolot*, 4:507–17).

Hitler's doctors were an odd pair of healers. Brandt had the rank of lieutenant general in the Waffen SS. In 1948 he was tried and sentenced to death for his lethal medical practices by the Nuremburg "Doctors Case" Tribunal. Dr. Ellen Gibbels, citing the internist and chemist Dr. Günther Schenck writes that most of Morell's injections consisted of diluted grape-sugar solutions sometimes strengthened with vitamins and similar mild substances; only rarely did he use stronger medication (Ellen Gibbels, "Hitlers Nervenkrankheit," 216).

44. Speer, *Inside the Third Reich,* 436.

45. Percy Ernst Schramm, *Kriegstagebuch des Oberkommandos der Wehrmacht 1940–1945,* 7.

46. Hanna Reitsch was a test pilot and captain in the German air force. She had been badly injured during experimental work on the V weapons.

47. Michaelis and Schraepler, *Ursachen und Folgen,* 23:183. Hitler had long been able to explain everything to people who needed to believe him. A former general on the staff of OKW said after the war that he had more than once observed Hitler's remarkable powers of persuasion. A soldier, he said, returning on leave from the eastern front, seething with a fury accumulated over months of receiving orders that could not possibly be carried out, would be determined to put his case before Hitler. Granted an interview he would emerge regenerated, convinced that Hitler and his grand strategy were right after all and the complaints trivial (Horst Treusch von Buttler-Brandenfels, interview by author, Cassel, Germany).

48. In the autumn of 1944 the first jet fighters were sent into action by the Luftwaffe and were in short supply (Schramm, *Kriegstagebuch,* 970).

The German inspector of fighter planes, General Galland, estimated Allied air superiority in the autumn of 1944 at twenty to one (Michaelis and Schraepler, *Ursachen und Folgen,* 22:241).

49. Guderian, *Erinnerungen eines Soldaten,* 375.

50. Michaelis and Schraepler, *Ursachen und Folgen,* 23:171.

51. One general who moved his command post was General Helmuth Weidling who commanded Berlin and to whom, the year before, Hitler had awarded the Knight's Cross with oak leaves. Weidling's life was spared, and he was restored to command only when he was able to confront Hitler in his bunker and convince him that he had followed orders.

52. The number who died at Dresden is not known—estimates range up to 135,000 (ibid., 1).

53. No matter that shipping skilled Jews to Auschwitz from remaining ghetto factories in Poland would lose the Reich hundreds of irreplaceable workers whom the army declared essential—all Jews, even including a few specialized craftsmen working for the survival of the Reich, had to be destroyed.

54. Ibid., 19:550–59 (from Peter Kleist, *Zwischen Hitler und Stalin 1939–1945*); Alexander Fischer, *Sowjetische Deutschlandpolitik im Zweiten Weltkrieg 1941–1945,* 40–42.

Alexandra Kollontai was the daughter of a Czarist general. She had joined the Bolshevik party before it came to power and was a member of its Central Committee. She remained ambassadress in Stockholm until the end of World War II.

55. Neither Claus nor Alexandrov, as Schulenburg pointed out, was a Jew.

56. On October 19, 1942, Stalin sent a telegram to Soviet Ambassador Ivan Maiski, declaring: "All of us in Moscow have gained the impression that Churchill is holding to a course leading to the defeat of the USSR in order then to come to terms with the Germany of Hitler or Brüning at the expense of our country" (Jonathon Haslam, "Litvinov, Stalin and the Road Not Taken," *Soviet Foreign Policy 1917–1990: A Retrospective*).

To put pressure on London, an official of Tass suggested that a Soviet transmitter broadcast, in the name of a group of German generals, programs praising the

Bismarckian policies of partnership with Russia and opposition to British imperialism (Steven Merritt Miner, "His Master's Voice: Viacheslav Mikhailovich Molotov as Stalin's Foreign Commissar," 84).

According to Marshal K. S. Moskalenko, as early as 1941 Stalin, Beria, and Molotov discussed the question of making peace with Germany and handing over the Baltic republics, Moldavia, a large part of the Ukraine, and White Russia (Volkogonov, *Triumph and Tragedy*, 412–13). They attempted to make contact with Hitler through the Bulgarian ambassador.

The story is more likely to be part of the post-Stalin revisionism in Soviet Russia than of an actual event for which there is, so far, no corroboration.

57. Hitler told Speer: "If the war is lost, the people will be lost also. It is not necessary to worry about what the German people will need for elemental survival. On the contrary, it is best for us to destroy even these things. For the nation has proved to be the weaker, and the future belongs solely to the stronger Eastern nation. In any case only those who are inferior will remain after this struggle, for the good have already been killed" (Speer, *Inside the Third Reich*, 440).

58. Göring never deserted Hitler. When he telegraphed the Führer for permission to negotiate with the Allies, he believed that Hitler, deprived of freedom of action in Berlin, would want him to deal with the Allies to gain some sort of reasonable peace. A furious Hitler thereupon ordered Göring's arrest, and he and his family became prisoners of the SS until they were freed after the death of Hitler by order of Hitler's appointed successor, Admiral Dönitz (Charles Bewley, *Hermann Göring and the Third Reich*, 405; Michaelis and Schraepler, *Ursachen und Folgen*, 23:154–55).

Himmler, oblivious to the contempt in which he, as the implacable Reichsführer SS, was universally held, did try to open negotiations with the Allies, but he had no success either with them or with Dönitz when he unexpectedly appeared at the latter's headquarters in Flensburg to take command. He had no luck with the Allies either. Although he had shaved off his mustache before being taken prisoner, his identity was soon established, and he swallowed a cyanide pill while his British interrogators were examining him (Michaelis and Schraepler, *Ursachen und Folgen*, 23:275).

59. Ibid., 172–73.

60. How Hitler died became a hotly disputed political issue; a Soviet commission found no evidence of a gunshot wound in May 1945, announcing that he had swallowed a cyanide pill. German witnesses in the bunker heard a single shot fired behind the closed doors of the room where he and his wife had retired to kill themselves. Two of them—his valet (Heinz Linge) and his chauffeur (Erich Kempa)—found his bloody corpse alongside the body of Eva when they entered the suite. Russian propaganda, always adept at twisting its account of any event to fit Soviet political aims (as would be manifest when a team of Soviet doctors staged an elaborate clinical charade to demonstrate how the Germans had committed the Katyn massacre), was from the beginning intent on proving that Hitler was a coward who had taken an easy way out of the havoc he had created. Post-Stalin, Russian, and Western researchers who are convinced Hitler shot himself disagree on how he did it. Apparently he bit into a cyanide capsule as he fired his pistol—but one historian says he shot himself in the mouth, one says in the left temple, another the right temple. In any event, the overwhelming weight of the evidence—the single shot heard, the eyewitness accounts of Hitler's bloody head, and forensic testimony after the

Soviet collapse—are far more convincing than the 1945 Soviet report (Lev Bezmenski, ed., *The Death of Adolf Hitler;* Gerhard Boldt, *Die Letzten Tage der Reichskanzlei;* Stephen Kinzer, "The Day Hitler Died: Even Now, New Details," *New York Times,* May 4, 1995; Ada Petrova and Peter Watson, *The Death of Hitler*).

61. East Germany, the former German Democratic Republic, after nearly a half-century of devastating Soviet occupation is being painfully but steadily revitalized (Jan S. Prybyla, "The German Cure for Trabies and Lesser Ills").

62. The North Vietnamese and North Koreans had Chinese and Soviet support in their wars against the United States. President Eisenhower joined Nikita Khrushchev in demanding Anglo-French withdrawal from Suez and from the campaign they, with Israel, had launched against Egypt.

63. In his Will of May 2, 1938, Hitler left one thousand marks a month each to his sister, Paula, and half-sister, Angela, and the sum of sixty thousand marks to his half-brother, Alois. They all outlived him but without any inheritance (Michaelis and Schraepler, *Ursachen und Folgen,* 11:517). See also ibid., 23:200.

Bibliography

Abendroth, Hans-Henning. "Die Deutsche Intervention im Spanischen Bürgerkrieg." *Vierteljahrshefte für Zeitgeschichte* 1 (1982): 117–29.

Abshagen, K. H. *Canaris.* Stuttgart: Union Verlag, 1959.

Absolon, Rudolf. *Die Wehrmacht im Dritten Reich.* Vol. 1. Boppard am Rhein: Harald Boldt Verlag, 1969.

Allied Control Authority for Germany. *Trial of the Major War Criminals before the International Military Tribunal, Nuremberg, 14 November 1945–1 October 1946.* Nuremberg: 1947–1949.

Augsburger Post Zeitung, February 19, 1933.

Aus dem Archiv des Deutschen Auswärtiges Amt. *Akten zur Deutschen Auswärtigen Politik 1918–1945.* Series C, vol. 5, book 1. Series D, vol. 3, book 2. Göttingen: Vanderhoeck & Ruprecht, 1977.

———. Series D, vols. 1, 2, 4, 5, 6, 7. Baden-Baden: Imprimerie Nationale, 1950–1956.

———. Series D, vols. 9, 10. Baden-Baden/Frankfurt a.M.: K. Keppler Verlag K.G., 1961–1963.

———. Series D, vol. 11, book 1. Bonn: Gebr. Hermes K.G., 1964.

Baehr, Walter, and Hans W. Baber. *Kriegsbriefe gefallener Studenten 1939–1945.* Tübingen: Rainer Wunderlich Verlag Hermann Leins, 1952.

Baumgart, Winfried. "Zur ansprache Hitlers vor den Führern der Wehrmacht am 22. August 1939." *Vierteljahrshefte für Zeitgeschichte* 2 (1968): 120–49.

Beard, Charles A. *American Foreign Policy in the Making 1932–1940.* New Haven, Conn.: Yale University Press, 1946.

Below, Nicolaus v. *Als Hitlers Adjutant 1937–45.* Mainz: v. Hase & Koehler Verlag, 1980.

Bennecke, Heinrich. "Die Memoiren des Ernst Röhm." *Politische Studien* (Munich) (1963).

Berndt, Alfred. "Zur entstehung des Reichstagsbrands." *Vierteljahrschefte für Zeitgeschichte* 1 (1975): 77–90.

Bewley, Charles. *Hermann Göring and the Third Reich.* New York: Devin-Adair, 1962.

Bezmenski, Lev, ed. *The Death of Adolf Hitler.* London: Michael Joseph, 1968.

Boehm, Eric H. *We Survived.* Santa Barbara, Calif.: ABC-Clio Information Services, 1985.

Boehm, Hermann. "Zur Ansprache Hitlers vor den Führern der Wehrmacht am 22. August 1939." *Vierteljahrshefte für Zeitgeschichte* 3 (1971): 294–304.

Boldt, Gerhard. *Die Letzten Tage der Reichskanzlei.* Hamburg: Rowohlt Verlag, 1947.

Bonnet, Georges. *De Washington au Quai d'Orsay.* Geneva: Les Éditions du Cheval Ailé Constant Bourquin, Editeur, 1946.

Boyd, Carl. *Hitler's Japanese Confidant: General Ōshima Hiroshi and MAGIC Intelligence 1941–1945.* Lawrence: University of Kansas Press, 1993.

Bracher, Karl Dietrich, Wolfgang Sauer, and Gerhard Schultz. *Die nationalsozialistische Machtergreifung.* 2d ed. Cologne and Oplanden: Westdeutscher Verlag, 1962.

Broszat, Martin. "Zum Streit um den Reichstagsbrand." *Vierteljahrshefte für Zeitgeschichte* 3 (1960): 275–79.

Brügel, J. W. *Stalin und Hitler.* Vienna: Europaverlag, 1973.

Brüning, Heinrich. *Memoiren 1918–1934.* Stuttgart: Deutsche Verlags-Anstalt, 1970.

Buchheit, Gert. *Ludwig Beck.* Munich: Paul List Verlag, 1964.

———. *Soldatentum und Rebellion.* Rastatt/Baden: Grote'sche Verlagsbuchhandlung, KG, 1961.

Buckreis, Adam. *Politik des 20. Jahrhunderts.* Vol. 1, *Weltgeschichte 1901–1936.* Nuremberg: Panorama-Verlag, n.d.

Burckhardt, Carl J. *Meine Danziger Mission 1937–1939.* Munich: Deutscher Taschenbuch Verlag GmbH., 1962.

Buttler-Brandenfels, Horst Treusch von. Interview by author. Cassel, Germany, 1965.

Cheuv, Felix. *Molotov Remembers: Inside Kremlin Politics.* Ed. Albert Resis. Chicago: Ivan R. Dee, 1993.

Churchill, Winston S. *The Gathering Storm.* Boston: Houghton Mifflin, 1948.

———. *Their Finest Hour.* Boston: Houghton Mifflin, 1949.

Ciano, Count Galeazzo. *Ciano's Hidden Diary 1937–1938.* New York: E. P. Dutton, 1953.

———. *Journal Politique 1939–1943.* Vols. 1, 2. Histoire et Société d'Aujourd'hui Éditions de la Baconnière-Neuchatel. n.d.

Dahlerus, Birger. *Der Letzte Versuch.* Munich: Nymphenburger Verlagshandlung, 1948.

Dallin, Alexander. *German Rule in Russia 1941–1945: A Study of Occupation Policies.* London: Macmillan, 1957.

Dallin, David J. *Soviet Russia and the Far East.* New Haven, Conn.: Yale University Press, 1948.

————. *Soviet Russia's Foreign Policy 1939–1942*. New Haven, Conn.: Yale University Press, 1947.

Davidson, Eugene. *The Making of Adolf Hitler*. New York: Macmillan, 1977.

————. *The Trial of the Germans*. New York: Macmillan, 1966.

Deutsch, Harold C. *The Conspiracy against Hitler*. Minneapolis: University of Minnesota Press, 1968.

————. *Hitler and His Generals*. Minneapolis: University of Minnesota Press, 1974.

Dietl, Gerda-Luise, and D. Kurt Herrmann. *General Dietl*. Munich: Münchner Buchverlag, 1951.

Dimitroff, Georg. *Georg Dimitroff, Leipzig 1933 Speeches, Letters, Documents*. N.p.: Sofia Press, 1968.

Domarus, Max. *Hitler Reden und Proklamationen 1932–1945*. Vols. 1, 2. Neustadt a.d. Aisch: Verlagsdruckerei Schmidt, 1962 and 1963.

Dönitz, Karl. *Zehn Jahre und Zwanzig Tage*. Bonn: Athenäum Verlag, 1958.

Ebray, Alcide. *Der unsaubere Frieden*. Trans. Grimm. Berlin: n.p., 1925. Originally published as *La Paix malpropre*.

Engel, Major. *Heeresadjutant bei Hitler 1938–1943*. Stuttgart: Deutsche Verlags-Anstalt, 1974.

Engelmann, Bernt. *Deutschland ohne Juden*. Munich: Deutsche Taschenbuch Verlag, 1974.

Eubank, Keith. *Munich*. Norman: University of Oklahoma Press, 1963.

Fabry, Philipp W. *Der Hitler-Stalin Pakt 1939–1941: Ein Beitrag zur Methode sowjetischer Aussenpolitik*. Darmstadt: Fundus Verlag, 1962.

Feiling, Keith. *The Life of Neville Chamberlain*. London: Macmillan, 1946.

Fest, Joachim C. *Hitler*. Berlin: Propyläen Verlag, 1973.

Fischer, Alexander. *Sowjetische Deutschlandpolitik im Zweiten Weltkrieg 1941–1945*. Stuttgart: Deutsche Verlags-Anstalt, 1975.

Fleischhauer, Ingeborg. "Der Deutsche-Sowjetische Grenz- und Freundschaftsvertrag vom 28. September 1939." *Vierteljahrshefte für Zeitgeschichte* 3 (1991): 457.

Florinsky, Michael T. *The Saar Struggle*. New York: Macmillan, 1935.

Foertsch, Hermann. *Schuld und Verhängnis*. Stuttgart: Deutsche Verlags-Anstalt, 1951.

François-Poncet, André. *Souvenirs d'une Ambassade à Berlin Septembre 1931–Octobre 1938*. Paris: Ernest Flammarion, 1946.

Frankreichs Saarpolitik: Ein Saar Interpellation im Bayerischen Landtag 14, 15 February 1922. Munich: Süddeutsche Verlag, 1922.

Freund, Michael, ed. *Geschichte des Zweiten Weltkrieges in Dokumenten*. Vol. 1. Freiburg: Verlag Herder, 1954. Vol. 2. Freiburg: Verlag Herder, and Freiburg/

Munich: Verlag Karl Alber, 1955. Vol. 3. Freiburg/Munich: Verlag Karl Alber, 1956.

Fröhlich, Elke, ed. *Die Tagebücher von Joseph Goebbels.* Part 1, vols. 1, 2, 3, 4. Munich: K. G. Saur, 1987. Part 2, vol. 7, Munich: K. G. Saur, 1993.

Gafencu, Grigore. *Last Days of Europe.* New Haven, Conn.: Yale University Press, 1948.

Gebhardt, Bruno. *Handbuch der Deutschen Geschichte.* Vols. 1, 2, 3, 4. Stuttgart: Union Verlag, vol. 1, 1964; vols. 2, 3, 4, 1965.

Geyer, Dietrich. "Sowjetrussland und die deutsche Arbeiterbewegung 1918–1932." *Vierteljahrshefte für Zeitgeschichte* 1 (1976): 2–37.

Gibbels, Ellen. "Hitlers Nervenkrankheit." *Vierteljahrshefte für Zeitgeschichte* 2 (1994): 155–220.

Gilbert, Martin, and Richard Gott. *The Appeasers.* Boston: Houghton Mifflin, 1963.

Gisevius, Hans Bernd. *Bis zum bitteren Ende.* Hamburg: Ruetten & Loening Verlag, n.d.

Glantz, David M. *Soviet Military Deception in the Second World War.* London: F. Cass, 1989.

Goebbels, Joseph. *Tagebücher 1945.* Hamburg: Hoffmann u. Campe Verlag, 1977.

Göhring, Walter, and Robert Machacek. *Start in den Abgrund.* Vienna: Kammer für Arbeiter und Angestellten, n.d.

Görlitz, Walter. *Der Deutsche Generalstab.* Frankfurt a.M.: Verlag der Frankfurter Hefte, n.d.

Gorlov, Sergei, preparer. "Soviet-German Military Cooperation." *International Affairs* (July 1990).

Gorodetsky, Gabriel. "Stalin und Hitlers Angriff auf die Sowjetunion." *Vierteljahrshefte für Zeitgeschichte* 4 (1989): 645–72.

Grimm, Friedrich. *Frankreich am Rhein.* Hamburg/Berlin: Hanseatische Verlagsanstalt, 1931.

Groscurth, Helmuth. *Tagebücher eines Abwehr-offiziers 1938–1940.* Stuttgart: Deutsche Verlags-Anstalt, 1970.

Guderian, Heinz. *Erinnerungen eines Soldaten.* Neckargemuend: Kurt Vowinkel Verlag, 1960.

Halder, Generaloberst. *Kriegstagebuch.* Vol. 2. Stuttgart: Kohlhammer Verlag, 1963.

Haslam, Jonathan. "Litvinov, Stalin and the Road Not Taken." In *Soviet Foreign Policy 1917–1990: A Retrospective,* ed. Gabriel Gorodetsky. Portland: Frank Cass, 1993: 55–62.

Heiber, Helmut. "Der Fall Grünspan." *Vierteljahrshefte für Zeitgeschichte* 1 (1957): 134–72.

Henderson, Nevile. *Failure of a Mission: Berlin 1937–1939*. New York: Putnam, 1940.

Hilberg, Raul. *The Destruction of the European Jews*. Chicago: Quadrangle, 1961.

Hilger, Gustav. *Wir und der Kreml*. Frankfurt a.M./Bonn: Athenäum Verlag, 1964.

Hillgruber, Andreas. *Germany and the Two Wars*. Cambridge: Harvard University Press, 1981.

Hoch, Anton. "Das Attentat auf Hitler im Münchner Bürgerbräukeller 1939." *Vierteljahrshefte für Zeitgeschichte* 4 (1969): 383–413.

Hoffmann, Joachim. *Die Geschichte der Wlassow-Armee*. Freiburg: Verlag Rombach, 1986.

Hoffmann, Peter. *The History of the German Resistance 1933–1945*. Cambridge: MIT Press, 1977.

Hossbach, Friedrich. *Zwischen Wehrmacht und Hitler 1934–1938*. Göttingen: Vanderhoeck & Ruprecht, 1965.

House, Edward Mandell, and Charles Seymour, eds. *What Really Happened at Paris*. New York: Scribner's, 1921.

Hüttenberger, Peter. *Die Gauleiter*. Stuttgart: Deutsche Verlags-Anstalt, 1969.

Internationaler Militärgerichtshof. *Der Prozess gegen die Hauptkriegsverbrecher vor dem Internationalen Militargerichtshof: Nürnberg, 14. November 1945–1. Oktober 1946*. Vols. 9, 10, 26, 27, 41. Nuremberg: 1947–1949.

International Military Tribunal, Nuremberg. *Nazi Conspiracy and Aggression*. 8 vols. and Supps. A and B. Washington: United States Government Printing Office, 1946–1948.

Jacobsen, Hans-Adolf. *1939–1945 Der Zweite Weltkrieg in Chronik und Dokumenten*. Darmstadt: Wehr und Wissen Verlagsgesellschaft, 1961.

Jagschitz, Gerhard. *Der Putsch*. Graz, Vienna, and Cologne: Verlag Styria, 1976.

Jaksch, Wenzel. *Europe's Road to Potsdam*. New York: Frederick A. Praeger, 1963.

Jochmann, Werner. *Adolf Hitler—Monologe im Führer Hauptquartier 1941–1944*. Hamburg: Albrecht Knaus Verlag, 1980.

Kempner, Robert M. W. *SS im Kreuzverhör*. Stuttgart: Union Deutsche Verlags, 1950.

Kempowski, Walter. *Das Echolot*. 4 vols. Germany: Albrecht Knaus, 1993.

Kertesz, Stephen D. *Between Russia and the West*. Notre Dame, Ind.: University of Notre Dame Press, 1984.

Kesselring, Albert. *Soldat bis zum letzten Tag*. Bonn: Athenäum-Verlag, 1953.

Kielmansegg, Johann Adolf. *Der Fritsch Prozess*. Hamburg: Hoffmann und Campe Verlag, 1947.

Kirkpatrick, Ivone. *The Inner Circle, Memoirs of Ivone Kirkpatrick*. London: Macmillan, 1959.

Kleist, Peter. *Zwischen Hitler und Stalin 1939–1945*. Bonn: n.p., 1950.

Knappe, Siegfried (with Ted Brusaw). *Soldat: Reflections of a German Soldier, 1936–1949.* New York: Dell, 1993.

Knieriem, August von. *The Nuremberg Trials.* Chicago: Henry Regnery, 1959.

Kordt, Erich. *Nicht aus den Akten . . .* Stuttgart: Union Deutsche Verlag, 1950.

———. *Wahn und Wirklichkeit.* Stuttgart: Union Deutsche Verlag, 1947.

Krautkrämer, Elmar. "Der Sturz Lavals im Dezember 1940." *Vierteljahrshefte für Zeitgeschichte* 1 (1979): 79–112.

Kuhn, Helmut, et al. *Die deutsche Universität im Dritten Reich.* Munich: R. Piper, 1966.

Litvinov, Maxim. *Notes for a Journal.* London: Andre Deutsch, 1955.

Lloyd George, David. *Memoirs of the Peace Conference.* New Haven, Conn.: Yale University Press, 1939.

Lossberg, Bernhard von. *Im Wehrmachte Führungs Stab.* Hamburg: H. H. Noelke Verlag, 1950.

MacDonald, Callum. *The Killing of SS Obergruppenführer Reinhard Heydrich.* New York: Free Press, 1989.

Manstein, Erich von. *Verlorene Siege.* Bonn: Athenäum-Verlag, 1959.

Maser, Werner. *Adolf Hitler.* Munich/Esslingen: Bechtle Verlag, 1971.

McSherry, James. *Stalin, Hitler, and Europe.* Cleveland and New York: World Publishing, 1968.

Meissner, Hans Otto, and Harry Wilde. *Die Machtergreifung: Ein Bericht über die Technik des nationalsozialistischen Staatsstreichs.* Stuttgart: J. G. Cotta'sche Buchhandlung Nachf., 1958.

Meissner, Otto. *Staatssekretär unter Ebert-Hindenburg-Hitler.* Hamburg: Hoffmann und Campe Verlag, 1950.

Michaelis, Herbert, and Ernst Schraepler, eds. *Ursachen und Folgen.* Vols. 9–19, 21, 22, 23. Berlin: Dokumenten-Verlag Dr. Herbert Wendler & Co., n.d.

Militärgeschichtliches Forschungsamt. *Das Deutsche Reich und der zweite Weltkrieg.* Vols. 1, 2. Stuttgart: Deutsche Verlags-Anstalt, 1979.

———. *Handbuch zur deutschen Militärgeschichte 1648–1939.* Vol. 7. Munich: Bernard & Graefe Verlag für Wehrwesen, 1977.

Miner, Steven Merritt. "His Master's Voice: Viacheslav Mikhailovich Molotov as Stalin's Foreign Commissar." In *The Diplomats 1939–1979*, ed. Gordon A. Criag and Francis L. Loewenheim. Princeton, N.J.: Princeton University Press, 1994.

Münchner Neueste Nachrichten. January 31, 1933.

Nadolny, Rufolf. *Mein Beitrag.* Wiesbaden: Limes Verlag, 1955.

New York Times. January 31, 1933; March 22, 1933; May 4, 1995.

Noakes, Jeremy, and Geoffrey Pridham, eds. *Documents on Nazism 1919–1945.* New York: Viking, 1974.

Osborne, Sidney. *The Saar Question.* London: Allen and Unwin, 1923.

Papen, Franz von. *Der Wahrheit eine Gasse*. Munich: Paul List Verlag, 1952.

Parliamentary Debates, House of Commons. 5th series, vol. 345, cols. 435–39.

Petrova, Ada, and Peter Watson. *The Death of Hitler*. New York: W. W. Norton, 1995.

Ploetz, A. G. *Geschichte des Zweiten Weltkrieges*. Wuerzburg: A. G. Ploetz Verlag, 1960.

Poliakov, Leon, and Josef Wulf. *Das Dritte Reich und seine Diener*. Berlin-Grunewald: Arani Verlags-GmbH., 1956.

"Promemoria eines Bayerischen Richters zu den Juni-Morden 1934." *Vierteljahrshefte für Zeitgeschichte* 1 (1957): 102–4.

Prybyla, Jan S. "The German Cure for Trabies and Lesser Ills." Working paper no. 11-95-11, Department of Economics, Pennsylvania State University.

Raeder, Erich. *Mein Leben: V. 2 1935 bis Spandau 1955*. Tübingen-Neckar: Verlag Fritz Schlichtenmayer, 1957.

Read, James Morgan. *Atrocity Propaganda 1914–1919*. New Haven, Conn.: Yale University Press, 1941.

Recktewald, Johann. *Woran hat Adolf Hitler gelitten?* Munich/Basel: Ernst Reinhardt Verlag, 1963.

Reichstag. *Das Saargebiet unter der Herrschaft des Waffenstillstandsabkommens und des Vertrags von Versailles*. Berlin: Verlag von Georg Stilke, 1921.

Ritthaler, Anton. "Eine Etappe auf Hitlers Weg zur ungeteilten Macht/Hugenbergs Rücktritt als Reichminister." *Vierteljahrshefte für Zeitgeschichte* 2 (1960): 193–219.

Röhm, Ernst. *Die Geschichte eines Hochverräters*. Munich: Verlag Franz Eher Nachf., 1933.

Roos, Hans. "Die 'Präventivkriegspläne' Pilsudskis von 1933." *Vierteljahrshefte für Zeitgeschichte* 4 (1955): 344–63.

Rühle, Gerd. *Das Dritte Reich*. Vols. 2, 3, 4, 5. Berlin: Hummelverlag, n.d.

Runzheimer, Jürgen. "Der Überfall auf den sender Gleiwitz im Jahre 1939." *Vierteljahrshefte für Zeitgeschichte* 4 (1962): 408–26.

Das Saargebiet und die Frankenwährung. Berlin: Bund Saar Vereine, n.d.

Scheidewin, Wolfgang, ed. *Die Saar und Ruhr-Frage im Englischen Unterhaus* (English Commons debate on the Saar, May 10, 1923). Potsdam: n.p., 1923.

Schmidt, Paul. *Statist auf diplomatischer Bühne 1923–1945*. Frankfurt a.M./Bonn: Athenäum-Verlag, 1961.

Schmidt, Rainer F. "Der Hess-Flug und das Kabinett Churchill." *Vierteljahrshefte für Zeitgeschichte* 1 (1994): 1–38.

Schnabel, Franz. *Deutsche Geschichte im 19 Jahrhundert*. Vol. 2. Freiburg: n.p., 1948 and 1949.

Schneider, Hans. "Das Ermächtigungsgesetz vom 24. März 1933." *Vierteljahrshefte für Zeitgeschichte* 3 (1953): 197–221.

Schneider, Heinrich. *Das Wunder an der Saar.* Stuttgart: Seewald, 1974.

Schramm, Percy Ernst. *Kriegstagebuch des Oberkommandos der Wehrmacht 1940–1945.* Vol. 4. Frankfurt a.M.: Bernard & Graefe Verlag für Wehrwesen, 1961.

Seymour, Charles, ed. *The Intimate Papers of Colonel House.* Vol. 4. Boston: Houghton Mifflin, 1928.

Sir, F. A., ed. *Dokumente der Deutschen Politik.* Vols. 1, 2. Berlin: Junker und Dünnhaupt Verlag, 1942.

Smelser, Ronald M. *The Sudeten Problem 1933–1938.* Middletown, Conn.: Wesleyan University Press, 1975.

Sokolov, Vladimir. "Peoples Commissar Maxim Litvinov." *International Affairs* (May 1991).

Speer, Albert. *Inside the Third Reich.* New York: Macmillan, 1970.

Stieve, Friedrich, ed. *Der Diplomatische Schriftwechsel Iswolskis aus den Jahren 1914–1917.* Vols. 1–6. Berlin: Deutsche Verlagsgesellschaft für Politik und Geschichte, 1925.

Stratz, Hans-Wolfgang. "Die Studentische 'Aktion wider den undeutschen Geist' im Frühjar 1933." *Vierteljahrshefte für Zeitgeschichte* 4 (1968): 347–72.

Strawson, John. *Hitler's Battles for Europe.* New York: Charles Scribner's, 1971.

Streit, Christian. *Keine Kameraden.* Stuttgart: Deutsche Verlags-Anstalt, 1978.

Suworow, Viktor. *Der Eisbrecher: Hitler in Stalins Kalkül.* Stuttgart: Klett-Cotta, 1989.

Sweet, Paul R. "Der Versuch amtlicher Einflussnahme auf die Edition der 'Documents on Foreign Policy, 1933–1941.'" *Vierteljahrshefte für Zeitgeschichte* 2 (1991): 265–303.

Talbott, Strobe, ed. *Khrushchev Remembers.* Boston and Toronto: Little, Brown, 1970.

Tardieu, André. *The Truth about the Treaty.* London: Hodder and Stoughton, 1921.

Temperley, H. W. V., ed. *A History of the Peace Conference of Paris.* Vol. 2. London: Hodder and Stoughton, 1920.

Thürauf, Ulrich, ed. *Schulthess' Europäischer Geschichtskalender.* Vol. 74. Munich: C. H. Beck'sche Verlagsbuchhandlung, 1934.

Tobias, Fritz. *Der Reichstagsbrand.* Rastatt/Baden: Grote'sche Verlagsbuchhandlung KG., 1962.

Toland, John. *Adolf Hitler.* New York: Doubleday, 1976.

Trachtenberg, Jakow. *Die Greuelpropaganda ist eine Lügenpropaganda sagen die deutschen Juden selbst.* Berlin: Jakow Trachtenberg Verlag, 1933.

Treve, Wilhelm. "Rede Hitlers vor der Deutschen Presse." *Vierteljahrshefte für Zeitgeschichte* 2 (1958): 175–91.

Trevor-Roper, H. R. *The Last Days of Hitler.* London: Macmillan, 1962.

Vaksberg, Arkady. *Stalin's Prosecutor.* New York: Grove Weidenfeld, 1991.

Vanwelkenhuyzen, Jean. "Die Niederlande und der 'Alarm' in Januar 1940." *Vierteljahrshefte für Zeitgeschichte* 1 (1960): 17–36.

Vogel, Th., ed. *Der Saar Befreiungskampf im Reich 1918–1935*. Berlin: Bund der Saarvereine, n.d.

Volkogonov, Dimitri. *Stalin: Triumph and Tragedy*. London: Weidenfeld and Nicolson, 1991.

Wagenlehner, Günther. *Staat oder Kommunismus*. Stuttgart: Seewald Verlag, 1971.

Wagner, Walter. *Die deutsche Justiz und der Nationalsozialismus*. Vol. 3. Stuttgart: Deutsche Verlags-Anstalt, 1974.

Warlimont, Walter. *Inside Hitler's Headquarters 1939–45*. New York: Frederick A. Praeger, 1964.

———. *Im Hauptquartier der deutschen Wehrmacht 1939–1945*. Frankfurt a.M.: Bernard & Graefe Verlag für Wehrwesen, 1962.

Watts, Franklin, ed. *Voices of History*. New York: Franklin Watts, 1942.

Weissbuch über die Erschiessungen des 30. Juni 1934. Paris: Éditions du Carrefour, 1935.

Wieder, Joachim. *Stalingrad und die Verantwortung des Soldaten*. Munich: Numphenburger Verlagshandlung, 1962.

Woodward, E. L., and Rohan Butler, eds. *Documents on British Foreign Policy 1919–1939*. 2d series, vols. 5, 6; 3d series, vols. 1, 2, 3, 4, 5, 7. London: His Majesty's Stationery Office, 1947–1960.

Wulf, Joseph. *Literatur und Dichtung im Dritten Reich*. Gütersloh: Sigbert Mohn Verlag, 1963.

———. *Presse und Funk im Dritten Reich*. Gütersloh: Sigbert Mohn Verlag, 1964.

Yerofeyev, Vladimir. "Ten Years in PCFA Secretariat." *International Affairs* (October 1991): 88–97.

Zawodny, J. K. *Death in the Forest*. Notre Dame, Ind.: University of Notre Dame Press, 1962.

Zelzer, Maria. *Weg und Schicksal der Stuttgarter Juden*. Stuttgart: Ernst Klett Verlag, 1964.

Zhukov, G. K. *The Memoirs of Marshal Zhukov*. New York: Delacort, 1971.

Index

Abetz, Otto, 480*n31*
Abwehr, 77
Academy for German Law, 117
Adam, Gen. Wilhelm, 39, 84, 149, 216
Africa, 441–42
Agriculture, 116–17
Air force. *See* German air force; and other
   countries
Albania, 362, 418
Alexandrov, 450, 486*n55*
Alliance of German Officers, 443–44
Altmark, 403
Amery, Leopold, 306
Amnesty, 108–9
Andlauer, Gen., 143
Anschluss, 87–88, 93, 130, 158–60, 191–92,
   223, 224, 314, 470*n1*
Anti-Comintern Pact, 172, 341
Anti-Semitism: Jewish newspapers
   suspended, 9, 14; in Germany, 14–15,
   26–29, 40–44, 47–48, 117–18, 213,
   320–25; of Hitler, 26, 27, 40, 56, 213,
   218, 309, 321–22, 330, 337–39, 444–45,
   475*n24;* and Göring, 27, 315–16, 322,
   325; of Goebbels, 27, 321, 325; Law for
   the Restoration of Career Officialdom,
   28, 39, 41; violence against Jews, 41;
   Germans disturbed by, 41–42; Jewish
   organizations' instructions to foreigners
   not to intervene, 42–43; concentration
   camps, 47; and churches, 64, 65;
   and Reichs Association of German
   Industry, 121; and Nuremberg laws,
   161; Kristallnacht, 259, 320, 321,
   324, 325; and immigration of Jews,
   323–25, 475*n27;* in German Poland,
   401; Madagascar plan for Jewish
   settlement, 412, 414, 435, 480*n31;*

extermination of Jews, 435, 444–45. *See
   also* Concentration camps
Ardennes, 446, 447
Ark Royal, 412–13
Army. *See* German army; and other
   countries
Arnim, Gen. Hans-Jürgen von, 442
Asquith, Herbert Henry, 144
Association of National German Jews, 43
Astakov, Georgi, 382
Attolico, Bernardo, 296 98, 302
Augsburger Postzeitung, 9
Austria: National Socialism in, 26, 86,
   88–93, 158, 187, 464*n2;* German
   territorial claims on, 50; Dollfuss
   government in, 51, 56, 86–97; coup
   against Dollfuss government, 51, 56,
   93–103, 188; and Mussolini, 51, 88,
   93, 102–3, 127, 131, 158, 164, 314;
   economy of, 52, 87, 88; opposition
   to Dollfuss government in, 86–87,
   91–93; and *Anschluss,* 87–88, 93, 130,
   158–60, 190–92, 223, 224, 314, 470*n1;*
   Social Democrats in, 88; and League of
   Nations, 88, 93; government oppression
   in, 88–89, 90, 91; Hitler's policy on,
   89–90, 92–93, 102, 152, 166–69, 187–92;
   SA in, 91–93, 94, 95, 97–101; and Rome
   Protocols, 93, 159; SS in, 93–94, 95;
   rebellion in Vienna, 93–99; SA rising
   in countryside, 99–101; and Italy's
   attack on Ethiopia, 130; Gentlemen's
   Agreement with Germany, 158–60, 187;
   in Hossbach protocol, 166–69; and
   Berchtesgaden agreement, 188–91, 231;
   German invasion of, 190–92, 470*n23;*
   plebiscite on support for Schuschnigg
   and independence, 191, 469–70*n20;*
   "flower war" in, 192